AUTOCOURSE

The World's Leading Grand Prix Annual

HAZLETON PUBLISHING

ap RACING

FIT TO WIN

Check the record books.
No other manufacturer of racing brakes
or clutches even comes close.

AP Lockheed and AP Borg & Beck
components have become a byword for
performance - the standard by which
all others are judged.

AP Racing, Wheler Road,
Seven Stars Industrial Estate,
Coventry CV3 4LB. Tel: 01203 639595
International: +44 1203 639595
Fax: +44 1203 639559

CONTENTS

Autocourse 1995-96
is published by
Hazleton Publishing Ltd,
3 Richmond Hill,
Richmond, Surrey
TW10 6RE.

Colour reproduction by
Barrett Berkeley Ltd, London.

Printed in England by
Butler and Tanner Ltd,
Frome, Somerset.

© Hazleton Publishing Ltd 1995.
No part of this publication may be reproduced, stored in a retrieval system or transmitted, in any form or by any means, electronic, mechanical, photocopying, recording or otherwise, without prior permission in writing from Hazleton Publishing Ltd.

ISBN: 1-874557-36-5

DISTRIBUTORS
UNITED KINGDOM
Bookpoint Ltd
39 Milton Park
Abingdon
Oxfordshire OX14 4TD
Telephone: 01235 400400
Fax: 01235 861038

NORTH AMERICA
Motorbooks International
PO Box 1
729 Prospect Ave.
Osceola
Wisconsin 54020, USA
Telephone: (1) 715 294 3345
Fax: (1) 715 294 4448

AUSTRALIA
Technical Book and
Magazine Co. Pty
295 Swanston Street
Melbourne
Victoria 3000
Telephone: (03) 9663 3951
Fax: (03) 9663 2094

NEW ZEALAND
David Bateman Ltd
PO Box 100-242
North Shore Mail Centre
Auckland 1330
Telephone: (9) 415 7664
Fax: (9) 415 8892

SOUTH AFRICA
Motorbooks
341 Jan Smuts Avenue
Craighall Park
Johannesburg
Telephone: (011) 325 4458/60
Fax: (011) 325 4146

FOREWORD by Michael Schumacher	5
EDITOR'S INTRODUCTION	6
THE TOP TEN DRIVERS OF 1995	15
FANGIO A tribute to Juan Manuel Fangio by Denis Jenkinson	28
MICHAEL SCHUMACHER A profile of the 1995 World Champion by Tony Dodgins	32
THE STATE OF FORMULA 1 by Alan Henry	36
FORMULA 1 REVIEW by Bob Constanduros, Maurice Hamilton and Alan Henry	41
1995 GRANDS PRIX by Alan Henry	83
1995 FORMULA 1 STATISTICS compiled by David Hayhoe and Nick Henry	232
FORMULA 3000 REVIEW by Andrew Benson	234
FORMULA 3 REVIEW by Gary Watkins	236
SPORTS CAR RACING REVIEW by Adam Cooper	238
BRITISH TOURING CAR CHAMPIONSHIP by Laurence Foster	242
INTERNATIONAL TOURING CAR RACING REVIEW by Laurence Foster	248
UNITED STATES RACING REVIEW by Gordon Kirby	254
OTHER MAJOR 1995 RESULTS compiled by David Hayhoe	265

PUBLISHER
Richard Poulter

EDITOR
Alan Henry

MANAGING EDITOR
Peter Lovering

ART EDITOR
Steve Small

PRODUCTION MANAGER
Steven Palmer

BUSINESS DEVELOPMENT MANAGER
Simon Maurice

SALES PROMOTION
Clare Kristensen

RESULTS AND STATISTICS
David Hayhoe
Nick Henry

F1 ILLUSTRATIONS
Ian Hutchinson
Nicola Fox

CHIEF CONTRIBUTING PHOTOGRAPHERS
Allsport
Diana Burnett
Paul-Henri Cahier
Lukas Gorys
LAT Photographic
Matthias Schneider
Nigel Snowdon
Sutton Photographic
Words & Pictures

Cover photos:
The main photo of World Champion Michael Schumacher in the Benetton-Renault is by Darren Heath/Zooom Photographic.

Bottom left: **The podium at Silverstone was the stage for three drivers who were all to score their maiden Grand Prix wins during the 1995 season. Jean Alesi *(left)* and David Coulthard hoist Johnny Herbert on their shoulders after the Briton had won his home Grand Prix.**
Photo: Steve Etherington/Empics

Bottom right: **Although he notched up four wins, Damon Hill once again had to settle for second place behind Schumacher in the battle for the drivers' crown.**
Photo: John Marsh/Action Images

ACKNOWLEDGEMENTS

The Editor of *Autocourse* wishes to thank the following for their assistance in compiling the 1995-96 edition:
France: ACO, Automobiles Ligier (Frank Dernie, Richard Grundy, Tom Walkinshaw and Chris Williams), Fédération Française du Sport Automobile, FIA (Bernie Ecclestone, Max Mosley, Francesco Longanesi-Cattani, Alistair Watkins and Charlie Whiting), Peugeot Sport (Jean-Pierre Jabouille and Jean-Claude Lefebvre), Renault Sport (Jean-Jacques Delaruwiere, Bernard Dudot and Christine Marquilie); **Germany:** Mercedes-Benz (Martin Geers, Norbert Haug and Wolfgang Schattling), Oberste Nationale Sportkommission; **Great Britain:** *Autocar* (Michael Harvey and Janice Stephens), Benetton Formula (Maria Bellanca, Ross Brawn, Flavio Briatore, Rory Byrne, Jessica Salisbury and Patrizia Spinelli), Timothy Collings, Bob Constanduros, Cosworth Engineering (Dick Scammell), Arrows Grand Prix International (Alan Jenkins and Jackie Oliver), Ben Edwards, Ford (Peter Gillitzer, Cliff Peters, Sophie Sicot and Martin Whitaker), Mike Greasley, Mo Hamilton, Brian Hart Ltd (Jane Brace and Brian Hart), John Hogan, Ian Hutchinson, Ilmor Engineering (Mario Illien and Paul Morgan), Tony Jardine, Denis Jenkinson, the trustees of the estate of the late Edgar Jessop, Jordan Grand Prix (Gary Anderson, Louise Goodman, Tim Holloway, Eddie Jordan and Ian Phillips), John Judd, Lola Cars, McLaren International (Jocelyne Bia, Justine Blake, Ron Dennis, Norman Howell, Neil Oatley, Jo Ramirez and Peter Stayner), Pacific Grand Prix (Ian Dawson, Mark Gallagher and Keith Wiggins), Stan Piecha, RAC MSA (Derek Tye), Nigel Roebuck, Shell International, Eric Silbermann, Silverstone Circuits, Simtek, Tyrrell Racing Organisation (Vincent Franchesini, Rupert Manwaring, Harvey Postlethwaite and Ken Tyrrell), Professor E. S. 'Syd' Watkins, Williams Grand Prix Engineering (Ann Bradshaw, Jane Gorard, Patrick Head, Adrian Newey, Richard West and Frank Williams), John Watson; **Italy:** Commissione Sportiva Automobilistica Italiana, Forti Corse (Carlo Gancia), Scuderia Ferrari (John Barnard, Giancarlo Bacchini, Antonio Ghini, Niki Lauda and Jean Todt), Minardi Scuderia Italia (Leopoldo Canetoli and Giancarlo Minardi); **Japan:** Yamaha ('Herbie' Blash and Rob Faulkner); **Switzerland:** Marlboro Motorsport (Agnes Carlier), Sauber (Gustav Busing and Peter Sauber); **USA:** Daytona International Speedway, Goodyear (Barry Griffin, Cal Lint, Leo Mehl, Ron Pike and Tony Shakespeare), IMSA, IndyCar, Indy Lights, NASCAR, Roger Penske, SCCA, USAC.

Photographs published in *Autocourse 1995-96* have been contributed by:
Action Images/John Marsh, *Allsport*/Pascal Rondeau/Mike Hewitt, James Barron, Gérard Berthoud, *Bothwell Photographic*/Mark Bothwell, Michael C. Brown, Diana Burnett, Paul-Henri Cahier, Steve Domenjoz, *Empics*/Steve Etherington/Claire Mackintosh, Lukas Gorys, *GP Photo*/Peter Nygaard, Joseph J. Jiran, Nigel Kinrade, *LAT Photographic*/Steve Tee, Pamela Lauesen/*FOSA*, Dominique Leroy, *Steve Mohlenkamp Photography*, John Overton, Matthias Schneider, Nigel Snowdon, *Sporting Pictures (UK) Ltd*, *Sutton Photographic*/Keith Sutton/Mark Sutton, Denis L. Tanney, *Words & Pictures*/Colin McMaster/Bryn Williams, Tony Di Zinno and *Zooom Photographic*/Darren Heath.

FOREWORD

by Michael Schumacher

Winning my second consecutive World Championship has given me enormous satisfaction, as has the fact that I managed to win nine of the seventeen races which made up this varied season. Grand Prix motor racing today is an extremely complex affair, relying as it does not only on a highly competitive performance from the driver, but also on a commitment to high standards of professionalism from the team with which he works.

In that respect, I must pay tribute to the sheer professionalism of the Mild Seven Benetton team which has supported me so superbly throughout my endeavours. All the mechanics, engineers and personnel back at the factory have worked ceaselessly to help me win not only the drivers' title, but also Benetton's first-ever constructors' championship.

I would also like to record my thanks to all my fans throughout the world. I have been deeply touched by their support, which has always been an inspiration for me.

This was a year in which Grand Prix racing swallowed hard and did its best to digest some of the painful lessons forced on it by the acutely tragic events of 1994. Although outwardly the business seemed much the same, one got the impression that Formula 1 was making a big effort somehow to rediscover itself with the impetus for change not only focusing on improved long-term safety, but with the governing body also attempting to impose more discipline on driving tactics and cracking down on any remaining scope for technical rule infringements.

It is difficult to assess precisely how much worthwhile progress was made on either of these fronts. One of the problems of an annual review is that, while it provides an instant snapshot of recent events, there is not always sufficient time for them to assume an accurate historic perspective before it is necessary to commit them to print. However, it would be nice if the 1995 season comes to be regarded as a year of transition during which the Grand Prix fraternity made a (not always successful) attempt to pick up the thread of its own credibility.

The FIA began the year in a robust frame of mind, signalling that it had the technical wherewithal to police each and every aspect of its own rules with sufficient detailed vigilance to make it impossible for any team to get away with any clandestine infringement. Under the circumstances, it was therefore unfortunate that the opening race in Brazil ended in controversy over the question of gas chromatograph readings of the fuel samples taken from Michael Schumacher's winning Benetton and the second-placed Williams of David Coulthard.

Thankfully, the matter was speedily resolved, but on the face of it the whole episode, together with Schumacher's rather tiresome 'gamesmanship' at the pre-season weigh-in, understandably made those outside the intense F1 paddock milieu stand back and wonder whether the sport had really inherited any additional wisdom from the lessons of 1994.

As far as the cars were concerned, they had considerably less downforce. They slid around more and were harder to drive on the outer limit of adhesion. They were only fractionally slower, if at all, and while considerable safety upgrading had been done on many circuits across the world in the aftermath of the Senna and Ratzenberger fatalities, F1 continued to be a high-risk business with refuelling stops remaining an integral part of the Grand Prix fabric.

We were once again reminded of the dangers implicit in such strategies when Eddie Irvine's Jordan was enveloped in flames at a pit stop during the Belgian GP at Spa. The incident may not have received the frenzied tabloid media coverage which surrounded Jos Verstappen's fiery misfortune at Hockenheim just over 12 months earlier, but it yet again raised the issue of whether such a perilous practice was merely pandering to television viewing figures while adding nothing in real terms to the sport apart from disrupting an otherwise perfectly straightforward motor race.

As far as the championship battle itself was concerned, the contest between Michael Schumacher's Benetton – now powered by Renault – and Damon Hill's similarly propelled Williams picked up where it had left off in Adelaide the previous year. The two men spent the first half of the season scrapping cleanly to gain the upper hand, but their rivalry took a turn for the worse after the French GP at Magny-Cours where Michael accused Hill of giving him a brake test as they lapped a slower car early in their battle for the lead.

This spilled over into very public acrimony when the two collided while battling for the lead at Silverstone, incivilities were exchanged in public and their personal relationship strayed into the volatile area previously explored by Prost/Senna and Mansell/Piquet – although, it must be emphasised, without the personal venom which made those rivalries so bitterly unpleasant.

Hill's critics would say he overdrove beyond his limits to keep in touch with the man who, increasingly, was maturing into the best driver of the post-Senna era. Schumacher and Benetton worked as a team, brilliantly harnessing race strategy time and again to gain the upper hand over the technically superior Williams-Renaults. From the standpoint of Michael's second drivers' championship, subjugating Johnny Herbert's requirements was probably a significant factor which enabled the German ace to clinch the title with two races still to run.

As far as the constructors' championship was concerned, it was less of an issue. Benetton had the reliability Williams so sorely lacked and if the FW17s were not rolling to a halt at the side of the track, or in the pits, then Hill and David Coulthard were making too many driving errors. As a collective entity, Williams effectively threw away their fourth successive constructors' championship simply because, on this rare occasion, they were not good enough.

In terms of engine power, Renault decisively retained the upper hand. Challenges from Ferrari, Mercedes and Peugeot all yielded less than expected. The Maranello cars were often within a whisker of the front-running pace, but suffered from appalling mechanical unreliability. The first year of McLaren's alliance with Mercedes-Benz was disappointing, delivering less by far than had been expected by the German company's management, and at times it seemed as though neither Jordan nor Peugeot had quite grasped what was needed to compete in F1's absolute front line.

Further back, while our political lords and masters in the wider world might have been talking in terms of economic regeneration, life down at the back of the F1 bus remained a precarious way of earning a living. The cash-strapped Simtek team bowed out owing in excess of $6 million just before the Canadian GP, while Pacific and Minardi also eked out a precarious existence close to the financial low-water mark. Life for these teams in the future

THE UPPER HAND...

EDITOR'S INTRODUCTION

Left: Grand Prix racing has endeavoured to profit from the lessons of the disastrous 1994 San Marino Grand Prix. Michael Schumacher and Damon Hill pause for a moment's public reflection prior to the start of this year's race.

Below: Renault power separated the title contenders from the rest of the F1 field.

will be made potentially difficult by the imposition of a 107 per cent qualifying cut-off requirement from the start of 1996.

In other words, if you're not quick enough, don't bother to come because Bernie and Max don't want you. Put simply, F1 power broker Ecclestone would rather have smaller, better-quality grids. On the face of it, this might seem a commercially cavalier approach, but once you think how many cars have usually fallen by the wayside within the first 30 laps of most Grands Prix, you can see his point. The also-rans bring little to the show, apart from the blindingly obvious fact that everybody must start somewhere.

Elsewhere on the scene, Nigel Mansell arrived back to the accompaniment of fanfares from McLaren, Marlboro and Mercedes – and drifted away again, virtually unnoticed, after only two races. Heinz-Harald Frentzen consolidated his position as the most promising driver yet to score his first F1 victory, Michael Schumacher opted to switch to Ferrari at the end of the season – and Eddie Irvine somehow contrived to go with him. Lucky boy.

As far as the formulae feeding F1 are concerned, Formula 3000 came to the end of its life in 1995 to be replaced by a one-make category next season. Whether this will be any better at producing closely contested racing remains to be seen, but F3 continued to throw up promising new talent in the form of Norberto Fontana, Ralf Schumacher, Oliver Gavin and Ralph Firman, all of whom could arguably make the jump straight into F1, particularly if their debuts were preceded by a year occupying the increasingly fashionable, if necessary, role of test driver.

However, the performances of former British F3 pacesetters Jan Magnussen and Dario Franchitti in the German touring car arena have reminded us that this high-tech environment is another world in which stars of the future can nurture their talents. Of course, the profile of international touring car racing has been raised considerably in 1995 with television patronage from Bernie Ecclestone and the FIA for the newly instigated ITC series. Race organisers throughout the world please note: if you haven't the money to order from Bernie's expensive à la carte menu for F1, there is a less costly table d'hôte touring car alternative now available.

Sports car racing achieved a degree of regeneration with the global GT series and McLaren found a worthwhile use for some of its unsold F1 supercars, winning Le Mans to give its million-dollar baby an instant, high-profile competition heritage. On the other side of the Atlantic, Jacques Villeneuve took the Indy Car title and won the Indy 500 in a year which saw all three works Penske-Mercs fail to make the grid at the Brickyard. Next year Villeneuve comes to F1 with Williams, turning his back on the Indy Car business at the start of what promises to be potentially its most troubled season ever thanks to its ongoing confrontation with Indianapolis boss Tony George's Indy Racing League.

Taken as a whole, though, 1995 was a promising season which threw up pointers to suggest that the next two years might offer even better racing and more variety in the winner's circle. On a more thoughtful note, the formation of the FIA Expert Advisory Committee under the Presidency of Professor Syd Watkins promises accelerated high-technology progress on safety issues, such as air bags, barrier design and impact resistance. Next year's cars will be even safer and more secure than before and the process of improvement seems set to continue into the future. A more positive way of countering any potential future critics of our sport would somehow be difficult to envisage.

Alan Henry
Tillingham, Essex
November 1995

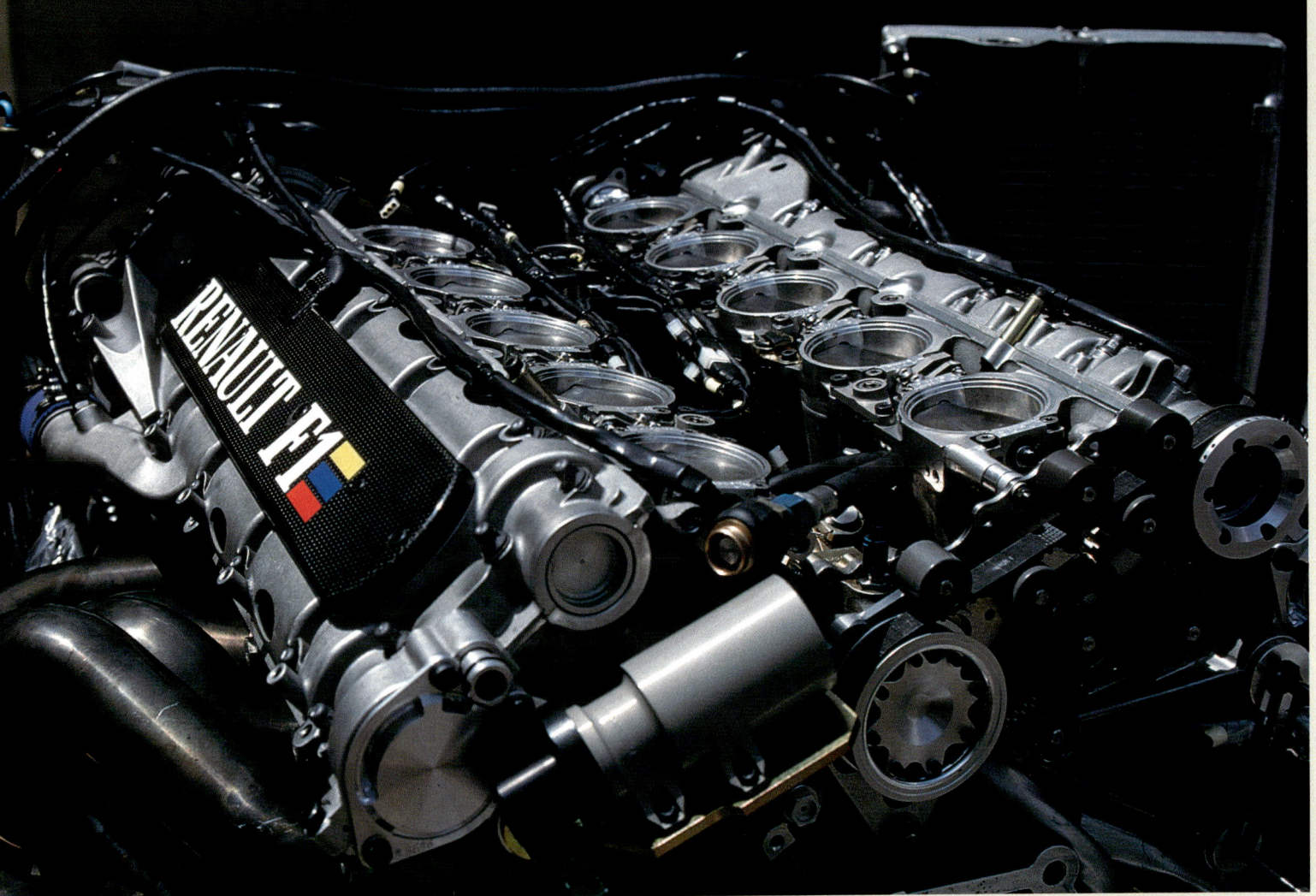

FROM TRACK TO ROAD

For Goodyear, Formula 1 is the experience, the most modern enthusiasm of engineers gua

The Goodyear Eagle F 1 road tyre is a direct result of Goodyear's racing rain-tyre technology

ADVERTISEMENT FEATURE

:trictest test laboratory. Many years of
echnology and the never-flagging
antees success.

GOODYEAR'S CONTINUING commitment to Grand Prix motor racing as a technical proving ground for its future road car products received yet another ringing endorsement in 1995 when the new Goodyear Eagle F1 road tyre made its premier at the Geneva Motor Show.

Its design innovations are derived from the company's 30 year involvement with Formula 1 Grand Prix tyres and confirmed Goodyear's place on pole position in the high performance market.

Goodyear's continuing conviction that the technical knowledge derived from participating in Formula 1 produces a substantial contribution to the quality and performance levels of the latest generation of high performance tyres is dramatically illustrated by the Goodyear Eagle F1 road tyre.

> There is no doubt that Goodyear's engineering expertise and innovation will continue in the foreseeable future

Unlike racing drivers, the everyday motorist cannot make pit stops to change tyres when the weather changes. Passenger car tyres have to deal with all road conditions and the new Eagle F1 road tyre, developed at Goodyear's Technical Centre at Luxembourg, illustrates the graphic benefits for road car users when the lessons of the track are transferred direct to the streets.

Pierre Kummer, the company's manager of passenger tyre development based at Luxembourg, explains: "Much of what we learn with race tyres in terms of handling, cornering and overall response, we can transfer to the design of tyres that operate at lower speeds and in a less demanding environment.

"For us, motor sport is the strictest test laboratory. Only many years of experience, the most modern technology and the never-flagging enthusiasm of our engineers and researchers guarantees success."

Leo Mehl, Goodyear's General Manager of Worldwide Racing, confirmed the new tyre's racing heritage. "There is no doubt that our involvement in Formula 1 and the lessons we learn gives us the extra edge in designing road tyres.

"These new tyres have a great affinity with the Aquatro wet weather Grand Prix tyres we supply to the Formula 1 teams, such as Ferrari, McLaren, Williams and Benetton."

The design includes a striking directional tread with natural flow grooves giving improved water evacuation. This offers superior resistance to aquaplaning and better safety. A new silica-based tread compound provides exceptionally high levels of grip in wet and dry conditions.

The multi-radius tread profile gives the Eagle F1 an even pressure distribution across the entire footprint. This leads

ADVERTISEMENT FEATURE

to longer tyre life and better handling throughout the speed spectrum.

"The rewards of Grand Prix racing are pretty well split 50/50 between advertising benefits and the technical feedback," explained Leo Mehl. "Of course, we sometimes encounter an element of opposition, 'all we're doing is beating ourselves', but this attitude is only valid if you've stopped developing the product. It might be right if you are no longer contributing, so we've learned that we had better not stop contributing."

Milestones in Goodyear's Grand Prix history are many and varied. Niki Lauda won the company's 100th victory at the wheel of a Ferrari in the 1977 German Grand Prix at Hockenheim. The 200th came up at Adelaide in 1987 when Gerhard Berger emerged victorious, again at the wheel of a Ferrari.

In 1979 the manufacture of all racing tyres reverted to Akron, but Wolverhampton remained the home of the Formula 1 service division, and there was a major hiccup in Goodyear's Formula 1 involvement at the end of 1980 when the company withdrew for six months at the height of a political battle within the sport.

By 1983, Akron was ready with its first radial F1 tyre, since when the company has consistently met the challenge of adapting its products to suit changes in chassis regulations and the varying requirements of engine power.

"In that respect, there is no doubt that Formula 1 will continue to stretch our engineering expertise and innovation in the foreseeable future," confirms Leo Mehl. "Which is, of course, what Goodyear's involvement in Grand Prix racing has traditionally been all about."

By the end of the 1994 season, Goodyear had surpassed the 300 Grand Prix win barrier, proving that, pushing tyre technology to the outer limit of its performance, motor racing continues to supply the company with a consistently demanding and reliable test ground.

If a component or material can be seen to function depend-

Benetton tyre man inspecting the team's Goodyear tyre allocation for a typical race weekend

Goodyear's new road tyre has great affinity with the wet weather F1 tyre used by all the teams

ADVERTISEMENT FEATURE

Goodyear support is calculated in over 20,000 tyres used in an average season

ably in a highly-stressed racing environment, it can generally be assumed that it will display a significant safety margin when dealing with the normal operating conditions encountered on the road.

Goodyear's matchless success in Formula 1 has not only trained engineers and technicians in the disciplines required for long-term success in the racing world, where deadlines are tight and unyielding, but has also resulted in valuable technical transfer into road car tyre manufacturing. This has not only re-

sulted in a range of superior products, but also ensures that the company is pushing the outer edges of the performance envelope when it comes to evaluating and assessing new developments for the future.

It is through this on-going experience in the demanding and challenging technical crucible of Grand Prix racing, where the Goodyear Eagle Formula 1 tyres have powered a long list of drivers to Grand Prix victories, that the lessons have been absorbed which contributed to the successful development of the latest Goodyear Eagle F1 road tyre.

This state-of-the-art product, developed for Europe's most prestigious vehicle manufacturers, decisively advances automotive progress by significantly improving the resistance to aquaplaning.

Yet the practical benefits of these high-speed endeavours on some of the most demanding racing circuits in the world continue to be available to the private motorist through tyres such as the Goodyear Eagle F1 road tyre, again underlining the matchless benefits which accrue from Goodyear's worldwide commitment to this most challenging of sports.

Our fastest moving parts.

The piston in the Ford Zetec-R Formula One engine accelerates from 0-100 miles per hour in just one thousandth of a second.

Moving quickly on, the turbo in the Ford Cosworth engine which won the 1995 Indy 500 and PPG Indy Car Championship spins at 80,000rpm.

And yet, from 1996, Cosworth's fastest moving parts will be castings. Up to one million castings per year will be produced using the patented Cosworth process at a new, highly automated UK foundry in which £25 million has been invested.

Phase A alone has already produced full order books to supply high quality, precision engine castings to companies such as General Motors, Jaguar, Ford and many other manufacturers around the world.

This is all part of our fast moving success in the field of automotive technology.

CASTINGS • ENGINEERING • MANUFACTURING • RACING

St James Mill Rd   Northampton NN5 5JJ   United Kingdom   Tel: + 44 1604 732100   Fax: + 44 1604 732113

Cosworth is a registered trade mark belonging to Vickers PLC.

Vickers
A division of Vickers PLC

FIA FORMULA ONE WORLD CHAMPIONSHIP 1995

TOP TEN DRIVERS

Chosen by the Editor, taking into account their racing performances and the equipment at their disposal

Photographs by Matthias Schneider

top ten

michael schumacher 1

- *michael schumacher*
- *Date of birth: 3 January 1969*
- *Team: Mild Seven Benetton Renault*
- *Grand Prix starts in 1995: 17*
- *World Championship placing: 1st*
- *Wins: 9; Poles: 4; Points: 102*

If the cynics had even a sliver of doubt about Michael Schumacher's status within the Formula 1 community, such reservations were utterly and completely expunged by the end of the 1995 World Championship season. Michael now stands poised to assume the mantle so tragically discarded by the late Ayrton Senna. Precisely at which point history will judge that the torch has finally passed between the two generations is as yet unclear. But it is only a matter of when rather than if.

Schumacher this year underlined that he possesses all the qualities to gain admittance to that select élite of all-time greats: blinding speed, overwhelming commitment, ruthlessness and an almost ethereal second sense when it comes to racecraft. The season began on a difficult note for the German driver, but his nerve never wavered. The controversy which surrounded his approach to the drivers' weigh-in at São Paulo, followed by the complex issues involved in his initial disqualification from the Brazilian GP win, conspired to place him in an unfortunate light.

In Argentina, Schumacher finished a distant third after being troubled by tyre performance inconsistencies, and he followed this up by crashing heavily while in the lead at Imola. With three races gone, Damon Hill led the championship, having scored two wins in the Williams FW17. Yet Schumacher reversed this trend in brilliant style, dominating the Spanish GP at Barcelona to open a run of success which would see him notch up a total of nine wins out of the season's seventeen races.

The fact that the German *wunderkind* qualified on pole position only four times did not seem to matter in the slightest. Watching Schumacher and the Benetton team apply all their tactical acuity to the business of turning the tables on their rivals at Williams – the occupants of pole position on no fewer than twelve occasions – was rather like witnessing F1's equivalent of synchronised swimming. It wasn't quite telepathy, but it looked pretty close.

Schumacher brought the title within his grasp with a truly brilliant victory in the Grand Prix of Europe, an occasion which may fall into focus as the day on which he confirmed his move to another level above his peers. If there was a downside to his on-track behaviour, it was a Senna-like inclination to push driving etiquette to the outer limits of acceptability. The defensive tactics he employed against Hill at Spa during his superb drive to victory from 16th place on the grid were the most vivid example of this.

top ten

damon hill

2

Hill's critics will doubtless say that this rating deeply flatters the 35-year-old British driver's 1995 performances. They will argue that he all too frequently squandered the performance of the Williams FW17 – widely acclaimed as the best car of the season – and really should have won the World Championship. But these are too frequently the critics who hail Schumacher as a God-like figure in a class of his own.

Well, the critics can't have it both ways; it is no disgrace to be second in such a situation, and Damon Hill was the only driver who consistently carried the fight to the Benetton ace. Without him, there would have been precious little in the way of serious motor racing in 1995. Hill started the season with high hopes, but after dominating the opening stages of the Brazilian GP found himself spinning off when the left-rear suspension broke. It set the tone for a run of technical failures which were as much responsible for blunting his title challenge as his own driving errors.

Damon's victories at Buenos Aires and Imola served to remind everybody that there is a definite knack to keeping out of trouble and winning races. Thereafter, a bad run of technical unreliability and poor pit strategy on the part of the Williams team took the edge off his performances. Then came the collision with Schumacher at Silverstone and the second-lap spin at Hockenheim: big errors, by any standards. He atoned with a fine win at Budapest, where the high-downforce circuit requirements suited the Williams just fine, but was beaten hollow by Michael at Spa and then got bogged down in a terrible trough with poor performances through to Suzuka.

Watching Hill struggle with himself and his team was a rather uncomfortable sight. It was not helped by his own rather plaintive voice requesting that the FIA clarify what is and is not permissible in terms of driving tactics – a totally reasonable inquiry, bearing in mind the inconsistencies all too frequently displayed by race stewards throughout the season. Inevitably, though, it cast Damon in the light of a whinger.

At the end of the season he finally put the wheels back on his personal reputation with an apparently straightforward victory in the Australian GP which, in reality, was made psychologically more difficult by the total absence of pressure in the second half of the race. It was a popular success, for Hill is a pleasant man who has shown himself to be more anxious about and constrained by rules of conduct on the circuit than many of his contemporaries. This should not necessarily be construed as a weakness.

- **damon hill**
- Date of birth: 17 September 1960
- Team: Rothmans Williams Renault
- Grand Prix starts in 1995: 17
- World Championship placing: 2nd
- Wins: 4; Poles: 7; Points: 69

top ten

3 heinz-harald frentzen

Heinz-Harald Frentzen proved in 1995 that he may be the only driver with the same degree of basic natural flair as his compatriot and former Mercedes Group C colleague Michael Schumacher. So how can one reach such a conclusion, apart from the obvious reality that he has done an extremely consistent job in what, quite frankly, is a mid-ranging racing car, the Sauber C14?

Like Schumacher, Frentzen has this year exerted a significant advantage over his teammate, whether Karl Wendlinger or the much-touted and, as things transpired, highly disappointing Jean-Christophe Boullion. Like Schumacher, with similar equipment he has usually been light years ahead of his team-mate. Not for Sauber the situation which existed at Ferrari or Williams where the two drivers were very evenly matched in terms of qualifying and potential race performances.

Although Ford's Zetec-R V8 in 3-litre form perhaps did not have the performance Cosworth hoped for (witness their decision to make their first V10 for 1996), Frentzen never qualified lower than 14th all season and from Hungary onwards was never out of the top ten grid positions after an uprated version of the engine was made available. His run to fourth place at Spa, where he overtook Blundell's McLaren in the closing stages, and his steady drive to gain his first podium position with third place at Monza, were evidence of his maturing talent and consistency.

Fifth in Portugal was his best qualifying position of the season, but the last four races yielded no more points, although he climbed as high as second behind Hill's Williams at Adelaide before the gearbox broke.

Frentzen's name had been linked with several rival teams before Ford put their financial shoulder to the wheel and helped secure his place at Sauber for 1996. Yet there are some who already believe that Heinz-Harald has outgrown his position with the Swiss-based team and is now more than ready to take a front-running seat with one of the established 'top three'. He has a delicate touch, displays consistency and tactical awareness, and is steadily smoothing out the rough edges of his driving style which saw him involved in several silly incidents during his first year with Sauber in 1994.

Although Frentzen remains with the team next season, the real question is just who secures his services for 1997. Schumacher must be fervently hoping that it is not Williams, Benetton or even McLaren, for the quiet and unobtrusive 28-year-old from Moenchengladbach is certainly made of the Right Stuff.

- *heinz-harald frentzen*
- *Date of birth: 18 May 1967*
- *Team: Red Bull Sauber Ford*
- *Grand Prix starts in 1995: 17*
- *World Championship placing: 9th*
- *Wins: 0; Poles: 0; Points: 15*

top ten

gerhard berger

4

- *gerhard berger*
- *Date of birth: 27 August 1959*
- *Team: Scuderia Ferrari*
- *Grand Prix starts in 1995: 17*
- *World Championship placing: 6th*
- *Wins: 0; Poles: 1; Points: 31*

If there was an injustice in 1995 it was that Gerhard Berger failed to win a single Grand Prix. This was cruelly ironic as, fleetingly, in the aftermath of the Interlagos race, the Austrian believed that he had inherited his first win of the season as a result of the Benetton/Williams fuel specification debacle. But Schumacher was reinstated on appeal and Gerhard pushed back to his original third place.

The Ferrari team is a traditionally volatile environment, but Berger worked well with Jean Todt to smooth out the emotional peaks and troughs which all too frequently seem to be an integral part of Maranello's *modus operandi*. He out-qualified Alesi twelve times to five – perhaps surprising, bearing in mind the perception of the Frenchman as one of F1's absolute fastest performers – and might well have triumphed in the San Marino GP had he not stalled his 412T2 at a pit stop when he was running ahead of eventual winner Damon Hill.

At Monaco, Gerhard could have been forgiven for being extremely annoyed with the team's practice strategy. The Ferrari was a serious front row contender, as emphasised by Alesi's first-session provisional pole, but when Jean hit trouble in second qualifying and was debarred by the rules from any further use of his race car, Gerhard had to rush through his own runs to permit the Frenchman a completely abortive late-session try in his car. The net result was that neither Ferrari made the front row and, after Alesi triggered a first-corner accident at the start of the race, Gerhard had to take a spare car fitted with a lower-specification engine and finished third. It might well have been a lot better.

Disappointments followed thick and fast. He ran out of fuel on the in lap prior to his sole refuelling stop at Montreal, then rammed Brundle's Ligier off the track almost within sight of the chequered flag. At Magny-Cours he had problems with his refuelling rig, a loose wheel caused him to retire an otherwise healthy car at Silverstone and any chance of victory at Monza was wiped out when the wing-mounted camera fell off Alesi's sister car and broke one of his Ferrari's steering arms. A handful of third places hardly amounted to much consolation, particularly as his late-season races were blighted by engine sensor problems and his final outing for Maranello ended in the mother-and-father of blow-ups at Adelaide.

Throughout all this mayhem, Berger remained philosophical, steady and a team player of the first rank. In his heart of hearts he wanted to stay at Ferrari in 1996, as much as anything to reap the benefit of all his work since rejoining the team in 1993. But he had no intention of being cast in the supporting role to Michael Schumacher, so when the chance of a Benetton-Renault drive came his way, he grasped it with both hands. Few would dispute that Maranello is the loser.

top ten

jean alesi

5

Dynamic, inspired, unpredictable, volatile, brilliant and immature: Jean Alesi's season yet again saw him display the full range of his emotions, although he at last managed to score his first Grand Prix victory when Schumacher's Benetton faltered briefly in Montreal. For the historians, it couldn't have been better: Ferrari number 27 winning at the Circuit Gilles Villeneuve in the French Canadian's spiritual home. Yet the sum total of the season amounted to less by far than Alesi had been hoping for.

One of Jean's best drives came in the second race of the season in Buenos Aires, where he kept Damon Hill on his toes right to the end of the Argentine GP, finishing a strong second. On the strength of that performance, you felt that perhaps he just might, after all, be in a position to challenge for the championship. An outsider, perhaps, but a contender nevertheless. He followed that up with second at Imola, retired in Spain and Monaco and won in Montreal. Thereafter, his season progressively fell apart, the lowest point being at Monza where a wheel bearing failure deprived him of possible victory with only eight laps to the chequered flag. It was the story of his life.

At Estoril, he lost his temper with Jean Todt and told an Italian TV interviewer how he had been screwed by Maranello's Sporting Director. This landed him with a huge fine from the team, but his morale was clearly not dented, as witness a brilliant run on slicks at the Nürburgring which almost earned him a famous victory in the Grand Prix of Europe. He was jumped by Schumacher only three laps from the end and many within his team accused him of going to sleep in the closing stages of the race.

Ferrari had a truly dismal time in the last three races of the season and Alesi rounded off the year by driving Schumacher off the road at Adelaide in what must rank as one of the most blatantly deliberate displays of bad driving seen all season. Extraordinarily, the stewards did not even make a move to impose any penalty for what seemed nothing more than an astoundingly petulant manoeuvre.

Next year Alesi moves to Benetton where he will again be paired with Gerhard Berger. The French driver's fans believe that he is now poised on the verge of a World Championship challenge. Yet the adjectives used in the first sentence of this profile could well prevent him from realising that great ambition.

- *jean alesi*
- *Date of birth: 11 June 1964*
- *Team: Scuderia Ferrari*
- *Grand Prix starts in 1995: 17*
- *World Championship placing: 5th*
- *Wins: 1; Poles: 0; Points: 42*

top ten

david coulthard

6

- *david coulthard*
- *Date of birth: 27 March 1971*
- *Team: Rothmans Williams Renault*
- *Grand Prix starts in 1995: 17*
- *World Championship placing: 3rd*
- *Wins: 1; Poles: 5; Points: 49*

Although David Coulthard is rightly regarded as one of the most promising new talents to emerge in recent years, the stark facts of the matter are that this pleasant Scot made too many mistakes in his first full season of Grand Prix racing – and increasingly displayed a worrying tendency to accept responsibility for precious few of them.

It is all very well to defend Coulthard by pointing to his team-mate's catalogue of errors, but Hill generally made his mistakes while in the thick of the front-running action. Coulthard's gaffes included spinning on the parade lap at Monza, his out lap at the Nürburgring and the second lap of the race at Montreal and, finally, clouting the pit wall at Adelaide while leading. On each occasion David convincingly rationalised his mistakes with a lucid fluency which sometimes took scant account of the obvious fact that he was the man behind the wheel at the time.

That said, his performance in the Portuguese GP at Estoril demonstrated just what a high level of potential Coulthard will be taking to the McLaren-Mercedes team in 1996. He is a genuine front-runner with absolutely the correct temperament, both in and out of the car, to establish himself as a formidably successful driver.

It was unfortunate that the first half of Coulthard's season was undermined not only by Williams's technical unreliability, but also by the lingering effects of tonsillitis which were not resolved until he went into hospital for an operation immediately after the Canadian GP.

Coulthard should have won the British GP, but a fault with the electronic speed limiting device on his car resulted in his incurring a stop-go penalty for exceeding the pit lane limit, a delay which dropped him to third.

With a succession of retirements and problems behind him, it was perhaps understandable that he took a slightly prudent approach to the German GP at Hockenheim, preferring a strategic second place to Schumacher to risking going off the road. This was something of a turning point in his relationship with the Williams team management, which concluded – wrongly – that he was not quick enough. Not that this really mattered, of course, because it seems that McLaren had an option on David's services in 1996 dating back to before Christmas 1994. His switch to the red and whites was duly confirmed at the Nürburgring.

A single win was certainly much less than Coulthard's talent deserved in 1995, but he did enough to underline that he has a flair which should duly earn him considerable success in the future. His self-assurance sometimes made it difficult to believe that this was only his first full season of F1 competition.

top ten

johnny herbert

7

Keeping out of trouble and not making many mistakes were the hallmarks of Johnny Herbert's season, even though it was sometimes difficult to reconcile the fact that this was the Englishman's best F1 year by far with the firmly defined subordinate role he found himself playing as Michael Schumacher's number two in the Benetton-Renault squad.

After starting the season with a retirement in Brazil, Herbert did not fail to finish until Montreal, where Häkkinen pushed him off on the opening lap. He then suffered a similar fate at Alesi's hands early in the French GP, after which he ran all the way through to Adelaide with only two finishes outside the top six. Had he survived to finish second in Australia, he would have leap-frogged ahead of Coulthard to take third place in the Drivers' World Championship. Some say that would have been no more than he deserved.

Of course, the high spot of Herbert's season came with his two wins at Silverstone and Monza, both achieved in the wake of Hill/Schumacher tangles. He was obviously delighted to have triumphed in front of his home crowd at Silverstone and the glee with which Jean Alesi and David Coulthard, the second- and third-placed finishers, raised the pint-sized Essex lad on their shoulders during the podium ceremony served as an indication of just how popular Herbert is among his peers.

However, Johnny rightly regarded Monza as a more convincing performance. He was much closer to the front-running pace on this occasion and felt, overall, he drove a better, more rounded race and benefited from a well-judged refuelling strategy to move ahead of Häkkinen's McLaren in the closing stages. In the second half of the season, his consistency and reliability when it came to scoring regular top-six finishes were a key factor in Benetton's first-ever victory in the constructors' championship.

Despite this, it was difficult for Johnny to feel anything other than a second-class citizen within the Benetton team environment. After a particularly disappointing performance at Spa, he went public with his complaints and received a very severe put-down from Schumacher, who, in effect, accused him of sour grapes.

Only later, when being interviewed for the *Autocourse* team profile, did Benetton Technical Director Ross Brawn acknowledge, after all, that Johnny perhaps did not get all the attention that he deserved. Yet the bottom line is that the man who won two Grands Prix in 1995 is struggling to get a drive next season. Perhaps Herbert's chirpy character gives the impression that he is not always as serious as he needs to be in F1's front line.

- *johnny herbert*
- *Date of birth: 25 June 1964*
- *Team: Mild Seven Benetton Renault*
- *Grand Prix starts in 1995: 17*
- *World Championship placing: 4th*
- *Wins: 2; Poles: 0; Points: 45*

top ten

mika häkkinen

8

- *mika häkkinen*
- *Date of birth: 28 September 1968*
- *Team: Marlboro McLaren Mercedes*
- *Grand Prix starts in 1995: 15*
- *World Championship placing: 7th*
- *Wins: 0; Poles: 0; Points: 17*

Mika Häkkinen's season began on a highly promising note, the McLaren driver all but challenging the two Williamses and Schumacher's Benetton in the early stages of the Brazilian GP, and ended in near-disaster with that serious accident in first qualifying at Adelaide. In between, the popular Finn had a roller-coaster year highlighted by two second places while at the same time punctuated by several silly incidents which were unacceptable for a driver of his experience.

Many F1 insiders firmly believe that Mika is the only driver today who has the sheer speed to take on Michael Schumacher in a straight fight on equal footing. In his third season with McLaren, he continued to display an unwavering loyalty to his employers and enjoys the total confidence of team chief Ron Dennis.

Mika started the season superbly to finish a strong fourth at Interlagos, but chopped across Eddie Irvine's Jordan and collected a punctured rear tyre which sent him straight into the gravel trap in the second race at Buenos Aires. This was followed by a fine fifth at Imola – where he was stupendously quick on slicks in the damp early stages – but he retired in Spain and Monaco and blotted his copybook in a big way in Montreal with an absurdly over-ambitious first-lap overtaking manoeuvre which eliminated both Herbert and himself from the contest.

A second-lap spin at Spa was equally unfortunate, but this was followed up by a very respectable second at Monza – the best result thus far for the McLaren-Mercedes partnership. Along with the rest of the team, Mika was understandably frustrated by the drop-off in form displayed at both Estoril and the Nürburgring, but he bounced back from an appendix operation which caused him to miss the Pacific GP to post a terrific second place to Schumacher's Benetton at Suzuka, where the MP4/10B really worked well.

Yet none of this could conceal the basic disappointment that McLaren had not yet managed to furnish Mika with a car capable of carrying the Finn to his first Grand Prix victory. Häkkinen is fundamentally one of those dazzling seat-of-the-pants talents which remind one of Ronnie Peterson, Gilles Villeneuve or, indeed, his own manager Keke Rosberg. His performances in 1995 again signalled that the likeable Mika has the speed and ability to win races, but whether he can be sufficiently consistent to win a World Championship is another matter altogether.

top ten

9 eddie irvine

This gregarious Ulsterman hit the headlines more for his recruitment by Ferrari for 1996 than for any great feats on the circuit with his Jordan-Peugeot. In fact, the most one could really say about him was that he generally looked more convincing than Rubens Barrichello, an achievement which, in itself, looked progressively less remarkable as the season unfolded.

Yet there is a spark about Irvine's character which suggests that his best days are yet to come. Only five times did he fail to out-qualify his Brazilian team-mate, whose credentials amassed in the junior formulae were ostensibly more convincing. Irvine's best result came in Montreal, where the Jordans outlasted many of their fastest rivals, but to Eddie's credit he was not unduly impressed. He rightly pointed out that they had only made it to the finish by dint of pussyfooting along in an attempt to eke out their fuel load to the finish. Privately he was forming the opinion that the Silverstone-based team was not making the sort of progress it should have been and, by the middle of the year, wanted out on almost any basis.

Not that Irvine was without his own performance shortcomings. According to his team he could lose interest midway through a race if there was little hope of a decent result, yet his drives to fourth place at Suzuka and sixth at the Nürburgring could be regarded as barometers of his real potential. His laid-back attitude was maddening to some, yet Irvine shrugged aside misfortune and certainly never bore a grudge towards any rivals who may or may not have short-changed him on the circuit.

The cheerful insouciance with which he acknowledged his promotion to the Ferrari ranks was in some way tempered by the knowledge that he would be playing second fiddle to Michael Schumacher, and the manner in which he dealt with the media at the Nürburgring when it was announced that he was switching to the Maranello team was enough to make seasoned Ferrari-watchers shudder.

Irvine has a lot to learn about the politics involved in being an employee of the Prancing Horse. Yet it may be that by closing his mind to that aspect of the job, and simply concentrating on the racing, he will breeze through the experience without any trouble. Maybe.

- *eddie irvine*
- *Date of birth: 10 November 1965*
- *Team: Total Jordan Peugeot*
- *Grand Prix starts in 1995: 17*
- *World Championship placing: 12th*
- *Wins: 0; Poles: 0; Points: 10*

top ten

mark blundell

10

- *mark blundell*
- *Date of birth: 8 April 1966*
- *Team: Marlboro McLaren Mercedes*
- *Grand Prix starts in 1995: 15*
- *World Championship placing: 10th*
- *Wins: 0; Poles: 0; Points: 13*

This popular Englishman may not have been as quick as his team-mate Mika Häkkinen, but the hard facts show that he scored only four fewer championship points than the highly rated Finn. It is also arguable that without his contribution, McLaren-Mercedes might well have been seventh in the constructors' championship rather than fourth.

Blundell started the year as McLaren's test driver, but was immediately pressed into action for the first two races of the season after it was found necessary to build an enlarged MP4/10B monocoque to accommodate prestige-signing Nigel Mansell. He then missed the San Marino and Spanish races, only to be reappointed to the team after Mansell's decision to absent himself from the remainder of the season. He celebrated his return with an excellent fifth place through the streets of the Principality, but continued to be employed only on a race-to-race basis, which was understandably unsettling for his confidence level.

Mark took fifth places at Silverstone and Spa, and fourth at Monza and Adelaide, but possibly his best race of all came at Suzuka, where he qualified 24th and last after a huge accident in the Saturday free practice session. Despite feeling bruised and shaken, he drove steadily through the field to finish seventh, less than two seconds behind Mika Salo's sixth-placed Tyrrell at the chequered flag.

Blundell was resilient and undemanding, fitting neatly into the McLaren camp and proving enormously popular with the mechanics and engineers, who found him straightforward and willing in his approach. It was unfortunate that his final race with the team was highlighted by his balking of Heinz-Harald Frentzen's Sauber when the Ford-engined car was poised to lap him, an episode which lasted for three laps and attracted a vigorous response from the German driver once he finally pulled level with the McLaren.

Nevertheless, to post a top-six finish on the weekend of Häkkinen's terrible practice accident was as good a way as any to round off his association with the McLaren team. Blundell deserves to stay in F1, even if he is not an obvious winner, and one must hope that his unfortunate treatment of Frentzen does not compromise his prospects of joining the Sauber ranks in 1996.

JUAN MANUEL FANGIO

FANGIO

A personal tribute by Denis Jenkinson

Left: Denis Jenkinson and Juan Manuel Fangio share a solemn moment at the tomb of the legendary Italian driver, Tazio Nuvolari, in 1955.

Right: Fangio offers a few words of fatherly advice to former Ferrari team-mate Peter Collins during the 1957 British Grand Prix meeting at Aintree.

I first saw Juan Manuel Fangio race in 1949 when he won the Pau Grand Prix on the street circuit round the Basco-Bearnais city in south-west France, within sight of the Pyrenean mountains. I had gone to Pau not to see a future five-times World Champion, but to race a motor cycle. The Grand Prix was traditionally held on Easter Monday, with motor cycle racing the day before. We practised on Saturday morning and the Grand Prix cars practised in the afternoon, so naturally I stayed behind to watch.

Fangio did not disappoint, for he was known as a natural winner before he left Argentina, being champion in that country's national races with home-made specials and a winner of marathon stock car events in which he displayed remarkable stamina and endurance. More important was the impression he made on good European Grand Prix drivers of the time when they went out to the winter races in South America. They returned to Europe with the simple words: 'he is good, a future champion.'

At first, Fangio's driving style was not very good to watch. Though it had all the speed and panache of Raymond Sommer, it did not have the elegance of Ascari or Farina, or the delicacy and finesse of Maurice Trintignant or Prince Bira. Nevertheless he won his first Grand Prix in Europe, with a Maserati at San Remo, his second at Pau and his third at Perpignan. He then changed to a Gordini and won at Marseilles, followed by a victory at Monza with a Ferrari before completing his European tour with another win at Albi, by now back in a Maserati.

Fangio came to Europe with a pretty good CV, but went back to Argentina about halfway through the '49 season with a much better one!

At the end of that season, I wrote in one of my motor racing books, 'to those of us who have been fortunate enough to see this Fangio in action, the fact that he scored a hat-trick with his first three appearances in European racing does not come as such a surprise, for he really "motor races" with his Maserati in a manner that is a joy to behold.'

An incident in the Pau Grand Prix which really endeared 'this Fangio' to me occurred near the end of the race. Like all the Maseratis, his car was losing oil, so he stopped at the pits to replenish his tank as you were allowed to do in those days. He was in the lead at the time, and the rules in France decreed that engines must be stopped when at the pits and could only be restarted by a portable electric starter or by the starting handle. In other words, push-starting was forbidden.

While oil was poured in, Fangio sat motionless in the cockpit. Then a mechanic inserted a handle and wound away, but the engine would not start. Another mechanic tried, but still nothing. Then they both wound away to no avail.

Fangio was still sitting there calmly, even though his lead was being frittered away. Without a word, he climbed out, went to the front of the car, quietly took the handle from the mechanics, inserted it and gave a determined and sharp pull-up. The engine burst into life. He was back into the cockpit and gone, without losing his lead, before anyone fully realised what had happened. Had I not been standing in the pit lane by the car, I would never have believed it.

Some years later, I asked him about that incident. He explained that, knowing racing engines in general and Maserati engines in particular, he realised that the engine was not responding to being turned over at a constant speed. The magneto was not giving its best spark, so by jerking the engine over compression the magneto gave the effect of an impulse starter. He smiled when he told me this and said, 'It is a good thing for a racing driver to "know" his engine.'

He did not always win with a sick car, but he would invariably finish, and that indomitable quality which never allowed him to give up was Fangio The Man. Another trait I admired in him at that Pau Grand Prix incident was his ability to keep calm under the greatest strain. He was to display it throughout his life, both inside and outside motor racing. No wonder he was accepted worldwide in later years as an unofficial ambassador for his country.

His greatest demonstration of that ability to keep calm in times of crisis was during the 1951 Belgian Grand Prix on the very fast Spa-Francorchamps circuit when he was driving for the Alfa Romeo team. Two stops for fuel and tyres were planned and, after setting a new lap record at over 120 mph, Fangio made his first stop while in the lead.

Drama then intervened when the left-rear wheel would not come off its hub. It was fourteen and a half minutes before Fangio rejoined the race, during which time the Alfa mechanics had to remove the entire wheel, hub and rear brake from the driveshaft, take the assembly into the pits, remove the tyre from the rim, fit and inflate a new tyre, and then fit the whole assembly back on the rear axle.

Throughout this, Fangio stood by, watching but not saying a word to anyone and displaying no outward emotion, cleaning his goggles, cleaning the windscreen of the car and, above all, not making a fuss like some well-known drivers of that and even the current era.

When he rejoined, all hope of regaining the lead was gone, but he was determined to finish the race and protect his lap record if need be, thus preserving the World Championship point earned by fastest lap in those days. His big handicap now was that he could not make his second scheduled tyre change and had to preserve the rubber on his car for the rest of the race as well as going fast enough to be classified as a finisher. He finished ninth and retained his lap record.

In later life, when telling us about this incident, he said, 'That day people said how calm I was in the pits as I saw my chances of a win slipping away. It was not me they were slipping away from. I had done everything as it should be done, and made no mistakes. I believe that someone might well get nervous, or at least uneasy, when he has made a mistake. That was not the case with me. I was calm, even though Farina was at the top of the championship table. The second race of the championship was soon to come.'

I watched that drama from the grandstand opposite the Alfa pits, not on a television screen, and joined in the applause and cheers from the spectators as this remarkable man from the Argentine went back into the race.

During his ten years of racing in Europe, Fangio seemed to create at least one magical legend each year. Many racing drivers would have been content to win one World Championship in that time, but Fangio won five. He entered motor races to win; if you won more than anyone else, you were justified in being called World Champion. He said, 'If you are World Champion, it is up to you to always be the best and to show that you are champion.'

The interesting thing about Fangio during that time was the way in which he would return to Argentina as soon as the Grand Prix season was finished. No world publicity tours, no hype and bullshit in those days. If you did not know who the World Champion racing driver was, then you were not paying attention to your sport. He was born in Balcarce in 1911 and Argentina was his home; when he finished his season of work, he went home. He had no desire to live in Monte Carlo, or in a tax haven, or even in a beautiful part of Europe. It was always 'better in Balcarce, where my friends and family are'.

In 1955, when Stirling Moss joined Fangio in the Mercedes-Benz team, he took me along to help with the sports car element of his contract and I had the opportunity of becoming part of the team, and getting to know Fangio from the inside looking out rather than simply as a spectator looking in.

During practice for the Mille Miglia, we were in a Mercedes-Benz 300SL Gullwing coupé and Fangio caught us up in an SLR open racer and overtook us as we went into the Abruzzi mountains, where speed and power were not that important. Rising to the challenge as any good racing driver would, Stirling tucked in behind and drove on the limit to stay with 'the Old Boy'. That was exciting, but the open car gradually pulled away from us!

On another practice run, Fangio was in his pale blue Mercedes cabriolet touring car and we were in Stirling's 220 saloon. We were going down the Adriatic coast road, in and out of the normal daily traffic, and were astounded by the way Fangio was carving his way through gaps with this big, dignified cabriolet.

After about ten minutes of this, Stirling backed off and said, 'Bugger me – if I try and keep this pace, we'll collect a donkey cart or a truck!' Then he grinned and added, 'Or collect the Old Boy when he bounces back off a rock.' But inwardly we both knew that Fangio would not be doing that.

One night at Modena, as darkness was falling and we had finished for the day, there was a roaring noise outside the hotel so we went out to take a look. There was Fangio in the SLR 'practice car' with only one headlamp working, saying that he was pressing on back to Brescia – 'only three more hours . . .' He had started out that morning and was completing a whole lap of the 1000-mile route without a break, something we never managed.

After he retired, Fangio would often return to Europe on business trips, principally connected with his Mercedes-Benz dealership in Buenos Aires. If it could be combined with a visit to a Grand Prix, he would take the opportunity and arrive at Monza, for example, before Saturday practice, often accompanied by his old sparring partner Froilan Gonzalez. Ten or fifteen years after his last race his presence

28

was magical and *'Fangio!'* was the word that rippled through the crowd and along the pit lane.

He and Gonzalez would greet me cordially, not as a journalist or race reporter, but as a familiar figure they remembered from their European racing days; a figure who always seemed to be at the races and who was still on the scene. I don't think for a moment they knew my name, and Fangio's nearest approach to pronouncing it was 'Gekinson' but he would greet me in the pit lane as 'Barbetta' (the little bearded one) or 'Carozzino' (the crazy man in the racing sidecar) or, more simply, 'Il compagne di Moss'.

In the 1970s I got to know Fangio more intimately when Count Volpi persuaded him to co-operate in making a very serious colour film production of his racing life. The brilliant director Hugh Hudson, maker of the classic Pirelli film *The Tortoise and the Hare* and subsequently *Chariots of Fire*, took the job on with unlimited backing.

In spite of their communication being entirely through an interpreter, Hudson and Fangio got on well, and when they returned to Volpi's studio in Rome, I joined them as Hudson's motor racing adviser – a chance of a lifetime which gave me a wonderful opportunity to get to know Fangio The Man. Fangio The Driver, I had seen for myself already.

My final contact with this man of many parts – always a gentleman by anybody's standards, deep in thinking and perception – was when he published his autobiography in Buenos Aires in 1986 at the age of 75 years. Naturally it was written in Spanish, but when Patrick Stephens Ltd arranged to make an English translation in 1990, I was greatly honoured to be asked to keep an editorial eye on the whole project.

I wrote to Fangio at his home in Balcarce to tell him how honoured I was to be given this job, saying he would probably remember me from the great days when racing cars had their engines in front of the driver. I received a most charming reply, written from his Mercedes-Benz office in Buenos Aires. I quote:

'Dear Jenkinson. I was gratefully surprised when you tell me in your letter you're working to ensure the correct manuscript translation of *Fangio: cuando el hombre es mas que il mito*. I was worried about that, but not more since then.

'Of course I remember you from those "good old times" of front-engined Grand Prix cars. And mostly always I keep you in mind because I've 'Fangio' the book you edited on the talks I had with Hugh Hudson for the film. It is behind me here in this office. In the day before Christmas I wish you and yours the best. Sincerely: (signed) J.M. Fangio'

Note that he addressed me simply as Jenkinson; typical of South American, Spanish and Italian people who only use the family name in friendly relationships. When he was racing, he was merely Fangio – like his contemporaries Ascari, Villoresi, Farina, Behra, Musso, Castellotti et al.

Fangio was Fangio. There was no need to embellish his name. It was powerful enough on its own.

162 GRAND PRIX WINS, 18 WORLD CHAMPIONSHIPS ON SHELL. CONCLUSIVE PROOF NOT ALL FUELS ARE THE SAME.

1953, Alberto Ascari, Ferrari.

1956, Juan Manuel Fangio, Lancia-Ferrari.

1958, Mike Hawthorn, Ferrari.

1968, Graham Hill, Lotus.

1970, Jochen Rindt, Lotus.

1984, Niki Lauda, McLaren.

1989, Alain Prost, McLaren.

1990, Ayrton Senna, McLaren.

1991, Ayrton Senna, McLaren.

SHELL'S SPONSORSHIP OF McLAREN ENDED IN 1994.

MICHAEL SCHUMACHER PROFILE

the class act
by Tony Dodgins

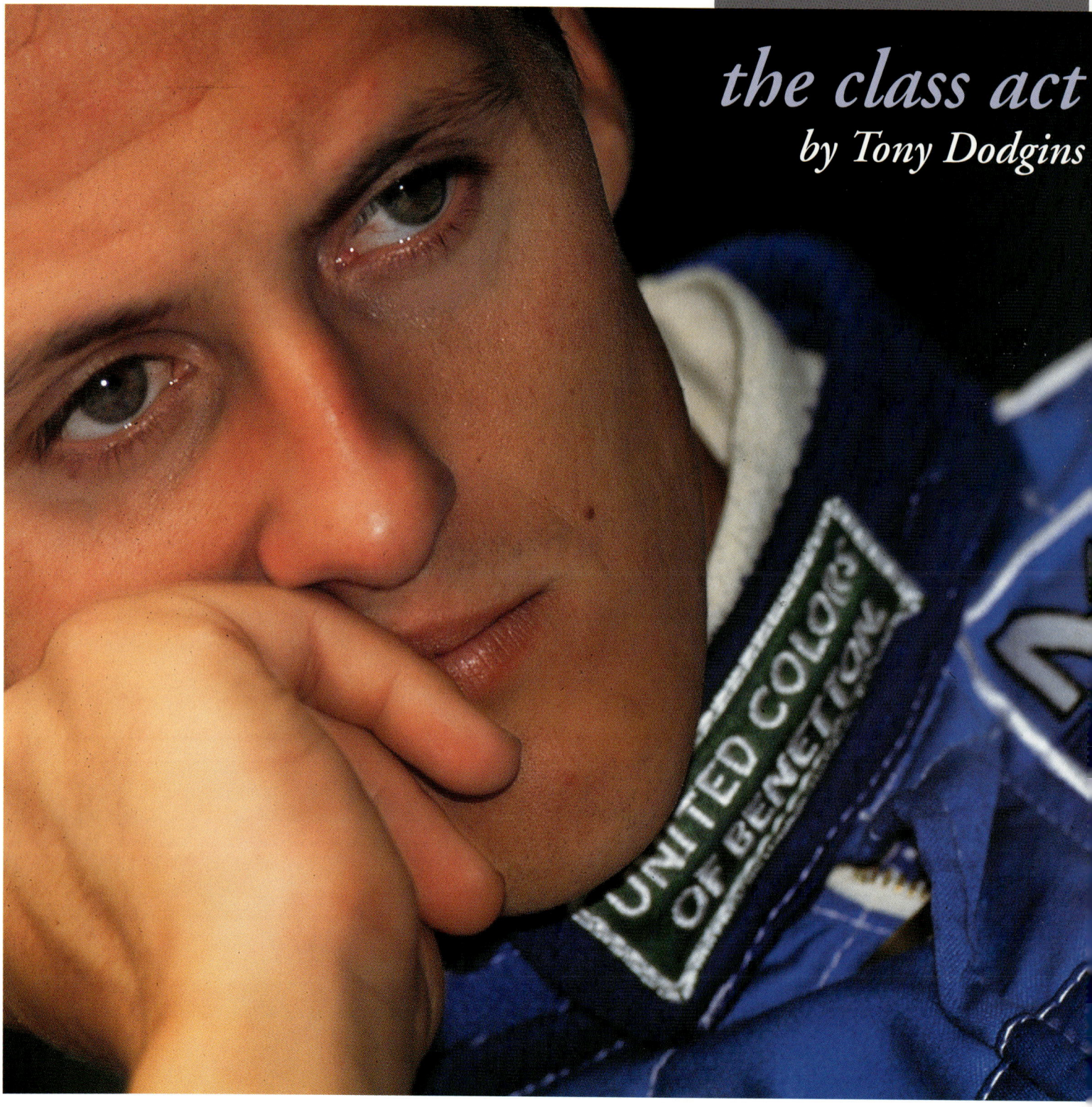

Arrogant or merely confident? Boring or merely focused? An intimidator or merely hard? It depends who you speak to, of course, but on one thing everyone is agreed: Michael Schumacher is in a class of his own.

Schumacher does not like to talk about 1 May 1994. At the time of his death, Ayrton Senna stood alone. But you had the feeling the situation was about to change. Senna was the target for Schumacher and when the great Brazilian was lost, so was Michael's personal measuring stick.

Damon Hill, with respect, is no replacement. Sadly, the popular British perception of Schumacher is fashioned by the endless screeds of pulp fiction served up by the tabloid rags. The Horrible Hun undermining Demon Damon, and like that. The reality? There is no contest. Schumacher has never regarded Hill as remotely in his class and nothing has changed.

Why is Schumacher so good?

'Something I hardly ever get a chance to do is to see these guys out on the circuit actually driving,' Ron Dennis said at Suzuka. 'But if you watched Schumacher in Aida you knew exactly why he was going to be on the front row and why he would win the race. He was mind-blowing. He just changes his style to suit the nature of the circuit, as Ayrton did, to such an extent. If it requires a track to be driven clean he will drive it clean. If it requires the car to be thrown in and put sideways to scrub speed as opposed to hitting the brakes and destabilising it, that's what he does. Monaco, for instance, has to be driven as if you are in a kart, but it takes so much car control. You have to get close to the barriers and use all the road.'

Interesting. Schumacher won his second Monaco Grand Prix in 1995 and because he did it with a single refuelling stop, fingers were pointed at the Williams strategy. But Benetton Technical Director Ross Brawn said: 'Michael is brilliant at Monaco and we were able to do that because he could drive just as quickly as Hill with a heavier fuel load.'

That is the whole point. Undeniably, Benetton has done a superb job this year, but much of their strategic flexibility is possible *because* Schumacher is in the cockpit. It was the same in Aida. Williams was panned again for running Coulthard through on two stops while Schumacher made three and overhauled him. Yet, average out the pair's lap times to the end of the race from the point Coulthard made his first stop and you discover that Schumacher was 0.75s a lap quicker. No amount of strategy can overcome that.

One intriguing aspect of the season has been the superiority of the Williams in qualifying and Schumacher in the race. You might have expected the opposite. Given Schumacher's ability it would be reasonable to expect him to be able to wring one special lap out of a more difficult car and then struggle when he had to do it for 70 laps on Sunday afternoon.

'It's an interesting question,' Brawn says. 'I guess you have to say that qualifying has become a lot less critical. It's nice to be on pole but it's not quite as important as it used to be. You have to balance qualifying against race performance. It's the race that counts and I think Michael has decided that qualifying isn't that important. Mentally he concentrates on the race. If qualifying passes him

by he doesn't seem too bothered, but he's fantastic in a race situation. He is very fit and given a new set of tyres will immediately be quick. It may only be fractions of seconds for a few laps, but he gets the very best out of every situation.' The consummate racer.

On the regular treadmill of travel and work schedules involved in covering Formula 1, it needs more to set the pulses racing than when visiting as an enthusiast, without commitment. Senna used to have the magic spell. You knew to expect something special, as the rule rather than the exception. The same is true of Schumacher. You left the Nürburgring this year with the same feeling you had leaving Donington in 1993. A buzz. Genuine excitement. It reminded you again why you love the sport.

Schumacher admits that his second championship was more satisfying than the first, spoiled as it was by the controversial disqualifications and whisperings of Benetton foul play. The mutterings followed the team into 1995, especially when the super-fit Schumacher weighed in some seven kilos heavier than the year before. Drivers step on the scales in race kit, complete with helmet, at the start of the season. At the end of each race, car and driver must not weigh more than 575 kilos. The heavier the driver, therefore, the lighter the team can run the car. Patrick Head calculated that seven kilos was worth around 14 seconds over 70 laps of Interlagos. In the Benetton back room that weekend was a Schumacher crash helmet marked: 'Take this to Brazil.' A heavier one for the weigh-in perhaps?

Schumacher himself admitted to eating before the weigh-in, drinking copious amounts of mineral water and refraining from the loo. The fuss over the whole thing was hugely out of proportion and Schumacher was vilified. But was it not just a case of team and driver pushing everything to the extreme which, we are repeatedly told, is the only way of achieving success in such a competitive environment? Had Hill and Williams tried it, would there not just have been wry smiles all round? Was it really so very different from the boxer who, as a matter of course, weighs in bang on the division limit two days before the contest and then fights at six pounds over? Or different from Jody Scheckter oiling the toes of his training shoes to do the squat thrusts in the World Superstars final all those years ago?

With Michael's great ability, he didn't need to do it. Anyone with a pound for every time that opinion was voiced would be wealthy indeed. But that is to misunderstand Schumacher and Benetton. Both sought to extract the absolute maximum from every situation and, increasingly, the paddock came to accept that here was a driver and team operating on a different level.

Johnny Herbert, Schumacher's own team-mate, became a victim of it just as JJ Lehto and Jos Verstappen had been the year before. Benetton was Schumacher's team and, allegedly, Herbert wasn't even allowed his own pedal set-up in case his car was needed for Schumacher. But such things don't explain the two-second qualifying gap between them apparent at more than a third of the season's races.

'I just can't drive the car the way Michael likes it set up,' Herbert said. 'He has the car very twitchy and you need a lot of confidence to drive it like that on the limit. That confidence comes with testing and he doesn't allow me much of that, so it's a bit of a Catch 22.'

Schumacher is the youngest double World Champion in the sport's history. Like almost every other true ace, he seemed born to Formula 1 the moment he arrived. Immediately he was quicker than triple World Champion Nelson Piquet. In 1992, an amazed Martin Brundle was stunned by the young German's confidence and bearing for one of such little experience. 'In a debrief he would press a point with engineers who had been in the game years, even if he was wrong. I had never seen that before with someone so young.'

But what about the arrogance?

It is there for sure, but by no means is it overbearing. Schumacher has come from a modest upbringing in Kerpen-Mannheim, is from working-class stock and now lives, newly married, in Monte Carlo, with his jet, boat, Ferrari 355, Mercedes SL, Harley and his $25 million a year Ferrari contract.

At just 26, he could be forgiven for being a total pain in the butt. But he's not. Perhaps *because* of his roots, he doesn't suffer prima donna syndrome, is almost always unfailingly polite, and has a ready smile and, contrary to popular perception, a sense of humour. Humility, however, is fairly well buried.

That smile sometimes becomes a smirk. When it does, you either smirk with him or it irritates. More than once during 1995 there was a difference of opinion, let's say, with Hill. At many a press conference Damon, with thunderous dark expression, spoke in measured tones while Schumacher sat alongside wearing the smirk. He took great pleasure in Damon, the pole man remember, trying to explain his trouncing at Monaco. The smirk, a shrug, a quick shake of the head as he leaned back in his seat accompanied Hill's opinion that this was Formula 1 and that karting tactics did not fit. 'Perhaps you should try karting sometime . . .' Schumacher replied, tangibly smug. This is the trait some find offensive.

Boring?

He lists karting as his hobby, cycling and mountain-biking as his active sports and Michael Jackson, Phil Collins, Tina Turner and Whitney Houston as his favourite singers. He likes Italian food. Apple juice with mineral water is his favourite drink. His dream is to become World Champion again and to start a family. The family, you can see, is important and there is a sensitive side. Even his boat is called Jenny, after the dog.

Whereas Hill is a well-educated, intelligent, dignified and rounded individual to whom the family came first and success later, Schumacher is a blazing talent whose entire life has been fashioned around motor racing success. And it still is. He's almost ten years younger and perhaps it would be more meaningful to assess his personality ten years hence.

Schumacher's detractors say he will never be a star in the way Senna was. He doesn't have the same depth, the mystique. True, perhaps. But neither does he betray the sullen, boorish, almost contemptuous indifference of which Ayrton was capable. You never see the 'Same shit, different day' body language on a Grand Prix podium, even if it has got something to do with the Benetton marketing machine playing to the cameras.

Schumacher, perhaps, is more like Mansell but without the insecurities: an uncomplicated family man who is abnormally gifted at anything which captures his interest. Add in the confidence that comes with knowing it, an almost Sennaesque passion for racing, and you have a most potent cocktail. A cocktail like no other and with a price to match.

It doesn't help Schumacher that he is German. But stereotyped descriptions of Michael as a Teutonic, soulless automaton are undeserved and unfair. Anybody at Spa or the Nürburgring knows that. And, as for that Monza banner 'Better one Alesi today than 100 Schumachers tomorrow', let's ask the *tifosi* again in September '96 . . .

Goldline Bearings Ltd
Proven Quality and Performance is our commitment to excellence

The suppliers of high quality bearings for high performance cars.

Ampep Goldline* generation of self-lubrication rod end and spherical bearings established in 1987 to meet the requirements of higher load rate, improved life and maintenance free features demanded by designers and operators of high performance cars.

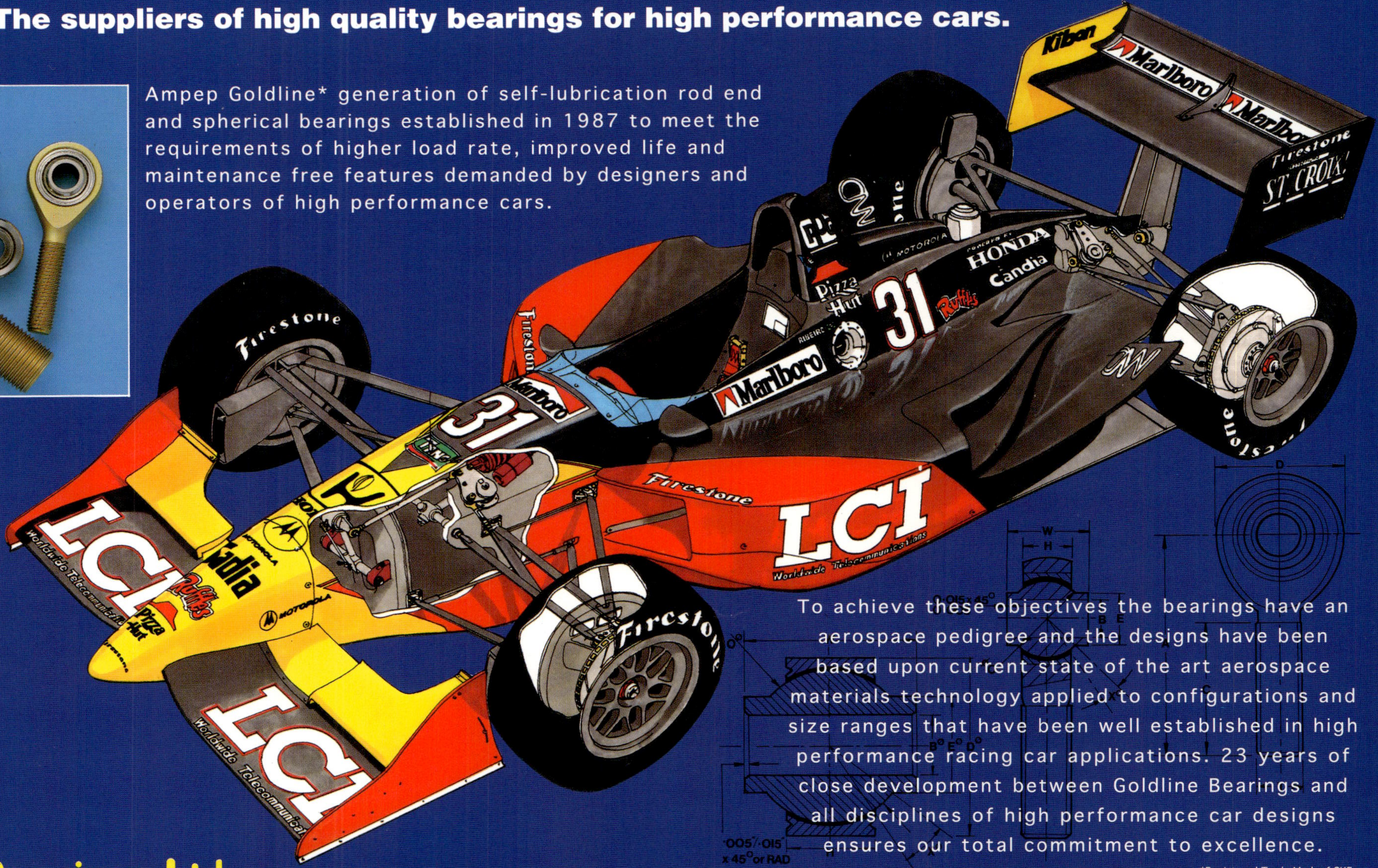

To achieve these objectives the bearings have an aerospace pedigree and the designs have been based upon current state of the art aerospace materials technology applied to configurations and size ranges that have been well established in high performance racing car applications. 23 years of close development between Goldline Bearings and all disciplines of high performance car designs ensures our total commitment to excellence.

*Registered Trade Mark of SKF

U.S.A. DISTRIBUTOR:
CONTACT: Bob Long, Truechoice Inc
4180 Weaver Court, Hilliard, Ohio 43026
Tel No 614 8763483 / Fax No 614 8769292

24 Hour Delivery Worldwide Export Service

Goldline Bearings Ltd

CONTACT: Mike Jones, Ryan Currier, Richard Brunning
Stafford Park 17, Telford TF3 3BN, England.
Tel No 01952 292401 / Fax No 01952 292403

STORM CLOUDS

Photo: Lukas Gorys

Paul-Henri Cahier

Bryn Williams/Words & Pictures

GATHER?
by Alan Henry

THE STATE OF FORMULA ONE

Main photo: Michael Schumacher sweeps to victory under threatening skies at Magny-Cours, a state-of-the-art circuit recently redeveloped at enormous cost. Race promoters are naturally keen to safeguard their multi-million-pound investments.

Bottom, left to right: The all-seeing eye. Television coverage has become a key factor in the development of Grand Prix racing. In-car cameras have put the viewer in the driver's seat.
A ban on carbon brakes is not the panacea some suppose.
Sink or swim. Max Mosley listens to Nick Wirth at Monaco. No lifebelt was forthcoming for Simtek.

Technical rule changes introduced for the 1995 World Championship Formula 1 season may have gone some way towards addressing concerns over safety, but wider preoccupations continued to linger just below the surface of what has long since become a TV-dependent, multi-million-dollar global sport. Put simply, is the racing close enough and sufficiently competitive to justify Grand Prix motor racing's continued existence in this televised super league?

In many ways, this is a highly contentious political minefield through which to stray. There is a solid body of opinion which believes that romantic notions of 'close fought' Grand Prix racing are nothing more than soft-focus nostalgia. Certainly, the writer was taken aback to hear one respected team chief yearning for the 'Good Old Days' of the mid-1970s when everybody, well, apart from Ferrari *almost* everybody, had Cosworth Ford engines and the racing was terrific.

The reality, of course, is somewhat different. The racing in those days was generally as dreary as the exhaust note of a field of Cosworth V8s was monotonous. Truly, this was a trough in F1 history. Today's Grand Prix fields have more technical variety and interest than ever before, with the possible exception of the turbo era a decade ago.

On the other had, the 1995 season ended with Damon Hill winning the last Australian GP to be held at Adelaide by the crushing margin of more than two laps, the race having fallen apart behind him. Only the 1969 Spanish GP at Barcelona, where Jackie Stewart's Matra beat Bruce McLaren's McLaren, had been won by a similar margin since the official World Championship was instigated.

The issue of closer racing is also inextricably interwoven with the need to somehow keep control over the performance of today's generation of F1 cars. As FIA President Max Mosley told the constructors early in 1995, there are several potential new F1 venues across the world where the promoters are prepared to make the multi-million-dollar investment required to upgrade their circuits to the latest standards.

Naturally enough, in return for such investment, these promoters not only want long-term contracts for their races, but also some sort of undertaking from the sport's governing body that a sudden upsurge in the performance of the cars will not place them in a position where more massive investment will be required two or three years down the road. It is a delicate matter to balance out.

Amidst the periodic clamour to control spiralling lap speeds and ensure better racing, one of the most familiar suggestions is the banning of carbon brakes in an effort to open out F1 braking distances with a view to encouraging more frequent overtaking. But as Williams Technical Director Patrick Head emphasised this year, it is not quite as simple as that.

'We've been told that we've got to come up with ideas to keep the cars' performance under control, and that's fine,' he says. 'It's better than sitting back and having other people decide. So I thought we should have a look at various things; one of the things might be banning carbon brakes.

'It was ten years ago that we last used cast-iron brakes, and then we were using asbestos-based pads and now we're on sintered carbon metallic pads. I rang AP and asked if they could provide some brakes, they said no problem, and we ran them during a test at Silverstone in July.

'Damon did his fastest lap of the day on them and thought they were really great. On the carbon brakes we were getting 4.2G longitudinal and 4G with the cast-iron brakes, Damon reporting there was a nice relationship between load on the pedal and stopping power, so he could control the car better going into the corners.' So basically there was little to be gained on this front in terms of potential for closer racing.

However, there is a cost consideration here. Carbon brakes are enormously expensive and Head admits that he blanches at the prospect of using up four or six sets of discs at £3500–£4000 per set in a two- or three-day test. 'I just say to myself this is silly,' he admits, 'but I don't think that necessarily banning carbon brakes is the answer. The only thing you can really do is [for the FIA] to supply everybody with the same brakes, and the next thing you might see is one of the companies going off to the European court and so on.'

So what about a change in engine regulations? In 1993, the teams suggested a 2.5-litre V6 formula – pegging the power output to around 600 bhp – yet the very day after that meeting, the FIA confirmed stability of the current engine regulations until the year 2000.

'This is a complex situation,' notes F1 engine specialist Brian Hart. 'I personally can't see much of a future

THE STATE OF FORMULA ONE

Left: Marlboro's red army on the march. The wishes of the multinational sponsors will determine F1's future.

Right: Do trackside spectators really matter? Contrast the almost inaccessible TI Circuit, built in a remote mountain location, with the Adelaide street circuit, which hosted the Australian Grand Prix for the last time after a successful run of eleven years and attracted a huge crowd to its farewell party.

in a 2.5-litre V6. It would require a huge amount of investment on the huge pistons, the cost of making it reliable at the sort of revs you'll need to run it at to get the sort of bhp per litre we're currently developing with the 3-litre engines.'

Yet the cost of engine development remains an acutely concerning element within the contemporary F1 equation, whether or not regulations on this front are changed within the foreseeable future. Back in 1978, when Frank Williams and Patrick Head were seriously starting together in F1, they could purchase a race-winning Cosworth DFV engine for around £12,500.

In 1995, also-rans such as Pacific and Minardi were paying in excess of £3 million for lease deals on Cosworth ED V8s which didn't have a hope in hell of powering them to race victories. And Brian Hart, for example, estimates the ballpark figure for the cost of manufacturing one of his type 830 3-litre V8s at around £200,000 apiece.

In this respect, F1 racing costs have dramatically outstripped inflation and left an almost impossible mountain to scale for those ambitious newcomers, such as Pacific and Forti, who are seeking to establish a Grand Prix bridgehead. Yet balancing out this situation where the rich get dramatically richer and the poor can barely get a look-in seems a virtual impossibility.

Yet, by the same token, Patrick Head believes there is no way of imposing any sort of general budgetary constraints in the F1 business. 'There is a law of natural selection which generally tends to sort these things out,' he claims.

'If to run the cars costs more than people can generally find budgets to support, then the top team chiefs tend to get together and propose banning using spare cars, intercontinental testing and so on. You cannot artificially apply such constraints.'

Ian Phillips, the Jordan team's Commercial Director, agrees. 'It's a team's responsibility to manage its own resources,' he says. 'If you can't work out the budget, you can't complain. People go crying to Bernie saying, "It's not fair, it's not fair." But it's nonsense. People take the decision to come into F1 with their eyes open, they know what the rules are.

'We have been very lucky, perhaps because Eddie was always very cost-conscious. We watched everything. It may be that Simtek, for example [which went under in 1995], was headed by a very enthusiastic young engineer who had no business experience. But everybody knows what the rules of the game are.'

Phillips also believes that there are few other designers in the F1 pit lane who can design and produce a car on a financially more efficient basis than Jordan's Technical Director Gary Anderson. That, says Phillips, reflects his practical background as a mechanic and small-time F3 constructor in his own right. He avoids the obvious F1 trap which seems to dictate that a component must be complex and costly simply because it is being produced for an F1 application.

Patrick Head basically agrees with this, pointing out that he has seen components on minor-league F1 cars so costly and complex to manufacture that a well-funded team like Williams would think twice before producing similar parts.

Yet, for all the costs involved, when the F1 cars arrive at the circuits their operation is governed by restrictions which many people find strangely at odds with the outlay involved in developing them in the first place. Many argue that we can't have it both ways. If F1 is international motor racing's major league category, then restrictions on the number of laps which are permitted in qualifying – and indeed the sets of tyres allowed per car over a race weekend – are uncomfortably at odds with the image it should project.

FIA President Max Mosley firmly refutes such a conclusion. 'In a nutshell, it's wrong,' he says. 'All sports have a restriction on various things you can and you can't make use of. To allow unlimited laps and tyres would simply increase the performance gap between the top teams and the smaller ones.'

Neither does he think that such restrictions are in any way at odds with the 107 per cent qualifying requirement which will be imposed from the start of the 1996 season. 'Any small team which is properly organised will be able to get within the 107 per cent margin,' he insists. 'This figure successfully takes into account the disadvantages and shortcomings with which those teams will have to deal.'

Clearly, there is a feeling within the upper echelons of the governing body that there may be one or two teams in F1 who do not, on the basis of their performance in 1995, deserve to be there. On the other hand, if they raise the standard of their game to successfully perform within the 107 per cent envelope, then the FIA will be satisfied that they have justified their candidature. Yet the underlying problem may be that to impose regulations which threaten to cut back fields to around the 20-car mark is not to leave much surplus fat in the event of an unexpected economic crisis jeopardising the position of ostensibly better-funded teams further up the grid.

At the end of the day, this debate may in fact be permitting emotion to get in the way of hard statistics. Between 1950 and 1986 no fewer than 23 races were won by margins in excess of a lap. Yet in the last ten seasons there have been only two comparable episodes: Schumacher's 1994 victory over Hill at Interlagos and Damon's success at Adelaide this season.

Moreover, of the forty recorded occasions since 1950 of races being won by less than a second, nine have occurred in the last decade. Thus, on a purely statistical basis, the obvious conclusion is that the racing in F1 is probably no better and no worse than it has always been. It is simply the fact that television coverage tends to focus attention on the poor races because it is so easy for casual TV viewers to 'roam' the channels in search of something more interesting to tickle their fancy.

None of this should unduly concern the dyed-in-the-wool enthusiast, you might say. And quite rightly so. But the multinational corporations whose colours bedeck the flanks of the Benettons, Williamses, Ferraris and McLarens see things from a different perspective. It is up to the F1 community to decide whether it's necessary further to jazz up the show in the years to come to keep those high spenders opening their cheque books.

SUCCESS.
IT'S A
MIND
GAME.

For further information: TAG Heuer UK, P.O. Box 59, Manchester, M28 3BD. Telephone: 01204 862179.   S/el Series.

CONTRIBUTORS
Bob Constanduros • Maurice Hamilton • Alan Henry

F1 ILLUSTRATIONS
Ian Hutchinson

1
2
BENETTON

MICHAEL SCHUMACHER

JOHNNY HERBERT

Benetton may have won the first race of the season in Brazil, but that could not hide the fact that they were in some difficulty. Michael Schumacher's success at Interlagos came only after Damon Hill had dropped out with broken suspension. Two weeks later in Argentina, and again in Imola a month after that, the reigning World Champion was struggling as Hill and Williams hammered home a clear advantage. Then Benetton began to edge back.

The recovery and subsequent run of success by Schumacher and his team has been an object lesson for the rest of the pit lane, a sign of Benetton's very impressive strength in depth. The B195 may not have been the most consistently competitive car but the team from Oxfordshire and their number one driver made the best use of it on Sunday afternoons.

Superb race tactics were complemented by a very slick pit stop routine and aggressive performances from the driver, but none of that would have amounted to anything if the car had not been so reliable. That was the most striking aspect of Benetton's season, particularly after going through the frequently underestimated difficulty of changing engine supplier. Switching from Ford to Renault made sense on paper since the French V10 continued to be head and shoulders above the rest, both in terms of performance and consistency, but the very act of leaving a company in the next county for one across the Channel brought unavoidable pressures, never mind the technical considerations necessary when accommodating a ten-cylinder engine for the first time.

'We underestimated that, partly because we had not changed engine supplier for so long,' admits Ross Brawn. 'Our 1994 car had been a good one because we had been together as a group at Benetton for three years, plus a much longer period with Cosworth. We had a nice package all round. Renault have been fantastic and it's no disrespect to them whatsoever when I say that any transition is difficult.

'Things didn't work out at first as we had hoped. At the beginning of the season we had a problem with the hydraulic pump drives. There was also a problem with gearbox cases cracking due to vibrational stress. That really set us back quite a bit and the first few races were spent finding our feet. Williams quite clearly had the advantage.'

Every team, of course, had been affected by the late changes to the technical regulations but, for Mild Seven Benetton Renault, the delayed build programme had come at a bad time. In the winter of 1994/95, Benetton needed to have the new car running sooner than usual, if only to check fundamental points such as the fuel and oil systems relative to an unfamiliar engine.

'There is always a fine balance between the conceptional period of a car and having it run in time to get it sorted,' says Brawn. 'I had to finalise the B195 much sooner than I would have liked in order to deal with any unforeseen problems, the sort of things that Williams would have met early on in their relationship with Renault and then dealt with accordingly.'

That said, Brawn and a technical team including Benetton stalwarts such as Rory Byrne and Pat Symonds dealt effectively with initial problems. From there on, progress was aided significantly by the kind of reliability which other teams would kill for. It didn't happen by chance, of course.

'Our philosophy', says Brawn, 'is that performance comes from good design and research and development. Reliability comes from design, manufacturing and systems. The part has to be designed properly for it to be fundamentally reliable. It has to be made to a high standard. Then it must be looked after properly. We have some very good systems, some very good people at Benetton. We have built a good team, and that's where the reliability comes from. There's no great secret to it.'

As Benetton set off for Japan and Australia at the end of the season, they had only suffered two major problems in the races. In Montreal, the gearbox control software had

BENETTON B195-RENAULT

Sponsors: Mild Seven, Renault, Elf, Bitburger, Kickers, Technogym

Team Principal: Flavio Briatore **Designers:** Ross Brawn, Rory Byrne **Team Manager:** Joan Villadelprat **Chief Mechanic:** Mick Ainsley-Cowlishaw

ENGINE **Type:** Renault RS7/RS7B/RS7C **No. of cylinders/vee angle:** V10 (67°) **Sparking plugs:** Champion **Electronics:** Magneti Marelli **Fuel:** Elf **Oil:** Elf

TRANSMISSION **Gearbox:** Benetton six-speed transverse **Driveshafts:** Benetton **Clutch:** AP

CHASSIS **Front suspension:** pushrod **Rear suspension:** pushrod **Suspension dampers:** WP **Wheel diameter:** front: 13 in. rear: 13 in. **Wheel rim widths:** front: 11.5 in. rear: 13.7 in. **Tyres:** Goodyear **Brake pads:** Carbone Industrie **Brake discs:** Carbone Industrie **Brake calipers:** Brembo **Steering:** Benetton **Radiators:** Secan **Fuel tanks:** ATL **Battery:** Benetton **Instruments:** Benetton

DIMENSIONS **Formula weight:** 1311.7 lb/595 kg including driver

FORMULA 1 REVIEW

Left: The architects of another triumphant season for Benetton *(left to right)*: Flavio Briatore, Joan Villadelprat and Technical Director Ross Brawn.

Below left: The latest Benetton was not an easy car to drive, but the combination of bullet-proof reliability, a total mastery of race strategy and the matchless virtuosity of Michael Schumacher allowed the team to win both the drivers' and constructors' championships.

Bottom: Johnny Herbert is chaired by his mechanics after winning the British Grand Prix. Although the former Lotus driver's season with Benetton was largely frustrating, there were a few moments to look back on with satisfaction.

unexpectedly gone haywire, a pit stop curing the problem and dropping Schumacher from the lead to an eventual fifth place. In Hungary, the failure of a fuel pump drive cost Michael second place.

'When we looked through the data after the Canadian Grand Prix,' explains Brawn, 'we found that the software had been presented with a set of circumstances – clutch positioning and certain other factors which we had never anticipated – and the software became scrambled and more or less didn't know what to do. Michael got to the pits, where we turned it off and then on again – and that cleared it. But we now know about that potential problem.

'After Hungary, a thorough investigation led to Renault responding by making a stronger and more durable part. But, really, I am not attributing blame to either party because Renault supply the piece and we look after it. The shaft should never have failed; it doesn't take much load. Maybe it got a knock somewhere along the line. It was one of those unfortunate things.'

Hungary was also one of the few

FORMULA 1 REVIEW

Left: Despite a switch to the dominant Renault V10, the Benetton B195 bore a close resemblance to its title-winning predecessor. Johnny Herbert never really came to terms with the car's nervous handling.

Bottom: Michael Schumacher has made an immense contribution to the Benetton team's rise to pre-eminence over the last four seasons. Now Ferrari looks expectantly to its Messiah.

Opposite: The German became the youngest driver to win successive World Championships. A majestic victory at Monaco confirmed his status as the best of his generation.

occasions when Benetton's race strategy fell foul of an unexpected technical malaise when Schumacher's refuelling rig failed to deliver the full load first time round. Apart from that, however, the team's pit stop strategy was usually close to perfection. Brawn, who made the final decisions each time, plays down the advantage the team appeared to have.

'There are three points,' he says. 'The first is that my job was made easier by having a driver such as Michael. He understood what we were trying to do. He could build his race around it, know when to push hard, come in without question. You can't underestimate the role a driver like Michael can play.

'Second, it is my belief that we have the quickest crew in the pit lane. They really are remarkable. Even if there is a problem, they know how to deal with it very quickly.

'And the third point is that I really don't think we are particularly clever – but I am surprised by some of the decisions other teams make. We have a good discussion about what we are going to do, make decisions and then run them with a fairly iron fist. If you deliberate, you are lost. Your decisions may not always be right, but they should be clear. That's what we have tried to do.'

In fact, the team has been accused of total inflexibility when it comes to dealing with Johnny Herbert in order to accommodate the needs of their number one driver. For Herbert, back with the team with which he had made a shaky start to his career six years before, this was seen as his last chance after a long period in the doldrums with Lotus. Johnny became a race winner for the first time at Silverstone, where everyone was delighted for the chirpy Essex man. Victory at Monza was more meritorious after Johnny had run with the leaders throughout and was on hand to take advantage of their misfortunes. And yet Herbert's year as a whole did little to enhance his reputation. Brawn has every sympathy.

'Quite honestly, it was an unfortunate time for Johnny to join the team. If he had been with us last year, he would have enjoyed a happier season. The fact is that the car has not been as good as we would have liked. When faced with those circumstances, it's difficult to be fair about the response you have to make to try and sort out the car. Given the situation we were in, I think it was proper that we used Michael to try and solve the problems as quickly as possible; he has been driving for us for four years; he's the quicker driver, the one with the most experience.

'If we had started the season with a very good car, then the issue of which driver did the most testing would have been much easier. In fairness to Johnny, the comments he made about the car were correct. It's not that we didn't believe him; we were simply unable to address the things which troubled Johnny as quickly as we should have done because those problems in some ways did not trouble Michael. Confidence level in the car is not a problem for Michael, which meant there were other things that we could get on with sorting out. Giving Johnny confidence in the car was not always our highest priority.

'I won't pretend that we have done a fantastic job for Johnny Herbert; we did the right job for the team under the circumstances we were faced with. As a result, we had a good crack at both championships, Johnny won two races, he was third in the drivers' championship after Monza. Maybe it could have been better for him – but he scored more points than ever before. There's a lot in Johnny but we were not in a position to get the most out of him. He deserves a lot more credit for what he has done – particularly at Monza. It was a shame that was overlooked in the fuss surrounding Michael and Damon.

'That's what people will remember most about 1995 in general and Monza in particular. As far as Benetton is concerned, the car has not been as good as I had hoped but the move to Renault was essential for the long-term competitiveness of the company.' It was a difficult transition but no one expected it to be easy. Winning 11 races out of 17 and both championships was even more satisfying as a result.

Maurice Hamilton

TYRRELL 3/4

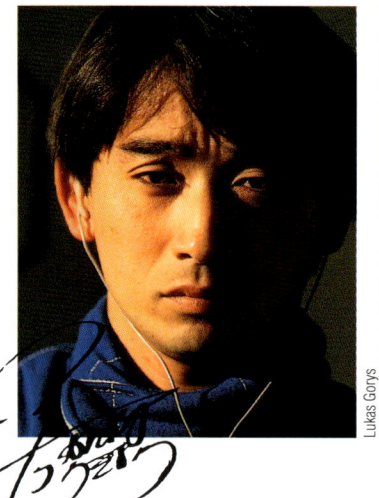

UKYO KATAYAMA — **GABRIELE TARQUINI** — **MIKA SALO**

Arguably, the most disappointing team of the season, if only because of the promise shown in 1994. In a preview, *Autosport* predicted that Tyrrell would have 'the best season for a very long time' in 1995; and rightly so. Nine months later, that forecast appeared asinine.

It was not until Monza in September that Nokia Tyrrell Yamaha managed to scrape together their first points of the season, and then only because the leading runners had either tripped over themselves or had parts of one car fall off and take out the other. It was inconceivable that, 12 months before, Tyrrell had been sixth in the championship. It was even harder to believe that Ukyo Katayama had regularly been pushing the Williams-Renaults and talking with confidence about the chance of podium finishes. In 1995, the only thing he saw of the quick boys was a waved fist as they tried to lap the blue and white Tyrrell.

So what went wrong? Harvey Postlethwaite takes care in choosing the right words. 'I don't want to give a lot of lame excuses,' he says finally. 'We spend our money very wisely but we are not a wealthy team. And if you are not a wealthy team and you have a bad year, you will come ninth; in a good year, you might come fifth. If you have a healthy budget then, if things go right, you might win the championship; if you have a bad year, you will come fifth. That's the difference.

'If there are too many compromises, then you have a struggle on your hands. We have had to do too many things without a sufficient budget. I know that's a poor excuse, because we really should have done better.'

That may be so but Postlethwaite surely made a rod for his own back by returning to Tyrrell at the end of 1993 and producing a car – presumably under the same constraints evident in 1995 – which was much more competitive than the 023.

'That's true, up to a point,' agrees Postlethwaite. 'Mike Gascoyne and I put our heads down, more or less ignored everything else, and did what turned out to be a reasonable car. The Yamaha engine was in a good state of development, our drivers were motivated and the whole thing gelled.

'In the winter of 1994/95, however, I had many more things to do and, if I'm honest, I probably took my eye off the ball. Mike also had to spend too much time doing things other than what he does best and we ended up with a car which, for the want of a better description, was a bit of an orphan. We've been paying the price ever since.'

That penalty clause came into play when the technical team attempted to make the best of their Hydrolink front suspension, a novel concept designed to ease the setting-up of the car and reduce some of the traditional compromise. It was – and still is – a very worthwhile system. The only mistake the team made was to put it on a mediocre car. When backs were up against the former wood-yard wall down in Ockham, the Hydrolink was removed mid-season through no fault of its own.

One disappointment had built on another, each problem not calamitous in isolation but, collectively, a spiralling sequence of dissatisfaction. Engine reliability problems early in the year caused a glitch in development of the V10 and, although Postlethwaite will not say as much, it is possible to detect a hint of disappointment with the performance of the Yamaha. Added to which, Mika Salo was making every mistake in the F1 book during his first full season. Even so, his speed and huge depth of potential were enough to knock the previously ascendant Katayama seriously off course. In fact, Ukyo disappointed even more than the car he was struggling to drive.

'Unfortunately,' says Postlethwaite, 'Ukyo has the terrible tendency to drive around problems. If the car doesn't do what he wants, then he simply changes the way he drives it. That's all very well during final qualifying, but you mustn't do it at 9.30 on a Friday morning!

'We've also had the additional

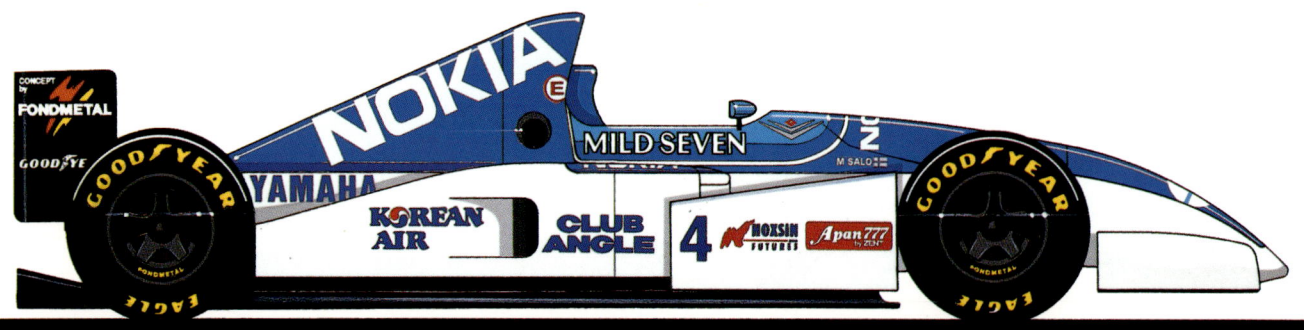

TYRRELL 023-YAMAHA

Sponsors: Nokia, Mild Seven, Fondmetal, Apan 777, Club Angle, Agip, Calbee, Korean Air, Hoxsin

Team Principal: Ken Tyrrell **Designer:** Harvey Postlethwaite **Team Manager:** Steve Nielsen **Chief Mechanic:** Chris White

ENGINE **Type:** Yamaha OX10C **No. of cylinders/vee angle:** V10 (72°) **Sparking plugs:** NGK **Electronics:** Zytek/Pi Research **Fuel:** Agip **Oil:** Agip

TRANSMISSION **Gearbox:** Tyrrell six-speed transverse **Driveshafts:** Tyrrell **Clutch:** AP

CHASSIS **Front suspension:** Tyrrell Hydrolink **Rear suspension:** Tyrrell Hydrolink **Suspension dampers:** Koni **Wheel diameter:** front: 13 in. rear: 13 in. **Wheel rim widths:** front: 11 in. rear: 13.5 in. **Tyres:** Goodyear **Brake pads:** AP/Hitco **Brake discs:** AP/Hitco **Brake calipers:** AP **Steering:** Tyrrell **Radiators:** Tyrrell/Secan **Fuel tanks:** ATL **Battery:** Tyrrell **Instruments:** Pi Research/Tyrrell

DIMENSIONS **Wheelbase:** 113.9 in./2895 mm **Track:** front: 78.7 in./2000 mm rear: 78.7 in./2000 mm **Formula weight:** 1311.7 lb/595 kg including driver

FORMULA 1 REVIEW

Left: More than a decade after his team's last Grand Prix victory, Ken Tyrrell is still at the helm.

After displaying impressive verve in 1994, little Ukyo Katayama *(below)* seems to have lost his way.

Although Tyrrell's results were bitterly disappointing in 1995, considerable progress has been made in other areas. Team manager Rupert Manwaring *(below centre)* remains a key figure.

Bottom right: An open-air debriefing session for Mika Salo at Monaco. The Finn was unable to maintain his barnstorming start to the season but his talent is unquestioned.

problem of working with drivers who like set-ups which are totally different. If they mistook which car they were getting into, one would fly off backwards at the first corner and the other would shoot straight on; their driving styles are that different. It meant that we were floundering a bit because a clear picture was not emerging. Then there was the fact that Mika was a bit of a shock for Ukyo and it caused him to overdrive. But the spark is definitely still there; if we had given Ukyo a better car, it would have been a very different story.

'Mika has struggled too, because he didn't know the circuits and he's made the mistakes you'd expect of a novice. In fact, he's fed up with having to go and see the stewards because of various misdemeanours! But he's a terrific talent. I have absolutely no doubt about that.'

That much was obvious when Salo qualified twelfth and then seventh for the first two races. Had he not developed cramp in Brazil because of an ill-fitting seat, and tangled with a back-marker in Argentina, the Finn would have scored points both times. But at least the season finished with a couple of consolation prizes as Salo finished sixth at Suzuka and then fifth in the Adelaide finale.

'Points in our first two races would

have got us off to a much better start,' admits Postlethwaite 'But I don't want to paint a gloomy picture because there have been other things which have been super. The team as a whole works very well indeed and the production side, which I spent much of the winter reorganising, works brilliantly. The cars don't break down any more – which was the big problem in 1994. Unfortunately, there is not much point in droning round and round when you are off the pace! So, yes, we have underperformed, but we know what to do to put it right.

Maurice Hamilton

5 6 WILLIAMS

DAMON HILL

DAVID COULTHARD

By the Williams team's high standards, 1995 was a disappointing year. The new Renault-propelled FW17 was, taken across the season, the most competitive car in the business and yet the team finished the season with only five wins to its credit. Benetton had amassed eleven.

The truth of the matter is that Damon Hill and David Coulthard frequently failed to get the best out of their machinery, yet that is only part of the story. Williams also suffered an unusually bad time with mechanical unreliability which almost certainly cost them victory at Silverstone as well as a string of top-six finishes during the course of the year.

The new technical regulations for 1995 represented a totally fresh start, as Chief Designer Adrian Newey explained: 'The flat bottomed regulations came in at the start of 1983, so we had thirteen seasons of more or less stable aerodynamic regulations, and then a very major change.

'Some parts of the car were not really much affected by the regulation changes and others were heavily affected. Given the amount of time available from when we started researching the car from the new regulations, it was a matter of intelligent guesswork, of trying to judge which areas to concentrate on.'

As far as suspension configuration was concerned, Newey retained much the same front torsion bar suspension package as employed on the previous year's FW16, but the anti-roll bar arrangement was altered in order to position the steering wheel slightly higher, to get it further away from the brake pedal to provide more room for Damon's feet!

The front suspension incorporated a third spring into the design from the start, 'although we didn't manage to find any sort of gain out of it until later in the season', explained Newey. As far as the rear suspension was concerned, it became evident pretty quickly that, with the stepped bottom aerodynamics, the FW16-style carbon top wishbone arrangement was not really the correct solution. The intention was to run the revised B-spec rear end from the start of the season, although for a variety of development and manufacturing reasons this did not come on stream until the Portuguese GP.

'We took the decision that this was how we would start the year, because we wanted a back end which was reliable, tried and tested,' says Newey. Compromise or not, the season began on an upbeat note with Hill leading commandingly at Interlagos before spinning out of the race when a rear suspension pushrod turn buckle – the clevis on the end of the pushrod which goes onto the bellcrank – broke.

'This was a manufacturing problem,' said Newey. 'The component was a tried and tested part which we had been using all the previous season. It was physically the same design as we'd used on FW16, now coping with rather less downforce, so it should have been well in. Sure, it was aggravated by the bumpy track surface at Interlagos, but it stood up all right the previous year on a car which hadn't been good over the bumps.'

Damon made up for this disappointment with wins at Buenos Aires and Imola, Coulthard having qualified on pole in Argentina only to pull off with electronic problems when also challenging for the lead. But then Goodyear made a front tyre construction change at Imola which took Williams some time to get to grips with.

'It seemed to affect our car more than some of the others,' said Newey. 'It had seemed OK in testing, but when we started using it in anger, for some reason it definitely didn't suit our car as well as some of the others. But Goodyear are certainly not silly; they introduced it, so they must have thought the bulk of the field would benefit from it.'

This led the FW17 into something of a performance trough at a time when other minor problems arose to bug the team's progress. Hydraulic problems intervened to sideline Coulthard at Barcelona and Hill at Montreal, while a differential problem in the warm-up at Monaco sent the team off in the wrong direction as far as Damon's race strategy was concerned.

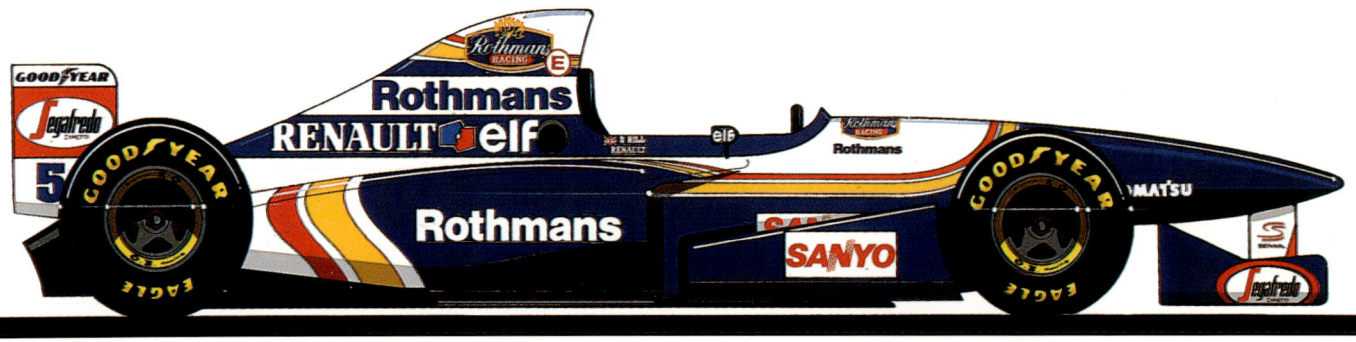

WILLIAMS FW17-RENAULT

Sponsors: Rothmans, Renault, Elf, Segafredo, Sanyo

Team Principal: Frank Williams **Designers:** Patrick Head, Adrian Newey **Team Manager:** Dickie Stanford **Chief Mechanic:** Carl Gaden

ENGINE **Type:** Renault RS7/RS7B/RS7C **No. of cylinders/vee angle:** V10 (67°) **Sparking plugs:** Champion **Electronics:** Magneti Marelli **Fuel:** Elf **Oil:** Elf

TRANSMISSION **Gearbox:** Williams six-speed transverse **Driveshafts:** Williams **Clutch:** AP

CHASSIS **Front suspension:** pushrod, bellcrank, torsion spring **Rear suspension:** pushrod, bellcrank, coil spring **Suspension dampers:** Williams/Penske **Wheel diameter:** front: 13 in. rear: 13 in. **Wheel rim widths:** front: 11.5 in. rear: 13.7 in. **Tyres:** Goodyear **Brake pads:** Carbone Industrie or Hitco **Brake discs:** Carbone Industrie or Hitco **Brake calipers:** AP **Steering:** Williams **Radiators:** Secan **Fuel tanks:** ATL **Battery:** Williams **Instruments:** Williams

DIMENSIONS **Wheelbase:** 114.9 in./2920 mm **Formula weight:** 1311.7 lb/595 kg including driver

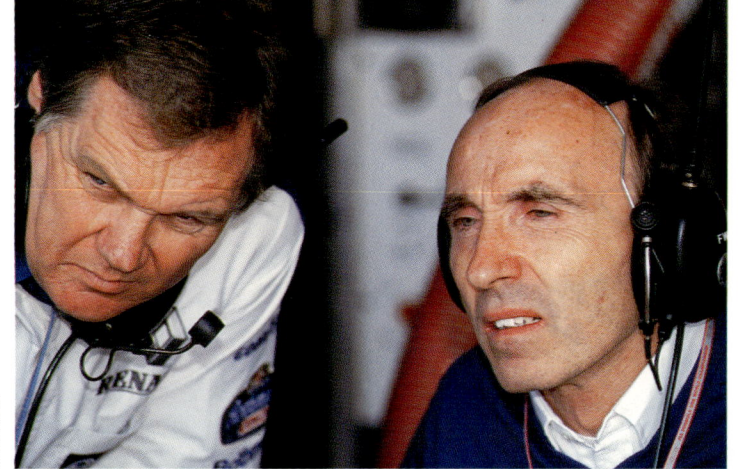

Diana Burnett

Left: The Williams FW17 was the car of the year; to the undisguised dismay of Patrick Head *(left)* and Frank Williams, the silverware went to Benetton.

Below: Damon Hill tries to trace those missing fractions of a second in the Williams pit garage at Estoril. There were times when the team seemed to lose confidence in its number one driver.

Bottom left: Adrian Newey ponders the poor reliability that blunted the Williams title challenge.

David Coulthard *(bottom right)* is moving to McLaren with a single Grand Prix victory on his CV. With a little good fortune, it could easily have been more.

Diana Burnett

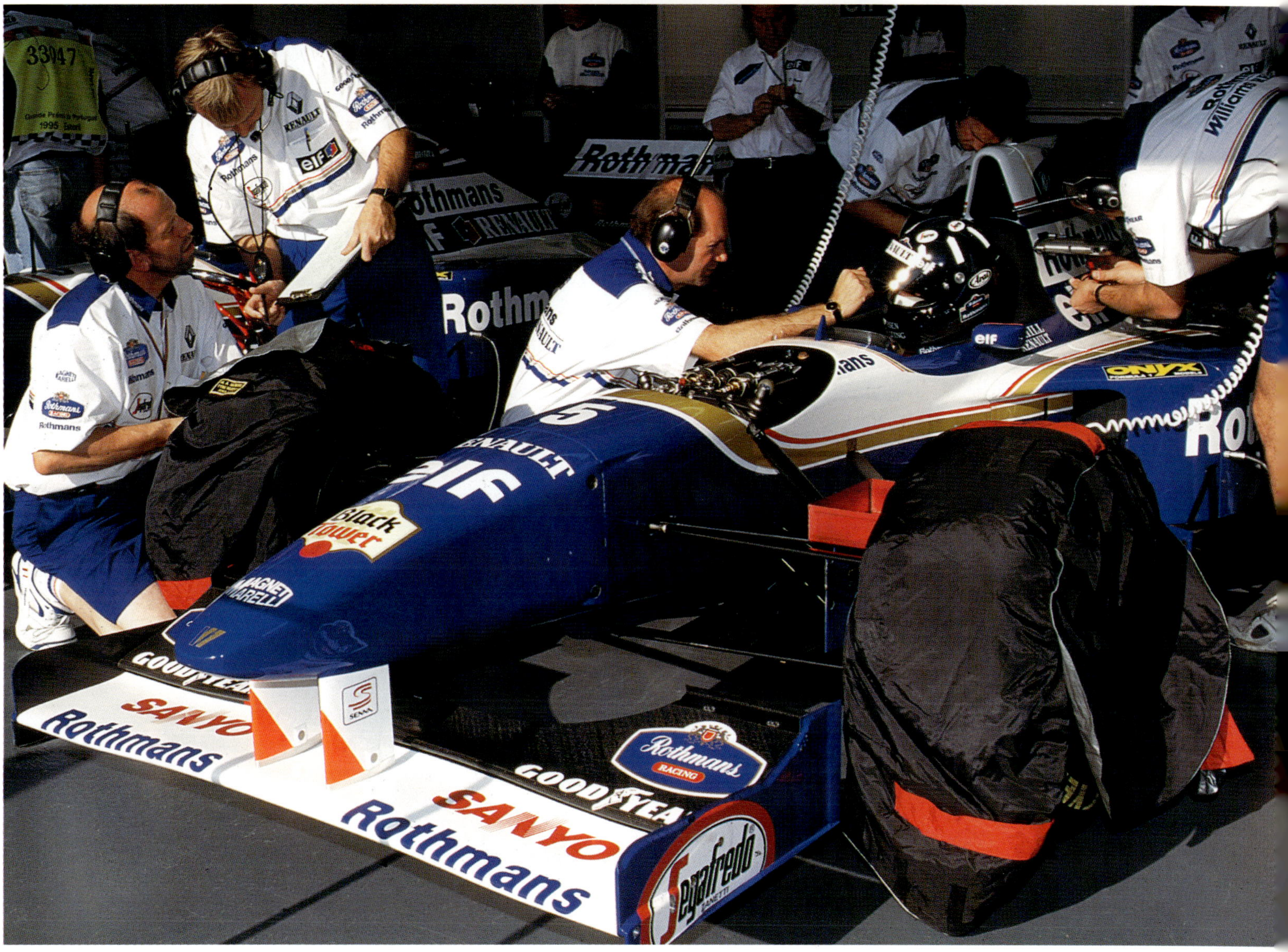

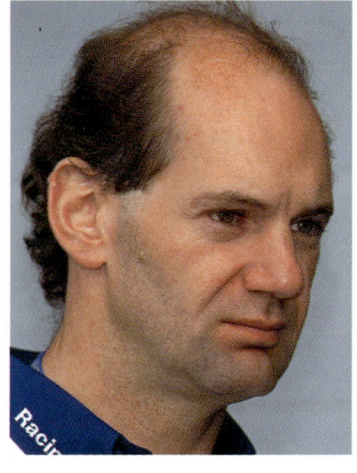

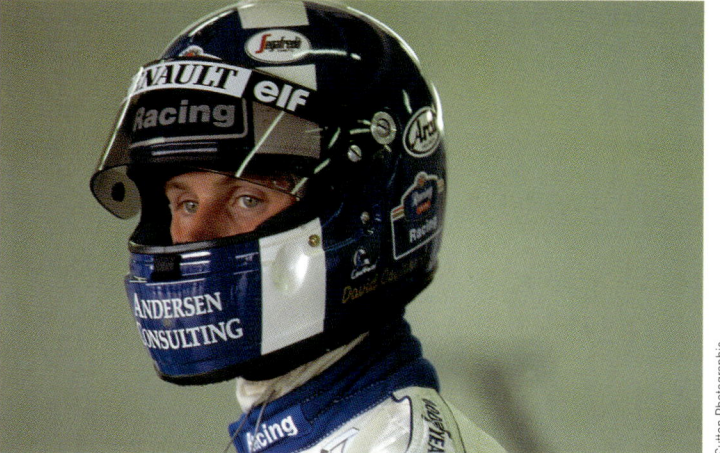

'Our lack of performance in the warm-up panicked us into two stops because we thought everybody else must have been going for two, to be going as quickly as they did,' says Newey. 'The car was dreadful in the warm-up and we concluded, "Oh Christ, the car's not good on half fuel, we'll have to revert back down." But it was the differential which was the problem and we went down the wrong avenue.

'Montreal, we made a complete hash of, although David spun off early. I don't think he would have beaten Schumacher, but I think he might have beaten Alesi.' The spate of hydraulic pump problems had its roots in a lot of pre-season testing

Diana Burnett

Sutton Photographic

FORMULA 1 REVIEW

Damon Hill *(below)* was eclipsed by his rival Michael Schumacher; silly mistakes marred David Coulthard's first full season in Formula 1 *(bottom)*; but in Hungary they could celebrate a Williams 1-2 *(right)*.

problems with belts. This was eventually sorted out partly by ducting far more cooling air to the belts themselves, partly by changing the belt material. Despite the fact that Williams did all the development work, Benetton also secured supplies of these revised belts. 'All of which was a little irritating,' said Newey with masterly understatement.

Extra revs and accompanying vibration produced by the smaller 3-litre engines used in 1995 was at least partly the cause, so Williams had to go into an intense development programme with Vickers, who made changes to the pump, and that seemed to solve the problem.

'The reliability of the car has really been very disappointing,' admitted Newey, 'although the hardware has generally been reasonably reliable. The gearbox, although having the same rear suspension on it, incorporated changes to the internals of the gears which gave some problems early on. Coupled with hydraulic problems and some electrical glitches, it was all pretty unfortunate.'

Coulthard lost a possible victory in Buenos Aires with a failure of the electronic throttle blipper control, while a similar electronic problem at Silverstone caused his electronic speed limiter to pack up in the British GP, which meant that he incurred a ten-second stop-go penalty for exceeding the pit lane limit. For much of the first part of the season, the young Scot also suffered from the lingering effects of tonsillitis and it was only after an operation immediately after the Canadian race that he began to display representative form.

However, his failure to take on Michael Schumacher in a battle for the lead at Hockenheim was regarded as a Black Mark by the Williams management. He would not be re-signed for 1996, his place being taken by Indy Car star Jacques Villeneuve in a driver selection which was made in mid-August – absurdly early in the season.

Coulthard's position as regards any possible ongoing involvement with Williams was always clouded in contractual complexity: it now seems clear that there was a residual obligation to McLaren stemming from his appearance in front of the FIA Contract Recognition Board at the end of 1994. The Scot's management company, IMG, always insisted that he chose to leave Williams for McLaren which, if the case, could be regarded as a somewhat eccentric career strategy when one considers the comparative performances of the two teams.

Either way, once it became clear that David was moving, he put in a series of blistering performances at Spa and Monza, culminating in a dominant victory at Estoril. However, his spins on the parade lap at Monza and the first warm-up lap at the Nürburgring, as well as hitting the Adelaide pit wall, were uncharacteristically cack-handed demonstrations on the part of this very skilled young driver, proof perhaps of a talent which has yet to fully mature.

Damon, meanwhile, had hoped for much more from the 1995 season. His biggest disappointments were failing to win at Monaco and Silverstone, although his over-exuberant dive down the inside on his home turf was aggravated by Schumacher's unyielding determination to turn into the corner, no matter what.

More serious by far was Hill's spin at Hockenheim which wrote him out of a race he showed every sign of dominating. Then there was Monza and the disappointment of two poor starts at Estoril and the Nürburgring, permitted Schumacher to seize the initiative and control the outcome of their own personal championship battle from the word go.

Overwhelmingly, though, Damon Hill showed himself to be a decent man with a sense of motor racing ethics which sometimes seems strangely out of place in today's high-pressure F1 environment. Williams don't always show him as much understanding as they might; fine in a season when the cars from Didcot display their traditional bullet-proof reliability, but perhaps not so helpful in a year when the team's World Championship challenge is jeopardised as much by the cars' failure to finish races as the shortcomings of the men behind the wheel.

Alan Henry

AVAILABLE IN THE FINEST SHOPS. FOR DETAILS TEL. DOERGE AGENCY, 0171 4080223

7 McLAREN 8

MARK BLUNDELL

NIGEL MANSELL

MIKA HÄKKINEN

McLaren's new partnership with Mercedes-Benz was not cemented until October 1994 and the technical challenge of accommodating the team's fourth change of engine in as many years put considerable strain on the Woking company's resources from the outset.

The first technical information relating to the all-new Mercedes FO110 3-litre V10 was communicated to McLaren's design department in mid-October '94, although by that time the team under Chief Designer Neil Oatley and aerodynamicist Henri Durand were already well under way with other aspects of the MP4/10 chassis concept.

To maximise the opportunities provided by the new 50 mm stepped undertray regulations, McLaren boss Ron Dennis had insisted that Ilmor Engineering, the Mercedes racing engine division, adopt a completely fresh approach to the architecture of its new engine. The introduction of the 50 mm undertray rules meant that the undertray profile would make considerable inroads into the amount of space available alongside the engine itself, complicating the challenge of packaging such ancillaries as the exhaust manifold and oil, water and hydraulic pumps.

To cater for this, Ilmor made a fundamental change in configuration when designing the new V10, opening out the vee angle from 72 to 75 degrees in order to position the hydraulic pump between the two banks of cylinders. This in turn demanded an exceedingly compact exhaust system, Mario Illien choosing to abandon the conventional fan-shaped manifold in favour of a tightly curved spiral, this leaving room for the oil and water pumps below.

Sustaining Ilmor's reputation for compact packaging, the V10's dimensions were smaller than some of its eight-cylinder opposition, allowing the McLaren team maximum installational flexibility.

'The engine was a little bit smaller than the Peugeot V10 which we'd used before,' said Neil Oatley, 'so there was no problem installing them in the space available. We requested the raised ancillaries from the outset because initially we were uncertain how the underside of the car would look, so the raised position gave us the option of trying several solutions underneath.'

The distinctive McLaren MP4/10 was officially unveiled at London's Science Museum on 17 February, the new machine distinguished by its high-nose configuration and small wing atop the engine cover for added downforce. This exploited a provision in the F1 technical regulations which permits the body to extend 25 cm to either side of the car's centre line at this point.

The Mercedes V10 drove through a six-speed transverse semi-automatic gearbox, using a hand clutch mounted on paddles behind the steering wheel, and relying on electrical controls supplied by TAG Electronics. Oatley admits that some consideration was given to a longitudinal gearbox, 'but we didn't think in the time we had available we could do a sensible job on a longitudinal 'box, because the aerodynamic concept wasn't finalised at the point we would have had to make a decision.

'So although logic would tell us that a longitudinal 'box would offer more options – although it has its downsides – we thought the most practical approach was to revamp the previous year's gearbox to suit the new rules and engine.'

As far as the driver line-up was concerned, Mika Häkkinen was starting the second season of a three-year contract with McLaren, but pressure from the team's sponsors for a high-profile name brought Nigel Mansell into the equation once he had been passed over in favour of David Coulthard for the vacant Williams-Renault seat.

The announcement of Mansell's recruitment was made amidst outpourings of mutual admiration from both Ron Dennis and Nigel himself, but seasoned F1-watchers simply kept their fingers crossed. A time bomb was ticking away here; it was only a question of when or how it

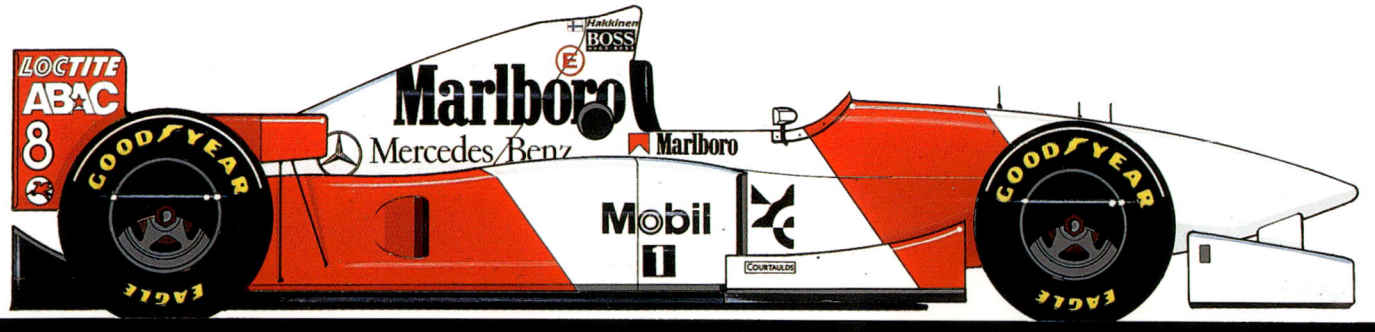

McLAREN MP4/10-MERCEDES

Sponsors: Marlboro, Mobil, Courtaulds, Boss, Goodyear, Loctite, Sun, ABAC, Kenwood, Computervision, TAG Heuer

Team Principal: Ron Dennis **Designers:** Neil Oatley, Henri Durand, Matthew Jeffreys, Dave Neilson, Dave North, Tim Goss **Team Manager:** Dave Ryan **Chief Mechanics:** Mike Negline, Paul Simpson

ENGINE **Type:** Mercedes-Benz FO110 **No. of cylinders/vee angle:** V10 (75°) **Electronics:** TAG Electronics **Fuel:** Mobil **Oil:** Mobil

TRANSMISSION **Gearbox:** McLaren six-speed transverse **Driveshafts:** McLaren **Clutch:** Sachs

CHASSIS **Front suspension:** unequal length wishbones, pushrod, inboard spring/damper **Rear suspension:** unequal length wishbones, pushrod, inboard spring/damper **Suspension dampers:** Bilstein **Wheel diameter:** front: 13 in. rear: 13 in. **Wheel rim widths:** front: 11.75 in. rear: 13.7 in. **Tyres:** Goodyear **Brake pads:** Carbone Industrie or Hitco **Brake discs:** Carbone Industrie or Hitco **Brake calipers:** AP **Steering:** McLaren **Radiators:** McLaren/Calsonic **Fuel tanks:** ATL **Battery:** GS **Instruments:** TAG Electronics

DIMENSIONS **Wheelbase:** 115.1 in./2925 mm **Track:** front: 66.5 in./1690 mm rear: 63.1 in./1605 mm **Formula weight:** 1311.7 lb/595 kg including driver

FORMULA 1 REVIEW

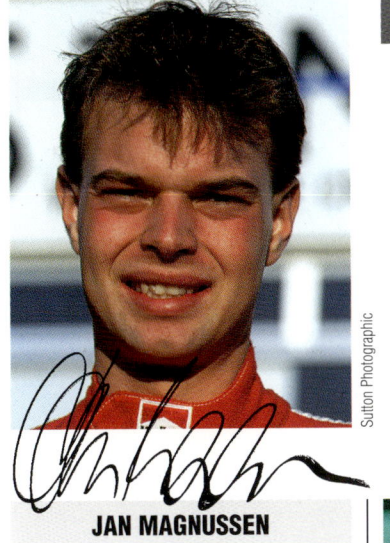
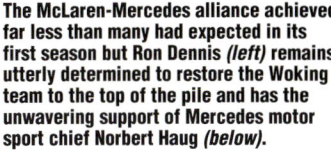

JAN MAGNUSSEN

The McLaren-Mercedes alliance achieved far less than many had expected in its first season but Ron Dennis *(left)* remains utterly determined to restore the Woking team to the top of the pile and has the unwavering support of Mercedes motor sport chief Norbert Haug *(below)*.

Below left: Mario Illien of Ilmor *(left)* and McLaren designer Neil Oatley are the men who have to come up with a winning package.

Bottom: Gloom in the McLaren pit at Imola as Nigel Mansell contemplates the gap separating the MP4/10B from the front-runners.

would be detonated. Approaching his 41st birthday, Mansell knew he needed a competitive car from the outset if he was to make a full-time F1 return stick. The real question was whether McLaren could provide him with an instantly competitive package from the outset.

From the first pre-race test, it was clear that the MP4/10 was suffering from a major handling imbalance. Despite predictions from other designers that the new '95 breed of F1 challenger would be somewhat less pitch sensitive than their predecessors, Oatley correctly predicted this would not necessarily be the case. But he could hardly have anticipated the problems in this area from which his new design would suffer.

Worse still, Mansell and Häkkinen also found that the cockpit dimensions lacked sufficient elbow room for them to steer properly, the problem being particularly acute for the Englishman. Even before the season began the team thus found itself facing a major crisis and, after considerable detailed deliberation, decided there was no alternative but to design and build a slightly wider monocoque for Nigel's use. In the meantime, Mansell had to stand down from the first two races of the season and his place alongside Häkkinen was taken by Mark Blundell.

Front-end grip was the key problem with the MP4/10 from the outset, although the new Mercedes-engined challenger proved promising in its first two outings in Brazil and Argentina. Häkkinen took fourth place at Interlagos, Blundell sixth, and the Finn ran particularly strongly in the opening stages of the race, losing only fractionally to the Renault-propelled trio of Hill, Schumacher and Coulthard in front of him.

In Buenos Aires, Häkkinen qualified fifth only to spin off at the first corner after his left-rear tyre was punctured against the nose of Irvine's Jordan, while Blundell stopped with an oil leak from a cracked gearbox casing. For the third race at Imola, Mansell returned at the wheel of the revised MP4/10B, the car having been substantially

FORMULA 1 REVIEW

Left: Mika Häkkinen charges up the hill at Monaco. The McLaren's engine cover-mounted wing may well have offered additional downforce, but it did nothing for the car's visual appeal.

Below left: On our way. Häkkinen's second place at Monza confirmed the great progress that had been made since the start of the season.

Mark Blundell *(opposite)* took over from the disenchanted Mansell and soon became a firm favourite with the team.

redesigned from the dash bulkhead to the rear seat back. The process had take only 33 days – just over half the 65 days which the team would normally allocate for such a major transformation.

Once Mansell fitted the car, it quickly became clear that the team had to face up to more problems. The MP4/10B's handling was still beset by understeer and Mansell made no bones about the fact that he felt uncomfortable with a car which so demonstrably lacked front-end grip.

He managed to qualify within half a second of Häkkinen at Barcelona, but the Finn easily outclassed him in the race and Nigel opted for retirement after a couple of lurid slides across a gravel trap. Before the next race at Monaco, Mansell and Ron Dennis had agreed to terminate the ill-starred partnership with as much dignity as they could muster. By any objective standards, it had been a fiasco.

With Blundell now restored to the full-time driver line-up in place of the hard-to-please Mansell, team morale bucked up considerably from the Monaco GP onwards. Mark's equable temperament and willing approach made him enormously popular with the McLaren mechanics and factory workforce, almost as a counterpoint to Häkkinen's increasingly preoccupied mood. Even so, Dennis continued to employ Blundell on a race-to-race basis for the balance of the season, a strategy which the McLaren boss clearly believed was calculated to get the best out of the Englishman.

A fuel system problem at Barcelona had prevented Häkkinen from scoring a strong fourth place in the Spanish GP, after which the MP4/10B's performance tailed off steadily to bottom out at the French GP, where both cars were hopelessly off the pace. The British GP at Silverstone saw a major step forward in power and driveability from Ilmor, a revised version of the Mercedes V10 allowing Häkkinen to set fastest time in the race morning warm-up, and at Hockenheim both cars ran in the top six before suffering engine failures.

Throughout the balance of the season Ilmor concentrated on improving the engine's mid-range torque and driveability while at the same time inching forward in terms of power output. The need to progress more quickly than the opposition in an effort to catch up resulted in Dennis pushing his entire workforce to the outer limits of endurance throughout the season.

Yet it was here that McLaren and Mercedes displayed the sheer strength in depth of their commitment. After engine failures in Hungary, Ilmor stripped the V10s, assessed the problem, made and installed fresh components and bench-tested the revised engines in time for a test at Silverstone a week later. In parallel, McLaren produced a revised gearbox casing to accommodate new rear suspension geometry at Spa, where Häkkinen qualified third and then blotted his copybook with an absurd second-lap spin at La Source.

Blundell came home fifth at Spa, but the team achieved its best result so far at Monza with second and fourth, although both Ferraris, both Williamses and Schumacher's Benetton had retired while running ahead of the MP4/10Bs. Determined to sustain the tempo of development, McLaren pushed ahead with the development of a revised C-spec car for Estoril and the Nürburgring, but design problems with yet another new rear geometry package left them in disarray. The strategy of running slicks on a damp track at the Nürburgring may have worked for Ferrari, but not for McLaren, so the European season finale was a low point of the year.

For the Pacific Grand Prix at Aida, Häkkinen was hospitalised following an appendectomy and his place taken impressively by test driver Jan Magnussen. Häkkinen then returned for the Japanese GP at Suzuka, qualifying third and finishing a superb second only twenty seconds behind Schumacher's Benetton. The MP4/10B's performance at the smooth, low-downforce Suzuka track was an enormous encouragement to the whole team. But disaster was to follow at Adelaide, where Häkkinen crashed at high speed when a rear tyre punctured on debris and he suffered head injuries from which he is now thankfully recovering.

Characteristically, Ron Dennis has implacable faith in his company's ability to turn the corner and keep his partners at Mercedes and Philip Morris satisfied in the future. With that in mind, the season finished in a mood more upbeat and optimistic than the results might seem to justify at first glance. McLaren may have been down in 1995, but only the reckless would even begin to count them out.

Alan Henry

1940: the first crashworthy floor unit. Cross members provided good lateral protection.

Support from the steering wheel? The test sledge showed the limits.

At 50 km/h against the wall: the occupant cell of the 1951 170 S remained largely intact.

Catch up on 5 research in It would

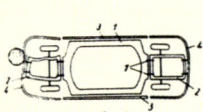
As early as 1951, we patented the principle of the safety passenger cell.

The landing was also excellent: the 220 SE at the start of the 1960's.

▶ When, many years ago, we began to assess vehicles systematically in crash tests, more than a few eyebrows were raised. Nobody used to think much about the safety of cars in those days.

▶ Today, things are quite different. And because we make important research discoveries available to all other manufacturers too, and thus to all car drivers, Mercedes-Benz developments such as crumple zones, the safety steering column, ABS and the airbag can now be found in many of our competitors' cars – in many cases, only

The computer-calculated forked front members disperse impact energy.

By the end of the 1950's, we were already working on seatbelts.

Acceleration skid control ensures tyre-to-road adhesion.

The hot water rocket accelerated the test car to its crash speed.

Side impact was on our agenda as early as the 1970's.

What would in reality be too dangerous, we assess in the driving simulator.

0 years' safety a few years? be nice.

a few years after these safety features started to find extensive application in our own car range.

▶ However, we shall maintain our leading edge in future, too, and certain safety innovations will appear first in a Mercedes-Benz. There is a quite simple reason for this: the first to start thinking is the first with the new ideas.

Mercedes-Benz
Engineered like no other car in the world

Since 1958, wedge-pin door locks have prevented doors from flying open in an accident.

The most common type of accident: the offset crash. It has been a part of our test programme since the 1970's.

eather head restraints afford protection in an accident.

As early as the 1950's, we removed all sharp edges on the dashboard.

The smallest people receive our greatest attention.

At the end of the 1960's, our airbag was still widely ridiculed.

9 ARROWS
10

GIANNI MORBIDELLI

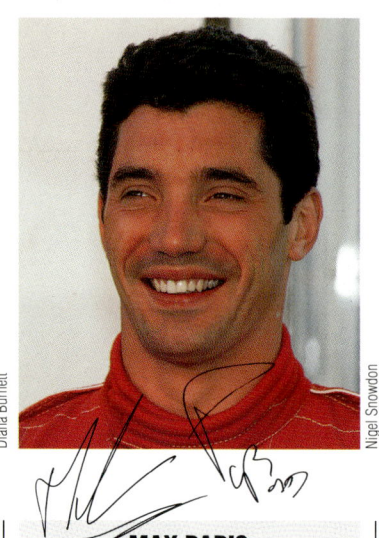
MAX PAPIS

TAKI INOUE

The sight of Gianni Morbidelli eating up the gap between his brand-new Footwork and Jean Alesi's much-tested Ferrari in the closing laps of the Brazilian Grand Prix probably represented the Arrows team's best memory of 1995. Things never seemed quite the same again and when, at mid-season, Morbidelli was replaced by F1 debutant Max Papis, the prospects of adding more World Championship points to the one scored by Gianni in Canada receded dramatically.

Fate saved the best until last, however. Morbidelli returned to the team for the last three races and survived to finish third in Adelaide, earning Jack Oliver's lads their first podium since Eddie Cheever at Phoenix in 1989.

Arrows team principal Jackie Oliver had done all he could to ensure that things would be better than during the previous year, although Christian Fittipaldi had crossed the Atlantic to the Indy Car scene and the team had lost some of its vital backing. But Oliver had at least managed to step off the customer Ford rung of the ladder by ensuring an exclusive deal with Brian Hart, who had chopped two cylinders off his successful V10 to make a superb, compact jewel of a V8. Together with Hart had come South Africa's fuel supplier Sasol, but the team was still desperately short of funds.

For that reason, Japan's Taki Inoue would continue the F1 career he had started with Simtek at Suzuka the previous year, although the learning curve would continue to be very steep. However, he secured his position by bringing much-needed finance to the team.

What was so immensely pleasing was that Alan Jenkins's FA16 worked so well so quickly. When it arrived at Interlagos for the first race, it had completed just two days' shakedown. 'The idea was not to repackage last year's car to the new rules, even if it looks like it from the grandstand,' explained Jenkins at the start of the year.

'The main idea was to have as much development potential in the car as possible. We went for a fairly complicated rear suspension and a fairly big step for us on the [six-speed longitudinal] gearbox, allowing for a few variables on the aerodynamics. There are also more variables in the rear suspension than may be apparent to the eye in terms of springs and dampers.'

Hopes that the car would be good straight out of the box were certainly borne out by Morbidelli's performance in Brazil, sadly cut short by fuel pressure problems ten laps from the chequered flag. Then at Imola Gianni was running seventh for a while and battling with Barrichello and Panis. The likeable Italian was where it mattered to pick up a point in Canada, having earlier fought off the attentions of Blundell's McLaren.

But the frustrations had already surfaced as far as the technical side was concerned. 'Initially the performance was at a good level, only a little bit shy of that attained by the top engines,' summarised Jenkins. 'But the basic disappointment over the season has been our inability to develop either the engine or the car, mainly for budgetary reasons.

'Brian has been more than capable of improving the engine dramatically. For example, we have a version which Gianni used at Imola which was 6–8 km/h quicker everywhere and which Max ran at Monza, where it was 10 km/h quicker at the end of the straight. But it was only possible to have one or two experimental engines. That side of things has been a bit depressing.'

In retrospect, Jenkins admitted that his philosophy of leaving as much development potential in the chassis as possible was perhaps too ambitious, given the budget for testing: 'We tried to do too much and gave ourselves too many options.'

The team employed a triple-spring suspension system; the central springs controlled ride height, pitch and dive while the outer ones controlled roll, so they could be varied independently. 'We got a bit lost about Magny-Cours time,' confessed Jenkins, 'and that became more dif-

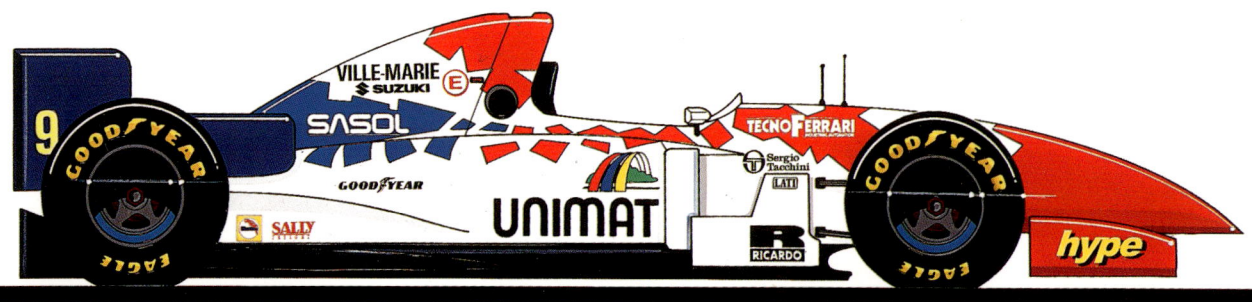

FOOTWORK FA16-HART

Sponsors: Unimat, Sasol, Hype

Team Principals: Jackie Oliver, Alan Rees **Designer:** Alan Jenkins **Team Manager:** Alan Harrison **Chief Mechanic:** Ken Sibley

ENGINE **Type:** Hart 830 **No. of cylinders/vee angle:** V8 (72°) **Sparking plugs:** Champion **Electronics:** TAG Electronics **Fuel:** Sasol **Oil:** Sasol

TRANSMISSION **Gearbox:** Arrows/Xtrac six-speed longitudinal **Driveshafts:** Arrows **Clutch:** AP

CHASSIS **Front suspension:** double wishbones, pushrod **Rear suspension:** double wishbones, pushrod **Suspension dampers:** Arrows **Wheel diameter:** front: 13 in. rear: 13 in.

Wheel rim widths: front: 11.5 in. rear: 13.7 in. **Tyres:** Goodyear **Brake pads:** SEP **Brake discs:** SEP **Brake calipers:** Brembo **Steering:** Arrows **Radiators:** Secan

Fuel tanks: APT **Battery:** FIAMM **Instruments:** Pi Research

DIMENSIONS **Chassis weight (tub):** 105.8 lb/48 kg **Formula weight:** 1311.7 lb/595 kg including driver

FORMULA 1 REVIEW

Japanese novice Taki Inoue *(left)* drove sensibly but is currently best known for his unfortunate misadventures with course cars in Monaco and Hungary.

Budgetary constraints prevented Alan Jenkins *(below)* exploiting the full potential of his neat design but the team maintained an impressive standard of preparation and presentation *(centre)*.

Bottom left: Inoue leads Max Papis in Hungary. The Italian endured a difficult Formula 1 baptism.

Bottom right: Gianni Morbidelli gave the team a massive boost with his third-place finish in Australia.

ficult because we lost continuity when Gianni stopped racing for us. But we began to understand it [the car] again and towards the end of the European season we were probably where we should have been a couple of months before.'

Jenkins therefore wasn't unhappy about the work done over the winter, simply the way things had developed since then. But it came to the point where, for budgetary reasons, the team's most talented and experienced driver was reduced to the role of tester, sorting out the car for two colleagues who were racing because they had brought financial help to the team.

Max Papis made his debut at the British Grand Prix, and although the F3000 race winner was initially quicker than Inoue, this was scarcely a Clash of the Titans. Oliver would admit that Papis was under pressure, particularly as he succeeded the popular Morbidelli, and a lot of things went wrong for him. 'Mistakes have been made either with the equipment or its use,' said Oliver. 'It hasn't gone all that well for him. But he's likeable, enthusiastic and potentially could do well.'

Inoue, meanwhile, initially looked hugely out of his depth, although he didn't make too many mistakes. 'He has been a consistently moderate performer,' concluded Oliver. 'His learning curve has been steep, but his performance very flat.'

It will be a shame, given the technical possibilities in 1995, if the Arrows team's year is remembered more for Inoue's two bizarre incidents with the course car – in Monaco and Hungary – than for Morbidelli's third place in Australia.

Bob Constanduros

11 SIMTEK 12

MIMMO SCHIATTARELLA

JOS VERSTAPPEN

Bottom left: As Nick Wirth discovered to his cost, sound engineering is no guarantee of F1 viability.

Below: Jos Verstappen heads for 12th place in Spain, the ill-fated Simtek team's best result of the year.

Nick Wirth's Banbury-based Simtek team began the year on an upbeat note, hoping to capitalise on the steady progress achieved throughout the second half of its maiden F1 programme in 1994. After the tragedy of Roland Ratzenberger's death during qualifying for the San Marino GP, Simtek had been shaken to its core. But Wirth and his colleagues had displayed considerable resilience in coming to terms with this disaster and were determined to establish a firm F1 bridgehead in their second season.

The team's new S951 chassis was a straightforward and uncomplicated Cosworth ED-engined machine and an arrangement to secure the services of Benetton test driver Jos Verstappen gained Simtek use of Benetton's 1994 six-speed semi-automatic gearbox. The new Simteks were the last of the '95 generation to be completed, arriving at the opening race at Interlagos with scarcely any testing under their belt. This was to set the tone for what followed.

The second car was due to be shared between Domenico Schiattarella and Hideki Noda, but Verstappen was the star of the show from the outset, qualifying an excellent 14th in Argentina, 17th for the San Marino GP and then 16th on the grid at Barcelona.

Early-season transmission unreliability undermined the team's efforts and Verstappen's best result was 12th in Spain, but by that stage the team was facing potentially ruinous financial problems as a promised major sponsor seemed to be stalling on an undertaking to make agreed funds available. Matters came to a head at Monaco, where Wirth admitted that the team had little prospect of competing in Canada unless the promised sponsorship materialised by the end of the following week.

Nothing happened and Simtek duly went into voluntary receivership with debts of the order of £6 million. The assets of the team raised a paltry £250,000, closing the book on the history of this gallant little F1 operation after barely eighteen months in the business and proving that enthusiasm and technical competence alone are insufficient in today's highly commercialised F1 environment.

Alan Henry

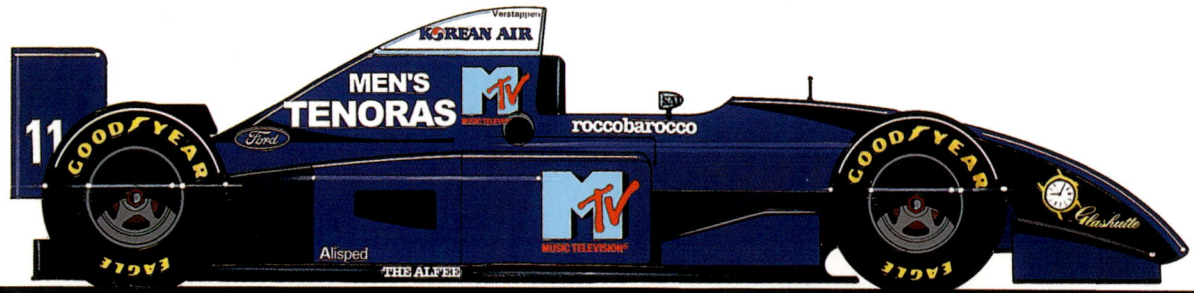

SIMTEK S951-FORD

Sponsors: MTV, Barbara MC, Korean Air, XTC

Team Principal: Nick Wirth **Designer:** Paul Crooks **Team Manager:** Charlie Moody

ENGINE **Type:** Cosworth ED **No. of cylinders/vee angle:** V8 (75°) **Sparking plugs:** Champion **Electronics:** Cosworth **Fuel:** Elf **Oil:** Elf

TRANSMISSION **Gearbox:** Benetton six-speed transverse **Driveshafts:** Xtrac **Clutch:** AP

CHASSIS **Front suspension:** double wishbones, pushrod **Rear suspension:** double wishbones, pushrod **Suspension dampers:** Penske **Wheel diameter:** front: 13 in. rear: 13 in.
Wheel rim widths: front: 11.5 in. rear: 13.7 in. **Tyres:** Goodyear **Brake pads:** AP/Hitco **Brake discs:** Carbone Industrie **Brake calipers:** Brembo **Radiators:** Secan
Fuel tanks: ATL

DIMENSIONS **Formula weight:** 1311.7 lb/595 kg including driver

UNIPART
Commitment to Continuous Improvement

Jordan Grand Prix and sponsors Unipart – organisations committed to continuous improvement

Unipart has a long history of involvement in Formula 1 racing, which continues right up to the present day with the sponsorship of and the supply of products to Jordan Grand Prix

JORDAN and the Rampant Lion ... something

Rubens and Eddie
... healthy rivalry

Peugeot power for 1995 through 1996 and 1997 as well ...
a long term commitment to continual improvement

The best looking car in F1?
...valeted with the Unipart Car Care Range

Canadian Grand Prix, Rubens 2nd, Eddie 3rd

UNIPART

o prove

Dedicated to continuous improvement...
    choose Unipart products
        whatever make or model your car

> "*Eddie Irvine . . . you had to be blind not to notice his potential . . .*"
>
> **Michael Schumacher**

> "*I'm looking forward to racing this car, it's the most competitive I've had*"
>
> **Rubens Barrichello**

the Brand in Action

*The Answer is YES,
Now What's the Question?*

14 JORDAN 15

RUBENS BARRICHELLO — **EDDIE IRVINE**

This was the big step. After four years of frequently impressive progress through the middle order, Jordan Grand Prix seemed ready to attack the major league when the deal with Peugeot was announced in September 1994.

Of course, life is never as simple as that but, with Eddie Jordan, it was difficult not to be upbeat. In one breath, he would play it down; with another, he would remind you that his team had hoped to score 20 points in 1994 and actually came away with 28. Then, in a moment of typical enthusiasm, he would speak out of the side of his mouth and talk about maybe 'sneaking in a win' in 1995. And why not? Anything seemed possible.

By round 14 of the 1995 championship, Total Jordan Peugeot had a mere 18 points. The figure should have been 50 – maybe more. After all, the cars had been qualifying inside the top ten; they were perfectly placed, not to win races, but to regularly collect points. And, time after time, the neat little car would roll to a halt with some fault or other. Gary Anderson, the Technical Director at Total Jordan Peugeot, does not need reminding of what might have been.

'Reliability has been the biggest problem,' he says ruefully. 'The trouble is that, when you are the size we are, your attention is focused on establishing reliability. Monza was a good example. Rubens [Barrichello] qualified sixth and he even led briefly. Then he went out with clutch trouble. In actual fact, he was on borrowed time because of a hydraulic leak which was about to raise its head and he wouldn't have finished the race in any case. So, looking at it positively, we recognised two problems in one race.

'But the point is that I then spent the whole of the following week trying to find a solution to the clutch problem. So there we were, trying to design the 1996 car, keep the current one competitive – and a week is spent on reliability. The thing that hurts us most is that we are not big enough to keep up the development programme and also have to deal with unreliability. We had this problem in 1993, and it was back again in 1995.'

That may seem a retrograde step in view of the success enjoyed in 1994. In fact, it was a typical product of the upheaval brought about by working with a different engine manufacturer and, to a certain extent, a vastly different business culture to the one established so successfully by Anderson and Brian Hart. Because of the compact nature of Hart's operation in Harlow, Anderson and the engine builder could work by an intuitive and informal method whereby a decision could be reached during a five-minute conversation over the telephone, both men being racers who understood precisely what the other was thinking. Anderson has had to adapt to the more time-consuming methods of a major manufacturer which does not take a step of any importance without having at least one meeting to discuss it.

'It's been a change of direction for us,' says Anderson. 'Everything is different; you have to learn all over again. I am a big believer in communication but you don't need to spend a day talking about something which could be dealt with in a matter of minutes. Peugeot have a lot of people and it's not so important if some of them are tied up in a meeting. I miss a day out of my time very badly.'

More time was spent testing than ever before thanks to the establishment of a test team, but that in itself was not the passport to success which many had imagined it to be. Again, it was a case of adapting to the changing circumstances and making the most of them. At first, Jordan seemed to have a handle on the entire operation when pre-season tests consistently produced very competitive times. Reality set in at the very first race in Brazil.

'We were confident going to Brazil,' agrees Anderson, 'but then we found that the car wasn't very good on the bumps. I attributed that to the fact that we did not do enough testing on different types of circuits. We did a lot of running at Estoril and Silverstone, and a little at

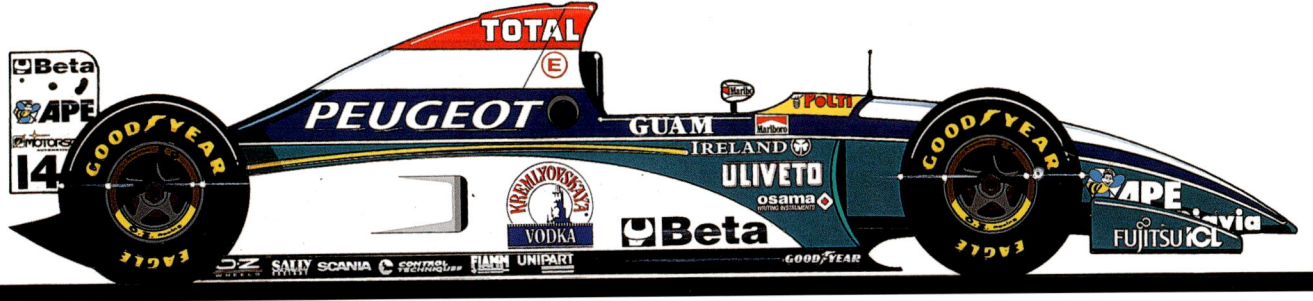

JORDAN 195-PEUGEOT

Sponsors: Total, Marlboro, APE, Beta, Cadtek, Diavia, GUAM, Polti, Uliveto, Unipart

Team Principal: Eddie Jordan **Designer:** Gary Anderson **Team Manager:** John Walton **Chief Mechanic:** Jim Vale

ENGINE **Type:** Peugeot A10 **No. of cylinders/vee angle:** V10 (72°) **Sparking plugs:** NGK **Electronics:** TAG Electronics **Fuel:** Total **Oil:** Total

TRANSMISSION **Gearbox:** Jordan seven-speed longitudinal **Driveshafts:** Jordan **Clutch:** AP

CHASSIS **Front suspension:** double wishbones, pushrod **Rear suspension:** double wishbones, pushrod **Suspension dampers:** Jordan **Wheel diameter:** front: 13 in. rear: 13 in.

Wheel rim widths: front: 11.5 in. rear: 13.7 in. **Tyres:** Goodyear **Brake pads:** SEP **Brake discs:** SEP **Brake calipers:** Brembo **Steering:** Jordan **Radiators:** Jordan

Fuel tanks: Jordan/ATL **Battery:** FIAMM **Instruments:** TAG Electronics

DIMENSIONS **Wheelbase:** 116.1 in./2950 mm **Track:** front: 66.9 in./1700 mm rear: 63.7 in./1618 mm **Gearbox weight:** 116.8 lb/53 kg **Chassis weight (tub):** 83.7 lb/38 kg

Formula Weight: 1311.7 lb/595 kg including driver **Fuel capacity:** 27.2 gallons/124 litres

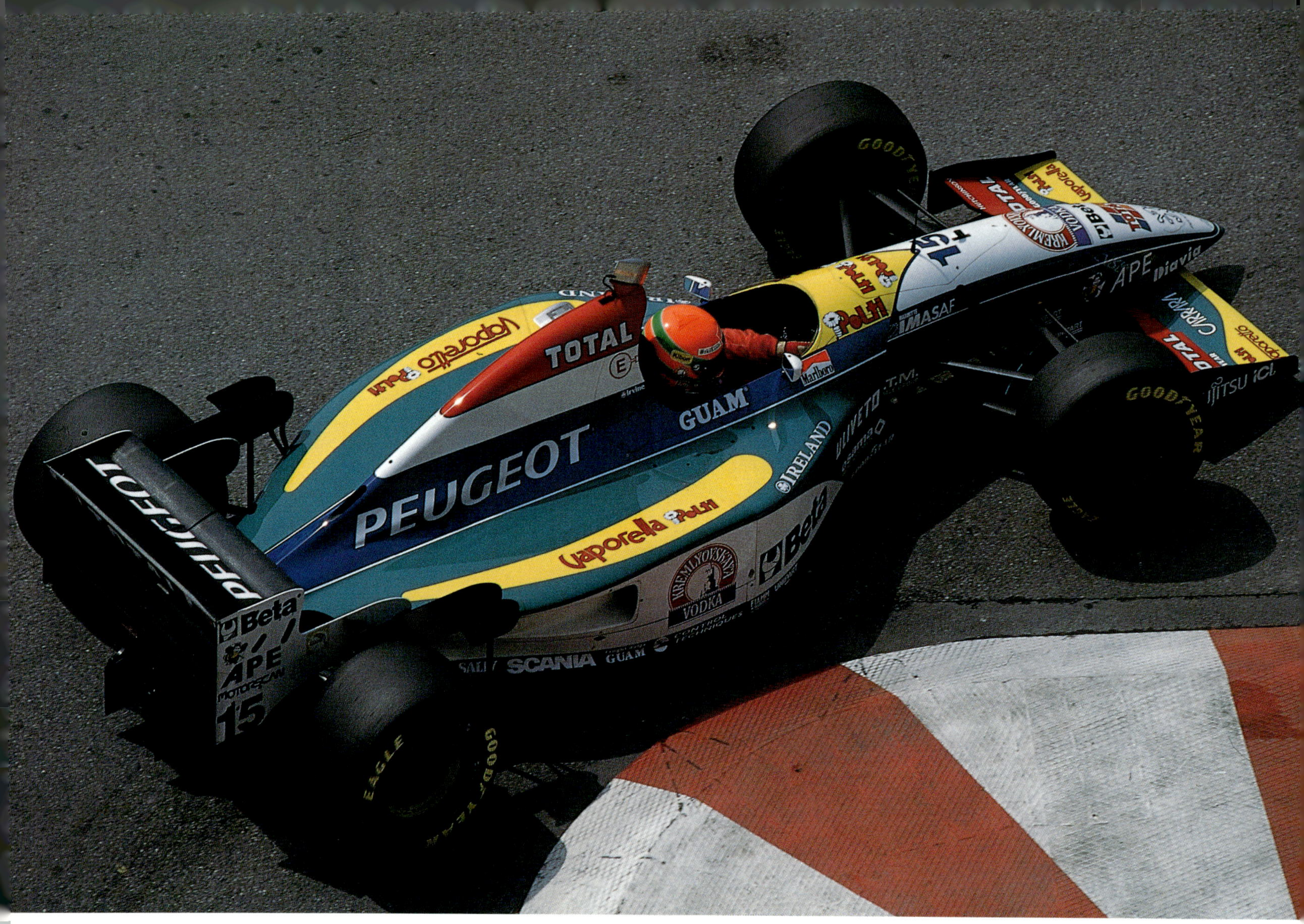
PEUGEOT
PEUGEOT
TOTAL
GUAM
SCANIA
IRELAND
Beta
APE
15
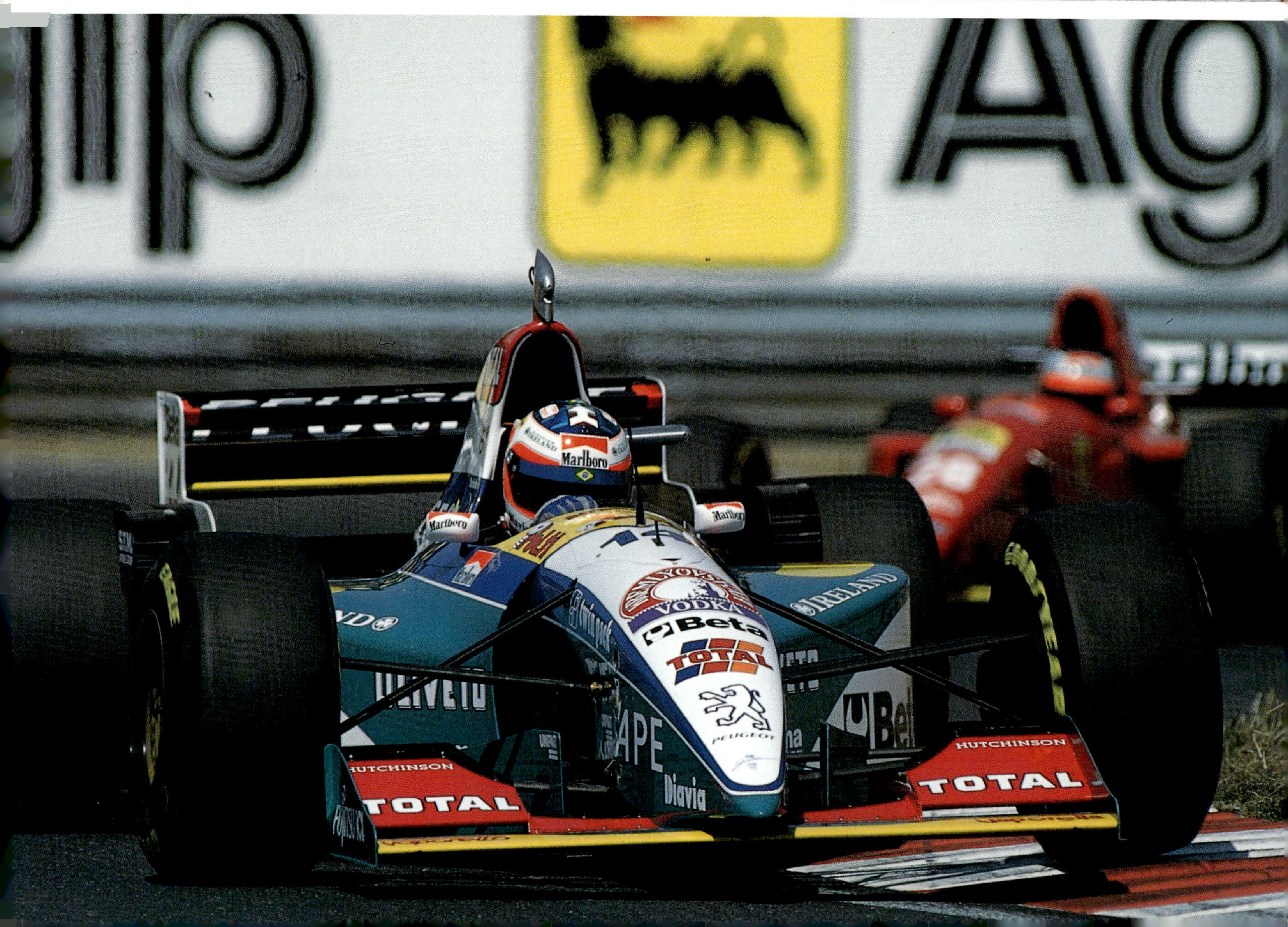
VODKA
Beta
TOTAL
TOTAL
TOTAL
HUTCHINSON
HUTCHINSON
IRELAND
APE
Diavia
PEUGEOT

FORMULA 1 REVIEW

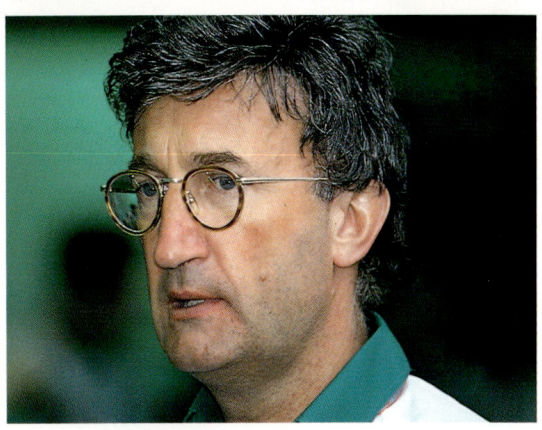

Eddie Irvine *(left)* posted a number of impressive qualifying performances but became disheartened by the Jordan-Peugeot's woeful unreliability.

Seemingly disconcerted by the pace of his self-assured team-mate, **Rubens Barrichello** *(below left)* has failed to maintain his initial meteoric progress.

Right: Both Jean-Pierre Jabouille of Peugeot and Eddie Jordan had expected a little more from their first year together.

Below right: Technical Director Gary Anderson *(right)* still has faith in Barrichello's potential. Meanwhile Eddie Irvine *(bottom right)* will measure himself against Schumacher at Ferrari in 1996.

Jerez, but we now recognise that we need to go further afield to cover all eventualities.

'From there on, we tried to pick ourselves up and improve – and we did that for a reasonable amount of time. We qualified better and Peugeot produced more power, particularly at the top end, even if the mid-range was not as strong as it could have been. By mid-season, I felt we were in a good position.'

That certainly seemed to be the way of it when Barrichello and Irvine finished second and third in Canada, the first time that two Jordan drivers had reached the podium. Luck had played its part but the Jordan drivers were there at the end to pick up the reward. They seemed ready to collect more points on circuits which would suit the Jordan 195. Then the unreliability problems arrived in earnest and Anderson watched 30 points and more fall into the hands of others. Why, then, had the extra testing not caught some of these failures in advance?

'By September, we had done maybe 20 tests,' says Anderson, 'but I could count on one hand the number which had been productive. There are many reasons for that but it was apparent that we needed to manage them a lot better. For instance, we do a lot of work at Silverstone but the attitude that we are just across the road from the factory prevails too much. If we are going testing then we should leave the factory as if it is a serious operation thousands of miles away and not the "it's no big drama, it's only Silverstone" approach. Again, this is connected with the size we are and the need for a more professional understanding of the job we are trying to do.'

The link with Peugeot was not the widely perceived end to all financial worries. Certainly, the Jordan budget may have been reasonable, but it was not top drawer, a fact underlined at Monza where the Jordans appeared festooned with stickers for tuppeny-ha'penny deals – a colourful hint to Peugeot to open their chequebook a bit wider. At least the team was not burdened by excessive retainers for their drivers.

Barrichello and Irvine took part in their second full season together and, along with Berger and Alesi at Ferrari, they were regarded as one of the most competitive pairings on the grid. Not that it was a partnership in the strict sense of the word since reputations were at stake and Barrichello, the slightly more experienced of the two, suffered at the hands of Irvine during qualifying in the first two-thirds of the season. Anderson was more concerned about getting his drivers to work for the team rather than for themselves.

'That was a bit of a stumbling block,' he admits. 'It was a struggle to keep the two of them focused together. There is no doubt that Eddie is bloody quick on a one-lap run. But, in a race situation, I think Rubens is the better of the two. His biggest problem was coming to terms with the fact that Eddie is quick. The day Rubens accepts and understands that, the day he believes that the team is doing everything it can for both drivers, then he will move a step ahead. He has a lot of potential which I don't believe even he knows he has. He has done a good job, although he can be lazy at times and if, say, he's tenth, then he will stay tenth.

'Eddie is more a seat-of-the-pants driver. If the car is reasonable, then he will do a good job. But, to be honest, I think he sometimes gets bored in the race. He will do a few laps, have a bit of a fling and then perhaps not bother if there is not a lot happening. Eddie needs to see the whole picture a bit more; think of the entire race rather than just the lap he is on.'

The team as a whole could do with the experience of running consistently – and finishing – in the top three. Pit stop strategy, for instance, has fallen down occasionally purely because of a lack of a reasoned approach which comes through knowing how to win races, the very reason why McLaren have been able to steal the edge on Jordan despite having an inferior car. It has been part of the education which is an essential aspect of the growing process which both Jordan and Peugeot must go through if they are to think seriously about joining Williams, Benetton and Ferrari.

'I'm pleased with where we are going in 1996,' says Anderson. 'But it's been a massive fight so far. People have been right to have expectations because of our step forward with Peugeot; but these people don't understand what is involved. We have been building in 1995 and I believe that next year is when those expectations should start to come good.

Maurice Hamilton

16 PACIFIC
17

BERTRAND GACHOT

GIOVANNI LAVAGGI

JEAN-DENIS DELETRAZ

ANDREA MONTERMINI

It was McLaren which kindly gave Keith Wiggins's Pacific team one of their happiest moments in 1995. During the opening laps of the European Grand Prix, Andrea Montermini was running 16th, well ahead of the two red and white cars...

All in all, however, it was a difficult second season for Pacific. 'This was our first year really,' said designer Frank Coppuck. 'We didn't have one single drawing from last year's car to even look at.' Indeed, Pacific was trying hard totally to erase the memory of the unloved Reynard-based '94 car.

Even though the new Ford ED-powered PR02 was launched relatively early, it was only just about shaken down by the time it left for Brazil and did most of its testing at the races themselves. 'We boxed ourselves into a corner on quite a few things,' admitted Coppuck. 'Some of the suspension geometry hasn't been quite right and consequently we've had some instability under braking.

'We had a lot of problems at the beginning of the year with hydraulics and I'm not really happy with the car aerodynamically. It's not too bad at high speed, but we have a problem on low- and medium-speed corners, which is where we lose the bulk of our time.

'Furthermore, we don't have some of the other bits and pieces that other teams have. We didn't have a throttle blipper for most of the season; we instigated the electronic clutch and a few other bits and pieces on the differential. We were basically building on what we have.'

Coupled to this was a difficult financial situation which eventually saw the drivers reducing the number of laps they did in practice and qualifying. 'We had the same sponsors as in 1994,' explained commercial director Mark Gallagher. 'They came back with increased budgets, but as we had increased our effort four or five fold, they knew it wouldn't be enough. It was very important for the drivers to bring money, and in the end we spent between eight and nine million dollars.

'After Magny-Cours, we had to prove to Cosworth that we were serious about controlling costs and engine mileage when cash-flow became difficult. So we ran restricted mileage up to Spa.'

Andrea Montermini spearheaded the team's effort and acquitted himself reasonably against experienced team-mate Bertrand Gachot. 'Andrea's done a good job,' said Wiggins. 'He's a racer. He's not too complicated, he is a quick driver with a basic, natural Italian feeling. Not necessarily technical, but a good driver.'

Thankfully, he didn't cost the team too much in broken cars either; nor did Gachot's successors Giovanni Lavaggi and Jean-Denis Deletraz. However, Bertrand returned for the last three races and picked up an eighth-place finish in Australia.

It was, from many viewpoints, a year for survival and building for the future. 'We're all learning in this team,' said Wiggins, 'but we're making steady progress.'

Bob Constanduros

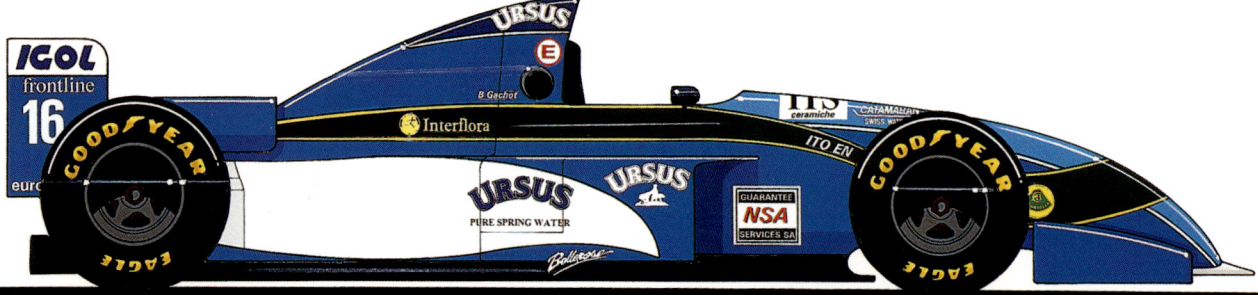

PACIFIC PR02-FORD

Sponsors: Ursus, Catamaran, Igol, Quest, Hewlett Packard, ITS

Team Principal: Keith Wiggins **Designer:** Frank Coppuck **Team Manager:** Ian Dawson **Chief Mechanic:** Jerry Bond

ENGINE **Type:** Ford ED **No. of cylinders/vee angle:** V8 (75°) **Electronics:** Cosworth/Pi Research **Fuel:** Elf **Oil:** Elf

TRANSMISSION **Gearbox:** Pacific/Hewland six-speed transverse **Driveshafts:** Tripod **Clutch:** AP

CHASSIS **Front suspension:** double wishbones, pushrod **Rear suspension:** double wishbones, pushrod **Suspension dampers:** Penske **Wheel diameter:** front: 13 in. rear: 13 in. **Wheel rim widths:** front: 11.5 in. rear: 13.7 in. **Tyres:** Goodyear **Brake pads:** Carbone Industrie **Brake discs:** Carbone Industrie **Brake calipers:** AP **Steering:** Jack Knight **Radiators:** Secan **Fuel tanks:** ATL **Battery:** FIAMM **Instruments:** Pi Research

DIMENSIONS **Wheelbase:** 113.2 in./2877 mm **Track:** front: 66.4 in./1688 mm rear: 62.9 in./1600 mm **Gearbox weight:** 114.6 lb/52 kg **Chassis weight (tub):** 88.1 lb/40 kg **Formula weight:** 1311.7 lb/595 kg including driver **Fuel capacity:** 19.7 gallons/90 litres

21 FORTI 22

PEDRO DINIZ

ROBERTO MORENO

This year's newcomers were Forti Corse, who graduated from Formula 3000 thanks to a healthy three-year contract with Pedro Paulo Diniz and his backers. Diniz, like the team, was a newcomer to F1, but experience was added by team-mate Roberto Moreno and, briefly, former Brabham and Fondmetal engineer Sergio Rinland.

The team never seemed to lack for budget, which allowed them to work steadily at gaining experience, both on the track and off. With Ford's customer ED power units and a team which almost doubled during the year to 42 people, they were never going to set the world alight, but their cars did finish on a fairly regular basis and they strove hard to catch up with the rest of the Ford opposition.

The Forti team did more testing than many more established operations before the season started, which increased their experience, but, as designer Giorgio Stirano explained, they then had to redesign the car during the course of the year: 'It simply wasn't efficient and we had to restart it. We took off more

than 60 kg from the first version to the last and by Silverstone we were on the weight limit. During the year we also had to re-homologate the nose and side pods, develop the semi-automatic gearbox, which was worth about half a second a lap, and redesign the monocoque, not in terms of shape but in terms of the lay-up of the skins.'

Stirano, who admittedly lacked F1 experience, was to be helped by Rinland, who was asked to act on a consultancy basis to lay down guide-lines, shape and mechanical concept. However, it seems that there was a problem with the value of these guidelines, so the team went ahead without him.

With everyone involved learning about the F1 business, there were not too many worrying about the team's performance, but even that improved during the year to the point that they were on a par with the somewhat poorer Pacific team, although Forti was admittedly using more-advanced-specification engines.

Diniz didn't make too many mistakes and generally kept his nose clean, staying out of the way of his peers. Moreno may have contributed in terms of experience, yet surprisingly he began to be out-qualified by his team-mate. A finish rate of around 50 per cent was impressive for newcomers; Forti may have been the butt of a few jokes at the start, but they certainly established a base on which to build for the forthcoming two years of the contract.

Bob Constanduros

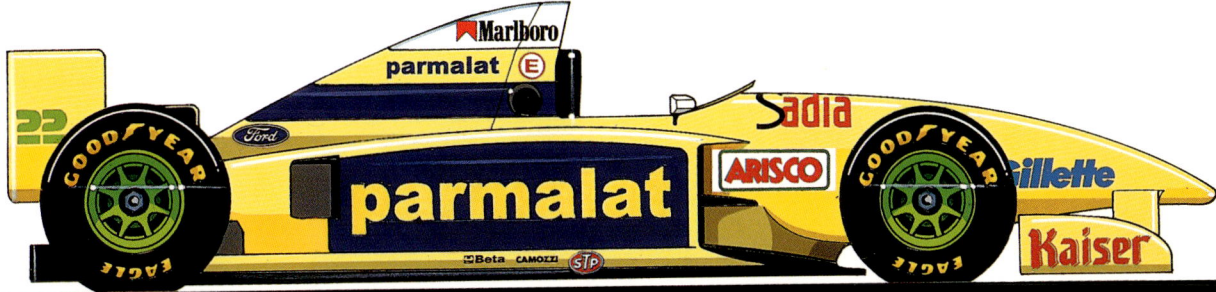

FORTI FG01-FORD

Sponsors: Parmalat, Marlboro, Sadia, Kaiser, Arisco

Team Principals: Guido Forti, Carlo Gancia **Designer:** Giorgio Stirano **Chief Mechanic:** Paolo Guerci

ENGINE **Type:** Ford ED **No. of cylinders/vee angle:** V8 (75°) **Sparking plugs:** Champion **Electronics:** Cosworth **Fuel:** Elf **Oil:** Elf

TRANSMISSION **Gearbox:** Hewland **Driveshafts:** Forti **Clutch:** AP

CHASSIS **Front suspension:** double wishbones, pushrod **Rear suspension:** double wishbones, pushrod **Suspension dampers:** Dynamic **Wheel diameter:** front: 13 in. rear: 13 in.

Wheel rim widths: front: 11.5 in. rear: 13.7 in. **Tyres:** Goodyear **Brake pads:** Carbone Industrie **Brake discs:** Carbone Industrie **Brake calipers:** AP **Steering:** Forti

Radiators: Behr **Fuel tanks:** Premier **Battery:** FIAMM **Instruments:** Pi Research

DIMENSIONS **Wheelbase:** 116.1 in./2950 mm **Track:** front: 66.9 in./1700 mm rear: 62.9 in./1600 mm **Chassis weight (tub):** 92.5 lb/42 kg **Formula weight:** 1311.7 lb/595 kg including driver

Fuel capacity: 28.5 gallons/130 litres

23 MINARDI 24

PIERLUIGI MARTINI

PEDRO LAMY

LUCA BADOER

Perhaps the saddest sight of the season was that of the Minardi team's trucks and motorhomes being escorted out of the paddock on the evening after the French Grand Prix to a truck park 5 km down the road where, like some naughty children, they were to be locked away for who knew how long.

To the outsider – and we're all outsiders because the matter remains confidential – Giancarlo Minardi's little team had its tuck pinched by those heavyweight seniors Flavio Briatore and Tom Walkinshaw, and the Italian team was still being bullied because it sneaked that this was unfair. Or they wanted justice, as it is known in the grown-up world.

Put bluntly, Minardi thought it had finally got itself out of the customer engine doldrums when they began negotiating for the Mugen V10 which had shown so well, albeit briefly, in the Lotus at Monza in 1994. Quite suddenly, on 30 November, they were told that they didn't have the Mugen and Ligier did. For a moment or two, Minardi considered quitting F1 altogether.

From then on, a series of court cases led not to Ligier having trouble in Italy, but to Minardi's equipment initially being seized by bailiffs at Magny-Cours and then held for several days after the race. Shortly afterwards the situation was resolved quite suddenly – yet, according to one source, the terms agreed in July could quite as easily have been agreed in January.

The whole saga meant that Minardi was obliged to map out two different cars. Designer Aldo Costa started on a customer Ford ED-powered chassis, switched to a Mugen V10 car and then reverted to the Ford project when the Mugen deal disappeared. That said, the main differences were with the gearbox and cooling, the rear end being dramatically different.

However, Minardi was fortunate on two counts. A supply of Cosworth's customer ED V8 was available due to the abstention of DAMS and the collapse of Larrousse's aspirations. Minardi, moreover, was a trusted Cosworth customer, and the non-participation of DAMS also meant that the new team's Xtrac-developed gearbox was available as a short-cut to an instant unit. Having said that, it was not without its problems during the course of the year, causing several retirements.

The 1995 car was to be Aldo Costa's last for the team. After seven years, he left in September for family reasons and joined Ferrari. But in his time he had established a firmly based design department; there were never any major problems with the M195. Its handling was quite neutral, reported the drivers, and well suited to the power of the ED engine.

The Cosworth-built V8 was very much a customer engine, reliable and as powerful as it could be to suit the price demanded by teams on low budgets. Once this 3-litre derivative of the HB was established, the main development was the adoption of high-pressure injectors during the year, although the life between rebuilds was extended by 150 km in the course of the season.

While Minardi could consider itself a cut above newcomers such as Forti and Pacific, it was very much on a par financially. Italy's tax investigators had made potential motor racing sponsors feel somewhat nervous, and with over 90 per cent of its finance flowing from Italian sources, Minardi had to make do with even less money than during the previous year.

For the same reason, Minardi decided not to be quite so nationalistic, appreciating that running the two Italian drivers with whom they started the season wasn't actually generating any more publicity at home – Ferrari get all that. Consequently, with mid-season cash-flow becoming tight, Pierluigi Martini was replaced by Pedro Lamy.

Prior to his departure, Martini had only been quicker than team-mate Luca Badoer five times to four. The Minardi veteran, in his eighth season with the team, had lost some of his motivation and the former F3000 champion, after a year's enforced sabbatical, was retained in prefer-

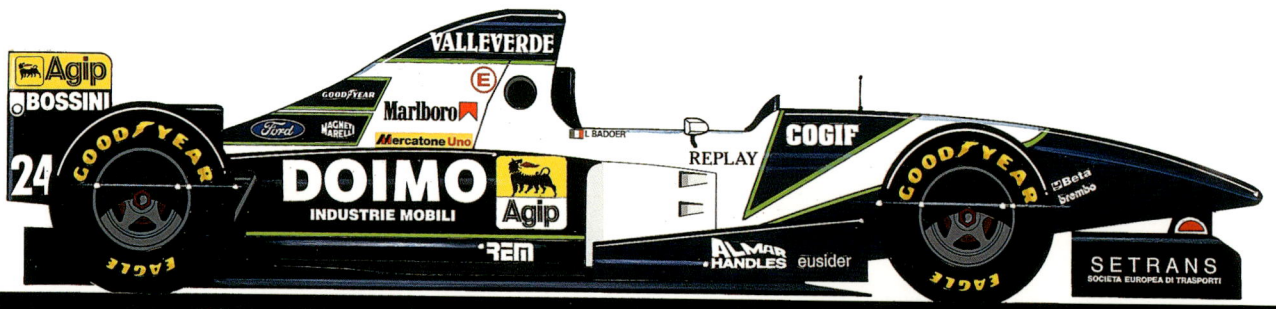

MINARDI M195-FORD

Sponsors: Marlboro, Doimo, Agip, Valleverde, Cocif, Berco

Team Principals: Giancarlo Minardi, Paolo Stanzani **Designer:** Aldo Costa **Team Manager:** Giancarlo Minardi **Chief Mechanic:** Gabriele Pagliarini

ENGINE **Type:** Ford EDM **No. of cylinders/vee angle:** V8 (75°) **Sparking plugs:** Magneti Marelli **Electronics:** Magneti Marelli **Fuel:** Agip **Oil:** Agip

TRANSMISSION **Gearbox:** Minardi/Xtrac six-speed transverse **Driveshafts:** Minardi **Clutch:** AP

CHASSIS **Front suspension:** double wishbones, pushrod, inboard spring/damper **Rear suspension:** double wishbones, pushrod, inboard spring/damper **Suspension dampers:** Penske
Wheel diameter: front: 13 in. rear: 13 in. **Wheel rim widths:** front: 11.5 in. rear: 13.7 in. **Tyres:** Goodyear **Brake pads:** Carbone Industrie **Brake discs:** Carbone Industrie
Brake calipers: Brembo **Steering:** Minardi **Radiators:** Secan **Fuel tanks:** ATL **Battery:** Magneti Marelli **Instruments:** Magneti Marelli

DIMENSIONS **Wheelbase:** 111.8 in./2840 mm **Track:** front: 66.3 in./1686 mm rear: 63.7 in./1620 mm **Formula weight:** 1311.7 lb/595 kg including driver **Fuel capacity:** 24.1 gallons/110 litres

FORMULA 1 REVIEW

Even shorn of its ungainly central wing *(bottom left)*, the M195 was scarcely elegant, but the biggest handicap facing Giancarlo Minardi *(bottom right)* and designer Aldo Costa *(centre)* was the lack of a works engine deal.

ence to the elder statesman. But Lamy certainly provided Badoer with plenty of motivation. In his first qualifying session at the Hungaroring, the Portuguese driver, making his return after suffering severe injuries testing for Lotus in 1994, was quicker than the Italian and the duo would go on to share honours. They were very evenly matched.

Such competition did have its drawbacks, however, for Badoer had more off-track incidents in the second half of the season than in the first. He crashed spectacularly under braking for the Ascari chicane during qualifying at Monza and again during the race on cold tyres. Yet, curiously, it was on this high-speed circuit that Minardi had one of its best races. Hockenheim was also good, despite the cars' lack of power.

Points, however, were inevitably going to be hard to come by. Martini and Badoer were heading for seventh and eighth at Monaco when Luca damaged his suspension, and consistency also proved beneficial at Silverstone, where Martini was again seventh at the end. It was not until the last race of the season in Adelaide that Lamy finally scored the team's sole point of the year.

In both Monaco and Britain Piero had followed home Heinz-Harald Frentzen in the Zetec-powered Sauber, a point which was not lost on the Minardi hierarchy, who usually made useful propaganda from any close encounters with teams running works engines, particularly Ford's.

It was always at the back of their minds that the team had the potential to be just as good as those others who had works engines. Unsurprisingly, they never forgot that this was the year in which they should have really made a mark in F1 after so many seasons of trying and surviving.

Bob Constanduros

25 LIGIER 26

AGURI SUZUKI

MARTIN BRUNDLE

OLIVIER PANIS

After the previous year's lack of stability, the Ligier team settled down in 1995 under its new management structure with Tom Walkinshaw at the helm, assisted by some of his long-time colleagues such as Tony Dowe and Ian Reed, formerly of TWR USA. With the addition of Operations Director Dowe, who had already had one brief stint with the team in 1994, it was no surprise to see team manager Cesare Fiorio departing at the conclusion of his contract mid-season.

However, other factors within the team were not quite so stable. To begin with, the decision on an engine supply contract with Mugen was only finalised late in 1994, which meant that the car design was late being completed. The team also signed three drivers for its two cars, prompting some slight destabilising musical chairs in the car alongside Olivier Panis. At the same time, the team was fighting for its traditional financial life-blood in the form of continued support from long-term Ligier partner/sponsors Gitanes, Elf and Loto. For the first time since 1986, Ligier was France's only F1 team.

Even so, circumstances had already seen the transfer of Renault engines from one Flavio Briatore-controlled team to another – Benetton being the fortunate and successful recipient. So what engines would Ligier use? The question mark hovered for several months, but negotiations with Mugen were well under way by the '94 Australian GP and finalised at the end of November, much to the disadvantage of Minardi, who felt they already had an agreement in place with the Japanese company. Thus in December began a legal saga which eventually came to a head after all Minardi's equipment was impounded at this year's French GP.

Due to the late decision on engines, Frank Dernie had already started designing the new car 'from the front' and had three refugee Lotus designers to help him, men already familiar with the Mugen power unit and aware of relevant short cuts. Asked about the theme of the new car shortly after the start of the season, Dernie would confess that the main aim was 'just getting it finished'.

The first Mugen V10 arrived at Ligier's Magny-Cours base on 17 December with 'Happy Christmas' emblazoned on the cam covers. Some 76 days later the new JS41 ran for the first time and the team embarked on an intensive test programme. While the car was quick straight out of the box in the dry, it was, in Dernie's words, 'really horrendous in the wet, with a propensity to oversteer into corners in an uncontrollable, unexpected and unpredictable manner'. Thankfully, that was soon cured.

What initially attracted critical attention to the new Ligier was its apparent similarity to the Benetton, a fact which was not denied. Indeed, the gearbox internals, shift mechanism and control system came directly from the Enstone-based sister team.

'The car is aerodynamically very, very similar,' added Walkinshaw. 'Mechanically it is totally different and structurally it is quite different as well. Aerodynamically, it's as close as we can make it the same. I don't know how you would end up with anything else if you take a core of engineers who have been working on the Benetton. Of course the damn thing looks the same.

'But if you go into the detail of the car, there is nothing interchangeable. When you crash-test the car, you get a totally different signature.' Dernie went on to explain that, apart from the fact that they used totally different engines, Benetton and Ligier have different CAD systems and even their alogorithms are different, so it wasn't physically possible for everything to be designed by one and manufactured by the other. There were downsides to using even the same gearbox components: suppliers were stretched to manufacture twice the number of parts.

However, the two cars progressively differed outwardly as development took place. Ligier looked for

LIGIER JS41-MUGEN HONDA

Sponsors: Gitanes, Elf, Loto Sportif

Team Principal: Tom Walkinshaw **Designer:** Frank Dernie **Team Manager:** Tony Dowe **Chief Mechanic:** Robert Dassaud

ENGINE **Type:** Mugen Honda MF301 **No. of cylinders/vee angle:** V10 (72°) **Sparking plugs:** NGK **Electronics:** Honda PGM/FI **Fuel:** Elf **Oil:** Elf

TRANSMISSION **Gearbox:** Benetton six-speed transverse **Driveshafts:** Ligier **Clutch:** AP

CHASSIS **Front suspension:** double wishbones, pushrod **Rear suspension:** double wishbones, pushrod **Suspension dampers:** Dynamic/WP **Wheel diameter:** front: 13 in. rear: 13 in. **Wheel rim widths:** front: 11 in. rear: 16.5 in. **Tyres:** Goodyear **Brake pads:** Carbone Industrie **Brake discs:** Carbone Industrie **Brake calipers:** AP/Brembo **Steering:** Ligier **Radiators:** Secan **Fuel tanks:** ATL **Battery:** FIAMM **Instruments:** Ligier

DIMENSIONS **Wheelbase:** 115.7 in./2940 mm **Formula weight:** 1311.7 lb/595 kg including driver

FORMULA 1 REVIEW

Under the guidance of Tom Walkinshaw *(right)* the Ligier team achieved a measure of stability, even if progress was steady rather than spectacular.

The reshaped team had a strong British flavour, with former Benetton engineer Frank Dernie *(below right)* responsible for the design of the new JS41 and Martin Brundle *(bottom)* sharing the second car with Japan's Aguri Suzuki. However, Jacques Laffite *(below centre right)*, the driver who epitomised the team's unique character in its early days, returned to ensure that its traditional identity was not betrayed, as well as keeping an eye on fellow countryman Olivier Panis.

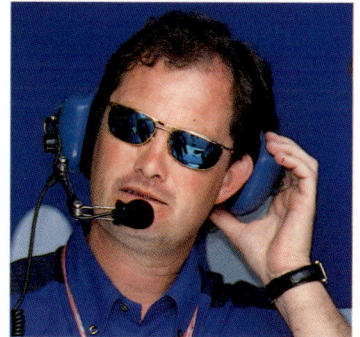

improved aerodynamic stability after their initial problems in the wet and over the bumps. They also undertook several tests on damping and springing which quickly yielded substantial results, so they could usually achieve a reasonable balance. The team also did its own fly-by-wire throttle system.

Mugen produced their first evolution engine at Monza, scene of an engine revision the year before. But comparing the Benetton's performance to the Ligier on Hockenheim's straights, Dernie found that the car was still too slow despite running very little wing. Even with revisions, the JS41 was still 17 km/h too slow on the straight at Monza, raising a question mark over the Mugen V10's power ouput. But the team's reliability was once again remarkable, only an annoying water leak and a single engine problem causing mechanical retirements.

Sadly, the sum total of the team's performances was slightly less than the previous year when Ligier did so well in the face of three management changes. Certainly the team had hoped to be more competitive with the addition of Martin Brundle to the driving strength, originally to share the second car with the returning Aguri Suzuki.

Yet by no means did the veteran Brit eclipse his younger French colleague. In qualifying, Brundle was more often than not quicker but, faced with his first strong F1 teammate, Panis still kept his end up. But Olivier made more mistakes, notably in the opening race of the year, matching his '94 retirement record (one) within a hundred metres of the first green light of '95. Furthermore, as contract time approached towards the end of the season, there was a trio of uncharacteristic spins to mar Panis's progress, although second place in Adelaide proved a timely bonus.

Brundle, meanwhile, put in a typically workmanlike job even though Suzuki's inclusion sometimes saw him on the sidelines. His chase of Coulthard at Magny-Cours was surely one of his best performances and he got on the rostrum at Spa after another fine effort. Suzuki had a mixed season, unhappy not to get more testing, which led to a reduced programme, but at least he scored a point in Germany.

Suggestions that Ligier would abandon its French roots continued to prove unwarranted and it was amusing to see that both former owners, Guy Ligier and Cyril de Rouvre, attended some races. Meanwhile Jacques Laffite rejoined the team to strengthen its national PR in an attempt to maintain the valuable French commercial contracts.

Bob Constanduros

27 FERRARI 28

JEAN ALESI

GERHARD BERGER

The Ferrari 412T2 was probably the best-looking car of 1995 from the purely aesthetic standpoint, and drivers Jean Alesi and Gerhard Berger generally had few complaints about its handling and stability. The 412T2 was the latest product of John Barnard's UK-based design armoury as the famous Maranello team sought to build on its promising 1994 season with a view to challenging for the World Championship in 1996.

While Jean Todt continued in his role as Ferrari's Sporting Director, Barnard tended to keep away from most of the races, concentrating on R&D work for the future at Ferrari Design & Development. Giorgio Ascanelli joined from McLaren as senior race engineer and the technical team was further strengthened by former Benetton aerodynamicist Wilhelm Toet. However, by season's end Ferrari had won only a single race – Jean Alesi's fortuitous victory at Montreal, inherited when Schumacher's Benetton was delayed by technical problems. It was a lot less than they had expected.

Yet the 412T2s had been quick from the outset. At Interlagos, Gerhard Berger finished third, and was briefly promoted to first after Schumacher and Coulthard were excluded for an apparent fuel irregularity. The Benetton and Williams were subsequently reinstated, much to Maranello's indignation, but Alesi helped cool the embers of the team's indignation by finishing a close second behind Hill at Buenos Aires.

Come the San Marino GP at Imola, Ferrari should have come close to winning, at worst. Unfortunately Gerhard Berger stalled his car at a refuelling stop, allowing Damon Hill's Williams through to an unchallenged victory. Another one which got away was Monaco, where John Barnard believes that Alesi had a genuine chance of winning had he not had his efforts in second qualifying blighted by a hydraulic pump failure, incurred a push-start and been obliged to take over Berger's car later in the session.

'Alesi was deeply unlucky there,' admits Barnard, 'because had he been able to start from the front row, there was a good chance of him winning. I think he might even have put it across Schumacher in a straight fight.'

Barnard's attitude towards the process of continual development, never allowing a design to 'freeze' at a specific point in time, meant that he was always pushing for improvement, regarding every development as a staging post on the journey to something better next season.

'We underestimated certain factors on the aerodynamic side,' admits Barnard. 'Although we had what we regarded as fundamentally a good car, we were pushing hard on development from mid-season, although we didn't really find anything new. We ran OK in Canada, despite Berger running low on fuel on his in lap prior to refuelling, but then Renault came out with a significant step forward on engine development for Magny-Cours which set us back a little.

'For Silverstone we began to look at revised quarter-panels for the rear bodywork, but I suppose the bottom line was that we died a bit on the aerodynamic side mid-season. We were fiddling with different Coke-panels [waisted rear bodywork] and had a new front wing package which we initially tried at Spa. We also kept on changing the rear geometry a few times.

'In general, I suppose, what surprised us most was that we started developing higher downforce loadings on the wheels than we saw before, even though the new rules were primarily intended to cut downforce. But the change of regulations also allowed us to do a small fuel tank, which enabled us to design a more compact car which the drivers felt quite confident throwing around.'

On the engine development side, Ing. Martinelli's group at Maranello concentrated on driveability as much as top-end power, all of which pleased Barnard, the smaller seven-bearing 3-litre V12 revving at around 16,500 rpm with generally impressive reliability.

There were disappointments, of

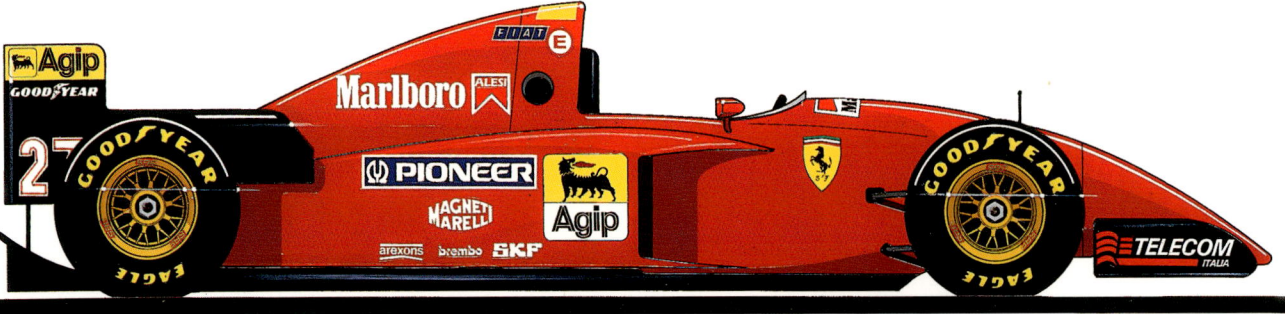

FERRARI 412T2

Sponsors: Marlboro, Agip, Pioneer

Team Principal: Luca di Montezemolo **Designer:** John Barnard **Team Manager:** Jean Todt **Chief Mechanic:** Nigel Stepney

ENGINE **Type:** Ferrari 044 **No. of cylinders/vee angle:** V12 (75°) **Sparking plugs:** Champion **Electronics:** Magneti Marelli **Fuel:** Agip **Oil:** Agip

TRANSMISSION **Gearbox:** Ferrari six-speed transverse **Driveshafts:** Ferrari **Clutch:** Daikin

CHASSIS **Front suspension:** double wishbones, pushrod, torsion spring **Rear suspension:** double wishbones, pushrod, torsion spring **Suspension dampers:** Ferrari
Wheel diameter: front: 13 in. rear: 13 in. **Wheel rim widths:** front: 12 in. rear: 13.7 in. **Tyres:** Goodyear **Brake pads:** SEP and Hitco **Brake discs:** SEP and Hitco
Brake calipers: Brembo **Steering:** Ferrari **Radiators:** Secan **Fuel tanks:** ATL **Instruments:** Magneti Marelli

DIMENSIONS **Wheelbase:** 115.3 in./2930 mm **Formula weight:** 1311.7 lb/595 kg including driver **Fuel capacity:** 27.4 gallons/125 litres

FORMULA 1 REVIEW

Right: John Barnard hears Niki Lauda's side of the story. While the English designer has endeavoured to steer clear of Maranello politics, Lauda has been at the centre of endless speculation regarding his future at Ferrari.

Centre: The Ferrari pit crew monitor progress during practice. The burden of expectation on the legendary Italian team is almost unbearable.

Bottom: Masterminding Ferrari's return to the top: Sporting Director Jean Todt and President Luca di Montezemolo.

course, most acute of which was at Monza, where Alesi and Berger were running in 1-2 formation at the head of the pack before disaster intervened. Gerhard dropped out when the wing-mounted camera on Alesi's car fell off and smashed his 412T2's left-front steering arm, after which Jean seemed on course for an emotional home victory when a rear wheel bearing packed up with only eight laps left to run.

'Nobody could blame the drivers for what happened at Monza,' conceded Barnard, 'although I'm bound to wonder how Alesi could cover 2500 km in testing there and have no problems.' Privately, Barnard feels that Jean's extrovert use of the destructive kerbs at the Italian circuit could have played a significant role in his downfall in this year's home race.

Early in the season, Barnard concluded that Alesi had come on extremely well, making highly positive contributions to the testing process and generally projecting himself as something of a reformed character. Unlike in previous years, Alesi was now the man who seemed cool and confident, while Berger, who had previously played that role, seemed less certain and secure.

True enough, Berger had more than his fair share of problems. A major refuelling glitch at Magny-Cours dropped him well down the field, he stopped with a loose wheel immediately after a pit stop at Silverstone and suffered electronic problems at the Nürburgring which prevented him from being in with a shout at the end of the European GP.

Barnard accepts that Alesi drove brilliantly for much of that race, where both 412T2s were started on slicks on a still-damp track surface, but reckons that, while concerns about fuel consumption were a factor,

77

FORMULA 1 REVIEW

Left: Gerhard Berger attacks the harbourfront chicane at Monaco with characteristic exuberance. The 412T2 was undoubtedly the most attractive F1 car to appear in 1995 as well as one of the most effective.

Italian engineer Giorgio Ascanelli *(right)* switched to Ferrari from McLaren, joining a cosmopolitan racing department that also includes English team co-ordinator Nigel Stepney *(far right)* and Japanese engine wizard Osamu Goto *(below right).*

Bottom: Jean Alesi and Gerhard Berger will be team-mates again in 1996. After three seasons together at Ferrari, both are joining Benetton.

he threw it away in the closing stages when he sat behind Häkkinen's much slower McLaren for many laps, allowing Schumacher to eat up his advantage. Had Alesi kept up the pressure, Barnard contends, he could have built up a sufficient cushion to have kept ahead to the chequered flag.

From a political standpoint, Ferrari remained its usual individualistic and highly volatile environment. Niki Lauda's role as team consultant was put very firmly on the line after he made some typically outspoken observations to the media mid-season.

Todt interpreted this as somehow trespassing on his own personal sphere of interest, and Niki was dismissed. Except, of course, he wasn't. Word has it that Lauda went straight to Fiat President Romiti, above Luca di Montezemolo's head, to get the matter straightened out and himself reinstated. This drama threatened to intensify as, in the closing weeks of the season, the German media began running stories hinting that incoming star Michael Schumacher had expressed a reluctance to work with Niki, all of which bodes well for a lively 1996 season.

Barnard has kept well out of the political arena, happy to be tucked away in Britain's F1 'Silicon Valley' where his outstation makes all the F1 suspension, gearbox spacers and nose boxes, and plans to expand to even more long-term development work in 1996, even perhaps increasing Ferrari Design & Development's component manufacturing capability. Barnard is also extremely happy with the way that Ferrari's wind tunnel, at British Aerospace's Filton facility, is now contributing to the competitiveness of the programme.

Michael Schumacher's recruitment for 1995 and '96 on a contract which will reputedly earn him almost $50 million for that period is being seen by some observers as the final element in the jigsaw required to push Maranello back into a World Championship-winning position. John Barnard has another new chassis under development to cater for the promising new 3-litre V10 engine which underwent its first circuit test at Fiorano during October '94.

Building a winning Formula 1 car is a complex, time-consuming and highly expensive operation. Whether a single driver can raise the standard of Maranello's on-track game to the point where the team can win its first constructors' championship since 1983 remains to be seen. Certainly, having missed out on the opportunity of working with Prost at Ferrari, Barnard is looking forward to seeing what Schumacher can bring to the party. Stars of that calibre don't pass by very often.

Alan Henry

29 SAUBER
30

KARL WENDLINGER

JEAN-CHRISTOPHE BOULLION

HEINZ-HARALD FRENTZEN

The world looked at Ford's Zetec-R installed in a Sauber and thought 'what happened to the World Championship-winning engine from last season?' Was it the engine, reduced to 3 litres? Was it the team, not as experienced as Benetton? Or the lead driver – highly regarded, but without Schumacher's seasoned edge? Or the management, lacking either the experience or clout of those in charge at Enstone?

Of course, it was all these and more. Sauber had enjoyed a special relationship with a major manufacturer right from its F1 debut. But now Mercedes had ditched them in favour of McLaren – and Benetton had ditched Ford for Renault. So the wallflowers joined forces.

Nobody was very certain that the new alliance would work. After all, Sauber had been a Mercedes team far longer than it had been competing in F1, having been regarded as a quasi-works organisation from its endurance racing days. But all that had come to an end, as had the additional sponsorship conjured up by Mercedes when the mythical *Broker* magazine came to nought. Sauber would now have to stand on its own feet.

They did this by taking on Red Bull, makers of the Austrian health drink, as a majority shareholder, although Peter Sauber kept control of his company by retaining the lion's share of voting rights. Joining Red Bull was the Malaysian petroleum giant, Petronas, so the team was no worse off than during the previous year. The Fritz Kaiser Group was retained to look after sponsorship contacts.

Ford, spurned by Benetton, had considered several other teams but eventually threw in its lot with Sauber. There were mixed blessings. Sauber had already initiated a chassis design to accommodate Mario Illien's compact and light new 3-litre Mercedes V10. In the end, they would run Ford's Zetec-R which, still having the bore of a 3.5-litre, was between 10 and 15 kg heavier and, says Sauber, 35 mm longer than the previous year's Mercedes V10, and a bit higher too. All in all, the engine didn't suit the chassis, the weight distribution was wrong and the car suffered from inherent understeer.

The team did as much as they could to improve the situation. After Imola, a magnesium gearbox casing replaced the original aluminium one in order to save weight at the rear. There was also a switch to a high-nose specification, plus revised undertray, rear wings, turning vanes, springs and dampers post-Brazil. These helped reduce the C14's understeer and lack of efficiency, and at least the car was reliable from the start.

In the meantime, the team faced the delicate task of re-introducing Karl Wendlinger to F1 after his dreadful accident the year before at Monaco. Sadly, it seemed that he wasn't up to it. This wasn't a problem for the team, only for Karl; after three races, his place was taken by Williams test driver Jean-Christophe Boullion.

It wasn't easy for the Frenchman either. Boullion made a spectacular debut at Monaco, crashing at the chicane in an almost identical re-run of Wendlinger's accident just twelve months earlier. He then raced to eighth place, but had to learn the many circuits which were new to him and found it difficult swapping back and forth from the Williams he tested to the Sauber he raced.

Yet as the season progressed, several developments prompted an overall improvement in the Sauber team performance. Firstly, Frentzen was developing into a fine technical driver, able to tell engineers exactly what the car was doing and what improvements were required. Secondly, Max Welti rejoined as team director, the conductor of the Sauber orchestra directing operations fairly, analytically and positively. Thirdly, the team was now gathering experience, able to make improvements expediently. Fourthly, given some direction, the whole programme began to gather its own momentum with everyone enthusiastic that progress was being made.

SAUBER C14-FORD

Sponsors: Red Bull, Petronas

Team Principals: Peter Sauber, Max Welti **Designers:** Leo Ress, André de Cortanze **Team Manager:** Beat Zehnder **Chief Mechanic:** Daniel Christ

ENGINE **Type:** Ford Zetec-R **No. of cylinders/vee angle:** V8 (90°) **Electronics:** Ford **Fuel:** Elf **Oil:** Elf

TRANSMISSION **Gearbox:** Sauber/Xtrac six-speed transverse **Driveshafts:** MAT **Clutch:** Sachs

CHASSIS **Front suspension:** double wishbones, pushrod **Rear suspension:** double wishbones, pushrod **Suspension dampers:** Sachs **Wheel diameter:** front: 13 in. rear: 13 in.

Wheel rim widths: front: 11.5 in. rear: 13.7 in. **Tyres:** Goodyear **Brake pads:** SEP **Brake discs:** SEP **Brake calipers:** Brembo **Steering:** Sauber **Radiators:** Behr/Secan

Fuel tanks: ATL **Battery:** Sauber **Instruments:** Ford

DIMENSIONS **Wheelbase:** 114.9 in./2920 mm **Track:** front: 66.1 in./1680 mm rear: 63.3 in./1610 mm **Gearbox weight:** 116.8 lb/53 kg **Chassis weight (tub):** 90.3 lb/41 kg

Formula weight: 1311.7 lb/595 kg including driver **Fuel capacity:** 27.4 gallons/125 litres

FORMULA 1 REVIEW

Right: Chief Designer Leo Ress *(left)* discusses progress with Peter Gillitzer of Ford. The loss of the Mercedes backing which had helped his team to graduate to Grand Prix racing obliged Peter Sauber *(far right)* to seek a new partner.

There were signs during the season that the technical team led by Ress and André de Cortanze *(below right)* was beginning to come to terms with the demands of Formula 1, but Sauber's greatest single asset is possibly gifted German driver Heinz-Harald Frentzen *(bottom),* who scored the first podium finish of his Grand Prix career with third place at Monza.

In fact, progress was achieved right from the beginning of the year. Although Frentzen's ninth on the grid in Argentina was his best qualifying performance until Portugal, his fifth-place finish at Buenos Aires was followed up with sixths at Imola, Monaco and Silverstone, a fifth in Hungary, fourth at Spa and then his first podium when he took third place at Monza.

In terms of qualifying, Frentzen started off just inside the top 15, then gradually pulled up to around the sixth row of the grid and regularly moved up into the top ten after Cosworth's mid-season hike in engine power which originally appeared at Hockenheim.

Cosworth increased the Zetec's maximum speed by 500 rpm as well as working on throttle response and the inlet manifold; although the engine which appeared for Hockenheim was principally used for qualifying, it was intended as a race engine. It was no surprise for Cosworth that Sauber commented on their rate of development. 'Everyone wants more development, don't they?' pointed out Cosworth's Dick Scammell.

The cars proved remarkably reliable, with neither driver having too many retirements despite some mistakes which would not have been made by more experienced hands. Frentzen, however, still had an enviable reputation to defend as a contemporary of Schumacher's and this was difficult for him. Both he and Boullion made elementary errors, although usually reserving them for free practice sessions, and the team proved adept at preparing reliable cars.

As ever, Sauber tended to err on the side of caution in terms of race strategy. Frentzen was always keen on a single stop rather than risking too many pit visits for fuel and tyres. Boullion scored his first points in Germany while Italy was the apogee in terms of performance, with both drivers scoring.

By the end of the year, Sauber had been confirmed as the recipient of Ford's new V10 engine for 1996. At least the team would now benefit from continuity, despite shouldering the responsibility of a new engine to develop.

Bob Constanduros

BENETTON'S FIRST

1995. Benetton's first World Constructor's Championship.

SCHUMACHER'S SECOND

Michael Schumacher's second World Driver's Championship.

CHAMPION'S 18TH

Champion's 18th World Championship. The greatest track record in Formula One.

324 Grand Prix wins

World-beating technology you can drive on the road.

1995 GRANDS PRIX

BRAZILIAN GRAND PRIX	84
ARGENTINE GRAND PRIX	94
SAN MARINO GRAND PRIX	104
SPANISH GRAND PRIX	112
MONACO GRAND PRIX	120
CANADIAN GRAND PRIX	130
FRENCH GRAND PRIX	138
BRITISH GRAND PRIX	146
GERMAN GRAND PRIX	156
HUNGARIAN GRAND PRIX	166
BELGIAN GRAND PRIX	174
ITALIAN GRAND PRIX	182
PORTUGUESE GRAND PRIX	192
GRAND PRIX OF EUROPE	200
PACIFIC GRAND PRIX	208
JAPANESE GRAND PRIX	216
AUSTRALIAN GRAND PRIX	224

WORLD CHAMPIONSHIP • ROUND 1

Brazilian Grand Prix

| SCHUMACHER |
| COULTHARD |
| BERGER |
| HÄKKINEN |
| ALESI |
| BLUNDELL |

BRAZILIAN GRAND PRIX

Michael Schumacher endured a weekend of wildly fluctuating fortunes. A disturbing high-speed crash in first qualifying *(main picture)* failed to shake the German's steely resolve and he opened his title defence with a comfortable win, only for victory to be handed to Ferrari's Gerhard Berger *(inset)* when Schumacher and second-place finisher David Coulthard were both disqualified.

It looked like a bad start to a troubled weekend. It had been raining, sure enough, but the track was dry by the time the Benetton B195 came slamming into the 140 mph Ferra Dura right-hander at Interlagos. It was Friday's first qualifying session and Michael Schumacher had just moved up to set fourth-fastest time when the Renault-engined car seemed to twitch suddenly, midway through the corner. At this point on the circuit, a driver is faced with braking hard immediately his car is pointing in a straight line again, in preparation for another, much sharper right-hander. But Michael never got that far.

The Benetton lurched outwards onto the grass, snapped sideways and was momentarily launched into the air before slamming backwards into the retaining wall. The rear end of the Benetton seemed quite badly damaged, but the German driver walked away suffering from only slight bruising.

The session was red-flagged to a halt so that the debris could be cleared up, but there was no question of Michael taking over Johnny Herbert's car for the balance of the session. Nor would Johnny go out either. Both Benetton drivers were grounded for the remainder of the day as it quickly became clear that Michael's accident had been caused by some sort of steering failure.

'There was a little movement in the steering wheel at the previous corner and at the next it went completely,' explained Schumacher. 'I spun the car backwards into the tyre barrier and the safety structure behind my head did a good job of protecting me.

'For sure I am not very happy about this, but I believe that the team will spend a lot of time investigating the situation for tomorrow and they will find the problem.' Subsequent examination revealed an apparent partial failure of a joint in the steering column at the point where it angles to enter the steering rack, but the matter was speedily rectified and both B195s duly appeared on parade for Saturday morning's free practice session. Replacement components were manufactured by a company in São Paulo located by Benetton engineer Tim Wright and no further problems were encountered.

Some observers in the pit lane could not avoid shuddering ever so slightly. Mention of steering problems inevitably threw people's minds back to that dark day at Imola the

TECHNICAL CHANGES FOR THE NEW SEASON

The long-term legacy of the fatal accidents to Ayrton Senna and Roland Ratzenberger during the 1994 San Marino Grand Prix meeting provided sustained impetus for more revisions to the F1 technical regulations into 1995, continuing a process which had started at the FIA's initiative only a few weeks after that disastrous weekend.

However, the bottom line was that this would now be another battle between the rule makers and car designers. The most basic change was the reduction of engine capacity from 3.5 to 3 litres, accompanied by stringent measures to check fuel specifications.

This involved the competing fuel companies lodging with the FIA a sample of any fuel specification they wished to employ at an individual race or races. What amounted to a DNA-style 'fingerprint' would be produced, unique to each fuel sample, and subsequent samples taken from the governing body would be submitted to a gas chromatograph test to ensure that the 'fingerprint' matched. As the Brazilian Grand Prix served to emphasise, this strategy was set to cause trouble from the outset.

Other key steps designed to rein in F1 car performance included:
- Introduction of 50 mm step in chassis floor in addition to 10 mm 'plank' to reduce contribution of under-car aerodynamics.
- Smaller front wings. Except for brake cooling ducts, in plan view there was to be no bodywork in the area formed by two longitudinal lines 400 mm and 1000 mm from the car centre line and two transverse lines, one 350 mm forward of and one 800 mm behind the front wheel centre line.
- Smaller and lower rear wings. Any bodywork positioned behind the rear wheel centre line more than 500 mm above the 'reference plane' not allowed to occupy a surface area greater than 70 per cent of a rectangle whose edges are 500 mm either side of the car centre line and 500 mm and 800 mm above that reference plane.
- Further-enhanced crash testing. Further update of frontal impact test against a solid barrier, first introduced in 1985. Involves nose box attached to a complete survival cell, fuel tank full of water and a 75 kg dummy strapped into the cockpit. During the impact, deceleration in the chest of the dummy must not exceed 60G for more than three milli-seconds. Frontal deformation confined to nose box and no damage sustained to fire extinguishers or seat belts (harness width of which increased from 50 to 75 mm for 1995).

In addition, chassis also submitted to a static load test on main roll structure, on side of nose, and a dramatic impact test of 780 kg travelling at 5 m/second against impact absorbing structures either side of the complete survival cell.

The neat Pacific PR02 (right) represented a huge advance over its Reynard-dervied predecessor but that alone was no guarantee of competitiveness.

Above right: Eddie Jordan's ambitious team had once again embraced the benefits of a factory engine deal, forsaking Brian Hart's tiny concern for the might of Peugeot.

BENETTON-RENAULT
All-new Benetton B195 chassis from Ross Brawn's design group, now fitted with 3-litre Renault RS7 V10 engine driving through six-speed semi-automatic transverse gearbox and retaining three-pedal set-up for the start of the season. Car equipped with 150-litre fuel tank to give team flexibility and scope for possible one-stop race strategy. Reigning World Champion Michael Schumacher continuing to lead the team partnered by former Lotus number one Johnny Herbert. Frenchman Emmanuel Collard signed as the team's test driver.

TYRRELL-YAMAHA
Ukyo Katayama now partnered by highly rated F1 novice Mika Salo in promising Harvey Postlethwaite-designed type 023, featuring new 'Hydrolink' suspension system designed to enhance mechanical grip and claw back some of the performance benefits of active suspension, which was banned at the end of the 1993 season. Latest-spec 3-litre Yamaha OX10C V10-cylinder engine driving through six-speed transverse semi-automatic gearbox using pneumatic activation from reservoir also feeding engine's air-valve mechanism.

WILLIAMS-RENAULT
Striking new car breaking with recent Williams design tradition by having Benetton-style raised nose, although Chief Designer Adrian Newey retained side pod configuration similar to immediate FW16 predecessor. Powered by 3-litre Renault RS7 V10 driving through lighter and narrower six-speed transverse semi-automatic gearbox with driveshafts encased in aerodynamic CFC upper rear wishbone as on previous year's car. Torsion bar springing at front, coil-spring dampers at rear. Damon Hill and David Coulthard retained in all-British driver line-up with highly rated 1994 FIA F3000 Champion Jean-Christophe Boullion signed as test driver.

McLAREN-MERCEDES
Visually dramatic new McLaren MP4/10 chassis powered by 3-litre Ilmor-made Mercedes-Benz FO110, a 75-degree pneumatic-valve V10 with narrow bottom end specifically designed to suit new 50 mm stepped undertray regulations. McLaren transverse six-speed semi-automatic gearbox with electronic activation developed by associate company, TAG Electronic Systems. Two-pedal configuration with hand-operated clutch control behind steering wheel. Distinctive aerodynamics incorporating secondary aerofoil on trailing edge of engine cover, apparently to enhance airflow through rear vent of engine airbox. Nigel Mansell signed to drive alongside Mika Häkkinen, although Mark Blundell called in to start the season when preliminary testing revealed that Mansell's hips could not be accommodated within existing monocoque; intensive development programme instigated to produce new, slightly wider MP4/10B chassis in time for third race of season. Blundell thereafter confirmed as team's test driver.

ARROWS-HART
Surely the most strikingly innovative and superbly packaged car of the 1995 F1 generation, the Arrows team's Alan Jenkins-designed Footwork FA16 featured an ultra-slim monocoque and mono-shock suspension, front and rear, powered by Brian Hart's brilliantly compact new type 830 3-litre, 72-degree V8 engine driving through a six-speed longitudinal gearbox. Gianni Morbidelli signed to start the season as team leader on an eight-race deal, with Japanese F3000 exponent Taki Inoue providing the finance necessary to gain access to the second car.

SIMTEK-FORD
Brand-new S951 chassis based heavily on lessons learned with 1994 chassis from this small Banbury-based constructor. Powered by 3-litre Cosworth ED V8 engine driving through Benetton six-speed transverse gearbox as part of a deal which saw Jos Verstappen joining Simtek together with Hideki Noda and Mimmo Schiattarella, who both had sponsorship available to secure a limited number of races.

JORDAN-PEUGEOT
All-new Gary Anderson-designed 195 chassis package powered by 72-degree Peugeot A10E V10-cylinder engine derived from A6 3.5-litre unit previously used by McLaren, but with new

cylinder head and crankshaft and revised bore and stroke. Car featured seven-speed longitudinal Jordan semi-automatic gearbox with electronically operated hydraulic sequential change and pushrod suspension all round. Potentially very strong driver line-up of Rubens Barrichello and Eddie Irvine retained for new season.

PACIFIC-FORD
The small Thetford-based team started with a clean sheet of paper following disastrous maiden F1 season in 1994 with Ilmor-powered, Reynard-originated design. All-new Frank Coppuck-designed PR02 monocoque powered by 3-litre Cosworth ED V8 engine and featuring smallest fuel tank of current F1 generation at 90 litres, requiring two refuelling stops at every race on the calendar. Bertrand Gachot stayed on to lead driver line-up partnered by Italy's Andrea Montermini. Fielded under Pacific Team Lotus banner following arrangement with Lotus MD David Hunt after the famous Hethel-based team closed its doors after 37 seasons in F1.

BRAZILIAN GRAND PRIX

Left: The 1995 Formula 1 technical regulations were framed to reduce aerodynamic downforce and limit cornering speeds. In addition to the 50 mm step in the chassis floor shown in the diagram, the cars were again fitted with the 10 mm 'plank' introduced in 1994.

KEY
Area F: Bodywork which is more than 250 mm from the centre line of the car may not lie outside these boxes on each side of the car; Area H: Bodywork which is more than 150 mm from the centre line of the car is not permitted in these areas on each side of the car; Area D: Bodywork is not allowed in this area more than 150 mm from the centre line of the car.

With thanks to Williams Grand Prix Engineering

The raised nose pioneered by Benetton had become the latest Formula 1 design orthodoxy; none was more dramatically contoured than McLaren's *(below)*.

Bottom: Ligier Technical Director Frank Dernie *(left)* confers with Benetton counterpart Ross Brawn. The marked similarity between the French team's latest offering and the new Benetton prompted speculation that its origins owed more to Enstone than Magny-Cours.

Weight fluctuations prompt paddock whispers

New regulations requiring the all-up weight of a car and driver together to be not less than 595 kg triggered another slice of potential controversy at Interlagos when suspicions were raised that certain drivers might have been attending the official pre-season weigh-in carrying some form of ballast.

With cars now weighed after the race with the driver not strapped in the cockpit, a heavier 'officially registered' driver weight would offer potential for running the car itself lighter in the individual race. Doubts as to whether several drivers were playing fair were inevitably triggered when Michael Schumacher tipped the scales at 77 kg – 8 kg heavier than last year. He was weighed again after the race, when he was found to be 71.5 kg.

Schumacher was trenchant in his defence of this weight increase, explaining that he had pursued a revised training regime which was responsible for turning fat into muscle. Sceptics understandably pointed out that, with a physique like a greyhound, it was not immediately obvious that the 1994 World Champion had fatty tissue to spare.

Among other drivers to display unexpected increases in weight were Gerhard Berger and Heinz-Harald Frentzen, both of whom were apparently heavier by 6.5 kg. However, when they were weighed again following the race, the figures were still the same.

MINARDI-FORD
Amidst accusations that the Mugen Honda company had reneged on a deal to supply them with V10 engines in 1995, the Minardi team settled down at the end of November '94 to redesign the new M195 challenger. This accommodated a customer Cosworth Ford V8, officially designated the EDM to indicate its use of Magneti Marelli electronic engine management system. Neat, evolutionary Aldo Costa design using Minardi electro-hydraulic control system for Xtrac semi-automatic gearbox. Pierluigi Martini stayed on as *de facto* team leader, partnered by F1 returnee Luca Badoer, while '94 Italian F3 champ and Monaco F3 winner Giancarlo Fisichella signed as official test driver.

LIGIER-MUGEN
Now under the operational management of former Benetton engineering director Tom Walkinshaw, the Ligier team benefited from Mugen Honda 3-litre V10 engines installed in the all-new Frank Dernie-designed JS41, which looked a bit too much like a blue Benetton B195 for the liking of several rival chief designers when it rolled out for scrutineering at Interlagos. Olivier Panis, Martin Brundle and Aguri Suzuki signed to drive, with the Frenchman scheduled for a full programme and Suzuki opening the season in the second car.

FERRARI
Distinctive new John Barnard-designed 412T2 powered by new 3-litre steel-block V12 engine positioned further forward in chassis thanks to the use of smaller 140-litre fuel cell under the new regulations. Torsion bar suspension all round with transverse six-speed semi-automatic gearbox and two-pedal control with manual clutch. Gerhard Berger and Jean Alesi remain on driving strength with Nicola Larini retained as test driver. Engine department, now under the direction of Paolo Martinelli, working on V10 programme for possible use later in the season installed in the same chassis.

SAUBER-FORD
Ford's factory-backed team for the '95 F1 season using 3-litre Zetec-R V8s after similar deal with Benetton came to an end. Neatly engineered and unspectacular Leo Ress-designed C14 chassis for Heinz-Harald Frentzen and Karl Wendlinger, with Argentine driver Norberto Fontana, a '94 German F3 Championship contender, signed as test driver.

LARROUSSE
Acute financial problems force the French team to miss the first two races of the season while discussions continue regarding possible partnership with Junior Team principals Jean Messaoudi and Laurent Barlesi. Initial plans to update LH94 chassis come to nothing and team officially withdraws from F1 just prior to San Marino GP.

---

previous May when Ayrton Senna was killed while leading the San Marino GP. Steering failure had been mentioned as a possible cause behind the accident which cost the life of the world's leading F1 driver. And here we were, nine months later, at Ayrton's home circuit, still waiting for the official inquiry to stumble towards some sort of definitive conclusion, and we were – yet again – talking about broken steering.

Yet this was only the second of three chapters in the troubled story of Schumacher's Brazilian GP weekend. He'd got off on the wrong foot by attracting suspicion at the official weigh-in, where he was revealed to have ballooned by 9 kg since last season (see sidebar). The uncharitably minded concluded it was a scam to cheat the 595 kg car-and-driver minimum weight limit, but Michael put it down to a change in his training regime which had transformed surplus fat into muscle.

If FIA Technical Delegate Charlie Whiting's smile became ever so slightly fixed at this point, it was perhaps understandable. Schumacher's whippet-like frame hardly seemed burdened by any unwanted flab. But other drivers also displayed similar, if less extreme, discrepancies in the avoirdupois department. Whiting let it pass, but Schumacher was weighed again after the race. No problem; he and his Benetton tipped the scales at 599 kg. Quite legal.

But that wasn't to be the end of the story. Schumacher's winning Benetton B195 and David Coulthard's Williams FW17 would be found using Elf fuel the specification of which did not match the sample originally lodged with the FIA prior to the meeting (see sidebar again). As a result, they were disqualified from the race and victory fell to Gerhard Berger's Ferrari 412T2, which had been one lap down at the chequered flag. For the moment, it seemed as though the 1995 season would pick up where '94 left off. The transition from one controversy to another appeared absolutely seamless.

Meanwhile, back to Friday afternoon. The unspoken sub-text to everybody's overwhelming relief was that Schumacher had been extremely lucky. There were plenty of other places at Interlagos where such a crucial malfunction could have proved simply disastrous for the reigning World Champion. But everybody tried to keep their thoughts privately filed in a mental card-index.

And you couldn't help noticing that the track was pretty bumpy.

Try that again. Appallingly bumpy! Interlagos had been resurfaced since the 1994 race, but to an extremely unsatisfactory standard. 'Bumpy as hell, quite unbelievable,' shrugged Brazilian first-timer David Coulthard. The mood in Senna's home town was also somewhat uncertain. Would there be a backlash against F1 in general? Frank Williams, for one, was taking no chances, Ayrton's old team chief surrounded by a posse of burly bodyguards wherever he went. But there was no aggravation whatsoever, and the apparent lack of spectator interest during the two days of qualifying was corrected when a capacity 40,000-strong crowd turned out on race morning.

On the face of Friday's events it would have been easy to conclude that Damon Hill was set to start the new season as he'd finished the last – hustling Schumacher into an uncharacteristic error. Damon finished first qualifying 0.9s faster than Gerhard Berger's pretty new Ferrari 412T2, the Austrian just nipping in ahead of Hill's team-mate David Coulthard in the other Williams FW17.

The young Scot's performance was pretty impressive given that this was his first experience of Interlagos and he was also shrugging off the after-effects of tonsillitis, which had disrupted his physical preparation for the first race of the year. 'The car feels pretty good,' said David, 'but I'm just a little bit concerned that I may lack stamina for the race as I've not been able to do any training for two weeks.'

On Saturday, Schumacher was quickest in the morning's free practice session, which started in heavy rain, the track drying out almost completely before the end. The overnight modifications to the steering column joint ensured that he was now in a considerably more relaxed frame of mind, although the main factor behind Michael's decisive recovery was a change in the B195's ride height.

This was duplicated by Johnny Herbert and, while Michael pushed his way ahead of Coulthard to join Hill on the front row, Benetton's number two completed the second row to make it three British drivers in the top four. 'At least from that point of view, the English have got Michael surrounded,' smiled Damon wryly. Herbert's success was achieved at a price; one of the skids

87

BRAZILIAN GRAND PRIX

Diary

December 1994

FIA Contract Recognition Board rules that Williams, not McLaren, has prior claim to David Coulthard's services for 1995.

David Hunt takes control of beleaguered Team Lotus and lays off staff until end of the year.

Yoshio Nakamura, former Honda F1 chief engineer, dies aged 76.

Damon Hill clinches new contract with Williams for 1995, reputedly worth over £1 million.

January 1995

Williams confirms David Coulthard as Damon Hill's team-mate for the 1995 F1 World Championship season.

Karl Wendlinger, now recovered from injuries sustained at Monaco in 1994, is confirmed as Sauber team driver alongside Heinz-Harald Frentzen.

Team Lotus finally abandons struggle to continue independent F1 operation.

New Jordan 195-Peugeot is the first 1995 F1 challenger to be unveiled.

February

Nigel Mansell confirmed as Mika Häkkinen's McLaren team-mate.

New McLaren MP4/10-Mercedes launched at London's Science Museum.

McLaren find Mansell unable to fit comfortably in new car. Intensive programme to build enlarged monocoque set in hand, as Mark Blundell stands in for Nigel at first two Grands Prix of season.

---

had come off the underside, punching a hole in the bottom of the monocoque which required an all-nighter to repair, including removing the car's fuel cell.

Hill had been less happy with his FW17 in second qualifying, having made a slight chassis set-up change after the morning's free practice. The handling didn't feel quite so sharp and he also lost time running wide on oil dropped by Berger's Ferrari at the chicane immediately after the pits.

Had there been a contest for the best-looking new F1 car of the 1995 generation, Maranello's gorgeous low-nosed 412T2 would surely have swept the board. Moreover, despite the need for some minor changes in engine mapping on Friday, both Berger and Jean Alesi were well satisfied with the promise displayed by their new machines.

Gerhard, using a two-pedal set-up with hand-operated clutch, took an excellent second place on the first day, with Alesi, using a three-pedal set-up, fourth after a slight tyre pressure discrepancy on his first run. At his second try, the Frenchman was balked by a slower car, but he was still pretty pleased with the end result.

'Within another couple of races, I think we should be able to catch the Williams,' said Berger confidently, even though he suffered a setback in the form of an engine failure in second qualifying. He slipped to fifth in the final order, one place ahead of Alesi.

Holidaying in the Caribbean, Nigel Mansell might have been forgiven for feeling quite satisfied that he had made the correct decision when he opted to pass up the chance of squeezing himself into the new McLaren MP4/10 cockpit, preferring to wait until a new, enlarged chassis was built up specifically to accommodate him.

His stand-in, Mark Blundell, reported that the new McLaren's handling still felt rather unstable and unpredictable, particularly as it built up speed coming out of the corners. Regular team man Mika Häkkinen also had problems, being slowed early on Friday morning when the steering began to stiffen up due to a partially seized front wishbone joint.

However, the MP4/10's handling had definitely been improved since its initial pre-season testing by the adoption of revised rear suspension geometry, incorporating repositioned lower rear wishbones, which had been tested by Häkkinen at Silverstone just before the cars were loaded up for the flight to Brazil.

Blundell eventually qualified ninth, two places behind Mika and separated from his team-mate only by Irvine's Jordan and 0.4s. Mark was pretty happy with that, but the Finn made no bones about the fact that he was still disappointed with the chassis balance and expected much more.

A sense of great anticipation had surrounded the elegant Jordan-Peugeots throughout the whirl of pre-season testing, but Rubens Barrichello would claim the unwanted distinction of experiencing the first engine failure of the year 'on active service'. The Brazilian's Jordan emitted a thin trail of smoke from one exhaust pipe before rolling to a halt out on the circuit early in first qualifying. It seemed pretty clear that a valve or piston failure had been to blame, but Peugeot Sport boss Jean-Pierre Jabouille couldn't quite bring himself to utter the words. 'Our first session has been difficult, we have had quite a few problems,' he said euphemistically.

Rubens abandoned his 195 out on the circuit, grabbed his seat and ran back to the pits to take over Eddie Irvine's sister car. 'I had very little time to sit in Eddie's car before going out onto the circuit,' he explained later. 'We couldn't put my seat in or change the pedals, so I was quite uncomfortable and it was difficult to see the track properly.' Under the circumstances, 11th-fastest time wasn't too bad.

Unfortunately, there was more disappointment in store for Jordan on Saturday. Irvine suffered a gearbox oil pressure problem in the morning, then spun off after setting eighth-fastest time in second qualifying. Barrichello, meanwhile, had a problem with his gearbox electronics early in the afternoon and could count himself lucky when the session was red-flagged to a halt after Mimmo Schiattarella crashed his Simtek.

This enabled the Jordan crew to resolve the problem and Rubens returned to the track soon after the session was restarted. Unfortunately he then began to over-drive, lost control over a bump and spun into a gravel trap. 'The pressure just got to me,' he admitted honestly, fighting back the tears. To have ended up 16th on the grid for his home Grand Prix was nothing short of a bitter disappointment.

Completing the top ten was Olivier Panis after a steady run in the Benetton-lookalike Ligier JS41, team-mate Aguri Suzuki getting back into the swing of F1 motoring with several spins on his way to 15th place in the other car. It was his first F1 outing since handling a Jordan in the 1994 Pacific GP.

Ukyo Katayama and Mika Salo proved encouragingly well matched in the new Tyrrell 023-Yamahas, qualifying 11th and 12th. Ukyo lost any chance of improving with a spin in the final session while Salo, who spun twice on Friday, was not totally satisfied with the chassis set-up. Technical Director Harvey Postlethwaite admitted that the team had failed to get the best out of the cars under the circumstances.

The new Footwork FA16 attracted many favourable comments from rival teams, particularly the compact dimensions of its all-new Hart V8 engine, which was being tried in competitive anger for the first time. The slim lines of the car's rear end were enhanced by the use of a longitudinal

Left: The class assembles for the start-of-term photo. How many pupils would have dropped out by the end of the year?

His thinning hair miraculously reinvigorated, Roberto Moreno *(below left)* was back in F1 after a two-year absence.

Centre: 'Yen or dollars?' Taki Inoue *(left)* talks business with Arrows boss Jackie Oliver.

A contemplative Eddie Irvine *(bottom)* considers the prospects for the new Jordan-Peugeot alliance.

Below: Damon Hill follows the progress of his impressive young team-mate David Coulthard from the cockpit of his Williams.

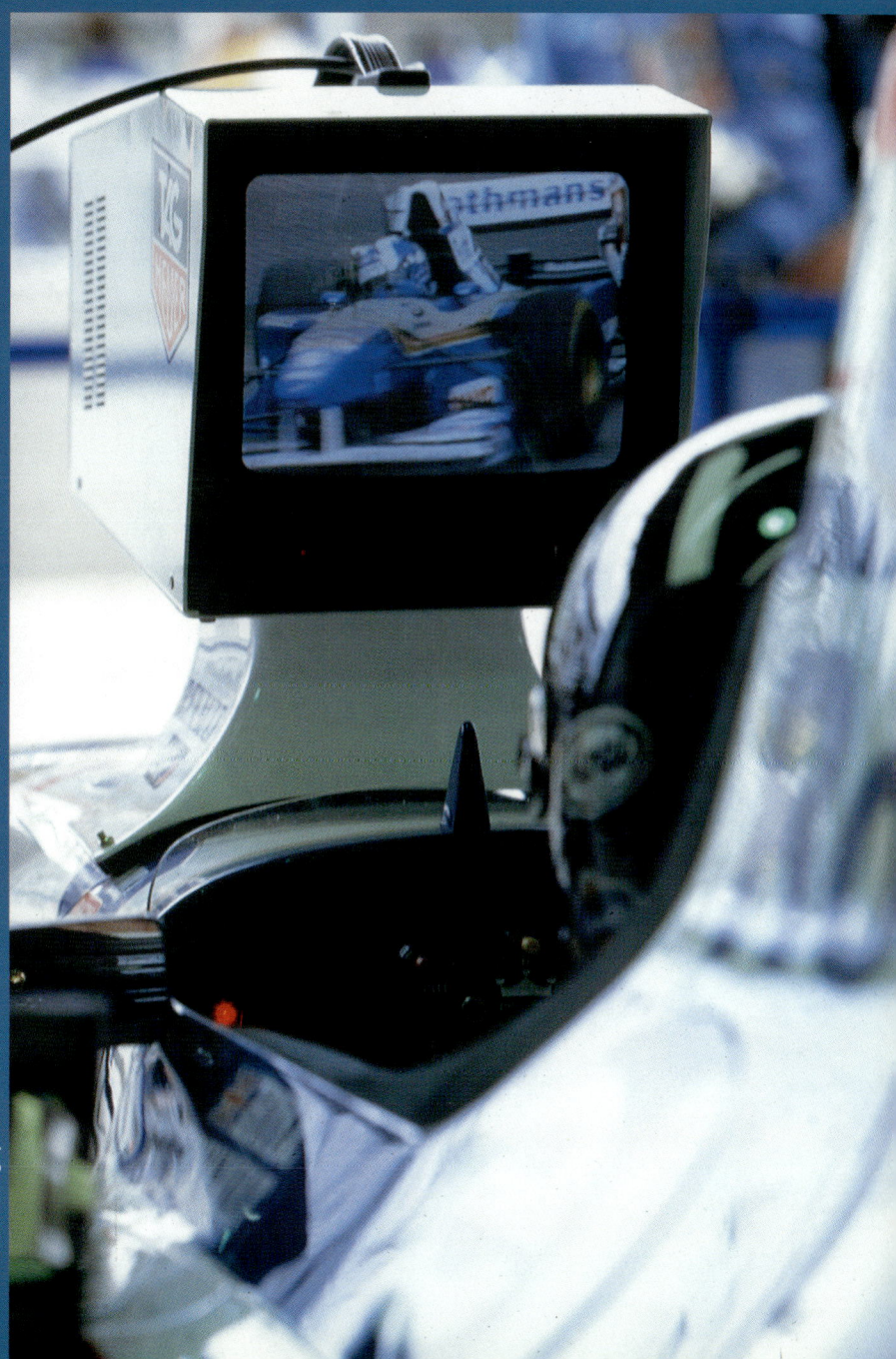

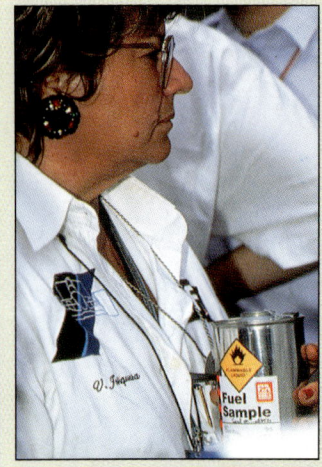

The fuel row

After Michael Schumacher and David Coulthard crossed the line in first and second places at the end of the Brazilian GP, further samples of their Elf fuel were examined by the FIA-appointed chemist using a Hewlett Packard gas chromatograph. Once again, it was found that the fuel did not match the sample lodged with the governing body prior to the race; the discrepancy was duly reported to the stewards and both cars were disqualified.

The implications of all this were obvious: namely, that with Elf only bringing one type of fuel to Interlagos, if the sample taken after Friday qualifying was found to be non-approved, then it logically followed that the same outcome would flow from a post-race examination.

It was clear from the outset, however, that nobody was saying that the Elf fuel was illegal in the sense that it transgressed any of the rules concerning the chemical components it was permitted to contain. The infringement was that it simply did not match the 'fingerprint' of its previously lodged sample.

Elf's Valerie Jorquera *(above)* responded trenchantly to the ruling. 'Elf is a big company,' she said. 'Can you imagine we would be stupid enough to wait for the agreement of Fuel A and then send Fuel B for the race? We knew we would have samples taken and we do not feel guilty at all. We have done a proper job.'

Meanwhile, Williams Technical Director Patrick Head expressed his concerns about the accuracy of the FIA's trackside fuel-testing equipment – even though the tests were run no fewer than six times, leaving FIA Technical Delegate Charlie Whiting with no doubt over their failure to match. But Head insisted that Williams would certainly have withdrawn Hill and Coulthard from the race had they believed that there was any question of disqualification on the day.

'We were only informed that there was a problem with our qualifying fuel only minutes before the pit lane opened prior to the race,' he explained. 'As there was only one type of Elf fuel available to us in Brazil, there was obviously no point in risking the drivers if we were going to be excluded.

'We understood [from an FIA representative] that, although Coulthard's car was running provisionally, as was Schumacher's Benetton, there was absolutely no question of disqualification until the fuel samples had been returned to Europe for detailed analysis.'

However, FIA President Max Mosley commented: 'We ran the test which everybody agreed. Two of the fuel samples – the Agip used by Ferrari and Mobil used by McLaren – matched and one, Elf, did not. Faced with that eventuality, we had to take action.'

Benetton and Williams quickly lodged a formal appeal against the disqualifications and an FIA Appeal Court hearing was set for Thursday 13 April, just after the Argentine Grand Prix.

---

gearbox and while Gianni Morbidelli had a promising qualifying session on Friday, he felt he could have improved on his eventual 13th after being dogged by excessive oversteer on Saturday afternoon. This was eventually traced to damper trouble, but insufficient time remained to correct the problem.

Further back, Taki Inoue spent most of his time simply learning about the new car, inadvertently balking Hill's Williams on a couple of occasions during second qualifying. Even so, the Japanese novice didn't do a bad job to qualify 21st, sandwiched by the promising new Pacific PR02s of Bertrand Gachot and Andrea Montermini.

Less convincing were the Sauber C14-Fords of Heinz-Harald Frentzen and Karl Wendlinger, which seemed to be battling harder with the Interlagos bumps than most of their rivals on the way to 14th and 19th places respectively.

Pierluigi Martini and Luca Badoer earned 17th and 18th places in their Cosworth EDM-engined Minardis, both suffering from flat spots in their V8s' power curve during qualifying, while the Forti Corse entries of Roberto Moreno and Pedro Diniz at least managed to match the pace of the new Simtek S951s, which arrived at Interlagos with no test mileage at all under their belts. For the moment, at least.

As the final touches were put to the competing cars for the first Grand Prix of the new season, the general mood on race morning was a sense of relief that a possible strike over the terms of the F1 drivers' superlicences had been averted in the run-up to the Brazilian fixture. Many drivers had been reluctant to sign their superlicence forms due to lingering concerns about third-party insurance liability and possible promotional demands made on their time by the FIA. Happily, the governing body moved to allay these concerns and the threat, however unlikely, of a boycott faded.

There were other worries, however. Following the pit fire involving Jos Verstappen's Benetton in the 1994 German Grand Prix, Intertechnique, the company entrusted with the manufacture of the FIA refuelling rigs, had redesigned this equipment for the new season. With that in mind, it was not reassuring to hear that McLaren had experienced a quite significant leakage with the new rig while carrying out a test outside its Woking factory. It transpired that a retaining spring in the fuel valve had been incorrectly fitted, but Intertechnique moved to rectify the problem before Interlagos. Even so, it was difficult to feel comfortable about the refuelling business under the circumstances.

Just before the race came another bombshell. Benetton and Williams were formally advised by the stewards that samples of fuel taken from Schumacher's and Coulthard's cars were found not to match the 'fingerprint' of the samples lodged with the FIA prior to the meeting. Accordingly, the two drivers would be competing provisionally and a fine of $30,000 apiece was imposed on the teams, both of whom, very shrewdly, opted not to inform their drivers of the problem as they didn't want to unsettle them only 30 minutes before the start.

At the green light, Hill's pole-position Williams looked set to get the jump on Schumacher's Benetton, but Michael left his braking as late as possible and nipped inside to take the lead as the pack jostled into the first ess-bend. Coulthard was third, but Herbert, who had been forced to take the spare Benetton after a problem with the gearbox control on his race car during the warm-up, found his new mount overheating even before the start. Frustratingly, he dropped back and was swallowed by

Right: Damon Hill spun out of the lead on lap 31 due to a suspension breakage. Michael Schumacher inherited the spoils.

McLaren's new alliance with Mercedes got off to a promising start, with both cars finishing in the points. Mika Häkkinen *(below)* took fourth place despite delays at both his scheduled pit stops and a potentially disastrous bird-strike.

the pack while Häkkinen made a great start and vaulted ahead of the two Ferraris to take fourth place. Panis spun off at the first corner after a tap from Katayama's Tyrrell, the Frenchman being effectively the second casualty of the race since Martini's Minardi had broken its gearbox on the formation lap.

At the end of the opening lap Schumacher was 0.5s clear of Hill with Coulthard close behind, but a gap was already opening to Häkkinen, Berger and Alesi, with Herbert seventh ahead of Irvine and the two Tyrrell-Yamahas. Mark Blundell was well back in 14th place, his McLaren having suffered gearchange problems on its warm-up lap. The problem was traced to a glitch with the finger-tip change mechanism, so the steering wheel was replaced on the grid only for the box to change from first to third as he accelerated away from the line.

Schumacher may have been leading, but Hill seemed able to control the gap as he wished. On lap four, Michael chopped Damon quite dramatically as the Williams driver went to poke the FW17's nose inside the Benetton on a fast left-hander, causing Hill to lose momentum and allowing Coulthard to pull level on the outside. But David signalled Damon to take the line as he knew he couldn't quite keep pace with his two faster colleagues and, wisely, preferred to settle into his own rhythm in third place rather than push his luck too hard.

Now the race began to settle down. Still shadowing Schumacher, Hill eased clear of Coulthard, while Häkkinen found himself alone in fourth place ahead of the two evenly matched Ferraris. In seventh place Irvine was embroiled in a wheel-to-wheel battle with his old Japanese F3000 sparring partner Mika Salo, the Jordan-Peugeot and Tyrrell-Yamaha running virtually side by side as they came past the pits.

Damon really had the hammer down, closing the gap to 0.2s by lap 18, when Michael headed for the pits only to find the entrance lane blocked by Barrichello, who, having taken the spare Jordan, had rolled to a stop with a gearchange actuator failure and was being pushed out of the way. Nevertheless, it was a quick 7.6s stop, confirming that Benetton was pursuing its familiar three-stop strategy, but when Damon came in for a 10.8s stop at the end of lap 21, he was able to get back out ahead of Schumacher and then went back into the lead when Coulthard pitted at the end of the following lap.

Thereafter, Hill began to edge away confidently, building up a 3.4s advantage until fortune turned against him after 30 laps. 'Things were looking good, but I lost second gear coming out of one of the hairpins at the end of the lap,' explained Hill. 'Then going into the first turn at the start of lap 31, I selected third gear and suddenly the thing just locked up and I went off.' Subsequent detailed examination of the Williams FW17 revealed that the left-rear suspension pushrod had broken at its upper end, causing that corner to sit down and the car to snap out of control.

Coulthard's first stop dropped him back briefly to fifth place, promoting Häkkinen to second. But Mika's first refuelling stop saw him demoted to seventh place after being stationary for no less than 18.6s as the McLaren mechanics wrestled with a refuelling hose which proved reluctant to detach itself from the car-mounted filler. That allowed Berger to move into third place, but he too dropped back to seventh when he was delayed by a sticking left-front wheel nut during his first stop at the end of lap 27.

Schumacher, now free of Hill's presence, made a second refuelling stop at the end of lap 35, allowing Coulthard to go through to take a 12.1s lead. The impressive Salo was now briefly third ahead of his compatriot Häkkinen, but the Tyrrell driver was suffering increasingly with cramp and was attempting to control the Tyrrell with one hand as a result. That caused him to spin under pressure from Häkkinen on lap 38, after which he came straight in for tyres, dropping back to eighth. His mate Irvine was by now long gone with gearchange actuator problems.

Schumacher had trimmed Coulthard's advantage back to 5.9s by the time David came in for his second refuelling stop at the end of lap 47, the surviving Williams resuming 22.5s behind the World Champion. That meant Michael had sufficient in hand to make a third refuelling stop at the end of lap 53 and retain the lead, squeezing back into the race 3.4s ahead of Coulthard, and he stayed there to the end, confidently pulling away again to pass the chequered flag 8.06s ahead.

Berger wound up a lap down in third place ahead of the dogged Häkkinen, whose second refuelling stop was as protracted as the first – for the same reason. The McLaren also hit a bird, removing a rear wing flap, which made the handling a bit lurid in the second half of the race.

Alesi came home fifth ahead of Blundell and the very promising Salo. Aguri Suzuki's Ligier plodded home eighth, having earlier accounted for Herbert after a light collision with the Benetton number two, while Andrea Montermini's Pacific and Pedro Diniz's slow Forti completed the list of finishers.

It was a bitterly disappointing day for Morbidelli in particular, the Footwork-Hart storming along in sixth place when a blocked fuel line caused its retirement with only nine laps to go, while the Sauber-Fords had a disastrous time. Frentzen's engine cut out and Wendlinger stopped with a broken battery cable – not quite the sort of performance Ford had been hoping for after its glorious 1994 partnership with the Benetton team.

Then came the rub. Further fuel samples were taken from Schumacher's Benetton and Coulthard's Williams. Again the FIA's gas chromatograph check revealed that they didn't match the pre-race sample and the matter was reported to the stewards. Later in the evening the two cars were disqualified, promoting Berger to an apparent victory.

The 1995 season had kicked off embroiled in as much controversy as surrounded the last race of 1994. But Berger was not destined to enjoy his success for long. As darkness fell over Interlagos, it was not the end of the Brazilian Grand Prix story by any stretch of the imagination.

FIA FORMULA ONE WORLD CHAMPIONSHIP ROUND 1

GRANDE PRÊMIO DO BRASIL
INTERLAGOS
24–26 MARCH 1995

Autodromo Jose Carlos Pace, Interlagos, São Paulo
CIRCUIT LENGTH: 2.687 miles/4.325 km

Race distance: 71 laps, 190.807 miles/307.075 km
Race weather: Warm and overcast

Place	Driver	Nat.	No.	Entrant	Car/Engine	Laps	Time/Retirement	Speed (mph/km/h)
1	**Michael Schumacher**	D	1	Mild Seven Benetton Renault	Benetton B195-Renault RS7 V10	71	1h 38m 34.154s	116.145/186.919
2	**David Coulthard**	GB	6	Rothmans Williams Renault	Williams FW17-Renault RS7 V10	71	1h 38m 42.214s	115.988/186.665
3	**Gerhard Berger**	A	28	Scuderia Ferrari	Ferrari 412T2 044 V12	70		
4	**Mika Häkkinen**	SF	8	Marlboro McLaren Mercedes	McLaren MP4/10-Mercedes FO110 V10	70		
5	**Jean Alesi**	F	27	Scuderia Ferrari	Ferrari 412T2 044 V12	70		
6	**Mark Blundell**	GB	7	Marlboro McLaren Mercedes	McLaren MP4/10-Mercedes FO110 V10	70		
7	Mika Salo	SF	4	Nokia Tyrrell Yamaha	Tyrrell 023-Yamaha OX10C V10	69		
8	Aguri Suzuki	J	25	Ligier Gitanes Blondes	Ligier JS41-Mugen Honda MF301 V10	69		
9	Andrea Montermini	I	17	Pacific Grand Prix Ltd	Pacific PR02-Ford ED V8	65		
10	Pedro Diniz	BR	21	Parmalat Forti Ford	Forti FG01-Ford ED V8	64		
	Gianni Morbidelli	I	9	Footwork Hart	Footwork FA16-Hart 830 V8	62	Fuel pump	
	Taki Inoue	J	10	Footwork Hart	Footwork FA16-Hart 830 V8	48	Fire	
	Luca Badoer	I	24	Minardi Scuderia Italia	Minardi M195-Ford EDM V8	47	Gearbox	
	Roberto Moreno	BR	22	Parmalat Forti Ford	Forti FG01-Ford ED V8	47	Spun off	
	Karl Wendlinger	A	29	Red Bull Sauber Ford	Sauber C14-Ford Zetec-R V8	41	Electrics	
	Damon Hill	GB	5	Rothmans Williams Renault	Williams FW17-Renault RS7 V10	30	Suspension	
	Johnny Herbert	GB	2	Mild Seven Benetton Renault	Benetton B195-Renault RS7 V10	30	Collision with Suzuki	
	Bertrand Gachot	F	16	Pacific Grand Prix Ltd	Pacific PR02-Ford ED V8	23	Gearbox	
	Rubens Barrichello	BR	14	Total Jordan Peugeot	Jordan 195-Peugeot A10 V10	16	Gearbox	
	Jos Verstappen	NL	12	MTV Simtek Ford	Simtek S951-Ford ED V8	16	Clutch	
	Ukyo Katayama	J	3	Nokia Tyrrell Yamaha	Tyrrell 023-Yamaha OX10C V10	15	Spun off	
	Eddie Irvine	GB	15	Total Jordan Peugeot	Jordan 195-Peugeot V10	15	Gearbox	
	Domenico Schiattarella	I	11	MTV Simtek Ford	Simtek S951-Ford ED V8	12	Steering box	
	Heinz-Harald Frentzen	D	30	Red Bull Sauber Ford	Sauber C14-Ford Zetec-R V8	10	Electrics	
	Olivier Panis	F	26	Ligier Gitanes Blondes	Ligier JS41-Mugen Honda MF301 V10	0	Spun off	
DNS	Pierluigi Martini	I	23	Minardi Scuderia Italia	Minardi M195-Ford EDM V8	0	Gearbox	

Fastest lap: Schumacher, on lap 51, 1m 20.921s, 119.557 mph/192.409 km/h.
Lap record: Michael Schumacher (F1 Benetton B194-Ford V8), 1m 18.455s, 123.315 mph/198.457 km/h (1994).

All cars used Goodyear tyres

All results and data © FIA 1995

STARTING GRID

1 **SCHUMACHER** (1m 20.382s) Benetton	5 **HILL** (1m 20.081s) Williams
2 **HERBERT** (1m 20.888s) Benetton	6 **COULTHARD** (1m 20.422s) Williams
27 **ALESI** (1m 21.041s) Ferrari	28 **BERGER** (1m 20.906s) Ferrari
15 **IRVINE** (1m 21.749s) Jordan	8 **HÄKKINEN** (1m 21.399s) McLaren
26 **PANIS** (1m 21.914s) Ligier	7 **BLUNDELL** (1m 21.779s) McLaren
4 **SALO** (1m 22.416s) Tyrrell	3 **KATAYAMA** (1m 22.325s) Tyrrell
30 **FRENTZEN** (1m 22.872s) Sauber	9 **MORBIDELLI** (1m 22.468s) Footwork
14 **BARRICHELLO** (1m 22.975s) Jordan	25 **SUZUKI** (1m 22.971s) Ligier
24 **BADOER** (1m 24.443s) Minardi	23 **MARTINI*** (1m 24.383s) Minardi
16 **GACHOT** (1m 25.127s) Pacific	29 **WENDLINGER** (1m 24.723s) Sauber
17 **MONTERMINI** (1m 25.886s) Pacific	10 **INOUE** (1m 25.225s) Footwork
12 **VERSTAPPEN** (1m 26.323s) Simtek	22 **MORENO** (1m 26.269s) Forti
11 **SCHIATTARELLA** (1m 28.106s) Simtek	21 **DINIZ** (1m 27.792s) Forti

* did not start

FOR THE RECORD

First Grand Prix start
Pedro Diniz
Andrea Montermini

TIME SHEETS

Friday free practice
Dry, hot

Pos.	Driver	Laps	Time
1	Damon Hill	19	1m 21.664s
2	David Coulthard	22	1m 21.666s
3	Michael Schumacher	15	1m 22.468s
4	Jean Alesi	14	1m 22.568s
5	Gerhard Berger	18	1m 22.953s
6	Mark Blundell	17	1m 23.053s
7	Mika Salo	23	1m 23.567s
8	Johnny Herbert	8	1m 24.246s
9	Gianni Morbidelli	16	1m 25.229s
10	Olivier Panis	10	1m 25.515s
11	Rubens Barrichello	20	1m 25.664s
12	Heinz-Harald Frentzen	15	1m 25.739s
13	Aguri Suzuki	8	1m 25.923s
14	Mika Häkkinen	13	1m 26.018s
15	Eddie Irvine	16	1m 26.152s
16	Luca Badoer	22	1m 26.314s
17	Ukyo Katayama	13	1m 27.495s
18	Karl Wendlinger	15	1m 27.537s
19	Roberto Moreno	9	1m 30.657s
20	Bertrand Gachot	12	1m 33.743s
21	Pedro Diniz	11	1m 36.246s
22	Andrea Montermini	5	1m 37.349s
23	Taki Inoue	10	1m 42.199s
	Pierluigi Martini	0	no time
	Domenico Schiattarella	0	no time
	Jos Verstappen	0	no time

Saturday free practice
Wet at first, then dry

Pos.	Driver	Laps	Time
1	Michael Schumacher	16	1m 23.607s
2	Gerhard Berger	15	1m 23.960s
3	Damon Hill	21	1m 24.119s
4	Mika Häkkinen	21	1m 24.483s
5	Jean Alesi	9	1m 24.711s
6	Olivier Panis	21	1m 24.881s
7	Ukyo Katayama	19	1m 26.119s
8	Mark Blundell	17	1m 26.622s
9	Pierluigi Martini	16	1m 29.052s
10	Mika Salo	20	1m 29.332s
11	Johnny Herbert	19	1m 30.625s
12	David Coulthard	13	1m 31.198s
13	Bertrand Gachot	7	1m 32.685s
14	Gianni Morbidelli	13	1m 32.736s
15	Rubens Barrichello	19	1m 33.703s
16	Andrea Montermini	8	1m 34.169s
17	Heinz-Harald Frentzen	13	1m 35.356s
18	Luca Badoer	12	1m 36.363s
19	Pedro Diniz	13	1m 36.417s
20	Aguri Suzuki	17	1m 36.563s
21	Domenico Schiattarella	12	1m 36.687s
22	Karl Wendlinger	15	1m 37.248s
23	Roberto Moreno	14	1m 37.604s
24	Jos Verstappen	18	1m 39.403s
25	Taki Inoue	7	1m 44.495s
26	Eddie Irvine	1	3m 27.666s

Friday qualifying
Dry, hot

Pos.	Driver	Laps	Time
1	**Damon Hill**	12	**1m 20.081s**
2	Gerhard Berger	10	1m 21.015s
3	David Coulthard	10	1m 21.343s
4	Jean Alesi	10	1m 21.655s
5	Mika Häkkinen	11	1m 22.017s
6	Michael Schumacher	2	1m 22.131s
7	Olivier Panis	11	1m 22.208s
8	Eddie Irvine	9	1m 22.370s
9	Mark Blundell	11	1m 22.821s
10	Aguri Suzuki	11	1m 23.251s
11	Rubens Barrichello	8	1m 23.350s
12	Gianni Morbidelli	11	1m 23.403s
13	Mika Salo	6	1m 23.470s
14	Heinz-Harald Frentzen	8	1m 24.065s
15	Ukyo Katayama	6	1m 24.165s
16	**Luca Badoer**	12	**1m 24.443s**
17	**Karl Wendlinger**	11	**1m 24.723s**
18	Bertrand Gachot	11	1m 25.819s
19	Taki Inoue	12	1m 27.036s
20	Roberto Moreno	12	1m 27.204s
21	Andrea Montermini	5	1m 27.440s
22	Pierluigi Martini	2	1m 56.532s
23	Jos Verstappen	4	2m 01.610s
	Johnny Herbert	0	no time
	Domenico Schiattarella	0	no time
	Pedro Diniz	0	no time

Saturday qualifying
Overcast, dry

Pos.	Driver	Laps	Time
1	**Michael Schumacher**	12	**1m 20.382s**
2	**David Coulthard**	11	**1m 20.422s**
3	Damon Hill	12	1m 20.429s
4	**Johnny Herbert**	12	**1m 20.888s**
5	Gerhard Berger	7	1m 20.906s
6	**Jean Alesi**	12	**1m 21.041s**
7	**Mika Häkkinen**	12	**1m 21.399s**
8	Eddie Irvine	10	1m 21.749s
9	**Mark Blundell**	10	**1m 21.779s**
10	**Olivier Panis**	12	**1m 21.914s**
11	**Ukyo Katayama**	10	**1m 22.325s**
12	**Mika Salo**	12	**1m 22.416s**
13	**Gianni Morbidelli**	10	**1m 22.468s**
14	**Heinz-Harald Frentzen**	10	**1m 22.872s**
15	**Aguri Suzuki**	11	**1m 22.971s**
16	**Rubens Barrichello**	5	**1m 22.975s**
17	Pierluigi Martini	11	1m 24.383s
18	Bertrand Gachot	11	1m 25.127s
19	Karl Wendlinger	11	1m 25.161s
20	Luca Badoer	4	1m 25.205s
21	**Taki Inoue**	12	**1m 25.225s**
22	**Andrea Montermini**	12	**1m 25.886s**
23	**Roberto Moreno**	12	**1m 26.269s**
24	**Jos Verstappen**	6	**1m 26.323s**
25	**Pedro Diniz**	7	**1m 27.792s**
26	**Domenico Schiattarella**	2	**1m 28.106s**

WARM-UP
Dry, hot

Pos.	Driver	Laps	Time
1	David Coulthard	11	1m 21.581s
2	Damon Hill	14	1m 21.599s
3	Michael Schumacher	10	1m 22.124s
4	Olivier Panis	10	1m 22.256s
5	Jean Alesi	10	1m 22.263s
6	Mika Häkkinen	12	1m 22.314s
7	Johnny Herbert	5	1m 22.675s
8	Rubens Barrichello	13	1m 22.702s
9	Eddie Irvine	11	1m 22.731s
10	Gerhard Berger	11	1m 23.034s
11	Heinz-Harald Frentzen	11	1m 23.266s
12	Mika Salo	13	1m 23.461s
13	Ukyo Katayama	12	1m 23.674s
14	Mark Blundell	11	1m 23.708s
15	Aguri Suzuki	12	1m 23.867s
16	Pierluigi Martini	10	1m 25.644s
17	Karl Wendlinger	10	1m 25.789s
18	Bertrand Gachot	11	1m 25.822s
19	Luca Badoer	15	1m 25.932s
20	Taki Inoue	11	1m 26.709s
21	Pedro Diniz	11	1m 27.522s
22	Gianni Morbidelli	5	1m 34.262s
23	Roberto Moreno	3	1m 38.108s
24	Andrea Montermini	2	6m 55.785s
	Jos Verstappen	0	no time
	Domenico Schiattarella	0	no time

Fastest race laps
Warm, overcast

Driver	Time	Lap
Michael Schumacher	1m 20.921s	51
Damon Hill	1m 20.982s	25
David Coulthard	1m 21.543s	39
Mika Häkkinen	1m 22.495s	35
Gerhard Berger	1m 22.679s	30
Gianni Morbidelli	1m 22.818s	61
Mika Salo	1m 22.979s	25
Johnny Herbert	1m 23.009s	18
Aguri Suzuki	1m 23.049s	25
Jean Alesi	1m 23.207s	16
Mark Blundell	1m 23.252s	38
Rubens Barrichello	1m 23.346s	13
Eddie Irvine	1m 23.355s	11
Ukyo Katayama	1m 23.718s	4
Heinz-Harald Frentzen	1m 24.087s	10
Karl Wendlinger	1m 24.387s	23
Jos Verstappen	1m 26.017s	3
Luca Badoer	1m 26.349s	13
Taki Inoue	1m 26.470s	34
Bertrand Gachot	1m 26.826s	22
Andrea Montermini	1m 27.447s	7
Roberto Moreno	1m 27.829s	31
Domenico Schiattarella	1m 28.467s	9
Pedro Diniz	1m 28.811s	49

CHASSIS LOG BOOK

	Driver	Chassis
1	Schumacher	Benetton B195/4
2	Herbert	Benetton B195/1
spare		Benetton B195/3
3	Katayama	Tyrrell 023/1
4	Salo	Tyrrell 023/2
spare		Tyrrell 023/3
5	Hill	Williams FW17/1
6	Coulthard	Williams FW17/2
spare		Williams FW17/3
7	Blundell	McLaren MP4/10/2
8	Häkkinen	McLaren MP4/10/3
spare		McLaren MP4/10/4
9	Morbidelli	Footwork FA16/2
10	Inoue	Footwork FA16/1
11	Schiattarella	Simtek S951/2
12	Verstappen	Simtek S951/1
14	Barrichello	Jordan 195/1
15	Irvine	Jordan 195/3
spare		Jordan 195/2
16	Gachot	Pacific PR02/1
17	Montermini	Pacific PR02/2
21	Diniz	Forti FG01/1
22	Moreno	Forti FG01/2
23	Martini	Minardi M195/1
24	Badoer	Minardi M195/6
spare		Minardi M195/3
25	Suzuki	Ligier JS41/2
26	Panis	Ligier JS41/1
spare		Ligier JS41/3
27	Alesi	Ferrari 412T2/157
28	Berger	Ferrari 412T2/159
spare		Ferrari 412T2/156
29	Wendlinger	Sauber C14/2
30	Frentzen	Sauber C14/3
spare		Sauber C14/1

POINTS TABLES

Drivers

1	Michael Schumacher	10
2	David Coulthard	6
3	Gerhard Berger	4
4	Mika Häkkinen	3
5	Jean Alesi	2
6	Mark Blundell	1

Constructors

1	Ferrari	6
2	McLaren	4

Points and results reflect outcome of FIA Court of Appeal hearing on 13 April

WORLD CHAMPIONSHIP • ROUND 2

ARGENTINE GRAND PRIX

HILL
ALESI
SCHUMACHER
HERBERT
FRENTZEN
BERGER

The familiar arch at the entrance to the circuit *(far left)* now bears the name of one of Argentina's greatest drivers.

Below: Track conditions during the two days of official practice were often appalling, with poor visibility adding to the hazards, but Carlos Reutemann *(centre)* was obviously pleased to be back in the cockpit of a Ferrari.

A circumspect Mika Häkkinen *(below left)* splashes through the puddles, anxious to avoid the fate that has befallen Olivier Panis *(bottom)*.

ARGENTINE GRAND PRIX

Diary

The FIA changes its technical rules for Buenos Aires with the result that ram effect is now once again allowed to be developed by the engine airboxes.

FIA President Max Mosley makes visit to China during which he visits the Zhuhai circuit, fuelling rumours of a Chinese GP as early as 1997.

Nicola Foulston sells control of Brands Hatch, Mallory Park, Oulton Park and Snetterton in a £15.5 million deal which sees her retain a 10 per cent stake in the newly formed Brands Hatch Leisure Group, which she continues to run as Managing Director.

Top F1 teams show limited enthusiasm for possible 17th Grand Prix fixture.

Emmanuel Collard confirmed as Benetton test driver.

Damon Hill scored a decisive victory in the first Argentine Grand Prix to be held in 14 years, taking the tenth win of his career after a well-judged and strategically astute drive at the Buenos Aires Autodrome. The race took place in dry conditions after two days of almost ceaseless rain had left the field with precious little experience in setting up their cars for anything less than a near-flooded track surface. This situation clearly worked against Michael Schumacher in the race when his chances of victory were seriously undermined by dramatically inconsistent performance from his successive sets of tyres.

The reigning World Champion could only finish the afternoon a distant third behind Jean Alesi's Ferrari, but it was clear that the Benetton team leader's performance was not a totally accurate representation of the B195's long-term potential. As at Interlagos a fortnight earlier, the Argentine race saw the leading contenders flexing their muscles; but quite where this left them in an overall competitive perspective, in relation to one another, had yet to be firmly established.

The F1 community arrived in Buenos Aires in a mood of enthusiastic anticipation. The Argentine Grand Prix was one of the most enjoyable races on the calendar until circumstances caused it to be dropped from the F1 teams' itinerary in 1982.

Argentina has a unique motor racing tradition and, despite many changes to the topography, atmosphere still oozes from the paddock at the Buenos Aires Municipal Autodrome. This is pretty well the same stretch of tarmac where the legendary Juan Manuel Fangio had won the Argentine GP in a Mercedes W196 forty years earlier on a day when most of his rivals fell like flies in the searing 100-degree heat.

In addition to Fangio, the five-times World Champion, this is the country which gave us Froilan Gonzalez – 'El Cabazon' (Fat Head!) – the roly-poly giant who scored Ferrari's first-ever World Championship Grand Prix win at Silverstone back in 1951. And, of course, more recently, the great Carlos Reutemann, a man who surely deserved to win a world title but somehow never quite managed to string it all together. Reutemann, who finished second for Williams in the '81 Argentine race, revived memories of his glittering career with some impressive demonstration laps in a 3.5-litre 1994 Ferrari 412T1B.

Since 1981, the Buenos Aires circuit had been renamed the Autodromo Oscar Galvez, in memory of the great Argentine national champion who was a rival of Fangio's in the immediate post-war years. He died only a few years ago and it was also sad that Fangio himself, gravely ill at the age of 83, was unable to visit the circuit over this Grand Prix weekend.

Unfortunately, from the moment the F1 fraternity arrived in Buenos Aires, the early-autumn weather turned out to be inhospitably unsettled. Instead of the blazing sunshine recalled so fondly, it was humid, overcast and the rain was simply pouring down.

Understandably, such conditions tended to cloud some drivers' perceptions of the revised circuit. Some thought it too tight, too acrobatic. The surface didn't drain well enough and the straights didn't seem to be long enough.

'It's possible to get into quite a nice rhythm,' said David Coulthard, 'but it's too tight. Just as you get into sixth gear, it's time to go onto the brakes again.' Yet there were others who were really lapping it up.

'I think it's really good,' enthused Mika Häkkinen. 'It's difficult and quite demanding. It's a circuit which tests the drivers and that's what I like.'

As things transpired, it was Coulthard who coped magnificently with the treacherous track surface on Saturday afternoon, confidently handling his Williams FW17 on a perfectly timed run in the closing moments of a chaotic session. He had already finished Friday's first qualifying session 0.5s ahead of Ferrari's Jean Alesi, the Sauber-Ford of Heinz-Harald Frentzen and his Williams team-mate Damon Hill after a frantic shoot-out during the final ten minutes of a session which at one point seemed as though it would never end.

'We had enough fuel in the car for me to stay out to the chequered flag,' explained the Scot at the end of the first day, 'although I have to say this place doesn't exactly dry out as quickly as somewhere like Silverstone. It must be something to do with the humidity. It would certainly be nice to start from pole position, but that's only part of the weekend's equation. Winning the race is what it's all about.'

Friday qualifying looked in severe risk of being washed into the River Plate by a thunderstorm of Wagnerian proportions. Car after car spun off the near-flooded circuit before the red flag came out after only 15 minutes.

'Conditions when the rain was at its heaviest were just impossible,' shrugged Hill. 'There was so much surface water that it was possible to spin my rear wheels in any gear on the back straight.'

Hill had earlier lost time when he spun over a kerb in the Friday morning free practice session, damaging his Williams's undertray. 'I was so furious with myself that I punched the steering wheel really hard in frustration and hurt my thumb,' he admitted. 'I've been carrying round a bag of frozen prawns ever since trying to get the swelling down!'

After marshals had spent half an hour sweeping away the worst of the puddles, the session resumed with the Jordan-Peugeots of Eddie Irvine and Rubens Barrichello soon establishing themselves at the head of the field. Unfortunately for the Jordan squad, Japanese novice Taki Inoue then spun his Footwork-Hart and the session had to be stopped again when it was found that the wayward machine had jammed in gear and steadfastly resisted all efforts by the marshals to move it.

The Footwork was eventually retrieved from its position on the racing line on the back of a rescue truck. Inoue's entrant, Arrows, was fined $20,000 for not fitting its car with a device whereby the driven wheels could be de-coupled in the event of its coming to rest with the engine stopped. Jack Oliver's explanation to the stewards that the gearbox was meshed between second and third didn't seem to cut any ice.

Sure enough, when the cars returned to the circuit, the rain had at last stopped and the skies were brightening, although the track surface continued to glisten treacherously. Mika Häkkinen briefly pushed the McLaren MP4/10-Mercedes onto provisional pole, but he was soon ousted by the fearless Jean Alesi, the Frenchman hurling his Ferrari about with characteristic abandon, sawing away at the steering wheel with great armfuls of opposite lock.

With four minutes to go, Hill and Coulthard moved up into second and third places behind the Ferrari, but were then immediately dislodged as Heinz-Harald Frentzen moved up to second in his Sauber-Ford. Finally, Coulthard pulled the quickest lap out of the bag and, with Gianni Morbidelli's Footwork spinning on the racing line less than 30 seconds

95

ARGENTINE GRAND PRIX

Ferrari fury as Schumacher and Coulthard reinstated in Brazil result

Gerhard Berger's one-point lead in the Drivers' World Championship lasted barely four days after he took sixth place in the Argentine Grand Prix. The following Thursday, an FIA Court of Appeal reinstated Michael Schumacher and David Coulthard in first and second places in the Brazilian GP – but disallowed their teams the constructors' points for those positions.

This provoked a blistering response from the Ferrari team which, while acknowledging that the Benetton and Williams drivers gained no advantage from the non-approved Elf fuel used at the Interlagos race, expressed the view that the FIA decision was fundamentally flawed.

'The decisions made by the FIA International Court of Appeal seem to imply that a driver may win a Formula 1 Grand Prix even if racing with a car not complying with the technical regulations,' noted an official statement from Maranello.

Berger, who was now deprived of his inherited victory in the Brazilian race by this decision, adopted an even-handed tone. 'I respect the decision of the FIA,' he observed, 'but to admit that the car specification was non-homologated and punish the team, yet accept the drivers' results, shows that we at Ferrari are stupid if we have new things and do not use them in a race simply because they are non-approved.'

However, Ferrari adviser Niki Lauda did not beat about the bush. Interviewed in the *Salzburger Nachrichten* newspaper two days after the decision, he really let fly.

'The verdict is the greatest joke of all time,' he stormed. 'I cannot separate car and driver completely. If this is the new rule, that you can build an illegal car and let the team pay for victory, the whole thing is [now] only commercial and has nothing to do with sport any more.

'The next time, we could build a car with a five-litre engine, win and pay. It's like scoring a half-goal in soccer – it's not possible. Either you score a goal or not. The decision for me is the biggest defeat for the FIA, who cannot govern the sport any longer.'

At the Appeal Court hearing, submissions were heard by lawyers acting for both Benetton and Williams, with assistance from Elf's Gilbert Chapelet and Professor Sandra from Leiden University, while the FIA's case was presented by Secretary General Pierre de Coninck, assisted by Technical Delegate Charlie Whiting and chemist Dr Robert Large.

While there was no doubt that a 'quantitive difference' existed between the Elf fuel homologated by the FIA and the fuel used in Brazil, the teams maintained that this discrepancy offered no performance advantage. The anomalous nature of the situation was further emphasised by the fact that Hill's Williams used the same specification Elf fuel to win in Buenos Aires a fortnight later – it having subsequently been resubmitted and given the all-clear prior to this event.

However, although the FIA recorded the fact that 'experts heard during the hearing are in disagreement on this point [whether or not the Brazilian GP discrepancy offered enhanced car performance]' there was some evidence to suggest that variations in fuel test results produced by different makes of gas chromatograph were a factor taken into account when reaching the decision.

It was also important to make the point that the FIA Appeal Court merely changed the penalty applicable. Benetton and Williams remained guilty of the offence as originally charged.

Having triggered the multiple accident that caused the race to be stopped on the first lap, Jean Alesi *(right)* took the spare Ferrari 412T2 and maintained the team's promising start to the year with an impressive second place.

Happily recovered from the injuries sustained in the 1994 Monaco Grand Prix that had left him in a coma for almost three weeks, Karl Wendlinger *(below right)* had made a courageous return to Formula 1 with Sauber but had yet to recapture his old sparkle.

---

before the end of the session, the chequered flag appeared at last.

Behind Hill came Gerhard Berger's Ferrari, Häkkinen, Irvine, Barrichello and a highly disappointed Michael Schumacher, who had several off-track excursions with his Benetton-Renault.

Friday evening found every team manager scanning the local weather forecasts with varying degrees of trepidation. The indications were that the weather would be slightly better on Saturday, but there was still the unpredictable possibility of at least some heavy rain. The problem was to know quite when.

In fact, Saturday dawned bright and sunny, enabling the teams to tackle the circuit in dry conditions for the first time. But, as the session unfolded, the skies darkened and ominous thunder clouds rolled in across the Buenos Aires skyline from the west.

The need to check out dry-weather chassis settings meant that Saturday morning's free practice was conducted with all the enthusiastic frenzy of an official qualifying session. Hill quickly established the dry-weather benchmark on 1m 32.230s with Coulthard only 0.4s behind just after the mid-session break.

Schumacher was initially experimenting with his Benetton's chassis set-up as well as adjusting the Renault V10's mapping before taking time out for a quick spin. Thereafter he began to up the pressure in spectacular style, hurling the Benetton from lock to lock in a succession of lurid slides on the still-dusty track surface to post a quickest time of 1m 31.376s literally seconds before the end of the session.

Nevertheless, Hill and Coulthard remained close behind in second and third places, Damon having lost time with a slight gearchange electrical control problem, and both Williams drivers used only a single set of tyres for most of the session, only scrubbing in one fresh set apiece right at the end. The pity was, they wouldn't need them until race day.

This session also provided a clear indication that the new McLaren-Mercedes partnership was making positive progress. For this race the MP4/10s sported revised rear wings and a new front aerodynamic package together with slight suspension modifications. From Ilmor came a few small changes to the inlet system of the FO110 engine, offering both a small increment in top-end power and enhanced driveability lower down the rev range – a factor which made the cars a little easier to handle in the wet.

At the start of Saturday free practice, Mika briefly managed to post second-fastest time before fading to fifth, admitting that he had made his quickest run a little too early 'and helped clean up the track for the others'. Of course, all this effort proved of little avail as the rain returned with a vengeance about 20 minutes before the start of second qualifying. We then faced the quite remarkable possibility that no cars at all would venture out onto the circuit. The conditions were truly appalling and, although Mimmo Schiattarella bravely went out in his Simtek, the rain's intensity could be gauged from the fact that he couldn't get within 2.4s of his Friday best.

As the session drew to a close, it seemed as though the skies were brightening and there was a slight possibility of producing some quicker times. With ten minutes left, Schumacher accelerated out of the pits and the World Champion's presence on the circuit triggered a flood of activity from his front-line rivals.

Hill and Coulthard were soon out again, then Mika Salo's Tyrrell, Frentzen's Sauber – and suddenly the track became as crowded as usual. The faintest trace of a racing line was beginning to appear and Hill posted a 1m 55.057s to take pole. Häkkinen got up to what was now third – matching Hill's best to three decimal places – and the McLaren ace pushed on through to second on 1m 54.529s before Coulthard timed everything to perfection, stealing pole with a 1m 53.241s – a full 0.8s faster than Damon.

Coulthard admitted that his performance reflected a great deal of credit on Williams's team-work. 'At one point I virtually stopped on the back straight trying to guarantee myself a clear lap,' he explained, 'even though it is impossible to guarantee that nobody will come out of the pits ahead of you. Under the circumstances, it was just a question of keeping going to the flag.' He also had a brief excursion through one of the gravel traps, which seemed to cause him no problems.

Hill was happy to have improved to second place, content at least with a front-row starting position, and Schumacher seemed similarly content with third. 'I think we are a bit quicker than the Williams in dry conditions,' he speculated, 'and it will be a long, hard race tomorrow. I was aquaplaning all over the place, the conditions were awful and I couldn't see anything. If I'd had one more lap I think I could have done it, but in the end I told the team "forget it".'

Elsewhere, Jordan had come to Argentina determined to make up for its disappointing first race using Peugeot engines in Brazil. Redesigned hydraulic actuators in the gearchange system had been fitted to both cars and Irvine celebrated by speeding to fourth place, his best-ever grid position. By contrast, Barrichello wound up a trifle disappointed. His car suffered a pneumatic valvegear malfunction during Saturday's dry session and he then complained of being balked by Berger in the rain, ending up in tenth place.

Häkkinen was moderately satisfied with fifth place ahead of Alesi, the Ferrari driver slipping back from second, then came the outstanding Salo, Berger and Frentzen in the best-placed Sauber. Gerhard had a disappointing time in second qualifying, for while his team-mate made the most of one of the six new revised-specification V12s available to the team at this race, the Austrian found their enhanced mid-range torque of academic interest as he was beset by overheating brakes.

The works-Ford-engined Saubers had been the subject of much damper development work since Interlagos and displayed generally much-enhanced handling qualities on the smooth Buenos Aires track surface. Frentzen was quite satisfied to be starting only one place behind a Ferrari at this second race of the season.

Johnny Herbert was highly disappointed to have ended up a distant 11th, spinning off on the start/finish straight during final qualifying, but Morbidelli produced another strong performance in the Footwork-Hart and Jos Verstappen left the Simtek lads almost hugging each other with joy after taking 14th place overall, by far the team's best qualifying position to date.

Ukyo Katayama seemed to have been psychologically unnerved by Salo in much the same was as Barrichello had apparently taken a firm second place to Irvine in the Jordan ranks. The pleasant Japanese driver could not better 15th-fastest time in the tricky conditions, but at least this was better than Taki Inoue, who was not allowed out in second qualifying as he crashed during the morning as he entered the pit lane and the team was getting worryingly short of spares.

As far as the rest of the grid order was concerned, Mark Blundell was acutely disappointed with his 17th place qualifying position, having failed to work out a decent chassis balance on his McLaren-Mercedes, while both the Ligier-Mugens also failed to demonstrate any vestige of their anticipated form.

At the back of the pack, Andrea Montermini was fortunate to escape a hugely spectacular off-course excursion which left his Pacific trailing a broken nose section and badly damaged undertray. Karl Wendlinger was also continuing to have trouble getting into the swing of things after recovering from his 1994 Monaco

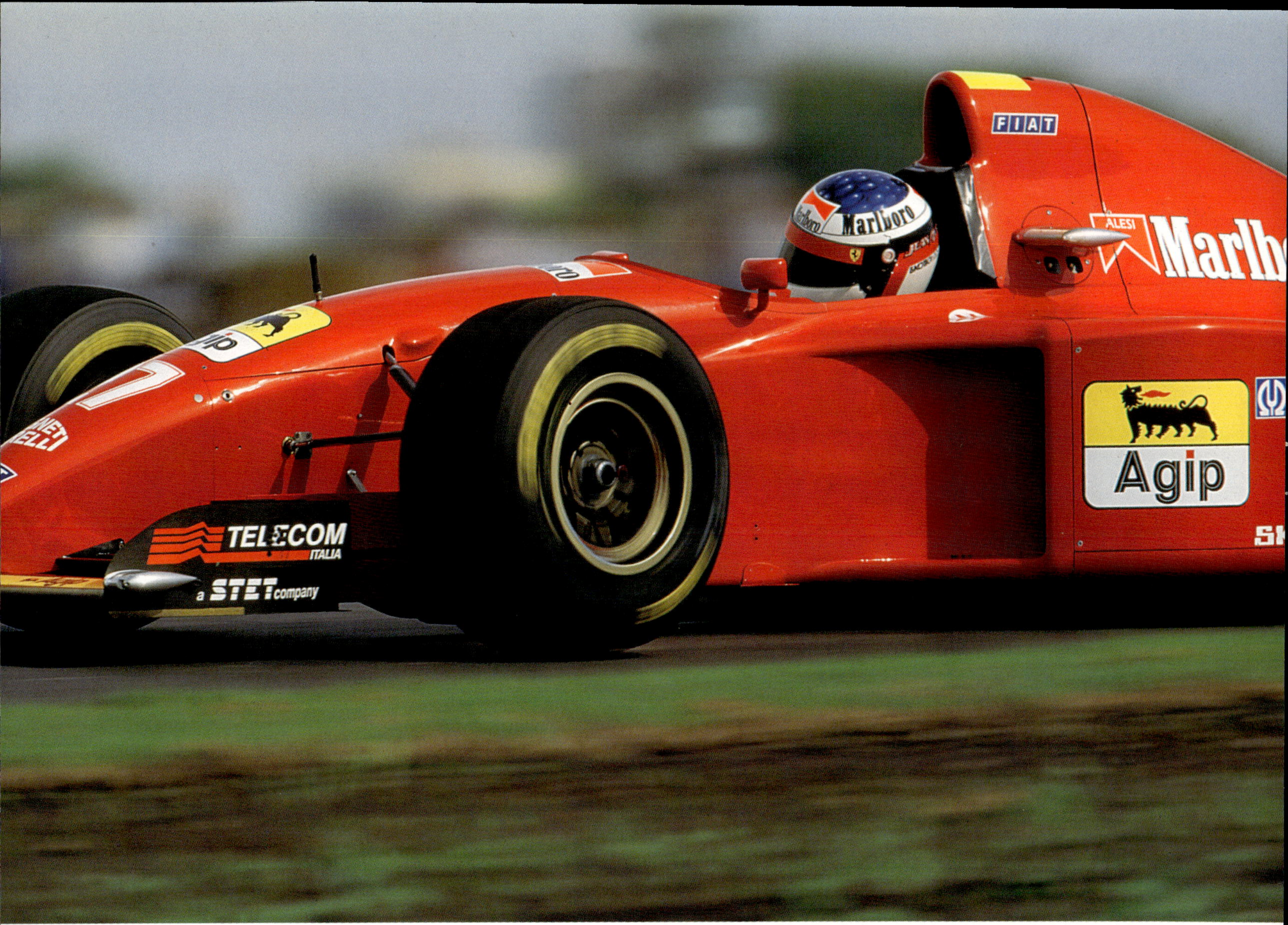
FIAT
ALESI
Marlboro
Agip
TELECOM
ITALIA
a STET company

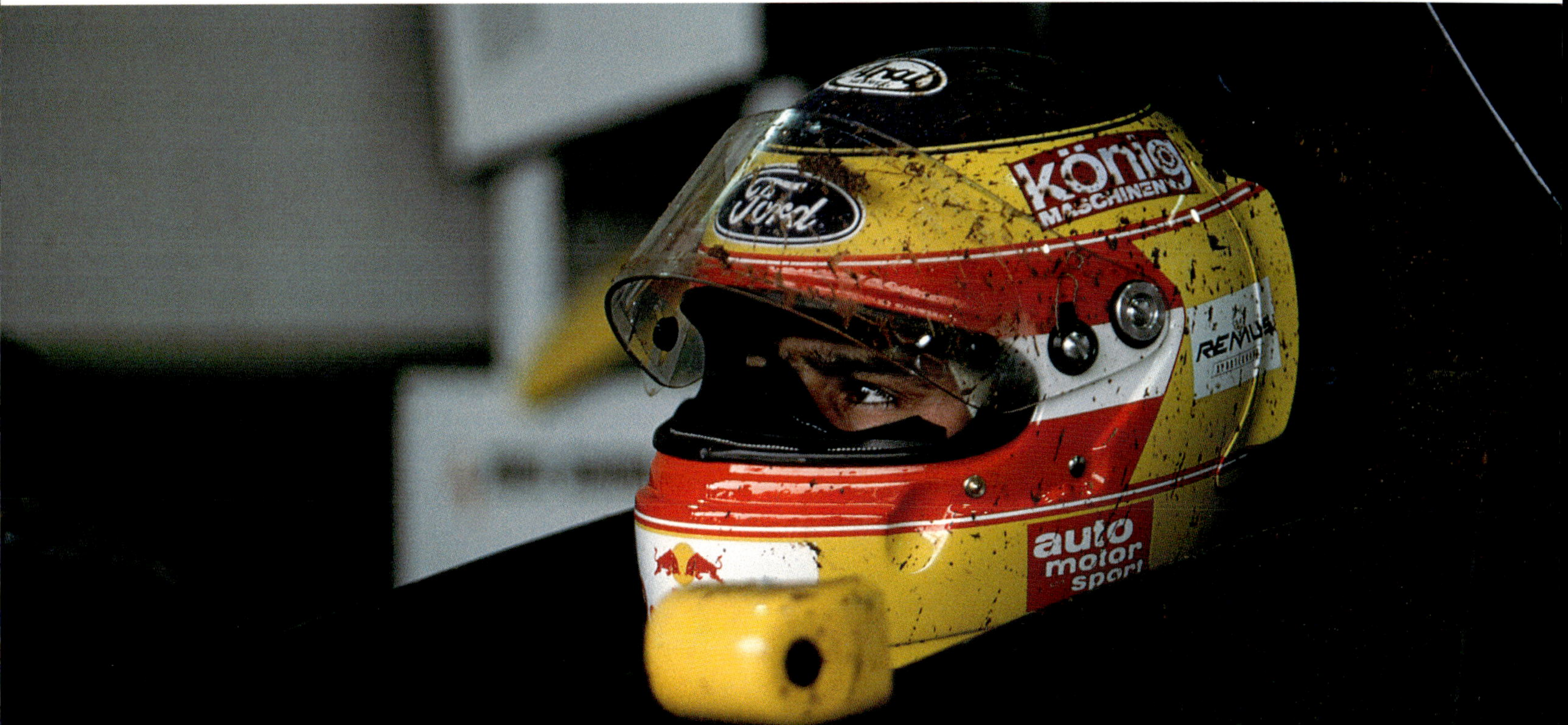
Ford
König
MASCHINEN
auto
motor
sport

ARGENTINE GRAND PRIX

Left: Olivier Panis, one of the victims of the first-corner mayhem, races back to the pits in readiness for the restart with the man who set it in motion, Jean Alesi, a safe distance ahead.

Inset: In a separate incident, further round the opening lap, Johnny Herbert locked the brakes of his Benetton and ran into the back of Rubens Barrichello's Jordan amid a cloud of tyre-smoke.

While Jos Verstappen describes his part in the drama to his manager, former Grand Prix driver Huub Rothengatter, the Simtek mechanics set about replacing a damaged suspension wishbone on the grid.

accident. Admittedly it was early days yet, but his tentative approach and extreme nervousness in the wet were all too uncomfortably obvious from the touchlines.

The race morning warm-up saw Hill fastest ahead of Berger, Alesi, Schumacher and Coulthard. Alesi tried both 412T2s to check all was well – a shrewd move, as things transpired. Then it was Coulthard's job to lead the pack away on its parade lap, the young Scot facing his first pole-position start since his F3 days. His reputation for blistering starts from lowly grid positions was well established. The question now was, could he do the same with an empty track in front of him?

Could he? Not half! As the starting light blinked green, David made an absolutely copybook getaway, leading by at least three lengths into the first tight right-hander. Hill slotted into an immediate second place while Häkkinen made a brilliant getaway to slice cleanly – if closely – inside Schumacher's Benetton as they arrived in the braking area. It was all simmering up nicely for a cracking race.

Not so! Down the inside came Jean Alesi's Ferrari after a poor start. 'The track was slippery on the tight line and I just lost it,' shrugged the Frenchman. In a split-second, all hell seemed to break loose. Mika Salo, right behind the Ferrari, had to brake hard as Alesi spun sideways and his Tyrrell was rammed from behind by the hapless Luca Badoer's Minardi. Panis then collected Martini, knocking him into Herbert, and, two corners later, Johnny hit the rear of Barrichello's Jordan, damaging the Benetton's steering. But with Alesi's Ferrari stranded broadside across the inside kerb, its water and oil radiators fractured, the organisers had no choice but to put out the red flag.

Coulthard, advised over the radio from his pit, simply couldn't believe it. Now he had it all to do again! Alesi was fortunate that it was his turn to have first call on the spare Ferrari at this race, but Barrichello had to take a spare Jordan set up for Irvine and it took so long to adjust the cockpit for the shorter Brazilian that he was forced to take the restart from the pit lane.

Herbert took over the spare Benetton and the Tyrrell mechanics did a fantastic job repairing Salo's car, but there was only bad news for Badoer. His car damaged beyond immediate repair, and with no spare Minardi yet to hand, the Italian had to spend the rest of the afternoon spectating from the pits. Jos Verstappen's Simtek had tagged Häkkinen in the midst of this débâcle, breaking a suspension wishbone, but this was easily replaced in time for the second start.

So off they went again. Coulthard once more made a splendid getaway to lead into the first turn, but this time Schumacher got the jump on Damon and slipped the Benetton into an immediate second place. There was more drama just behind as the left tyre of Häkkinen's McLaren made very firm contact with the right-front wing of Irvine's Jordan. The net result was that Mika came barrelling into the first turn on three wheels and a cascade of flailing rubber, pirouetting straight into the gravel trap on the outside of the turn, while Eddie headed for the pits at the end of the opening lap for a fresh nose cone to be fitted.

Häkkinen didn't mince his words. 'I had a good fight with Schumacher in the first corner at the first start,' he explained. 'It was good professional racing; we were close, but we did not touch each other. Accelerating out of the first corner, I was in third place and everything was going well. Then the red flag came out and the race was stopped. The second start was very similar. I was heading for third position again into the first corner, when I felt Irvine touch my rear tyre. It exploded immediately and I went off.'

That was certainly not the way Irvine saw it, simply regarding it as a repeat of Häkkinen's squeezing tactics which saw him given a one-race suspension after being held responsible for the first-lap multiple pile-up at Hockenheim the previous July. And this wasn't the end of the drama. Midway round the opening lap, Wendlinger's Sauber somehow contrived to take out both Pacifics even before Coulthard had tripped the timing beam to lead across the line by a full two seconds at the end of the first flying lap of the afternoon.

Schumacher was second with Hill fending off the superb Salo, then Alesi, Frentzen, Katayama, Herbert and Blundell, the surviving McLaren-Mercedes driver making a stupendous start from 17th on the grid, while the impressive Verstappen completed the top ten. By contrast, Gerhard Berger had made a simply rotten getaway, dropping from eighth to 12th first time round after being wrong-footed by the Häkkinen/Irvine drama at the first corner.

Coulthard pulled out a healthy 4.3s advantage over Schumacher by the end of the fifth lap, but then everything went wrong.

'Coming into the hairpin before the pits, my engine suddenly died and I thought that was it,' he said. 'But I flicked down through the gears and the engine just fired up when I got down into first – which is why I suddenly got violent wheelspin and laid rubber all the way back out onto the startline straight!'

This left Schumacher leading from Hill by 0.6s with Coulthard third, then a long gap back to Alesi, Salo, Frentzen and Herbert. Hill was now pressuring Schumacher relentlessly, finally diving inside the Benetton to take second place under braking for the first corner going into lap 11. The World Champion was apparently suffering an unexpectedly premature deterioration in grip from his first set of tyres and was in no position to defend his place when Coulthard came scything by on the outside at the same point five laps later, the Scot's task aided slightly by the fact that they were coming up to lap Martini's Minardi at that point.

'I knew I had only three laps left before making my first refuelling stop,' said Coulthard, 'so I wanted to make a point by passing Michael. Unfortunately, shortly afterwards I had problems with inconsistent response from the electronic throttle mechanism. Then the engine cut, and that was it.' The Williams rolled to a halt midway round lap 17. By this stage the luckless Irvine was also out, having succumbed to engine failure, while Blundell's great charge in the McLaren had come to an end after nine laps when gearbox overheating caused by a loss of lubricant from a crack in the casing resulted in damage to the Mercedes V10.

Hill came in for his first refuelling stop (13.5s) at the end of lap 16, briefly allowing Schumacher into the lead, but when Michael came in for a 7.4s stop next time round, Alesi's Ferrari took over at the head of the field. Thus by lap 20 it was Jean just 0.4s ahead of Hill, with a long gap back to Schumacher, who was at least finding that his second set of rubber worked rather better than the first.

Fourth was Herbert, not totally happy with the handling of the spare Benetton, then Frentzen, the remarkable Verstappen, Morbidelli, Salo (who'd already made his first stop) and the hard-charging Barrichello.

On lap 26, two laps after Verstappen's gallant run ended with a broken gearbox, Alesi came in for the first of his two refuelling stops, dropping to second but emerging from the pits still just ahead of Schumacher. But Hill was now not to be denied and successfully emerged from his second refuelling stop at the end of lap 34 with his advantage intact. Schumacher stopped again on lap 35, only to find that he was back to square one: his third set of rubber was dreadful, effectively ending any chance of his staying on terms with Alesi.

By lap 48, Alesi had moved to within five seconds of Hill's leading

99

Williams and it seemed possible that the Ferrari was going to mount a very genuine challenge for the lead. At that point he came in for his second refuelling stop, Hill taking the cue to come in for his third next time round. On lap 51 the gap between the two cars was a whisker under four seconds, but then Damon reasserted his control – 4.1s, 4.4s, 6.2s, 6.8s, 7.4s, 8.4s – and by lap 60, with 12 left to run, it was all over bar the shouting.

Controlling the race to perfection, Hill eventually won by 6.407s. 'The car was absolutely superb over the whole weekend, and I haven't enjoyed driving a car through a Grand Prix as much as that before,' he enthused.

'I didn't make a good start and I was biding my time behind Michael, but I could see that David was getting away so I had to think what to do about it. I had a good race with Michael; he was very difficult to pass here, but I managed to get a tow into the first corner and then with a clear bit of track I got away.

'Jean was always a worry and I wasn't sure I was safe until I was eight seconds ahead with two laps to go. It's easy to crack under pressure, but the team gave me three perfect stops and the car didn't miss a beat.'

Alesi was philosophical, yet pretty satisfied with the way his day ended – bearing in mind how it had started. It also proved that there was nothing wrong with Ferrari's standards of preparation, for the spare 412T2 had run faultlessly. By contrast, Schumacher was extremely disappointed, and not a little perplexed, by the inconsistent tyre performance which had bedevilled his Benetton all afternoon. With 19 laps to go he had made his third refuelling stop, retaining third place, and went like the wind to set the fastest lap of the race. His fourth set of tyres had been perfect.

Behind Herbert, fifth place should have gone to Salo's Tyrrell, but he was taken out of the race with 24 laps to run by the antics of erratic back-marker Aguri Suzuki, the Ligier driver having earlier caused some strife to Gerhard Berger.

'I was on the radio telling them that they should get some blue flags put out, or he was going to take me off,' fumed the Finnish new boy, 'and that's just what happened. He was locking brakes and going wide in the corners, then coming straight back across my nose. Perhaps he thought he was on the same lap.'

Williams seemed to have an edge over Benetton on this occasion and Damon Hill took full advantage to score a commanding victory that put his World Championship challenge back on course after his disappointment in Brazil.

Salo's fraught afternoon ended with him cutting his hand on a rusty nail as he scaled a fence in order to find his way back to the pits. Small wonder, under the circumstances, that there was a frank exchange of views between the two men immediately after the race.

'I'm glad they're replacing him with Martin [Brundle] for the next race,' said Salo in conclusion, 'because we need professional drivers. It is dangerous with guys like that.' In fact, the Tyrrell driver would have to wait until Spain before competing in a Suzuki-free zone.

Salo's late-race retirement elevated Heinz-Harald Frentzen's Sauber C14 to fifth place, albeit two laps behind Hill's winning Williams. Completing the top six was Gerhard Berger's Ferrari, the Austrian having a disappointing run after his poor start which left him bogged down in traffic during the opening stages of the race.

After taking almost a dozen laps to battle his way past Verstappen's Simtek, Gerhard radioed in to say that the car felt almost undriveable. Believing he had a serious damper problem, he pitted on lap 14 and the car was just on the point of being pushed away when Chief Mechanic Nigel Stepney noticed that the right-front tyre was partly deflated. Berger's machine was pushed back into place, refettled and sent back into the race after losing a whopping 81 seconds. He resumed 16th and spent the rest of the afternoon battling back into contention.

Olivier Panis finished seventh for Ligier ahead of Ukyo Katayama's Tyrrell and Domenico Schiattarella's Simtek, while the Fortis of Pedro Diniz and Roberto Moreno were both still running at the end, albeit having completed insufficient laps to be classified.

Damon Hill and the Williams team came away from the Argentine Grand Prix in a confident frame of mind. Although the winner had reported a degree of inconsistency in his tyres' performance, that looked like fine detail. It seemed that both Williams FW17s could go deeper into the corners than either of the Benettons as well as putting their power down more decisively.

The only fly in the ointment was Schumacher's fastest lap on his Benetton's fourth set of tyres. It was 0.7s faster than the best Hill could manage. A fleeting one-off? Or a marker for the future? Time alone would tell.

FIA FORMULA ONE WORLD CHAMPIONSHIP ROUND 2

GRAN PREMIO DE ARGENTINA

BUENOS AIRES 7-9 APRIL 1995

Race distance: 72 laps, 190.541 miles/306.648 km
Race weather: Warm and overcast

AUTODROMO OSCAR ALFREDO GALVEZ, BUENOS AIRES

CIRCUIT LENGTH: 2.646 miles/4.259 km

Place	Driver	Nat.	No.	Entrant	Car/Engine	Laps	Time/Retirement	Speed (mph/km/h)
1	**Damon Hill**	GB	5	Rothmans Williams Renault	Williams FW17-Renault RS7 V10	72	1h 53m 14.532s	100.901/162.385
2	**Jean Alesi**	F	27	Scuderia Ferrari	Ferrari 412T2 044 V12	72	1h 53m 20.939s	100.806/162.232
3	**Michael Schumacher**	D	1	Mild Seven Benetton Renault	Benetton B195-Renault RS7 V10	72	1h 53m 47.908s	100.408/161.592
4	**Johnny Herbert**	GB	2	Mild Seven Benetton Renault	Benetton B195-Renault RS7 V10	71		
5	**Heinz-Harald Frentzen**	D	30	Red Bull Sauber Ford	Sauber C14-Ford Zetec-R V8	70		
6	**Gerhard Berger**	A	28	Scuderia Ferrari	Ferrari 412T2 044 V12	70		
7	Olivier Panis	F	26	Ligier Gitanes Blondes	Ligier JS41-Mugen Honda MF301 V10	70		
8	Ukyo Katayama	J	3	Nokia Tyrrell Yamaha	Tyrrell 023-Yamaha OX10C V10	69		
9	Domenico Schiattarella	I	11	MTV Simtek Ford	Simtek S951-Ford ED V8	68		
NC	Pedro Diniz	BR	21	Parmalat Forti Ford	Forti FG01-Ford ED V8	63		
NC	Roberto Moreno	BR	22	Parmalat Forti Ford	Forti FG01-Ford ED V8	63		
	Mika Salo	SF	4	Nokia Tyrrell Yamaha	Tyrrell 023-Yamaha OX10C V10	48	Collision with Suzuki	
	Aguri Suzuki	J	25	Ligier Gitanes Blondes	Ligier JS41-Mugen Honda MF301 V10	47	Collision with Salo	
	Pierluigi Martini	I	23	Minardi Scuderia Italia	Minardi M195-Ford EDM V8	44	Spun off	
	Gianni Morbidelli	I	9	Footwork Hart	Footwork FA16-Hart 830 V8	43	Electrics	
	Taki Inoue	J	10	Footwork Hart	Footwork FA16-Hart 830 V8	40	Spun off	
	Rubens Barrichello	BR	14	Total Jordan Peugeot	Jordan 195-Peugeot A10 V10	33	Oil leak	
	Jos Verstappen	NL	12	MTV Simtek Ford	Simtek S951-Ford ED V8	23	Gearbox	
	David Coulthard	GB	6	Rothmans Williams Renault	Williams FW17-Renault RS7 V10	16	Clutch	
	Mark Blundell	GB	7	Marlboro McLaren Mercedes	McLaren MP4/10-Mercedes FO110 V10	9	Engine	
	Eddie Irvine	GB	15	Total Jordan Peugeot	Jordan 195-Peugeot A10 V10	6	Engine	
	Andrea Montermini	I	17	Pacific Grand Prix Ltd	Pacific PR02-Ford ED V8	1	Suspension damage	
	Mika Häkkinen	SF	8	Marlboro McLaren Mercedes	McLaren MP4/10-Mercedes FO110 V10	0	Collision with Irvine	
	Bertrand Gachot	F	16	Pacific Grand Prix Ltd	Pacific PR02-Ford ED V8	0	Collision with Wendlinger	
	Karl Wendlinger	A	29	Red Bull Sauber Ford	Sauber C14-Ford Zetec-R V8	0	Collision with Gachot	
DNS	Luca Badoer	I	24	Minardi Scuderia Italia	Minardi M195-Ford EDM V8	0	Accident damage	

Fastest lap: Schumacher, on lap 55, 1m 30.522s, 105.245 mph/169.377 km/h (record).
New circuit. No previous lap record.

All cars used Goodyear tyres

All results and data © FIA 1995

STARTING GRID

5 **HILL** (1m 54.057s) Williams	6 **COULTHARD** (1m 53.241s) Williams
15 **IRVINE** (1m 54.381s) Jordan	1 **SCHUMACHER** (1m 54.272s) Benetton
27 **ALESI** (1m 54.637s) Ferrari	8 **HÄKKINEN** (1m 54.529s) McLaren
28 **BERGER** (1m 55.276s) Ferrari	4 **SALO** (1m 54.757s) Tyrrell
14 **BARRICHELLO*** (1m 56.114s) Jordan	30 **FRENTZEN** (1m 55.583s) Sauber
9 **MORBIDELLI** (1m 57.092s) Footwork	2 **HERBERT** (1m 57.068s) Benetton
12 **VERSTAPPEN** (1m 57.231s) Simtek	24 **BADOER**** (1m 57.167s) Minardi
23 **MARTINI** (1m 58.066s) Minardi	3 **KATAYAMA** (1m 57.484s) Tyrrell
26 **PANIS** (1m 58.824s) Ligier	7 **BLUNDELL** (1m 58.660s) McLaren
11 **SCHIATTARELLA** (1m 59.539s) Simtek	25 **SUZUKI** (1m 58.882s) Ligier
17 **MONTERMINI** (2m 01.763s) Pacific	29 **WENDLINGER** (2m 00.751s) Sauber
22 **MORENO** (2m 04.481s) Forti	16 **GACHOT** (2m 04.050s) Pacific
10 **INOUE** (2m 07.298s) Footwork	21 **DINIZ** (2m 05.932s) Forti

* took restart from pit lane
** did not take restart

FOR THE RECORD

First Grand Prix pole position
David Coulthard
50th Grand Prix start
Mika Häkkinen

TIME SHEETS

Friday free practice
Heavy rain

Pos.	Driver	Laps	Time
1	Jean Alesi	14	1m 58.207s
2	Heinz-Harald Frentzen	16	1m 58.381s
3	Eddie Irvine	10	1m 59.124s
4	Michael Schumacher	14	1m 59.276s
5	David Coulthard	15	1m 59.701s
6	Rubens Barrichello	11	2m 00.306s
7	Mika Häkkinen	11	2m 00.313s
8	Mika Salo	6	2m 00.611s
9	Gerhard Berger	9	2m 00.675s
10	Jos Verstappen	7	2m 01.293s
11	Luca Badoer	9	2m 01.864s
12	Gianni Morbidelli	7	2m 01.947s
13	Mark Blundell	14	2m 02.411s
14	Ukyo Katayama	9	2m 03.547s
15	Domenico Schiattarella	7	2m 03.603s
16	Pierluigi Martini	9	2m 03.763s
17	Karl Wendlinger	12	2m 04.039s
18	Johnny Herbert	5	2m 05.229s
19	Andrea Montermini	6	2m 08.805s
20	Bertrand Gachot	11	2m 11.024s
21	Taki Inoue	4	2m 11.683s
22	Roberto Moreno	11	2m 13.848s
23	Aguri Suzuki	2	2m 16.107s
24	Pedro Diniz	2	2m 17.042s
25	Damon Hill	4	4m 29.056s
	Olivier Panis	0	no time

Saturday free practice
Dry and bright

Pos.	Driver	Laps	Time
1	Michael Schumacher	21	1m 31.376s
2	Damon Hill	20	1m 31.595s
3	David Coulthard	20	1m 32.136s
4	Jean Alesi	22	1m 32.383s
5	Mika Häkkinen	21	1m 32.440s
6	Eddie Irvine	23	1m 33.510s
7	Gerhard Berger	20	1m 33.554s
8	Rubens Barrichello	8	1m 34.080s
9	Olivier Panis	18	1m 34.174s
10	Mika Salo	19	1m 34.310s
11	Mark Blundell	22	1m 34.317s
12	Heinz-Harald Frentzen	23	1m 34.876s
13	Aguri Suzuki	20	1m 35.129s
14	Johnny Herbert	13	1m 35.372s
15	Gianni Morbidelli	13	1m 35.502s
16	Taki Inoue	20	1m 35.637s
17	Karl Wendlinger	23	1m 35.659s
18	Ukyo Katayama	16	1m 35.669s
19	Jos Verstappen	11	1m 37.034s
20	Pierluigi Martini	14	1m 37.336s
21	Andrea Montermini	18	1m 37.388s
22	Luca Badoer	6	1m 38.162s
23	Roberto Moreno	13	1m 38.319s
24	Bertrand Gachot	19	1m 38.355s
25	Domenico Schiattarella	14	1m 38.633s
26	Pedro Diniz	23	1m 39.211s

Friday qualifying
Heavy rain

Pos.	Driver	Laps	Time
1	David Coulthard	10	1m 54.670s
2	Jean Alesi	12	1m 55.213s
3	**Heinz-Harald Frentzen**	12	**1m 55.583s**
4	Damon Hill	9	1m 55.677s
5	Gerhard Berger	11	1m 56.260s
6	Mika Häkkinen	12	1m 56.449s
7	Eddie Irvine	7	1m 56.615s
8	Rubens Barrichello	12	1m 56.746s
9	Michael Schumacher	10	1m 57.056s
10	**Johnny Herbert**	8	**1m 57.068s**
11	**Luca Badoer**	11	**1m 57.167s**
12	Gianni Morbidelli	7	1m 57.684s
13	Mika Salo	5	1m 57.738s
14	**Pierluigi Martini**	8	**1m 58.066s**
15	**Mark Blundell**	8	**1m 58.660s**
16	Olivier Panis	10	1m 59.204s
17	Ukyo Katayama	9	1m 59.909s
18	Aguri Suzuki	10	2m 01.446s
19	**Andrea Montermini**	12	**2m 01.763s**
20	Karl Wendlinger	10	2m 01.774s
21	Jos Verstappen	6	2m 02.410s
22	Domenico Schiattarella	7	2m 02.806s
23	**Bertrand Gachot**	9	**2m 04.050s**
24	**Roberto Moreno**	11	**2m 04.481s**
25	**Pedro Diniz**	10	**2m 05.932s**
26	**Taki Inoue**	4	**2m 07.298s**

Saturday qualifying
Rain, drying slightly

Pos.	Driver	Laps	Time
1	**David Coulthard**	6	**1m 53.241s**
2	**Damon Hill**	8	**1m 54.057s**
3	**Michael Schumacher**	7	**1m 54.272s**
4	**Eddie Irvine**	8	**1m 54.381s**
5	**Mika Häkkinen**	8	**1m 54.529s**
6	**Jean Alesi**	10	**1m 54.637s**
7	**Mika Salo**	11	**1m 54.757s**
8	**Gerhard Berger**	6	**1m 55.276s**
9	**Rubens Barrichello**	8	**1m 56.114s**
10	Heinz-Harald Frentzen	7	1m 56.168s
11	**Gianni Morbidelli**	5	**1m 57.092s**
12	**Jos Verstappen**	8	**1m 57.231s**
13	Johnny Herbert	7	1m 57.341s
14	**Ukyo Katayama**	11	**1m 57.484s**
15	Luca Badoer	5	1m 57.657s
16	Mark Blundell	7	1m 58.767s
17	**Olivier Panis**	6	**1m 58.824s**
18	**Aguri Suzuki**	5	**1m 58.882s**
19	**Domenico Schiattarella**	10	**1m 59.539s**
20	**Karl Wendlinger**	7	**2m 00.751s**
21	Pierluigi Martini	3	2m 01.059s
22	Bertrand Gachot	7	2m 09.359s
23	Roberto Moreno	4	2m 15.398s
	Andrea Montermini	0	no time
	Pedro Diniz	0	no time
	Taki Inoue	0	no time

Warm-up
Dry and bright

Pos.	Driver	Laps	Time
1	Damon Hill	14	1m 31.679s
2	Gerhard Berger	10	1m 31.933s
3	Jean Alesi	13	1m 32.144s
4	Michael Schumacher	9	1m 32.176s
5	David Coulthard	10	1m 32.843s
6	Rubens Barrichello	12	1m 32.881s
7	Eddie Irvine	11	1m 33.131s
8	Mark Blundell	13	1m 33.326s
9	Olivier Panis	15	1m 33.370s
10	Heinz-Harald Frentzen	11	1m 33.609s
11	Mika Häkkinen	11	1m 33.641s
12	Johnny Herbert	13	1m 33.941s
13	Mika Salo	11	1m 34.614s
14	Ukyo Katayama	12	1m 34.971s
15	Gianni Morbidelli	12	1m 35.108s
16	Karl Wendlinger	12	1m 35.301s
17	Pierluigi Martini	14	1m 35.537s
18	Aguri Suzuki	13	1m 35.576s
19	Jos Verstappen	10	1m 35.735s
20	Bertrand Gachot	11	1m 37.082s
21	Domenico Schiattarella	9	1m 37.466s
22	Taki Inoue	10	1m 37.654s
23	Andrea Montermini	8	1m 38.590s
24	Roberto Moreno	11	1m 40.518s
25	Pedro Diniz	10	1m 42.014s
26	Luca Badoer	1	2m 38.406s

Fastest race laps
Warm, overcast

Driver	Time	Lap
Michael Schumacher	1m 30.522s	55
Damon Hill	1m 31.253s	21
Jean Alesi	1m 31.453s	25
Gerhard Berger	1m 31.868s	65
David Coulthard	1m 32.095s	3
Johnny Herbert	1m 33.082s	32
Mika Salo	1m 33.636s	28
Rubens Barrichello	1m 33.810s	26
Olivier Panis	1m 33.953s	27
Aguri Suzuki	1m 34.049s	26
Ukyo Katayama	1m 34.106s	5
Heinz-Harald Frentzen	1m 34.331s	4
Gianni Morbidelli	1m 34.396s	26
Mark Blundell	1m 34.963s	5
Eddie Irvine	1m 35.070s	4
Taki Inoue	1m 35.325s	30
Jos Verstappen	1m 35.353s	5
Pierluigi Martini	1m 35.837s	5
Domenico Schiattarella	1m 35.945s	27
Pedro Diniz	1m 40.683s	4
Roberto Moreno	1m 40.730s	4

CHASSIS LOG BOOK

1	Schumacher	Benetton B195/4
2	Herbert	Benetton B195/3
spare		Benetton B195/1
3	Katayama	Tyrrell 023/1
4	Salo	Tyrrell 023/2
spare		Tyrrell 023/3
5	Hill	Williams FW17/1
6	Coulthard	Williams FW17/2
spare		Williams FW17/3
7	Blundell	McLaren MP4/10/2
8	Häkkinen	McLaren MP4/10/3
spare		McLaren MP4/10/4
9	Morbidelli	Footwork FA16/2
10	Inoue	Footwork FA16/1
11	Schiattarella	Simtek S951/1
12	Verstappen	Simtek S951/2
16	Gachot	Pacific PR02/1
17	Montermini	Pacific PR02/2
21	Diniz	Forti FG01/1
22	Moreno	Forti FG01/2
23	Martini	Minardi M195/2
24	Badoer	Minardi M195/2
25	Suzuki	Ligier JS41/2
26	Panis	Ligier JS41/1
spare		Ligier JS41/3
27	Alesi	Ferrari 412T2/157
28	Berger	Ferrari 412T2/159
spare		Ferrari 412T2/156
29	Wendlinger	Sauber C14/2
30	Frentzen	Sauber C14/3
spare		Sauber C14/1

POINTS TABLES

Drivers

1	Michael Schumacher	14
2	Damon Hill	10
3	Jean Alesi	8
4	David Coulthard	6
5	Gerhard Berger	5
6 =	Mika Häkkinen	3
6 =	Johnny Herbert	3
8	Heinz-Harald Frentzen	2
9	Mark Blundell	1

Constructors

1	Ferrari	13
2	Williams	10
3	Benetton	7
4	McLaren	4
5	Sauber	2

Points and results reflect outcome of FIA Court of Appeal hearing on 13 April

WORLD CHAMPIONSHIP • ROUND 3

SAN MARINO GRAND PRIX

HILL
ALESI
BERGER
COULTHARD
HÄKKINEN
FRENTZEN

Above: Surrounded by a rather unseemly scrum of photographers, the drivers observed a minute's silence in memory of Ayrton Senna and Roland Ratzenberger before the start.

The mood on the rostrum after the race was altogether different as Damon Hill celebrated his second win in succession with Ferrari team-mates Jean Alesi *(left)* and Gerhard Berger.

SAN MARINO GRAND PRIX

Diary

Maurizio Passarini, the magistrate entrusted with investigating Ayrton Senna's fatal accident, reveals it may be another six months before he is ready to issue his findings.

Minardi initiates legal action against Mugen over collapse of agreed 1995 engine supply deal.

Cosworth racing director Dick Scammell receives an MBE in the Queen's birthday honours list.

Gérard Larrousse abandons all hope of a late start to season at Imola and withdraws his Paul Ricard-based team from F1.

It seemed the same. Yet somehow it never could or would be the same. Coming back to Imola was difficult for Williams, no question about it. Twelve months earlier, David Coulthard had been driving an F3000 car at Silverstone, wondering where the money was coming from to finance his next race. He'd received a 'good luck' message from Ayrton Senna to celebrate the start of his third season in the Second Division.

Now the Scot was at Imola himself. Not as a makeweight in F1's supporting cast, but as a proven, front-line member of the Williams squad. Motor racing's capacity for regeneration had produced another young talent after the passing of the brightest star in the constellation.

Yet from the moment Ayrton Senna's Williams-Renault had plunged off the road at Tamburello with such catastrophic consequences on 1 May 1994, it was obvious that there would be no question of Formula 1 racing returning to the Autodromo Enzo e Dino Ferrari unless wide-ranging safety improvements were implemented.

Thankfully, the circuit owners moved decisively and willingly to accommodate the concerns of both motor racing's governing body and the competing drivers. The bottom line was sampled for the first time on the Thursday prior to this year's race when two additional sessions of unofficial testing revealed that the track had been skilfully reprofiled without completely losing its distinctive character.

The most obvious change was the addition of chicanes at the flat-out Tamburello and Villeneuve corners which had claimed the lives of Senna and the Austrian novice, Roland Ratzenberger, in the previous year's race. Tamburello, of course, had previously been flat out with no problems in a Grand Prix car – until something went horribly wrong for Senna.

Now the cars had to brake from just over 170 mph in sixth gear to enter a flowing new chicane at just over 70 mph in fourth. Once past this new deviation, it was back up to around 165 mph in fifth before slowing again for a 100 mph, fourth-gear chicane at Villeneuve.

As if to balance these speed restrictions, the absurdly tight chicane which had previously marred the medium-speed Acque Minerali corner had been removed. In addition, gravel traps and run-off areas all round the track had been considerably enlarged.

Yet, for all these improvements, memories of the 1994 race remained indelibly stamped on all the drivers' memories. 'It is not just another race, no way you can say that,' reflected Damon Hill, Senna's former team-mate.

'It is not easy to escape the memories of last year's event. But the circuit now offers a new challenge. From the viewpoint of driving technique, it bears no resemblance to the old track and requires a very different approach.'

As far as the action on the circuit was concerned, Nigel Mansell wasn't about to perform miracles on his first competitive outing for the McLaren-Mercedes team. He knew it. They knew it. But neither was prepared for the sight of the former F1 and Indy Car champion pirouetting wildly off the track after only a handful of laps in the specially arranged Thursday morning acclimatisation session.

Yet there were no expressions of frustration from Britain's most successful F1 driver, even though he had to sit out the remainder of the session.

'It was totally my fault,' he grinned. 'I went for the clutch – and forgot where it was!' Mansell, braking hard for the downhill Rivazza left-hander, momentarily overlooked the fact that the MP4/10B was equipped with a hand-operated clutch, rather than the regular third pedal – and the team's totally new car, with its specially enlarged cockpit, was left skidding inelegantly through the gravel trap.

Happily, Mansell's impromptu excursion failed to jeopardise the results of the McLaren team's 33-day marathon to build the new car. Mansell only had his first fitting in the cockpit the previous Friday and it was as late as the day prior to testing at Imola that the second MP4/10B monocoque passed the FIA side-impact test without which it could not have been signed off for racing.

Mansell ended up eighth fastest, moderately optimistic about his prospects for the weekend. 'The McLaren-Mercedes team has done a sensational job building this new car,' he enthused, 'so we are now at the point where we can start developing it. I feel happy and comfortable in the cockpit – I can even apply opposite lock, something which was impossible in the original car as there was just no room to move my arms.'

Nevertheless, Mansell still had some way to progress in order to close the 2.5s gap separating his best time from Jean Alesi's pace-setting Ferrari.

Not since 1983, when Frenchman Patrick Tambay scored an immensely popular victory, had Ferrari managed to win at the circuit which carries the name of their founder. But Alesi signalled that he aimed to change all that come race day, even though he was only a scant 0.36s ahead of David Coulthard's Williams FW17 at the end of preliminary testing.

Ferrari had a slightly more powerful, revised-specification V12 engine available for use by Alesi and Gerhard Berger in Friday's first qualifying session. But with both Michael Schumacher and Damon Hill concentrating on setting up their cars for much of the Thursday test, any over-optimism on the part of the fiercely patriotic local crowds could be seen as premature.

Maranello's initial strategy had been to prepare two fresh engines, each to slightly different specifications, for Berger and Alesi to use on Friday and Saturday. Somewhat theatrically, perhaps, they intended to replace the first day's engines with units developing around 5 bhp more in preparation for second qualifying.

Unfortunately, Berger's scheduled 'Friday spec.' engine developed a problem shortly after it was installed on Thursday evening, so his slightly more powerful unit designated for Saturday was installed instead for first qualifying.

This enabled Gerhard to get within 0.008s of Schumacher's provisional pole position in the closing moments of the session. This promised a worthwhile confrontation come race day as the two men had recently exchanged stern words in the media over the matter of the Benetton team leader's disqualification, and subsequent reinstatement, at the Brazilian GP.

On the technical front, the Benetton and Williams teams both benefited from the first significantly uprated Renault RS7 engine specification of the new season, the French V10 now featuring a modified valve timing system and revised inlet ducts, strengthening its power curve at low- and medium-range engine speeds.

From the outset, it was clear that the field was divided into two distinct segments – the Benettons, Williamses and Ferraris, and the rest of the field. Through the fast chicanes and medium-speed swerves, these six cars looked stable, secure and immensely quick. Quite simply, they were in a class of their own.

Schumacher, fresh from a five-day test at Jerez, was very happy with the overall performance of his Benetton, but this was in sharp contrast to Johnny Herbert's feelings about his B195. The Englishman ended the first day 2.12s slower than his team-mate, which could in no way be interpreted as an accurate reflection of his comparative ability.

Increasingly, Herbert seemed to have become marginalised amidst what, in the absence of any concrete explanation from Benetton, was looking more and more like a one-car team. Michael's only slight setback in preparation for the race came on Saturday morning when he clipped a kerb at the Variante Alta and took off one of his B195's front wheels against the retaining wall.

'There was no danger at all, in my view,' said Michael reassuringly. 'I was very slow going against that wall, and just ripped off the tyre, which bounced away.

'I just touched the kerb on the inside, and the car got out of control, spun round, went onto the grass and hit the wall. It was nothing dramatic. The problem was that I went at a bad angle into the wall; the car kept pushing against the wheel and that's why it ripped off in this way and jumped over the car.'

At the end of Friday qualifying Coulthard was in third place, 0.1s behind Berger, with Damon Hill fourth ahead of Alesi. Damon would be quickest in the free practice session on Saturday morning, despite a trip across a gravel trap when he momentarily caught the throttle pedal as he braked for the new Tamburello chicane. A heavy overnight shower had washed away much of the rubber laid on Thursday and Friday but both Williams drivers reckoned they were in with a chance. Damon's Friday best had been 1m 27.537s, and when he got down to 1m 27.512s on Saturday, he thought fleetingly in terms of a front row position.

'The car felt very good in race trim and when I did that, I thought, "right, I can pick up some time here,"' he explained. 'My next run was in traffic, so that was no good and in the end I couldn't make it. But, no, I don't think Benetton have caught up. I believe we still have the best engine/chassis combination around.'

Coulthard was similarly upbeat, the split-timing showing him to be 0.03s up on Schumacher's pole time on the approach to Tosa, about one-third of the way round the lap. But he lost a few tenths going through

105

that climbing left-hander, then found himself with a great armful of oversteer at Rivazza, so he failed to improve. Prior to that, David had been chasing a touch too much understeer. Generally, though, the Scot was pretty pleased with life.

Berger, meanwhile, quickly realised that there was no chance of taking pole and set off to scrub in some tyres in preparation for the race. Suddenly he heard his pit advising him – erroneously, as things turned out – that Coulthard had snatched pole. He piled on the pressure, and slid off briefly at Tamburello, having to be satisfied with second in the eventual grid order. Despite improving his time Hill remained in fourth place overall ahead of Alesi, Jean having a lurid moment exiting Rivazza which prevented him registering any improvement in the second session.

The pursuing pack was led by the McLaren-Mercedes of Mika Häkkinen, who didn't bother to run in second qualifying. He had made some worthwhile progress on chassis set-up during Saturday morning's free practice, but knew there was no chance of improving on sixth place. It made more sense to conserve tyres for the race.

Nigel Mansell, meanwhile, ended up ninth. He had lost time on Saturday morning when an oil cooler split, forcing him to abandon the car out on the circuit in a re-run of Häkkinen's experiences during Thursday testing. Yet Nigel remained relaxed and conservative in his predictions, correctly judging just how much work was still ahead.

Over in the Jordan camp, concerns over Peugeot engine unreliability remained after a Silverstone test blighted by crankshaft breakages and problems with the air-valve system. Irvine spun off after setting his best time on Friday, then had clutch problems the following day. He qualified seventh ahead of Herbert and Mansell, with Rubens Barrichello a disappointed tenth.

The Brazilian raised memories of his qualifying accident a year earlier by crashing heavily at the fast Piratella double left-hander in the closing moments of second qualifying. It was a big shunt, but Rubens was given a clean bill of health after a check-up at the circuit hospital.

Gianni Morbidelli again did a good job to qualify 11th with the neat Footwork-Hart, although he lost any prospect of bettering his time on Saturday when he spun off at Acque Minerali, scattering gravel all over the racing line. Taki Inoue picked up speed to qualify 19th, the Japanese novice looking a lot more capable on this occasion, although some observers felt this said more about the excellent Alan Jenkins-designed FA16 chassis than the F3000 graduate's inherent ability.

Olivier Panis emerged a moderately promising 12th fastest overall, four places ahead of his team-mate Aguri Suzuki, Ligier being the only two-car team whose drivers both registered an improvement in the second session. By contrast, the Tyrrell-Yamahas were abjectly disappointing. Ukyo Katayama and Mika Salo both suffered failures of high-mileage engines in Thursday testing and both complained of excessive understeer in Friday's first qualifying session, although Salo was one of the handful of drivers to improve his time on Saturday.

The Finn finally lined up in 13th place with Katayama, still unhappy about his chassis balance, two places further back. Splitting the two Tyrrells was Heinz-Harald Frentzen in the faster of the two Sauber C14s, although a revamp to high-nose configuration, which had been tested at Mugello the previous week, yielded no significant improvement to the Ford works team's prospects.

Frentzen's abiding problem continued to be understeer, while team-mate Karl Wendlinger ended up in a disappointing 21st place. The pleasant Austrian driver's performance again suggested that a return to his pre-Monaco '94 potential represented a forlorn hope.

Jos Verstappen did a good job to qualify his Simtek S951 in 17th place, the Dutchman feeling that he might have gone even quicker had there been sufficient time to change gear ratios prior to second qualifying. Pierluigi Martini's Minardi – which suffered two gearbox hydraulic pump failures on Friday – was next, ahead of Inoue's Footwork. Luca Badoer's Minardi completed the top 20 with Wendlinger next up, followed by Bertrand Gachot in the quicker Pacific, ahead of Schiattarella's Simtek and Andrea Montermini, who did a good job considering he underwent keyhole surgery to remove his appendix on the Wednesday prior to the race. Right at the back, as usual, were the two Fortis, Roberto Moreno being the quicker of the two – but still nine seconds away from pole position.

Weather conditions for the race were the big concern on Saturday evening. The forecast for Sunday predicted light, intermittent showers, but the warm-up took place in impossible conditions of torrential rain.

SAN MARINO GRAND PRIX

Left: FIA President Max Mosley *(left)* shares his thoughts with F1 supremo Bernie Ecclestone.

Opposite: Squeezed snugly into a cockpit bristling with electronic wizardry, Ferrari's Gerhard Berger prepares for action. The Austrian lost all chance of victory when he stalled his engine at his second pit stop after problems with the hand-operated clutch.

The Saubers now sported fashionable raised noses but there was no discernible improvement in their form. While Heinz-Harald Frentzen at least picked up a championship point, Karl Wendlinger *(below)* continued to struggle.

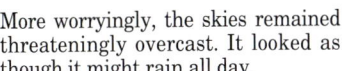
Mosley calls for 'more adult approach'

World Champion Michael Schumacher and the Elf fuel company both received an outspoken dressing-down from Max Mosley at Imola during a press conference in the course of which the FIA President called for a 'more adult approach' to Formula 1.

In particular, he focused on the question of Schumacher's attitude towards the pre-season drivers' check at Interlagos where a remarkable discrepancy in his weight was apparently registered.

'I think it is unfortunate if a World Champion gets involved in a "misunderstanding" over how much he may or may not weigh at any time in a weekend,' said Mosley firmly. 'It reflects very poorly on the sport and again shows a lack of an adult attitude towards it.

'It is not extraordinary that someone should have put on six kilos or more in one year, especially if weight no longer matters and if he has been training hard. What is extraordinary is that he should have lost it in the space of three days.'

Mosley was also uncompromising over the reinstatement of Schumacher and David Coulthard after their fuel was found not to conform with the regulations in Brazil. He made it quite clear that, had the matter been left to his sole judgement, the original Brazilian GP results would have stood.

'I understand that this would be unfair on the drivers, but I believe in the maxim that hard cases make bad law,' he explained. 'If you do something to overcome an obvious unfairness, you put yourself in a position which is not logically consistent.'

He then moved on to address a scathing attack on Elf on the subject of their mis-matched fuel in Brazil: 'I am sorry to have to say this about Elf, which is a big company, but once again, it was childish to continue pretending for two whole weeks that the petrol was the same, that the FIA technicians did not know what they were doing and that the machines we used [to check the fuel] were out of date.

'That company must have known, within 24 hours of the race in Brazil, that the two petrols were different. If we were able to get this result confirmed – as we did – by the Swiss Federal Laboratories, by an independent laboratory in Germany, and by an independent British laboratory – one must be absolutely sure that Elf, too, got that result rapidly confirmed.'

In Mosley's view, this was not the sort of behaviour to be expected from a major international company. He added: 'When they know something, they should admit it, and not keep a campaign going for nearly three weeks – notably in the French press – pretending something everybody knew was not true.'

He acknowledged that the FIA did not always get everything right 'but we do make honest attempts to do so, and I suggest that [elsewhere in the sport] an honest and adult attitude is required.'

More worryingly, the skies remained threateningly overcast. It looked as though it might rain all day.

Alesi and Berger topped the time sheets at the end of the 30-minute session, with Schumacher third and Mansell – using a lower-downforce aerodynamic set-up than Häkkinen – fourth in the McLaren-Mercedes. Hill and Coulthard had several spins, reporting that the conditions were absolutely diabolical and that a lot of work needed to be done on the FW17's wet-weather chassis set-up.

Thankfully, the rain had stopped well before the pit lane opened prior to the start, but the track surface was still glistening ominously as the cars set out on their warm-up laps. Those who chose to start on rain tyres were Schumacher, Berger, Coulthard, Hill and Barrichello. The rest, including both the McLarens, opted for slicks. It proved a disastrous strategy which eliminated all hopes of even keeping the leaders in sight.

Just prior to the start, the drivers assembled at the front of the starting grid to share one minute's silence in honour of Senna and Ratzenberger. Once these respects had been paid, it was back to their cars and on with the action.

At the green light, Schumacher made a clean getaway to lead into the first chicane from Berger, Coulthard and Hill. The whole field managed to muscle through intact, although Mansell nudged Morbidelli's Footwork, causing the Italian to head straight into the pit lane at the end of the opening lap with a puncture and a damaged suspension joint. Gianni resumed with a fresh set of unscrubbed slicks and the labels were still visible on the front tyres eight laps later, an indication of how cold and reluctant to dry out the track surface remained.

Berger came through 0.7s behind Schumacher at the end of the opening lap with Coulthard, Hill and Alesi following on and Häkkinen's slick-shod McLaren hanging on gamely in sixth place. Further back, Jos Verstappen had stormed the Simtek through from 17th on the grid to 13th, while Luca Badoer was facing a nerve-racking race, his Minardi's left-hand mirror having vibrated off shortly after the start.

At the end of lap two, Aguri Suzuki spun his Ligier at Rivazza, briefly forcing Martini's Minardi onto the edge of the gravel as he swerved to avoid the Mugen-engined machine. Both continued, but the

107

SAN MARINO GRAND PRIX

incident rather broke up the queue further back down the field, while Badoer collided with Wendlinger at Piratella, forcing the Sauber driver into the pits at the end of lap three. Karl then inadvertently exceeded the pit lane speed limit and had to come in for a stop-go penalty.

By lap five, the leaders were already lapping the slick-shod tail-enders and Badoer's badly restricted rearward vision caused him to chop Berger's Ferrari as the Austrian came up to pass him. The track was drying steadily by now and Gerhard was the first to opt for a switch to slicks, the Ferrari coming in for an 8.8s stop at the end of lap six, dropping briefly to fifth.

On lap seven, Herbert spun under braking for the Tamburello chicane, but quickly got going again, although he was soon anxious to come in for fresh rubber, having flat-spotted his tyres during this unscheduled gyration. At the end of his ninth lap, he aimed for the pit lane, only to be waved straight through as Schumacher was expected for his switch onto slicks.

Michael duly stopped on lap ten, as did Hill, and when Coulthard came in at the end of lap 11, the way was clear for the World Champion to regain his lead. But Schumacher never completed the lap. Resuming just ahead of Berger, he lost control on cold slicks when he hit a puddle approaching the second Piratella left-hander, slamming into the barrier before bouncing to a halt in the gravel trap.

The car was badly damaged, but Michael was not quick to shoulder sole responsibility for the accident, feeling that perhaps something had locked up at the back of the car. Subsequent detailed examination of the B195 revealed that there had apparently been no such failure.

Schumacher's abrupt departure left Berger leading comfortably ahead of the Williams duo, Hill dodging ahead of Coulthard when David made his tyre change at the end of lap 11. Alesi, who had changed to slicks on lap eight, was still right on the tail of the two FW17s, but Häkkinen was now way back and destined to make his first fuel stop of the day on lap 16, just as Alesi and Coulthard squeezed through Tosa absolutely side by side, locked in their ferocious battle over third place.

Getting through the slower traffic to best effect seemed likely to be one of the key factors in resolving the lead battle. The Minardis – whether with both mirrors still attached or not – made life particularly stressful for the front-runners, but it was all great stuff with plenty of lurid ducking and diving in traffic to keep the television viewers on the edge of their seats.

On lap 22, Berger came in for his second stop, but stalled the Ferrari

Left: **The unexpected arrival of Eddie Irvine's Jordan-Peugeot in the Ligier pit area caused understandable consternation among the French team's mechanics, who had been expecting a blue car.**

After the inevitable media fanfare, Nigel Mansell *(right)* **made a low-key debut for McLaren, bringing the specially built MP4/10B home in tenth place.**

David Coulthard *(bottom)* **had an eventful race, finishing fourth after a spin, a stop-go penalty, a protracted pit stop and a furious battle with Ferrari's Jean Alesi.**

and lost the lead to Hill. 'That was enormously frustrating,' said Gerhard afterwards. 'During the warm-up, I had been worried about the feel of the hand clutch and the engine just stalled when I was in for the second time. That lost me all chance of competing for a position at the front of the pack. I think the Williams-Renault was still more competitive, but we might have had a chance.'

Just prior to taking the lead, Hill ran slightly wide at Rivazza as he lapped Katayama's Tyrrell, momentarily allowing the Japanese driver to repass and Coulthard to close right up onto his tail. David was determined to keep the pressure on his team-mate, but on lap 28 he spun exiting the Villeneuve chicane, ploughing sideways over the kerb but thankfully still managing to keep his engine running.

Coulthard came straight into the pits for fresh rubber, resuming without losing second place, but now with Alesi right on his tail. Thereafter, the Scot found himself grappling with understeer, having damaged a front wing end plate in that earlier spin. Unfortunately, as he accelerated back into the race, Coulthard exceeded the pit lane speed limit and was back into the pits for a ten-second stop-go penalty at the end of lap 36, dropping to third. At his final pit stop eight laps later, the FW17 would be fitted with a replacement nose section – the 19.7s delay dropping him firmly to fourth place behind Berger.

Coulthard finished the day somewhat critical of his own personal performance. But he shrugged aside criticism from Alesi to the effect that his behaviour at the height of their battle was 'incorrect' – although when Jean came down the outside into Rivazza at one point and David's right-rear wheel made very firm contact with the Ferrari's left-front, perhaps David was being a little over-exuberant.

'I always deal with these things in a private way,' said Coulthard robustly, declining to be drawn into a public exchange with the Ferrari driver. 'If Jean has a problem, I'm sure, like a nice man, he'll come along and square it with me. Otherwise, no problem. I'm quite happy how I drove, but disappointed I spun . . .'

Once Coulthard had suffered his initial delay, the contest for the top four positions was never in doubt, with Hill never putting a wheel out of place to win by 18.5s from the slightly disappointed Alesi. However, Maranello could draw considerable consolation from the fact that they now shared the constructors' championship lead with Williams after another reliable performance from both cars.

Fifth place eventually fell to Häkkinen's McLaren, although Mansell could well have taken those two points after an unspectacular run. Since tapping Morbidelli on the opening lap, Nigel had run steadily at the bottom of the top ten, planning a two-stop strategy, and by lap 23 he was up to sixth place, although on the point of being lapped by the leaders.

Mansell made his first routine refuelling stop on lap 28 and his second on lap 43 when his McLaren's nose section was replaced after reports from marshals out on the circuit correctly suggesting that one of the end plates had worked loose. After his second stop he accelerated out of the pit again only to be slightly wrong-footed under braking for Tosa, when he couldn't quite work out which way one of the slow Fortis was going to move.

Quite late on, he cut in towards the apex – by which time Eddie Irvine's Jordan was coming up the inside. In the ensuing contact, Irvine's car lost its nose section and Mansell found himself heading straight back to the pits again to replace a punctured left-rear tyre.

That left Mika to retake fifth place ahead of Frentzen, Herbert and the frustrated Irvine, who spun again eight laps from the finish after his unscheduled stop to fit a fresh nose section. It was the last straw for Eddie in a race which had seen him 'wrong slot' into the Ligier pit for his first tyre change. But with Barrichello succumbing to gearbox failure, it was another bad day for the Jordan-Peugeot squad, which was hard pressed to see the funny side of it all.

Frentzen, by contrast, had a good run after a precarious first few laps on slicks. By the end of the race the Sauber's chassis balance felt much better than at any stage during qualifying, so gaining a single championship point was a worthwhile bonus. By contrast, Wendlinger's rotten luck continued; when he came in for his second stop at the end of lap 44, the locking device on the left-rear wheel jammed completely. It proved impossible to remove, so that was the end of his race.

Mansell wound up in tenth place, his disappointing 1995 F1 debut being rounded off in some pain when a Ferrari-mad photographer somehow managed to hit him on the head with a telephoto lens as he rushed past the McLaren garage. It had been a bad day for McLaren, but Ron Dennis didn't attempt to dodge the reality that it had been absolutely the wrong decision to start both cars on slicks.

Yet for Damon Hill and the Williams team, it had been a truly memorable afternoon. Twelve months earlier, the San Marino GP had ended on a note of bleak, despairing tragedy, but now Hill's fine win could be regarded as a final, symbolic exorcising of those painful memories. It was also his 11th Grand Prix win in 37 races, a record of which anybody could have been proud.

FIA FORMULA ONE WORLD CHAMPIONSHIP ROUND 3

GRAN PREMIO DI SAN MARINO
IMOLA
28-30 APRIL 1995

IMOLA – Autodromo Dino e Enzo Ferrari
CIRCUIT LENGTH: 3.041 MILES/4.895 KM

Race distance: 63 laps, 191.621 miles/308.385 km
Race weather: Cool, cloudy

Place	Driver	Nat.	No.	Entrant	Car/Engine	Laps	Time/Retirement	Speed (mph/km/h)
1	**Damon Hill**	GB	5	Rothmans Williams Renault	Williams FW17-Renault RS7 V10	63	1h 41m 42.552s	113.040/181.921
2	**Jean Alesi**	F	27	Scuderia Ferrari	Ferrari 412T2 044 V12	63	1h 42m 01.062s	112.698/181.371
3	**Gerhard Berger**	A	28	Scuderia Ferrari	Ferrari 412T2 044 V12	63	1h 42m 25.668s	112.247/180.645
4	**David Coulthard**	GB	6	Rothmans Williams Renault	Williams FW17-Renault RS7 V10	63	1h 42m 34.442s	112.087/180.387
5	**Mika Häkkinen**	SF	8	Marlboro McLaren Mercedes	McLaren MP4/10-Mercedes FO110 V10	62		
6	**Heinz-Harald Frentzen**	D	30	Red Bull Sauber Ford	Sauber C14-Ford Zetec-R V8	62		
7	**Johnny Herbert**	GB	2	Mild Seven Benetton Renault	Benetton B195-Renault RS7 V10	61		
8	**Eddie Irvine**	GB	15	Total Jordan Peugeot	Jordan 195-Peugeot A10 V10	61		
9	**Olivier Panis**	F	26	Ligier Gitanes Blondes	Ligier JS41-Mugen Honda MF301 V10	61		
10	**Nigel Mansell**	GB	7	Marlboro McLaren Mercedes	McLaren MP4/10B-Mercedes FO110 V10	61		
11	Aguri Suzuki	J	25	Ligier Gitanes Blondes	Ligier JS41-Mugen Honda MF301 V10	60		
12	Pierluigi Martini	I	23	Minardi Scuderia Italia	Minardi M195-Ford EDM V8	59		
13	Gianni Morbidelli	I	9	Footwork Hart	Footwork FA16-Hart 830 V8	59		
14	Luca Badoer	I	24	Minardi Scuderia Italia	Minardi M195-Ford EDM V8	59		
NC	Pedro Diniz	BR	21	Parmalat Forti Ford	Forti FG01-Ford ED V8	56		
NC	Roberto Moreno	BR	22	Parmalat Forti Ford	Forti FG01-Ford ED V8	56		
	Karl Wendlinger	A	29	Red Bull Sauber Ford	Sauber C14-Ford Zetec-R V8	43	Stuck wheel nut	
	Bertrand Gachot	F	16	Pacific Grand Prix Ltd	Pacific PR02-Ford ED V8	36	Gearbox	
	Domenico Schiattarella	I	11	MTV Simtek Ford	Simtek S951-Ford ED V8	35	Suspension	
	Rubens Barrichello	BR	14	Total Jordan Peugeot	Jordan 195-Peugeot A10 V10	31	Gearbox	
	Ukyo Katayama	J	3	Nokia Tyrrell Yamaha	Tyrrell 023-Yamaha OX10C V10	23	Spun off	
	Mika Salo	SF	4	Nokia Tyrrell Yamaha	Tyrrell 023-Yamaha OX10C V10	19	Engine	
	Andrea Montermini	I	17	Pacific Grand Prix Ltd	Pacific PR02-Ford ED V8	15	Gearbox	
	Jos Verstappen	NL	12	MTV Simtek Ford	Simtek S951-Ford ED V8	14	Gearbox	
	Taki Inoue	J	10	Footwork Hart	Footwork FA16-Hart 830 V8	12	Spun off	
	Michael Schumacher	D	1	Mild Seven Benetton Renault	Benetton B195-Renault RS7 V10	10	Accident	

Fastest lap: Berger, on lap 57, 1m 29.568s, 122.250 mph/196.744 km/h (record for new 3.041-mile/4.895-km circuit).
Previous lap record: Damon Hill (F1 Williams FW16-Renault V10), 1m 24.335s, 133.682 mph/215.141 km/h (1994 – on old 3.132-mile/5.040-km circuit).

All cars used Goodyear tyres

All results and data © FIA 1995

STARTING GRID

1 SCHUMACHER (1m 27.274s) Benetton
28 BERGER (1m 27.282s) Ferrari

6 COULTHARD (1m 27.459s) Williams
5 HILL (1m 27.512s) Williams

27 ALESI (1m 27.813s) Ferrari
8 HÄKKINEN (1m 28.343s) McLaren

15 IRVINE (1m 28.516s) Jordan
2 HERBERT (1m 29.350s) Benetton

7 MANSELL (1m 29.517s) McLaren
14 BARRICHELLO (1m 29.551s) Jordan

9 MORBIDELLI (1m 29.582s) Footwork
26 PANIS (1m 30.760s) Ligier

4 SALO (1m 31.035s) Tyrrell
30 FRENTZEN (1m 31.358s) Sauber

3 KATAYAMA (1m 31.630s) Tyrrell
25 SUZUKI (1m 31.913s) Ligier

12 VERSTAPPEN (1m 32.156s) Simtek
23 MARTINI (1m 32.445s) Minardi

10 INOUE (1m 32.710s) Footwork
24 BADOER (1m 33.071s) Minardi

29 WENDLINGER (1m 33.494s) Sauber
16 GACHOT (1m 33.892s) Pacific

11 SCHIATTARELLA (1m 33.965s) Simtek
17 MONTERMINI (1m 35.169s) Pacific

22 MORENO (1m 36.065s) Forti
21 DINIZ (1m 36.624s) Forti

TIME SHEETS

Friday free practice
Bright, light cloud

Pos.	Driver	Laps	Time
1	David Coulthard	23	1m 27.685s
2	Michael Schumacher	23	1m 28.469s
3	Mika Häkkinen	22	1m 28.941s
4	Damon Hill	17	1m 29.084s
5	Jean Alesi	23	1m 29.304s
6	Eddie Irvine	22	1m 29.477s
7	Gerhard Berger	19	1m 29.606s
8	Rubens Barrichello	23	1m 29.617s
9	Nigel Mansell	23	1m 29.775s
10	Johnny Herbert	23	1m 30.258s
11	Mika Salo	22	1m 30.937s
12	Ukyo Katayama	20	1m 30.988s
13	Heinz-Harald Frentzen	21	1m 31.219s
14	Olivier Panis	22	1m 31.533s
15	Gianni Morbidelli	14	1m 31.815s
16	Aguri Suzuki	16	1m 32.753s
17	Karl Wendlinger	22	1m 33.583s
18	Luca Badoer	23	1m 33.983s
19	Taki Inoue	23	1m 34.264s
20	Jos Verstappen	22	1m 34.299s
21	Bertrand Gachot	23	1m 34.765s
22	Andrea Montermini	22	1m 35.069s
23	Domenico Schiattarella	9	1m 35.500s
24	Pierluigi Martini	4	1m 35.628s
25	Roberto Moreno	22	1m 38.470s
26	Pedro Diniz	14	1m 38.715s

Saturday free practice
Sunny and warm

Pos.	Driver	Laps	Time
1	Damon Hill	22	1m 28.251s
2	David Coulthard	23	1m 28.339s
3	Mika Häkkinen	19	1m 28.913s
4	Jean Alesi	22	1m 29.080s
5	Michael Schumacher	14	1m 29.153s
6	Gerhard Berger	20	1m 29.497s
7	Rubens Barrichello	22	1m 29.598s
8	Eddie Irvine	22	1m 29.925s
9	Olivier Panis	23	1m 30.864s
10	Gianni Morbidelli	11	1m 31.476s
11	Johnny Herbert	13	1m 31.481s
12	Ukyo Katayama	23	1m 31.603s
13	Nigel Mansell	8	1m 31.716s
14	Aguri Suzuki	23	1m 31.910s
15	Heinz-Harald Frentzen	16	1m 32.107s
16	Jos Verstappen	20	1m 32.237s
17	Mika Salo	20	1m 32.435s
18	Luca Badoer	21	1m 33.532s
19	Domenico Schiattarella	11	1m 33.726s
20	Andrea Montermini	14	1m 33.766s
21	Karl Wendlinger	23	1m 34.155s
22	Roberto Moreno	22	1m 35.277s
23	Pierluigi Martini	7	1m 35.473s
24	Bertrand Gachot	7	1m 35.715s
25	Pedro Diniz	15	1m 37.133s
26	Taki Inoue	2	1m 58.327s

Friday qualifying
Bright, light cloud

Pos.	Driver	Laps	Time
1	**Michael Schumacher**	**10**	**1m 27.274s**
2	**Gerhard Berger**	**12**	**1m 27.282s**
3	**David Coulthard**	**11**	**1m 27.459s**
4	Damon Hill	12	1m 27.537s
5	**Jean Alesi**	**12**	**1m 27.813s**
6	**Mika Häkkinen**	**11**	**1m 28.343s**
7	**Eddie Irvine**	**8**	**1m 28.516s**
8	Johnny Herbert	12	1m 29.403s
9	**Nigel Mansell**	**11**	**1m 29.517s**
10	Rubens Barrichello	12	1m 29.580s
11	**Gianni Morbidelli**	**12**	**1m 29.582s**
12	Olivier Panis	11	1m 30.801s
13	Mika Salo	10	1m 31.221s
14	**Heinz-Harald Frentzen**	**12**	**1m 31.358s**
15	**Ukyo Katayama**	**11**	**1m 31.630s**
16	**Jos Verstappen**	**11**	**1m 32.156s**
17	Aguri Suzuki	11	1m 32.297s
18	**Pierluigi Martini**	**8**	**1m 32.445s**
19	Taki Inoue	12	1m 32.988s
20	**Luca Badoer**	**12**	**1m 33.071s**
21	**Karl Wendlinger**	**11**	**1m 33.494s**
22	**Bertrand Gachot**	**12**	**1m 33.892s**
23	**Domenico Schiattarella**	**9**	**1m 33.965s**
24	**Andrea Montermini**	**11**	**1m 35.169s**
25	Pedro Diniz	12	1m 36.686s
26	Roberto Moreno	5	1m 37.612s

Saturday qualifying
Sunny and warm

Pos.	Driver	Laps	Time
1	Michael Schumacher	8	1m 27.413s
2	**Damon Hill**	**12**	**1m 27.512s**
3	David Coulthard	10	1m 27.600s
4	Jean Alesi	11	1m 28.431s
5	**Johnny Herbert**	**10**	**1m 29.350s**
6	**Rubens Barrichello**	**11**	**1m 29.551s**
7	Nigel Mansell	10	1m 29.966s
8	**Olivier Panis**	**12**	**1m 30.760s**
9	**Mika Salo**	**12**	**1m 31.035s**
10	Gianni Morbidelli	5	1m 31.147s
11	Heinz-Harald Frentzen	12	1m 31.423s
12	Ukyo Katayama	12	1m 31.736s
13	**Aguri Suzuki**	**12**	**1m 31.913s**
14	Jos Verstappen	11	1m 32.425s
15	**Taki Inoue**	**12**	**1m 32.710s**
16	Luca Badoer	12	1m 33.430s
17	Karl Wendlinger	12	1m 33.554s
18	Pierluigi Martini	12	1m 33.832s
19	Domenico Schiattarella	11	1m 34.064s
20	Bertrand Gachot	7	1m 35.253s
21	Andrea Montermini	9	1m 35.282s
22	**Roberto Moreno**	**12**	**1m 36.065s**
23	**Pedro Diniz**	**12**	**1m 36.624s**
24	Gerhard Berger	8	1m 38.801s
25	Eddie Irvine	3	1m 41.247s
26	Mika Häkkinen	0	no time

Warm-up
Torrential rain

Pos.	Driver	Laps	Time
1	Jean Alesi	12	1m 59.555s
2	Gerhard Berger	7	2m 01.591s
3	Michael Schumacher	8	2m 02.359s
4	Nigel Mansell	11	2m 03.381s
5	Mika Häkkinen	11	2m 03.809s
6	Rubens Barrichello	9	2m 04.179s
7	Olivier Panis	11	2m 05.318s
8	David Coulthard	8	2m 05.530s
9	Gianni Morbidelli	10	2m 06.767s
10	Damon Hill	8	2m 07.644s
11	Mika Salo	6	2m 08.145s
12	Johnny Herbert	6	2m 08.252s
13	Jos Verstappen	6	2m 08.309s
14	Ukyo Katayama	8	2m 10.504s
15	Domenico Schiattarella	8	2m 11.692s
16	Luca Badoer	8	2m 12.485s
17	Pierluigi Martini	7	2m 12.892s
18	Heinz-Harald Frentzen	6	2m 14.416s
19	Karl Wendlinger	4	2m 19.873s
20	Roberto Moreno	8	2m 20.615s
21	Taki Inoue	7	2m 21.009s
22	Pedro Diniz	7	2m 24.904s
23	Bertrand Gachot	5	2m 27.122s
24	Aguri Suzuki	4	2m 35.135s
25	Eddie Irvine	2	5m 20.549s
26	Andrea Montermini	2	7m 48.835s

Fastest race laps
Track damp, drying out

Driver	Time	Lap
Gerhard Berger	1m 29.568s	57
Damon Hill	1m 29.710s	42
Jean Alesi	1m 30.008s	42
David Coulthard	1m 30.049s	59
Johnny Herbert	1m 30.055s	60
Eddie Irvine	1m 30.868s	53
Mika Häkkinen	1m 31.029s	54
Olivier Panis	1m 31.135s	44
Nigel Mansell	1m 31.251s	41
Heinz-Harald Frentzen	1m 31.754s	60
Aguri Suzuki	1m 32.280s	55
Pierluigi Martini	1m 32.280s	59
Gianni Morbidelli	1m 33.415s	54
Rubens Barrichello	1m 33.540s	30
Karl Wendlinger	1m 33.617s	43
Luca Badoer	1m 33.838s	49
Domenico Schiattarella	1m 35.534s	31
Bertrand Gachot	1m 36.136s	35
Ukyo Katayama	1m 37.243s	23
Roberto Moreno	1m 37.529s	52
Pedro Diniz	1m 37.872s	52
Mika Salo	1m 39.837s	17
Jos Verstappen	1m 44.585s	12
Michael Schumacher	1m 45.701s	8
Andrea Montermini	1m 47.102s	12
Taki Inoue	1m 59.717s	11

CHASSIS LOG BOOK

1	Schumacher	Benetton B195/4
2	Herbert	Benetton B195/5
	spare	Benetton B195/1
3	Katayama	Tyrrell 023/4
4	Salo	Tyrrell 023/2
	spare	Tyrrell 023/3
5	Hill	Williams FW17/4
6	Coulthard	Williams FW17/2
	spare	Williams FW17/3
7	Mansell	McLaren MP4/10B/1
8	Häkkinen	McLaren MP4/10/3
	spare	McLaren MP4/10/2
9	Morbidelli	Footwork FA16/2
10	Inoue	Footwork FA16/1
11	Schiattarella	Simtek S951/1
12	Verstappen	Simtek S951/2
14	Barrichello	Jordan 195/4
15	Irvine	Jordan 195/3
	spare	Jordan 195/1
16	Gachot	Pacific PR02/1
17	Montermini	Pacific PR02/2
21	Diniz	Forti FG01/1
22	Moreno	Forti FG01/2
23	Martini	Minardi M195/3
24	Badoer	Minardi M195/2
25	Suzuki	Ligier JS41/1
26	Panis	Ligier JS41/4
	spare	Ligier JS41/2
27	Alesi	Ferrari 412T2/157
28	Berger	Ferrari 412T2/159
	spare	Ferrari 412T2/156
29	Wendlinger	Sauber C14/2
30	Frentzen	Sauber C14/3
	spare	Sauber C14/1

POINTS TABLES

Drivers

1	Damon Hill	20
2	Michael Schumacher	14
3	Jean Alesi	14
4 =	David Coulthard	9
4 =	Gerhard Berger	9
6	Mika Häkkinen	5
7 =	Johnny Herbert	3
7 =	Heinz-Harald Frentzen	3
9	Mark Blundell	1

Constructors

1 =	Williams	23
1 =	Ferrari	23
3	Benetton	7
4	McLaren	6
5	Sauber	3

WORLD CHAMPIONSHIP • ROUND 4

SPANISH GRAND PRIX

SCHUMACHER
HERBERT
BERGER
HILL
IRVINE
PANIS

SPANISH GRAND PRIX

Michael Schumacher *(left)* scored an imperious victory after radical overnight changes to the set-up of his Benetton-Renault had transformed its handling in time for final qualifying.

Far left: A bitterly frustrated Damon Hill makes his way back to the Williams pit garage after losing second place – and his lead in the World Championship – due to a last-lap hydraulic failure.

Johnny Herbert *(below left)* profited from Damon's misfortune to complete a Benetton 1-2, a timely boost for the former Lotus driver, who had hitherto seemed somewhat isolated within the team.

Diary

Bernie Ecclestone is jointly ranked at 196 in a Sunday Times *supplement on the 500 richest people in Britain.*

Scott Brayton qualifies on pole position for Indy 500 at 231 mph in Menard team's Lola-Buick, while Mercedes-powered Penskes of Al Unser Jr and Emerson Fittipaldi fail to make the race.

Cosworth chief engine designer Geoff Goddard to leave the famous Northampton company and join TWR.

Financially strapped Simtek F1 team denies rumours of possible merger with Dave Richards's Prodrive operation.

In Friday qualifying, Michael Schumacher's Benetton hadn't looked any great shakes. Jean Alesi and Gerhard Berger set the pace for Ferrari in the first qualifying session for the Spanish GP and it seemed quite possible that we would witness an all-Maranello front row for the first time since Hockenheim, 1994.

You might have been forgiven for thinking that Schumacher was on the run. Perhaps he was still below par following his high-speed accident at Imola. Then again, perhaps not. In Saturday qualifying, Michael and Benetton turned the tables and set the agenda. Pole by 0.6s and then a copybook run to victory in Sunday's race, a success which catapulted him back into the drivers' championship points lead.

Right enough, Williams had a catastrophic race day, but the fact remains that Schumacher was on top of the job. The opposition would slink away home on Sunday night with the overwhelming feeling that F1's balance of power had shifted. Decisively, if not for good.

Yet, from the moment Ferrari's scarlet 412T2s accelerated out onto the Circuit de Catalunya, it seemed as though Maranello might be poised to sustain the momentum of its recent F1 revival with Jean Alesi and Gerhard Berger out-running their key rivals to set fastest times in Friday's first qualifying session. Admittedly, theirs was a slender advantage, for David Coulthard, despite still suffering from a bout of secondary tonsillitis, made a stern bid for provisional pole position in his Williams-Renault, the young Scot failing in his quest by 0.4s on the first anniversary of his F1 debut.

Furthermore, Berger was quick to counsel caution. 'I must admit that I'm a bit surprised at this result,' said the Austrian candidly. 'I still feel that, especially in race trim, we are not yet at the level of our strongest opponents. But we are closing on them, step by step.'

At the end of the day, however, although Ferrari to some extent benefited from the minor problems experienced by their fellow front-runners, it was the way in which the prospect of the Prancing Horse winning its first constructors' championship since 1983 seemed to be steadily evolving from fanciful dream to distinct possibility which really held people's attention.

Alesi and Berger, of course, were aiming even higher. Both had set their sights on becoming Ferrari's first World Champion driver since Jody Scheckter in 1979. By the same token, Schumacher, Hill and Coulthard would not have it so.

For the moment, however, these were dreams for the future. The immediate challenge of the Circuit de Catalunya seemed set to be pretty stimulating for the latest breed of 3-litre F1 machinery. The Nissan chicane on the return leg of the track had now been bypassed by a new section of straight, which made the approach to the Caixa left-hander significantly more challenging – as well as providing another overtaking opportunity.

'It is a good circuit,' said championship points leader Damon Hill, 'an excellent example of how to incorporate quick corners on a modern track. There are a couple of opportunities to get a tow and overtake, and it doesn't seem to suffer too badly from varying grip levels when you get off the racing line.'

That said, Damon finished the day struggling with his Williams FW17 in fifth place, a fraction behind Michael Schumacher's similarly powered Benetton B195.

'I can't find a balance,' he complained. 'All my laps were very messy – locked wheels, oversteer and so on. We've got the car wrong somewhere, so I will just have to work on the set-up. We are nowhere near where we should be.'

Short-term setbacks notwithstanding, Hill remained confident that fundamentally he still retained the upper hand over Schumacher – for the moment, at least. The fine-handling Williams FW17 had proved versatile and consistently competitive on every circuit so far this season and nobody was betting against Hill as a potential winner come Sunday. Not yet.

'We [Williams] have a perceptible but fine advantage and we're going to capitalise on that now,' said Damon. 'It is less painful than it will be at the end of the year as the championship will close up by then.' When he voiced those words on Friday, he could hardly have imagined just how dramatically the picture would change over the following two days.

Despite a lurid spin just ahead of Alesi's Ferrari, Johnny Herbert felt he was making worthwhile progress with his Benetton, ending up seventh ahead of Eddie Irvine's Jordan-Peugeot.

Further back, Nigel Mansell found himself battling a McLaren-Mercedes handling imbalance sufficiently precarious to pitch him into a wild spin early in first qualifying. Of the British contingent, only Martin Brundle, making his 1995 F1 debut alongside Olivier Panis in the Ligier-Mugen Honda squad, was slower at the end of the first day.

'It went from sheer oversteer to sheer understeer,' explained Nigel. 'I have to go and have a long think about this. I have no doubt in my mind that this is a fundamental car problem. Having said that, I have no doubt that McLaren will get it right – it's just a question of how much time and how many races go by before they do.' The reality, in fact, was somewhat worse: Mansell could already see that the MP4/10B, enlarged cockpit or not, was not going to be capable of challenging for the lead. He was already losing interest and Ron Dennis was having to work overtime behind the scenes in order to sustain Nigel's flagging motivation.

Mansell finished first qualifying a disappointed 12th, six places and 1.8s away from his team-mate Mika Häkkinen, whose handling problems, while broadly similar, seemed less pronounced than those experienced by the English veteran.

Damon's optimism returned on Saturday morning when he set fastest time, 0.2s ahead of Coulthard. But he knew only too well that the FW17 was operating within a worryingly tight performance envelope. 'It's an elusive kind of feeling,' he confessed. 'We're struggling to get a balance and it only came right over the last few laps when we used new tyres. We're just chipping away at it.'

His remarks seemed to be concealing a deeper-rooted concern as to what might happen in second qualifying. Sure enough, his worst fears were soon to be confirmed. Schumacher, his Benetton's chassis set-up having again been changed dramatically overnight, stormed round in 1m 21.452s to throw pole position beyond anybody else's realistic reach. The B195 looked simply transformed, its razor-sharp handling contrasting vividly with the precarious balance displayed at Interlagos, Buenos Aires and Imola.

'I have to say "well done" to the team,' admitted Schumacher with a gleeful grin. 'I think I must have caused them a few more grey hairs overnight, but it has been worthwhile and I am surprised that there is such a big gap between myself and the opposition. I went out again at the end of the session because we had made a change to the car, and I thought that I could improve by maybe a tenth or two. We also had a chance to try the car in race trim this morning and I was quite happy with it.'

Ferrari responded robustly, with Alesi clipping his best down to 1m 22.052s, a scant 0.019s ahead of third-placed Berger, who reported being balked briefly by Schiattarella's Simtek. Maranello was strong, admittedly, but not quite strong enough. The 412T2s were benefiting from enhanced front-end grip by using 11.5 in. front rims for this race for added tyre sidewall stiffness.

Hill then duly made his bid, reporting that he felt quite satisfied with the FW17's handling on his first run, although he confessed to pushing too hard too soon and went wide at one corner, getting dirt on his tyres. He eased back to clean up his rubber, then put the hammer down again. That earned him a morale-boosting 1m 22.378s on his first run – good enough for second place – but then the two Ferraris went ahead and Coulthard vaulted past to clinch his place on the outside of the second row. So Damon wound up fifth. It was less, by far, than he had been hoping for.

'Well, it looks like the party is over for the moment,' he shrugged. 'We've been relegated to the bottom of the First Division, at least as far as qualifying is concerned. Yes, I am worried about the race – we will try to pull something out of the hat, but we need better performance in all areas.

'You just can't afford to concede any advantage to these guys. In the first few races we managed to get away with it, but I must admit that I'm a bit surprised at the speed at which Benetton and Ferrari came back at us.'

Coulthard also ended the day in a rather disappointed mood. 'This morning, I thought we had some front row potential,' he reflected, 'but we've got quite a problem working out a good balance between the fast and medium-speed corners. What worries me is that if Michael gets off the line first, he will get away while we are working to get ahead of the Ferraris.'

Eddie Irvine was fortunate to extricate his Jordan from a gravel trap on Friday afternoon, improving his 195's set-up sufficiently to qualify a solid sixth on Saturday, separated from team-mate Rubens Barrichello by Herbert's seventh-placed Benetton. Irvine didn't use new tyres in

113

SPANISH GRAND PRIX

Eye contact. Damon Hill looks up into the face of one of the Williams team's engineers as they discuss the handling of his car over the intercom before he returns to the track. Meanwhile, the sceptical gaze of Frank Williams is everywhere as he monitors the running of his team from his position at the back of the pit garage.

the second qualifying session and admitted that new 'barge boards' behind the front wheels – extending forward to shield the lower front suspension wishbone – definitely enhanced the car's performance. Barrichello lost time with an oil leak in second qualifying, but generally felt more confident.

That was more than Herbert could admit to, however. 'I am disappointed overall, obviously, but on both sets of tyres I was balked very badly at the first corner,' he explained. 'The first time it was Alesi and then it was a Sauber which had just finished [its run] and a Ligier coming out of the pits. They went through the corner together and that messed up my lap. The car seems a bit more driveable, but there is still work to do.'

Behind Barrichello, Mika Häkkinen and Nigel Mansell qualified a solid ninth and tenth. Nigel felt this emphasised that he was as quick as Häkkinen, but the truth was that Mika had messed up his best lap – yet was still faster than the English veteran. Either way, for the McLaren-Mercedes to end up almost 2.5s slower than Schumacher's pace-setting Benetton gave an indication of how far the new partnership needed to progress before it could have a hope of winning races.

The Ilmor-made Mercedes V10s at least continued their habit of trouble-free running, but neither driver was happy with the chassis balance. The McLaren behaved unpredictably, yawing from oversteer to understeer. The team could go some way towards minimising the problem – and Mansell admitted the car was 'more controllable' on Saturday morning – but the second qualifying session ended with Nigel talking in terms of revised suspension components. 'All of which take time to manufacture and test,' he said reflectively. 'So I would have to say that, realistically, Damon still remains favourite for the championship, followed by Schumacher and the Ferraris.'

Martin Brundle at last made his debut for the Ligier-Mugen squad, the Englishman finding that the JS41 Benetton-lookalike was a far more difficult-to-handle prospect over the bumps and ripples at Barcelona than it had originally seemed during preliminary testing on the smooth track surface at Magny-Cours.

He looked slow, almost out of his depth, on Friday, but asserted his F1 credentials with a strong run to 11th place on Saturday. Team-mate Olivier Panis, who had originally set the Ligier pace, was disappointed to wind up 15th, feeling that insufficient progress had been made on his chassis set-up between the first and second days.

Heinz-Harald Frentzen claimed 12th place in the revised, high-nose Sauber C14, the team having made some really worthwhile progress trying a new undertray at the Imola test immediately after the San Marino GP. It was therefore disappointing that Karl Wendlinger still found himself grappling with understeer right through to the closing moments of second qualifying. By the time he was comfortable with his set-up, the session was almost at an end and he was left trailing in 20th place.

Mika Salo spent much of Friday battling handling problems with his Tyrrell-Yamaha, but then had to relinquish his 023 to team-mate Ukyo Katayama during second qualifying after the Japanese driver's engine – freshly installed after a previous breakage in the morning session – blew up as he braked for the first corner. This was frustrating for both men. It meant that Salo was unable to run in the closing stages of the session when the track was at its fastest, while Katayama was left driving a car whose cockpit wasn't properly tailored for him. Yet despite finding the controls all rather far away, he managed to improve to 17th, only four places behind the young Finn.

Gianni Morbidelli was an excellent 14th after curing a vibration and understeer problem which had slowed him on Friday, while Taki Inoue, trying an F1 car on a track where he had previous racing experience for the first time, looked quite respectable on his way to 18th place.

Jos Verstappen did a fine job to line up 16th for Simtek, despite problems on both days synchronising the clutch and throttle 'blipper' operation, which resulted in damaged dog rings, with Pierluigi Martini taking 19th, separated from team-mate Luca Badoer by Wendlinger's Sauber. The two Minardis had a close call during second qualifying after Martini, who'd taken off some downforce in an effort to pick up straightline speed, spun on the double right-hander before the pits and was almost collected by Badoer.

Schiattarella wound up 22nd ahead of the two Pacifics and the tail-end Forti-Fords. The FG01s sported a revised, lower engine cover and a more steeply raked diffuser for this event.

The race morning warm-up saw Schumacher again fastest from a confident Alesi, followed by Berger, who suffered a problem with the gearchange electronics, Häkkinen, Hill and Coulthard. Damon reported that the car didn't feel too bad, but Coulthard was still a little under the weather. Neither man needed reminding that nothing other than a Williams-Renault had won the Spanish Grand Prix since the race first came to the Circuit de Catalunya in 1991. They were keeping their fingers crossed.

You had to hand it to Alesi; he tried. The start was chaotic, for although the red lights went off, no green lights ever came on, so the pack got away in rather ragged formation. Jean tried everything he knew on the sprint to the first corner, but Schumacher was clearly ahead. Moreover, Berger suspected his team-mate was already mechanically doomed. He'd noticed a trail of coolant from the rear of Alesi's car from the time they set out on the formation lap, which had seen the demise of Montermini, who scuttled into the pits with hydraulic pressure problems and failed to start.

At the end of the opening lap Schumacher led by a whopping 1.05s from Alesi with Hill up to third after a magnificent getaway. Next up was Berger from Irvine, Häkkinen, Coulthard, Herbert, Barrichello, Frentzen and Brundle. Nigel Mansell was down in 14th place behind the two Tyrrell-Yamahas and with Olivier Panis snapping at his heels, the Frenchman moving past the McLaren high roller second time round.

Schumacher was making it an absolute cakewalk. By lap three, the World Champion had 2.8s to spare over Alesi, although Hill and Berger were now tight on the Frenchman's tail. Irvine was a solid fifth, but Coulthard was now ahead of Häkkinen and closing in on the Jordan-Peugeot. Mansell retook Panis on the sixth lap and slipped ahead of Katayama's Tyrrell on lap eight to reach 13th – although only after Ukyo slid wide over the kerb exiting the right-hander before the pits.

Hill was really pressuring Alesi in the opening stages, but rather than stay boxed in behind the Ferrari, he elected to come in for a first (10.3s) refuelling stop at the end of lap 13, by which time Schumacher was 8.1s ahead and going away all the time.

That left Alesi and Berger briefly running 2-3, while Coulthard stopped at the end of lap 14, dropping from fourth to ninth, and Irvine dropped from sixth to 11th next time round.

Lap 15 also saw Mansell trail into the pits for a 7.4s refuelling stop. He resumed on fresh tyres and then ran wide over a gravel trap just as Schumacher came up to lap him. At the end of lap 18, Nigel came in for good, swinging the McLaren straight into its garage and walking away without even bothering to debrief with his engineer Steve Hallam. As Jordan's Gary Anderson, watching from the adjacent pit, observed: 'He had the body language of a man who was walking away from F1 for good.' This proved to be a perspicacious remark, by any standards.

'I had a problem with the car's balance from the start,' said Mansell. 'It was oversteering a lot initially, then it went into understeer after a few laps. But at least it was driveable. After I stopped for tyres, the car was all right and then it went into understeer. In the fast and medium-speed corners, the car was virtually impossible to drive.' But, as Ron Dennis would later observe, 'Nigel chose not to continue.' To all intents and purposes, the Mansell/McLaren alliance had run out of road for good.

At the end of lap 16, Berger made his first refuelling stop, briefly promoting Häkkinen to third place, and then Alesi stopped at the end of lap 19, resuming just ahead of Hill. But the second-place Ferrari lasted only until the end of lap 25, when its V12 blew up spectacularly crossing the start/finish line. Jean pulled over to the right as Damon surged through into second place. He walked away from the car almost in tears of frustration.

Further back, there would be more drama as Gachot's Pacific caught fire as fuel leaked from a sticking valve on the PR02 as he accelerated back into the race after his second stop. He pulled off for good at the end of the pit lane. Taki Inoue also stopped with an engine bay fire soon after developing a gearbox downchange problem; the fuel and hydraulic lines were burnt, together with the wiring loom, but the conflagration was quickly doused by the Arrows mechanics.

Schumacher waited until all his key rivals had refuelled, staying out until lap 21 before making an 8.1s stop, resuming clearly in the lead. By the time Alesi's departure gave

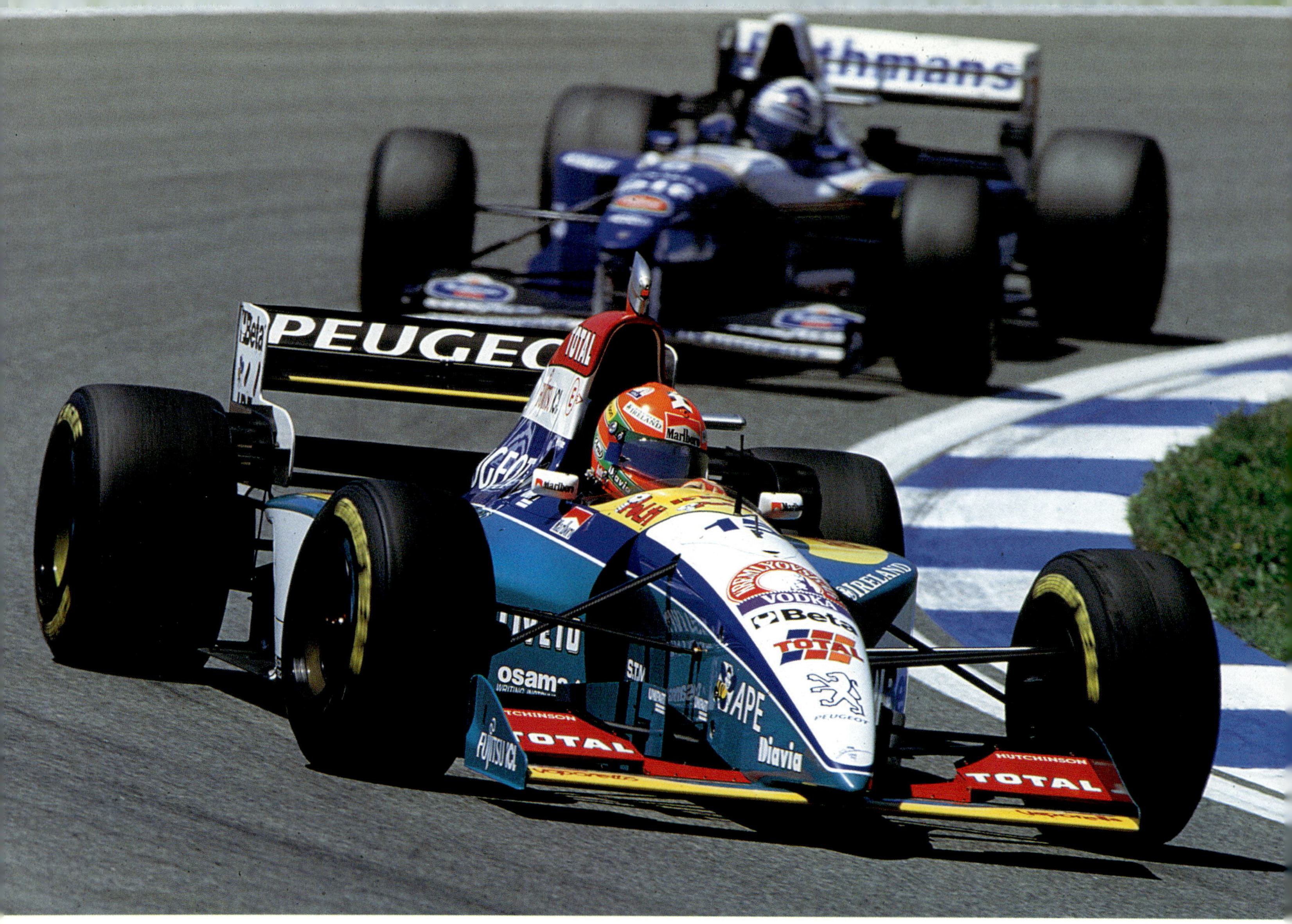
PEUGEO
TOTAL
osama
TOTAL
Diavia
HUTCHINSON
TOTAL

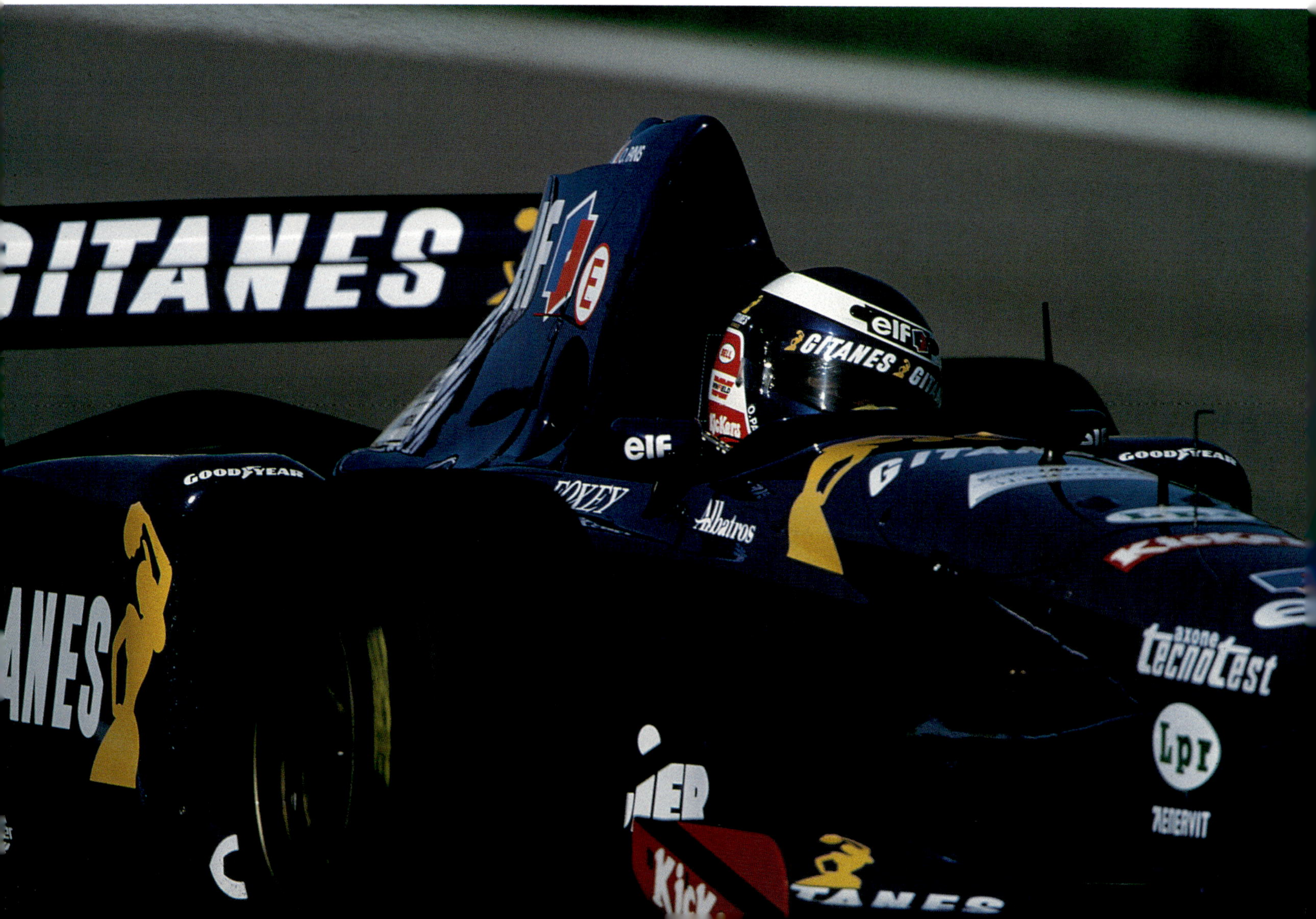
GITANES
GOODYEAR
elf
Albatros
GOODYEAR
tecnotest
Lpr

Eddie Irvine *(left)* picked up fifth place for Jordan, the first top-six finish of the season for the Silverstone-based team. David Coulthard follows.

The second Jordan-Peugeot of Rubens Barrichello was set to follow the Ulsterman home until a throttle problem allowed Ligier's Olivier Panis *(below left)* to nip past on the last lap and score *his* team's first point of the year.

Right: A pensive Nigel Mansell ponders his future at McLaren. The prospect evidently didn't appeal.

Mansell bows out on a low note

The realisation that Nigel Mansell and McLaren were reaching the end of their partnership began to dawn when the 1992 World Champion attended a media conference after qualifying at Barcelona. Mansell's body language was that of a man who was distracted, whose impatience with the McLaren MP4/10B was obviously wearing thin. Everybody involved in the partnership seemed to be desperately looking for the odd grain of comfort with which to console themselves.

Mansell's subsequent performance in the race, where he gave up after running well down the field, was hardly calculated to impress the senior Mercedes executives attending the event during their visit to Spain for the Barcelona Motor Show. Mercedes chief executive Helmut Werner and Daimler Benz AG chief executive-designate Jurgen Schrempp must have been deeply concerned over what they saw.

'It is quite clear that our performance here is inadequate for our own objectives,' said Ron Dennis with masterful understatement. 'Whatever the capabilities of our car, we haven't exploited it yet. In final qualifying we clearly went in the wrong direction.

'This track highlights our car's deficiency in long, sweeping curves. The problem is also exaggerated by characteristics of the engine in a certain rev range, but it is mainly the car. We should be sixth and seventh on the grid, but at the moment we don't have a car capable of taking on the lead Benetton, the two Williams and the Ferraris.

'There is only one way to remove these problems and that is hard work, nothing else. There is no magic in motor racing – it's all numbers and understanding what the car and drivers require. And getting on with it.'

During the week immediately following the Spanish Grand Prix, McLaren stayed on at the Circuit de Catalunya for an intensive programme of testing. Mansell was not present, his absence explained by the fact that risking another special 'wide' MP4/10B monocoque in the run-up to Monaco 'would have been derogatory [sic] to the racing programme.' As things turned out, Mansell would not be racing at Monaco. Or anywhere else.

The following weekend, Dennis journeyed to Mansell's home in the West Country, close to the Woodbury Golf and Country Club which had increasingly become the focal point of his driver's business life over the preceding 12 months. 'Extensive and open discussions' followed and it was decided to end their current F1 agreement.

'The performance of the 1995 F1 car has not met the expectations of both parties so far this year,' said Dennis in an official McLaren communiqué issued on the Wednesday prior to the Monaco race.

'Nigel has not felt confident within the car and this has affected his ability to commit fully to the programme. In these circumstances I believe that we have determined the most appropriate course of action. The relationship has been short and has obviously not achieved the results anticipated by either party.

'However, I have found Nigel to be entirely straightforward and totally professional in his business conduct. Whilst this decision brings to an end our current relationship, I would certainly not preclude us working together in the future.'

Mansell's official response was similarly cordial. 'I am obviously disappointed that the relationship with McLaren and Mercedes, which could have achieved so much, has been concluded early,' he noted. 'At this stage of my career, I had expected, on joining McLaren, that the total package would have given me the possibility to be competitive with the other top teams.

'I have certainly enjoyed many aspects of the relationship with the team and working with them has been a unique experience. They are undoubtedly building a future which will, I am sure, be successful in the long-term. I have no immediate plans in Formula 1, but have welcomed the opportunity to keep in touch with the team, with whom I have parted on the best possible terms.'

Speculation suggested that Mansell walked away from the deal with around $1.2 million, his fees for the first four races of the season – including the two from which he was excluded from participation through no fault of his own.

The story of Mansell and McLaren had been a total fiasco from which neither party emerged with much credibility – and Philip Morris must have been hanging its corporate head in despair at having insisted on bringing the two together in the first place.

SPANISH GRAND PRIX

Hill a clear track to the leading Benetton, Michael was a comfortable 12.3s to the good. It was a lost cause for Williams. Damon stopped for the second time on lap 30, allowing Coulthard into second place for a lap before the Scot also came in. Berger was now second for a lap, then made his second stop on lap 33. By the time Hill took up station again in second place, Schumacher was 37 seconds away down the road.

Now Herbert was up into third place, but the second Benetton was on schedule to make its second refuelling stop at the end of lap 40. By this stage, Johnny's sense of excitement and anticipation was running at such fever pitch that he accelerated back into the fray towing his rear trolley jack the length of the pit lane – fortunately it flew off, to be retrieved by the marshals, before he regained the circuit.

'I heard them telling me "stop, stop, stop" on the radio,' he explained, 'and I just had time to say "what?" when suddenly I heard "go, go, go" – it was all a bit confusing!'

On lap 43, Schumacher came in for a second refuelling stop, resuming a handy 7.7s ahead of Hill. It was now all over bar the shouting, for Williams had opted for a three-stop strategy and Damon duly came in at the end of lap 47, followed by Coulthard next time round. Hill resumed in second place, with Coulthard trailing Berger until Gerhard made his third stop at the end of lap 50. With ten laps to run, Schumacher was 23.4s ahead.

Still, it looked promising for Williams as far as constructors' championship points were concerned, their cars running strongly in second and third places. But suddenly Herbert received an unexpected bonus, being elevated to third place on lap 55 as Coulthard ground to a smoking halt with hydraulic failure out on the circuit.

'I had a small fire,' said David, 'obviously caused by oil leaking onto the exhaust, and it took away third place. Before that, I had been running fairly comfortably, even though I didn't feel great, and there would have been no problem getting to the finish.'

Then came the most bitter blow of all. As Damon went past into his final lap, confident that six points would allow him to retain a slender lead in the drivers' championship, the hydraulics went wrong on his Williams too.

'I went to pull for sixth gear, it didn't happen and something went wrong in the hydraulic system which runs the gearbox,' he explained in tones of disbelief. 'At first, it was OK, as it was stuck in fifth and you can do a lap round here in fifth [as Schumacher proved in 1994!] and I still had the throttle. But unfortunately the throttle system works off the hydraulic pump . . .'

Two corners from home, the FW17's engine cut and Hill was jumped by Herbert and Berger as he coasted round to take the chequered flag in an eventual fourth place. 'It was a tough race, but I would have taken second place, kept the lead in the championship and that would have been good enough for me, because we didn't have a good weekend,' he reflected. 'Our strategy was OK, but we just couldn't live with Michael's speed.'

Herbert was absolutely exhilarated to have rounded off a Benetton 1-2, at a stroke taking his first podium finish and his best-ever F1 result. Third place, under the circumstances, was poor consolation for Ferrari on a weekend which had originally seemed to hold out so much promise. And Gerhard was only moderately satisfied.

'To be honest, I wasn't very happy how I drove in the race,' he admitted. 'I had a bad start and couldn't get things quite right. I didn't really know whether two stops or three was the right strategy and I seemed to be on the radio to the pit all the time. As it was, we did three stops, but I think we should have only made two.'

Behind Hill, Eddie Irvine scored the first points of the season for the Jordan-Peugeot squad after Häkkinen's McLaren rolled to a halt with a loss of fuel pressure with 12 laps left to run. 'I made a good start, despite the fact that the green light didn't come on,' said Irvine. 'Then I got held up lapping one of the Fortis and was forced to go on the dirt to get past.

'That was just before the first pit stop, but I made the position back again on the third stop. The result wasn't brilliant, though it is good to get some points. What is really positive, though, is I think we've finally cured the problem of rear-end grip. The car understeered a lot in the high-speed corners, but at low speed it was really great.'

Team-mate Rubens Barrichello was on course for sixth until his throttle mechanism went haywire and he dropped behind Panis's Ligier on the very last lap. 'I don't know why, but all the problems seem to be happening to me at the moment,' he mused.

Heinz-Harald Frentzen dropped behind Panis at his first stop to finish eighth for Sauber, while Martin Brundle had been ahead of them both only to lose a huge chunk of time at his first stop due to a problem with the refuelling rig. 'From the corner of my eye, I could see that the guys were having difficulty getting the fuel to flow,' he said. 'It is extremely frustrating that all the weekend's hard work should be wasted by such a small detail outside our control. I am certain I was on target for at least a point.'

Mika Salo had a lonely race to tenth place, the sole Tyrrell finisher after Katayama had succumbed to a loss of air pressure to his Yamaha V10's pneumatic valvegear, while Gianni Morbidelli was 11th for Footwork ahead of Verstappen, Wendlinger, Martini and Schiattarella.

Hill's last-lap misfortune had lost Williams the lead of the constructors' championship to Ferrari while Benetton's 1-2 result meant that they were now only four points behind the Italian team in this particular contest. Schumacher led the drivers' title chase by a single point.

More worryingly, on the strength of his performance at Barcelona, he had appeared totally inviolate. What could Damon and Williams do now?

117

FIA FORMULA ONE WORLD CHAMPIONSHIP ROUND 4

GRAN PREMIO MARLBORO DE ESPAÑA
CATALUNYA 12-14 MAY 1995

CATALUNYA CIRCUIT – BARCELONA

CIRCUIT LENGTH: 2.937 MILES/4.727 KM

Race distance: 65 laps, 190.919 miles/307.255 km
Race weather: Dry, warm and sunny

Place	Driver	Nat.	No.	Entrant	Car/Engine	Laps	Time/Retirement	Speed (mph/km/h)
1	**Michael Schumacher**	D	1	Mild Seven Benetton Renault	Benetton B195-Renault RS7 V10	65	1h 34m 20.507s	121.365/195.320
2	**Johnny Herbert**	GB	2	Mild Seven Benetton Renault	Benetton B195-Renault RS7 V10	65	1h 35m 12.495s	120.261/193.542
3	**Gerhard Berger**	A	28	Scuderia Ferrari	Ferrari 412T2 044 V12	65	1h 35m 25.744s	119.982/193.094
4	**Damon Hill**	GB	5	Rothmans Williams Renault	Williams FW17-Renault RS7 V10	65	1h 36m 22.256s	118.810/191.207
5	**Eddie Irvine**	GB	15	Total Jordan Peugeot	Jordan 195-Peugeot A10 V10	64		
6	**Olivier Panis**	F	26	Ligier Gitanes Blondes	Ligier JS41-Mugen Honda MF301 V10	64		
7	Rubens Barrichello	BR	14	Total Jordan Peugeot	Jordan 195-Peugeot A10 V10	64		
8	Heinz-Harald Frentzen	D	30	Red Bull Sauber Ford	Sauber C14-Ford Zetec-R V8	64		
9	Martin Brundle	GB	25	Ligier Gitanes Blondes	Ligier JS41-Mugen Honda MF301 V10	64		
10	Mika Salo	SF	4	Nokia Tyrrell Yamaha	Tyrrell 023-Yamaha OX10C V10	64		
11	Gianni Morbidelli	I	9	Footwork Hart	Footwork FA16-Hart 830 V8	63		
12	Jos Verstappen	NL	12	MTV Simtek Ford	Simtek S951-Ford ED V8	63		
13	Karl Wendlinger	A	29	Red Bull Sauber Ford	Sauber C14-Ford Zetec-R V8	63		
14	Pierluigi Martini	I	23	Minardi Scuderia Italia	Minardi M195-Ford EDM V8	62		
15	Domenico Schiattarella	I	11	MTV Simtek Ford	Simtek S951-Ford ED V8	61		
	Ukyo Katayama	J	3	Nokia Tyrrell Yamaha	Tyrrell 023-Yamaha OX10C V10	56	Engine	
	David Coulthard	GB	6	Rothmans Williams Renault	Williams FW17-Renault RS7 V10	54	Gearbox	
	Mika Häkkinen	SF	8	Marlboro McLaren Mercedes	McLaren MP4/10-Mercedes FO110 V10	53	Fuel pressure	
	Taki Inoue	J	10	Footwork Hart	Footwork FA16-Hart 830 V8	43	Engine fire	
	Bertrand Gachot	F	16	Pacific Grand Prix Ltd	Pacific PR02-Ford ED V8	43	Fire	
	Roberto Moreno	BR	22	Parmalat Forti Ford	Forti FG01-Ford ED V8	39	Water pump	
	Jean Alesi	F	27	Scuderia Ferrari	Ferrari 412T2 044 V12	25	Engine	
	Luca Badoer	I	24	Minardi Scuderia Italia	Minardi M195-Ford ED V8	21	Gearbox	
	Nigel Mansell	GB	7	Marlboro McLaren Mercedes	McLaren MP4/10B-Mercedes FO110 V10	18	Gave up	
	Pedro Diniz	BR	21	Parmalat Forti Ford	Forti FG01-Ford ED V8	17	Gearbox	
DNS	Andrea Montermini	I	17	Pacific Grand Prix Ltd	Pacific PR02-Ford ED V8	0	Gearbox	

Fastest lap: Hill, on lap 46, 1m 24.531s, 125.089 mph/201.313 km/h.
Lap record: Michael Schumacher (F1 Benetton B193B-Ford V8), 1m 20.989s, 131.113 mph/211.006 km/h (1993 on old circuit).

All cars used Goodyear tyres

All results and data © FIA 1995

STARTING GRID

1 SCHUMACHER (1m 21.452s) Benetton	**27 ALESI** (1m 22.052s) Ferrari
28 BERGER (1m 22.071s) Ferrari	**6 COULTHARD** (1m 22.332s) Williams
5 HILL (1m 22.349s) Williams	**15 IRVINE** (1m 23.352s) Jordan
2 HERBERT (1m 23.536s) Benetton	**14 BARRICHELLO** (1m 23.705s) Jordan
8 HÄKKINEN (1m 23.833s) McLaren	**7 MANSELL** (1m 23.927s) McLaren
25 BRUNDLE (1m 24.727s) Ligier	**30 FRENTZEN** (1m 24.802s) Sauber
4 SALO (1m 24.971s) Tyrrell	**9 MORBIDELLI** (1m 25.053s) Footwork
26 PANIS (1m 25.204s) Ligier	**12 VERSTAPPEN** (1m 25.827s) Simtek
3 KATAYAMA (1m 25.946s) Tyrrell	**10 INOUE** (1m 26.059s) Footwork
23 MARTINI (1m 26.619s) Minardi	**29 WENDLINGER** (1m 27.007s) Sauber
24 BADOER (1m 27.345s) Minardi	**11 SCHIATTARELLA** (1m 27.575s) Simtek
17 MONTERMINI* (1m 28.094s) Pacific	**16 GACHOT** (1m 28.598s) Pacific
22 MORENO (1m 28.963s) Forti	**21 DINIZ** (1m 29.540s) Forti

* did not start

FOR THE RECORD

50th Grand Prix start
Ukyo Katayama

TIME SHEETS

Friday free practice
Wet initially, steadily drying

Pos.	Driver	Laps	Time
1	Michael Schumacher	19	1m 24.083s
2	Gerhard Berger	21	1m 25.216s
3	Jean Alesi	21	1m 25.377s
4	Mika Häkkinen	20	1m 26.173s
5	Damon Hill	22	1m 26.362s
6	Eddie Irvine	21	1m 26.411s
7	Heinz-Harald Frentzen	18	1m 27.094s
8	Olivier Panis	22	1m 27.343s
9	David Coulthard	15	1m 27.388s
10	Ukyo Katayama	21	1m 27.736s
11	Rubens Barrichello	23	1m 27.859s
12	Jos Verstappen	19	1m 28.907s
13	Taki Inoue	20	1m 28.984s
14	Nigel Mansell	19	1m 29.162s
15	Mika Salo	23	1m 29.311s
16	Domenico Schiattarella	17	1m 29.534s
17	Pierluigi Martini	23	1m 29.646s
18	Gianni Morbidelli	19	1m 29.921s
19	Karl Wendlinger	11	1m 30.403s
20	Martin Brundle	23	1m 30.552s
21	Bertrand Gachot	16	1m 31.216s
22	Luca Badoer	22	1m 31.897s
23	Pedro Diniz	19	1m 33.299s
24	Roberto Moreno	23	1m 34.324s
25	Johnny Herbert	13	1m 37.809s
26	Andrea Montermini	3	4m 02.032s

Friday qualifying
Dry and bright

Pos.	Driver	Laps	Time
1	Jean Alesi	9	1m 23.104s
2	Gerhard Berger	11	1m 23.458s
3	David Coulthard	10	1m 23.496s
4	Michael Schumacher	8	1m 23.535s
5	Damon Hill	9	1m 24.356s
6	Mika Häkkinen	12	1m 24.427s
7	Johnny Herbert	10	1m 24.461s
8	Eddie Irvine	12	1m 24.891s
9	Heinz-Harald Frentzen	12	1m 25.655s
10	Olivier Panis	12	1m 25.902s
11	Ukyo Katayama	12	1m 26.033s
12	Nigel Mansell	11	1m 26.246s
13	Rubens Barrichello	3	1m 26.413s
14	Mika Salo	10	1m 26.462s
15	Martin Brundle	12	1m 26.747s
16	Taki Inoue	12	1m 26.846s
17	Gianni Morbidelli	11	1m 27.280s
18	Jos Verstappen	6	1m 27.666s
19	Pierluigi Martini	12	1m 28.008s
20	Karl Wendlinger	12	1m 28.305s
21	Domenico Schiattarella	11	1m 28.312s
22	Luca Badoer	12	1m 28.563s
23	Andrea Montermini	10	1m 29.942s
24	Bertrand Gachot	10	1m 30.429s
25	Pedro Diniz	12	1m 30.578s
26	Roberto Moreno	11	1m 31.063s

Saturday free practice
Dry and bright

Pos.	Driver	Laps	Time
1	Damon Hill	23	1m 22.465s
2	David Coulthard	21	1m 22.666s
3	Michael Schumacher	21	1m 22.938s
4	Gerhard Berger	16	1m 23.413s
5	Jean Alesi	11	1m 23.821s
6	Johnny Herbert	23	1m 24.115s
7	Nigel Mansell	23	1m 24.209s
8	Mika Häkkinen	21	1m 24.482s
9	Rubens Barrichello	21	1m 24.546s
10	Gianni Morbidelli	22	1m 24.551s
11	Martin Brundle	23	1m 25.277s
12	Eddie Irvine	22	1m 25.476s
13	Mika Salo	23	1m 25.709s
14	Olivier Panis	23	1m 25.755s
15	Heinz-Harald Frentzen	23	1m 26.056s
16	Ukyo Katayama	14	1m 26.146s
17	Jos Verstappen	17	1m 26.851s
18	Pierluigi Martini	23	1m 27.291s
19	Taki Inoue	10	1m 27.420s
20	Domenico Schiattarella	23	1m 27.514s
21	Luca Badoer	22	1m 27.591s
22	Karl Wendlinger	22	1m 27.648s
23	Andrea Montermini	18	1m 28.261s
24	Roberto Moreno	20	1m 28.570s
25	Bertrand Gachot	16	1m 29.719s
26	Pedro Diniz	23	1m 30.206s

Saturday qualifying
Dry and bright

Pos.	Driver	Laps	Time
1	Michael Schumacher	11	1m 21.452s
2	Jean Alesi	9	1m 22.052s
3	Gerhard Berger	8	1m 22.071s
4	David Coulthard	11	1m 22.332s
5	Damon Hill	12	1m 22.349s
6	Eddie Irvine	11	1m 23.352s
7	Johnny Herbert	12	1m 23.536s
8	Rubens Barrichello	12	1m 23.705s
9	Mika Häkkinen	10	1m 23.833s
10	Nigel Mansell	12	1m 23.927s
11	Martin Brundle	11	1m 24.727s
12	Heinz-Harald Frentzen	11	1m 24.802s
13	Mika Salo	12	1m 24.971s
14	Gianni Morbidelli	12	1m 25.053s
15	Olivier Panis	11	1m 25.204s
16	Jos Verstappen	11	1m 25.827s
17	Ukyo Katayama	9	1m 25.946s
18	Taki Inoue	12	1m 26.059s
19	Pierluigi Martini	9	1m 26.619s
20	Karl Wendlinger	12	1m 27.007s
21	Luca Badoer	12	1m 27.345s
22	Domenico Schiattarella	12	1m 27.575s
23	Andrea Montermini	12	1m 28.094s
24	Bertrand Gachot	12	1m 28.598s
25	Roberto Moreno	12	1m 28.963s
26	Pedro Diniz	12	1m 29.540s

Warm-up
Dry and bright

Pos.	Driver	Laps	Time
1	Michael Schumacher	12	1m 23.432s
2	Jean Alesi	13	1m 24.065s
3	Gerhard Berger	9	1m 24.550s
4	Mika Häkkinen	12	1m 24.065s
5	Damon Hill	14	1m 24.724s
6	David Coulthard	10	1m 24.734s
7	Johnny Herbert	14	1m 25.267s
8	Eddie Irvine	10	1m 25.290s
9	Rubens Barrichello	14	1m 25.411s
10	Nigel Mansell	12	1m 25.850s
11	Heinz-Harald Frentzen	13	1m 26.082s
12	Olivier Panis	13	1m 26.294s
13	Martin Brundle	13	1m 26.388s
14	Gianni Morbidelli	12	1m 26.793s
15	Taki Inoue	13	1m 26.880s
16	Jos Verstappen	10	1m 27.084s
17	Andrea Montermini	12	1m 27.440s
18	Ukyo Katayama	15	1m 27.503s
19	Pierluigi Martini	11	1m 27.568s
20	Karl Wendlinger	14	1m 27.728s
21	Luca Badoer	13	1m 27.850s
22	Mika Salo	13	1m 28.072s
23	Bertrand Gachot	10	1m 30.468s
24	Roberto Moreno	11	1m 31.274s
25	Pedro Diniz	13	1m 32.758s
26	Domenico Schiattarella	2	29m 03.968s

Fastest race laps
Dry, warm and sunny

Driver	Time	Lap
Damon Hill	1m 24.531s	46
Michael Schumacher	1m 24.787s	36
David Coulthard	1m 25.409s	11
Johnny Herbert	1m 25.521s	36
Jean Alesi	1m 25.671s	15
Mika Häkkinen	1m 25.771s	31
Gerhard Berger	1m 25.794s	48
Eddie Irvine	1m 25.868s	43
Rubens Barrichello	1m 26.246s	45
Olivier Panis	1m 26.369s	22
Martin Brundle	1m 27.039s	25
Nigel Mansell	1m 27.054s	17
Gianni Morbidelli	1m 27.284s	57
Heinz-Harald Frentzen	1m 27.328s	24
Ukyo Katayama	1m 27.467s	42
Mika Salo	1m 27.823s	58
Jos Verstappen	1m 27.923s	39
Karl Wendlinger	1m 27.991s	50
Taki Inoue	1m 28.204s	16
Pierluigi Martini	1m 28.828s	21
Luca Badoer	1m 29.032s	17
Domenico Schiattarella	1m 29.712s	44
Bertrand Gachot	1m 29.924s	35
Roberto Moreno	1m 31.783s	7
Pedro Diniz	1m 32.423s	4

CHASSIS LOG BOOK

No.	Driver	Chassis
1	Schumacher	Benetton B195/1
2	Herbert	Benetton B195/5
	spare	Benetton B195/4
3	Katayama	Tyrrell 023/4
4	Salo	Tyrrell 023/3
	spare	Tyrrell 023/2
5	Hill	Williams FW17/4
6	Coulthard	Williams FW17/2
	spare	Williams FW17/3
7	Mansell	McLaren MP4/10B/1
8	Häkkinen	McLaren MP4/10/3
	spare	McLaren MP4/10/2
9	Morbidelli	Footwork FA16/2
10	Inoue	Footwork FA16/1
	spare	Footwork FA16/3
11	Schiattarella	Simtek S951/1
12	Verstappen	Simtek S951/2
14	Barrichello	Jordan 195/4
15	Irvine	Jordan 195/3
	spare	Jordan 195/1
16	Gachot	Pacific PR02/1
17	Montermini	Pacific PR02/2
21	Diniz	Forti FG01/1
22	Moreno	Forti FG01/2
23	Martini	Minardi M195/3
24	Badoer	Minardi M195/2
25	Brundle	Ligier JS41/1
26	Panis	Ligier JS41/4
	spare	Ligier JS41/2
27	Alesi	Ferrari 412T2/161
28	Berger	Ferrari 412T2/159
	spare	Ferrari 412T2/160
29	Wendlinger	Sauber C14/4
30	Frentzen	Sauber C14/3
	spare	Sauber C14/2

POINTS TABLES

Drivers

1	Michael Schumacher	24
2	Damon Hill	23
3	Jean Alesi	14
4	Gerhard Berger	13
5=	David Coulthard	9
5=	Johnny Herbert	9
7	Mika Häkkinen	5
8	Heinz-Harald Frentzen	3
9	Eddie Irvine	2
10=	Mark Blundell	1
10=	Olivier Panis	1

Constructors

1	Ferrari	27
2	Williams	26
3	Benetton	23
4	McLaren	6
5	Sauber	3
6	Jordan	2
7	Ligier	1

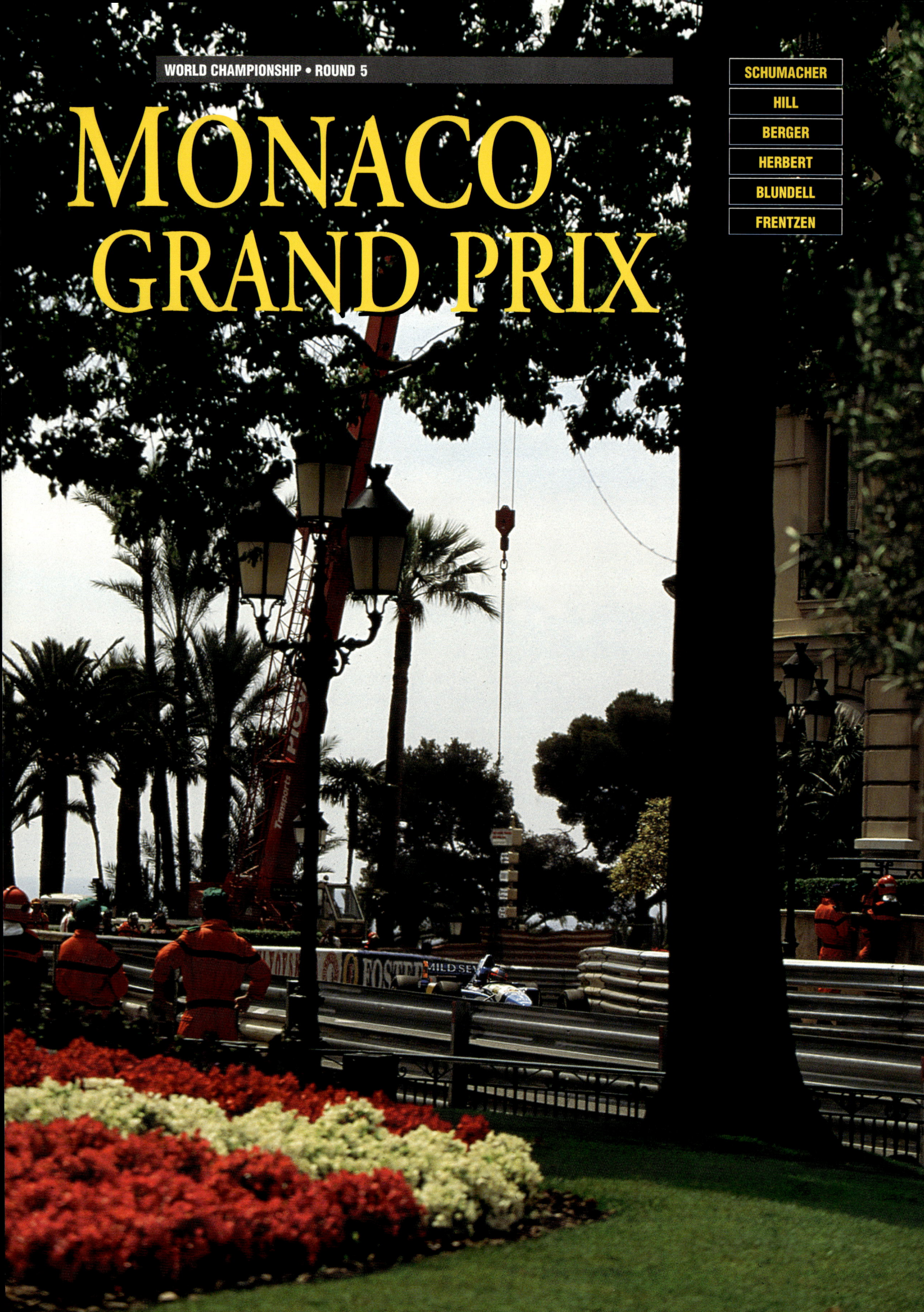

MONACO GRAND PRIX

Left: No other circuit possesses a fraction of the charm and challenge of Monaco but it has to be recognised that safety standards rigorously enforced elsewhere can never be attained in the Principality. Michael Schumacher hurtles through Massenet on his way to another commanding victory for Benetton.

Japanese novice Taki Inoue was fortunate to escape without serious injury when his Footwork-Hart was struck by a course car while being towed to the pits during the mid-session break on Saturday morning.

Diary

Plans for a round of the PPG Indy Car World Series to be held at Rio de Janeiro's Autodromo Riocentro in 1996 are announced.

Beijing bids for possible Chinese Grand Prix in 1997.

Martin Brundle confirmed as Olivier Panis's partner in Ligier team at least until the British Grand Prix.

Vincenzo Sospiri wins F3000 Pau Grand Prix in Super Nova team's Reynard-Cosworth.

Nigel Mansell may well have taken his leave of Grand Prix racing, but the image of the former World Champion's fleeting involvement with the McLaren-Mercedes team continued to watch over the F1 fraternity from dozens of advertising hoardings across the famous Mediterranean Principality, paradoxically one of the few venues on the title trail where Nigel never quite managed to unleash a winning performance.

Yet it had to be said that such ironic symbolism certainly didn't seem to bother the McLaren personnel as they toiled away in the absurdly confined Monaco pit lane and, even though Mansell's successor Mark Blundell celebrated his return to the cockpit with an accident in the closing moments of Thursday's first qualifying session, it was difficult to discern any pangs of nostalgia for the previous incumbent.

Mark perhaps pressed a little too hard on cool tyres and went rattling down the barrier. 'My fault entirely,' he acknowledged with refreshing candour on his return to the pits.

'Unfortunately I maybe gave it a little bit too much throttle on low-pressure rear tyres and damaged the front of the car when I hit the side of the barrier.'

It would perhaps have been uncharitable to suggest that such an accident might have prompted a subtly different response from the cockpit had Mansell still been the custodian of car number seven. It was undeniable that the McLaren MP4/10B still remained some way from the winning pace, but there was an obvious spring in the steps of the team mechanics. It almost seemed irrelevant that Mika Häkkinen finished the first day in fifth place ahead of Johnny Herbert's Benetton, while Blundell wound up eighth.

Although only confirmed as the team's second driver for the next two races, Blundell was nevertheless strongly tipped to fill the McLaren berth for the remainder of the season. The general consensus was that rumours suggesting Mansell might return for a final guest performance at the British Grand Prix, should the MP4/10B be massaged into front-running form, had no basis in truth.

Meanwhile Jean Alesi's stirring performance for Ferrari again underlined the Italian team's role as a potential winning force, even on a circuit where the V12's inherent lack of torque was expected to be a disadvantage through the many tight corners. Jean's performance was inspirational. Shaving close to the double-layer guard rails, he radiated an irrepressible confidence at the wheel of a car which was performing perfectly. Ferrari certainly came well-equipped; in addition to a spare car on hand for each driver, the Maranello squad also brought along a revised rear suspension set-up which was kept in reserve on the first day.

'I actually kissed the guard rail a couple of times on my best lap,' admitted Alesi. 'Once coming out of Ste Dévote and then again out of Portier, just before the tunnel. But it was no big problem, honestly.'

Jean thus finished first qualifying with a 1m 23.754s best, 0.39s ahead of Michael Schumacher's Benetton B195 and Gerhard Berger's Ferrari. Schumacher had been less than totally satisfied with his B195's handling during Thursday morning's free practice session and the car's rear end was stripped down for a precautionary check before first qualifying.

In the afternoon, Schumacher was disappointed that a brief rain shower interrupted his rhythm, preventing him from completing his full 12-lap allocation. Pole position, he felt, would have been well within his grasp. 'We should close the gap on Saturday as there is still more to come,' he predicted. 'I feel quite confident for final qualifying.'

Berger was also in terrific form with the second 412T2, time and again hurtling over the brow out of Casino Square in huge opposite-lock slides which raised echoes of the legendary Gilles Villeneuve. Although Gerhard ended up feeling pretty content with his efforts, he reported that he had been held up by slower traffic on what he had hoped might be his best lap.

'It looked like a red car,' he noted acidly and, sure enough, on this occasion the culprit had been his own team-mate!

Damon Hill finished first qualifying with his Williams FW17 a solid fourth at the track where his late father Graham had won five times between 1963 and 1969.

'I had no real problems with the car,' he said, 'but on my first run I caught Blundell as I came through the section by the swimming pool and I thought the track lost some of its pace after the rain shower.

'That said, I think we could have matched Alesi's time, but at Monaco everything is down to the final qualifying session on Saturday and I was keeping a little in reserve for then.'

Hill's team-mate David Coulthard was tackling Monaco for the first time, never having competed here in any of the junior formulae, and that lack of experience was dramatically underlined as he finished the day a modest 11th, one place behind Martin Brundle's Ligier.

'I think when I stop trying to remember what corner comes next, I will start to make some progress,' he shrugged. 'While other people are concentrating on setting up their cars, I am still learning the circuit.'

There was no F1 practice at Monaco on the Friday, so Coulthard had a day to dwell on where he might pick up the 2.8s separating him from provisional pole position. Alesi, alone among the front-runners, might have been forgiven for hoping for rain on Saturday as the most certain means of protecting his advantage.

Coulthard, who was still suffering slightly with tonsillitis, was certainly disappointed not to have recorded the best 'rookie' time through the streets of the Principality, at least on the first day. That distinction fell to Jordan first-timer Eddie Irvine, who did an excellent job to post ninth-fastest time, four places ahead of his team-mate Rubens Barrichello. The young Brazilian continued to play a psychologically subservient role to his team-mate, this time complaining that he never managed to get a clear lap in traffic.

On Saturday morning, Hill demonstrated his true capabilities by posting a 1m 23.468s – good enough for pole if reproduced in an official qualifying session. Alesi was second ahead of the much-improved Coulthard, with Mika Häkkinen driving the McLaren-Mercedes like a rally car on opposite lock to produce fourth-fastest time.

Schumacher certainly had his problems on Saturday morning. He damaged his suspension in a collision with Frentzen's Sauber on the exit from Casino Square, which cost him a lot of time. Later, Frentzen crashed heavily into the barrier at Massenet and, although he escaped unhurt, his Sauber C14 was quite badly damaged.

However, this was a minor incident when compared with that which befell Taki Inoue's Footwork. The Japanese driver had spun at Mirabeau, stalling his engine, and was duly retrieved by a tow-truck at the mid-session break. He was well on his way back to the pits when the course car, being driven at absurdly excessive speed by rally ace Jean Ragnotti, slammed into the back of the FA16 at the swimming pool esses.

The impact flipped the Footwork over, dropping its hapless, unbelted driver – who was fortunate to be wearing his helmet – out onto the track surface. Luckily, after being taken to hospital for a check-up, he was found not to have sustained any injuries.

The stewards went some way towards tacitly acknowledging the incident was not Inoue's fault by authorising Footwork to use its spare chassis for second qualifying. However, this indulgence was all slightly academic, for Taki was not given clearance by the doctors to take part, although he would get a clean bill of health on race morning. It remained to be seen what compensation would be offered to Footwork by the AC de Monaco in respect of the team's wrecked chassis after Ragnotti's unconscionably reckless performance.

MONACO GRAND PRIX

A quick lap at Monaco requires utter precision, ceaseless concentration and unfailing aggression. Gerhard Berger *(left)* and Damon Hill *(below left)* demonstrate all three as they thread their way between the intimidating steel barriers that line the track.

Right: Just to add to Simtek's misfortunes, Domenico Schiattarella was handed a $20,000 fine, suspended for three races, when his attempts to perform a spin-turn at the blind Rascasse hairpin incurred the displeasure of the stewards.

Second qualifying turned out to be absolutely electrifying, one of those memorable days when every spectator is poised to the edge of their seat for the entire session. Brundle and Olivier Panis in the Ligiers set the ball rolling with some impressively quick times, but Schumacher looked as though he had regained the initiative for Benetton when he posted a 1m 23.6s best about 20 minutes into the session.

Michael retired to the pits to await a response from the opposition. It wasn't long coming as Berger moved up to third on 1m 24.139s. Then Hill stormed round in 1m 23.294s to dislodge Schumacher from pole, his Williams looking smooth, crisp and secure all round the lap.

Then Alesi went out in a bid to regain his pole position only for his Ferrari to roll to a halt at Rascasse, sidelined when its engine stalled due to a problem with the hydraulic pressure to the semi-automatic gearchange mechanism. The marshals pushed him to one side of the circuit, but Jean dropped the clutch and bump-started the engine.

This was a clear breach of the rules and the stewards decided to ban him from using his race car for the balance of the session. That left the frustrated Frenchman sitting around in the pits waiting for Berger to hurry through his runs more quickly than he would have liked, the Austrian having carefully conserved four fresh sets of tyres for this final hour.

Steadily, Alesi's chances of a top grid position were slipping away. Häkkinen took the McLaren-Merc round in 1m 23.857s to take fourth place, then Brundle improved to sixth on 1m 24.712s. Then it was Schumacher's turn to raise the stakes. Shaving 0.4s off Hill's best at the first timing split, Michael produced a 1m 22.742s best to take back pole – 0.9s inside his own best from his first run. But Hill wasn't worried, trumping Michael's efforts with a 1m 22.115s.

Schumacher tried to respond, but the Benetton was a little too tail-happy for his tastes. Then Hill hammered home his advantage with a 1m 21.952s to prove that he still had a little more in hand.

'When Michael did his quick lap early in the session, I thought Benetton was seriously back in the groove again and we would be in trouble,' admitted Damon, 'but it all unfolded for me. My last run was the nearest to a perfect lap I think I have ever produced. Now I've got my sixth pole and I want to follow that with the sixth win for the Hill family at Monaco.'

Coulthard, meanwhile, was delighted with his third place in the other Williams FW17. Commented Patrick Head: 'It was one of those rare days when every little change to the car seemed to register an improvement. It's a good start to the weekend.'

Schumacher shrugged aside the disappointment. 'Obviously we struggled this afternoon as a result of this morning's incident with Heinz-Harald which spoiled our whole day,' he explained.

'I was going slowly and kept over to the left coming out of Casino Square, but as Heinz-Harald was overtaking me, he lost control for a moment and hit my right-front wheel with his left-rear. That pushed me into the barrier quite hard, bending the suspension, and the balance of the car was not so good this afternoon.'

Berger tried hard, but couldn't improve on fourth place, leaving Alesi to commandeer his car only for the last few moments of the session once the pedal positions had been changed. Jean, remarkably well under control, tore into his final lap only 13 seconds before the chequered flag fell. But he couldn't improve and finished the day 0.3s away from his Thursday best. Given the circumstances, it was heart-rending that he should find himself only fifth fastest overall.

In the closing moments of the session, Irvine crashed heavily at Tabac, ripping two wheels off his Jordan after a lap which had seen him 0.5s up on his previous best at the first timing split. The resultant yellow flags and debris all over the circuit prevented Häkkinen from making his hoped-for improvement in the McLaren MP4/10B.

As a result, the Finn wound up a somewhat philosophical sixth, four places ahead of Blundell's sister car, which had spun into the barrier at Rascasse during the morning's free practice session. The car needed a new rear wing, bodywork, right-rear suspension and undertray, and Mark subsequently survived a trip into the Ste Dévote escape road on Saturday afternoon.

'I think perhaps I should have spent less time experimenting with chassis set-ups and a little more just concentrating on getting used to the car,' he said thoughtfully.

Blundell wound up behind Johnny Herbert's Benetton, the impressive Martin Brundle's Ligier-Mugen and the luckless Irvine. In 11th place was Rubens Barrichello's Jordan ahead of Panis, the Ligier driver caught in traffic after flat-spotting his first set of tyres under braking for Ste Dévote, while Gianni Morbidelli took 13th place in his Footwork-Hart.

Frentzen was unable to take part after crashing his own Sauber during the morning, a feat duplicated at the same spot by new boy Jean-Christophe Boullion, who had taken over Karl Wendlinger's place in the works Ford squad. Frentzen was thus unable to take over the Frenchman's car and slipped to 14th place while Boullion himself was consigned to a disappointed 19th in the grid order for his F1 race debut.

Ukyo Katayama's Tyrrell-Yamaha was beset by wheelspin over the bumps, poor handling and traffic. He qualified 15th, two places ahead of his similarly afflicted team-mate Mika Salo. Both Tyrrell drivers complained that their cars felt unstable over the bumps and simply couldn't get the job done.

Luca Badoer was satisfied with 16th place, reporting that his Minardi M195 felt quite well balanced, but Pierluigi Martini was unhappy with the brake balance on his sister car and lined up two places further back.

Behind Boullion came Mimmo Schiattarella's Simtek, then Bertrand Gachot's Pacific and Pedro Diniz in the faster of the two Fortis. He had a quick spin and then, with only five minutes to go, relinquished his car to team-mate Roberto Moreno, whose own car had developed a serious misfire. Roberto emerged in 24th place, sandwiched by Jos Verstappen's Simtek and Andrea Montermini, while the bruised Inoue was understandably slowest after failing to take part in the second session.

The race morning warm-up saw Alesi and Berger first and second for Ferrari, both men trying their race and spare cars. Schumacher was third from Häkkinen and Herbert with Hill down in sixth place, worried about an unexpected touch of understeer which seemed to have blunted the fine edge of his Williams's handling. Over in the Jordan camp Irvine's damaged 195 had been rebuilt round a fresh monocoque but there was some understandable concern as Barrichello's car suffered a broken wheel rim. Meanwhile Taki Inoue was out in the spare Footwork, and Frentzen planned to take his rebuilt chassis for the race only for it to develop an oil leak on the warm-up lap, forcing him to switch to the spare.

Simtek on the brink

Simtek boss Nick Wirth signalled that his fledgling team was close to the end of the F1 road with his candid admission at Monaco that the organisation needed a financial lifeline of 'several million dollars' if it was to have any chance of making it to the Canadian Grand Prix, the next race on the championship schedule.

'Throughout the weekend we held endless meetings with our sponsors, partners and potential backers,' he explained, 'and while all have urged us to continue, the reality is that none have yet committed the necessary funding to allow us to do so. I am not prepared to limp from race to race like a wounded animal, telling the world that everything is OK, when it is not.'

Simtek's plight highlighted the financial problems which bedevil the smaller teams at the back of the starting grid who find themselves in a situation where the expenditure on a Cosworth ED 'customer' engine deal – estimated by *Autosport* magazine as being of the order of £370,000 every six weeks throughout the season – can represent around 75 per cent of their total operating budget.

However, Bernie Ecclestone firmly played down the notion that Simtek's problems represented the tip of a financial crisis in Formula 1. He told *Autosport*: 'People have always been struggling. When I owned Brabham we were struggling. So long as I have been in motor racing there have been people looking for sponsorship. Nothing is new.'

As things transpired, Simtek eventually decided against going to Montreal, hopeful that a backer could be found to save the team in time for a return at the French GP – and mindful of the FIA's assurances that any team which wanted to miss one race, should there eventually turn out to be 17 rounds of the championship, could do so without penalty.

Sadly, there was to be no reprieve. During the week following the Canadian Grand Prix, Wirth's two companies – Simtek Grand Prix and Simtek Research Ltd – went into receivership.

'With the French GP the next on the calendar, there isn't much time to try and get the show back on the road,' said Lindsay Denney, the receiver of Simtek Grand Prix. 'However, the cars have already proved themselves to be capable of doing well, providing the team has the stability of sufficient financial resources to continue the development work.'

In the event, that backing was not forthcoming and Simtek did not appear at Magny-Cours, writing *finis* to an audacious F1 challenge which had already survived the body-blow of Roland Ratzenberger's death at Imola in 1994. Sadly, its financial problems turned out to be a mountain Wirth and his colleagues simply could not climb.

123

Nigel Snowdon

Pascal Rondeau/Allsport

Colin McMaster/Words & Pictures

Pascal Rondeau/Allsport

Lukas Gorys

Pascal Rondeau/Allsport

Steve Domenjoz

G.P. Photo/Peter Nygaard

Clockwise, from top left: Nigel Mansell's brief fling with McLaren appeared to be at an end, but the memory lingered on; celebrated photographer Nigel Snowdon stalks his prey in the F1 jungle; levers mounted behind the steering wheel have taken the place of a conventional gearshift but Ferrari's Gerhard Berger still needs to tape up his hands before tackling the streets of Monte Carlo; a close-up view for one privileged spectator as Roberto Moreno sweeps past in the uncompetitive Forti; unable to defend his pole position in Saturday's final qualifying session, Jean Alesi attempts to control his emotions while he waits for the Ferrari mechanics to prepare Berger's car; Mika Salo gets to grips with the Monaco bumps while Tyrrell team-mate Ukyo Katayama opts for a novel solution to his problems with traffic; Mark Blundell took over Mansell's McLaren-Mercedes and lifted the Woking team's flagging spirits with a steady run to fifth place.

MONACO GRAND PRIX

Reigning European F3000 Champion Jean-Christophe Boullion *(left)* had been called into the Sauber team to replace the unfortunate Karl Wendlinger and took eighth place on his Grand Prix debut despite a last-lap clash with Footwork's Gianni Morbidelli.

Below left: Jos Verstappen locks a wheel in the Simtek. Gearbox maladies prevented him from taking the restart, and the impending closure of Nick Wirth's financially distressed team meant that, for the present at least, the young Dutchman's promising Formula 1 career was on hold.

The drivers were originally given to understand that, in the event of a first-corner shunt at Ste Dévote, the safety car would be deployed rather than the race stopped. At the green light, Hill duly accelerated cleanly into the lead ahead of Schumacher, but Coulthard was a little slow off the mark and Alesi came slamming up the inside from his third-row starting position, making it three abreast with the Williams and Berger's Ferrari as they aimed for the narrowing funnel at the tricky uphill right-hander.

'It was difficult, as I had Gerhard come along on the outside,' explained Coulthard in what was subsequently seen to be the most lucid account of what happened next. 'I gave him some room, as the barrier comes out going down to the first corner, and Jean stayed on the inside, sort of half a car length behind. Basically, the circuit narrows and I was sandwiched in the middle . . .'

Alesi's left-front wheel began rubbing against the Williams's right-hand side pod, then suddenly Coulthard was launched into the air as his right-rear wheel rode over the Ferrari, bouncing into Berger as he spun to a halt in the middle of the corner. Both Ferraris were out on the spot, while also involved were the two Tyrrells, the Footworks and Schiattarella's Simtek.

The one man who seemed to be laughing all the way to the bank was Brundle, who dodged his Ligier through the debris to emerge third behind Hill and Schumacher as they sprinted up the hill towards Casino Square. Then out came the red flag as the track was quite clearly badly blocked. Now everybody had to do it all a second time.

Both Ferrari drivers took their spare cars for the restart, although Gerhard's mount for the rest of the afternoon was fitted with a less powerful, slightly earlier-specification engine. After Schiattarella's involvement in the first-corner shunt, there was more bitter disappointment in store for the financially beleaguered Simtek squad as Verstappen's S951 was pushed away from the grid with gearbox problems. It would be the last time we saw one of Nick Wirth's cars lining up to do battle.

At the restart, Hill again stormed away into an immediate lead, completing the opening lap 0.5s ahead of Schumacher. Coulthard was playing himself in steadily, holding third place in the spare Williams FW17, while Alesi and Berger were next ahead of Herbert, Häkkinen, Irvine, Brundle, Barrichello, Blundell and Panis. At the end of lap six, Morbidelli was the first pit visitor: a section of a tie-rope from a tyre-heating blanket had somehow got jammed between a rear wheel and the hub, setting up a dangerous vibration.

The problem was duly rectified, but ten laps later Gianni was back in again to receive a ten-second stop-go penalty for a jump start – as were Brundle, Frentzen, Barrichello, Panis and Montermini at around the same time. Meanwhile, Hill was easing away from Schumacher at the head of the pack; not quickly enough, perhaps, but it would all depend on the Benetton driver's refuelling strategy. Hill was stopping twice, so if Michael was running a one-stop strategy and could almost keep pace with the Williams, then Damon was clearly in big trouble.

By lap 17, Hill had pulled out 2.3s over his rival, but then the Williams driver was held up very badly by one of the dawdling Fortis and his advantage was cut back to 1.8s by the time he pulled in for his first refuelling stop at the end of lap 24. Damon's car was stationary for only 8.5s, but not only did Schumacher go through into the lead, he continued right through to the end of lap 36 before coming in for a 10.2s stop for fuel and tyres. Damon's nightmare had become a reality – Michael was only stopping once.

To add to Hill's woes, his Williams was still beset by too much time-consuming understeer in the slow corners. He had briefly dropped to fourth after his first stop, but was immediately promoted to third when Berger made a 6.7s first refuelling stop at the end of lap 25. Alesi, meanwhile, took the lead momentarily on lap 37 before making his own single refuelling stop, further frustrating Damon by getting back into the race ahead of him in second place.

Alesi's great drive ended on lap 42 when he crashed heavily at Tabac trying to avoid Brundle's spinning Ligier which he was just coming up to lap. That enabled Hill to dodge through into second place.

'I was pushing very hard,' said Alesi later, 'and I think I could have fought for the lead. But as had happened on previous occasions, I found myself stuck behind Brundle, who slowed me down for two laps even though he was a lap down and much slower than me.

'Despite being shown the blue flag, Brundle was driving so much on the limit to block me that he eventually touched the guard rail at Tabac and spun in front of me. I was so close, I could not avoid the accident.' Brundle crisply dismissed Alesi's complaints by pointing out that he was running in seventh place and making ground on Blundell's sixth-place McLaren-Mercedes. His view was that he had his own race to run.

Hill, meanwhile, found himself simply unable to make any meaningful ground on Schumacher. The understeer was a real killer and, even after fitting fresh tyres at his second refuelling stop on lap 52, there was simply nothing he could do. He ran out the race a dejected second, unable to fathom out how things had gone so badly wrong.

'I am bitterly disappointed not to have won here,' he reflected. 'The car was very good in qualifying and unfortunately didn't match up to that performance today. I cannot explain why that should be.

'We got caught out again by our pit stop strategy and I am pretty cheesed off. It's making life too easy for Michael. The way things went I would have finished third behind Jean Alesi – but for his accident – and he also had two stops.

'It is my final choice as the driver, but you cannot point the finger at any individual. Everyone contributes, it is a team decision, and we got it wrong. I knew it was going to be tough when I was not making any impression on Michael at the start. I knew then he had only one stop planned, yet I could not get away from him.

'When a guy with more fuel aboard his car can keep up, you know it is going to be a long, hard race. We just got it horribly wrong.' Only much later, when the cars were stripped down on their return to the factory, did one possible reason for Hill's understeer problem become apparent when it was found that his FW17's differential had partially seized.

At least he got to the finish. Coulthard's FW17 retired with a gearbox problem at the end of lap 17 while lying third. 'At the restart there had been a panic to get me out in the spare car and we didn't have time enough to calibrate the throttle,' explained the Scot. 'I had a lot of oversteer initially, but got used to that and started to pull away from Jean. Then I lost third gear, first, and then fourth and fifth. And that was it!'

Berger came home a philosophical third. 'Considering how things went, I think this was a good result,' he acknowledged. 'My spare car had the least powerful engine of the four we had here and I couldn't hope for much more. Even though I don't normally like to say it, I think Ferrari was unlucky this weekend and the result does not reflect the true potential of our cars.

'I had a two-stop strategy and I think that Michael's strategy of one stop was correct. I was a bit stuck behind Herbert after my first stop, so I couldn't really get the best out of my fresh tyres.' Gerhard eventually got ahead of the Englishman's Benetton when Johnny made his single refuelling stop on lap 39, but by then the Ferrari had dropped 26 seconds adrift of Hill's Williams with no prospect of closing the gap.

Behind Herbert's Benetton, Mark Blundell steadied McLaren's nerves with a solid fifth place despite a slight gearbox problem with the MP4/10B. The Englishman's performance went some way to compensate for the early retirement of Mika Häkkinen's car, the Finn holding seventh place when he retired with an engine problem on his ninth lap.

Frentzen took sixth place for Sauber, despite his C14 being jammed in fourth gear for the last few laps, with Martini finishing just outside the points, while Boullion was classified in eighth place ahead of Morbidelli in his first Grand Prix despite being pitched into a spin by the Footwork on the final lap.

Pedro Diniz was the last of the ten finishers in a race which had been distinguished by a high level of attrition, mechanical and otherwise. Jordan encountered more disappointment with Irvine succumbing to a broken wheel and Barrichello's car stopping with a malfunction of its throttle mechanism. Panis crashed his Ligier, as did Katayama the Tyrrell, while Mika Salo, who had started the spare Tyrrell from the pit lane after damaging his race car in the first-corner fracas, suffered an engine failure after 63 laps.

For Hill, failing to win Monaco was a psychological body-blow even though there may have been quantifiable technical reasons for the Williams's handling imbalance. Despite this, it was difficult to argue against Benetton's refuelling strategy for Schumacher. Yet again this winning partnership had displayed almost uncanny prescience as far as tactics were concerned.

For the opposition, it was all rather demoralising.

FIA FORMULA ONE WORLD CHAMPIONSHIP ROUND 5

GRAND PRIX DE MONACO

MONTE CARLO 25–28 MAY 1995

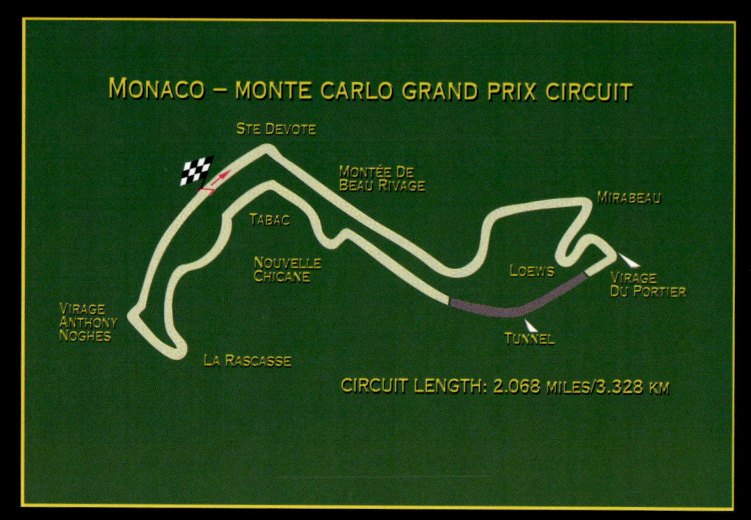

MONACO – MONTE CARLO GRAND PRIX CIRCUIT

CIRCUIT LENGTH: 2.068 MILES/3.328 KM

Race distance: 78 laps, 161.297 miles/259.584 km
Race weather: Warm, sunny

Place	Driver	Nat.	No.	Entrant	Car/Engine	Laps	Time/Retirement	Speed (mph/km/h)
1	**Michael Schumacher**	D	1	Mild Seven Benetton Renault	Benetton B195-Renault RS7 V10	78	1h 53m 11.258s	85.502/137.603
2	**Damon Hill**	GB	5	Rothmans Williams Renault	Williams FW17-Renault RS7 V10	78	1h 53m 46.075s	85.066/136.901
3	**Gerhard Berger**	A	28	Scuderia Ferrari	Ferrari 412T2 044 V12	78	1h 54m 22.705s	84.612/136.171
4	**Johnny Herbert**	GB	2	Mild Seven Benetton Renault	Benetton B195-Renault RS7 V10	77		
5	**Mark Blundell**	GB	7	Marlboro McLaren Mercedes	McLaren MP4/10B-Mercedes FO110 V10	77		
6	**Heinz-Harald Frentzen**	D	30	Red Bull Sauber Ford	Sauber C14-Ford Zetec-R V8	76		
7	Pierluigi Martini	I	23	Minardi Scuderia Italia	Minardi M195-Ford EDM V8	76		
8	Jean-Christophe Boullion	F	29	Red Bull Sauber Ford	Sauber C14-Ford Zetec-R V8	74	Collision with Morbidelli	
9	Gianni Morbidelli	I	9	Footwork Hart	Footwork FA16-Hart 830 V8	74		
10	Pedro Diniz	BR	21	Parmalat Forti Ford	Forti FG01-Ford ED V8	72		
	Luca Badoer	I	24	Minardi Scuderia Italia	Minardi M195-Ford EDM V8	68	Suspension	
	Olivier Panis	F	26	Ligier Gitanes Blondes	Ligier JS41-Mugen Honda MF301 V10	65	Accident	
	Mika Salo	SF	4	Nokia Tyrrell Yamaha	Tyrrell 023-Yamaha OX10C V10	63	Engine	
	Rubens Barrichello	BR	14	Total Jordan Peugeot	Jordan 195-Peugeot A10 V10	60	Throttle	
	Bertrand Gachot	F	16	Pacific Grand Prix Ltd	Pacific PR02-Ford ED V8	42	Gearbox	
	Jean Alesi	F	27	Scuderia Ferrari	Ferrari 412T2 044 V12	41	Accident	
	Martin Brundle	GB	25	Ligier Gitanes Blondes	Ligier JS41-Mugen Honda MF301 V10	40	Spun off	
	Taki Inoue	J	10	Footwork Hart	Footwork FA16-Hart 830 V8	27	Gearbox	
	Ukyo Katayama	J	3	Nokia Tyrrell Yamaha	Tyrrell 023-Yamaha OX10C V10	26	Accident	
DQ	Andrea Montermini	I	17	Pacific Grand Prix Ltd	Pacific PR02-Ford ED V8	23	Disqualified	
	Eddie Irvine	GB	15	Total Jordan Peugeot	Jordan 195-Peugeot A10 V10	22	Broken wheel rim	
	David Coulthard	GB	6	Rothmans Williams Renault	Williams FW17-Renault RS7 V10	16	Gearbox	
	Roberto Moreno	BR	22	Parmalat Forti Ford	Forti FG01-Ford ED V8	9	Brake pipe	
	Mika Häkkinen	SF	8	Marlboro McLaren Mercedes	McLaren MP4/10B-Mercedes FO110 V10	8	Engine	
DNS	Domenico Schiattarella	I	11	MTV Simtek Ford	Simtek S951-Ford ED V8	0	Accident	
DNS	Jos Verstappen	NL	12	MTV Simtek Ford	Simtek S951-Ford ED V8	0	Gearbox	

Fastest lap: Alesi, on lap 36, 1m 24.621s, 87.974 mph/141.581 km/h.
Lap record: Michael Schumacher (F1 Benetton B194-Ford V8), 1m 21.076s, 91.821 mph/147.772 km/h (1994).

All cars used Goodyear tyres

All results and data © FIA 1995

STARTING GRID

1 SCHUMACHER (1m 22.742s) Benetton	**5 HILL** (1m 21.952s) Williams
28 BERGER (1m 23.220s) Ferrari	**6 COULTHARD** (1m 23.109s) Williams
8 HÄKKINEN (1m 23.857s) McLaren	**27 ALESI** (1m 23.754s) Ferrari
25 BRUNDLE (1m 24.447s) Ligier	**2 HERBERT** (1m 23.885s) Benetton
7 BLUNDELL (1m 24.933s) McLaren	**15 IRVINE** (1m 24.857s) Jordan
26 PANIS (1m 25.125s) Ligier	**14 BARRICHELLO** (1m 25.081s) Jordan
30 FRENTZEN (1m 25.661s) Sauber	**9 MORBIDELLI** (1m 25.447s) Footwork
24 BADOER (1m 25.969s) Minardi	**3 KATAYAMA** (1m 25.808s) Tyrrell
23 MARTINI (1m 26.913s) Minardi	**4 SALO*** (1m 26.473s) Tyrrell
11 SCHIATTARELLA** (1m 28.337s) Simtek	**29 BOULLION** (1m 27.145s) Sauber
21 DINIZ (1m 29.244s) Forti	**16 GACHOT** (1m 29.039s) Pacific
22 MORENO (1m 29.608s) Forti	**12 VERSTAPPEN**** (1m 29.391s) Simtek
10 INOUE (1m 31.542s) Footwork	**17 MONTERMINI** (1m 30.149s) Pacific

* took restart from pit lane
** did not take restart

FOR THE RECORD

First Grand Prix start
Jean-Christophe Boullion

TIME SHEETS

Thursday free practice
Bright and sunny

Pos.	Driver	Laps	Time
1	Jean Alesi	22	1m 25.457s
2	Michael Schumacher	15	1m 25.771s
3	Damon Hill	23	1m 25.832s
4	Mika Häkkinen	21	1m 26.210s
5	Mark Blundell	23	1m 26.536s
6	Johnny Herbert	23	1m 27.170s
7	David Coulthard	22	1m 27.404s
8	Rubens Barrichello	23	1m 27.562s
9	Gerhard Berger	21	1m 27.883s
10	Olivier Panis	19	1m 28.084s
11	Gianni Morbidelli	22	1m 28.459s
12	Martin Brundle	23	1m 28.684s
13	Eddie Irvine	23	1m 29.011s
14	Luca Badoer	21	1m 29.279s
15	Ukyo Katayama	23	1m 29.365s
16	Domenico Schiattarella	24	1m 29.737s
17	Pierluigi Martini	23	1m 29.915s
18	Heinz-Harald Frentzen	13	1m 30.171s
19	Mika Salo	23	1m 30.787s
20	Bertrand Gachot	22	1m 30.803s
21	Roberto Moreno	23	1m 30.923s
22	Andrea Montermini	21	1m 31.354s
23	Jean-Christophe Boullion	11	1m 31.742s
24	Jos Verstappen	5	1m 33.821s
25	Pedro Diniz	18	1m 33.941s
26	Taki Inoue	22	1m 36.169s

Thursday qualifying
Bright, interrupted by rain shower

Pos.	Driver	Laps	Time
1	**Jean Alesi**	**8**	**1m 23.754s**
2	Michael Schumacher	9	1m 24.146s
3	Gerhard Berger	8	1m 24.509s
4	Damon Hill	12	1m 24.659s
5	Mika Häkkinen	11	1m 24.831s
6	Johnny Herbert	10	1m 25.623s
7	**Heinz-Harald Frentzen**	**11**	**1m 25.661s**
8	Mark Blundell	7	1m 26.017s
9	Eddie Irvine	12	1m 26.447s
10	Martin Brundle	6	1m 26.457s
11	David Coulthard	11	1m 26.556s
12	Olivier Panis	12	1m 26.579s
13	Rubens Barrichello	12	1m 26.787s
14	Gianni Morbidelli	11	1m 26.828s
15	Luca Badoer	12	1m 27.615s
16	Pierluigi Martini	10	1m 27.714s
17	Mika Salo	12	1m 28.123s
18	Ukyo Katayama	11	1m 28.439s
19	**Jos Verstappen**	**4**	**1m 29.391s**
20	Domenico Schiattarella	5	1m 29.439s
21	Jean-Christophe Boullion	11	1m 30.014s
22	**Andrea Montermini**	**12**	**1m 30.149s**
23	Roberto Moreno	6	1m 30.461s
24	**Taki Inoue**	**8**	**1m 31.542s**
25	Pedro Diniz	5	1m 34.963s
26	Bertrand Gachot	1	13m 33.570s

Saturday free practice
Bright and warm

Pos.	Driver	Laps	Time
1	Damon Hill	23	1m 23.468s
2	Jean Alesi	21	1m 24.252s
3	David Coulthard	23	1m 24.491s
4	Mika Häkkinen	23	1m 24.540s
5	Gerhard Berger	23	1m 24.887s
6	Olivier Panis	22	1m 25.115s
7	Michael Schumacher	11	1m 25.120s
8	Martin Brundle	23	1m 25.307s
9	Eddie Irvine	20	1m 25.660s
10	Johnny Herbert	23	1m 26.188s
11	Rubens Barrichello	22	1m 26.251s
12	Gianni Morbidelli	23	1m 26.326s
13	Mark Blundell	12	1m 27.094s
14	Mika Salo	23	1m 27.180s
15	Heinz-Harald Frentzen	11	1m 27.232s
16	Pierluigi Martini	23	1m 27.372s
17	Luca Badoer	22	1m 27.740s
18	Ukyo Katayama	22	1m 28.768s
19	Jean-Christophe Boullion	22	1m 29.145s
20	Bertrand Gachot	17	1m 29.316s
21	Roberto Moreno	22	1m 29.612s
22	Domenico Schiattarella	23	1m 30.495s
23	Pedro Diniz	23	1m 30.613s
24	Andrea Montermini	13	1m 30.715s
25	Jos Verstappen	7	1m 31.265s
26	Taki Inoue	6	1m 35.625s

Saturday qualifying
Bright and warm

Pos.	Driver	Laps	Time
1	Damon Hill	11	1m 21.952s
2	Michael Schumacher	12	1m 22.742s
3	David Coulthard	12	1m 23.109s
4	Gerhard Berger	9	1m 23.220s
5	Mika Häkkinen	11	1m 23.857s
6	Johnny Herbert	12	1m 23.885s
7	Jean Alesi	4	1m 24.023s
8	Martin Brundle	12	1m 24.447s
9	Eddie Irvine	10	1m 24.857s
10	Mark Blundell	12	1m 24.933s
11	Rubens Barrichello	12	1m 25.081s
12	Olivier Panis	12	1m 25.125s
13	Gianni Morbidelli	12	1m 25.447s
14	Ukyo Katayama	12	1m 25.808s
15	Luca Badoer	12	1m 25.969s
16	Mika Salo	12	1m 26.473s
17	Pierluigi Martini	12	1m 26.913s
18	Jean-Christophe Boullion	10	1m 27.145s
19	Domenico Schiattarella	12	1m 28.337s
20	Bertrand Gachot	12	1m 29.039s
21	Pedro Diniz	11	1m 29.244s
22	Roberto Moreno	7	1m 29.608s
23	Jos Verstappen	4	1m 30.015s
	Taki Inoue	0	no time
	Andrea Montermini	0	no time
	Heinz-Harald Frentzen	0	no time

Warm-up
Bright and warm

Pos.	Driver	Laps	Time
1	Jean Alesi	16	1m 24.356s
2	Gerhard Berger	11	1m 25.014s
3	Michael Schumacher	13	1m 25.230s
4	Mika Häkkinen	15	1m 25.246s
5	Johnny Herbert	14	1m 26.480s
6	Damon Hill	13	1m 26.768s
7	Olivier Panis	17	1m 26.845s
8	Eddie Irvine	11	1m 26.893s
9	Mark Blundell	17	1m 27.118s
10	Martin Brundle	12	1m 27.282s
11	David Coulthard	10	1m 27.534s
12	Gianni Morbidelli	15	1m 27.610s
13	Pierluigi Martini	15	1m 27.832s
14	Heinz-Harald Frentzen	9	1m 27.982s
15	Rubens Barrichello	10	1m 28.077s
16	Luca Badoer	11	1m 28.560s
17	Ukyo Katayama	14	1m 28.800s
18	Mika Salo	10	1m 29.830s
19	Jean-Christophe Boullion	15	1m 30.659s
20	Jos Verstappen	4	1m 31.045s
21	Domenico Schiattarella	10	1m 31.427s
22	Roberto Moreno	12	1m 31.955s
23	Bertrand Gachot	7	1m 32.120s
24	Andrea Montermini	4	1m 32.248s
25	Pedro Diniz	16	1m 32.399s
26	Taki Inoue	7	1m 34.177s

Fastest race laps
Warm and sunny

Driver	Time	Lap
Jean Alesi	1m 24.621s	36
Michael Schumacher	1m 24.773s	33
Damon Hill	1m 24.790s	54
Gerhard Berger	1m 25.3/9s	49
David Coulthard	1m 25.884s	15
Martin Brundle	1m 25.985s	39
Rubens Barrichello	1m 26.279s	51
Mark Blundell	1m 26.717s	33
Heinz-Harald Frentzen	1m 26.741s	49
Olivier Panis	1m 26.819s	62
Johnny Herbert	1m 26.923s	8
Eddie Irvine	1m 26.933s	19
Mika Häkkinen	1m 27.091s	5
Luca Badoer	1m 27.359s	60
Gianni Morbidelli	1m 27.532s	45
Ukyo Katayama	1m 27.568s	10
Pierluigi Martini	1m 27.761s	60
Mika Salo	1m 27.914s	45
Jean-Christophe Boullion	1m 28.417s	57
Andrea Montermini	1m 29.548s	20
Taki Inoue	1m 30.174s	21
Pedro Diniz	1m 30.193s	55
Bertrand Gachot	1m 30.394s	7
Roberto Moreno	1m 30.532s	6

CHASSIS LOG BOOK

1	Schumacher	Benetton B195/6
2	Herbert	Benetton B195/3
spare		Benetton B195/1
3	Katayama	Tyrrell 023/4
4	Salo	Tyrrell 023/2
spare		Tyrrell 023/3
5	Hill	Williams FW17/4
6	Coulthard	Williams FW17/2
spare		Williams FW17/3
7	Blundell	McLaren MP4/10B/1
8	Häkkinen	McLaren MP4/10B/3
spare		McLaren MP4/10B/2
9	Morbidelli	Footwork FA16/2
10	Inoue	Footwork FA16/1
spare		Footwork FA16/3
11	Schiattarella	Simtek S951/1
12	Verstappen	Simtek S951/2
14	Barrichello	Jordan 195/4
15	Irvine	Jordan 195/3
spare		Jordan 195/1
16	Gachot	Pacific PR02/1
17	Montermini	Pacific PR02/2
21	Diniz	Forti FG01/1
22	Moreno	Forti FG01/2
23	Martini	Minardi M195/3
24	Badoer	Minardi M195/2
spare		Minardi M195/1
25	Brundle	Ligier JS41/5
26	Panis	Ligier JS41/4
spare		Ligier JS41/2
27	Alesi	Ferrari 412T2/161
28	Berger	Ferrari 412T2/159
spares		Ferrari 412T2/160 & 156
29	Boullion	Sauber C14/4
30	Frentzen	Sauber C14/3
spare		Sauber C14/2

POINTS TABLES

Drivers

1	Michael Schumacher	34
2	Damon Hill	29
3	Gerhard Berger	17
4	Jean Alesi	14
5	Johnny Herbert	12
6	David Coulthard	9
7	Mika Häkkinen	5
8	Heinz-Harald Frentzen	4
9	Mark Blundell	3
10	Eddie Irvine	2
11	Olivier Panis	1

Constructors

1	Benetton	36
2	Williams	32
3	Ferrari	31
4	McLaren	8
5	Sauber	4
6	Jordan	2
7	Ligier	1

WORLD CHAMPIONSHIP • ROUND 6

CANADIAN GRAND PRIX

ALESI
BARRICHELLO
IRVINE
PANIS
SCHUMACHER
MORBIDELLI

CANADIAN GRAND PRIX

After enduring long spells of frustration punctuated by occasional cruel disappointments since joining Ferrari in 1991, Jean Alesi finally scored the first Grand Prix win of his career. On the rostrum afterwards he basked in the adulation of the adoring crowd.

Diary

FIA President Max Mosley tries a BTCC 2-litre Alfa Romeo at Brands Hatch.

Indianapolis 500 not included in the official list of PPG Indy Car World Series races for 1996 published at Detroit Grand Prix.

Zandvoort granted Dutch government approval to revamp its circuit into a facility suitable for Formula 1 use.

Even when it all goes wrong for Michael Schumacher, he manages to grasp a worthwhile consolation prize. Fifth place wasn't quite what he was looking for, but to manage it after a gearchange problem had been rectified seemed to prove that Lady Luck had blessed his Benetton. Yet again.

Make no mistake, nobody begrudged Jean Alesi the first victory of his Grand Prix career when, at his 91st attempt, the Frenchman finally cast aside his apparent jinx to lead past the chequered flag for Ferrari. That it was also in a scarlet car carrying the emotive number 27 on the aptly named Circuit Gilles Villeneuve was another symbolic bonus. Yet given the state of contemporary Formula 1, it almost went without saying that Jean won only because Michael Schumacher's Benetton faltered. Albeit momentarily.

Put simply, Schuey had it in the bag from the word go. From the start, the World Champion was in a class of his own. He waited just long enough for his key rivals to make their sole refuelling stops before making his own, emerging from a 12.9s single pit visit on lap 38 of the 69-lap race with his lead intact. At that point it was Birthday Boy Alesi, 31 that very day, whom he had to keep tabs on in second place as Damon Hill's ill-handling Williams was by then battling to keep pace in third.

On lap 51, Damon finally succumbed to another Williams hydraulic pump failure, stopping right in front of the pits. His body language as he stalked away to speak to Frank Williams was not promising. Even the sight of Schumacher heading for the pits for an unscheduled stop on lap 58 offered only fleeting consolation.

The leading Benetton had developed a gearchange glitch, but the problem was quickly rectified and Michael went back into the race like the wind. He made it back to fifth place, to claim two crucial championship points, almost catching Olivier Panis's Ligier JS41 on the final lap.

Jordan had a terrific result with Rubens Barrichello and Eddie Irvine nursing their fuel-starved Peugeot-propelled machines through to second and third places. At a stroke, the Silverstone team vaulted ahead of the hapless McLaren squad to take fourth place in the constructors' championship. It was a delicious moment of irony for Eddie as Ron's rival red and white racers both retired from the fray, Häkkinen on the opening lap after a wildly intemperate attempt to overtake Johnny Herbert's Benetton at the tight, first-gear hairpin.

Hill's efforts to loosen Schumacher's arm lock on the 1995 World Championship contest received yet another apparent setback from the outset when Benetton's German ace confidently assumed control in the first qualifying session at Montreal.

It was a performance which added further spice to the frenzy of pit lane speculation that as many as three rival teams – Ferrari, Williams and McLaren – might be poised to bid in excess of $20 million to tempt the 26-year-old away from his current employers for 1996.

Schumacher set the pace from the start of the first morning's free practice session, thrusting ahead of Jean Alesi's Ferrari and Williams teammates Hill and David Coulthard. Yet with all the competitors complaining of poor grip and a bruising ride over the bumps of the Montreal track, Michael yet again displayed his unerring flair for extracting a fraction more from his machinery than most of his rivals.

'I feel quite happy with the car here,' said Schumacher, 'although we need to do some more work on its performance under hard braking. I think it is particularly important to try to get pole position today as some rain is forecast for Saturday.'

At the start of Friday's hour-long qualifying session, Michael stayed in the seclusion of the Benetton garage until taking to the track with only 25 minutes to go. By this time Alesi had underlined the market attraction of Ferrari's current technical package by posting fastest time ahead of Hill and Coulthard.

With 20 minutes to go, Hill dislodged Alesi from his position at the top of the timing screens, but by then Schumacher was well into his stride and, despite being balked by Pedro Diniz's Forti on his first run, slammed in the fastest time by over half a second with 15 minutes left.

Gerhard Berger followed that up with a last-ditch effort to rescue the day for Ferrari, despite having lost most of the morning session after an engine failure. As Schumacher watched impassively from the cockpit of his Benetton, snug in the pit lane garage, the Austrian pushed back ahead of Hill to take second place in the provisional grid order.

But Hill successfully counter-attacked, regaining second place ahead of Berger, Alesi, Coulthard, Eddie Irvine's Jordan and Johnny Herbert's Benetton before the end of the session. Herbert, in particular, had experienced an acutely frustrating day, losing time in the morning after a faulty driveshaft had to be replaced, and then having a change of springs midway through the timed session.

Berger tried to respond to Damon's challenge, but he was delayed by a sticking valve on the refuelling rig when the 412T2 was being topped up just prior to its final run, so he caught the chequered flag going into what would have been his last flying lap of the day.

Hill, meanwhile, was far from delighted with the performance of his Williams FW17. 'It was no more than a satisfactory start to the weekend,' he said. 'The car is a bit of a fight, to be honest, and very tricky to balance. I'm also suffering a bit from a head cold caused by the hotel's air conditioning.'

Coulthard, who lost time early in Friday free practice with a clutch problem, continued to be bugged by a troublesome gearbox downchange mechanism. 'I've been battling slow-speed grip,' shrugged the Scot. 'I'm now not as confident as I felt I would be before I came here.'

Over in the McLaren camp, Mika Häkkinen and Mark Blundell were finding the MP4/10B still quite a handful through the corners, although a switch from Bilstein to Penske dampers had gone some way to enhancing its potential in this respect. 'But the rear end doesn't stick going into the corners,' explained Mika, 'so I just can't carry sufficient speed onto the straights.' Häkkinen's problems were compounded when he collected a $10,000 fine for ignoring the red light at the pit exit on Saturday afternoon, having committed a similar offence at Monaco.

Blundell was using an earlier-specification Mercedes V10 to finish the first day two places behind Häkkinen in 11th place, his position as Nigel Mansell's successor in the McLaren-Mercedes squad yet again the focal point of media scrutiny.

Formally confirmed as Häkkinen's running mate for Monaco and Montreal only, it was being suggested that Mercedes might prefer that he be replaced by their protégé Heinz-Harald Frentzen, currently the Sauber team leader. But the rumour was firmly quashed, being denied emphatically by McLaren, Mercedes and Frentzen himself.

Further down the pack, Martin Brundle had a dismal afternoon,

131

Top F1 teams monopolise television viewing figures

The television viewing figures for the first five Grands Prix of the 1995 season provided cold comfort for all but the trio of front-running F1 teams when they were circulated informally at Montreal. In graphic fashion, they reflected the rewards which go with sustained success and the painful cost of failure.

Produced by Bernie Ecclestone's FOCA TV organisation, they showed that Williams, Benetton and Ferrari monopolised the total air time with around one and a half hours each. By contrast, McLaren's fading form was rewarded with only 16 minutes' coverage – well ahead of the rest of the pack, but very modest for a team with such a respected pedigree and long-established high profile, reflecting a lack of competitiveness which was clearly painful to team chief Ron Dennis.

The bottom line was that Williams, Benetton and Ferrari grabbed a massive 83 per cent of the overall coverage, leaving McLaren taking a paltry 4.5 per cent and the other nine teams sharing out the remaining 12.5 per cent.

This breakdown also highlighted the uphill financial struggle faced by smaller F1 teams, a concern voiced by Pacific Grand Prix team boss Keith Wiggins. 'I have heard it said that if the new teams cannot field a competitive package, attract media attention and therefore fail to find sponsorship, we should stop doing F1,' he commented. 'I do not accept that defeatist argument. Far from the new teams not being up to the task of competing in F1, I would argue that sponsors, motor manufacturers and the sport's administrators should look to us as the future of the sport.

'Three teams have dominated F1 for more than a decade, and I would point out that many so-called established teams have failed to deliver a competitive assault on the championship in spite of having strong sponsorship, often works engines and good driver line-ups.

'It is therefore time that sponsors and manufacturers examined the results achieved by certain teams and evaluated how their support could benefit a new team with proven potential. A wider supply of engines from a variety of manufacturers would have benefits for teams, the manufacturers themselves and F1 as a whole.'

Brave words, but none calculated to cut any ice with the ruling classes in Grand Prix racing. Within weeks of Wiggins's well-reasoned plea, the FIA would announce measures to make participation at the back of the grid more difficult – not easier – with the imposition of a qualifying cut-off point for all 1996 Grands Prix pegged at 107 per cent of the pole-position time.

Without major sponsorship and manufacturer-backed engines, it is almost impossible for the small teams to obtain the results that will earn them the advantages they lack. As a Pacific shareholder, Bertrand Gachot was acutely aware of the almost insoluble dilemma facing Keith Wiggins's gallant band.

removing his Ligier-Mugen's nose wing with an inelegant slide into a gravel trap after two slow laps. Only three years earlier, as Schumacher's team-mate at the wheel of a Benetton-Ford, Brundle had dodged ahead of the future World Champion to hold a fleeting second place in the Canadian race on this same circuit. With this in mind, the shifting sands of motor racing fortune must have seemed particularly cruel to Martin, but he took over team-mate Olivier Panis's car in the closing moments of the session to vault from 23rd in the order to a more respectable 15th. Even so, it was far from what he had been expecting.

On Saturday, Schumacher continued to set the pace, although failing by 0.1s to match his Friday best. He survived a spin at the first corner, reversing back off the grass to regain the circuit in what appeared a somewhat dangerous move, but kept the upper hand over the rather dejected Hill. It was Michael's ninth pole position and the 100th achieved by a Renault-powered F1 car.

'Yes, I feel confident for the race,' said Schumacher, although he acknowledged that he would be worried in the event of rain. 'When I spun this afternoon I had gone a bit wide on the previous corner and picked up some dirt on the tyres, then went too strong on the throttle, got wheelspin and went off.'

Together with Damon, Michael had some uncomplimentary remarks to make concerning the retention of the absurdly tight, artificial chicane which had been introduced in time for the '94 race. In the opinion of the two front-runners, with the reduced performance of the new 3-litre F1 generation, there was no further need for this acrobatic section of track.

The farcical air surrounding the whole business was heightened when Race Director John Corsmit announced to the drivers: 'During the race, for safety reasons, there shall be no overtaking from the beginning of the left-side chicane kerb until after the chicane.

'Further, if during the race, the chicane is blocked, for whatever reason, you will be shown a panel informing you that it is blocked and permitting you to go straight on under yellow flag conditions.'

Coulthard improved on Saturday, slicing half a second off his Friday best to line up third. 'I am very happy to be in front of the Ferraris,' he admitted. 'If I can make a good start, I shall feel quite happy for the race. The car still feels quite difficult to balance, although we have improved a bit since yesterday.'

Frustratingly, the Ferrari challenge faded slightly on the second day. Berger's efforts were thwarted when the session was red-flagged to a halt with just over two minutes to go after Luca Badoer's Minardi spun to rest in the middle of a corner after clipping a kerb and deflating a rear tyre.

Gerhard still had one run left to go and went out when the session was fleetingly resumed, only to exceed the prescribed 12-lap allocation and have all his Saturday times initially disallowed as a result. Thankfully, this slip did not affect his overall grid placing as he would have retained fourth place on the strength of his Friday best. Eventually, his Saturday times were reinstated. Meanwhile Coulthard's effort relegated Alesi to fifth fastest overall.

Herbert was reasonably content with his sixth place in the final grid order, despite being slightly disappointed that his second set of tyres failed to endow his Benetton with the extra grip he'd been hoping for. He lined up immediately ahead of Mika Häkkinen's McLaren, the Finn talking in terms of 'a much improved chassis balance which enabled us to make the car considerably quicker'.

To be frank, viewed from the roll-bar-mounted camera, Häkkinen's quick lap looked luridly precarious compared with the rival Benetton and Ferrari. But you couldn't argue with the bare facts – Mika matched the level of Coulthard's day-to-day improvement by shaving half a second off his Friday best.

Blundell, whose car was fitted with a fresh Mercedes V10 after the Saturday morning session, also registered a 0.6s improvement to clinch tenth place in the final line-up. It was satisfactory, but not really good enough.

Meanwhile the Peugeot-engined Jordan 195s were benefiting from a new rear suspension set-up which had first been tried by the Silverstone squad's newly established test team at the Northampton circuit the previous Friday. Fitted to Rubens Barrichello's car on Friday morning, then also to Eddie Irvine's in time for first qualifying, it yielded appreciably enhanced rear-end grip.

Irvine slipped from sixth on Friday to eighth in the final order, spinning without damage in second qualifying. 'The car wasn't as good as yesterday,' shrugged Eddie. 'It was bad this morning – very nervous – and no better this afternoon. I'm not really sure why. It was hard work to drive anyway. As far as the spin was concerned, I just lost it – the engine can be a bit peaky when you put the power down and it caught me a bit by surprise.'

Rubens wound up ninth, losing time with a broken electrical wire on the first day, then crashing heavily on Saturday morning when he lost downforce following too closely behind one of the Fortis on a particularly bumpy section of the circuit. The rear end of the Brazilian's car was quite badly damaged, so the whole rear end of the spare 195 – complete with revised suspension – was grafted on in time for final qualifying. Under the circumstances, Barrichello did a very respectable job.

'Our car was quite critical over the bumps and it snapped to oversteer,' said Rubens. 'The car was quite badly damaged and the boys did a really good job to fix it so quickly.'

Behind Blundell, Olivier Panis was slightly disappointed to have netted only 11th in his Ligier-Mugen, but at least he was immediately ahead of Heinz-Harald Frentzen's Sauber C14 and Gianni Morbidelli's Footwork-Hart. The Italian lost second gear in Friday qualifying, but improved on the second day, in contrast to team-mate Taki Inoue, who lost gearbox hydraulic pressure and didn't run during the final hour.

Brundle was certainly not satisfied with 14th place on the grid, while Mika Salo and Ukyo Katayama again had a fraught time with the Tyrrell-Yamahas, both men finding the cars extremely difficult over the bumps and each having a spin in second qualifying. Ukyo was

Left: Mika Häkkinen's wildly optimistic attempt to dive inside Johnny Herbert's Benetton at the old pits hairpin eliminated them both on the first lap of the race.

With many of the leading runners sidelined by accidents, Gianni Morbidelli was able to pick up a valuable point for Footwork-Hart.

able to continue, but Mika ended up with his rear wheels firmly embedded in a gravel trap and went no further. It was a disappointing reward for the team's mechanics, who had completed an amazing 35-minute engine change on Salo's car between sessions!

Pierluigi Martini's Minardi was 17th ahead of a frustrated Jean-Christophe Boullion. The Frenchman's Sauber suffered a gearbox problem on Saturday morning, causing the engine to over-rev inadvertently and thus requiring the installation of a fresh Zetec-R V8 in time for second qualifying. Boullion found Frentzen's chassis settings not quite to his liking and felt he hadn't come close to doing himself justice.

Luca Badoer's Minardi claimed 19th place after its spin, while the Pacifics of Bertrand Gachot and Andrea Montermini were next up, trailed only by the hapless Inoue and the Forti Corse duo.

The race morning warm-up took place in torrential rain and Hill finished the half-hour session feeling pretty desperate. He suffered a gearbox problem with his race car and a sticking throttle which sent the spare FW17 sailing into a gravel trap. 'On this showing we'll finish 12th,' he shrugged. 'We're completely out of it.'

Damon ended the session a dismal 16th fastest with Alesi comfortably heading the times from Barrichello, Berger and Schumacher. Herbert spun off and broke his Benetton's gearbox oil cooler, while Irvine had fuel pressure problems, but both McLaren drivers reported that their MP4/10Bs felt quite good in the sodden conditions.

Happily, the rain stopped and the track was virtually dry in time for the start, but during the immediate pre-race warm-up laps, Blundell spun off and stalled his race car. This forced Mark to start in the spare McLaren which was set up for Häkkinen, so he had a slight disadvantage even before he took his place on the grid.

With Hill lining up on the right-hand side of the track, one might have been forgiven for thinking that he was better placed to take an immediate lead through the first long right-hander which leads into the braking area for a tight left, but Schumacher had that prospect well covered in his own mind. At the moment the green lights came on, the Benetton edged over to the right as it accelerated away from the grid, very firmly squeezing Hill's Williams into second place.

Everybody shuffled through the first turn intact and Michael came slamming through at the end of the opening lap with over a second in hand over his adversary. Coulthard was third ahead of Berger and Alesi, with Barrichello and Irvine next up. Already missing were Häkkinen's McLaren and Herbert's Benetton, the Finn having rammed his English rival at the far hairpin, a little over a mile from the start.

Johnny was fit to be tied. 'I am obviously extremely angry,' he said. 'I had made a good start, managed to get ahead of Alesi, then he managed to overtake me but I was quite happy with sixth place at that stage.

'I had what I thought was a nice gap behind me, then coming into the hairpin, Mika appeared from nowhere. He braked so late that the only way he was going to get round the corner properly was to hit me, which is exactly what he did. I thought I could have got out of it and was trying very hard, but we were interlocked and no matter what I did, we were stuck together. Anyway, the engine eventually stalled.'

Häkkinen, meanwhile, put a soft-focus innocence on his interpretation of events: 'As I entered the hairpin, trying to overtake Herbert on the inside, I braked late, but not too hard, otherwise I would have locked the wheels. Unfortunately, the track was damp at that spot and when Herbert started sliding in front of me, I couldn't avoid making contact with him.'

CANADIAN GRAND PRIX

Left: Martin Brundle lost fifth place when Gerhard Berger put two wheels on the grass in a desperate attempt to pass the Ligier and succeeded only in taking them both out of the race.

Right: Over-enthusiastic fans pour onto the track at the finish to celebrate Alesi's victory as the unfortunate Michael Schumacher trails back to the pits behind the Ligier of Olivier Panis, having narrowly failed to wrest fourth place from the Frenchman at the flag.

Below right: Rubens Barrichello *(left)* and Eddie Irvine took second and third places for Jordan after reliable runs to give the team its best result yet.

On the second lap, Coulthard spun wildly approaching the final ess-bend on the outward leg, just as Alesi ducked inside Berger. 'I lost the car under braking,' he explained frankly. 'It was just a combination of the car being difficult there all weekend and also I was under pressure from the Ferraris. I left my braking to the limit, went beyond it, hit a bump and lost the car. Even then I hoped that I could just spin and continue, but I tagged the gravel trap and that was that.'

By lap four, Schumacher was 4.2s ahead of Hill, with Alesi and Berger third and fourth ahead of the two Jordans. Frentzen was up to seventh in his Sauber ahead of Ligier twins Panis and Brundle. Damon was clearly struggling to keep pace with Schumacher and also starting to lose ground to the pursuing Ferraris, which would be scrambling all over his Williams by the end of lap six.

Further back down the field, the inevitable spate of jump-starters were coming in to take their ten-second stop-go medicine. These included both Tyrrell drivers, whose cars crept forward slightly as Katayama and Salo selected first gear, and Martini, who would later prove himself to be as much of a nuisance as ever when it came to letting the faster competitors lap his Minardi.

Montermini's trailing Pacific was out with gearbox hydraulic problems as early as lap six, after which there followed a 14-lap stint without any retirements. Meanwhile Hill was gradually worn down by Alesi and the Ferrari eventually slipped by into second place under braking for the first-gear hairpin on lap 17.

Berger had been keeping up with Alesi, but lost two seconds trying to get past Martini – a transgression which earned the Italian a ten-second stop-go penalty for blocking. Rightly so, most people thought, but that didn't prevent Giancarlo Minardi from issuing a highly indignant press release on the matter at the end of the race.

By lap 23, Schumacher was cruising round confidently 10.9s ahead of Alesi with Hill, still struggling for balance, battling to keep ahead of Berger. On lap 26, Gerhard duly went through into third place, and quickly edged away from the Williams.

A lap later Frentzen, who had been maintaining a constant gap to the Jordans, retired from seventh place when his engine cut out. Boullion was by then long gone, having spun into a gravel trap on lap 20 after putting a wheel in the dirt as he battled with Badoer's Minardi well down the field.

The Canadian race has always been extremely marginal on fuel consumption, with the Ferraris and Jordans in this case balanced on a knife-edge. The Ferraris planned to refuel as close to half-distance as possible, and it was agreed before the start that whichever car was ahead as they approached the race's midway point would come in on lap 34, followed by his team-mate next time round. Moreover, safety modifications to the FIA-supplied refuelling rigs, reducing the flow rate from 12 to 10 litres per second, would ensure that the pit stops were slightly longer all told.

Had Berger not been jumped by Alesi when Coulthard spun in front of them both early on, the Austrian would have had priority. As it was, Alesi made a 16.7s stop on lap 34, briefly promoting Berger to second, but Gerhard ran low on fuel and only just managed to stagger into the pit lane at walking pace when it came to his turn on lap 35.

The problem had been caused by a minor inaccuracy with the cockpit instrument display, but that was no consolation for Gerhard as he trailed back into the race now eighth between the two Ligiers. With all his rivals delayed or in disarray, Schumacher was now able to make a neat 12.9s stop on lap 38, rejoining with his lead intact.

Now it was Alesi, Hill, Barrichello and Irvine chasing the lead Benetton, but the Jordans gained further promotion when Damon rolled to a halt in front of the pits at the end of lap 51. 'We weren't competitive today, the car was not good to drive and finally we had a hydraulic problem,' he shrugged. 'I was stuck in fifth and then I lost the throttle. The car was handling badly so now we have got to go testing to see what we can do.'

Three laps earlier, the sole surviving McLaren-Mercedes dropped from ninth place when Blundell pulled up out on the circuit with an engine failure later attributed to a piston heat treatment problem.

Meanwhile, both Jordan drivers were also worried about their cars' fuel consumption – Eddie Irvine in particular. They had been told to lean off their fuel mixture early in the race, but Eddie turned it the wrong way to a richer setting, which he ran for ten laps before realising his mistake. From that point on, he had to pussyfoot his way back from a potentially parlous consumption condition, which at least took the heat off Barrichello in the closing stages of the race.

Suddenly, on lap 58, Schumacher was seen to slow up. His Benetton had jammed in third gear and, as he made for the pit lane, Alesi surged by into the lead.

The Benetton's GCU was going haywire trying to change gear even though it was jammed in third, but when Michael switched off the engine the problem cleared itself. The Benetton was restarted, but he immediately reported that the throttle seemed inoperative. Due to the high operating temperatures, the hydraulic pressure controlling this and the gearchange mechanism was taking longer than usual to build up, but when he switched off and restarted for a second time, all was well.

'I had been running second when, suddenly, as I came out of the last hairpin, I saw Schumacher's car on the big [television] screen,' said Alesi later. 'He was in the pits and they were taking off the steering wheel. I hardly dared to hope, but then the team came on the radio and told me he was out.

'With ten laps to go, I knew I could win – and I started to cry in the car. Every time I braked, my tears were hitting the visor. For about a lap I felt a bit disorientated, but then I said to myself "now you have to get back to driving" and after that I was OK.'

In fact, Schumacher was most certainly not out of the equation. The Benetton stormed back into the race in seventh place and Michael immediately began to set a row of fastest race laps. He was then handed a two-place bonus when Berger, uncharacteristically at the end of his tether, tried an absurdly ambitious overtaking manoeuvre on Martin Brundle's Ligier in an effort to wrest fifth place with only eight laps to go.

Berger put his Ferrari inside Brundle's car at impossible speed going into the first turn. 'I braked too late and got two wheels on the grass, so I couldn't slow down any more,' explained Gerhard, adding with masterful understatement, 'This has been a very bad day for me.'

Brundle certainly echoed those sentiments, as well as wondering what the hell Gerhard thought he was about. 'From the inside of the car, I didn't exactly understand what happened when Berger tried his ambitious manoeuvre,' he said dryly.

'I had kept well to the left all the way down the straight and didn't leave the slightest gap for him. I saw him in my mirror as we braked, then lost sight of him before spinning off.

'He was a bit out of order and just came across the grass and mounted me. I had better traction and he was quicker under braking.

'That was a real shame. I got off to a terrific start and made no mistakes, although I did struggle a bit with the heavier fuel load after refuelling. I must also have lost about eight seconds during the two laps before my stop due to traffic and other cars coming out of the pits. Then the car improved considerably as the weight came off and I was able to contain Berger. It was just a pity it all had to end the way it did.'

Thus they ran through to the finish, with Alesi easing back to win by just over half a minute from the delighted Jordan duo, Irvine following his team-mate across the line by less than a second. It was a measure of the popularity of the result that every team's pit crew was on the wall cheering madly as Jean came out of the final corner and accelerated up to the chequered flag.

Schumacher just failed to catch Panis for fourth place, by which time the enthusiasm of the crowd had run badly out of control and fans spilled out over the spectator fences onto the circuit, particularly around the start/finish line. Salo, heading for seventh place behind Gianni Morbidelli's Footwork, stopped within sight of the flag to avoid running down a large swathe of the paying public, but Badoer – who came from 50 seconds down – had no such reservations and charged past to displace the stationary Tyrrell.

The stewards rightly thought this was a very poor show and the results were subsequently amended to show the race order finalised at 68 laps – which put Badoer back into eighth place where he morally belonged.

Meanwhile, Alesi had stopped his Ferrari on the slowing-down lap, not because he was out of fuel but because, he said, he wanted to see the fans. Beaming broadly, he eventually took a lift back to the rostrum on the back of Schumacher's Benetton.

'I'm happy for Jean,' said the World Champion. 'Your first win, on your birthday, is special and well deserved by Jean. I couldn't have given him a better present!'

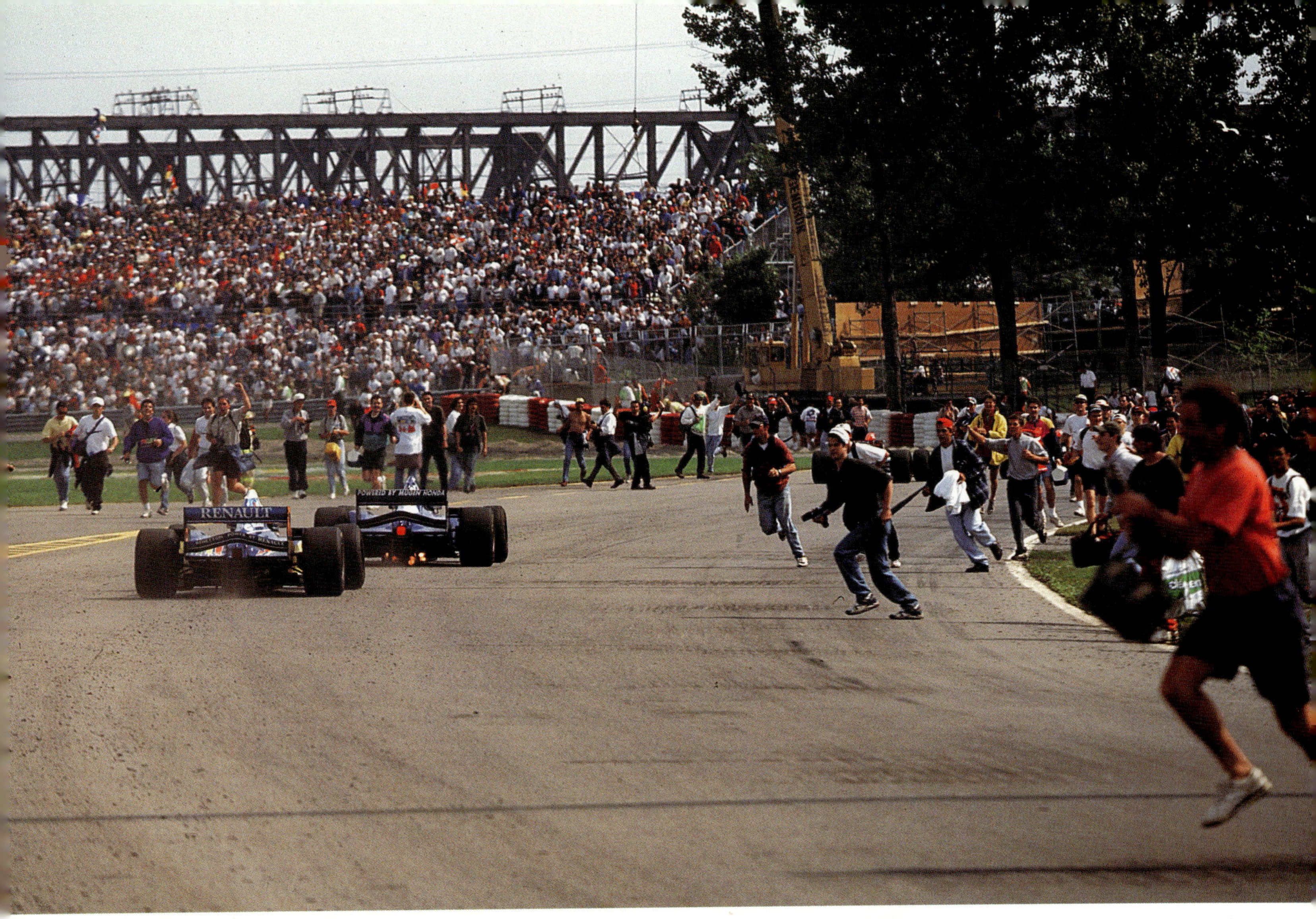
RENAULT
POWERED BY MUGEN HONDA

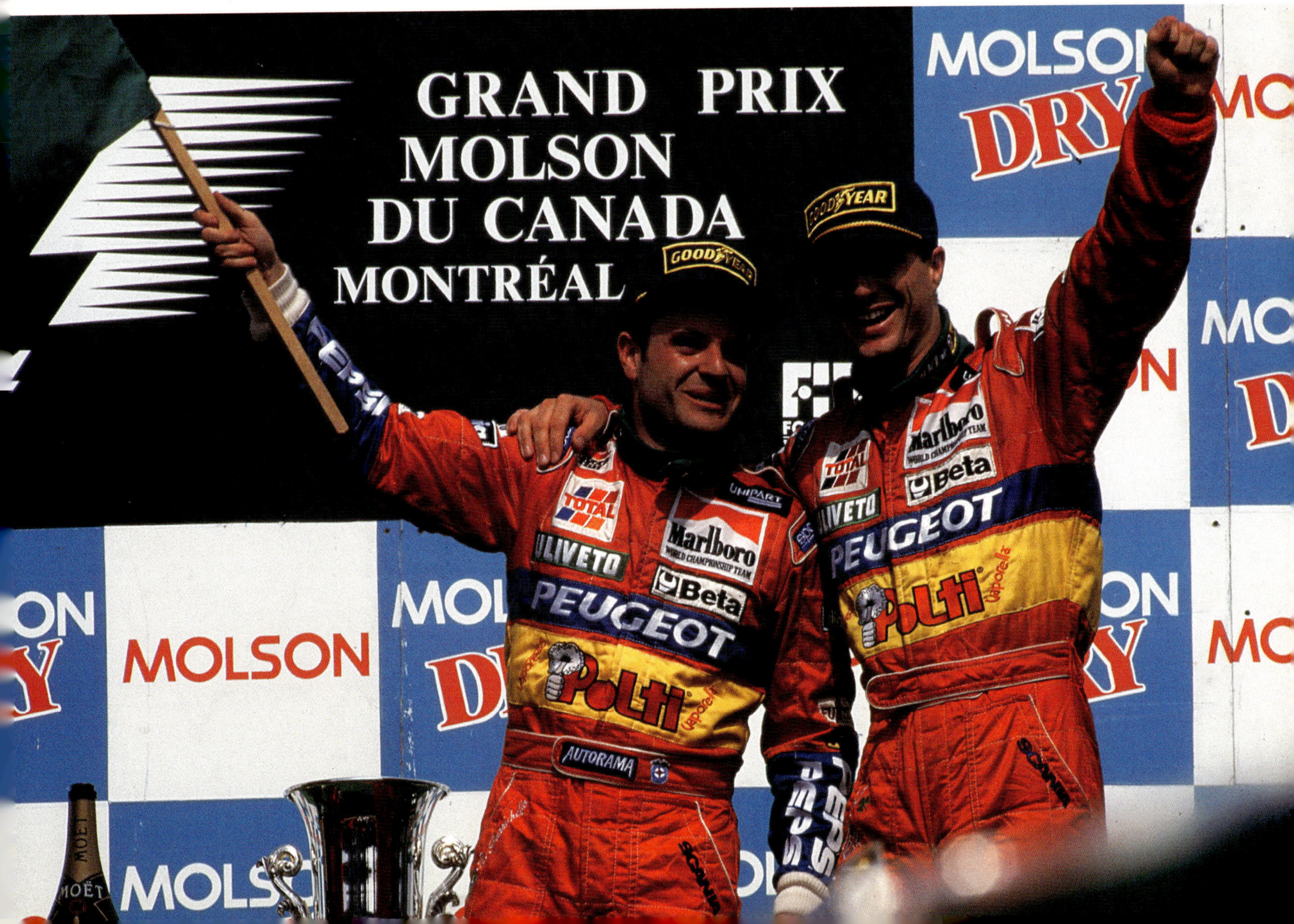
GRAND PRIX
MOLSON
DU CANADA
MONTRÉAL
MOLSON
DRY
MOLSON
GOODYEAR
TOTAL
Marlboro
ULIVETO
PEUGEOT
Beta
Polti
AUTORAMA

FIA FORMULA ONE WORLD CHAMPIONSHIP ROUND 6

GRAND PRIX MOLSON DU CANADA

MONTREAL
9-11 JUNE 1995

Race distance: 69 laps, 189.934 miles/305.670 km
(Official result declared after 68 laps)
Race weather: Cloudy, bright, dry

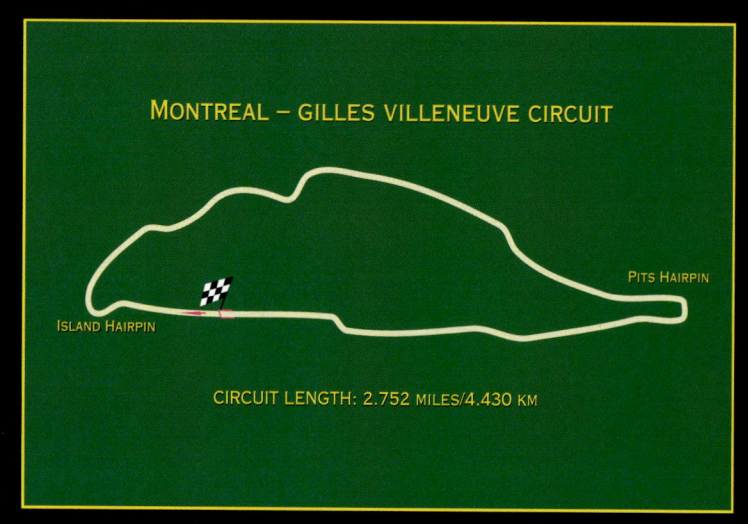

MONTREAL – GILLES VILLENEUVE CIRCUIT

CIRCUIT LENGTH: 2.752 MILES/4.430 KM

Place	Driver	Nat.	No.	Entrant	Car/Engine	Laps	Time/Retirement	Speed (mph/km/h)
1	**Jean Alesi**	F	27	Scuderia Ferrari	Ferrari 412T2 044 V12	68	1h 44m 54.171s	107.059/172.296
2	**Rubens Barrichello**	BR	14	Total Jordan Peugeot	Jordan 195-Peugeot A10 V10	68	1h 45m 25.648s	106.527/171.439
3	**Eddie Irvine**	GB	15	Total Jordan Peugeot	Jordan 195-Peugeot A10 V10	68	1h 45m 30.151s	106.451/171.317
4	**Olivier Panis**	F	26	Ligier Gitanes Blondes	Ligier JS41-Mugen Honda MF301 V10	68	1h 45m 35.485s	106.361/171.173
5	**Michael Schumacher**	D	1	Mild Seven Benetton Renault	Benetton B195-Renault RS7 V10	68	1h 45m 38.847s	106.305/171.082
6	**Gianni Morbidelli**	I	9	Footwork Hart	Footwork FA16-Hart 830 V8	67		
7	Mika Salo	SF	4	Nokia Tyrrell Yamaha	Tyrrell 023-Yamaha OX10C	67		
8	Luca Badoer	I	24	Minardi Scuderia Italia	Minardi M195-Ford EDM V8	67		
9	Taki Inoue	J	10	Footwork Hart	Footwork FA16-Hart 830 V8	66		
	Martin Brundle	GB	25	Ligier Gitanes Blondes	Ligier JS41-Mugen Honda MF301 V10	61	Collision with Berger	
	Gerhard Berger	A	28	Scuderia Ferrari	Ferrari 412T2 044 V12	61	Collision with Brundle	
	Pierluigi Martini	I	23	Minardi Scuderia Italia	Minardi M195-Ford EDM V8	60	Throttle	
	Roberto Moreno	BR	22	Parmalat Forti Ford	Forti FG01-Ford ED V8	54	Blocked fuel line	
	Damon Hill	GB	5	Rothmans Williams Renault	Williams FW17-Renault RS7 V10	50	Gearbox	
	Mark Blundell	GB	7	Marlboro McLaren Mercedes	McLaren MP4/10B-Mercedes FO110 V10	47	Engine	
	Ukyo Katayama	J	3	Nokia Tyrrell Yamaha	Tyrrell 023-Yamaha OX10C V10	42	Engine	
	Bertrand Gachot	F	16	Pacific Grand Prix Ltd	Pacific PR02-Ford ED V8	36	Battery	
	Heinz-Harald Frentzen	D	30	Red Bull Sauber Ford	Sauber C14-Ford Zetec-R V8	26	Engine	
	Pedro Diniz	BR	21	Parmalat Forti Ford	Forti FG01-Ford ED V8	26	Gearbox	
	Jean-Christophe Boullion	F	29	Red Bull Sauber Ford	Sauber C14-Ford Zetec-R V8	19	Spun off	
	Andrea Montermini	I	17	Pacific Grand Prix Ltd	Pacific PR02-Ford ED V8	5	Gearbox	
	David Coulthard	GB	6	Rothmans Williams Renault	Williams FW17-Renault RS7 V10	1	Spun off	
	Johnny Herbert	GB	2	Mild Seven Benetton Renault	Benetton B195-Renault RS7 V10	0	Collision with Häkkinen	
	Mika Häkkinen	SF	8	Marlboro McLaren Mercedes	McLaren MP4/10B-Mercedes FO110 V10	0	Collision with Herbert	

Fastest lap: Schumacher, on lap 67, 1m 29.174s, 111.126 mph/178.841 km/h.
Lap record: Michael Schumacher (F1 Benetton B194-Ford V8), 1m 28.927s, 111.937 mph/180.147 km/h (1994).

All cars used Goodyear tyres

All results and data © FIA 1995

STARTING GRID

1 SCHUMACHER (1m 27.661s) Benetton	5 HILL (1m 28.039s) Williams
6 COULTHARD (1m 28.091s) Williams	28 BERGER (1m 28.189s) Ferrari
27 ALESI (1m 28.474s) Ferrari	2 HERBERT (1m 28.498s) Benetton
8 HÄKKINEN (1m 28.910s) McLaren	15 IRVINE (1m 29.021s) Jordan
14 BARRICHELLO (1m 29.171s) Jordan	7 BLUNDELL (1m 29.641s) McLaren
26 PANIS (1m 29.809s) Ligier	30 FRENTZEN (1m 30.017s) Sauber
9 MORBIDELLI (1m 30.159s) Footwork	25 BRUNDLE (1m 30.255s) Ligier
4 SALO (1m 30.657s) Tyrrell	3 KATAYAMA (1m 31.382s) Tyrrell
23 MARTINI (1m 31.445s) Minardi	29 BOULLION (1m 31.838s) Sauber
24 BADOER (1m 31.853s) Minardi	16 GACHOT (1m 32.841s) Pacific
17 MONTERMINI (1m 32.894s) Pacific	10 INOUE (1m 32.995s) Footwork
22 MORENO (1m 34.000s) Forti	21 DINIZ (1m 34.982s) Forti

FOR THE RECORD

First Grand Prix win
Jean Alesi
50th Grand Prix start
Mark Blundell

TIME SHEETS

Friday free practice
Bright and breezy

Pos.	Driver	Laps	Time
1	Michael Schumacher	23	1m 28.145s
2	Jean Alesi	23	1m 28.487s
3	Damon Hill	20	1m 29.281s
4	David Coulthard	20	1m 29.537s
5	Mika Häkkinen	21	1m 29.641s
6	Rubens Barrichello	18	1m 29.798s
7	Eddie Irvine	21	1m 29.878s
8	Olivier Panis	19	1m 30.134s
9	Johnny Herbert	16	1m 30.175s
10	Gianni Morbidelli	20	1m 30.429s
11	Martin Brundle	23	1m 30.588s
12	Mark Blundell	18	1m 30.689s
13	Ukyo Katayama	21	1m 30.895s
14	Gerhard Berger	3	1m 30.991s
15	Heinz-Harald Frentzen	20	1m 31.265s
16	Mika Salo	23	1m 31.484s
17	Jean-Christophe Boullion	23	1m 31.923s
18	Pierluigi Martini	21	1m 32.201s
19	Luca Badoer	20	1m 33.161s
20	Andrea Montermini	22	1m 33.829s
21	Roberto Moreno	22	1m 35.036s
22	Taki Inoue	23	1m 35.188s
23	Bertrand Gachot	7	1m 35.834s
24	Pedro Diniz	18	1m 37.990s

Saturday free practice
Bright and cool

Pos.	Driver	Laps	Time
1	Damon Hill	22	1m 28.691s
2	Jean Alesi	22	1m 28.812s
3	Gerhard Berger	16	1m 28.887s
4	Michael Schumacher	22	1m 29.068s
5	Mika Häkkinen	21	1m 29.070s
6	Johnny Herbert	23	1m 29.097s
7	David Coulthard	17	1m 29.285s
8	Heinz-Harald Frentzen	23	1m 30.092s
9	Rubens Barrichello	13	1m 30.164s
10	Eddie Irvine	19	1m 30.406s
11	Mark Blundell	23	1m 30.439s
12	Martin Brundle	23	1m 30.627s
13	Gianni Morbidelli	11	1m 30.854s
14	Ukyo Katayama	20	1m 31.082s
15	Mika Salo	13	1m 31.763s
16	Pierluigi Martini	23	1m 31.831s
17	Luca Badoer	22	1m 32.142s
18	Jean-Christophe Boullion	15	1m 32.457s
19	Taki Inoue	20	1m 32.813s
20	Bertrand Gachot	23	1m 33.169s
21	Olivier Panis	8	1m 33.397s
22	Andrea Montermini	22	1m 33.683s
23	Roberto Moreno	23	1m 36.317s
24	Pedro Diniz	18	1m 36.851s

Friday qualifying
Sunny and bright

Pos.	Driver	Laps	Time
1	**Michael Schumacher**	**11**	**1m 27.661s**
2	**Damon Hill**	**12**	**1m 28.039s**
3	Gerhard Berger	9	1m 28.247s
4	Jean Alesi	8	1m 28.525s
5	David Coulthard	12	1m 28.590s
6	**Eddie Irvine**	**12**	**1m 29.021s**
7	Johnny Herbert	9	1m 29.295s
8	Rubens Barrichello	10	1m 29.393s
9	Mika Häkkinen	9	1m 29.406s
10	**Olivier Panis**	**10**	**1m 29.809s**
11	Mark Blundell	12	1m 30.279s
12	Heinz-Harald Frentzen	12	1m 30.285s
13	**Mika Salo**	**12**	**1m 30.657s**
14	Gianni Morbidelli	11	1m 30.854s
15	Martin Brundle	5	1m 30.880s
16	Pierluigi Martini	12	1m 31.859s
17	Jean-Christophe Boullion	12	1m 31.925s
18	Ukyo Katayama	6	1m 31.958s
19	Luca Badoer	12	1m 32.453s
20	**Taki Inoue**	**12**	**1m 32.995s**
21	Bertrand Gachot	12	1m 33.866s
22	Andrea Montermini	9	1m 33.910s
23	**Roberto Moreno**	**12**	**1m 34.000s**
24	Pedro Diniz	7	1m 36.187s

Saturday qualifying
Bright and warm

Pos.	Driver	Laps	Time
1	Michael Schumacher	10	1m 27.708s
2	**David Coulthard**	**12**	**1m 28.091s**
3	**Gerhard Berger**	**12**	**1m 28.189s**
4	**Jean Alesi**	**12**	**1m 28.474s**
5	**Johnny Herbert**	**12**	**1m 28.498s**
6	Damon Hill	11	1m 28.552s
7	**Mika Häkkinen**	**12**	**1m 28.910s**
8	**Rubens Barrichello**	**12**	**1m 29.171s**
9	Eddie Irvine	9	1m 29.259s
10	**Mark Blundell**	**12**	**1m 29.641s**
11	**Heinz-Harald Frentzen**	**11**	**1m 30.017s**
12	**Gianni Morbidelli**	**12**	**1m 30.159s**
13	**Martin Brundle**	**11**	**1m 30.255s**
14	Olivier Panis	11	1m 30.345s
15	Mika Salo	11	1m 30.695s
16	**Ukyo Katayama**	**12**	**1m 31.382s**
17	**Pierluigi Martini**	**11**	**1m 31.445s**
18	**Jean-Christophe Boullion**	**12**	**1m 31.838s**
19	**Luca Badoer**	**11**	**1m 31.853s**
20	**Bertrand Gachot**	**12**	**1m 32.841s**
21	**Andrea Montermini**	**12**	**1m 32.894s**
22	**Pedro Diniz**	**12**	**1m 34.982s**
23	Roberto Moreno	3	1m 35.559s
	Taki Inoue	0	no time

Warm-up
Torrential rain

Pos.	Driver	Laps	Time
1	Jean Alesi	15	1m 50.363s
2	Rubens Barrichello	11	1m 50.620s
3	Gerhard Berger	12	1m 51.805s
4	Michael Schumacher	14	1m 51.844s
5	Mika Häkkinen	12	1m 52.370s
6	Heinz-Harald Frentzen	11	1m 53.202s
7	Jean-Christophe Boullion	14	1m 53.444s
8	Luca Badoer	13	1m 53.462s
9	Mark Blundell	13	1m 53.761s
10	Johnny Herbert	12	1m 53.898s
11	Olivier Panis	13	1m 53.944s
12	David Coulthard	11	1m 54.586s
13	Martin Brundle	14	1m 54.755s
14	Mika Salo	13	1m 55.162s
15	Gianni Morbidelli	10	1m 55.985s
16	Damon Hill	9	1m 55.993s
17	Ukyo Katayama	12	1m 56.200s
18	Andrea Montermini	11	1m 57.665s
19	Bertrand Gachot	10	1m 59.980s
20	Pierluigi Martini	6	2m 00.145s
21	Taki Inoue	8	2m 03.906s
22	Roberto Moreno	7	2m 05.405s
23	Pedro Diniz	10	2m 08.923s
24	Eddie Irvine	3	2m 14.920s

Fastest race laps
Cloudy, bright and dry

Driver	Time	Lap
Michael Schumacher	1m 29.174s	67
Jean Alesi	1m 30.398s	33
Gerhard Berger	1m 30.491s	21
Rubens Barrichello	1m 30.626s	33
Damon Hill	1m 30.783s	9
Eddie Irvine	1m 30.874s	32
Heinz-Harald Frentzen	1m 31.155s	26
Martin Brundle	1m 31.496s	56
Mark Blundell	1m 31.527s	25
Olivier Panis	1m 31.654s	66
Gianni Morbidelli	1m 31.791s	31
Mika Salo	1m 32.153s	40
Ukyo Katayama	1m 32.435s	37
Pierluigi Martini	1m 32.855s	46
Jean-Christophe Boullion	1m 32.975s	13
Luca Badoer	1m 33.000s	15
Taki Inoue	1m 33.079s	31
Bertrand Gachot	1m 33.607s	21
Andrea Montermini	1m 35.588s	5
Roberto Moreno	1m 36.483s	51
Pedro Diniz	1m 38.055s	5
David Coulthard	1m 40.928s	1

CHASSIS LOG BOOK

1	Schumacher	Benetton B195/6
2	Herbert	Benetton B195/5
	spare	Benetton B195/1
3	Katayama	Tyrrell 023/4
4	Salo	Tyrrell 023/2
	spare	Tyrrell 023/3
5	Hill	Williams FW17/4
6	Coulthard	Williams FW17/5
	spare	Williams FW17/3
7	Blundell	McLaren MP4/10B/1
8	Häkkinen	McLaren MP4/10B/3
	spare	McLaren MP4/10B/2
9	Morbidelli	Footwork FA16/3
10	Inoue	Footwork FA16/2
14	Barrichello	Jordan 195/4
15	Irvine	Jordan 195/3
	spare	Jordan 195/1
16	Gachot	Pacific PR02/1
17	Montermini	Pacific PR02/2
21	Diniz	Forti FG01/3
22	Moreno	Forti FG01/2
	spare	Forti FG01/1
23	Martini	Minardi M195/3
24	Badoer	Minardi M195/2
	spare	Minardi M195/1
25	Brundle	Ligier JS41/5
26	Panis	Ligier JS41/4
	spare	Ligier JS41/2
27	Alesi	Ferrari 412T2/161
28	Berger	Ferrari 412T2/159
	spares	Ferrari 412T2/160 & 157
29	Boullion	Sauber C14/4
30	Frentzen	Sauber C14/3
	spare	Sauber C14/2

POINTS TABLES

Drivers

1	Michael Schumacher	36
2	Damon Hill	29
3	Jean Alesi	24
4	Gerhard Berger	17
5	Johnny Herbert	12
6	David Coulthard	9
7 =	Rubens Barrichello	6
7 =	Eddie Irvine	6
9	Mika Häkkinen	5
10 =	Heinz-Harald Frentzen	4
10 =	Olivier Panis	4
12	Mark Blundell	3
13	Gianni Morbidelli	1

Constructors

1	Ferrari	41
2	Benetton	38
3	Williams	32
4	Jordan	12
5	McLaren	8
6 =	Ligier	4
6 =	Sauber	4
8	Footwork	1

FRENCH GRAND PRIX

| SCHUMACHER |
| HILL |
| COULTHARD |
| BRUNDLE |
| ALESI |
| BARRICHELLO |

WORLD CHAMPIONSHIP • ROUND 7

Unable to match Damon Hill's pace in qualifying, Michael Schumacher slipped ahead of his rival during the first round of pit stops and controlled the race from the front thereafter.

FRENCH GRAND PRIX

Diary

Eddie Irvine raises eyebrows by describing the Silverstone circuit layout as 'atrocious' in the run-up to the British Grand Prix.

Ferrari confirms its new V10 Formula 1 engine is on schedule to have its first test in a chassis by September.

Gerhard Berger rumoured as a possible McLaren-Mercedes driver for 1996.

However you looked at it, Michael Schumacher and Benetton did a better job than Damon Hill and Williams when it came to their pit stop strategy in the French Grand Prix. Despite starting from pole position, Hill found himself 31.3s behind Schumacher at the chequered flag. With 7.8s of the World Champion's advantage seized at the first refuelling stop, the Williams squad was still left trying to work out where the 23.5s balance of Damon's overall deficit had been squandered.

Hill lost four crucial seconds among back-markers when Schumacher made his first pit stop, the Williams driver unable to come in on lap 20 as team-mate David Coulthard was already scheduled to arrive at that time.

Yet Hill's predictions of a Williams resurgence in France had seemed to be unfolding on course during first qualifying at the Circuit de Nevers when he and team-mate David Coulthard turned the contest for provisional pole into their own private battle.

Benefiting from significant suspension developments evaluated during test sessions at Barcelona and Silverstone during the three-week break since the Canadian GP, the Williams duo decisively kept the upper hand over Michael Schumacher's Benetton B195 in the sweltering 32-degree summer heat of central France.

According to the team's chief designer, Adrian Newey, the key to the FW17 handling breakthrough came when they tried a new wet-weather chassis set-up at Barcelona.

'That seemed to work pretty well,' he explained, 'so we adapted it for the dry and really started to make some progress. The whole process was mainly juggling with set-up, but we have got some aerodynamic changes – flick-ups ahead of the rear wheels and a revised diffuser – for this race.'

The end result was a major improvement in the FW17's slow-speed traction, its weakest area at Montreal, where Damon had really struggled off the pace.

'All the work we have done has improved the car, but we now have to put those changes to the test in the race,' said Hill. 'Renault have also provided us with a new-specification engine since Montreal, which will help us keep ahead of Ferrari, but not Schumacher, as Benetton, of course, use the same engines as us.

'It is obviously a very small margin because David is clearly keen to get a result – just as I was here last year against Mansell and in 1993 with Prost.'

Coulthard was feeling physically much fitter after an operation to remove his tonsils and reckoned that he might have beaten Hill to pole had it not been for a spectacular slide over the kerb at the tricky essbend just before the end of the lap.

'On my last run, I was ahead of Damon at the first two timing splits, but coming down to the last corner I ran wide,' he said. 'It's such a tight turn that I was thrown off-line and just couldn't get the power down.

'I feel we've made a lot of progress with the car, but it won't be until Sunday night that we really know whether or not those changes have worked.'

Despite this strong performance, the Williams drivers were reluctant to appear over-optimistic when assessing their race prospects. Schumacher finished first qualifying in third place, only 0.3s behind Coulthard, and was confident he could improve the handling of his car sufficiently to challenge for pole the following day.

For this race, the B195s shared the new Renault RS7B V10s used by Williams, as well as featuring revised airboxes and roll hoops, flick-ups ahead of the rear wheels and a modified front wing profile which had been evaluated exclusively by Schumacher at Silverstone the previous week.

The Ferrari 412T2s of Gerhard Berger and Canadian GP winner Jean Alesi finished the first day in fourth and fifth places, with Martin Brundle a very promising sixth in the Mugen-engined Ligier JS41, the French team celebrating its 300th Grand Prix outing at this race on its home circuit.

Further back, Johnny Herbert took eighth place after spinning his Benetton, Eddie Irvine 11th and Mark Blundell a frustrated 12th, battling handling problems with his McLaren MP4/10B.

Mika Häkkinen had a simply dreadful time in the other McLaren, losing the entire Friday morning free practice session with electronic problems which caused the gearchange mechanism to develop a mind of its own. A replacement gearbox and earlier-specification Mercedes V10 were installed for first qualifying – in which he used all three sets of tyres struggling to post tenth-fastest time. Late in the afternoon, Mika's car was loaded up and transported to the nearby Lurcy-Levis aerodrome where he ran for a couple of hours in the evening, enabling Ilmor to re-map his engine and check that all the electronic systems were working properly again.

Blundell's engine failure at the Canadian GP had been traced to incorrect heat treatment of the pistons, a fault which was confirmed after a subsequent failure at the Barcelona test. The problem had been duly rectified by Ilmor by the time the team arrived at Magny-Cours.

On Saturday afternoon the weather proved significantly cooler – air temperature dropped from 32 to around 27 degrees – which promised quicker lap times in second qualifying.

Hill was really confident after the Saturday morning free practice session. 'I was pretty pleased, the car felt magic,' he admitted. Then he went out to back up that contention by beating his Friday best with a 1m 17.878s midway through the session.

Schumacher responded with a 1m 17.512s, but Damon had the final say with a 1m 17.225s. Michael then waited until the final few minutes of the session in an effort to regain fastest time, but just failed after being balked momentarily by Häkkinen's McLaren.

Coulthard, meanwhile, was also into the 1m 17s bracket, qualifying third on 1m 17.925s with the admission that he had rather mistimed his runs. 'I didn't heat up my tyres sufficiently on my out lap,' he explained, 'and that caused me to lock up a couple of times going into the hairpin.'

However, Schumacher was clearly not happy. On Friday night it had become clear that the Goodyear technicians had inadvertently caused slow punctures to a total of five of Schumacher's tyres, and two of Herbert's, while they were in the process of taking their temperatures.

Even though Michael ended second qualifying with four fresh sets of rubber for race day, he did not look very pleased at all. Benetton asked the stewards whether Goodyear could replace the tyres, but the request was refused. Was this a big problem for Michael?

'At the moment, yes,' he replied curtly. 'The difficulty is that we don't have sufficient tyres for tomorrow. We can't run the old tyres because

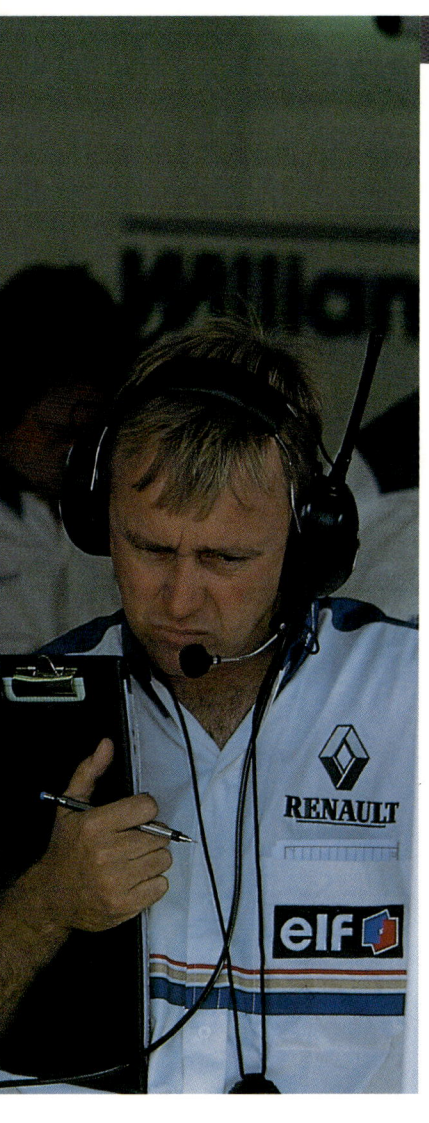

Left: Adrian Newey, Patrick Head and David Brown of Williams contemplate Damon Hill's narrow qualifying advantage and ponder their race strategy.

Below: Formula 1 veterans Tyler Alexander and Jo Ramirez can never have dreamed that one day they would have to don drivers' overalls in order to perform their pit lane duties.

Right: Sealed with a kiss? Giancarlo Minardi was reminded that Ligier boss Flavio Briatore is a formidable adversary.

Minardi temporarily sidelined by engine dispute

The Minardi Scuderia Italia team was almost prevented from taking part in the French Grand Prix when Ligier team chief Flavio Briatore took legal action against it for the alleged non-payment of Cosworth Ford HB engine leasing fees incurred in 1993 and '94.

The outstanding debt was to an engine supply company in which Briatore had an interest. The Minardi transporter and motorhome were put under lock and key by the legal authorities on the Thursday prior to the French race and only the intervention of a local judge enabled the team to participate on Saturday and Sunday.

The Dublin-based Grand Prix Engineering company was believed to be claiming £2.1 million from Minardi for the two-year deal to use the Cosworth HB V8s which previously powered the 3.5-litre TWR-run Group C Jaguars. However, Minardi said he had offered £430,000 to settle the debt, this being the amount he calculated was outstanding for 1993 as he claimed there was no deal for '94. However, it was understood that Briatore declined the offer, insisting on full payment of the larger figure.

The matter was complicated by the fact that Minardi was at the time suing the Japanese Mugen company, claiming it had gone back on a deal with the Faenza team in order to supply its powerful V10 engines to Ligier instead. This involved Minardi in a lot of expense as a result of having to redesign its 1995 F1 challenger to accommodate a Cosworth ED V8 engine.

Sources close to Minardi claim that the team did indeed sign a contract with Mugen. However, it is believed that this was contingent on certain bank guarantees being provided by the Italian team. These were not forthcoming and the deal was never legally activated as a result.

However, F1 insiders believed that the situation was quite clear-cut. Briatore would call off his action if Minardi did the same. For the moment, however, it was difficult to see how the stalemate could be broken.

---

over a kerb in the closing moments of Friday qualifying. He then had a slight hydraulic leak on Saturday morning and finished up seventh in the final order. 'No set-up, no good lap,' he shrugged.

In the Jordan camp there was an 'Evolution 2' version of the Peugeot A10 engine available for the first time, and Rubens Barrichello was delighted to qualify fifth ahead of Olivier Panis's Ligier and Berger.

'The car and engine were just fine,' enthused the Brazilian. 'I think Canada helped; getting a good result there has enabled me to relax a lot more and I feel like everything is back to normal.'

By contrast, Eddie Irvine simply could not explain why he emerged six places behind his team-mate. 'It's a bit of a mystery to me,' he admitted. 'We tried all sorts of things this morning, and every time we found something good for one particular corner, it seemed to have an adverse effect on another.'

Panis did an excellent job on Ligier's home circuit to show the Mugen V10 engine in a truly competitive light, even though the Frenchman confessed he didn't have a perfect chassis set-up for second qualifying.

By contrast, Martin Brundle crashed heavily at the long right-hander after the pits on his first lap in Saturday qualifying, thereafter being forced to wait until Panis had completed his quota of laps and he was able to take over the Frenchman's JS41. He slipped to ninth, unable to match his Friday best.

'It was all very frustrating,' said Martin. 'I got caught out by a slight crosswind. The car had been understeering at that point throughout the weekend and this time it just snapped round on me and swapped ends. I only just tapped the barrier, but that was it.'

Häkkinen vaulted from 11th to eighth in the closing moments of the session, taking full advantage of the cooler conditions, while Blundell had to be satisfied with 13th after an engine failure in the Saturday morning free practice session.

Johnny Herbert finished up a disappointed tenth, complaining of his Benetton's acute lack of grip, but Heinz-Harald Frentzen was encouraged by the performance of his Sauber C14 on his way to 12th, even though the crosswinds adversely affected its handling.

Mika Salo did a superb job to take 14th in the Tyrrell-Yamaha ahead of

we risk a problem. Because of the tyre situation, we can't make any more changes. We all know what happens when tyres explode.'

Under the circumstances, it was perhaps understandable that Michael's sense of humour stalled in the fast lane when Damon suggested that Williams might be generous enough to let him have some of its own worn rubber!

In fact, the Benetton team fully understood the dilemma the stewards faced in this situation and it was eventually agreed in principle that the team could have extra tyres in the race in the event of a puncture in the race. Such an occurrence would have to be verified by FIA Technical Delegate Charlie Whiting, however, and since Benetton didn't want to give away its pit stop strategy in advance of the race, they explained that they might make up to three tyre stops, in which case they might need that provision in an emergency. In fact, Schumacher would stop only twice on his run to victory.

Jean Alesi wound up a distant and frustrated fourth overall after a troubled time on Saturday. He lost the morning session with a gearchange hydraulic pump failure and, when the car was retrieved, the team opted to change both engine and gearbox in time for second qualifying. The resultant set-up wasn't ideal, but he would start from the second row – with a time 1.5s slower than Hill's pole winner.

Berger's car had to be rebuilt overnight round a new monocoque after he'd damaged its underside

141

FRENCH GRAND PRIX

Boullion in the second Sauber, the Williams test driver gradually ridding himself of frustrating understeer.

Gianni Morbidelli was 16th ahead of Luca Badoer, the Minardis permitted to take part after missing Friday's sessions altogether as the Faenza team was embroiled in a legal dispute with Flavio Briatore (see sidebar). They competed on the strict condition that the team transporter and motorhome were re-sealed under the jurisdiction of the court in nearby Nevers immediately after the race.

Taki Inoue performed respectably to line up 18th in the Footwork, one place ahead of Ukyo Katayama, who complained of poor handling balance after losing much of the morning session with an engine problem.

Pierluigi Martini lined up 20th ahead of Andrea Montermini, the best-placed Pacific driver having lost time with a broken front wishbone and gearbox failure on Saturday morning, while Gachot and the slow Fortis duly completed the grid.

The race morning warm-up started in heavy rain, but unlike Imola and Montreal, where Hill had been dismayed at the FW17's wet-weather feel, he was delighted with its set-up on this occasion. Even so, he made a premature switch to slicks as the track surface began to dry out, paying the penalty with a spin into one of the gravel traps. Coulthard posted second-fastest time behind Alesi, so both Williams drivers faced the start in a highly optimistic frame of mind.

At the green light it was Damon who got away cleanly from pole, leaning into the first left-hander clearly ahead of Schumacher's Benetton, the World Champion weaving to prevent his being jumped by Alesi or Barrichello as they jostled into the first turn.

At the tail of the field, Katayama tangled with Inoue, both Japanese drivers being eliminated on the spot, while Diniz was also wiped from the equation in a collision with Martini's Minardi. Montermini was involved as well, the Pacific coming straight into the pits first time round to lose almost seven laps while mechanics replaced the upper left-rear wishbone and track control arm.

Down the long back straight, Hill was about three lengths ahead of the Benetton with Barrichello jinking from side to side of the circuit in the third-placed Jordan to keep Coulthard from pulling alongside. Rubens was using an early-specification Peugeot V10, installed after his latest 'Evo2' unit suffered a slight loss of pressure from its air valve system during the morning warm-up and had to be replaced. Further back, Häkkinen dropped from seventh to tenth after taking to the gravel to avoid Alesi.

At the end of the opening lap, Damon had 0.4s in hand over Schumacher, the Renault-engined duo already pulling away from Barrichello, while the frustrated Coulthard was left boxed in behind his old F3 rival and just ahead of Panis's Ligier.

On the third lap, Herbert – running in sixth – left the door a little too far open as he swung into the right-hander at the end of the back straight. Alesi dived down the inside, pitching the Englishman into retirement just as Häkkinen had done in Montreal.

To heighten Johnny's disappointment, he was adjudged to have jumped the start and found himself rewarded with a $10,000 penalty which had been suspended from the Canadian GP, where he had committed the same offence. The punishment was a little unfair, perhaps, as in Montreal he had not lasted long enough to come in for his scheduled stop-go penalty.

Herbert had the consolation of Martin Brundle speaking out in his defence. A month earlier, Alesi had complained that Brundle had caused him to crash at Monaco by spinning in front of him. Now he replied in the same vein.

'Jean left Johnny to decide whether he wanted to move off the race track or have an accident,' he said firmly. 'But you cannot do that. If the guy is turning into a corner ahead of you, you cannot just put your car in a position where you are expecting him to decide whether he is going to give way or you are both going to have an accident.'

Barrichello's start had also been just a little too quick, but it wasn't until the end of lap nine that the Brazilian's ten-second stop-go penalty was made public. A similar penalty was incurred by Panis, so the Jordan and Ligier came in nose-to-tail at the end of lap 11 to receive their medicine. They resumed in ninth and tenth, leaving Coulthard's Williams in third place, six seconds shy of the leaders, and the Scot with his hands full fending off Brundle's Ligier.

There was now absolutely nothing to choose between Schumacher and Hill, Damon really under pressure from lap three onwards once Michael had got into his stride. On lap 13 there was almost a nasty moment as Hill, having eased off slightly as he came up to lap Moreno's Forti, was caught too quickly by the Benetton, which almost touched the rear of the FW17. At the time, it just seemed like a racing incident to be shrugged aside, but Michael would later increase the temperature of his rivalry with Hill by his references to the subject in his subsequent conversations with the German media.

'I was very angry with Damon,' he said. 'But I am not speaking to him about it until we have cooled off – maybe at a quiet moment later in the week. He seemed to lift off, or maybe even brake a little, and that was wrong. It was dangerous and unsporting. If he does it again, I know what to do with him.'

Whether that pay-off line represented a veiled threat to push Hill off the next time such an incident occurred was not really clear, but Damon handled the situation with characteristic dignity. Later in the week following the race he curtly dismissed complaints that he had in any way behaved in an unsporting manner.

FRENCH GRAND PRIX

David Coulthard takes the chequered flag ahead of the Ligier of Martin Brundle to clinch third place by less than half a second. Their hard-fought battle was the highlight of a largely disappointing race.

'Michael is a great driver and he is more than capable of looking after himself on the race track,' he stated firmly. 'I think he misjudged the manoeuvre in question on lap 13 and gave himself a bit of a fright. If he wants to talk to me about it then I will be more than happy to do so.'

Schumacher kept up the pressure until his first refuelling stop at the end of lap 19 and, when Hill came in after another two laps during which he was held up by slower traffic, the Williams team leader found himself resuming 7.8s down in second place.

'In those early stages, Michael's car seemed to be better under braking and he was lunging for the gaps,' said Damon after the race. 'Just before I came into the pits I lost a bit of time behind some slower cars, but even so, once he was ahead, there was nothing I could do.

'I was pushing as hard as I could to maintain the gap and hoping he was on a three-stop strategy, but that wasn't what actually happened. I am mystified because my car was really good in qualifying and I don't really understand why that form evaporated. It was pretty frustrating.

'Naturally, Michael has extended his points lead, but there is a long way to go and I still think the championship is wide open. I would like to think that I would start winning again at Silverstone.'

In the run through to the second spate of refuelling stops, Hill dropped back even further. From 9.3s adrift of the Benetton on lap 25, he faded to 11.3s down on lap 31 and 15.7s down on lap 40. Damon made his second refuelling stop on lap 43, leaving the way clear for Schumacher to come in a second time on lap 47. Michael was able to resume with 7.8s in hand over his rival, opening the gap to just over half a minute by the chequered flag.

Just before his second stop, Damon found himself in something of a communications dilemma. The skies had clouded over and a few drops of rain were already falling, so Hill had some difficulty making it clear that he was coming in for fresh slicks, not rain tyres. Moreover, there wasn't much flexibility in Damon's schedule by this stage; he'd somehow been short-changed slightly at his first refuelling stop, so there was no question of delaying his second stop for another lap or two. Either way, Schumacher was already well out of reach.

In their wake, Gerhard Berger briefly got up to third before making his first refuelling stop at the end of lap 22. It proved to be an absolute disaster. The nozzle on the refuelling hose initially refused to engage with the car-mounted valve and the Ferrari was stationary for an agonising 53.7s before the whole procedure was finally completed, dropping him back to a hopeless 17th.

That put Brundle through to third place, the Ligier driver running a three-stop strategy which proved to be an ideal formula. He had stopped initially on lap 19, then refuelled again on lap 34, when Coulthard went back ahead. David made his second stop on lap 46, when Martin popped ahead again, but Coulthard emerged just in front after Brundle made his third stop at the end of lap 55.

From then on, all bets were off in the battle for third. Brundle's Ligier had a touch of understeer in the faster corners, but that didn't bother him at all. The JS41 was simply flying on its home circuit and Martin never put a wheel wrong. By contrast, Coulthard found himself saddled with acute understeer for much of the race which cost him a lot of time, particularly through the long right-hand curve after the pits. The team changed his tyre pressures at his second refuelling stop, but it made no significant difference.

David revealed that the previous night he had dreamt that he'd spun on the final corner of the race, but managed to keep his cool to scramble home third by 0.4s. Martin frankly admitted that he had toyed with the idea of a do-or-die lunge down the inside 'but figured that, if I hit him, there was no way I would make it to the finishing line'.

Brundle was well chuffed. 'We chose a three-stop strategy and I think I drove the whole race without making a single mistake. The car went perfectly and I needed a result like this!'

Alesi took fifth in a Ferrari which was now clearly outclassed by the latest Renault RS7B engine. The Maranello lads were simply off the pace, Jean and Gerhard having run seventh and eighth in the early stages after poor starts.

Berger, meanwhile, made short work of the tail-enders and cut back through the field to latch onto the tail of Blundell's 11th-placed McLaren. Despite pulling alongside and rubbing wheels on a couple of occasions, Gerhard simply couldn't get by the determined Blundell, who was almost certainly remembering the two occasions in 1993 when Berger put his Ligier off the road.

Before long, Alesi pulled up onto Berger's tail, ready to lap him, so Gerhard let Jean go ahead, hoping that he might perhaps be able to nip by as Mark made way for the faster car. As it was, Alesi had to bump wheels with Mark before he got ahead, but Berger had to stay behind in 12th right to the flag.

Behind Alesi and Barrichello, Häkkinen finished seventh in his McLaren while the penalised Panis wound up eighth ahead of Irvine, the Jordan driver troubled throughout the race with steering which felt as if it was on the verge of seizing up. In all, there were a total of 16 finishers in what had been an extremely processional seventh round of the World Championship.

Yet there was still no explanation as to why the Williams FW17's dominant qualifying form had not been translated into a winning display on race day. It was beginning to look as though Benetton's B195 had now decisively made up its early-season performance deficit. And Michael Schumacher was looking unbeatable.

143

FIA FORMULA ONE WORLD CHAMPIONSHIP ROUND 7

GRAND PRIX DE FRANCE

MAGNY-COURS
30 JUNE – 2 JULY 1995

Race distance: 72 laps, 190.139 miles/306.000 km
Race weather: Warm, sunny, some cloud

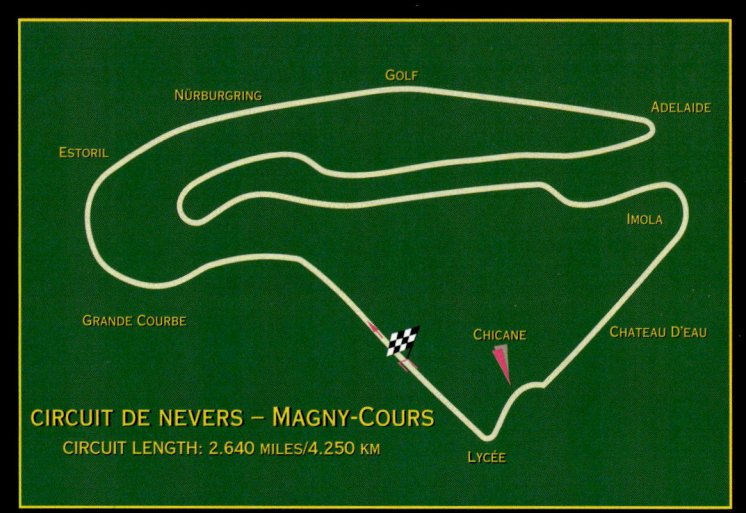

CIRCUIT DE NEVERS – MAGNY-COURS
CIRCUIT LENGTH: 2.640 miles/4.250 km

Place	Driver	Nat.	No.	Entrant	Car/Engine	Laps	Time/Retirement	Speed (mph/km/h)
1	**Michael Schumacher**	D	1	Mild Seven Benetton Renault	Benetton B195-Renault RS7B V10	72	1h 38m 28.429s	115.781/186.332
2	**Damon Hill**	GB	5	Rothmans Williams Renault	Williams FW17-Renault RS7B V10	72	1h 38m 59.738s	115.171/185.350
3	**David Coulthard**	GB	6	Rothmans Williams Renault	Williams FW17-Renault RS7B V10	72	1h 39m 31.255s	114.563/184.371
4	**Martin Brundle**	GB	25	Ligier Gitanes Blondes	Ligier JS41-Mugen Honda MF301 V10	72	1h 39m 31.722s	114.554/184.357
5	**Jean Alesi**	F	27	Scuderia Ferrari	Ferrari 412T2 044 V12	72	1h 39m 46.298s	114.275/183.908
6	Rubens Barrichello	BR	14	Total Jordan Peugeot	Jordan 195-Peugeot A10 V10	71		
7	Mika Häkkinen	SF	8	Marlboro McLaren Mercedes	McLaren MP4/10B-Mercedes FO110 V10	71		
8	Olivier Panis	F	26	Ligier Gitanes Blondes	Ligier JS41-Mugen Honda MF301 V10	71		
9	Eddie Irvine	GB	15	Total Jordan Peugeot	Jordan 195-Peugeot A10 V10	71		
10	Heinz-Harald Frentzen	D	30	Red Bull Sauber Ford	Sauber C14-Ford Zetec-R V8	71		
11	Mark Blundell	GB	7	Marlboro McLaren Mercedes	McLaren MP4/10B-Mercedes FO110 V10	70		
12	Gerhard Berger	A	28	Scuderia Ferrari	Ferrari 412T2 044 V12	70		
13	Luca Badoer	I	24	Minardi Scuderia Italia	Minardi M195-Ford EDM V8	69		
14	Gianni Morbidelli	I	9	Footwork Hart	Footwork FA16-Hart 830 V8	69		
15	Mika Salo	SF	4	Nokia Tyrrell Yamaha	Tyrrell 023-Yamaha OX10C V10	69		
16	Roberto Moreno	BR	22	Parmalat Forti Ford	Forti FG01-Ford ED V8	66		
NC	Andrea Montermini	I	17	Pacific Grand Prix Ltd	Pacific PR02-Ford ED V8	62		
	Jean-Christophe Boullion	F	29	Red Bull Sauber Ford	Sauber C14-Ford Zetec-R V8	48	Gearbox	
	Bertrand Gachot	F	16	Pacific Grand Prix Ltd	Pacific PR02-Ford ED V8	24	Gearbox	
	Pierluigi Martini	I	23	Minardi Scuderia Italia	Minardi M195-Ford EDM V8	23	Gearbox	
	Johnny Herbert	GB	2	Mild Seven Benetton Renault	Benetton B195-Renault RS7B V10	2	Collision with Alesi	
	Ukyo Katayama	J	3	Nokia Tyrrell Yamaha	Tyrrell 023-Yamaha OX10C V10	0	Collision with Inoue	
	Taki Inoue	J	10	Footwork Hart	Footwork FA16-Hart 830 V8	0	Collision with Katayama	
	Pedro Diniz	BR	21	Parmalat Forti Ford	Forti FG01-Ford ED V8	0	Collision with Martini	

Fastest lap: Schumacher, on lap 51, 1m 20.218s, 118.514 mph/190.730 km/h.
Lap record: Nigel Mansell (F1 Williams FW14B-Renault V10), 1m 17.070s, 123.355 mph/198.521 km/h (1992).

All cars used Goodyear tyres

All results and data © FIA 1995

STARTING GRID

1 SCHUMACHER (1m 17.512s) Benetton		**5 HILL** (1m 17.225s) Williams
27 ALESI (1m 18.761s) Ferrari		**6 COULTHARD** (1m 17.925s) Williams
26 PANIS (1m 19.047s) Ligier		**14 BARRICHELLO** (1m 18.810s) Jordan
8 HÄKKINEN (1m 19.238s) McLaren		**28 BERGER** (1m 19.051s) Ferrari
2 HERBERT (1m 19.555s) Benetton		**25 BRUNDLE** (1m 19.384s) Ligier
30 FRENTZEN (1m 20.309s) Sauber		**15 IRVINE** (1m 19.845s) Jordan
4 SALO (1m 20.796s) Tyrrell		**7 BLUNDELL** (1m 20.527s) McLaren
9 MORBIDELLI (1m 21.076s) Footwork		**29 BOULLION** (1m 20.943s) Sauber
10 INOUE (1m 21.894s) Footwork		**24 BADOER** (1m 21.323s) Minardi
23 MARTINI (1m 22.104s) Minardi		**3 KATAYAMA** (1m 21.930s) Tyrrell
16 GACHOT (1m 23.647s) Pacific		**17 MONTERMINI** (1m 23.466s) Pacific
22 MORENO (1m 24.865s) Forti		**21 DINIZ** (1m 24.184s) Forti

TIME SHEETS

Friday free practice
Sunny, very hot

Pos.	Driver	Laps	Time
1	Michael Schumacher	13	1m 19.535s
2	Olivier Panis	18	1m 19.663s
3	David Coulthard	23	1m 19.954s
4	Damon Hill	16	1m 19.987s
5	Jean Alesi	17	1m 20.051s
6	Martin Brundle	21	1m 20.213s
7	Gerhard Berger	15	1m 20.236s
8	Johnny Herbert	20	1m 20.721s
9	Rubens Barrichello	14	1m 20.974s
10	Eddie Irvine	16	1m 21.465s
11	Mark Blundell	21	1m 22.199s
12	Heinz-Harald Frentzen	22	1m 22.297s
13	Ukyo Katayama	21	1m 22.802s
14	Jean-Christophe Boullion	22	1m 22.884s
15	Gianni Morbidelli	12	1m 23.118s
16	Mika Salo	23	1m 23.133s
17	Andrea Montermini	21	1m 25.002s
18	Taki Inoue	23	1m 25.160s
19	Bertrand Gachot	17	1m 25.462s
20	Pedro Diniz	17	1m 26.407s
21	Roberto Moreno	6	1m 28.342s
22	Mika Häkkinen	7	1m 29.016s
	Pierluigi Martini	0	no time
	Luca Badoer	0	no time

Saturday free practice
Light cloud, very warm

Pos.	Driver	Laps	Time
1	Damon Hill	23	1m 18.561s
2	David Coulthard	23	1m 18.851s
3	Olivier Panis	23	1m 18.979s
4	Michael Schumacher	23	1m 19.134s
5	Martin Brundle	23	1m 19.135s
6	Gerhard Berger	15	1m 19.391s
7	Rubens Barrichello	21	1m 19.660s
8	Mika Häkkinen	21	1m 19.918s
9	Johnny Herbert	14	1m 20.023s
10	Eddie Irvine	20	1m 20.667s
11	Mark Blundell	16	1m 20.884s
12	Heinz-Harald Frentzen	18	1m 21.175s
13	Gianni Morbidelli	21	1m 21.511s
14	Luca Badoer	23	1m 21.542s
15	Pierluigi Martini	23	1m 21.769s
16	Jean-Christophe Boullion	22	1m 21.778s
17	Mika Salo	23	1m 21.887s
18	Taki Inoue	23	1m 22.787s
19	Ukyo Katayama	15	1m 22.863s
20	Bertrand Gachot	20	1m 23.934s
21	Pedro Diniz	15	1m 23.974s
22	Andrea Montermini	19	1m 24.100s
23	Roberto Moreno	23	1m 25.143s
24	Jean Alesi	1	1m 49.641s

Friday qualifying
Sunny, very hot

Pos.	Driver	Laps	Time
1	Damon Hill	12	1m 18.556s
2	David Coulthard	11	1m 18.585s
3	Michael Schumacher	12	1m 18.893s
4	Gerhard Berger	9	1m 19.051s
5	Jean Alesi	10	1m 19.254s
6	Martin Brundle	9	1m 19.384s
7	Olivier Panis	11	1m 19.466s
8	Johnny Herbert	9	1m 19.555s
9	Rubens Barrichello	12	1m 19.763s
10	Mika Häkkinen	10	1m 20.218s
11	Eddie Irvine	8	1m 20.713s
12	Mark Blundell	12	1m 20.804s
13	Heinz-Harald Frentzen	8	1m 21.111s
14	Gianni Morbidelli	12	1m 21.756s
15	Mika Salo	12	1m 21.921s
16	Jean-Christophe Boullion	11	1m 22.372s
17	Ukyo Katayama	4	1m 22.959s
18	Taki Inoue	12	1m 23.355s
19	Andrea Montermini	11	1m 24.172s
20	Bertrand Gachot	9	1m 24.509s
21	Pedro Diniz	9	1m 25.787s
22	Roberto Moreno	9	1m 26.445s
	Pierluigi Martini	0	no time
	Luca Badoer	0	no time

Saturday qualifying
Windy and bright

Pos.	Driver	Laps	Time
1	Damon Hill	11	1m 17.225s
2	Michael Schumacher	12	1m 17.512s
3	David Coulthard	10	1m 17.925s
4	Jean Alesi	10	1m 18.761s
5	Rubens Barrichello	10	1m 18.810s
6	Olivier Panis	11	1m 19.047s
7	Mika Häkkinen	12	1m 19.238s
8	Gerhard Berger	11	1m 19.295s
9	Martin Brundle	6	1m 19.524s
10	Eddie Irvine	11	1m 19.845s
11	Johnny Herbert	12	1m 20.000s
12	Heinz-Harald Frentzen	12	1m 20.309s
13	Mark Blundell	12	1m 20.527s
14	Mika Salo	10	1m 20.796s
15	Jean-Christophe Boullion	12	1m 20.943s
16	Gianni Morbidelli	12	1m 21.076s
17	Luca Badoer	12	1m 21.323s
18	Taki Inoue	12	1m 21.894s
19	Ukyo Katayama	12	1m 21.930s
20	Pierluigi Martini	12	1m 22.104s
21	Andrea Montermini	11	1m 23.466s
22	Bertrand Gachot	12	1m 23.647s
23	Pedro Diniz	10	1m 24.184s
24	Roberto Moreno	12	1m 24.865s

Warm-up
Rain initially, drying

Pos.	Driver	Laps	Time
1	Jean Alesi	14	1m 37.046s
2	David Coulthard	9	1m 37.613s
3	Rubens Barrichello	11	1m 37.688s
4	Michael Schumacher	15	1m 37.695s
5	Eddie Irvine	10	1m 37.727s
6	Olivier Panis	11	1m 37.822s
7	Gerhard Berger	9	1m 38.035s
8	Johnny Herbert	11	1m 38.238s
9	Martin Brundle	12	1m 38.303s
10	Damon Hill	10	1m 38.306s
11	Jean-Christophe Boullion	12	1m 38.541s
12	Luca Badoer	12	1m 38.981s
13	Heinz-Harald Frentzen	12	1m 39.468s
14	Mark Blundell	12	1m 39.870s
15	Mika Häkkinen	13	1m 40.300s
16	Ukyo Katayama	12	1m 40.718s
17	Pierluigi Martini	12	1m 41.204s
18	Bertrand Gachot	10	1m 41.557s
19	Mika Salo	4	1m 41.939s
20	Gianni Morbidelli	10	1m 42.153s
21	Andrea Montermini	12	1m 42.768s
22	Pedro Diniz	11	1m 42.845s
23	Roberto Moreno	10	1m 44.727s
24	Taki Inoue	7	1m 47.786s

Fastest race laps
Warm, sunny, some cloud

Driver	Time	Lap
Michael Schumacher	1m 20.218s	51
Damon Hill	1m 20.635s	9
Martin Brundle	1m 21.005s	60
David Coulthard	1m 21.235s	71
Jean Alesi	1m 21.360s	51
Olivier Panis	1m 21.398s	7
Rubens Barrichello	1m 21.455s	8
Eddie Irvine	1m 21.541s	54
Gerhard Berger	1m 21.782s	8
Mika Häkkinen	1m 22.058s	40
Heinz-Harald Frentzen	1m 22.688s	70
Mark Blundell	1m 22.698s	45
Jean-Christophe Boullion	1m 22.866s	46
Johnny Herbert	1m 23.080s	2
Mika Salo	1m 23.711s	50
Gianni Morbidelli	1m 24.256s	35
Pierluigi Martini	1m 24.354s	10
Luca Badoer	1m 24.546s	30
Andrea Montermini	1m 24.812s	39
Bertrand Gachot	1m 26.158s	7
Roberto Moreno	1m 26.748s	7

CHASSIS LOG BOOK

No.	Driver	Chassis
1	Schumacher	Benetton B195/6
2	Herbert	Benetton B195/3
	spare	Benetton B195/4
3	Katayama	Tyrrell 023/4
4	Salo	Tyrrell 023/3
	spare	Tyrrell 023/5
5	Hill	Williams FW17/5
6	Coulthard	Williams FW17/4
	spare	Williams FW17/2
7	Blundell	McLaren MP4/10B/5
8	Häkkinen	McLaren MP4/10B/3
	spare	McLaren MP4/10B/2
9	Morbidelli	Footwork FA16/3
10	Inoue	Footwork FA16/4
	spare	Footwork FA16/1
14	Barrichello	Jordan 195/4
15	Irvine	Jordan 195/3
	spare	Jordan 195/1
16	Gachot	Pacific PR02/1
17	Montermini	Pacific PR02/2
21	Diniz	Forti FG01/4
22	Moreno	Forti FG01/3
	spare	Forti FG01/2
23	Martini	Minardi M195/3
24	Badoer	Minardi M195/2
	spare	Minardi M195/1
25	Brundle	Ligier JS41/5
26	Panis	Ligier JS41/3
	spare	Ligier JS41/4
27	Alesi	Ferrari 412T2/161
28	Berger	Ferrari 412T2/157
	spare	Ferrari 412T2/160
29	Boullion	Sauber C14/4
30	Frentzen	Sauber C14/5
	spare	Sauber C14/1

POINTS TABLES

Drivers

1	Michael Schumacher	46
2	Damon Hill	35
3	Jean Alesi	26
4	Gerhard Berger	17
5	David Coulthard	13
6	Johnny Herbert	12
7	Rubens Barrichello	7
8	Eddie Irvine	6
9	Mika Häkkinen	5
10 =	Olivier Panis	4
10 =	Heinz-Harald Frentzen	4
12	Mark Blundell	3
12=	Martin Brundle	3
14	Gianni Morbidelli	1

Constructors

1	Benetton	48
2	Ferrari	43
3	Williams	42
4	Jordan	13
5	McLaren	8
6	Ligier	7
7	Sauber	4
8	Footwork	1

WORLD CHAMPIONSHIP • ROUND 8

BRITISH GRAND PRIX

HERBERT
ALESI
COULTHARD
PANIS
BLUNDELL
FRENTZEN

BRITISH GRAND PRIX

Diary

Juan Manuel Fangio dies in Buenos Aires at the age of 84.

Williams Chief Designer Adrian Newey revives the controversy surrounding the design similarities between the Benetton B195 and Ligier JS41, claiming that, as far as suspension geometry and aerodynamics are concerned, in his view they are identical.

The Japanese Dome team is rumoured to be readying an F1 challenge for 1996.

Ford confirms that Cosworth is to produce its first V10 F1 engine for Sauber to use in 1996.

Alain Prost tests DTM Mercedes C-class saloon at Magny-Cours, raising speculation that the four-times World Champion may be contemplating a return to racing.

A moving moment on the podium as a victorious Johnny Herbert is held aloft by his delighted rivals, Jean Alesi and David Coulthard. The Benetton driver's maiden Grand Prix win, seven years after a crash that very nearly ended his career, could not have been more popular.

Damon Hill's attempt to score a second successive home Grand Prix victory ended in disaster at Silverstone when he was involved in a controversial collision as he attempted to force his Williams ahead of Michael Schumacher's Benetton as they battled for the lead with only 15 laps left to run.

The incident provoked one hell of a furore, although it left both drivers with no more than red faces as they picked their way out of the gravel trap and walked – very separately – back to the pits. At a stroke, dozens of pit lane experts began offering their home-spun assessments of the situation, ranging from the vindictively critical to the mildly philosophical.

The reality, of course, is that it was a simple and straightforward racing accident. At worst, Hill could have been accused of a momentary touch of over-optimistic exuberance. Either way, he had to give it a try. Had he simply sat, visually transfixed by the Benetton's rear wing, all the way to the chequered flag, he would probably have deserved the uncharitable label of 'prat' which Frank Williams was alleged to have bestowed on him – something he vehemently denied – in the aftermath of the race.

Almost as a footnote, in the wake of all this excitement, Johnny Herbert kept his nose clean and charted a course through the debris to score his very first Grand Prix victory. It was an understandably emotional moment for the British driver who had suffered so many setbacks as he struggled to revive his professional career after suffering desperate leg injuries back in 1988.

David Coulthard summed it all up with great dignity at the post-race media conference when he said: 'I have to say, though, that in spite of me having lost the opportunity of winning after Damon and Michael crashed, I could not be any happier than I am to see Johnny win, especially after all he has been through.' At that, the press room filled with applause. Quite rightly too.

First qualifying saw Damon displaying a resolute determination to stop Michael Schumacher's World Championship bandwagon in its tracks, brilliantly eclipsing the German ace to set fastest time in dry, windy conditions in front of a 37,000-strong crowd.

Having won the previous year's race only after Schumacher was penalised for overtaking on the parade lap, Hill made it clear that it was his intention this time to remove all the ifs and buts which inevitably attached to his 1994 success. In so doing, he was aiming to make decisive inroads into Schumacher's 11-point lead as the championship battle neared its halfway point.

'It's a very good start, but as I've often said, Friday is fairly meaningless,' he admitted at the end of the session. 'The important thing is Sunday and the race. The way I feel at the moment, I'm more motivated than ever to win. Today was a good signal, a message to Michael that I'm not going to let him have it all his own way.

'After my fastest lap, I could see that I was P1 on the huge television screen alongside the circuit, and thought that was good news. As I drove round, there were fans waving flags all round the circuit and I appreciated that.'

Damon, whose wife Georgie was expecting their third child on the Silverstone race day, registered this psychological blow in the closing moments of an hour-long session in which Schumacher had initially seemed to be doing as he pleased at the head of the field. Seven minutes into the session, the World Champion had set the pace with a 1m 29.941s lap, Hill duly following with a best 0.2s slower.

Despite the blustery conditions which left the field battling against unpredictable crosswinds, Damon's Williams handled superbly on the faster outward leg of the circuit, most notably slamming through the sixth-gear Becketts ess-bend with a crisp precision that saw him 0.1s up through the first timing split at the end of the Hangar Straight.

Yet the remainder of the lap saw Hill's wafer-thin advantage slip away as his Williams struggled for grip on the tight second- and third-gear infield loop leading out onto the start/finish line. But in the middle of the session Hill made a minor, but crucial, spring change which decisively improved the car's handling.

Although Schumacher improved to 1m 28.397s, Hill was more than a match for him and stopped the clocks with an impressive 1m 28.124s. By then Schumacher had used up his allocation of laps and was unable to respond.

'The pressure is certainly on when Michael goes a second quicker,' said Hill. 'You know that you have to start to screw things down and concentrate to respond.

'My first run wasn't as good as I hoped it would be. Then we made some small changes to the car and went out to try them on a used set. The car felt OK and I was reasonably encouraged by that, and knew that we could go quicker again on a new set of tyres.

'That final run was more like how I knew it could be done. Just [a question of] digging a bit deeper and taking a few more risks. It got a bit sideways here and there, and I used too much kerb at the exit of the last corner, but there's no way you can lift even for a fraction of a second.

'You just have to keep your foot in it and hope you don't get the car completely on the grass.'

Hill's team-mate David Coulthard finished the day in a strong third place, the only other driver to break into the 1m 28s bracket. Yet the young Scot was disappointed not to have managed an even quicker time, reporting that his car seemed oversensitive to gusts of wind and wasn't handling at its best.

'The car felt a little bit bizarre to drive, partly because of the wind, although I did have a suspicion that [the set-up] was not quite one hundred per cent,' he explained. 'But we've done a lot of testing here over the past few weeks with a lot of fuel on board, so I feel quite optimistic.'

Ferrari led the pursuit of the Renault-engined brigade with Gerhard Berger in fourth place, while Johnny Herbert did a good job to set fifth-fastest time in his Benetton-Renault ahead of Jean Alesi's Ferrari. 'I am reasonably happy with my position,' said Herbert, 'but not with the performance of my car. It feels a little nervous at the moment, twitchy, a bit loose at the rear. When I accelerate, it has a lot of oversteer and then it is not smooth on the exit from the corners.'

Eddie Irvine's Jordan-Peugeot finished the Friday session a strong seventh, with Mika Häkkinen's McLaren-Mercedes eighth ahead of Rubens Barrichello's oversteering Jordan, Mark Blundell's McLaren and Martin Brundle's Ligier-Mugen. 'My only complaint was with the brake balance,' noted Irvine, 'an ongoing tendency to lock up, so you end up not using the brakes to the full.'

Yet Schumacher was far from dejected at the end of the day. Amidst the patriotic euphoria surrounding Hill's achievement, the Benetton team leader could point to some specifically quantifiable reasons for his inability to retain fastest time.

During the Friday morning free practice session, Schumacher had found his Benetton was understeering too much. To alleviate this, he increased downforce for first qualifying – and found himself handicapped by a lack of straightline speed. He also had a quick spin at Club Corner, but did not stall the engine and was able to continue.

'There is a small margin between Damon and myself like there was in France, but I'm not too bothered about it,' he said. 'The car is not behaving as it should, but we hope to sort that out. It's important to be on the front row and I'm optimistic for the race on Sunday.'

Clearly, the World Champion believed that the first day's showing represented no more than a fleeting setback in his quest to retain the title. Hill, however, saw it differently.

On Saturday, the weather conditions played firmly into Damon's hands, although his morning began on a disappointing note. It was raining during the free practice session when he spun coming out of the tight Priory left-hander and, in attempting to restart, broke a component in the transmission.

Luckily, Hill would get another opportunity to finalise his wet-weather chassis set-up when it rained again on Saturday afternoon, the delighted crowd being rewarded with their hero's guaranteed presence on pole position as there was no chance of improvement in second qualifying.

Coulthard posted fastest time by 0.19s in this wet session, the Scot being quite satisfied with his own performance although still slightly concerned whether or not his car's dry-weather handling imbalance had been rectified. Schumacher set second-fastest time again, this time locking up and sliding off the track at Stowe. With Herbert also crashing his B195 heavily at Copse, the Benetton lads faced a busy Saturday evening's work. On the face of it, this lapse by the Englishman did not seem calculated to increase his chances of keeping the second Benetton seat for the balance of the season.

There was consolation elsewhere in the field, however, with Mika Salo displaying his true potential by setting fourth-fastest time in the wet. It was a worthwhile morale-booster for the Tyrrell-Yamaha squad, but the young Finn still had to start from 23rd place on the grid after his Friday times were disallowed for missing the red light signalling him to stop for the pit lane weight check.

In the Ferrari camp, the 412T2s

BRITISH GRAND PRIX

Inset right: A mug's game? Not if you had your money on Johnny Herbert at 25-1.

Right: Jean Alesi's scorching start left Michael Schumacher trapped in third place ahead of David Coulthard as Damon Hill opened up a huge lead in the early stages of the race.

Below: Gerhard Berger and Niki Lauda don't look too optimistic about Ferrari's prospects at a circuit where the team was unable to carry out any pre-race testing.

were displaying excellent form bearing in mind that F1 regulations prevented them from testing at Silverstone prior to the race. With Berger and Alesi fourth and sixth by the end of the first day, both men made it clear that they wouldn't object to a wet race come Sunday afternoon.

Lack of recent testing experience was obviously something of a handicap, but a slightly revised aerodynamic package which included revisions to the side pods and diffusers looked promising. Gerhard's car was fitted with a fresh engine after he experienced a sudden loss of fuel pressure on Friday morning, but both men lacked straightline speed compared with the Renault brigade.

On Saturday morning, Jean set quickest time just before the mid-session break, but with yellow flags waving to signal Hill's spin, it all looked a touch risky. Later he had a tangle with Gachot's Pacific and then came tearing into the pit lane to find Montermini's Pacific being pushed by marshals, the Ferrari driver spinning as the only means of avoiding a collision.

After all this, the stewards were understandably anxious to discuss this sequence of events with the Frenchman. Unfortunately they mistakenly sent for Berger, which caused a few red faces at race control, and while Alesi was later seen, no sanction was imposed.

McLaren, meanwhile, had come to Silverstone with high hopes for yet another revision of the MP4/10B's front suspension geometry, this version having been tested at the circuit by Mika Häkkinen the previous Friday. But although he wound up eighth fastest in Friday qualifying, he did not seem to be in a particularly upbeat frame of mind.

'The situation is not very positive at the moment,' said the Finn, 'and I have to say I am naturally disappointed only to be eighth. The speed of the car is disappointing as we are experiencing the same problems as in Magny-Cours, with poor balance and understeer.'

Mark Blundell took tenth place on the grid, trying to put a more optimistic gloss on the latest changes. Ilmor duly produced a slightly revised Mercedes V10 for Häkkinen alone to try on Saturday, but the result was inconclusive as Mika only did three laps in the morning and didn't bother to go out at all in the wet second qualifying session.

Martin Brundle started from 11th place on the grid, Ligier trying power steering for the first time at a race. He was frustrated that the weather had effectively wiped out his second day getting accustomed to the Ligier JS41 at Silverstone, while Heinz-Harald Frentzen showed great form – and was briefly fastest on slicks towards the end of Saturday's damp free practice session – to qualify 12th in the Sauber C14, one place ahead of Olivier Panis in the second Ligier.

Ukyo Katayama was 14th for Tyrrell, ahead of Pierluigi Martini, who did a very creditable job considering that the Minardi team had not been able to return to its Faenza base since the French GP. Minardi's legal dispute with Flavio Briatore was only resolved on the Monday prior to the British race, as a consequence of which the team had to come directly to Silverstone.

Jean-Christophe Boullion was a disappointed 16th ahead of Arrows new boy Max Papis, who made quite a respectable debut as Gianni Morbidelli's successor in the Hart V8-en-

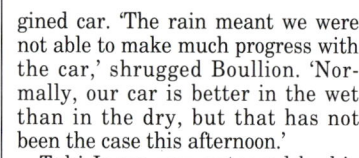

gined car. 'The rain meant we were not able to make much progress with the car,' shrugged Boullion. 'Normally, our car is better in the wet than in the dry, but that has not been the case this afternoon.'

Taki Inoue was outpaced by his new team-mate, clinching 19th place behind Luca Badoer, who spun his Minardi on Friday afternoon. Pedro Diniz completed the top twenty, despite losing time with electrical problems on Friday morning. The Brazilian novice was separated from team-mate Roberto Moreno by Gachot's Pacific, the more experienced Forti driver using a high-nose version of the FG01 chassis for the first time. Bertrand's Pacific suffered from gear selection problems and oversteer in the dry Friday qualifying session, but Andrea Montermini had to be content with last place on the grid behind Salo after losing Friday's qualifying session after the brake master cylinder failed.

On race morning, Hill was in a highly optimistic frame of mind from the outset, although he freely admitted that he was a little concerned as to precisely what refuelling strategy Schumacher might be running. Nevertheless, he got away perfectly from pole position to lead the sprint down to Copse Corner, with Jean Alesi

bursting through from the third row to slice inside Schumacher's Benetton as the pack jostled into the first right-hander.

This was a heaven-sent opportunity for Hill, who stormed out of Woodcote to lead the opening lap by 1.1s, leaving Schumacher effectively boxed in behind Alesi. Fourth was Coulthard ahead of Herbert, who was much happier with his Benetton after a failed shock absorber had been replaced after the warm-up, Mika Häkkinen's McLaren, Barrichello and Martin Brundle's Ligier.

Second time round and Hill was 2.1s ahead, then 3.3s, 4.7s and 6.2s by lap five. Further back, Irvine was already in trouble: his Jordan's clutch overheated on the starting grid and began slipping badly, so he eased off the throttle and was very slow away as a result, completing the opening lap down in 13th position.

Second time round he tried to pass Panis's Ligier under braking for the Abbey chicane and spun, soon after which his Peugeot V10 just cut out due to a problem with the crank sensor. 'I ended up parked at the same place as I did in last year's race,' shrugged Eddie. 'Maybe next year I will actually get to the finish.'

By the 12-lap mark, Hill was 12 seconds ahead, just as Panis came into the pits for a stop-go penalty, the Frenchman followed in by Barrichello at the end of lap 15. Both men had been adjudged to have jumped the start.

On lap 18, Hill was 19.5s ahead when Alesi came in for his first refuelling stop, allowing Schumacher through into second place. Damon made his first stop on lap 22, after which it became increasingly clear that Michael, now in the lead, was planning to run through the race refuelling only once.

Häkkinen, who had set fastest time in the race morning warm-up using the latest-specification Mercedes V10, ran a strong sixth from the start, moving up to fifth when Coulthard made his first stop on lap 15 and then fourth when Alesi came in to refuel three laps later. Unfortunately the car suffered hydraulic failure on lap 21 and he rolled to a halt out on the circuit.

It was also a bad day for Martin Brundle. Settling down in ninth place during the early laps, he began to close on Berger's Ferrari only for his Ligier to become increasingly difficult to handle over the bumps.

'I wondered whether I didn't have a broken shock absorber,' he said ruefully. 'Then on lap 17, with the first refuelling stops nearing, I lost the back end through Luffield and spun off, ending up a couple of metres into the gravel. Although I succeeded in keeping the engine going, I was stuck fast.'

Schumacher stayed out until lap 31, when he made a 13.4s stop, resuming in second place some 20.6s behind Hill. Now it was all a question of whether Damon could survive his second refuelling stop and return to the race ahead of the World Champion.

Meanwhile, Gerhard Berger had been battling his way up from eighth place after a very slow start, the Austrian moving through to fifth by the time he made his first refuelling stop on lap 20. He was stationary for 12.4s, but immediately after accelerating back into the race he had to pull up after detecting his left-front wheel wobbling ominously. It was a bitterly disappointing blow for Gerhard as he left an otherwise perfectly healthy car at the side of the track. He walked back to the pits where his mechanics did their best to hide their acute embarrassment over this dramatic lapse.

By lap 33, Hill was 21.3s ahead of Schumacher, gradually expanding the advantage to 22.62s on lap 35 and, eventually, to just under 27 seconds when he peeled off into the pit lane at the end of lap 41.

Hill was stationary for 11 seconds and would have caught Schumacher's Benetton in his peripheral vision as he reached the end of the pit lane, the World Champion now hard on the brakes as he slammed into the Copse right-hander. Michael was flying at racing speed and easily had sufficient momentum to carry himself safely ahead of Damon as the Williams driver accelerated hard onto his tail as they swooped through Becketts.

Now Hill had fresh tyres at his disposal, and the same fuel load as Schumacher's Benetton just three lengths ahead of him. It promised a tantalising race to the finish.

On lap 41 the gap was 1.57s, then Hill sliced it down to 0.72s next time round and on lap 44 there was effectively nothing between them, Benetton and Williams slamming across the line 0.496s apart. At the end of lap 45, Hill was climbing all over his rival and might well have got inside under braking at Stowe had it not been for the fact they were both lapping Boullion's Sauber.

Through the Abbey chicane they came, nose to tail, and out through the Bridge right-hander. Suddenly Damon decided to go for it. Schumacher seemed a little too far over to the right as he braked for Priory and,

149

in a flash, the Williams came powering up the inside of the Benetton.

Damon was now totally in Schumacher's hands. But Michael turned in and Hill, whisps of smoke coming from his front tyres as they locked up, went slamming into the side of the Benetton. The two cars spun off into the gravel trap, out of the race. The great confrontation was at an end.

Neither driver believed it was his responsibility. 'It was a racing accident,' shrugged Hill. 'I thought I saw an opportunity that I could take advantage of, but I am afraid Michael is a harder driver to pass than that and we had an accident.'

Schumacher branded Hill's manoeuvre as 'a crazy move' and attempted to draw a parallel with the incident at Adelaide in 1994, choosing to ignore the fact that, on that occasion, he had bounced off a wall before Damon made his move.

'What can I say?' shrugged the World Champion. 'I think what Damon did was totally unnecessary. In fact, it was really stupid. There was no room for two cars, and there is no place to overtake there.

'It is such a small straight and even if you brake in the first part, and you turn in, it is almost impossible and if I hadn't been there, I think he would have gone straight into the gravel. So he had absolutely no reason to attempt such an overtaking move at that time. It was all completely unnecessary!'

However, on examining the video evidence and taking into account the reports from observers out on the circuit, the stewards of the meeting issued a severe reprimand to both men. So, although Hill could be accused of being extremely over-ambitious in his assessment of the situation, the stewards' decision also indicated their belief that Schumacher deserved some of the blame.

The collision handed the lead to Herbert, only for Coulthard to force his Williams FW17 through into the lead three laps later. Unfortunately this turned out to be a futile gesture as David was soon signalled to come in for a ten-second stop-go penalty for exceeding the pit lane speed limit.

Ironically, this rule infringement was directly due to an electrical

BRITISH GRAND PRIX

Main picture: Exultation turns to dismay on the spectator banking as Damon Hill, anxious to capitalise on the performance advantage offered by fresh tyres, makes his ill-fated attempt to snatch the lead from Michael Schumacher.

David Coulthard *(left)* looked set to record his first Grand Prix win when he was handed a stop-go penalty for speeding in the pit lane.

Mark Blundell *(bottom)* gamely limped home on three wheels to take the final point after his McLaren was savaged by Barrichello's Jordan at Abbey on the penultimate lap.

Herbert found himself relieved of added pressure from Alesi as the Ferrari's oil pressure began to fade in the closing stages and the Frenchman was told to ease back over the radio link from his pit.

Coulthard duly recovered from his stop-go penalty to finish third, while Mark Blundell's McLaren-Mercedes looked on course for fourth place until it was rammed by Rubens Barrichello's Jordan on the penultimate lap. The Brazilian spun off, but Blundell limped home fifth on three tyres and a wheel rim, dropping a place to Olivier Panis's Ligier in the final mile. Rubens was absolutely furious with Blundell, taking the view that he had brake-tested his Jordan on a couple of occasions just before the two cars made contact.

'After my second stop I was catching Blundell really quickly again,' he explained. 'I was really going for it, but I was fair when I was overtaking people. Unfortunately Blundell wasn't so fair. Twice he brake-tested me on the exit of Club.

'I almost hit him, so I was a bit more careful next time. Then, coming into Abbey, I moved to overtake him and he suddenly moved to the left, leaving me no time to brake. I'm really upset – that's something I would never do.'

Blundell's interpretation of events was understandably different. 'I lost a place at the start, which is all down to me, but apart from that I kept a consistent pace throughout the race,' said Mark.

'However, I got a bit upset with the new blue flag rule; the flags were not used as I was trying to lap four or five people. I got stuck behind Martini for two and a half laps, which cost me a lot of time, and created the situation which saw Barrichello getting very close to me.

'In the end, I defended my line and Rubens hit the back of my car.'

Panis's last-lap promotion resulted in Ligier drawing level with McLaren in the constructors' championship battle, while Heinz-Harald Frentzen grabbed the final point on offer for sixth place in the Sauber-Ford.

As far as the World Championship battle was concerned, there were still 11 points between Hill and Schumacher as they headed for Hockenheim. But the signs at Silverstone were that Williams had really got a handle on the FW17's chassis set-up at long last. Life seemed set to get busier than ever for Schumacher in the weeks that followed.

problem which prevented the car's driver-activated speed limiter from working correctly. It also affected the electronic throttle 'blipper', which had been giving Coulthard problems on the downchange almost from the start of the race.

Coulthard later agreed with Alesi's contention that, with Silverstone in its current configuration, it is just not possible to get close enough to the car in front to have a realistic chance of overtaking. In the early stages of the race, David had been boxed in behind the Ferrari and Schumacher's Benetton, so the Williams team called him in early for his first refuelling stop, on lap 15.

'Immediately after I left the pits I had an electrical failure which meant I had no "blip" on the downchange, and on the upchange it felt as though the clutch was slipping,' he explained. 'At that point I was convinced my race was over.'

He added that the huge television screens around the circuit revealed the disappointing news of his penalty. 'In some cases it is good to have the big screens around the circuit,' he noted, 'but sometimes I hate them, because today I saw the message "Coulthard 10 Penalty". At that point the team hadn't told me about the penalty yet and I thought, "Maybe they won't tell me and it will just go away." Apparently they didn't want to disappoint me too early in the race and it was two laps before they told me!'

Herbert resumed the lead on lap 51 and held on to score a memorably sweet victory at a moment when his position within the Benetton ranks had seemed tenuous, amid speculation that he would soon be replaced by Jos Verstappen. It was a triumph which served dramatically to emphasise the unpredictable nature of topline motor racing, for Johnny had lost his first F1 seat after being dropped by Benetton midway through 1989 when it became clear that he had not fully recovered from leg injuries sustained in a Formula 3000 crash at Brands Hatch the previous summer. Six years later he had won the British Grand Prix.

'It is a fantastic feeling for me, especially as it is my home Grand Prix,' said Herbert. 'The support today was just fantastic and I really understand what Nigel and Damon mean when they talk about it.

'It really has been a long, hard slog for me. Thanks to my wife Rebecca, who has supported me all the way through since 1988 when I had the accident, and Peter Collins [MD of the now-defunct Lotus team] who got me into F1 twice, and to Flavio Briatore for giving me this drive this year.'

151

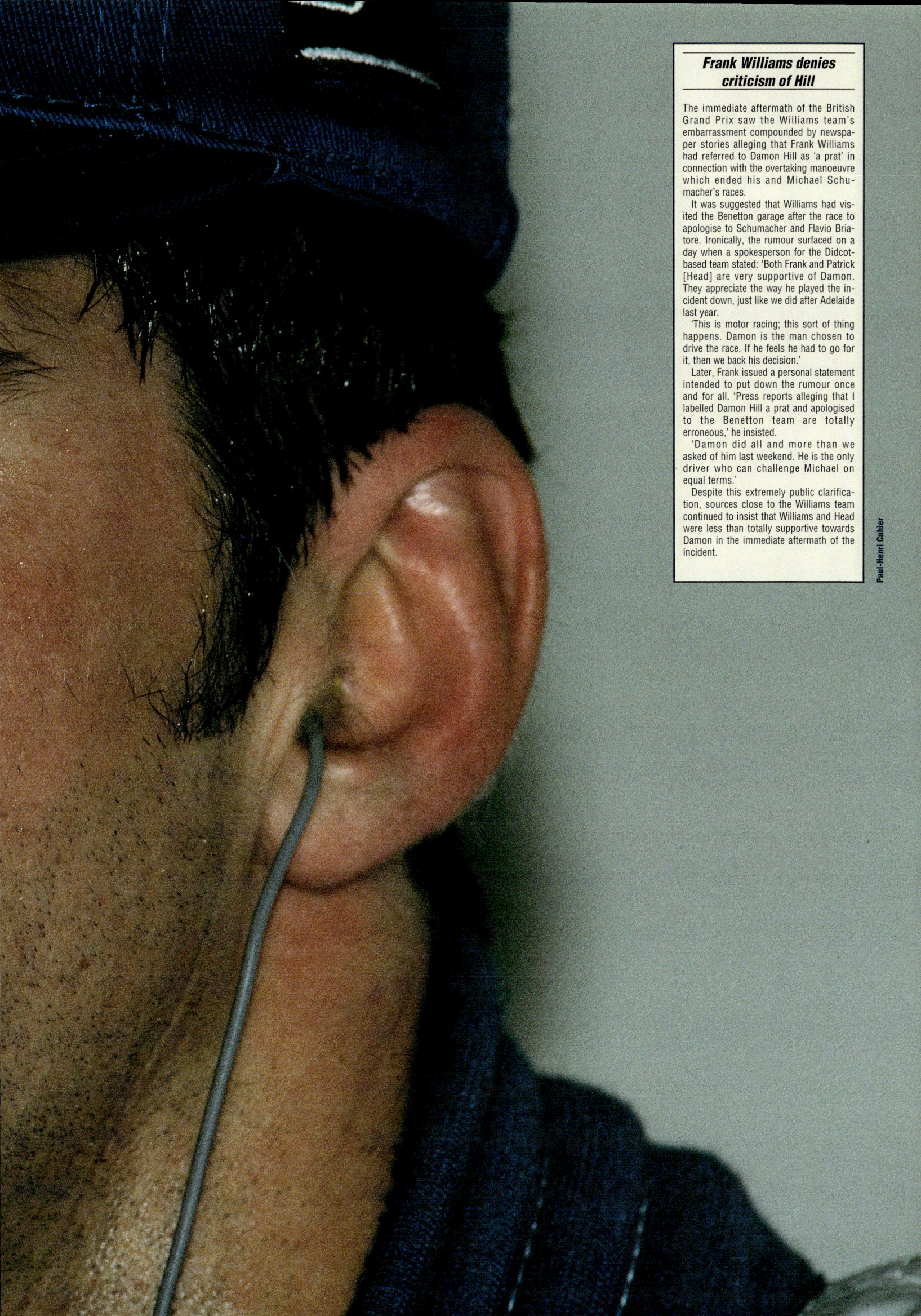

Frank Williams denies criticism of Hill

The immediate aftermath of the British Grand Prix saw the Williams team's embarrassment compounded by newspaper stories alleging that Frank Williams had referred to Damon Hill as 'a prat' in connection with the overtaking manoeuvre which ended his and Michael Schumacher's races.

It was suggested that Williams had visited the Benetton garage after the race to apologise to Schumacher and Flavio Briatore. Ironically, the rumour surfaced on a day when a spokesperson for the Didcot-based team stated: 'Both Frank and Patrick [Head] are very supportive of Damon. They appreciate the way he played the incident down, just like we did after Adelaide last year.

'This is motor racing; this sort of thing happens. Damon is the man chosen to drive the race. If he feels he had to go for it, then we back his decision.'

Later, Frank issued a personal statement intended to put down the rumour once and for all. 'Press reports alleging that I labelled Damon Hill a prat and apologised to the Benetton team are totally erroneous,' he insisted.

'Damon did all and more than we asked of him last weekend. He is the only driver who can challenge Michael on equal terms.'

Despite this extremely public clarification, sources close to the Williams team continued to insist that Williams and Head were less than totally supportive towards Damon in the immediate aftermath of the incident.

FIA FORMULA ONE WORLD CHAMPIONSHIP ROUND 8

BRITISH GRAND PRIX
SILVERSTONE 14-16 JULY 1995

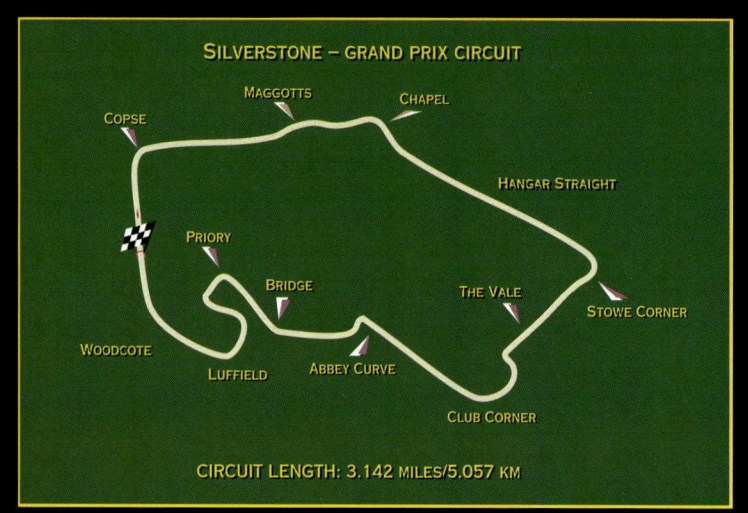

Race distance: 61 laps, 191.678 miles/308.477 km
Race weather: Warm, cloudy, windy

Place	Driver	Nat.	No.	Entrant	Car/Engine	Laps	Time/Retirement	Speed (mph/km/h)
1	**Johnny Herbert**	GB	2	Mild Seven Benetton Renault	Benetton B195-Renault RS7B V10	61	1h 34m 35.093s	121.591/195.682
2	**Jean Alesi**	F	27	Scuderia Ferrari	Ferrari 412T2 044 V12	61	1h 34m 51.572s	121.239/195.116
3	**David Coulthard**	GB	6	Rothmans Williams Renault	Williams FW17-Renault RS7B V10	61	1h 34m 58.981s	121.081/194.862
4	**Olivier Panis**	F	26	Ligier Gitanes Blondes	Ligier JS41-Mugen Honda MF301 V10	61	1h 36m 08.261s	119.627/192.522
5	**Mark Blundell**	GB	7	Marlboro McLaren Mercedes	McLaren MP4/10B-Mercedes FO110 V10	61	1h 36m 23.265s	119.317/192.022
6	**Heinz-Harald Frentzen**	D	30	Red Bull Sauber Ford	Sauber C14-Ford Zetec-R V8	60		
7	Pierluigi Martini	I	23	Minardi Scuderia Italia	Minardi M195-Ford EDM V8	60		
8	Mika Salo	SF	4	Nokia Tyrrell Yamaha	Tyrrell 023-Yamaha OX10C V10	60		
9	Jean-Christophe Boullion	F	29	Red Bull Sauber Ford	Sauber C14-Ford Zetec-R V8	60		
10	Luca Badoer	I	24	Minardi Scuderia Italia	Minardi M195-Ford EDM V8	60		
11	Rubens Barrichello	BR	14	Total Jordan Peugeot	Jordan 195-Peugeot A10 V10	59	Collision with Blundell	
12	Bertrand Gachot	F	16	Pacific Grand Prix Ltd	Pacific PR02-Ford ED V8	58		
	Roberto Moreno	BR	22	Parmalat Forti Ford	Forti FG01-Ford ED V8	48	Hydraulic pressure	
	Michael Schumacher	D	1	Mild Seven Benetton Renault	Benetton B195-Renault RS7B V10	45	Collision with Hill	
	Damon Hill	GB	5	Rothmans Williams Renault	Williams FW17-Renault RS7B V10	45	Collision with Schumacher	
	Massimiliano Papis	I	9	Footwork Hart	Footwork FA16-Hart 830 V8	28	Accident	
	Ukyo Katayama	J	3	Nokia Tyrrell Yamaha	Tyrrell 023-Yamaha OX10C V10	22	Fuel pressure	
	Andrea Montermini	I	17	Pacific Grand Prix Ltd	Pacific PR02-Ford ED V8	21	Spun off	
	Mika Häkkinen	SF	8	Marlboro McLaren Mercedes	McLaren MP4/10B-Mercedes FO110 V10	20	Electrics	
	Gerhard Berger	A	28	Scuderia Ferrari	Ferrari 412T2 044 V12	20	Loose wheel	
	Martin Brundle	GB	25	Ligier Gitanes Blondes	Ligier JS41-Mugen Honda MF301 V10	16	Spun off	
	Taki Inoue	J	10	Footwork Hart	Footwork FA16-Hart 830 V8	16	Spun off	
	Pedro Diniz	BR	21	Parmalat Forti Ford	Forti FG01-Ford ED V8	13	Gearbox	
	Eddie Irvine	GB	15	Total Jordan Peugeot	Jordan 195-Peugeot A10 V10	2	Electrics	

Fastest lap: Hill, on lap 37, 1m 29.752s, 126.037 mph/202.838 km/h.
Lap record: Damon Hill (F1 Williams FW16-Renault V10), 1m 27.100s, 129.875 mph/209.014 km/h (1994).

All cars used Goodyear tyres

All results and data © FIA 1995

Grid order	1	2	3	4	5	6	7	8	9	10	11	12	13	14	15	16	17	18	19	20	21	22	23	24	25	26	27	28	29	30	31	32	33	34	35	36	37	38	39	40	41	42	43	44	45	46
5 HILL	5	5	5	5	5	5	5	5	5	5	5	5	5	5	5	5	5	5	5	5	5	5	5	5	5	1	1	1	1	1	1	1	1	1	5	5	5	5	5	5	5	5	1	1	1	2
1 SCHUMACHER	27	27	27	27	27	27	27	27	27	27	27	27	27	27	27	27	27	1	1	1	1	1	5	5	5	5	5	5	5	5	5	5	5	5	1	1	1	1	1	1	1	1	5	5	5	6
6 COULTHARD	1	1	1	1	1	1	1	1	1	1	1	1	1	1	1	1	1	2	2	2	2	2	2	2	2	2	2	2	2	2	2	2	2	2	2	2	2	2	6	6	6	6	2	2	2	27
28 BERGER	6	6	6	6	6	6	6	6	6	6	6	6	6	6	2	2	2	27	8	8	7	7	27	27	27	27	27	27	27	27	27	27	27	27	27	27	27	27	27	6	2	2	2	2	2	14
2 HERBERT	2	2	2	2	2	2	2	2	2	2	2	2	2	2	6	6	6	8	28	28	27	27	6	6	6	6	6	6	6	6	6	6	6	6	6	6	6	6	2	2	27	27	27	27	27	5
27 ALESI	8	8	8	8	8	8	8	8	8	8	8	8	8	8	8	28	28	28	7	7	6	6	30	30	30	30	30	30	30	7	7	7	7	7	7	7	7	7	7	27	7	7	7	7	7	26
15 IRVINE	14	14	14	14	14	14	14	14	14	14	14	14	14	14	28	25	7	7	27	27	14	30	7	7	7	7	7	7	7	30	14	14	14	14	14	14	14	14	14	14	26	26	14	14	14	30
8 HÄKKINEN	25	28	28	28	28	28	28	28	28	28	28	28	28	28	25	7	6	6	6	6	30	3	14	14	14	14	14	14	14	14	30	30	30	26	26	26	26	26	26	26	14	14	30	26	26	23
14 BARRICHELLO	28	25	25	25	25	25	25	25	25	25	25	25	25	25	14	6	30	14	14	14	3	26	23	23	23	23	23	23	23	26	26	26	26	30	30	30	30	30	30	30	30	30	26	30	30	
7 BLUNDELL	30	30	30	7	7	7	7	7	7	7	7	7	7	7	7	30	14	30	30	30	26	14	26	26	26	26	26	26	26	24	4	4	4	4	4	4	4	29	23	23	23	23	23			
25 BRUNDLE	7	7	7	30	26	26	26	26	26	26	26	26	26	26	30	14	25	26	26	26	23	23	23	23	9	9	9	9	24	23	23	4	23	4	29	29	29	23	29	29	29	4	4			
30 FRENTZEN	26	26	26	26	3	3	3	3	3	3	3	3	3	3	3	3	26	26	26	26	9	9	24	24	24	24	24	24	4	4	29	29	29	29	23	23	23	4	4	4	4	29	29			
26 PANIS	15	23	23	23	23	23	23	23	23	23	23	23	29	29	29	29	29	29	29	29	4	4	4	4	4	4	4	4	29	29	24	24	24	24	24	24	24	24	24	24	24	24	24			
3 KATAYAMA	23	3	3	3	23	23	23	29	29	29	29	29	26	26	26	26	4	4	4	23	29	29	29	29	29	29	29	16	16	16	16	16	16	16	16	16	16	16	16	16	16					
23 MARTINI	3	29	29	29	29	29	29	23	23	23	23	23	23	23	23	4	23	23	23	4	16	16	16	16	16	16	16	22	22	22	22	22	22													
29 BOULLION	29	4	4	4	4	4	4	4	4	4	4	4	4	24	24	23	9	9	9	9	24	24	22	22	22	22	22																			
9 PAPIS	4	9	9	9	9	9	9	9	9	9	9	9	24	4	4	9	24	24	24	24	22	22																								
24 BADOER	9	10	10	10	10	10	10	10	10	10	10	10	10	9	9	24	16	16	16	22																										
10 INOUE	10	16	16	24	24	24	24	24	24	24	24	24	16	16	16	17	17	17	17																											
21 DINIZ	16	15	24	16	16	16	16	16	16	16	16	16	22	22	22	22																														
16 GACHOT	24	24	17	17	17	17	17	17	17	17	17	17	17	17																																
22 MORENO	21	17	21	22	22	22	22	22	22	22	22	22																																		
4 SALO	17	21	22	21	21	21	21	21	21	21	21	21																																		
17 MONTERMINI	22	22																																												

Pit stop
One lap behind leader

STARTING GRID

5 HILL (1m 28.124s) Williams	**1 SCHUMACHER** (1m 28.397s) Benetton
6 COULTHARD (1m 28.947s) Williams	**28 BERGER** (1m 29.657s) Ferrari
2 HERBERT (1m 29.867s) Benetton	**27 ALESI** (1m 29.874s) Ferrari
15 IRVINE (1m 30.083s) Jordan	**8 HÄKKINEN** (1m 30.140s) McLaren
14 BARRICHELLO (1m 30.354s) Jordan	**7 BLUNDELL** (1m 30.453s) McLaren
25 BRUNDLE (1m 30.946s) Ligier	**30 FRENTZEN** (1m 31.602s) Sauber
26 PANIS (1m 31.842s) Ligier	**3 KATAYAMA** (1m 32.087s) Tyrrell
23 MARTINI (1m 32.259s) Minardi	**29 BOULLION** (1m 33.166s) Sauber
9 PAPIS (1m 34.154s) Footwork	**24 BADOER** (1m 34.556s) Minardi
10 INOUE (1m 35.323s) Footwork	**21 DINIZ** (1m 36.023s) Forti
16 GACHOT (1m 36.076s) Pacific	**22 MORENO** (1m 36.651s) Forti
4 SALO (1m 48.639s) Tyrrell	**17 MONTERMINI** (1m 52.398s) Pacific

FOR THE RECORD

First Grand Prix win
Johnny Herbert

First Grand Prix start
Massimiliano Papis

TIME SHEETS

Friday free practice
Cloudy and windy

Pos.	Driver	Laps	Time
1	Michael Schumacher	16	1m 29.238s
2	Damon Hill	21	1m 29.272s
3	Jean Alesi	22	1m 29.661s
4	David Coulthard	19	1m 29.756s
5	Gerhard Berger	17	1m 30.467s
6	Johnny Herbert	20	1m 30.567s
7	Mika Häkkinen	20	1m 30.848s
8	Rubens Barrichello	21	1m 31.194s
9	Mark Blundell	22	1m 31.214s
10	Eddie Irvine	18	1m 31.419s
11	Martin Brundle	21	1m 31.866s
12	Ukyo Katayama	23	1m 32.236s
13	Olivier Panis	18	1m 32.364s
14	Heinz-Harald Frentzen	21	1m 32.729s
15	Mika Salo	22	1m 32.969s
16	Pierluigi Martini	19	1m 33.016s
17	Luca Badoer	20	1m 34.124s
18	Jean-Christophe Boullion	20	1m 34.351s
19	Massimiliano Papis	23	1m 34.973s
20	Andrea Montermini	7	1m 36.519s
21	Bertrand Gachot	7	1m 36.948s
22	Roberto Moreno	22	1m 37.001s
23	Taki Inoue	15	1m 37.194s
24	Pedro Diniz	21	1m 37.580s

Saturday free practice
Dry, wet, then steadily drying

Pos.	Driver	Laps	Time
1	Michael Schumacher	19	1m 31.390s
2	Jean Alesi	22	1m 31.908s
3	David Coulthard	15	1m 32.763s
4	Johnny Herbert	17	1m 33.062s
5	Olivier Panis	21	1m 33.637s
6	Heinz-Harald Frentzen	19	1m 34.169s
7	Mark Blundell	16	1m 34.321s
8	Rubens Barrichello	4	1m 34.353s
9	Pierluigi Martini	9	1m 35.795s
10	Massimiliano Papis	6	1m 36.638s
11	Mika Häkkinen	4	1m 38.251s
12	Luca Badoer	12	1m 38.898s
13	Pedro Diniz	18	1m 38.959s
14	Ukyo Katayama	19	1m 39.164s
15	Jean-Christophe Boullion	14	1m 39.500s
16	Andrea Montermini	6	1m 39.975s
17	Bertrand Gachot	7	1m 43.946s
18	Eddie Irvine	5	1m 46.416s
19	Martin Brundle	15	1m 47.087s
20	Mika Salo	9	1m 47.271s
21	Gerhard Berger	6	1m 49.320s
22	Damon Hill	2	1m 49.581s
23	Roberto Moreno	9	1m 53.474s
24	Taki Inoue	5	1m 54.364s

Friday qualifying
Windy and bright

Pos.	Driver	Laps	Time
1	**Damon Hill**	11	**1m 28.124s**
2	**Michael Schumacher**	11	**1m 28.397s**
3	**David Coulthard**	12	**1m 28.947s**
4	**Gerhard Berger**	8	**1m 29.657s**
5	**Johnny Herbert**	11	**1m 29.867s**
6	**Jean Alesi**	12	**1m 29.874s**
7	**Eddie Irvine**	9	**1m 30.083s**
8	**Mika Häkkinen**	12	**1m 30.140s**
9	**Rubens Barrichello**	12	**1m 30.354s**
10	**Mark Blundell**	11	**1m 30.453s**
11	**Martin Brundle**	11	**1m 30.946s**
12	**Heinz-Harald Frentzen**	11	**1m 31.602s**
13	**Olivier Panis**	11	**1m 31.842s**
14	**Ukyo Katayama**	12	**1m 32.087s**
15	**Pierluigi Martini**	12	**1m 32.259s**
16	**Jean-Christophe Boullion**	12	**1m 33.166s**
17	**Massimiliano Papis**	10	**1m 34.154s**
18	**Luca Badoer**	8	**1m 34.556s**
19	**Taki Inoue**	12	**1m 35.323s**
20	**Pedro Diniz**	12	**1m 36.023s**
21	**Bertrand Gachot**	7	**1m 36.076s**
22	**Roberto Moreno**	12	**1m 36.651s**
	Mika Salo	0	no time
	Andrea Montermini	0	no time

Saturday qualifying
Wet and cloudy

Pos.	Driver	Laps	Time
1	David Coulthard	8	1m 48.012s
2	Michael Schumacher	8	1m 48.204s
3	Jean Alesi	9	1m 48.205s
4	**Mika Salo**	9	**1m 48.639s**
5	Damon Hill	8	1m 48.800s
6	Rubens Barrichello	6	1m 49.152s
7	Martin Brundle	6	1m 49.414s
8	Luca Badoer	7	1m 50.959s
9	Eddie Irvine	4	1m 51.045s
10	Heinz-Harald Frentzen	6	1m 51.059s
11	Jean-Christophe Boullion	9	1m 51.086s
12	Olivier Panis	4	1m 51.657s
13	Gerhard Berger	6	1m 51.818s
14	Ukyo Katayama	6	1m 52.054s
15	**Andrea Montermini**	3	**1m 52.398s**
16	Massimiliano Papis	7	1m 53.097s
17	Johnny Herbert	4	1m 55.011s
18	Roberto Moreno	11	1m 56.374s
19	Pierluigi Martini	2	2m 13.471s
20	Pedro Diniz	2	5m 51.829s
21	Mark Blundell	1	56m 10.060s
	Mika Häkkinen	0	no time
	Taki Inoue	0	no time
	Bertrand Gachot	0	no time

Warm-up
Warm and bright

Pos.	Driver	Laps	Time
1	Mika Häkkinen	12	1m 29.685s
2	Damon Hill	12	1m 29.800s
3	David Coulthard	12	1m 29.901s
4	Jean Alesi	11	1m 30.002s
5	Gerhard Berger	14	1m 30.577s
6	Michael Schumacher	13	1m 30.665s
7	Rubens Barrichello	10	1m 30.848s
8	Martin Brundle	10	1m 30.905s
9	Eddie Irvine	12	1m 31.174s
10	Mark Blundell	13	1m 31.193s
11	Olivier Panis	14	1m 31.446s
12	Johnny Herbert	11	1m 31.843s
13	Mika Salo	9	1m 32.685s
14	Pierluigi Martini	10	1m 33.228s
15	Heinz-Harald Frentzen	10	1m 33.320s
16	Jean-Christophe Boullion	14	1m 33.471s
17	Ukyo Katayama	11	1m 33.535s
18	Luca Badoer	12	1m 34.033s
19	Massimiliano Papis	15	1m 34.605s
20	Andrea Montermini	6	1m 34.951s
21	Bertrand Gachot	11	1m 35.838s
22	Taki Inoue	12	1m 35.872s
23	Roberto Moreno	10	1m 37.242s
24	Pedro Diniz	10	1m 37.763s

Race fastest laps
Warm, cloudy, windy

Driver	Time	Lap
Damon Hill	1m 29.752s	37
Michael Schumacher	1m 30.271s	28
Jean Alesi	1m 30.768s	38
David Coulthard	1m 30.812s	42
Rubens Barrichello	1m 30.841s	38
Johnny Herbert	1m 31.149s	23
Olivier Panis	1m 31.393s	37
Gerhard Berger	1m 31.435s	16
Mark Blundell	1m 31.694s	54
Martin Brundle	1m 31.881s	9
Mika Häkkinen	1m 31.901s	17
Jean-Christophe Boullion	1m 32.588s	58
Heinz-Harald Frentzen	1m 33.012s	27
Mika Salo	1m 33.081s	41
Ukyo Katayama	1m 33.242s	20
Luca Badoer	1m 33.631s	31
Pierluigi Martini	1m 33.774s	53
Massimiliano Papis	1m 34.633s	21
Taki Inoue	1m 35.021s	15
Bertrand Gachot	1m 36.313s	8
Andrea Montermini	1m 36.445s	8
Roberto Moreno	1m 37.734s	4
Pedro Diniz	1m 37.859s	4
Eddie Irvine	1m 43.961s	2

CHASSIS LOG BOOK

1	Schumacher	Benetton B195/6
2	Herbert	Benetton B195/5
spare		Benetton B195/1
3	Katayama	Tyrrell 023/6
4	Salo	Tyrrell 023/5
spare		Tyrrell 023/3
5	Hill	Williams FW17/4
6	Coulthard	Williams FW17/5
spare		Williams FW17/2
7	Blundell	McLaren MP4/10B/1
8	Häkkinen	McLaren MP4/10B/5
spare		McLaren MP4/10B/2
9	Papis	Footwork FA16/3
10	Inoue	Footwork FA16/4
spare		Footwork FA16/1
14	Barrichello	Jordan 195/4
15	Irvine	Jordan 195/5
spare		Jordan 195/1
16	Gachot	Pacific PR02/1
17	Montermini	Pacific PR02/2
21	Diniz	Forti FG01/4
22	Moreno	Forti FG01/3
spare		Forti FG01/2
23	Martini	Minardi M195/3
24	Badoer	Minardi M195/2
spare		Minardi M195/1
25	Brundle	Ligier JS41/5
26	Panis	Ligier JS41/3
spare		Ligier JS41/4
27	Alesi	Ferrari 412T2/161
28	Berger	Ferrari 412T2/162
spare		Ferrari 412T2/160
29	Boullion	Sauber C14/4
30	Frentzen	Sauber C14/5
spare		Sauber C14/2

POINTS TABLES

Drivers

1	Michael Schumacher	46
2	Damon Hill	35
3	Jean Alesi	32
4	Johnny Herbert	22
5=	Gerhard Berger	17
5=	David Coulthard	17
7=	Rubens Barrichello	7
7=	Olivier Panis	7
9	Eddie Irvine	6
10=	Mark Blundell	5
10=	Heinz-Harald Frentzen	5
10=	Mika Häkkinen	5
13	Martin Brundle	3
14	Gianni Morbidelli	1

Constructors

1	Benetton	58
2	Ferrari	49
3	Williams	46
4	Jordan	13
5=	Ligier	10
5=	McLaren	10
7	Sauber	5
8	Footwork	1

Lap Chart

Lap	48	49	50	51	52	53	54	55	56	57	58	59	60	61	Pos
	2	6	6	2	2	2	2	2	2	2	2	2	2	2	1
	6	2	2	6	27	27	27	27	27	27	27	27	27	27	2
	27	27	27	27	6	6	6	6	6	6	6	6	6	6	3
	7	7	7	7	7	7	7	7	7	7	7	7	7	26	4
	14	14	14	14	14	14	14	14	14	14	14	14	26	7	5
	26	26	26	26	26	26	26	26	26	26	26	26	30		6
	30	30	30	30	30	30	30	30	30	30	30	30			
	23	23	23	23	23	23	23	23	23	23	23	4			
	4	4	4	4	4	4	4	4	4	4	4	29			
	24	24	24	24	24	24	24	29	29	29	29	24			
	29	29	29	29	29	29	29	24	24	24	24				
	16	16	16	16	16	16	16	16	16	16					
	22														

WORLD CHAMPIONSHIP • ROUND 9

GERMAN GRAND PRIX

Above: With firecrackers, flags and blaring horns creating a carnival atmosphere, Michael Schumacher acknowledges the cheers of his adoring fans after winning his home Grand Prix.

Right: Plans for Damon Hill to join Schumacher for the driver parade were dropped; instead the Benetton star and his team-mate Johnny Herbert found themselves sharing a car with Roberto Moreno and Pedro Diniz!

GERMAN GRAND PRIX

SCHUMACHER
COULTHARD
BERGER
HERBERT
BOULLION
SUZUKI

Diary

Jacques Villeneuve impresses the Williams team in a three-day test held at Silverstone in the week immediately following the German Grand Prix.

Former Lotus driver Pedro Lamy confirmed to replace Pierluigi Martini at Minardi for the balance of the season.

Alain Prost is linked to possible F1 return with McLaren-Mercedes.

Indy Car veteran Danny Sullivan breaks his pelvis in accident during Michigan 500.

McLaren announces plans for all-new, purpose-built technical headquarters on 120-acre site near Woking.

For Damon Hill, the 1995 German Grand Prix yielded the worst possible nightmare imaginable to round off a weekend during which he had attracted a level of retrospective criticism for his collision with Michael Schumacher only two weeks earlier.

Having completed the opening lap almost two seconds ahead of the World Champion, Hill's own title chances suffered a massive setback as he lost control at the first right-hander after the pits, his Williams FW17 spinning backwards across the gravel trap and into the retaining tyre barrier.

The tabloid media rushed forward to post the obituary notices on Hill's professional career. Yet those who scrutinised video tapes of his spin were left with a nagging suspicion that the car pirouetted out of control a little early in the corner for it to have been pure driver error. Sure enough, within days, Williams put out a communiqué acknowledging that a problem with a rear driveshaft joint could have contributed to the problem.

'We have identified a left-hand rear driveshaft joint showing unusual wear,' said Patrick Head. 'It is not beyond reasonable doubt that this could well have contributed to the spin.' Either way, the team thought it questionable that the FW17 would have lasted the full race distance suffering from such a problem.

After Hill's premature departure from the fray, Schumacher pulled steadily away from Coulthard, opening a five-second lead before making his first refuelling stop at the end of lap 19. Coulthard, running a one-stop strategy, briefly went ahead before making his single stop on lap 23, after which Schumacher really pushed hard, building up a sufficiently large cushion to allow himself the luxury of a tactically astute second stop on lap 34 without losing the lead.

Hill's crushing disappointment came after he had dominated the two official qualifying sessions in masterly style, with Schumacher hampered by handling problems and incorrect gear ratios on Friday and then unable to match the Englishman's time in the second timed session the following day.

The relationship between F1's two key players was hardly cordial in the aftermath of their previous tangle. Moreover, their Hockenheim weekend got off to an unfortunate start when a plan for Damon to ride with Michael in the pre-race driver parade was vetoed by F1 supremo Bernie Ecclestone.

'I think it's all hypocritical nonsense,' said Ecclestone, 'a load of rubbish. Damon could easily have apologised last week, but if he says it wasn't his fault, but somebody else's, why does he want to sit in the car beside him? They nearly sat together in the gravel at Silverstone, anyway. If they are together next year in the same team, then they can sit side by side then!'

Bernie also reminded everybody that there are a range of draconian sanctions available to the sport's governing body which can be applied against drivers who repeatedly become involved in collisions. However, this somehow became translated by certain sections of the media into a threat of a life ban on Hill if he became involved in another accident!

Hill replied trenchantly: 'There are rules applied to the sport which have always been there. The result of the inquiry after Silverstone was that both parties were to blame.

'I don't know what has changed by what Mr Ecclestone has said. Is it possible for him to apply penalties at his will? I don't know. Is that the way it works?' It subsequently transpired that Damon had sought out Bernie's advice over how to handle the aftermath of the Silverstone collision. He was advised to phone Michael and apologise, a course of action which Hill considered, then chose not to pursue.

After the Silverstone collision, Hill arrived in Germany to the accompaniment of much media-induced hysteria spiced with the occasional, wayward threat of physical retribution should he have the temerity to come between Schumacher and a possible home win.

Characteristically, Damon played down the prospect of any aggravation, shrewdly waving to the crowd in friendly fashion after spinning off during Friday morning's free practice session, held in conditions of intermittent rain on a damp track throughout.

Hill got caught out by the drying track surface. 'I had switched to slicks and just thought I would complete that lap and come in,' he explained, 'but the conditions just caught me out. But we had done enough work by that stage to get a good feel for the wet-weather set-up. I was pretty happy with it.'

Conditions remained much the same for first qualifying, in which Hill and Coulthard wound up 1-2 at the head of the field. 'It was bloody good fun,' said Damon. 'The majority of the circuit was definitely dry, and we were only about a second off last year's time, which is quite impressive when you think this is a horsepower circuit and we now have only 3 litres instead of 3.5. It certainly says quite a lot for the rate of progress from the cars and engines.

'I was pretty pleased because the conditions were changing all the time. We have a good strong front row – and I wouldn't cry if it was raining tomorrow, but the forecast is that it will be hotter.'

Despite the higher temperatures, Hill kept his advantage on Saturday, Schumacher improving to second place. The Williams FW17 looked fast and stable, with Damon proving particularly quick through the stadium section.

'It's very difficult to make up time on the rest of the circuit, especially between the four of us who are using the same engine,' he said. 'The differences are due to how [well] the car brakes – and the stadium is the only section with long corners. My car is handling beautifully, so the stadium is where I was able to take advantage of it.'

Schumacher was clearly disappointed, but at the same time seemed upbeat about the fact that he had challenged the Williams so closely. 'To be honest, I did not expect to get as close as I did,' he admitted. 'It was a plus to be able to fight so closely with Damon and with David and it was fun. Unfortunately, Damon did too good a job for me in the end!

'We improved the performance of the car significantly, including the balance, which is a good sign for the race after we had some problems finding the right compromise between speed and downforce.'

Behind Coulthard's third-place Williams, Gerhard Berger lined up fourth in the Ferrari 412T2, the Austrian appreciating that a repeat of his 1994 victory certainly looked a long-shot. He had spent three days testing at Imola with Nicola Larini prior to the German race and Gerhard came to Hockenheim confident that the team had a promising aerodynamic set-up available.

Unfortunately, while Berger worked out the optimum balance between downforce and speed, teammate Jean Alesi ran far too much downforce, paying for this error with a distant tenth place in the final grid

157

The dead of night. All seems quiet in the paddock, but in the pit garages many of the teams are still hard at work.

Paul-Henri Cahier

Left: Frank Williams and Damon Hill appear relaxed and confident during qualifying. It all went wrong on race day.

Watch the birdie. Max Papis *(below left)* looks the photographer straight in the eye as he negotiates one of the chicanes!

Below: Paddock guests included Nina Rindt, chatting with John Watson, and her daughter Natasha.

Middle: Heinz-Harald Frentzen hides in the back of his Ford Mondeo to escape the unwanted attentions of the fans.

Aguri Suzuki *(bottom)* struggled to the finish and was rewarded with sixth place.

GERMAN GRAND PRIX

It seemed unlikely that Jean Alesi and Ferrari Team Director Jean Todt would be working together in 1996.

order – his worst qualifying position of the season.

Fifth and sixth on the grid were the Jordan-Peugeots of Rubens Barrichello and Eddie Irvine, the Brazilian having a trouble-free run and reporting himself very happy with the feel of his 195. By contrast, Irvine was rather less satisfied. Having set fourth-quickest time in Saturday's free practice session, he made a minor set-up change to improve the car's rear-end grip after two runs in the afternoon and was confident of a second-row starting position.

'I made a mistake in the middle of my third run,' he said, 'but my fourth was going to be really good, until I came up behind one of the Minardis on an "out" lap. It's pretty easy to see when somebody's behind you on this circuit, so I couldn't believe it when he went into the chicane ahead of me. Then after that he just sat on the line. Unreal!'

Over in the McLaren camp, Ilmor had produced a further-revised 'Phase 2-1' version of the Mercedes FO110 V10 engine for this race, one step further advanced from the unit which displayed such promise in Mika Häkkinen's hands during the early stages of the British GP.

In addition, McLaren had made further changes to the front suspension geometry which, during testing the previous week at Barcelona, had helped Häkkinen to lap comfortably inside his Spanish GP qualifying time. The McLarens took seventh and eighth places on the grid, Häkkinen just ahead of Blundell, after Mika lost time with a major engine breakage on Saturday morning. 'That cost us a lot of time to work out the best qualifying set-up,' said the Finn.

Ninth place went to Johnny Herbert's Benetton. 'The car lacked mechanical grip this morning and did not improve for qualifying,' shrugged the Silverstone winner. 'We made various improvements, but none of them seemed to help me improve enough to move forward substantially.'

Sauber drivers Heinz-Harald Frentzen and Jean-Christophe Boullion had a revised, higher-revving Zetec-R V8 to hand on a weekend when Ford formally confirmed that Cosworth was developing a 3-litre V10 on its behalf for the 1996 season. Frentzen did a good job to qualify 11th, surviving a nasty moment when he clipped the left-rear wheel of Coulthard's Williams as the Scot nipped inside him into the right-

Montezemolo wants Schumacher – and signals Alesi's departure

Ferrari President Luca di Montezemolo gave a firm signal as to the Italian team's intentions in the run-up to the Hockenheim race by confirming that he had made approaches to both Michael Schumacher and Damon Hill for the 1996 season.

Speaking in *La Stampa*, the Italian newspaper regarded as the official mouthpiece of Fiat, Montezemolo was quoted as saying: 'To win in Formula 1, you need three things – a good organisation, a great car and a great driver. In my role as President, I have a duty to bring home the best. Schumacher is undoubtedly the best and I have a duty to think of him.

'We are likely to have a decision by mid-August. But I have been talking not only to Schumacher, but with others as well. With Hill, for example – a very serious type and decidedly faster than he appears to be.'

However, Montezemolo reserved some criticism for Jean Alesi, signalling – correctly – that he would be leaving the team at the end of the season. 'Alesi has been very clear,' continued Luca. 'He has said that the German's presence is not compatible with him.

'Alesi knows how much I admire him. But I have told him this and I say it again: it is important not to make accusations about treachery and not to behave like a little baby.'

Maranello watchers concluded that Montezemolo's words had, in effect, written *finis* to Alesi's five-year Ferrari career.

---

hander leading into the stadium on Saturday morning. Boullion benefited from the revised engine on the second day, the Frenchman reporting positive progress with the C14's handling balance after a test at Nogaro. He lined up 14th.

Olivier Panis took 12th place after a creditable effort, although he was a little disappointed not to have improved on his Friday best time. 'We are going to have a good look at the car to see whether there isn't a problem,' he shrugged. 'I was very with it this morning, running with low downforce, but this afternoon it felt more nervous and I had less grip.'

Aguri Suzuki replaced Martin Brundle in the second JS41, but it proved to be a somewhat troubled return to F1 for the popular Japanese driver. He managed only nine laps in the slippery conditions on Friday morning before thumping into the tyre barrier on the exit of the first turn. He then shunted again in the afternoon, this time suffering briefly from double vision which necessitated a hospital check-up in nearby Mannheim before he was given the all-clear to continue running on Saturday afternoon, qualifying a rather fraught 18th.

The Tyrrell team came to Hockenheim after testing at Magny-Cours without its Hydrolink suspension, which was shelved, both front and rear, for this race. Mika Salo was an impressive 13th fastest overall on his first visit to the circuit, but Ukyo Katayama had a gearbox problem after only five laps on Friday and was very disappointed with his car's handling balance the following day. Although he was only four places behind his Finnish colleague, his time deficit was almost two seconds.

Max Papis showed distinct promise with the Footwork FA15, lining up 15th, with team-mate Taki Inoue down in 19th place, the two Hart V8-engined cars split by Luca Badoer's Minardi, Katayama and Suzuki. Considering the relative power output of the Cosworth EDM V8 against the Mugen and Yamaha V10s, Badoer's performance was extremely respectable. Team-mate Pierluigi Martini emerged in 20th place, ahead of Pedro Diniz in the faster of the Forti FG01s, both of which had a slightly longer wheelbase and a more steeply raked undertray developed following tests in Fiat's Turin-based wind tunnel.

Roberto Moreno qualified the other Forti in 22nd place with the final row of the grid being filled by the Pacifics of Andrea Montermini and Giovanni Lavaggi, the former Porsche 962 racer taking over from Bertrand Gachot in an effort to boost the team's precarious financial position.

Schumacher was comfortably quickest in the race morning warm-up, ahead of Coulthard, Mika Häkkinen's McLaren and Hill, who had an unexpected surprise when he collected the debris from one of the many festive rockets set off by the spectators all round the circuit – in his FW17's cockpit. Thankfully, the projectile was spent and Damon came to no harm!

Immediately prior to the final parade lap, the Forti team ran into trouble when it became clear that the overheating problem experienced by Diniz during the warm-up had been caused by a water pump failure. He switched to the spare car, starting from the pit lane.

As he had done at both Magny-Cours and Silverstone, Damon made a scorching start from pole position, Schumacher tucking in behind as they set out for the first time down the long avenue of pine trees towards the first chicane. Leading from Schumacher in front of 128,000 German race fans, Hill's initial surge at the head of the pack promised an electrifying re-run of the ill-starred confrontation at Silverstone a fortnight earlier.

Braking for the third-gear right-hander which leads out of the stadium at the start of lap two, the rear end of the Williams snapped out of line almost before Damon had turned the car's nose into the corner. Seconds later, he was the most popular man in Germany, opening the way for a commanding victory for the local hero!

Hill was at a loss to explain his sudden loss of control. 'I'm very

161

GERMAN GRAND PRIX

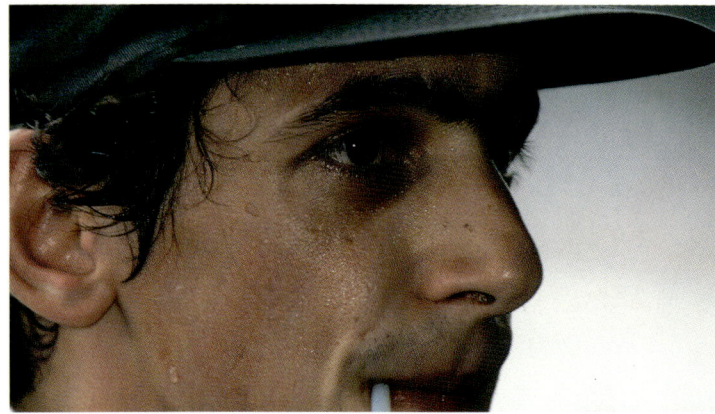

shocked about what happened, because I was very comfortable in the car,' he explained.

'I went into the corner and the rear suddenly locked up, and I went off. I don't have an explanation for it. It's possible that the track was slippery, but I was pushing hard, trying to pull out an advantage. But I must say I've been round that corner enough times this weekend to know whether I was within the limit of it.

'I'm just gutted completely. The first few laps of the race are always a bit tricky, and sometimes brakes come in at different rates. To me, it felt like that – the rear brakes suddenly came on a bit harder than they had done before, and caught me out.

'I was pitched into an oversteer very suddenly. I was not over-doing it. I came down into third gear and the back end went away from me.'

Damon said he had been aware of 'a lot of gunk' spewing from the rear end of his FW17 as the field was kept waiting a little longer than usual on the grid before the starting light came on. Yet he had made his third successive copybook start from pole to lead by almost two seconds at the end of the opening lap.

'The car felt terrific coming through the stadium for the first time,' he said later. However, Schumacher was destined to play second fiddle in front of his adoring crowd for just that single lap. Nor did he spare Hill when asked for his comments later.

'For sure, Damon made a big mistake,' he said firmly. 'He should have known that there would be some deposits on the track at this point. To be honest, I had thought about the first corner after the start. I knew that it would be slippery because everybody drops some oil on the first lap, so I braked early.

'Then I saw Damon suddenly go sideways and thought, "I can't believe this." Then he hit the wall, and I thought, "Fine, that's it."'

By the end of the second lap, Schumacher was 1.2s ahead of Coulthard, with a gap already opening to Berger's Ferrari. Then came Barrichello, Häkkinen, Irvine, Herbert, Blundell, Alesi, Panis and Frentzen. Max Papis had been left on the startline with transmission failure and Mika Salo's Tyrrell retired with clutch problems on the opening lap, so by the time Diniz crawled into the pits to abandon the spare Forti – which had not previously been run all weekend – he was the fourth retirement of the race.

With ten laps completed, Coulthard's Williams was 4.3s down with Barrichello now third for Jordan after an incredulous Berger had been flagged in at the end of lap five to receive a ten-second stop-go penalty for jumping the start.

'I am sure my car was still behind the line when the green light came on,' said Gerhard. 'I was told that when I put it into first gear, the car moved only seven centimetres. But I was still penalised. I think the electronic control system [which monitors the jump starts] is too sensitive.'

Berger resumed in 14th place to begin a long, hard charge back into contention. Meanwhile, by lap 12 Blundell had moved his McLaren into sixth place behind Häkkinen and Irvine after Alesi suddenly dived into the pits for an unscheduled stop, complaining that his Ferrari V12 had started to run ragged. He took on fresh tyres and some extra fuel, but returned for good to retire next time round.

On lap 15, Barrichello came in for what was due to be the first of two stops, promoting the hard-charging Häkkinen – another on a single-stop strategy – to third. Blundell was now fourth ahead of Barrichello and Irvine, but Mark would only last another three laps before his Mercedes V10 expired and he stopped out on the circuit. Meanwhile, Irvine began to report trouble with his brakes and his Peugeot V10 developed a misfire, so after his first scheduled stop on lap 22 he was called in again for an adjustment to be made to the engine's mapping.

On lap 19, it was Schumacher's turn to come in for his first refuelling stop, the Benetton remaining stationary for 8.9s before resuming in second place. Two laps later, Barrichello's engine failed after he had climbed back to fourth, a bitter disappointment for the Jordan squad, which had been aiming for a podium finish with some confidence.

Coulthard hung on in the lead until lap 23 when he made his single refuelling stop (15.3s), allowing Schumacher back ahead. Häkkinen was now a secure third, while the remarkable Berger was back to fourth ahead of Herbert's Benetton, Frentzen, Jean-Christophe Boullion in the second Sauber and Aguri Suzuki's Ligier.

On lap 24, the gap between Schumacher and Coulthard was 17.908s, close enough to make things marginal for the German if he was to keep ahead at his second refuelling stop. So Michael began to push hard. On lap 25, he extended his lead to 20.024s, but Coulthard trimmed it back slightly to 19.9s two laps later. But then Schumacher really got to grips with the Williams challenge, confidently asserting his superiority. By lap 29, the gap was up to 21.981s, then 23.24s and finally 25.076s over the next two laps.

Lap 34 saw Schumacher stop for the second time, his 24.1s advantage being reduced to 7.8s by the time he rejoined. On the same lap, Häkkinen retired with engine failure, while Frentzen had dropped from sixth on lap 33 when his Sauber's Ford Zetec-R blew up spectacularly.

By now, Schumacher had it in the bag, effectively home and dry on fresh tyres if he didn't make a slip. In the closing stages of the race, he paced himself with iron discipline, allowing his advantage over Coulthard to dwindle to 5.98s at the chequered flag.

Michael admitted that he had felt under pressure from Coulthard for much of the distance. 'I really had to push very hard in the beginning and middle stint to make sure I got out of my second stop ahead,' he admitted.

Even so, Coulthard was clearly disappointed by his apparent inability to pick up the winning gauntlet after Hill's early departure from the contest. 'I knew I would have to push very hard because we were only doing one stop,' he said, 'and perhaps I was a little more aware of getting to the finish rather than risking an off.'

Third place was well taken by Berger, while British GP winner Herbert survived a race of attrition to claim fourth place. All in all, this was a frustrating day for Johnny, who had to grapple with a throttle blipper working only intermittently on the downchange and a clutch which packed up shortly before the end. He did not finish the afternoon in a very happy frame of mind.

Fifth place fell to Boullion ahead of Suzuki's Ligier, that final point moving the French team ahead of McLaren in the constructors' points standings. The Japanese driver had an eventful race, sliding wide over the Ostkurve chicane with a punctured rear tyre just after half-distance and the JS41 later catching fire spectacularly on the slowing-down lap. 'Three laps from home, I smelled oil,' explained Aguri. 'I prayed for it to get to the finish and it finally caught fire just after the line. It couldn't have been closer!'

Williams test driver Jean-Christophe Boullion *(above left)* survived a race of attrition to open his World Championship account with fifth place for Sauber.

Above: Damon Hill's World Championship prospects were dealt a severe blow when, having made a perfect start from pole position, he spun out of the race at the start of the second lap.

David Coulthard *(right)* guided the second Williams to a secure second place but never looked likely to pose a serious threat to Schumacher's supremacy.

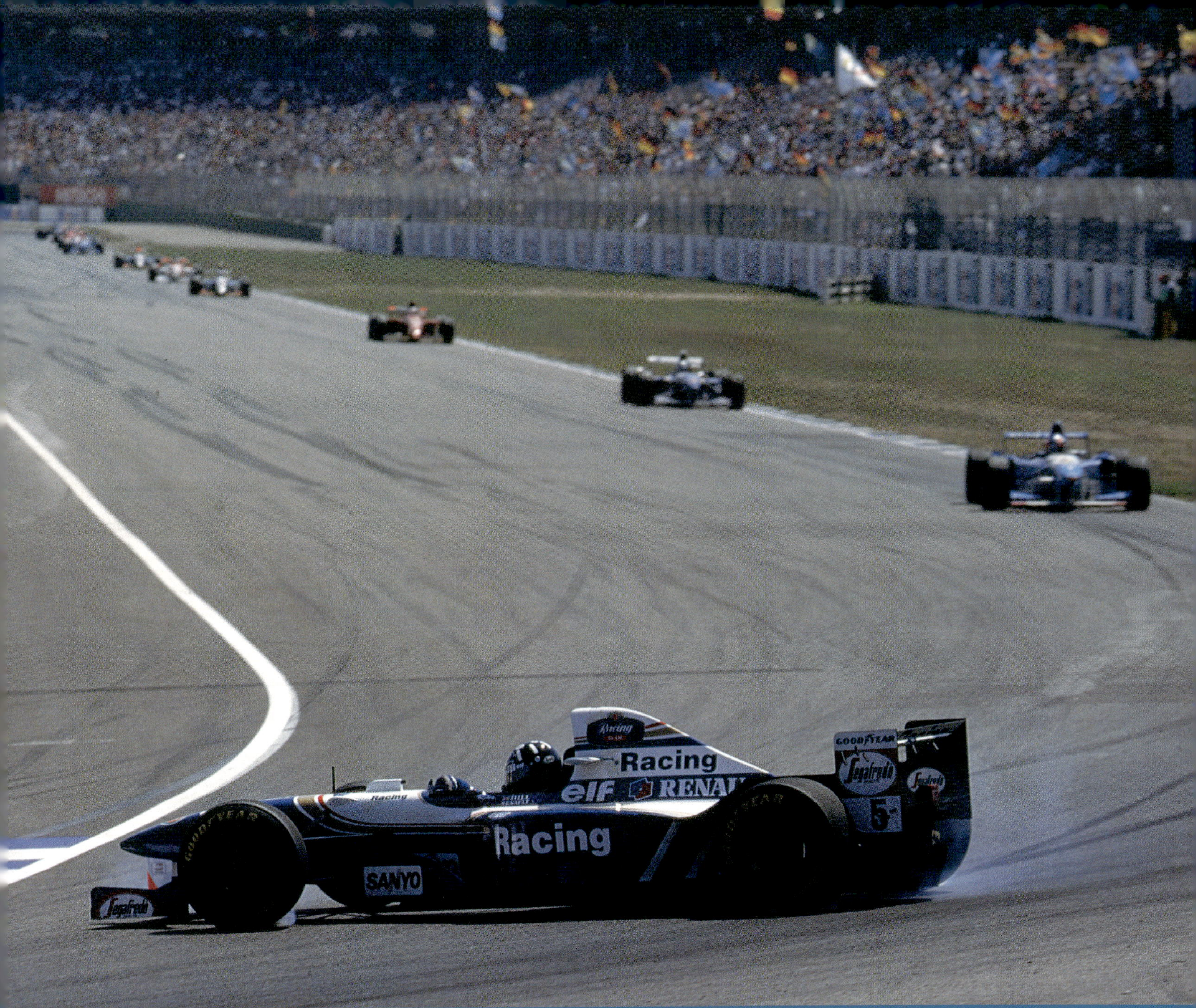

Darren Heath/Zooom Photographic

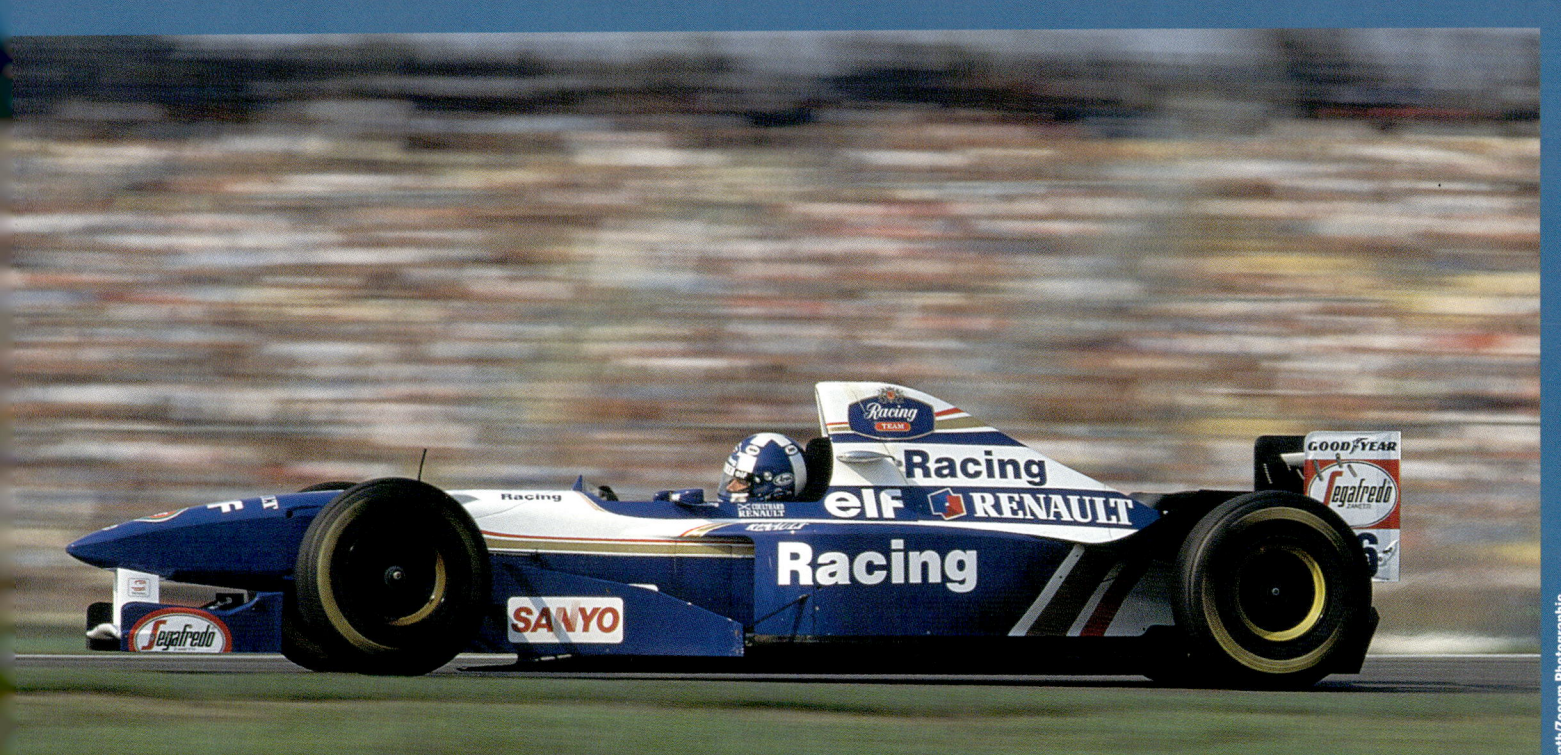

FIA FORMULA ONE WORLD CHAMPIONSHIP ROUND 9

GROSSER MOBIL 1 PREIS VON DEUTSCHLAND

HOCKENHEIM 28–30 JULY 1995

Race distance: 45 laps, 190.558 miles/306.675 km
Race weather: Hot, dry, sunny

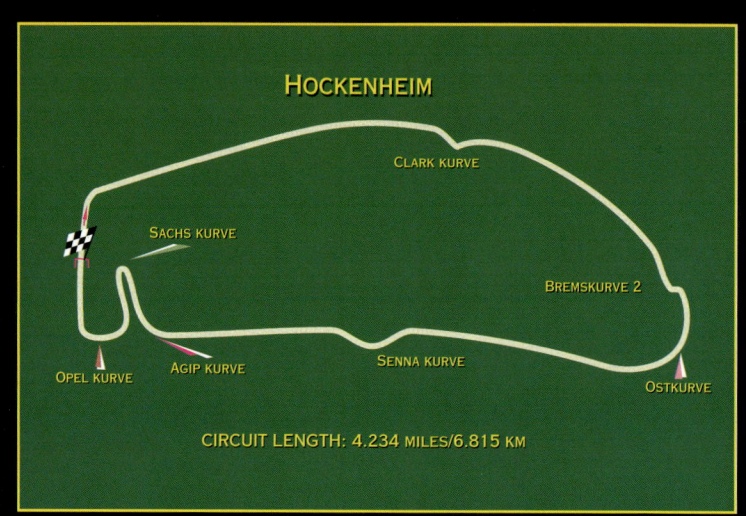

Place	Driver	Nat.	No.	Entrant	Car/Engine	Laps	Time/Retirement	Speed (mph/km/h)
1	**Michael Schumacher**	D	1	Mild Seven Benetton Renault	Benetton B195-Renault RS7B V10	45	1h 22m 56.043s	138.019/222.120
2	**David Coulthard**	GB	6	Rothmans Williams Renault	Williams FW17-Renault RS7B V10	45	1h 23m 02.031s	137.853/221.853
3	**Gerhard Berger**	A	28	Scuderia Ferrari	Ferrari 412T2 044 V12	45	1h 24m 04.140s	136.155/219.121
4	**Johnny Herbert**	GB	2	Mild Seven Benetton Renault	Benetton B195-Renault RS7B V10	45	1h 24m 19.479s	135.743/218.457
5	**Jean-Christophe Boullion**	F	29	Red Bull Sauber Ford	Sauber C14-Ford Zetec-R V8	44		
6	**Aguri Suzuki**	J	25	Ligier Gitanes Blondes	Ligier JS41-Mugen Honda MF301 V10	44		
7	Ukyo Katayama	J	3	Nokia Tyrrell Yamaha	Tyrrell 023-Yamaha OX10C V10	44		
8	Andrea Montermini	I	17	Pacific Grand Prix Ltd	Pacific PR02-Ford ED V8	42		
9	Eddie Irvine	GB	15	Total Jordan Peugeot	Jordan 195-Peugeot A10 V10	41	Engine	
	Mika Häkkinen	SF	8	Marlboro McLaren Mercedes	McLaren MP4/10B-Mercedes FO110 V10	33	Engine	
	Heinz-Harald Frentzen	D	30	Red Bull Sauber Ford	Sauber C14-Ford Zetec-R V8	32	Engine	
	Luca Badoer	I	24	Minardi Scuderia Italia	Minardi M195-Ford EDM V8	28	Gearbox	
	Giovanni Lavaggi	I	16	Pacific Grand Prix Ltd	Pacific PR02-Ford ED V8	27	Gearbox	
	Roberto Moreno	BR	22	Parmalat Forti Ford	Forti FG01-Ford ED V8	27	Driveshaft	
	Rubens Barrichello	BR	14	Total Jordan Peugeot	Jordan 195-Peugeot A10 V10	20	Engine	
	Mark Blundell	GB	7	Marlboro McLaren Mercedes	McLaren MP4/10B-Mercedes FO110 V10	17	Engine	
	Olivier Panis	F	26	Ligier Gitanes Blondes	Ligier JS41-Mugen Honda MF301 V10	13	Engine	
	Jean Alesi	F	27	Scuderia Ferrari	Ferrari 412T2 044 V12	12	Engine	
	Pierluigi Martini	I	23	Minardi Scuderia Italia	Minardi M195-Ford EDM V8	11	Engine	
	Taki Inoue	J	10	Footwork Hart	Footwork FA16-Hart 830 V8	9	Gearbox	
	Pedro Diniz	BR	21	Parmalat Forti Ford	Forti FG01-Ford ED V8	8	Brakes	
	Damon Hill	GB	5	Rothmans Williams Renault	Williams FW17-Renault RS7B V10	1	Spun off	
	Mika Salo	SF	4	Nokia Tyrrell Yamaha	Tyrrell 023-Yamaha OX10C V10	0	Clutch	
DNS	Massimiliano Papis	I	9	Footwork Hart	Footwork FA16-Hart 830 V8	0	Transmission	

Fastest lap: Schumacher, on lap 22, 1m 48.824s, 140.250 mph/225.711 km/h.
Lap record: David Coulthard (Williams FW16-Renault V10), 1m 46.211s, 143.700 mph/231.264 km/h (1994).

All cars used Goodyear tyres

FOR THE RECORD

First Grand Prix start
Giovanni Lavaggi

First Grand Prix points
Jean-Christophe Boullion

STARTING GRID

5 HILL (1m 44.385s) Williams		1 SCHUMACHER (1m 44.465s) Benetton	
6 COULTHARD (1m 44.540s) Williams		28 BERGER (1m 45.553s) Ferrari	
14 BARRICHELLO (1m 45.765s) Jordan		15 IRVINE (1m 45.846s) Jordan	
8 HÄKKINEN (1m 45.849s) McLaren		7 BLUNDELL (1m 46.221s) McLaren	
2 HERBERT (1m 46.315s) Benetton		27 ALESI (1m 46.356s) Ferrari	
30 FRENTZEN (1m 46.801s) Sauber		26 PANIS (1m 47.372s) Ligier	
4 SALO (1m 47.507s) Tyrrell		29 BOULLION (1m 47.636s) Sauber	
9 PAPIS* (1m 48.093s) Footwork		24 BADOER (1m 49.302s) Minardi	
3 KATAYAMA (1m 49.402s) Tyrrell		25 SUZUKI (1m 49.716s) Ligier	
10 INOUE (1m 49.892s) Footwork		23 MARTINI (1m 49.990s) Minardi	
21 DINIZ** (1m 52.961s) Forti		22 MORENO (1m 53.405s) Forti	
17 MONTERMINI (1m 53.492s) Pacific		16 LAVAGGI (1m 54.625s) Pacific	

* did not start
** started from pit lane

TIME SHEETS

Friday free practice
Intermittent rain, damp track throughout

Pos.	Driver	Laps	Time
1	Jean Alesi	17	1m 54.130s
2	Michael Schumacher	18	1m 59.504s
3	Damon Hill	15	2m 00.474s
4	David Coulthard	16	2m 00.779s
5	Luca Badoer	18	2m 01.028s
6	Gerhard Berger	15	2m 01.173s
7	Johnny Herbert	16	2m 01.716s
8	Jean-Christophe Boullion	15	2m 02.342s
9	Heinz-Harald Frentzen	12	2m 02.362s
10	Olivier Panis	21	2m 02.902s
11	Mika Salo	20	2m 03.379s
12	Rubens Barrichello	18	2m 03.631s
13	Ukyo Katayama	19	2m 03.816s
14	Massimiliano Papis	12	2m 04.862s
15	Pierluigi Martini	16	2m 05.086s
16	Eddie Irvine	6	2m 05.194s
17	Mika Häkkinen	14	2m 06.045s
18	Taki Inoue	12	2m 07.920s
19	Mark Blundell	13	2m 08.435s
20	Roberto Moreno	19	2m 08.613s
21	Giovanni Lavaggi	9	2m 12.617s
22	Aguri Suzuki	9	2m 13.438s
23	Pedro Diniz	10	2m 19.801s
24	Andrea Montermini	1	18m 32.469s

Saturday free practice
Hot and humid

Pos.	Driver	Laps	Time
1	David Coulthard	21	1m 44.689s
2	Damon Hill	23	1m 45.554s
3	Rubens Barrichello	19	1m 46.301s
4	Eddie Irvine	14	1m 46.320s
5	Mika Häkkinen	4	1m 46.638s
6	Michael Schumacher	17	1m 46.959s
7	Jean Alesi	17	1m 47.032s
8	Mark Blundell	16	1m 47.404s
9	Johnny Herbert	20	1m 47.431s
10	Olivier Panis	23	1m 47.758s
11	Jean-Christophe Boullion	23	1m 48.416s
12	Heinz-Harald Frentzen	16	1m 48.780s
13	Mika Salo	22	1m 49.103s
14	Massimiliano Papis	15	1m 49.218s
15	Ukyo Katayama	22	1m 49.229s
16	Gerhard Berger	5	1m 49.286s
17	Luca Badoer	23	1m 50.615s
18	Pierluigi Martini	17	1m 50.857s
19	Taki Inoue	11	1m 51.667s
20	Andrea Montermini	12	1m 53.068s
21	Roberto Moreno	15	1m 53.102s
22	Pedro Diniz	23	1m 53.808s
23	Giovanni Lavaggi	8	2m 00.248s
	Aguri Suzuki	0	no time

Friday qualifying
Damp, track drying steadily

Pos.	Driver	Laps	Time
1	Damon Hill	12	1m 44.932s
2	David Coulthard	12	1m 45.306s
3	Michael Schumacher	12	1m 45.505s
4	Mika Häkkinen	7	1m 46.291s
5	**Jean Alesi**	12	**1m 46.356s**
6	Johnny Herbert	12	1m 46.381s
7	Gerhard Berger	12	1m 46.482s
8	Eddie Irvine	11	1m 46.916s
9	**Olivier Panis**	12	**1m 47.372s**
10	Heinz-Harald Frentzen	11	1m 47.769s
11	Mark Blundell	8	1m 47.854s
12	Rubens Barrichello	9	1m 48.203s
13	Jean-Christophe Boullion	11	1m 48.526s
14	Mika Salo	12	1m 49.505s
15	Massimiliano Papis	12	1m 49.621s
16	Luca Badoer	12	1m 50.409s
17	Taki Inoue	12	1m 50.451s
18	Pierluigi Martini	12	1m 51.368s
19	Roberto Moreno	12	1m 53.456s
20	**Andrea Montermini**	5	**1m 53.492s**
21	Pedro Diniz	12	1m 54.303s
22	**Giovanni Lavaggi**	11	**1m 54.625s**
23	Ukyo Katayama	5	1m 56.518s
24	Aguri Suzuki	3	2m 04.193s

Saturday qualifying
Hot, humid, variable cloud

Pos.	Driver	Laps	Time
1	**Damon Hill**	10	**1m 44.385s**
2	**Michael Schumacher**	11	**1m 44.465s**
3	**David Coulthard**	11	**1m 44.540s**
4	**Gerhard Berger**	11	**1m 45.553s**
5	**Rubens Barrichello**	12	**1m 45.765s**
6	**Eddie Irvine**	12	**1m 45.846s**
7	**Mika Häkkinen**	12	**1m 45.849s**
8	**Mark Blundell**	11	**1m 46.221s**
9	**Johnny Herbert**	9	**1m 46.315s**
10	Jean Alesi	11	1m 46.475s
11	**Heinz-Harald Frentzen**	10	**1m 46.801s**
12	**Mika Salo**	12	**1m 47.507s**
13	Olivier Panis	11	1m 47.528s
14	**Jean-Christophe Boullion**	11	**1m 47.636s**
15	**Massimiliano Papis**	12	**1m 48.093s**
16	**Luca Badoer**	11	**1m 49.302s**
17	**Ukyo Katayama**	12	**1m 49.402s**
18	**Aguri Suzuki**	12	**1m 49.716s**
19	**Taki Inoue**	12	**1m 49.892s**
20	**Pierluigi Martini**	12	**1m 49.990s**
21	**Pedro Diniz**	12	**1m 52.961s**
22	**Roberto Moreno**	12	**1m 53.405s**
23	Giovanni Lavaggi	7	1m 56.335s
	Andrea Montermini	0	no time

Warm-up
Sunny and bright

Pos.	Driver	Laps	Time
1	Michael Schumacher	10	1m 47.452s
2	David Coulthard	8	1m 47.602s
3	Mika Häkkinen	9	1m 47.740s
4	Damon Hill	11	1m 48.131s
5	Rubens Barrichello	11	1m 48.499s
6	Jean Alesi	8	1m 48.640s
7	Johnny Herbert	12	1m 49.115s
8	Heinz-Harald Frentzen	11	1m 49.125s
9	Olivier Panis	12	1m 49.158s
10	Gerhard Berger	12	1m 49.181s
11	Eddie Irvine	10	1m 49.290s
12	Mark Blundell	8	1m 49.598s
13	Jean-Christophe Boullion	10	1m 49.991s
14	Mika Salo	9	1m 50.226s
15	Aguri Suzuki	11	1m 50.953s
16	Ukyo Katayama	10	1m 51.099s
17	Massimiliano Papis	12	1m 51.115s
18	Luca Badoer	11	1m 52.207s
19	Pierluigi Martini	11	1m 52.837s
20	Taki Inoue	10	1m 53.039s
21	Andrea Montermini	11	1m 53.114s
22	Roberto Moreno	9	1m 55.466s
23	Giovanni Lavaggi	9	1m 56.292s
24	Pedro Diniz	1	4m 40.009s

Race fastest laps
Hot, dry, sunny

Driver	Time	Lap
Michael Schumacher	1m 48.824s	22
David Coulthard	1m 49.787s	8
Mika Häkkinen	1m 49.900s	14
Gerhard Berger	1m 49.926s	20
Rubens Barrichello	1m 49.982s	12
Damon Hill	1m 49.989s	1
Eddie Irvine	1m 50.646s	30
Jean Alesi	1m 50.672s	10
Olivier Panis	1m 50.690s	7
Mark Blundell	1m 50.882s	9
Johnny Herbert	1m 50.929s	25
Heinz-Harald Frentzen	1m 51.426s	14
Aguri Suzuki	1m 51.760s	25
Jean-Christophe Boullion	1m 52.033s	20
Ukyo Katayama	1m 52.791s	25
Luca Badoer	1m 53.522s	12
Pierluigi Martini	1m 54.248s	11
Andrea Montermini	1m 54.341s	23
Taki Inoue	1m 55.047s	7
Roberto Moreno	1m 56.469s	6
Giovanni Lavaggi	1m 58.894s	8
Pedro Diniz	2m 02.176s	2

CHASSIS LOG BOOK

1	Schumacher	Benetton B195/6
2	Herbert	Benetton B195/5
	spare	Benetton B195/1
3	Katayama	Tyrrell 023/6
4	Salo	Tyrrell 023/5
	spare	Tyrrell 023/2
5	Hill	Williams FW17/4
6	Coulthard	Williams FW17/5
	spare	Williams FW17/2
7	Blundell	McLaren MP4/10B/6
8	Häkkinen	McLaren MP4/10B/5
	spare	McLaren MP4/10B/2
9	Papis	Footwork FA16/3
10	Inoue	Footwork FA16/4
	spare	Footwork FA16/1
14	Barrichello	Jordan 195/4
15	Irvine	Jordan 195/5
	spare	Jordan 195/1
16	Lavaggi	Pacific PR02/1
17	Montermini	Pacific PR02/2
21	Diniz	Forti FG01/4
22	Moreno	Forti FG01/3
	spare	Forti FG01/2
23	Martini	Minardi M195/3
24	Badoer	Minardi M195/2
	spare	Minardi M195/1
25	Suzuki	Ligier JS41/5
26	Panis	Ligier JS41/3
	spare	Ligier JS41/4
27	Alesi	Ferrari 412T2/161
28	Berger	Ferrari 412T2/162
	spare	Ferrari 412T2/160
29	Boullion	Sauber C14/5
30	Frentzen	Sauber C14/6
	spare	Sauber C14/2

POINTS TABLES

Drivers

1	Michael Schumacher	56
2	Damon Hill	35
3	Jean Alesi	32
4	Johnny Herbert	25
5	David Coulthard	23
6	Gerhard Berger	21
7 =	Rubens Barrichello	7
7 =	Olivier Panis	7
9	Eddie Irvine	6
10 =	Mika Häkkinen	5
10 =	Mark Blundell	5
10 =	Heinz-Harald Frentzen	5
13	Martin Brundle	3
14	Jean-Christophe Boullion	2
15	Gianni Morbidelli	1

Constructors

1	Benetton	71
2	Ferrari	53
3	Williams	52
4	Jordan	13
5	Ligier	11
6	McLaren	10
7	Sauber	7
8	Footwork	1

WORLD CHAMPIONSHIP • ROUND 10

HUNGARIAN GRAND PRIX

HILL
COULTHARD
BERGER
HERBERT
FRENTZEN
PANIS

HUNGARIAN GRAND PRIX

Diary

F3 front-runner Ralph Firman Jnr gets run in F1 McLaren-Mercedes.

Al Unser Jnr's Penske-Mercedes wins Indy Car race at Mid-Ohio.

Shell tipped to return to F1, replacing Agip as Ferrari's fuel sponsor.

Former Minardi aerodynamicist René Hilhorst switches to Sauber.

Master of all he surveys. Damon Hill needed to win in Hungary to revive his fading World Championship hopes and responded to the pressure in typically determined style, scoring a truly dominant victory from pole position.

Damon Hill's Williams FW17 may have looked a more comfortable car to drive than Michael Schumacher's Benetton B195, but that in no way detracted from the confident level of domination exerted by the English driver throughout the Hungarian Grand Prix weekend.

Frustrated by his retirements at Silverstone and Hockenheim, Hill came to Budapest knowing that this would be the crunch weekend. If he didn't win, then Schumacher's 21-point advantage in the drivers' title stakes was likely to become extended to unmanageable proportions. The only way for Damon to redress the balance was with a win on the second anniversary of his maiden F1 success round one of the most tiring and physically demanding tracks on the calendar.

Hill began his weekend in Budapest by setting course for his fourth successive pole position from the moment first qualifying started. There was no time to waste, and he knew it.

The Williams driver was in scintillating form, lapping 0.6s faster than team-mate David Coulthard to head the field on a day when Schumacher's Benetton was left trailing in fourth place behind Gerhard Berger's Ferrari. Damon really had the FW17 chassis working brilliantly in the sweltering conditions, despite the fact that he had grained one set of tyres during the morning's free practice session after making his first run a little too early.

In the afternoon he made his first run in spectacular style on the same worn tyres, posting a 1m 21.012s best to vault to the head of the timing sheets. Then Berger trumped that with a 1m 19.515s, followed by Schumacher, who took the Benetton round in 1m 19.490s. But Hill had their measure.

His Williams was fitted with fresh tyres and he flew round in 1m 18.374s to finish the first day in provisional pole position. 'This is a race where you have to be on the front row,' he said with satisfaction. 'I am very pleased with today's performance, which seemed pretty dominant and the sort of performance we are always expecting.

'I do not expect Michael to stay where he is tomorrow, but if he does then he's got problems. We need to display this sort of advantage if we are to win races. The fact is that I have a 21-point deficit and the only way out is to go forward.'

Coulthard reported that his FW17 still suffered a touch too much understeer. 'I tried to drive through it and that's why I had a quick spin,' he explained. 'I also had a brief problem with the throttle control – rather like I experienced in Argentina – but that was soon fixed.'

Berger was well satisfied with his Ferrari's feel, but Jean Alesi looked increasingly wayward from the very start of first qualifying. He had a tyre-smoking spin on the hairpin before the pits, then set fifth-fastest time before slamming off the road into a tyre barrier at around 120 mph. The Frenchman sustained slight whiplash injuries and was taken to hospital in Budapest for a precautionary check-up, but later released.

Commented Berger: 'I think I could even have got onto the front row had the engine not lost power on the second half of the lap. Modifications to the rear suspension, which we have developed in the last two weeks of testing, worked well and have allowed us to close up on the front-runners.'

Overtaking at the tortuous Hungaroring is more difficult than on possibly any other circuit apart from Monaco, relying as it does on a pursuer risking a collision or the driver in front making a mistake. With that in mind, a directive from the FIA's executive race director John Corsmit merely served to increase the uncertainty surrounding driver etiquette.

In essence, this was a rule clarification inviting stewards to apportion blame for any future F1 collisions on the basis that the car being overtaken should concede the corner once any part of the pursuing car has drawn level with 'any part of the car being overtaken'. On the face of it, this would have meant Schumacher being entirely to blame for the Silverstone collision. It was a development which caused a great deal of concern among the drivers. Understandably so.

'This is an unusual question, having to judge from a driver's point of view when another car is partly alongside you,' noted Coulthard. 'The new rule now states that when someone has part of his car alongside part of your car, then effectively he has the corner. I guess this rule is aimed at making everyone focus more [on what is happening behind] and to stop crazy manoeuvres.'

Hill added: 'I am mystified by these new rules.' Then he added an ironic reference to Adelaide last year: 'yet to my mind, it has come ten months too

HUNGARIAN GRAND PRIX

Hampered by oversteer in the early stages, David Coulthard *(left)* completed a good day for Williams with second place, but the Scot seemed destined for pastures new in 1996 . . .

Inset left: **Michael Schumacher battled long and hard to get on terms with Damon Hill's Williams only for fuel pump failure to eliminate his Benetton-Renault four laps from the flag.**

Villeneuve joins Williams

Indy 500 winner Jacques Villeneuve, son of the late Ferrari star Gilles, was confirmed as David Coulthard's successor in the Williams-Renault squad for the 1996 season immediately after the Hungarian Grand Prix. At the same time, Damon Hill was re-signed for another year in a deal reputed to be worth in the region of £6 million.

Damon's negotiating position with Williams had been enhanced not only by offers of a place in the Benetton-Renault line-up, but also by an invitation from the Newman-Haas Indy Car team to follow in Nigel Mansell's footsteps for 1996. 'I think any time you can have a choice of teams that are at the top, you have to consider yourself to be in a very privileged position, so I can't complain about that,' said Hill enigmatically at the Hungaroring, a couple of days before the continuation of his Williams deal was officially announced.

The confirmation of 24-year-old Villeneuve's recruitment came after an intensive three-day test programme at Silverstone during which the young French-Canadian impressed the Williams squad with his speed, commitment and maturity at the wheel of an FW17. In the immediate aftermath of the test, Frank Williams remarked: 'He's obviously got the right stuff. We will have to move quickly on this.'

Villeneuve's Indy Car entrant Barry Green said regretfully, 'Obviously we are sad to lose Jacques as a member of our team. He is one of the most talented drivers I have ever worked with and will be a star in F1.'

Meanwhile, David Coulthard and Williams failed to agree terms for 1996, the young Scot apparently having made his mind up that his career prospects would be better served by seeking pastures new for his second full season in F1. The confidence displayed by Coulthard's manager that 'David would be with a top team in 1996' tended to confirm paddock speculation that he had revived links with McLaren, the team which had originally made him a counter-offer for 1995, the validity of which was rejected by the FIA Contract Recognition Board in Lausanne.

---

late.' Thankfully, after energetic overtures from the team owners, the new rules were suspended on race morning. At least for this race.

Over in the McLaren camp, Mika Häkkinen took sixth place at the end of the first day, but the 2.2s deficit to Hill was certainly regarded with disappointment by Ron Dennis's crew. Both Mika and Mark Blundell used the small central aerofoil fitted on the tail of the engine cover in the quest for increased downforce. It was promising, but Häkkinen confessed that he could still not quite rid the car of its irritating understeer.

With track conditions speeding up as the rubber went down on Saturday morning, second qualifying turned out to be an absolutely electrifying affair. Coulthard set the ball rolling with a 1m 18.362s, then Hill trimmed this back to 1m 18.231s just after the session's midway point.

Coulthard was clearly out to enhance his F1 credentials in a week when his departure from Williams at the end of the season had been confirmed, storming round in 1m 17.588s on a fresh set of rubber. Then Berger went second fastest with a 1m 18.217s, followed by Schumacher, who claimed a place on the front row with a 1m 18.085s, despite a lurid slide at the final corner. Now Damon was down to fourth place.

Yet the Williams team leader was certainly not flustered. With just under ten minutes left, he dug deep into his personal resources to produce an amazing 1m 16.982s, throwing pole out of Coulthard's reach by three-tenths of a second. And then he spun off going into the first right-hander after the pits!

'I was just glancing down at my lap time read-out as I went into the braking area, and it just got away from me,' he explained, having kept the engine running and edged successfully back onto the circuit.

'I had a couple of bad runs and this just made me a bit more determined to get pole. Hats off to the team, though; they worked brilliantly under a lot of pressure.

'It was pretty exciting. I would say this is potentially the most important pole of my career. There are no two ways about it, I have to be at the front here to stand any chance of winning, but as we know we have had four poles without any success. I am pretty determined to put that right tomorrow.'

Schumacher then went out for a final run, but the World Champion's Benetton was short on front-end grip and rear-end stability. Coming through the final right-hander onto the pit straight, the B195 suddenly snapped into a tyre-smoking spin. Schuey kept his foot hard on the throttle, the car gyrated through 360 degrees and he completed the lap in 1m 19.7s – good enough for seventh place on the grid and quicker than the increasingly beleaguered Johnny Herbert could manage using a more conventional technique in the second Benetton.

'The car is quite unstable and just doesn't have as much mechanical grip [as the Williams],' said Schumacher. 'We are on the limit everywhere and the car feels critical. But we did run full tanks and it handles OK.

'We improved the car and got close, but it was still sliding and jumping over everything. In certain places it was understeering like hell and I was trying to overcome it with the throttle.'

Meanwhile, Berger was quite satisfied that he could have done no more with the Ferrari 412T2, describing his fourth-fastest lap as 'a moral pole position'. By contrast, Alesi's problems continued throughout Saturday. After being given a clean bill of health to return to the cockpit of a new car built up round a fresh monocoque, he was soon stranded out on the circuit with a gearbox failure during the morning. In the afternoon, he posted sixth-fastest time, then spun and stalled.

Häkkinen turned in McLaren's best dry-weather qualifying performance of the season, the Finn's MP4/10B lining up fifth in the final order – equalling his previous best in the rain at Buenos Aires. Unfortunately, Mark Blundell's Mercedes V10 blew up on only its third lap and he slipped to 13th place overall. 'In retrospect, we should have changed it after the morning session,' said Mark, 'because it didn't feel quite right then.'

Eddie Irvine's Jordan emerged in seventh place, his first Saturday run hampered by a throttle problem. 'I touched the throttle, the revs went crazy and then the engine cut out altogether,' he explained. 'Thankfully I was approaching the pit lane when it happened, so I was able to coast in.'

Irvine's second session times were subsequently disallowed because his car was deemed to have been pushed illegally out on the circuit as he eased his way into the pits, dropping him from seventh to 15th. However, they were then reinstated on a technicality – the original time sheet had not been marked 'provisional' so the stewards decreed that the original order should stand.

Rubens Barrichello, meanwhile, lost power and pulled into the pits with engine trouble, taking 14th place in the final grid order.

Over at Ligier, Martin Brundle's JS41 had to be fitted with a new wiring loom after Friday free practice when it was found that an unsoldered electrical lead was causing the gearbox to develop a mind of its own, changing up and down without warning. Things went much better for Martin in second qualifying and he vaulted forward to take eighth on the grid, two places ahead of team-mate Olivier Panis, whose progress was thwarted by unexpected understeer.

At Sauber, both Heinz-Harald Frentzen and Jean-Christophe Boullion started the weekend suffering from flu, which made life quite a struggle for the two works Ford-propelled drivers. Both spun in second qualifying, Frentzen winding up 11th and the Frenchman a rather undistinguished 19th.

Frentzen was quite satisfied. 'The balance of the car was good,' he admitted, 'but there was a lot of dirt on the track when I first went out and I was sure that it would improve. But then Montermini's Pacific, which was going very slowly, blocked me badly and I had to abandon the lap despite being 0.3s up at the first split. When I pushed hard again, the tyres had gone and I spun.'

Luca Badoer (12th) and new boy Pedro Lamy (15th) exploited the full potential of the Minardi M195s to good effect, the Portuguese former Lotus driver displacing old hand Pierluigi Martini by dint of an infusion of personal sponsorship. By contrast, Mika Salo and Ukyo Katayama had a simply dismal time with their Tyrrell 023s. Neither could make sense of the Yamaha-engined cars' handling over the bumpy track surface and had to work like hell to qualify 16th and 17th.

Taki Inoue managed 18th in the Footwork, team-mate Max Papis missing second qualifying after writing off his FA15 monocoque on Saturday morning. He slipped to 20th place overall, with the Pacific and Forti Corse lads taking their usual positions at the back.

With Coulthard alongside him on the front row of the grid and

HUNGARIAN GRAND PRIX

Right: As the luckless Rubens Barrichello (almost hidden) struggles towards the finish line, Gerhard Berger, Johnny Herbert and Heinz-Harald Frentzen sweep past to fill the places behind the victorious Williams-Renaults.

Below: Frentzen holds off the Ligier of Olivier Panis. Barrichello's misfortune enabled the Frenchman to pick up the final championship point on offer.

Bottom: Rubens walks away from his stricken Jordan-Peugeot, having had third place snatched away at the death.

Schumacher boxed in on the second row, Hill clearly found himself facing a golden opportunity to build up an early lead. Nor did he squander that opportunity. At the green light, everything went perfectly, with Hill accelerating cleanly into the lead while the Scot slotted into second place to neutralise Schumacher's immediate challenge.

At the end of the opening lap, Hill was already 1.3s ahead, chased by Coulthard, Schumacher, Berger, Häkkinen, Brundle, Alesi, Irvine, Herbert, Frentzen, Panis and Blundell. On the starting grid, Berger had changed his Ferrari's springs, a late adjustment which he soon regretted as the car began to understeer increasingly during the opening stages of the race. It was not long before he dropped away from Schumacher, but any pressure from Häkkinen quickly evaporated when the McLaren's engine failed on lap four, allowing Brundle's Ligier JS41 through onto the Austrian's tail.

Hill sprinted away impressively in the opening phase of the race, building up a 15.3s advantage by the time Schumacher found a gap and nipped ahead of Coulthard into second place midway round lap 13.

With only six laps completed, Hill had been 4.8s ahead of Coulthard, with a further 0.6s margin back to Schumacher. By lap eight, Damon was reeling off fastest laps in quick succession, looking totally unflustered and completely in command.

'I was amazed at the speed with which Damon disappeared,' said Coulthard, 'particularly as we were running the same race strategy. I had too much oversteer on my first set of tyres, and it caught me out at the chicane when Michael came by. Up until then, I thought I had him under control.'

On lap 16, Coulthard made his first refuelling stop, and next time round both Damon and Michael came in as well, Hill resuming with just over eight seconds in hand over his key rival.

Two laps later the gap had opened to 11.6s, Hill having made some ground in traffic, but then Michael had to make his second refuelling stop earlier than scheduled, coming in on lap 26 because he had not taken on as much fuel as intended at his first stop.

Schumacher's race strategy had been compromised by a malfunction with a valve in his refuelling rig which resulted in his Benetton being short-changed by approximately 15 litres. By the time he made his second stop, the team had discarded his original rig and opted to use the one allocated to Johnny Herbert to service both cars for the remainder of the race.

'That problem put us out of synchronisation with our stops,' explained Michael. 'I came back in just a few laps later and we had to put in a lot more fuel, plus we had to run a lot longer with the tyres, which was not the quickest way. We gave them as hard a time as we could, and it was just a bit unfortunate to stop four laps before the end.

'The car wasn't nice and you could see from the onboard cameras how hard I was working. To run our car quick and on the limit is tough. I think it would have been good enough to win, but Williams did a good job as well.'

As a result, Schumacher was now 28 seconds behind Hill, having just managed to squeeze back into the race ahead of Coulthard's third-placed Williams. By lap 30, Michael had trimmed Damon's advantage to 23.01s, and then reduced it to 19.96s on lap 32, before Hill began to open it out again. Damon set the fastest lap of the race so far on lap 34 and, by the time he came in for his second stop on lap 38, he was 27 seconds ahead.

Hill's FW17 was stationary for 9.4s before slipping back into the fray 1.27s ahead of Schumacher. Then, on lap 44, Hill got a little sideways coming out of the chicane in exactly the same way Coulthard had done. The Benetton edged alongside, but Hill kept the door firmly closed.

'It was a case of the boot being very firmly on the other foot,' he said with obvious satisfaction.

Behind the leaders, Alesi's Ferrari was briefly promoted to third during the first round of refuelling stops, but the Frenchman dropped back to seventh after making his own first stop on lap 19, allowing Coulthard to retake the place. Frentzen was now running fourth ahead of Blundell, with Rubens Barrichello – planning a two-stop run – up to sixth with his Jordan.

Other retirements by this stage included Lavaggi, who spun off in the Pacific, Moreno's Forti and the luckless Taki Inoue. The Japanese novice stopped his Footwork on the circuit when the engine failed and was then knocked down by the course car accelerating along the edge of the track to his assistance. Fortunately, Taki was not seriously hurt and escaped with some uncomfortable bruising.

As the battle continued out on the track, Benetton experienced another fuel leak as they attempted to repair Schumacher's original rig, causing Williams concern about the safety of bringing Coulthard in for his second stop while fuel was mopped up from the pit lane. Happily, with Williams fire extinguishers trained firmly at the Benetton lads, the spillage was duly contained in time for both Coulthard and Herbert to come in at the end of lap 36.

Alesi was running in fourth place when he made his second refuelling stop on lap 39, but his race was ended by engine failure three laps later. By lap 45, the order was Hill, leading by 2.09s from Schumacher, then Coulthard and Blundell, Barrichello, Berger and Brundle. Mark was still running strongly in sixth place, despite fuel pressure problems, when he came in to retire on lap 54.

'I am quite upset, because I think after such a poor weekend so far, the race would have given us a good result,' he said. 'The car was going well and the balance felt good, but unfortunately I had a fuel leak problem from very early on in the race which had a bad effect on my lap times.'

'Eventually the problem extended to the engine and we decided to get it back to the pits rather than lose it out on the circuit. It is a shame, because I felt I had a podium position within my grasp as I was on a two-stop strategy, with all the others in front having to stop one more time.'

Berger was now experiencing really acute understeer, having lost a nose wing end plate against Badoer's Minardi while lapping the Italian backmarker. 'I really had to use all my experience and the available track to keep in front of those who were pushing hard from behind,' he said.

Brundle would continue to chase the Austrian through to lap 67 when, with only ten laps to run, the Mugen's pneumatic valvegear gave out and he pulled in to retire. He had spent most of the race playing cat and mouse with the Ferrari and was frustrated to have encountered this disappointment so late in the day.

'I got off to a terrific start,' said Martin, 'even though I was on the dirty side of the track. The car was going really well, but then I got onto Berger's tail on lap nine, and that was to prove the story of my race. Except for a short period following my pit stops, when Herbert got between me and the Ferrari, I was right with him. But it just wasn't possible to pass because he had the advantage along the start/finish straight.'

Schumacher made his third stop on lap 48, the Benetton being stationary for 10.8s, but Hill successfully retained his advantage through his own third stop at the end of lap 58, resuming with 11.68s in hand over his German rival. From that moment onwards, he had victory in the bag as long as he didn't make a mistake.

Michael looked on course to finish a strong second, but the World Champion's Benetton was sidelined with a failure of its Renault engine's mechanical fuel pump with only four laps left to run. This promoted Coulthard to second, completing the Williams team's first 1-2 finish of the 1995 season.

David was satisfied with second place, even though he openly acknowledged he could not stay with Hill in the opening stages. His oversteer problem from the start was later traced to an incorrectly pressured first set of tyres, caused by a problem with the pre-heating blankets.

Berger's ill-handling Ferrari eventually overtook Rubens Barrichello's failing Jordan within sight of the chequered flag. Rubens had moved into fourth on lap 60 when Herbert made his third refuelling stop and then profited from Schumacher's retirement to take over third place in what seemed like a total vindication of his two-stop strategy.

Then, coming out of the final turn, Barrichello's Peugeot V10 shut down as it suffered a loss of air pressure to the pneumatic valvegear. He could do nothing but limp across the line, dropping to seventh as Berger, Herbert, Frentzen and Panis surged by in those agonising final few yards. It rounded off another bitterly disappointing day for the Jordan squad, as Irvine's 195 had also wilted with clutch failure.

'It was the best win of my F1 career,' said Hill, who had failed to finish the previous two races.

'It was a race I had to win, and I won it, so it was a bit of a pay-back day for me. I think we were pretty well in control throughout.

'Everything went to plan. It was not really clear, but after Schumacher's last stop, we needed a clean stop to get out ahead of him again. But traffic was a problem and it was not over until he dropped out.

'I was mighty relieved, but I think we had him beaten.'

171

FIA FORMULA ONE WORLD CHAMPIONSHIP ROUND 10

MARLBORO MAGYAR NAGYDÍJ
HUNGARORING
11-13 AUGUST 1995

HUNGARORING CIRCUIT
CIRCUIT LENGTH: 2.465 MILES/3.968 KM

Race distance: 77 laps, 189.850 miles/305.536 km
Race weather: Hot, sunny

Place	Driver	Nat.	No.	Entrant	Car/Engine	Laps	Time/Retirement	Speed (mph/km/h)
1	**Damon Hill**	GB	5	Rothmans Williams Renault	Williams FW17-Renault RS7B V10	77	1h 46m 25.721s	107.028/172.248
2	**David Coulthard**	GB	6	Rothmans Williams Renault	Williams FW17-Renault RS7B V10	77	1h 46m 59.119s	106.473/171.352
3	**Gerhard Berger**	A	28	Scuderia Ferrari	Ferrari 412T2 044 V12	76		
4	**Johnny Herbert**	GB	2	Mild Seven Benetton Renault	Benetton B195-Renault RS7B V10	76		
5	**Heinz-Harald Frentzen**	D	30	Red Bull Sauber Ford	Sauber C14-Ford Zetec-R V8	76		
6	**Olivier Panis**	F	26	Ligier Gitanes Blondes	Ligier JS41-Mugen Honda MF301 V10	76		
7	Rubens Barrichello	BR	14	Total Jordan Peugeot	Jordan 195-Peugeot A10 V10	76		
8	Luca Badoer	I	24	Minardi Scuderia Italia	Minardi M195-Ford EDM V8	75		
9	Pedro Lamy	P	23	Minardi Scuderia Italia	Minardi M195-Ford EDM V8	74		
10	Jean-Christophe Boullion	F	29	Red Bull Sauber Ford	Sauber C14-Ford Zetec-R V8	74		
11	Michael Schumacher	D	1	Mild Seven Benetton Renault	Benetton B195-Renault RS7B V10	73	Fuel pump	
12	Andrea Montermini	I	17	Pacific Grand Prix Ltd	Pacific PR02-Ford ED V8	73		
13	Eddie Irvine	GB	15	Total Jordan Peugeot	Jordan 195-Peugeot A10 V10	70	Clutch	
	Martin Brundle	GB	25	Ligier Gitanes Blondes	Ligier JS41-Mugen Honda MF301 V10	67	Engine	
	Mika Salo	SF	4	Nokia Tyrrell Yamaha	Tyrrell 023-Yamaha OX10C V10	58	Throttle	
	Mark Blundell	GB	7	Marlboro McLaren Mercedes	McLaren MP4/10B-Mercedes FO110 V10	54	Engine	
	Ukyo Katayama	J	3	Nokia Tyrrell Yamaha	Tyrrell 023-Yamaha OX10C V10	46	Accident	
	Massimiliano Papis	I	9	Footwork Hart	Footwork FA16-Hart 830 V8	45	Brakes	
	Jean Alesi	F	27	Scuderia Ferrari	Ferrari 412T2 044 V12	42	Engine	
	Pedro Diniz	BR	21	Parmalat Forti Ford	Forti FG01-Ford ED V8	32	Engine	
	Taki Inoue	J	10	Footwork Hart	Footwork FA16-Hart 830 V8	13	Engine	
	Roberto Moreno	BR	22	Parmalat Forti Ford	Forti FG01-Ford ED V8	8	Gearshift failure	
	Giovanni Lavaggi	I	16	Pacific Grand Prix Ltd	Pacific PR02-Ford ED V8	5	Spun off	
	Mika Häkkinen	SF	8	Marlboro McLaren Mercedes	McLaren MP4/10B-Mercedes FO110 V10	3	Engine	

Fastest lap: Hill, on lap 34, 1m 20.247s, 110.610 mph/178.010 km/h.
Lap record: Nigel Mansell (F1 Williams FW14B-Renault V10), 1m 18.308s, 113.349 mph/182.418 km/h (1992).
All cars used Goodyear tyres

STARTING GRID

5 HILL (1m 16.982s) Williams — **6 COULTHARD** (1m 17.366s) Williams

1 SCHUMACHER (1m 17.558s) Benetton — **28 BERGER** (1m 18.059s) Ferrari

8 HÄKKINEN (1m 18.363s) McLaren — **27 ALESI** (1m 18.968s) Ferrari

15 IRVINE (1m 19.499s) Jordan — **25 BRUNDLE** (1m 19.748s) Ligier

2 HERBERT (1m 20.072s) Benetton — **26 PANIS** (1m 20.160s) Ligier

30 FRENTZEN (1m 20.413s) Sauber — **24 BADOER** (1m 20.543s) Minardi

7 BLUNDELL (1m 20.640s) McLaren — **14 BARRICHELLO** (1m 20.902s) Jordan

23 LAMY (1m 21.156s) Minardi — **4 SALO** (1m 21.624s) Tyrrell

3 KATAYAMA (1m 21.702s) Tyrrell — **10 INOUE** (1m 22.081s) Footwork

29 BOULLION (1m 22.161s) Sauber — **9 PAPIS** (1m 23.275s) Footwork

22 MORENO (1m 24.351s) Forti — **17 MONTERMINI** (1m 24.371s) Pacific

21 DINIZ (1m 24.695s) Forti — **16 LAVAGGI** (1m 26.570s) Pacific

TIME SHEETS

Friday free practice
Sunny and hot

Pos.	Driver	Laps	Time
1	Michael Schumacher	15	1m 21.156s
2	David Coulthard	16	1m 21.234s
3	Gerhard Berger	20	1m 21.504s
4	Damon Hill	20	1m 21.864s
5	Jean Alesi	18	1m 21.933s
6	Olivier Panis	21	1m 22.269s
7	Mika Häkkinen	20	1m 22.446s
8	Eddie Irvine	11	1m 22.886s
9	Rubens Barrichello	8	1m 23.290s
10	Pedro Lamy	23	1m 23.447s
11	Johnny Herbert	21	1m 23.529s
12	Mark Blundell	19	1m 23.623s
13	Heinz-Harald Frentzen	20	1m 23.903s
14	Martin Brundle	16	1m 24.096s
15	Ukyo Katayama	23	1m 24.686s
16	Luca Badoer	23	1m 24.997s
17	Jean-Christophe Boullion	19	1m 25.036s
18	Mika Salo	23	1m 25.467s
19	Massimiliano Papis	20	1m 25.522s
20	Taki Inoue	20	1m 27.003s
21	Andrea Montermini	12	1m 27.623s
22	Pedro Diniz	20	1m 28.196s
23	Roberto Moreno	18	1m 28.591s
24	Giovanni Lavaggi	19	1m 30.087s

Saturday free practice
Hot, bright sunshine

Pos.	Driver	Laps	Time
1	Damon Hill	22	1m 18.682s
2	Mika Häkkinen	22	1m 18.726s
3	Michael Schumacher	20	1m 18.790s
4	David Coulthard	19	1m 18.876s
5	Gerhard Berger	20	1m 19.201s
6	Eddie Irvine	21	1m 19.782s
7	Olivier Panis	23	1m 19.973s
8	Jean Alesi	7	1m 20.021s
9	Rubens Barrichello	19	1m 20.251s
10	Johnny Herbert	23	1m 20.451s
11	Mark Blundell	21	1m 20.785s
12	Martin Brundle	22	1m 20.851s
13	Heinz-Harald Frentzen	17	1m 21.011s
14	Pedro Lamy	23	1m 21.638s
15	Luca Badoer	23	1m 21.754s
16	Mika Salo	22	1m 22.034s
17	Ukyo Katayama	22	1m 22.123s
18	Jean-Christophe Boullion	18	1m 22.518s
19	Taki Inoue	23	1m 23.173s
20	Massimiliano Papis	10	1m 23.325s
21	Roberto Moreno	13	1m 24.889s
22	Andrea Montermini	12	1m 25.081s
23	Pedro Diniz	21	1m 25.389s
24	Giovanni Lavaggi	14	1m 27.871s

Friday qualifying
Sunny and hot

Pos.	Driver	Laps	Time
1	Damon Hill	10	1m 18.374s
2	David Coulthard	12	1m 19.000s
3	Gerhard Berger	9	1m 19.033s
4	Michael Schumacher	11	1m 19.490s
5	Jean Alesi	4	1m 20.134s
6	Mika Häkkinen	10	1m 20.577s
7	Olivier Panis	6	1m 20.952s
8	Heinz-Harald Frentzen	6	1m 21.234s
9	Eddie Irvine	9	1m 21.246s
10	Mark Blundell	12	1m 21.663s
11	Martin Brundle	12	1m 21.818s
12	Rubens Barrichello	11	1m 21.874s
13	Johnny Herbert	12	1m 21.878s
14	Luca Badoer	12	1m 22.345s
15	Pedro Lamy	12	1m 22.600s
16	Jean-Christophe Boullion	7	1m 22.766s
17	Ukyo Katayama	11	1m 22.866s
18	**Massimiliano Papis**	10	**1m 23.275s**
19	Mika Salo	2	1m 24.440s
20	Taki Inoue	12	1m 24.656s
21	Andrea Montermini	7	1m 25.465s
22	Pedro Diniz	11	1m 25.934s
23	Roberto Moreno	12	1m 26.059s
24	Giovanni Lavaggi	12	1m 27.342s

Saturday qualifying
Sunny and hot

Pos.	Driver	Laps	Time
1	**Damon Hill**	11	**1m 16.982s**
2	**David Coulthard**	10	**1m 17.366s**
3	**Michael Schumacher**	12	**1m 17.558s**
4	**Gerhard Berger**	8	**1m 18.059s**
5	**Mika Häkkinen**	9	**1m 18.363s**
6	**Jean Alesi**	5	**1m 18.968s**
7	**Eddie Irvine**	11	**1m 19.499s**
8	**Martin Brundle**	9	**1m 19.748s**
9	**Johnny Herbert**	12	**1m 20.072s**
10	**Olivier Panis**	10	**1m 20.160s**
11	**Heinz-Harald Frentzen**	5	**1m 20.413s**
12	**Luca Badoer**	12	**1m 20.543s**
13	**Mark Blundell**	2	**1m 20.640s**
14	**Rubens Barrichello**	3	**1m 20.902s**
15	**Pedro Lamy**	12	**1m 21.156s**
16	**Mika Salo**	12	**1m 21.624s**
17	**Ukyo Katayama**	10	**1m 21.702s**
18	**Taki Inoue**	11	**1m 22.081s**
19	**Jean-Christophe Boullion**	2	**1m 22.161s**
20	**Roberto Moreno**	12	**1m 24.351s**
21	**Andrea Montermini**	12	**1m 24.371s**
22	**Pedro Diniz**	12	**1m 24.695s**
23	**Giovanni Lavaggi**	11	**1m 26.570s**
	Massimiliano Papis	0	no time

Warm-up
Sunny and hot

Pos.	Driver	Laps	Time
1	Michael Schumacher	12	1m 18.838s
2	Mika Häkkinen	11	1m 19.269s
3	Jean Alesi	12	1m 19.656s
4	Damon Hill	14	1m 19.793s
5	Olivier Panis	16	1m 19.940s
6	Eddie Irvine	14	1m 20.367s
7	David Coulthard	11	1m 20.654s
8	Martin Brundle	16	1m 20.784s
9	Mark Blundell	12	1m 20.863s
10	Johnny Herbert	16	1m 20.984s
11	Rubens Barrichello	11	1m 21.061s
12	Gerhard Berger	11	1m 21.159s
13	Heinz-Harald Frentzen	13	1m 21.234s
14	Jean-Christophe Boullion	11	1m 22.188s
15	Mika Salo	13	1m 22.372s
16	Ukyo Katayama	13	1m 22.551s
17	Pedro Lamy	13	1m 22.881s
18	Taki Inoue	12	1m 23.595s
19	Andrea Montermini	13	1m 24.177s
20	Massimiliano Papis	12	1m 24.798s
21	Roberto Moreno	13	1m 25.239s
22	Pedro Diniz	8	1m 28.012s
23	Giovanni Lavaggi	4	1m 29.455s
24	Luca Badoer	4	4m 59.758s

Race fastest laps
Sunny and hot

Driver	Time	Lap
Damon Hill	1m 20.247s	34
Michael Schumacher	1m 20.506s	22
David Coulthard	1m 21.126s	58
Olivier Panis	1m 21.343s	40
Gerhard Berger	1m 21.371s	38
Martin Brundle	1m 21.977s	40
Eddie Irvine	1m 22.211s	49
Mark Blundell	1m 22.235s	27
Jean Alesi	1m 22.276s	25
Johnny Herbert	1m 22.560s	6
Andrea Montermini	1m 22.663s	70
Rubens Barrichello	1m 22.677s	27
Mika Häkkinen	1m 22.720s	3
Heinz-Harald Frentzen	1m 23.146s	69
Jean-Christophe Boullion	1m 23.424s	53
Mika Salo	1m 23.556s	27
Luca Badoer	1m 23.608s	51
Ukyo Katayama	1m 23.994s	25
Pedro Lamy	1m 24.269s	16
Taki Inoue	1m 24.804s	9
Massimiliano Papis	1m 25.730s	8
Roberto Moreno	1m 26.556s	6
Pedro Diniz	1m 26.913s	6
Giovanni Lavaggi	1m 27.894s	3

CHASSIS LOG BOOK

No.	Driver	Chassis
1	Schumacher	Benetton B195/6
2	Herbert	Benetton B195/5
	spare	Benetton B195/1
3	Katayama	Tyrrell 023/5
4	Salo	Tyrrell 023/6
	spare	Tyrrell 023/2
5	Hill	Williams FW17/6
6	Coulthard	Williams FW17/5
	spare	Williams FW17/2
7	Blundell	McLaren MP4/10B/6
8	Häkkinen	McLaren MP4/10B/5
	spare	McLaren MP4/10B/2
9	Papis	Footwork FA16/3
10	Inoue	Footwork FA16/4
	spare	Footwork FA16/1
14	Barrichello	Jordan 195/4
15	Irvine	Jordan 195/5
	spare	Jordan 195/1
16	Lavaggi	Pacific PR02/1
17	Montermini	Pacific PR02/2
21	Diniz	Forti FG01/4
22	Moreno	Forti FG01/3
	spare	Forti FG01/2
23	Lamy	Minardi M195/3
24	Badoer	Minardi M195/2
	spare	Minardi M195/1
25	Brundle	Ligier JS41/5
26	Panis	Ligier JS41/3
	spare	Ligier JS41/4
27	Alesi	Ferrari 412T2/161
28	Berger	Ferrari 412T2/162
	spare	Ferrari 412T2/160
29	Boullion	Sauber C14/5
30	Frentzen	Sauber C14/6
	spare	Sauber C14/2

POINTS TABLES

Drivers

Pos	Driver	Pts
1	Michael Schumacher	56
2	Damon Hill	45
3	Jean Alesi	32
4	David Coulthard	29
5	Johnny Herbert	28
6	Gerhard Berger	25
7	Olivier Panis	8
8 =	Rubens Barrichello	7
8 =	Heinz-Harald Frentzen	7
10	Eddie Irvine	6
11	Mika Häkkinen	5
11 =	Mark Blundell	5
13	Martin Brundle	3
14	Jean-Christophe Boullion	2
15	Gianni Morbidelli	1
15 =	Aguri Suzuki	1

Constructors

Pos	Constructor	Pts
1	Benetton	74
2	Williams	68
3	Ferrari	57
4	Jordan	13
5	Ligier	12
6	McLaren	10
7	Sauber	9
8	Footwork	1

WORLD CHAMPIONSHIP • ROUND 11

BELGIAN GRAND PRIX

- SCHUMACHER
- HILL
- BRUNDLE
- FRENTZEN
- BLUNDELL
- BARRICHELLO

Below left: Running on slick tyres on a rain-soaked track surface, Michael Schumacher *(right)* resists Damon Hill's bid to seize the lead as the pair approach the braking area for Les Combes.

The Williams driver *(left)* was bitterly unhappy about the German's forceful tactics, but even a rostrum champagne shower from Martin Brundle, who finished third for Ligier, couldn't dampen Schumacher's spirits after a dazzling display of wet-weather virtuosity.

He won at Spa in '93, defeating Michael Schumacher's Benetton-Ford in a straight fight. He won again in '94, inheriting the win after Michael's car was disqualified in the 'worn plank' controversy. But this time Schumacher turned the tables decisively. The reigning World Champion stood firmly – some said too firmly – in the way of Damon Hill's hat-trick of Belgian Grand Prix victories, picking up one of the most memorable wins of his distinguished career.

He also collected a one-race ban, suspended for four races, for what the stewards clearly regarded as marginal driving tactics as he battled, on slicks in the wet, to keep Damon back in second place. The F1 paddock was divided in its assessment of his alleged malfeasance. Many people thought that Schumacher was guilty of dirty driving, nothing more nor less. Others took a more philosophical view, pointing out that it was a battle for the lead of a Grand Prix, not a vicarage garden party. For his part, Michael was mightily indignant about the whole affair.

Damon had kicked off the weekend fervently hoping that the notoriously fickle Ardennes summer weather would stay fine for Saturday qualifying at Spa-Francorchamps after losing out in a frantic last-lap lottery to finish the first timed session in a disappointing fourth place. Doused by hours of torrential rain, the treacherously slippery circuit gradually began to dry out in the last ten minutes of Friday qualifying, allowing Gerhard Berger to make a perfectly timed run and claim provisional pole position with his Ferrari 412T2.

It had been announced shortly after the Hungarian Grand Prix that the Italian team had been successful in its bid to lure Michael Schumacher away from Benetton for 1996, with Jean Alesi moving in the opposite direction, and the Austrian driver was no doubt hoping to celebrate his 36th birthday on race day by putting it over Maranello's new recruit.

Gerhard confessed that he had taken a slight gamble in terms of chassis set-up. 'Naturally, I'm very satisfied,' he said, 'especially as I made the right move at the right time. Towards the end of the session, I saw that there was less water on the track [than previously] and decided to run with less downforce to gain speed at the expense of a slight performance loss on the twisty parts of the circuit.'

Schumacher's Benetton B195 finished the first day second, ahead of Jean Alesi's Ferrari, leaving Hill with the not-too-concerning prospect of starting the 11th round of the title chase from the outside of the second row unless the weather took a turn for the better on Saturday.

'I got caught out by the end of the session,' explained Damon, 'because I ended up with a blistered rear tyre which slightly upset the car's handling. If it rains again, I'm in a bit of a tricky situation because it would be better to be on the front row. On the other hand, it is easier to overtake here than on just about any other circuit.'

Hill's team-mate David Coulthard finished the first session in fifth place, freely admitting that he was ever so slightly disappointed. Having cranked on more front wing to compensate for excessive understeer when the circuit was at its wettest, he found the car's handling translating into unnerving oversteer as the dry line gradually appeared.

Sixth place on the first day fell to Heinz-Harald Frentzen, the German Sauber driver again displaying impressive form as he squeezed every ounce out of the latest, higher-revving Ford Zetec-R V8 engine.

'Obviously, I am pleased to be sixth fastest on the provisional grid,' grinned Schumacher's old adversary, 'but, quite honestly, it was nothing special. We can improve the car even more. It felt good in the rain, but as the track dried out I began to have understeer.'

By contrast, things had gone badly for the Benetton team from the outset. On Friday morning, Johnny Herbert spun wildly coming out of the La Source hairpin, hitting the barrier on the right before bouncing across and rattling down the guard rail on the opposite side of the circuit.

There was no question of repairing Herbert's car for the afternoon, so he was obliged to sit out first qualifying; clearly, his perceived status in the team was not of an order which made it a worthwhile risk entrusting him with Schumacher's precious race car once the World Champion had completed his own allocation of laps.

As if that wasn't bad enough, on Saturday morning Michael was aiming for what he confidently believed would be the quickest time on a drying track surface when he clipped the inside apex kerb on the Malmedy right-hander immediately after Les Combes. The Benetton's front wheels momentarily lifted from the track surface and he went spearing across the circuit, fortunately just catching the end of the tyre barrier protecting the guard rail on the outside of the corner.

'That was a real shame, because I thought I would have set fastest time on that lap,' said Schuey. 'At the start of the session the car had felt really unstable, so we stiffened up the suspension and it felt really good, even though I had fuel aboard and was still using old tyres.'

Coulthard set fastest time on Saturday morning, while Hill collected a one-race suspended ban from the stewards after changing his mind at the last moment to cut across the grass into the pit lane entrance after some slight confusion with his pit-to-car radio communication.

The conditions dried progressively during the lunch break, but as the cars lined up to start second qualifying, the black clouds were already rolling in over the surrounding pine forests. As race director Roland Bruynseraede waved his green flag to indicate that the circuit was open, a huge queue of cars filed out onto the circuit, their drivers all anxious to post a decent time before the heavens opened yet again.

As it turned out, Gerhard Berger again judged things brilliantly, posting a 1m 54.392s best just as the rain returned. Alesi, who had suffered an engine failure during the morning's free practice session, also took the opportunity to vault up to second with Mika Häkkinen third and Eddie Irvine fourth.

This was the best-ever qualifying performance for the McLaren-Mercedes partnership and one which raised hopes for a really good race result from the Anglo-German alliance. The previous week had seen the Mercedes V10 cover over 370 km during testing at Silverstone and the cars appeared at Spa sporting a totally new gearbox casing, tailor-made to accept a revised suspension geometry.

Häkkinen's performance made up for the previous day's disappointment when he dropped to seventh place after being called into the pits with one lap still to go due to a communications misunderstanding with team chief Ron Dennis. 'My fault,' said Ron sheepishly.

As steady rainfall brought a sudden end to that initial flurry of activity, the cars retreated to the pits, where they stayed under cover until Roberto Moreno took his Forti out for an exploratory run just after 1.35 p.m.

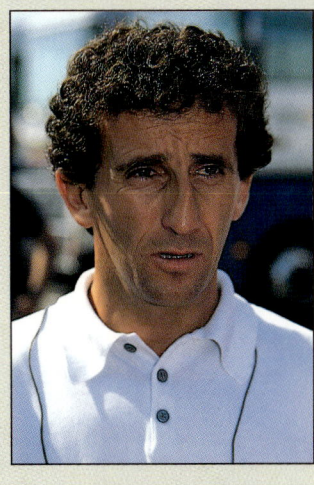

Prost enters 1996 F1 driver equation

Alain Prost's decision to test a McLaren MP4/10B-Mercedes in the week immediately following the Belgian race indicated that the veteran Frenchman was interested in further probing the possibility of a full-time F1 return for 1996.

'I believe that, in the way we will attack next year's programme, two drivers will not be enough,' said Ron Dennis at Spa, indicating that the team would confirm its driver line-up over the weekend of the European GP at the Nürburgring at the end of September. With speculation that David Coulthard was tied to McLaren under the terms of an option until that weekend, it seemed as though no firm decision as to the identity of Mika Häkkinen's partner for '96 would be made until Prost had reached his own personal conclusion.

In advance of Prost's first test, Dennis explained that the Frenchman's preliminary run would be nothing more than a 'comfort test' with a second, more intensive, outing scheduled for the week after the Italian GP.

Alain duly appeared at Silverstone the following week, completing some gentle laps in a McLaren completely devoid of any sponsorship identification. Asked to comment on the likelihood of a return, he commented: 'I cannot say there is no chance at all, but it is not part of the plan at the moment. I have no contract, but I am enjoying myself.

'The car is not difficult to drive, but, with no traction control and much less downforce, it is very different to the cars I last raced [in 1993].'

It was only to be expected that a sense of excitement and anticipation would surround Prost's first serious outing in an F1 car since he tried a McLaren-Peugeot at Estoril prior to the start of the '94 season. However, some McLaren insiders expressed the view that, with the team having just emerged from an unsuccessful relationship with Nigel Mansell, any attempt to revive the age-old partnership with Prost would be destined to end in a corresponding degree of disappointment.

Suddenly, another spurt of action signalled that the track surface was beginning to dry out again. Schumacher went out in his repaired Benetton and moved up to ninth, then Hill took a chance and moved through to sixth. With ten minutes left, Coulthard got up to fourth, but then we were treated to possibly the single most impressive performance of the day when Johnny Herbert timed his run to perfection to push the Scot out of fourth place in the final starting order.

Coulthard was disappointed not to have improved on fifth place. 'Yesterday I was fifth and today I'm fifth, that seems to be my number here,' he

BELGIAN GRAND PRIX

Diary

Niki Lauda arrives at Boeing's Seattle headquarters to take delivery of LaudaAir's latest 767 jet, which is named 'Ayrton Senna'.

Ligier finalises another two-year deal to keep Mugen Honda engines.

BTCC star Alain Menu tests Williams FW17 at Silverstone during the week following Belgian GP.

Vincenzo Sospiri extends FIA International F3000 Championship lead with convincing Spa victory.

Right: The horrific fire which engulfed Eddie Irvine's Jordan during the Ulsterman's second pit stop provided a shocking reminder of the dangers of refuelling. Fortunately, no one was hurt on this occasion.

Below: Mark Blundell leads Johnny Herbert and Heinz-Harald Frentzen. The German snatched fourth place from the McLaren driver with four laps left to run, but the Benetton number two had to settle for seventh after leading the race in the early stages.

pondered. 'I am not too disappointed as it isn't as bad as some places to overtake, and I don't intend to be fifth at the end of the first lap.

'It was a difficult decision when to go out, but we made the right one as it moved us up the grid [at the time]. I started from seventh last year and was challenging for the podium come the race. I'm sure that will be the case tomorrow.'

What David did not reveal was that he had sat down and undertaken a subtle reassessment of his personal driving style at the pre-Spa Silverstone test. He'd also taken some advice from his old mentor Jackie Stewart and amended his technique as a result. Rather than sustaining his image as the Last of the Late Brakers, he now decided to tackle things in a more moderated, early-on-the-brakes, early-on-the-throttle, Prost-like style. Over the next fortnight it would reap considerable dividends.

Mark Blundell's McLaren-Merc took sixth ahead of Irvine and a frustrated Damon Hill, who found himself relegated to an eventual eighth after a spin on the downhill Pouhon left-hander.

'It was a pretty disastrous day, really,' said Damon. 'The track surface was drying and I felt I had a good chance of improving my position. But the rear end stepped out at the bottom of the hill and I'm a little mystified as to why it did so. As far as the championship is concerned, this is not a total disaster, but from a performance viewpoint it was pretty messy.'

Hill's reference to his title prospects took into account the fact that Schumacher was left trailing in 16th place after suffering gearbox electronic problems at just the wrong moment, late in the session. On Michael's second run, the Benetton's gearbox had downchanged from sixth to fifth without bidding – then repeated this quirky performance on the straight at maximum revs, momentarily buzzing the Renault V10 to over 19,000 rpm. Even Renault Sport's engineering proved unable to survive such an overwhelming onslaught.

The bottom line was that Spa '95 turned out to be only the second occasion that one of Schumacher's team-mates had actually managed to out-qualify him! Herbert could now console himself that he had matched triple World Champion Nelson Piquet's achievement back in 1991 at the Australian GP.

Seventh and 12th for the Jordan-Peugeots was slightly disappointing as well. Irvine had spent the majority of the session praying for more rain after setting fourth-fastest time in the early stages. But the rain eventually came at the wrong moment.

'It's impossible to be smart here,' he shrugged. 'You've just got to go for it and pray you get lucky. It worked at the start of the session; I was looking really good for a while until the track started drying out. I waited until the last moment when it should have been drying – and then it started raining again. But I suppose, although the weather didn't do us any favours, it didn't do us any harm, either.'

Over in the Ligier camp, Olivier Panis, who had earlier suffered a simply massive Mugen Honda engine failure after only three laps in Saturday's untimed session, was well satisfied to qualify ninth ahead of Frentzen, the Sauber driver late out after his gearbox underwent repairs. Ligier had three examples of the latest-spec. Mugen Honda MF301H/B available for this Grand Prix, two being retained for the race and the third given to Martin Brundle for second qualifying after he proved the faster of the two JS41 drivers in Friday's timed session.

Mika Salo, relishing the additional stability conferred by revised rear suspension on his Tyrrell-Yamaha, ended up 11th after a performance which probably didn't quite do full justice to the car's potential. His team-mate Ukyo Katayama made an ill-timed pit stop to change his chassis set-up, rather than staying out on the circuit during a dry period, and the Japanese driver dropped to a disappointed 15th as a result.

Rubens Barrichello, balked by Frentzen on his best run, wound up 12th ahead of Martin Brundle's Ligier and Jean-Christophe Boullion's Sauber, the Frenchman's C14 repaired after he had crashed quite heavily on Saturday morning.

Behind Schumacher, Pedro Lamy ended up 17th for Minardi despite a slight off-track excursion during the final session, while Taki Inoue was next after a spin in his Footwork, followed by Luca Badoer's Minardi and Max Papis in the second FA15.

At the back, the two Pacifics and Fortis completed the final rows of the grid, but it hadn't been like that throughout the session. At one point, Giovanni Lavaggi had found himself provisionally lined up alongside Schumacher's Benetton. It wasn't a state of affairs seen before – nor one expected in the future.

The financial pressures facing both Minardi and, in particular, Pacific were thrown into sharp relief over the Spa weekend. The Norfolk-based team arrived in Belgium to find yet another problem awaiting

them in the form of an injunction from Swiss engine specialist Heini Mader, the man who maintained the Ilmor V10s used by the team in 1994.

Mader claimed an unpaid sum of £100,000 in connection with his work, Pacific chief Keith Wiggins asserting that the money was witheld because of defective workmanship. Eventually the two parties sat down to discuss the matter, Mader finally being persuaded to drop his injunction in return for Pacific withdrawing its defence to the matter.

'I think you would be right in saying that we have now reached a critical point,' admitted Pacific's commercial manager Mark Gallagher, 'and obviously the adverse publicity surrounding the Mader business hardly helps.'

Less pressing, but no less real, were rumours that Minardi was considering an amalgamation with the Forti Corse team for 1996 as a means of retaining an F1 presence. However, Minardi vigorously refuted rumours suggesting it might quit the World Championship stage at the end of the European season, turning its attention to preparing an Alfa Romeo Class 1 touring car programme instead.

Come race day, nobody quite knew what the weather was going to do, and there was rain in the air as the cars went out to the starting grid.

At the green light Johnny Herbert's Benetton burst through from the second row to momentarily edge alongside Alesi's Ferrari as they scrambled into the first turn. Going down into Eau Rouge, the two cars were side by side, but Jean's Ferrari had the inside line and managed to squeeze the Benetton aside. But Johnny came back at him under braking for Les Combes, running round the outside of the Ferrari to retake the initiative.

Herbert thus led the first lap from Alesi, Berger and Häkkinen, but the McLaren driver blotted his copybook with an inexplicable spin as he came out of La Source on the second lap, stalling his Mercedes V10 and being left with no choice but to retire on the spot.

Up to Les Combes for the second time, and Alesi ducked back inside to take the lead, completing lap two 1.3s ahead of Herbert's Benetton. Berger was now under pressure from Coulthard, with Hill fifth and Blundell's McLaren up to sixth.

'The start was very good,' reflected Herbert later, 'and I was helped by Gerhard blocking Mika, so I was able to get ahead of both of them.' Ferrari's hopes faded on lap four when Alesi came into the pits complaining about poor handling. He thought he'd picked up a puncture, so the left-rear tyre was changed, but as he accelerated back out of the pits again he realised that his car had suffered a suspension breakage and immediately pulled up at the exit of the pit lane. This put Herbert fleetingly back at the head of the pack on laps four and five, but Coulthard was steadily moving in for the kill.

On lap six, Herbert spun at Les Combes and dropped back to third, allowing David to dodge through into the lead, then spun again exiting the chicane before the pits. In so doing, he boxed in Blundell, forcing the McLaren to slow to a virtual stop, which dropped Mark from fifth to eighth.

Thereafter Coulthard ran strongly at the head of the pack, gradually inching away from team-mate Hill. He extended his advantage from 1.4s on lap six to 6.6s by lap 14, when technical problems blighted his challenge yet again, the Scot's FW17 rolling to a halt out on the circuit with an overheating gearbox.

'I had time in hand and was confident in the car all weekend, but sadly once again I didn't finish,' shrugged Coulthard. 'I saw some oil coming from my car about eight laps before and that cleared up, but maybe it pumped the oil out of the gearbox and eventually overheated.' It was later established that Coulthard had been tapped by Irvine in the first-lap scrum at La Source, fracturing an oil line to the Williams's gearbox.

At the end of lap 15, Berger made his first scheduled stop from third place, resuming in seventh. But he was back in the pits five laps later

177

BELGIAN GRAND PRIX

Revelling in the challenge posed by the daunting Ardennes circuit, Michael Schumacher climbed through the field from 16th place on the grid to score one of the best victories of his career.

Below right: Martin Brundle hurls the Ligier-Mugen Honda into the Bus Stop chicane. The former McLaren driver was unable to resist Damon Hill's late charge but fully deserved his first podium finish of the season.

Below left: Living with the past. Ron Dennis, never one to dwell on former glories, remained fully committed to the task of restoring the McLaren marque to winning ways.

for a new electronic control unit to be fitted in an attempt to cure a persistent misfire. He duly rejoined, but stopped for good after 22 laps when the problem refused to clear.

All this drama left us with a familiar situation at the head of the field. By lap 15 Hill and Schumacher were in command, running 1-2 at the front, but Damon made his first scheduled refuelling stop at the end of that same lap. Schumacher came in for the first time three laps later, allowing Damon to regain the advantage.

However, by this stage the rain was starting to fall again and Hill chose to duck back in for wet rubber at the end of lap 21, Michael preferring to stay out on slicks. Back in the fray, Hill quickly sliced into Schumacher's advantage and pulled up onto the Benetton's tail as they started lap 22.

But Michael certainly wasn't about to be ruffled, doggedly staying ahead in a demonstration of brilliant car control, but what Damon regarded as a somewhat lower standard of etiquette as he weaved around on the long straight up to Les Combes to keep Hill behind him. When Hill tried to dive inside at this point, Michael amazed everybody by keeping ahead on the outside line – on slicks in the wet! But Damon was less impressed when the Benetton clouted his Williams very firmly, pushing it up the kerb, on the exit to the corner.

This was a crucial stage in the race for Damon as his wet-tyre advantage was negated by what he clearly regarded as blatant blocking tactics from his key rival. Even so, at the end of the afternoon he would pick his words carefully after finishing in second place.

'If the rules do not prevent drivers from using cars as instruments to prevent other drivers from overtaking – in other words to forcibly drive at another car – then the rules are wrong, aren't they?' said Hill.

'If the rules say we can go out there and smash into each other as much as we want, then I'll make a decision whether or not I want to be in this sport.

'I have told Michael what I thought of his driving, but anyone who comes through from 16th to win deserves to be congratulated. But I could have won, but for a bit of bad luck. The conditions were very tricky and Michael drove a stupendous race. I'm just sorry that I wasn't able to be there at the end to give him some competition.

'We had some pretty hairy moments, and I must say I am not satisfied with being driven into. Michael drove very defensively to the point of touching wheels with me at the top of the hill.

'That's all well and good if it's accidental, but if it's meant on purpose, I would be pretty upset. These are F1 cars, not go-karts. Some things are acceptable, some are not, and Michael will have his own view about it, I expect.'

For his part, Schumacher diplomatically rebutted the implications behind Hill's razor-sharp observations.

'I think that is absolutely right,' he replied. 'Touching wheels in high-speed corners is not acceptable, but at the speed we were doing, I think you can do this. We are professional drivers and know how to keep these cars on the road.'

On lap 24, Hill forced his way ahead, but the track was drying now and the Williams's wet-weather rubber losing grip fast. Next time round, Damon slid wide at Stavelot, allowing Schumacher back through into the lead. On lap 26, Hill came in for a change back onto slicks only for the rain to start pouring down again almost immediately.

This time he kept at it, benefiting from the organisers' somewhat confusing decision to deploy the safety car. This was justified on the grounds that there were reports of standing water from post three on the circuit – Eau Rouge – even though cynics thought this looked like a good way of spicing up the action. On the same lap as the pace car was deployed, Katayama's Tyrrell spun off at Malmedy, having climbed as high as fourth after an excellent run.

Meanwhile, the Jordan team had earlier spiced up the race in spectacular style when Eddie Irvine's 195 caught fire at its second stop on lap 21. Eddie was running seventh at the time, but when the refuelling hose was removed, the car-mounted vent momentarily stuck open and a small amount of fuel escaped. This ignited on the Jordan's exhaust pipe, but prompt action by both the team's own mechanics and their vigilant colleagues in the adjacent Ligier garage snuffed out the conflagration before it could take hold.

It was a great shame that Irvine's race should have ended thus, for he had run magnificently ahead of Schumacher in the opening stages and certainly impressed the World Champion with the straightline speed of his Peugeot V10.

On lap 30, both Schumacher and Hill made scheduled refuelling stops under the cover of the safety car, resuming in nose-to-tail formation behind the Porsche coupé with its flashing lights. The green flag to resume racing was shown at the start of lap 33, but Damon's chances of a final challenge were dashed when he had to come back in again to receive a ten-second stop-go penalty for speeding in the pit lane on his previous visit.

That dropped him back to third behind Martin Brundle's Ligier, but he soon settled down to demolish his fellow Brit's advantage. From 9.5s on lap 38, Brundle's edge shrank to 1.8s with two laps to go and Damon eventually surged past the Mugen-engined car at Les Combes on the final lap.

Fourth place looked as though it was destined to go to Blundell, but Frentzen forced his way inside the McLaren-Merc at the chicane to take over the position only four laps from the chequered flag – an excellent effort.

Barrichello survived to take sixth ahead of Herbert, the Benetton number two frustrated over his team's pit work and general handling of his race. 'I should have been fourth at worst, not seventh,' he noted with as much dignity as he could muster.

FIA FORMULA ONE WORLD CHAMPIONSHIP ROUND 11

GRAND PRIX DE BELGIQUE

SPA-FRANCORCHAMPS
25-27 AUGUST 1995

Race distance: 44 laps, 190.671 miles/306.856 km
Race weather: Dry at first, then intermittent rain

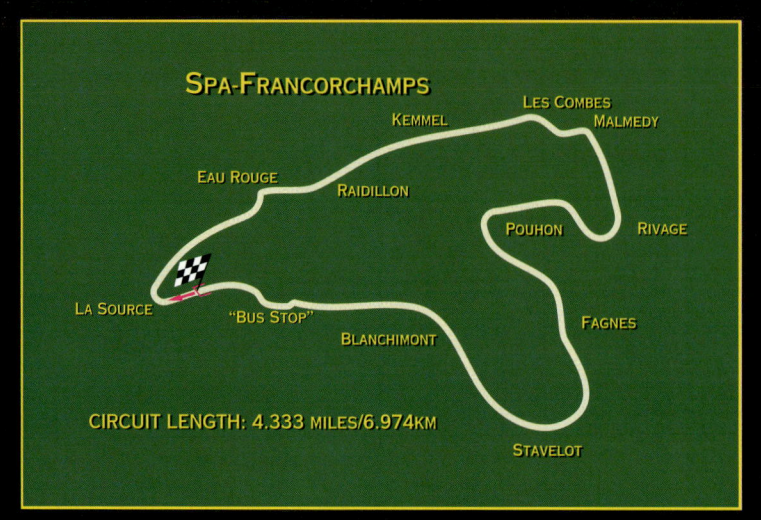

SPA-FRANCORCHAMPS

CIRCUIT LENGTH: 4.333 MILES/6.974KM

Place	Driver	Nat.	No.	Entrant	Car/Engine	Laps	Time/Retirement	Speed (mph/km/h)
1	**Michael Schumacher**	D	1	Mild Seven Benetton Renault	Benetton B195-Renault RS7B V10	44	1h 36m 47.875s	118.187/190.204
2	**Damon Hill**	GB	5	Rothmans Williams Renault	Williams FW17-Renault RS7B V10	44	1h 37m 07.368s	117.791/189.567
3	**Martin Brundle**	GB	25	Ligier Gitanes Blondes	Ligier JS41-Mugen Honda MF301 V10	44	1h 37m 12.873s	117.680/189.388
4	**Heinz-Harald Frentzen**	D	30	Red Bull Sauber Ford	Sauber C14-Ford Zetec-R V8	44	1h 37m 14.847s	117.640/189.324
5	**Mark Blundell**	GB	7	Marlboro McLaren Mercedes	McLaren MP4/10B-Mercedes FO110 V10	44	1h 37m 21.647s	117.504/189.104
6	**Rubens Barrichello**	BR	14	Total Jordan Peugeot	Jordan 195-Peugeot A10 V10	44	1h 37m 27.549s	117.385/188.913
7	Johnny Herbert	GB	2	Mild Seven Benetton Renault	Benetton B195-Renault RS7B V10	44	1h 37m 41.923s	117.097/188.450
8	Mika Salo	SF	4	Nokia Tyrrell Yamaha	Tyrrell 023-Yamaha OX10C V10	44	1h 37m 42.423s	117.087/188.434
9	Olivier Panis	F	26	Ligier Gitanes Blondes	Ligier JS41-Mugen Honda MF301 V10	44	1h 37m 54.045s	116.855/188.061
10	Pedro Lamy	P	23	Minardi Scuderia Italia	Minardi M195-Ford EDM V8	44	1h 38m 07.664s	116.585/187.626
11	Jean-Christophe Boullion	F	29	Red Bull Sauber Ford	Sauber C14-Ford Zetec-R V8	43		
12	Taki Inoue	J	10	Footwork Hart	Footwork FA16-Hart 830 V8	43		
13	Pedro Diniz	BR	21	Parmalat Forti Ford	Forti FG01-Ford ED V8	42		
14	Roberto Moreno	BR	22	Parmalat Forti Ford	Forti FG01-Ford ED V8	42		
	Ukyo Katayama	J	3	Nokia Tyrrell Yamaha	Tyrrell 023-Yamaha OX10C V10	28	Spun off	
	Giovanni Lavaggi	I	16	Pacific Grand Prix Ltd	Pacific PR02-Ford ED V8	27	Gearbox	
	Luca Badoer	I	24	Minardi Scuderia Italia	Minardi M195-Ford EDM V8	23	Spun off	
	Gerhard Berger	A	28	Scuderia Ferrari	Ferrari 412T2 044 V12	22	Electrics	
	Eddie Irvine	GB	15	Total Jordan Peugeot	Jordan 195-Peugeot A10 V10	21	Fire	
	Massimiliano Papis	I	9	Footwork Hart	Footwork FA16-Hart 830 V8	20	Spun off	
	Andrea Montermini	I	17	Pacific Grand Prix Ltd	Pacific PR02-Ford ED V8	18	Fuel pressure	
	David Coulthard	GB	6	Rothmans Williams Renault	Williams FW17-Renault RS7B V10	13	Gearbox	
	Jean Alesi	F	27	Scuderia Ferrari	Ferrari 412T2 044 V12	4	Suspension	
	Mika Häkkinen	SF	8	Marlboro McLaren Mercedes	McLaren MP4/10B-Mercedes FO110 V10	1	Spun off	

Fastest lap: Coulthard, on lap 11, 1m 53.412s, 137.555 mph/221.373 km/h.
Lap record: Alain Prost (F1 Williams FW15C-Renault V10), 1m 51.095s, 140.424 mph/225.990 km/h (1993).
All cars used Goodyear tyres

All results and data © FIA 1995

STARTING GRID

Pos	Driver	Time	Team
27	ALESI	(1m 54.631s)	Ferrari
28	BERGER	(1m 54.392s)	Ferrari
2	HERBERT	(1m 56.085s)	Benetton
8	HÄKKINEN	(1m 55.435s)	McLaren
7	BLUNDELL	(1m 56.622s)	McLaren
6	COULTHARD	(1m 56.254s)	Williams
5	HILL	(1m 57.768s)	Williams
15	IRVINE	(1m 57.001s)	Jordan
30	FRENTZEN	(1m 58.148s)	Sauber
26	PANIS	(1m 58.021s)	Ligier
14	BARRICHELLO	(1m 58.293s)	Jordan
4	SALO	(1m 58.224s)	Tyrrell
29	BOULLION	(1m 58.356s)	Sauber
25	BRUNDLE	(1m 58.314s)	Ligier
1	SCHUMACHER	(1m 59.079s)	Benetton
3	KATAYAMA	(1m 58.551s)	Tyrrell
10	INOUE	(1m 59.256s)	Footwork
23	LAMY	(1m 59.256s)	Minardi
9	PAPIS	(2m 01.685s)	Footwork
24	BADOER	(2m 01.013s)	Minardi
22	MORENO	(2m 03.817s)	Forti
17	MONTERMINI	(2m 02.405s)	Pacific
21	DINIZ	(2m 09.537s)	Forti
16	LAVAGGI	(2m 06.407s)	Pacific

Pacific's Andrea Montermini waits for the rain to ease during practice.

TIME SHEETS

Friday free practice
Heavy rain

Pos.	Driver	Laps	Time
1	Jean Alesi	17	2m 15.990s
2	Heinz-Harald Frentzen	17	2m 16.002s
3	David Coulthard	12	2m 16.940s
4	Mika Häkkinen	16	2m 17.091s
5	Olivier Panis	17	2m 17.304s
6	Rubens Barrichello	14	2m 17.398s
7	Eddie Irvine	17	2m 17.739s
8	Gerhard Berger	12	2m 17.976s
9	Michael Schumacher	12	2m 18.055s
10	Damon Hill	14	2m 18.302s
11	Martin Brundle	17	2m 18.885s
12	Jean-Christophe Boullion	15	2m 19.142s
13	Luca Badoer	18	2m 19.194s
14	Ukyo Katayama	18	2m 19.240s
15	Mark Blundell	10	2m 19.419s
16	Mika Salo	20	2m 20.025s
17	Pedro Lamy	20	2m 20.428s
18	Johnny Herbert	8	2m 20.829s
19	Massimiliano Papis	10	2m 23.753s
20	Roberto Moreno	17	2m 27.951s
21	Pedro Diniz	13	2m 28.125s
22	Taki Inoue	13	2m 35.815s
23	Giovanni Lavaggi	2	2m 58.874s
24	Andrea Montermini	1	50m 23.716s

Saturday free practice
Overcast and damp

Pos.	Driver	Laps	Time
1	David Coulthard	20	1m 52.474s
2	Mika Häkkinen	17	1m 52.876s
3	Michael Schumacher	19	1m 53.319s
4	Gerhard Berger	16	1m 53.343s
5	Damon Hill	20	1m 53.392s
6	Mark Blundell	20	1m 54.118s
7	Eddie Irvine	21	1m 54.283s
8	Mika Salo	23	1m 55.182s
9	Rubens Barrichello	20	1m 55.269s
10	Johnny Herbert	19	1m 55.786s
11	Martin Brundle	22	1m 55.887s
12	Ukyo Katayama	17	1m 56.062s
13	Heinz-Harald Frentzen	17	1m 56.309s
14	Jean Alesi	3	1m 56.959s
15	Jean-Christophe Boullion	16	1m 57.015s
16	Luca Badoer	21	1m 57.077s
17	Pedro Lamy	23	1m 57.669s
18	Massimiliano Papis	12	1m 57.814s
19	Taki Inoue	20	1m 59.206s
20	Andrea Montermini	7	2m 00.045s
21	Pedro Diniz	20	2m 01.630s
22	Roberto Moreno	18	2m 02.311s
23	Olivier Panis	3	2m 02.665s
24	Giovanni Lavaggi	5	6m 42.744s

Friday qualifying
Heavy rain, then slowly drying

Pos.	Driver	Laps	Time
1	Gerhard Berger	8	2m 14.744s
2	Michael Schumacher	7	2m 14.962s
3	Jean Alesi	10	2m 15.077s
4	Damon Hill	11	2m 15.143s
5	David Coulthard	9	2m 15.232s
6	Heinz-Harald Frentzen	12	2m 15.533s
7	Mika Häkkinen	11	2m 15.848s
8	Eddie Irvine	11	2m 16.540s
9	Rubens Barrichello	9	2m 17.144s
10	Martin Brundle	11	2m 17.207s
11	Luca Badoer	11	2m 17.335s
12	Jean-Christophe Boullion	12	2m 17.406s
13	Olivier Panis	11	2m 17.579s
14	Mika Salo	10	2m 18.104s
15	Mark Blundell	9	2m 18.136s
16	Ukyo Katayama	11	2m 18.194s
17	Pedro Lamy	12	2m 18.547s
18	Massimiliano Papis	12	2m 19.300s
19	Taki Inoue	10	2m 23.311s
20	Roberto Moreno	9	2m 23.417s
21	Andrea Montermini	5	2m 25.291s
22	Pedro Diniz	7	2m 25.699s
23	Giovanni Lavaggi	8	2m 26.311s
	Johnny Herbert	0	no time

Saturday qualifying
Variable damp/dry

Pos.	Driver	Laps	Time
1	Gerhard Berger	4	1m 54.392s
2	Jean Alesi	2	1m 54.631s
3	Mika Häkkinen	7	1m 55.435s
4	Johnny Herbert	8	1m 56.085s
5	David Coulthard	9	1m 56.254s
6	Mark Blundell	11	1m 56.622s
7	Eddie Irvine	6	1m 57.001s
8	Damon Hill	8	1m 57.768s
9	Olivier Panis	9	1m 58.021s
10	Heinz-Harald Frentzen	9	1m 58.148s
11	Mika Salo	5	1m 58.224s
12	Rubens Barrichello	6	1m 58.293s
13	Martin Brundle	8	1m 58.314s
14	Jean-Christophe Boullion	6	1m 58.356s
15	Ukyo Katayama	7	1m 58.551s
16	Michael Schumacher	6	1m 59.079s
17	Pedro Lamy	6	1m 59.256s
18	Taki Inoue	6	2m 00.990s
19	Luca Badoer	2	2m 01.013s
20	Massimiliano Papis	7	2m 01.685s
21	Andrea Montermini	7	2m 02.405s
22	Roberto Moreno	10	2m 03.817s
23	Giovanni Lavaggi	6	2m 06.407s
24	Pedro Diniz	8	2m 09.537s

Warm-up
Steady rain

Pos.	Driver	Laps	Time
1	Jean Alesi	10	2m 16.229s
2	Damon Hill	11	2m 16.339s
3	Michael Schumacher	9	2m 16.710s
4	David Coulthard	7	2m 17.081s
5	Mika Häkkinen	11	2m 17.412s
6	Rubens Barrichello	10	2m 18.326s
7	Gerhard Berger	8	2m 18.865s
8	Heinz-Harald Frentzen	8	2m 19.076s
9	Eddie Irvine	9	2m 19.334s
10	Jean-Christophe Boullion	8	2m 19.742s
11	Martin Brundle	8	2m 19.780s
12	Johnny Herbert	8	2m 20.573s
13	Mark Blundell	9	2m 21.000s
14	Mika Salo	8	2m 21.768s
15	Olivier Panis	10	2m 21.800s
16	Luca Badoer	9	2m 21.810s
17	Pedro Lamy	11	2m 22.305s
18	Ukyo Katayama	8	2m 22.771s
19	Massimiliano Papis	7	2m 24.032s
20	Taki Inoue	7	2m 26.584s
21	Roberto Moreno	8	2m 27.954s
22	Pedro Diniz	7	2m 29.752s
23	Andrea Montermini	3	2m 30.314s
24	Giovanni Lavaggi	4	4m 47.658s

Fastest race laps
Dry at first, then intermittent rain

Driver	Time	Lap
David Coulthard	1m 53.412s	11
Michael Schumacher	1m 53.613s	17
Damon Hill	1m 54.473s	14
Gerhard Berger	1m 55.462s	18
Eddie Irvine	1m 55.561s	14
Johnny Herbert	1m 55.630s	16
Mark Blundell	1m 55.972s	15
Heinz-Harald Frentzen	1m 56.261s	18
Martin Brundle	1m 56.502s	15
Olivier Panis	1m 56.696s	16
Jean Alesi	1m 56.853s	3
Rubens Barrichello	1m 56.967s	11
Ukyo Katayama	1m 57.229s	18
Mika Salo	1m 57.420s	17
Massimiliano Papis	1m 57.866s	15
Jean-Christophe Boullion	1m 57.927s	15
Pedro Lamy	1m 58.312s	17
Luca Badoer	1m 58.395s	14
Taki Inoue	1m 59.331s	15
Andrea Montermini	2m 00.136s	16
Pedro Diniz	2m 02.546s	17
Roberto Moreno	2m 02.603s	15
Giovanni Lavaggi	2m 04.196s	15
Mika Häkkinen	2m 07.082s	1

CHASSIS LOG BOOK

No.	Driver	Chassis
1	Schumacher	Benetton B195/6
2	Herbert	Benetton B195/5
	spare	Benetton B195/1
3	Katayama	Tyrrell 023/5
4	Salo	Tyrrell 023/6
	spare	Tyrrell 023/2
5	Hill	Williams FW17/6
6	Coulthard	Williams FW17/5
	spare	Williams FW17/2
7	Blundell	McLaren MP4/10B/6
8	Häkkinen	McLaren MP4/10B/5
	spare	McLaren MP4/10B/2
9	Papis	Footwork FA16/3
10	Inoue	Footwork FA16/4
	spare	Footwork FA16/1
14	Barrichello	Jordan 195/4
15	Irvine	Jordan 195/5
	spare	Jordan 195/1
16	Lavaggi	Pacific PR02/1
17	Montermini	Pacific PR02/2
21	Diniz	Forti FG01/4
22	Moreno	Forti FG01/3
	spare	Forti FG01/2
23	Lamy	Minardi M195/3
24	Badoer	Minardi M195/2
	spare	Minardi M195/1
25	Brundle	Ligier JS41/5
26	Panis	Ligier JS41/3
	spare	Ligier JS41/4
27	Alesi	Ferrari 412T2/163
28	Berger	Ferrari 412T2/162
	spare	Ferrari 412T2/160
29	Boullion	Sauber C14/5
30	Frentzen	Sauber C14/6
	spare	Sauber C14/2

POINTS TABLES

Drivers

1	Michael Schumacher	66
2	Damon Hill	51
3	Jean Alesi	32
4	David Coulthard	29
5	Johnny Herbert	28
6	Gerhard Berger	25
7	Heinz-Harald Frentzen	10
8 =	Rubens Barrichello	8
8 =	Olivier Panis	8
10 =	Martin Brundle	7
10 =	Mark Blundell	7
12	Eddie Irvine	6
13	Mika Häkkinen	5
14	Jean-Christophe Boullion	2
15 =	Gianni Morbidelli	1
15 =	Aguri Suzuki	1

Constructors

1	Benetton	84
2	Williams	74
3	Ferrari	57
4	Ligier	16
5	Jordan	14
6 =	McLaren	12
6 =	Sauber	12
8	Footwork	1

WORLD CHAMPIONSHIP • ROUND 12

ITALIAN GRAND PRIX

HERBERT
HÄKKINEN
FRENTZEN
BLUNDELL
SALO
BOULLION

Above: A delighted Johnny Herbert savours his second win of the season. Mika Häkkinen *(left)* and Heinz-Harald Frentzen also look pleased with their day's work, but Benetton boss Flavio Briatore *(right)* appears strangely preoccupied.

Although he was only eighth fastest in qualifying, Herbert *(right)* was well placed to inherit the spoils when a bizarre sequence of misfortunes eliminated the front-runners.

Johnny Herbert once again demonstrated the merits of running consistently and keeping out of trouble at Monza, that hotbed of Ferrari fervour just north of the famous Italian team's traditional heartland. Remaining cool and unflustered as others fell by the wayside, the Benetton number two picked his way through the debris to score his second win of the season. It was a success which moved him up to third place in the drivers' championship on a day when both Ferraris led – but failed – and Damon Hill rammed Michael Schumacher's Benetton in what, hysteria aside, could best be described as a most unfortunate set of circumstances.

Truth be told, the Italian Grand Prix had it all. David Coulthard was on pole but spun off during the parade lap, only to receive a heaven-sent second chance when the race was red-flagged after a multiple collision barely two miles into its distance. In the spare Williams he then led commandingly before spinning out with a seized front wheel bearing – the first in a bewildering sequence of retirements which left the most highly fancied runners littered around the circuit in various stages of disrepair. And Herbert tootling through to win.

Coulthard dramatically endorsed his candidature for any top-line seat which might be on offer for 1996 by absolutely dominating both qualifying sessions. From the moment the 24-year-old Scot accelerated out onto the circuit 23 minutes into Friday's hour-long first session, his Williams FW17 was never dislodged from the top of the timing screens, fending off firm challenges from both Gerhard Berger's Ferrari and his own teammate Damon Hill, who finished the day in second and third places respectively.

'It's a pity this wasn't Saturday, so I wouldn't have to worry about what is going to happen tomorrow,' said Coulthard. 'I was quick this morning, and then quick again in both my qualifying runs, so I feel pretty confident I can stay quickest tomorrow, although I know it will be an interesting battle.'

Coulthard's first session best was a 1m 25.516s – 0.6s inside the best Jean Alesi had managed during four days of pre-event testing for Ferrari the previous week, and less than two seconds away from the Frenchman's 1994 3.5-litre pole time. Considering Alesi had achieved that time with the benefit of more aerodynamic downforce and a slightly quicker circuit configuration, the Scot's achievement was praiseworthy indeed.

On Saturday, David was as good as his word. In hotter conditions, he went even quicker, causing some members of the Williams team to ponder the set of circumstances which had led to the young driver leaving the team at the end of the season. For the moment, at least, he was very much the F1 pacesetter.

From the start of Friday qualifying both Williams drivers, together with rivals Michael Schumacher and Johnny Herbert at Benetton, were using further-uprated C-specification Renault RS7 engines. This was seen as representing a robust response to the potential offered by the much-vaunted 'Evolution 3' version of Ferrari's 3-litre engine – the last such development before Maranello's new V10 underwent its preliminary testing prior to a planned race debut in 1996.

Although Berger grabbed second-quickest time in the closing moments of the first session, Hill remained confident that he would move forward to the front row in Saturday's second qualifying session. He also offered a well-timed reminder that Ferrari had enjoyed the luxury of immediate pre-race testing at a Monza track which had been extensively resurfaced as part of a programme of FIA-required safety improvements.

'Considering we don't get the chance to test here, I think we've done a good job and have more to come,' said Hill, referring to the fact that Monza is the designated test circuit for all the Italian teams in the same way as the British-based teams can use Silverstone in the run-up to their home race.

Coulthard's decisive display of precision driving had come at the end of a week in which the Italian media had whipped up a frenzy of speculation as to the identity of Michael Schumacher's 1996 partner at Ferrari. Much of this excitement had been triggered by Gerhard Berger's unexpected decision, announced after the Belgian GP, to join fellow Ferrari refugee Jean Alesi at Benetton. This surprise move by the veteran 36-year-old Austrian wrong-footed the Ferrari management which, hitherto, had felt confident that Gerhard would stay on alongside Schumacher in 1996.

In the event, Ferrari had to content itself with announcing that Shell would replace Agip as the company's fuel supplier in 1996, reviving a link first forged in 1929 when Enzo Ferrari originally established his independent team to race Alfa Romeo cars. It was also confirmed that Niki Lauda, the former World Champion who won two of his three titles for the Prancing Horse, would be relinquishing his role as a consultant to the legendary team.

However, Coulthard's position as a possible Ferrari candidate was complicated by the fact that McLaren retained an option on his services through to the end of September, at which point they would confirm their driver line-up at the Grand Prix of Europe. The paddock consensus at Monza suggested that if Alain Prost eventually agreed to make a full-time F1 return with McLaren, Coulthard would be released to pursue other career options. As things transpired, it didn't quite work out like that.

Either way, Coulthard's possible role as a candidate for the Ferrari drive certainly attracted Michael Schumacher's unofficial seal of approval, although the German driver seemed less happy with the prospect of Rubens Barrichello joining him in 1996, an option which was also considered earlier in the week.

Returning to the on-track action, the general feeling was that the Monza circuit authorities had done a good job uprating the safety provisions. Run-off areas at both the Curva Grande and the two Lesmo right-handers had been massively extended by cutting down a couple of hundred trees. The track had also been slightly reprofiled, the first Lesmo now being taken in third – rather than fourth – gear. By Saturday afternoon, the faster runners had obviously developed a clear feel for the track conditions, waiting until a handful of slower cars had ventured out before attempting to challenge Coulthard's provisional pole time.

At 13.22, Hill rolled out of the pit lane, quickly posting a 1m 25.802s which immediately moved him up to second place on the grid. But Coulthard, radiating a steely, focused commitment seldom seen before, raised the stakes by going even quicker to deliver a 1m 25.456s.

Hardly had everybody caught their breath when Coulthard went quicker again, slicing down to 1m 24.766s. This was serious stuff and even the rival Renault-equipped contenders were clearly going to be hard-pushed to match it.

With 20 minutes of the session left, Schumacher squared up to the task and turned in a 1m 26.843s on his first run. Clearly, this wasn't quick enough, so the World Champion came straight back into the pits for a slight set-up change and bided his time prior to launching a late-session challenge.

With only seven and a half minutes left to go, the track erupted into a flurry of activity. Suddenly, Ferrari bounced back into contention with

Benetton computer traces point finger at Hill

It was a trying week for Damon Hill in the aftermath of the Italian Grand Prix. To start with, both he and Michael Schumacher received a stern warning from Bernie Ecclestone that they could kill each other if they continued to be involved in collisions together – along with a hint at even tougher action from the FIA if these rough-house tactics were not shelved. Then Benetton went public with evidence from their telemetry which, it was claimed, firmly proved that Hill alone was to blame for the Monza incident.

Benetton went onto the defensive after being stung by media reports saying that Ecclestone had suggested that Schumacher might, conceivably, have been guilty of brake-testing Hill as they came up to lap Taki Inoue's Footwork. In their view, the data from Schumacher's car proved that Damon had simply misjudged his braking point.

Detailed examination of the telemetry traces showed that Hill's Williams was travelling almost 10 mph faster than Schumacher when he slammed into the back of the Benetton. 'The information we have analysed supports Michael's viewpoint,' said Ross Brawn, the team's Technical Director.

'We can trace each lap individually, either from the viewpoint of distance covered or time. This information is downloaded from the car after the event. I was curious that Damon suggested Michael braked early, so we decided to have a detailed look.'

Scrutiny of data from race laps 22, 23 and 24, the lap on which the collision occurred, left Brawn in no doubt about his findings. On lap 24, it was established that Schumacher was travelling quicker than he had been on the previous two tours.

The team was satisfied that Michael braked eight metres later than on the previous two laps and his rate of deceleration was the same on all three laps involved.

Former World Champion Alain Prost was slightly more philosophical as to the cause of the accident, although he certainly laid part of the blame at Hill's door.

'I think it is inevitable that when you have two drivers fighting for the championship you have one or two problems in the year.

'How can you avoid that? They want to win races, want to win championships. I think Damon just missed his braking point. That is a racing incident.'

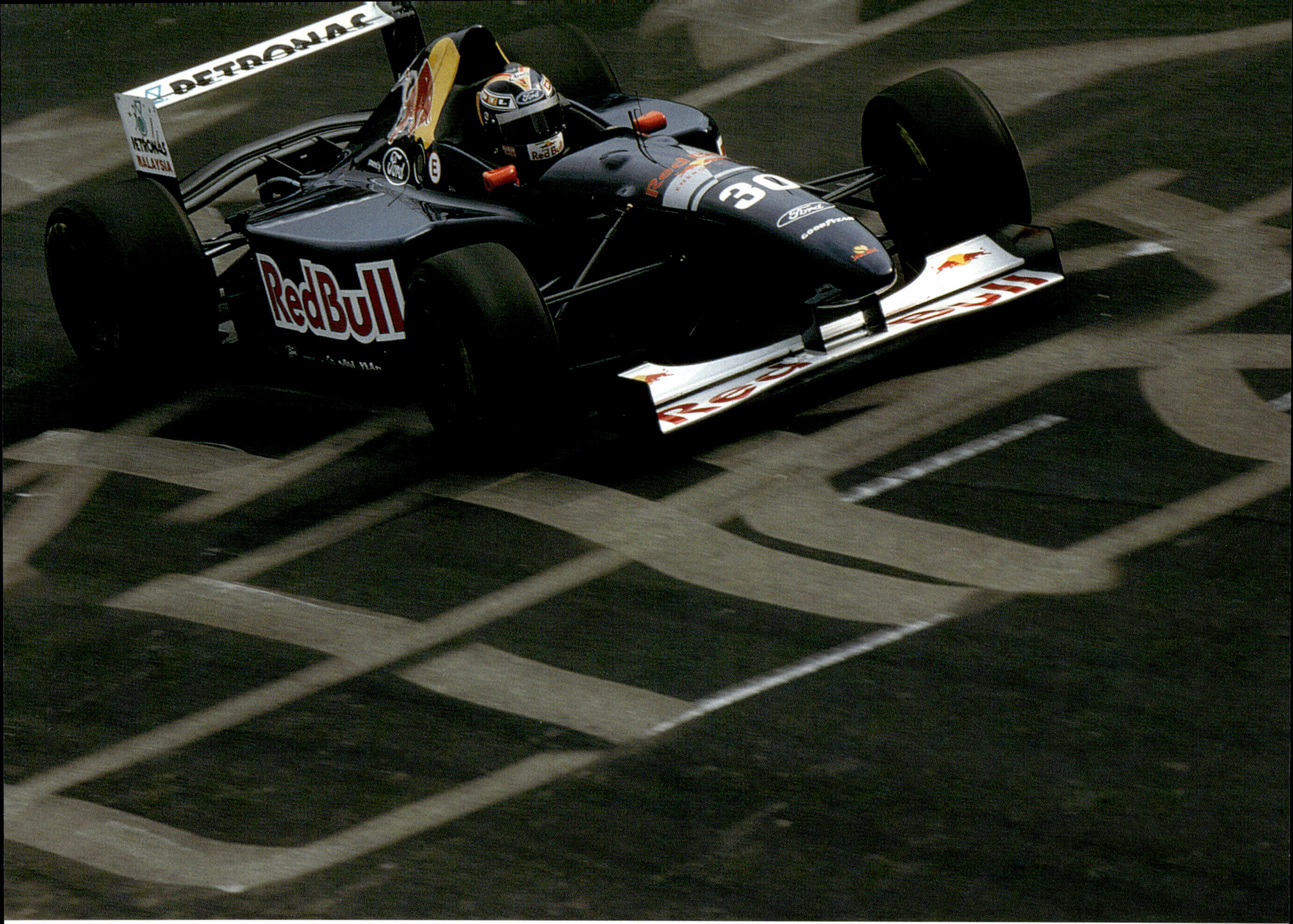
PETRONAS
PETRONAS MALAYSIA
RedBull
30
GOODYEAR

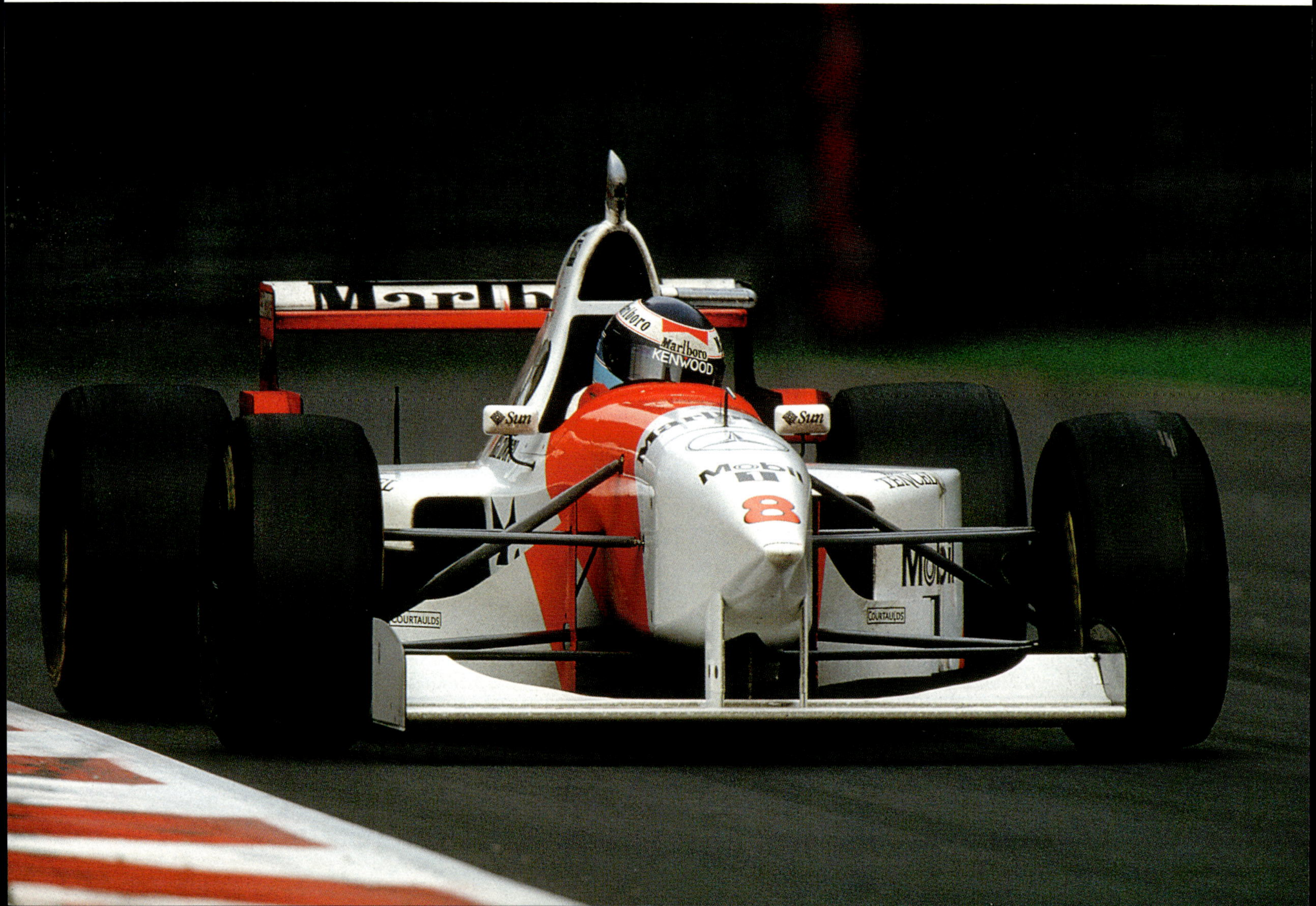
Marlboro
KENWOOD
Sun
Sun
Mobil
8
Mobil
COURTAULDS
COURTAULDS

ITALIAN GRAND PRIX

Enjoying some good fortune for once, the consistently impressive Heinz-Harald Frentzen *(left)* earned the first podium finish of his Grand Prix career with the steadily improving Sauber-Ford.

Below left: After months of struggle it seemed that McLaren were finally making worthwhile progress. Mika Häkkinen's second place was a fitting reward for the team's tireless efforts to regain competitiveness.

Mark Blundell *(below)* brought the second McLaren home in fourth place. The former Tyrrell driver's unfailing cheerfulness had helped sustain the Woking team's morale during a difficult season.

Diary

Touring car stalwart Kieth Odor killed after his Nissan Primera is T-boned by Frank Biela's Audi during race at Berlin's AVUS circuit.

Plans to allow top F1 teams to field three cars in 1996 Grands Prix is put on hold following F1 Commission meeting at Monza.

Gil de Ferran scores first Indy Car victory in season finale at Laguna Seca, where Jacques Villeneuve clinches the title.

Christian Fittipaldi confirmed as Michael Andretti's team-mate in the 1996 Newman-Haas Indy Car Lola-Ford squad.

Alesi producing a 1m 25.707s to move his scarlet steed onto the front row alongside Coulthard. The madly passionate crowds went frantic with delight, all round the circuit. But their joy was destined to be short-lived.

The amazing Coulthard came slamming back with a 1m 24.492s. Then Schumacher improved to 1m 25.230s, making it onto the front row. But the Williams driver was still firmly in charge, ending any vestige of debate by rounding off the day with a 1m 24.462s. Pole position was his by the substantial margin of half a second.

The best the Maranello brigade could salvage was third place for Gerhard Berger. Better than nothing, but in truth an acute disappointment for the home team, which had hoped for so much from this weekend. Gerhard had lost his first run due to an engine problem and the electronic control box was changed just in time for him to stage his late surge up to the second row.

Alesi also had a rotten time, his freshly installed V12 delivering its power in worryingly inconsistent fashion. It was shaping up to be far from the emotional farewell to the Ferrari fans that Jean had been hoping for. And there would be much worse to come on race day.

Fourth place was earned by Hill, the Englishman having a busy time indeed on Saturday. At the end of the morning's free practice session, Damon's Williams stopped out on the circuit with a rare Renault V10 engine failure. A replacement was fitted in double-quick time by his mechanics, but Damon could not get within 1.2s of his team-mate's best time.

'It was not the qualifying session I had been hoping for,' he said crisply, 'but it is not the end of the world. Congratulations to David, who did a great job all weekend. The team also did a great job changing the engine, but I understeered off at Lesmo – it was a scary moment when the car seemed to be turning right and heading straight for the barrier – but I just managed to get it back again!'

Alesi shared the third row with Rubens Barrichello, the Brazilian's Jordan 195 alone fitted with a revised exhaust system for this race. Eddie Irvine, by contrast, had several off-track excursions during the course of the two days' qualifying. On Saturday morning the Ulsterman's Peugeot V10 developed a leakage from its air-valve system and a fresh unit was installed between sessions. Then, in second qualifying, Eddie had a brake problem which ruined his first set of tyres, and still found the car oversteering more sharply than he felt was ideal. He went quicker, but dropped two places on the day to line up a very disappointed 12th.

Over in the McLaren camp, Mika Häkkinen managed to salvage seventh place in the final grid order after an action-packed time on Friday which saw him leave the road twice in his MP4/10B. Coming less than a fortnight after his second-lap spin at Spa, this seemed a very much less than satisfactory development for the Finn.

Mika freely admitted that he had made a driving error in the first accident, after which the entire left-hand suspension and associated componentry were changed. However, detailed investigation of Mika's second off-track excursion – which ruined his first qualifying bid – led to an admission that there was a '95 per cent chance' that a steering component failure had caused the accident.

An intensive programme of structural analysis was immediately instigated back at the team's Woking headquarters to examine similar components from the same batch, after which the McLaren factory was able to confirm that it would be safe to use replacement components available at Monza for the remainder of the weekend.

Häkkinen had thus been forced to take over Mark Blundell's car late in

185

ITALIAN GRAND PRIX

Staying focused. The Ligier pit crew are poised for action as Martin Brundle's JS41 limps towards them with a shredded tyre. Sadly the damage sustained as the Englishman made his way back to the pits forced him out of the race.

first qualifying, obliging the Englishman to rush through his own runs. Things were slightly better on Saturday when Mika and Mark ended up seventh and ninth, trading aerodynamic downforce for straightline speed and thus compromising their handling balance a little.

Herbert wound up a slightly dejected eighth in the number two Benetton, with Heinz-Harald Frentzen again doing a good job for Sauber to line up tenth ahead of Martin Brundle's Ligier. Olivier Panis was satisfied with 13th, praising the fly-by-wire throttle system being used on the Mugen Honda V10s for the first time, while Jean-Christophe Boullion recovered from a spate of braking problems on Saturday morning to get his Sauber C14 in the race in 14th spot.

Max Papis suffered seemingly endless gearbox maladies with his Footwork, but popped in a very respectable 15th-fastest time to line up ahead of the Tyrrells of Mika Salo and Ukyo Katayama, the Yamaha-engined contenders also using fly-by-wire throttles for the first time. Unfortunately, neither driver managed to work out a decent handling balance.

Minardi had a dismal time on home ground, Luca Badoer crashing heavily under braking for the Variante Ascari and rolling his M195 into the gravel trap after it bounced off the guard rail. Nevertheless, Badoer qualified 18th, one place ahead of team-mate Pedro Lamy, who slammed over the high kerb exiting the second Lesmo and wrecked his M195's nose cone in the process. Taki Inoue completed the top twenty for Footwork, followed by Pacific and Forti Corse, who shared the last two rows, as usual.

'Better one Alesi today than a thousand Schumachers tomorrow' announced a banner in the public enclosure immediately opposite the Ferrari pit. Perhaps Jean drew strength from this outpouring of support, for he was quickest in the race morning warm-up ahead of Coulthard, Berger, Schumacher and Hill. Even so, it would have taken a brave man to bet against Coulthard scoring his maiden GP win.

David duly took up his place on pole position and set out on the parade lap at the head of the pack, only for a bizarre helping of misfortune to befall him barely a mile before the starting grid proper. Exiting the Variante Ascari, the Williams unaccountably snapped into a spin and went bouncing roughly off the circuit across the outside kerb. Oil left from the Renault Clio race, or the historic single-seater event, was lamely cited as the possible cause. Schumacher could hardly believe his good fortune.

Round they came to the grid, with pole position now vacant. The green light came on and Schumacher's Benetton accelerated cleanly away from the line, weaving subtly and ominously as Berger attempted to edge his Ferrari level on the sprint towards the first chicane. At the end of the opening lap, Berger was perfectly poised to make a bid for the lead as he slammed past the pits towards that first chicane, but he needn't have bothered.

Further back down the pack, the Variante Ascari exit had claimed several more victims. Papis spun his Footwork, involving Montermini's Pacific, the two Fortis and Boullion's Sauber. With debris all over the circuit, there was no choice but to red-flag the event to a halt. Now it was Coulthard's turn to wonder at his good fortune.

The restart counted as a totally new race, so the Williams driver was entitled to take his original place on pole position, albeit driving the spare car, although Montermini and Moreno were less fortunate as their teams did not have such back-up equipment available.

Coulthard went in cold at the wheel of his replacement FW17, of course, as the rules forbid the use of spare cars throughout the two days of practice and qualifying. It didn't show, however, and David surged straight into the lead, with Berger this time forcing his way ahead of Schumacher as they scrambled for room into the first chicane.

Well down the pack, Salo's Tyrrell touched Panis's Ligier under braking for the Variante Ascari, the Finn spinning to the tail of the field as Coulthard led the pack out of Parabolica and up towards the timing line, completing the opening lap 0.3s ahead of Berger. Then came Schumacher and Hill, with a slight gap to Alesi, then Herbert, Barrichello, Häkkinen and Brundle.

It didn't take long for Coulthard to settle into the rhythm of things and within half a dozen laps he'd clearly got the feel of his new mount. On lap six he was 0.74s ahead, and he then stretched his advantage to 1.17s and 2.3s on consecutive laps. It seemed clear that David was the class of the field, but as he braked for the second chicane on lap 14, the Williams suddenly snapped out of control and spun into the gravel trap on the outside of the corner.

Coulthard managed to gather it all up and struggle round to the pits, where he slid straight past his prescribed stopping point, signalling that something had gone very badly wrong with his car. Closer examination revealed that the right-front wheel bearing had seized, pitching him violently out of control.

'A real shame,' he shrugged, 'because I was able to pull away, even though I had something in reserve. Suddenly I noticed a vibration from the front of the car, then the right-front wheel grabbed and spun me off.'

Now the crowd really had something to hold their attention. Berger was leading by 1.4s from Schumacher and extended his advantage to 2.3s by the time he completed his 20th lap. Hill was now right on the Benetton's tail, confident his Williams had the edge on its rival Renault-engined competitor and hopeful that he could leapfrog ahead of the German when it was time to come in for refuelling.

Meanwhile, Brundle lost much of his early momentum, dropping back behind Irvine and Blundell to trail along in 11th place by lap eight. The JS41 had picked up a slow puncture and his left-rear tyre soon disintegrated into shards of rubber as he limped back to the pits on three wheels. Nothing could be done, so the car was retired and Martin collected an official reprimand from the stewards for continuing to drive a car which was adjudged to be in a dangerous condition.

It was a bad day for Ligier, for Panis spun off at the first chicane at the start of his 21st lap, but this was small beer when compared with what was to follow as events clicked into place once more to re-ignite the seemingly perennial Hill/Schumacher rivalry.

With Alesi now closing steadily in fourth place, Michael and Damon came up to lap Taki Inoue's Footwork as they entered the Curva Grande. Perhaps trying to be helpful, Taki hugged the inside line through the fast right-hander, forcing Schumacher to lead Hill round the outside into the braking area for the second chicane.

Momentarily unsighted as Inoue dodged about – and worried that the Japanese novice had not seen his Williams – Damon left his braking extremely late and suddenly found himself surging into the back of Schumacher's Benetton as they slowed to negotiate the tight chicane.

The two cars went spearing off into the gravel trap and that was the end of the championship battle for another afternoon. Once out of his Benetton's cockpit, it seemed as though Michael was set to give Damon a piece of his mind there and then, but a marshal briefly intervened to steer him away from the Williams driver and they walked off stony faced, a few feet apart.

'I turned into the corner not expecting anything, just a normal entry into the corner,' said Schumacher. 'I was really into the corner and I was braking late compared to Gerhard and the other drivers. Suddenly I felt a big bang and Damon went into me. It was not a slight touch – he really crashed into me. I am certainly very upset about it, because it's the second time now and he's taken more points away from me which I could have gained by finishing in front of him.'

Hill, though apologetic, took a slightly defensive line in his response. 'There wasn't much conversation,' he admitted. 'Obviously Michael was very upset, but I'm upset too. I wanted to have a really good race to the end, but when you've got people out there who are really clueless as to what's going on around them [Inoue] then these things happen.

'I will never want to tangle deliberately or have an accident like that because it just ruins the race. Every time Michael got a bit of space I managed to pull him back.'

Just as Williams had at Spa, Benetton filed a protest against Hill's behaviour. The two drivers were called before the stewards and Damon received a one-race ban, suspended for one race. Schumacher was highly indignant because this was effectively a less severe punishment than the one-race ban suspended for four races he had received for rubbing wheels with the Williams driver at Spa, something he clearly regarded as a much lesser offence.

That left a Ferrari 1-2 at the head of the pack with Berger confidently leading across the timing line from Alesi, Barrichello, Häkkinen, Herbert and Irvine. On lap 25 Gerhard made a 17.7s refuelling stop – too long, delayed by a slight clutch problem. Thus when Alesi came in on the following lap, although his Ferrari

187

Nigel Snowdon

Sutton Photographic

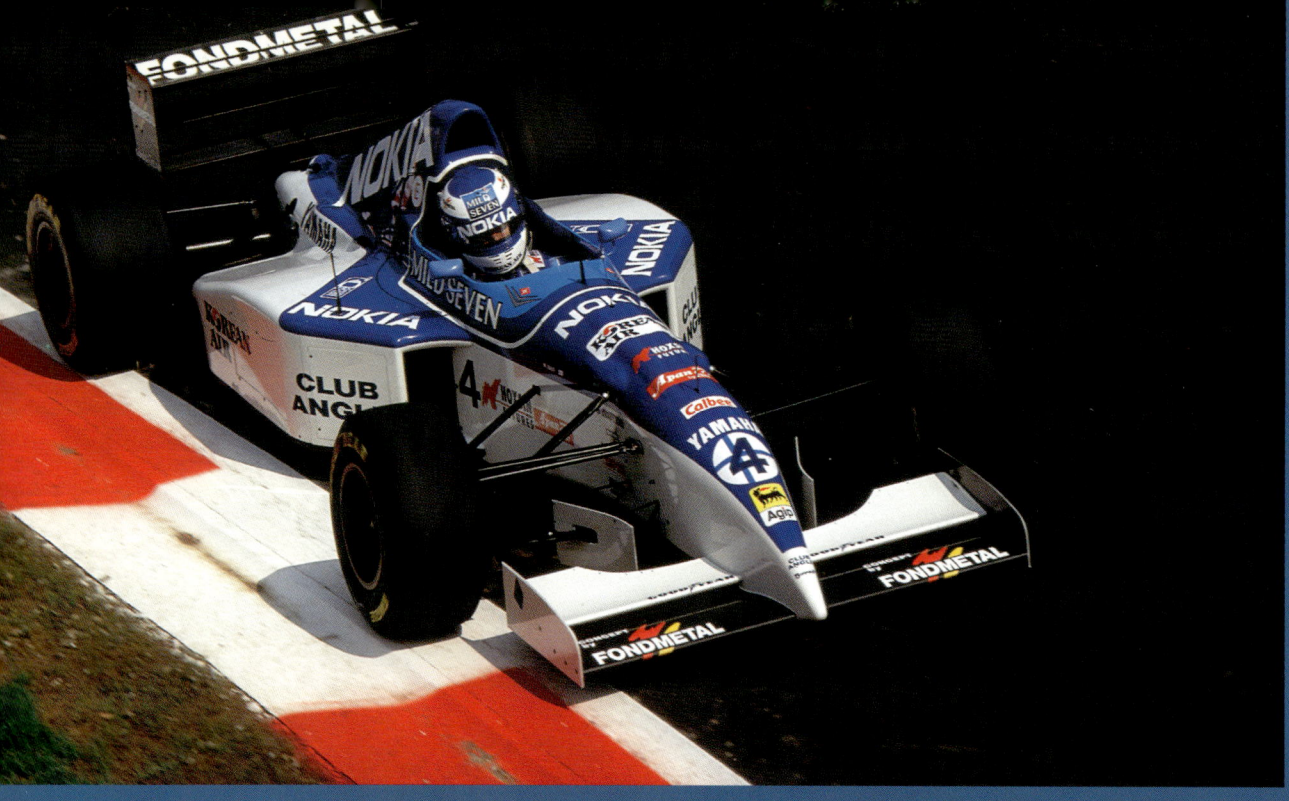

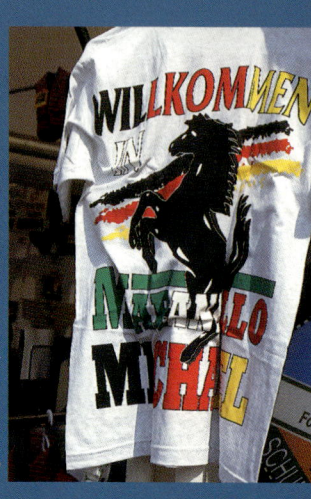

Denied by the reinstatement of Schumacher and Coulthard in Brazil, Mika Salo *(above)* finally scored his first World Championship points with fifth place for Tyrrell.

Right: It proved to be a disappointing weekend for Kumiko Goto, Jean Alesi's girlfriend, and for everyone else who had hoped to see the popular French driver crown his Ferrari career with a win in front of the adoring *tifosi*.

Below: Ferrari looked set for an emotional 1-2 on home ground as Alesi ran ahead of Gerhard Berger at the head of the field. However, the television camera attached to the rear wing of the Frenchman's car is already wilting and before long it will fall off, smashing the left-front suspension of Berger's 412T2.

Steve Etherington/Empics

Paul-Henri Cahier

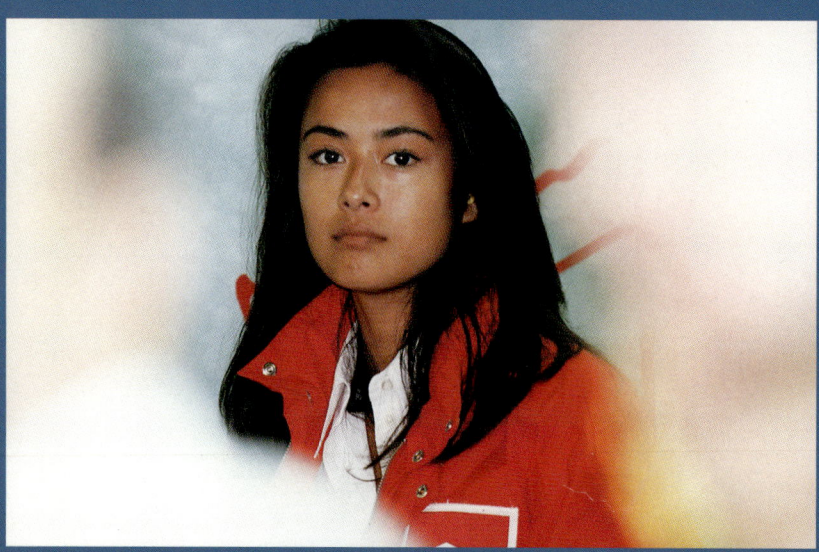

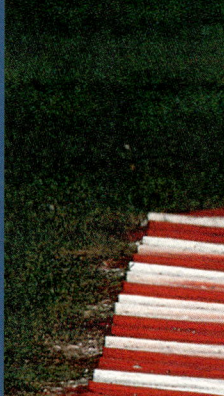

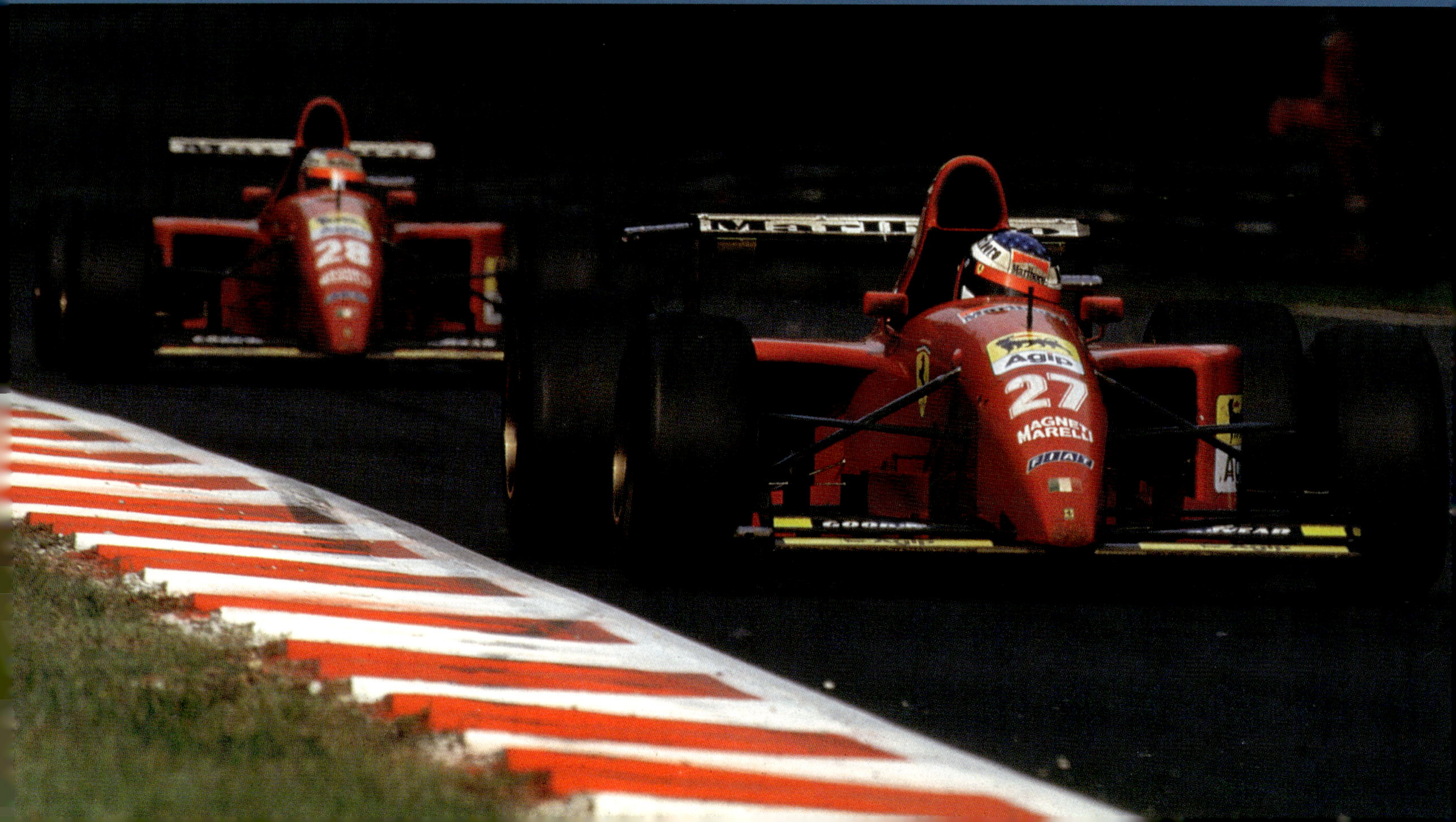

ITALIAN GRAND PRIX

Top centre: Contrary to many expectations, Michael Schumacher had yet to displace Jean Alesi in the hearts of the Ferrari faithful.

Top: Giovanni Lavaggi's Pacific spins out of the race after six laps, scattering gravel onto the track, but the Forti of Pedro Diniz slips past unscathed.

Above: David Coulthard leads Gerhard Berger, Michael Schumacher, Damon Hill, Johnny Herbert and Jean Alesi into the Variante Ascari. Only one of them would reach the finish.

Sutton Photographic

was stationary slightly longer, he got away cleanly and just squeezed out ahead of his team-mate.

On laps 26 and 27, Barrichello and Häkkinen briefly led before making their stops, resuming in fourth and fifth places with the Finn now ahead. However, Herbert stayed out until lap 30, which allowed him to consolidate third place. This proved to be the crucial turning-point in Johnny's fortunes, although at the time it seemed as though third was the best he could hope for.

The possibility of a Ferrari 1-2 was almost too much for the madly enthusiastic crowd to take aboard. But their joy was fleeting, lasting only three laps. Then the camera on the outer edge of Alesi's rear wing came adrift, bouncing down the road and slamming into the left-front suspension of his team-mate's car. The impact was sufficient to break Berger's left-hand steering arm and the Austrian slithered to a halt at the second chicane, thankful that it hadn't made contact with his helmet.

'This thing was coming for me at 180 mph and I just couldn't swerve,' he later explained. 'I'm just glad it hit the car, and not me.' Still, there was one Ferrari left at the head of the field. Jean remained comfortably in control until lap 45, when Maranello's great hopes began to unravel once and for all.

Alesi told his team over the radio that he thought he'd picked up a puncture. 'The car began to feel as though it was on three wheels,' he explained, 'but it wasn't a puncture, it was a wheel bearing failure.' Midway round lap 46 flames began to lick round the rear of the car and he trickled slowly into the pits. Alesi climbed out and sat down by the pit wall, head in hands. Like the crowd, he was stunned. There were only eight laps to go.

Thus Johnny Herbert won his second Grand Prix of the season. The Englishman explained it like this: 'I could see Jean ahead of me and then coming out of the Lesmo I noticed there was some smoke coming from his car. Then he started to go slowly, so at that point I realised I was going to take over the lead. I also knew the gap behind me and it was really a pleasant surprise.

'While I was behind Jean, I just felt I needed to press on, keep up and hope for some luck – and it happened. Our strategy for me to come in quite late also worked perfectly and I was delighted with that too. It has been a great day for me and everything went correctly – I was even wearing the same underpants that I wore at Silverstone!'

Only 17.7s further back, Mika Häkkinen gave McLaren its best result of the season with the MP4/10B. Mika was particularly happy with the driveability of the Mercedes FO110 engine in its latest specification, feeling that the whole package enabled him to push hard throughout the race without losing confidence.

With Mark Blundell coming home fourth, despite being slightly disappointed with the handling of his car when running with a heavier fuel load, it was clearly a morale-boosting day for McLaren. Mark had actually emerged from his refuelling stop on lap 26 ahead of Heinz-Harald Frentzen's Sauber-Ford, but the German – whose tyres were nicely warmed up after his own stop on the previous lap – was able to surge by under braking for the second chicane.

Frentzen was now seventh and quickly disposed of Eddie Irvine's Jordan to take what became fifth place as Berger retired, the Sauber now splitting the two Peugeot-engined cars. Then, on lap 41, Irvine retired from sixth place with engine failure, to be followed three laps later by Barrichello's sister car with an electrical problem. Now Frentzen was fourth, and when Alesi bowed out the German finally moved through to cement the first podium finish of his short career.

In fifth place, benefiting from a two-stop strategy, came Mika Salo's Tyrrell-Yamaha, the first helping of points for the young Finn and the first top-six finish for the team this season. The top six was completed by Jean-Christophe Boullion's Sauber, the Frenchman nipping ahead of Max Papis's Footwork only two laps from the chequered flag. The Arrows team had decided against fitting fresh rubber at Papis's sole refuelling stop, feeling that new tyres would make little difference to his cause. Some members of the team had second thoughts about that afterwards.

Inoue finished eighth ahead of Pedro Diniz and Ukyo Katayama, whose run was interrupted when his engine cut out with a sensor problem on lap 29 and he was lucky to coax his mount back to the pits. Unfortunately Salo's stop was due one lap later, so the Japanese driver waited patiently in the garage for his team-mate to be serviced before receiving attention. At the finish, he was six laps down and not classified in the final order.

FIA FORMULA ONE WORLD CHAMPIONSHIP ROUND 12

PIONEER 66° GRAN PREMIO D'ITALIA
MONZA AUTODROMO 8-10 SEPTEMBER 1995

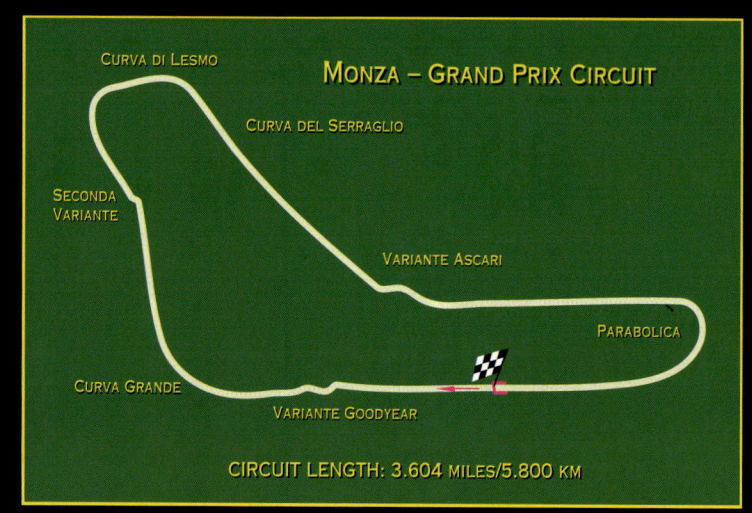

Race distance: 53 laps, 191.009 miles/307.400 km
Race weather: Warm, sunny

Place	Driver	Nat.	No.	Entrant	Car/Engine	Laps	Time/Retirement	Speed (mph/km/h)
1	**Johnny Herbert**	GB	2	Mild Seven Benetton Renault	Benetton B195-Renault RS7C V10	53	1h 18m 27.916s	145.285/233.814
2	**Mika Häkkinen**	SF	8	Marlboro McLaren Mercedes	McLaren MP4/10B-Mercedes FO110 V10	53	1h 18m 45.695s	144.738/232.934
3	**Heinz-Harald Frentzen**	D	30	Red Bull Sauber Ford	Sauber C14-Ford Zetec-R V8	53	1h 18m 52.237s	144.538/232.612
4	**Mark Blundell**	GB	7	Marlboro McLaren Mercedes	McLaren MP4/10B-Mercedes FO110 V10	53	1h 18m 56.139s	144.442/232.412
5	**Mika Salo**	SF	4	Nokia Tyrrell Yamaha	Tyrrell 023-Yamaha OX10C V10	52		
6	**Jean-Christophe Boullion**	F	29	Red Bull Sauber Ford	Sauber C14-Ford Zetec-R V8	52		
7	Massimiliano Papis	I	9	Footwork Hart	Footwork FA16-Hart 830 V8	52		
8	Taki Inoue	J	10	Footwork Hart	Footwork FA16-Hart 830 V8	52		
9	Pedro Diniz	BR	21	Parmalat Forti Ford	Forti FG01-Ford ED V8	50		
NC	Ukyo Katayama	J	3	Nokia Tyrrell Yamaha	Tyrrell 023-Yamaha OX10C V10	47		
	Jean Alesi	F	27	Scuderia Ferrari	Ferrari 412T2 044 V12	45	Wheel bearing	
	Rubens Barrichello	BR	14	Total Jordan Peugeot	Jordan 195-Peugeot A10 V10	43	Hydraulics	
	Eddie Irvine	GB	15	Total Jordan Peugeot	Jordan 195-Peugeot A10 V10	40	Engine	
	Gerhard Berger	A	28	Scuderia Ferrari	Ferrari 412T2 044 V12	32	Suspension	
	Luca Badoer	I	24	Minardi Scuderia Italia	Minardi M195-Ford EDM V8	26	Accident	
	Michael Schumacher	D	1	Mild Seven Benetton Renault	Benetton B195-Renault RS7C V10	23	Collision with Hill	
	Damon Hill	GB	5	Rothmans Williams Renault	Williams FW17-Renault RS7C V10	23	Collision with Schumacher	
	Olivier Panis	F	26	Ligier Gitanes Blondes	Ligier JS41-Mugen Honda MF301 V10	20	Spun off	
	David Coulthard	GB	6	Rothmans Williams Renault	Williams FW17-Renault RS7C V10	13	Wheel bearing	
	Martin Brundle	GB	25	Ligier Gitanes Blondes	Ligier JS41-Mugen Honda MF301 V10	10	Puncture	
	Giovanni Lavaggi	I	16	Pacific Grand Prix Ltd	Pacific PR02-Ford ED V8	6	Spun off	
	Pedro Lamy	P	23	Minardi Scuderia Italia	Minardi M195-Ford EDM V8	0	Differential	
DNS	Andrea Montermini	I	17	Pacific Grand Prix Ltd	Pacific PR02-Ford ED V8	0	Accident at first start	
DNS	Roberto Moreno	BR	22	Parmalat Forti Ford	Forti FG01-Ford ED V8	0	Accident at first start	

Fastest lap: Berger, on lap 24, 1m 26.419s, 149.354 mph/240.363 km/h (establishes record for revised circuit).
Previous lap record: Damon Hill (F1 Williams FW15C-Renault V10), 1m 23.575s, 155.241 mph/249.835 km/h (1993).
All cars used Goodyear tyres

All results and data © FIA 1995

Grid order		1	2	3	4	5	6	7	8	9	10	11	12	13	14	15	16	17	18	19	20	21	22	23	24	25	26	27	28	29	30	31	32	33	34	35	36	37	38	39	40
6	COULTHARD	6	6	6	6	6	6	6	6	6	6	6	6	6	28	28	28	28	28	28	28	28	28	28	28	27	14	8	2	2	27	27	27	27	27	27	27	27	27	27	27
1	SCHUMACHER	28	28	28	28	28	28	28	28	28	28	28	28	28	1	1	1	1	1	1	1	1	1	1	27	14	8	2	27	28	28	28	2	2	2	2	2	2	2	2	2
28	BERGER	1	1	1	1	1	1	1	1	1	1	1	1	1	5	5	5	5	5	5	5	5	5	5	14	8	2	15	28	28	2	2	8	8	8	8	8	8	8	8	8
5	HILL	5	5	5	5	5	5	5	5	5	5	5	5	5	27	27	27	27	27	27	27	27	27	27	8	2	27	27	8	8	8	8	14	14	14	14	14	14	14	14	14
27	ALESI	27	27	27	27	27	27	27	27	27	27	27	27	27	14	14	14	14	14	14	14	14	14	14	2	28	15	28	14	14	14	14	30	30	30	30	30	30	30	30	30
14	BARRICHELLO	2	2	14	14	14	14	14	14	14	14	14	14	14	8	8	8	8	8	8	8	8	8	8	15	15	28	14	15	30	30	30	15	15	15	15	15	15	15	15	15
8	HAKKINEN	14	14	2	8	8	8	8	8	8	8	8	8	8	2	2	2	2	2	2	2	2	2	2	7	7	7	30	30	15	15	15	7	7	7	7	7	7	7	7	7
2	HERBERT	8	8	8	2	2	2	2	2	2	2	2	2	2	15	15	15	15	15	15	15	15	15	15	30	30	30	7	7	7	7	7	9	9	9	9	9	9	9	9	9
7	BLUNDELL	25	15	15	15	15	15	15	15	15	15	15	15	15	7	7	7	7	7	7	7	7	7	7	24	9	10	10	4	4	4	9	4	4	4	4	4	4	4	4	4
30	FRENTZEN	15	25	25	25	25	25	25	7	7	7	7	7	7	30	30	30	30	30	30	30	30	30	30	9	10	29	4	3	9	9	4	29	29	29	29	29	29	29	29	29
25	BRUNDLE	7	7	7	7	7	7	7	25	25	25	25	25	30	3	26	26	26	26	26	26	26	26	24	10	29	4	9	9	10	10	10	10	10	10	10	10	10	10	10	10
15	IRVINE	30	30	30	30	30	30	30	30	25	25	25	3	3	26	24	24	24	24	24	24	24	9	9	29	4	9	29	10	29	29	29	21	21	21	21	21	21	21	21	21
26	PANIS	26	26	26	26	26	26	26	26	3	26	26	26	26	24	9	9	9	9	9	9	9	10	10	4	24	29	29	21	21	21	21	3	3	3	3	3	3	3	3	3
29	BOULLION	4	3	3	3	3	3	3	3	26	4	24	24	9	10	10	10	10	10	10	29	29	29	3	3	3	21	3	3	3	3										
9	PAPIS	3	24	24	24	24	24	24	4	4	9	9	9	10	29	29	29	29	29	29	4	4	4	21	21	21															
4	SALO	9	9	9	9	9	9	9	24	9	10	10	10	29	4	4	4	4	4	4	3	3	3																		
3	KATAYAMA	24	16	16	10	10	10	10	9	10	29	4	4	4	21	21	21	21	21	21																					
24	BADOER	16	10	10	4	16	10	10	10	29	4	21	21	21																												
23	LAMY	10	21	4	10	4	29	29	29	29	21	29	29																													
10	INOUE	21	29	21	21	29	21	16	21	21																																
17	MONTERMINI	29	4	29	29	29	21																																			
22	MORENO																																									
21	DINIZ																																									
16	LAVAGGI																																									

Pit stop
One lap behind leader

STARTING GRID

6 **COULTHARD** (1m 24.462s) Williams		1 **SCHUMACHER** (1m 25.026s) Benetton	
28 **BERGER** (1m 25.353s) Ferrari		5 **HILL** (1m 25.699s) Williams	
27 **ALESI** (1m 25.707s) Ferrari		14 **BARRICHELLO** (1m 25.919s) Jordan	
8 **HÄKKINEN** (1m 25.920s) McLaren		2 **HERBERT** (1m 26.433s) Benetton	
7 **BLUNDELL** (1m 26.472s) McLaren		30 **FRENTZEN** (1m 26.541s) Sauber	
25 **BRUNDLE** (1m 27.067s) Ligier		15 **IRVINE** (1m 27.271s) Jordan	
26 **PANIS** (1m 27.384s) Ligier		29 **BOULLION*** (1m 28.741s) Sauber	
9 **PAPIS** (1m 28.870s) Footwork		4 **SALO** (1m 29.028s) Tyrrell	
3 **KATAYAMA** (1m 29.287s) Tyrrell		24 **BADOER** (1m 29.559s) Minardi	
23 **LAMY** (1m 29.936s) Minardi		10 **INOUE** (1m 30.515s) Footwork	
17 **MONTERMINI**** (1m 30.721s) Pacific		22 **MORENO**** (1m 30.834s) Forti	
21 **DINIZ** (1m 32.102s) Forti		16 **LAVAGGI** (1m 32.470s) Pacific	

* started from pit lane
** did not start

FOR THE RECORD

First Grand Prix points
Mika Salo

TIME SHEETS

Friday free practice
Damp track, steadily drying

Pos.	Driver	Laps	Time
1	Jean Alesi	14	1m 30.218s
2	Johnny Herbert	18	1m 31.028s
3	David Coulthard	22	1m 31.124s
4	Michael Schumacher	14	1m 31.223s
5	Rubens Barrichello	19	1m 31.744s
6	Mark Blundell	15	1m 31.939s
7	Damon Hill	21	1m 32.251s
8	Heinz-Harald Frentzen	18	1m 32.380s
9	Gerhard Berger	15	1m 33.011s
10	Mika Häkkinen	13	1m 33.487s
11	Eddie Irvine	17	1m 34.112s
12	Martin Brundle	20	1m 34.960s
13	Mika Salo	23	1m 34.990s
14	Olivier Panis	16	1m 35.268s
15	Massimiliano Papis	18	1m 35.294s
16	Pedro Lamy	23	1m 36.188s
17	Ukyo Katayama	23	1m 36.972s
18	Luca Badoer	18	1m 37.359s
19	Pedro Diniz	14	1m 37.850s
20	Andrea Montermini	10	1m 38.801s
21	Roberto Moreno	13	1m 40.498s
22	Jean-Christophe Boullion	10	1m 40.987s
23	Taki Inoue	14	1m 43.362s
	Giovanni Lavaggi	0	no time

Saturday free practice
Dry, hot, sunny

Pos.	Driver	Laps	Time
1	Jean Alesi	19	1m 25.133s
2	David Coulthard	21	1m 25.135s
3	Gerhard Berger	20	1m 25.221s
4	Michael Schumacher	19	1m 25.919s
5	Mika Häkkinen	21	1m 26.186s
6	Damon Hill	22	1m 26.222s
7	Johnny Herbert	22	1m 26.387s
8	Eddie Irvine	20	1m 26.505s
9	Rubens Barrichello	22	1m 26.580s
10	Mark Blundell	19	1m 26.792s
11	Heinz-Harald Frentzen	20	1m 27.056s
12	Olivier Panis	15	1m 27.765s
13	Martin Brundle	23	1m 27.821s
14	Mika Salo	23	1m 28.471s
15	Massimiliano Papis	15	1m 28.553s
16	Ukyo Katayama	23	1m 29.391s
17	Luca Badoer	22	1m 30.084s
18	Taki Inoue	18	1m 30.268s
19	Andrea Montermini	11	1m 30.782s
20	Jean-Christophe Boullion	10	1m 30.973s
21	Roberto Moreno	14	1m 31.092s
22	Pedro Lamy	14	1m 31.205s
23	Pedro Diniz	22	1m 31.887s
24	Giovanni Lavaggi	15	1m 32.580s

Friday qualifying
Dry, hot, sunny

Pos.	Driver	Laps	Time
1	David Coulthard	12	1m 25.516s
2	Gerhard Berger	8	1m 25.904s
3	Damon Hill	12	1m 25.912s
4	Michael Schumacher	11	1m 26.098s
5	Jean Alesi	11	1m 26.323s
6	Johnny Herbert	12	1m 26.631s
7	Rubens Barrichello	12	1m 26.981s
8	Heinz-Harald Frentzen	12	1m 27.245s
9	Mark Blundell	12	1m 27.308s
10	Eddie Irvine	12	1m 27.573s
11	Olivier Panis	8	1m 28.418s
12	Mika Häkkinen	6	1m 28.895s
13	Martin Brundle	12	1m 29.200s
14	Mika Salo	12	1m 29.535s
15	**Pedro Lamy**	**12**	**1m 29.936s**
16	Taki Inoue	12	1m 30.632s
17	Luca Badoer	12	1m 30.731s
18	Jean-Christophe Boullion	8	1m 30.997s
19	Ukyo Katayama	8	1m 31.399s
20	Andrea Montermini	12	1m 32.121s
21	Roberto Moreno	12	1m 32.491s
22	Pedro Diniz	10	1m 32.540s
23	Giovanni Lavaggi	11	1m 32.935s
24	Massimiliano Papis	1	43m 10.257s

Saturday qualifying
Dry, hot, sunny

Pos.	Driver	Laps	Time
1	David Coulthard	12	1m 24.462s
2	Michael Schumacher	11	1m 25.026s
3	Gerhard Berger	7	1m 25.353s
4	Damon Hill	11	1m 25.699s
5	Jean Alesi	11	1m 25.707s
6	Rubens Barrichello	12	1m 25.919s
7	Mika Häkkinen	12	1m 25.920s
8	Johnny Herbert	12	1m 26.433s
9	Mark Blundell	12	1m 26.472s
10	Heinz-Harald Frentzen	12	1m 26.541s
11	Martin Brundle	12	1m 27.067s
12	Eddie Irvine	11	1m 27.271s
13	Olivier Panis	8	1m 27.384s
14	Jean-Christophe Boullion	12	1m 28.741s
15	Massimiliano Papis	10	1m 28.870s
16	Mika Salo	12	1m 29.028s
17	Ukyo Katayama	11	1m 29.287s
18	Luca Badoer	8	1m 29.559s
19	Taki Inoue	9	1m 30.515s
20	Andrea Montermini	12	1m 30.721s
21	Roberto Moreno	11	1m 30.834s
22	Pedro Lamy	3	1m 31.402s
23	Pedro Diniz	12	1m 32.102s
24	Giovanni Lavaggi	12	1m 32.470s

Warm-up
Dry, warm, overcast

Pos.	Driver	Laps	Time
1	Jean Alesi	12	1m 26.001s
2	David Coulthard	10	1m 26.439s
3	Gerhard Berger	13	1m 26.740s
4	Michael Schumacher	14	1m 27.021s
5	Damon Hill	13	1m 27.068s
6	Mika Häkkinen	15	1m 27.206s
7	Heinz-Harald Frentzen	16	1m 27.336s
8	Mark Blundell	12	1m 27.649s
9	Rubens Barrichello	14	1m 28.216s
10	Martin Brundle	15	1m 28.383s
11	Johnny Herbert	12	1m 28.412s
12	Olivier Panis	16	1m 28.465s
13	Ukyo Katayama	11	1m 28.999s
14	Eddie Irvine	9	1m 29.185s
15	Massimiliano Papis	17	1m 29.349s
16	Mika Salo	12	1m 29.457s
17	Jean-Christophe Boullion	14	1m 29.789s
18	Taki Inoue	10	1m 31.252s
19	Andrea Montermini	6	1m 31.916s
20	Luca Badoer	10	1m 31.964s
21	Roberto Moreno	14	1m 31.989s
22	Pedro Diniz	11	1m 32.446s
23	Pedro Lamy	14	1m 32.846s
24	Giovanni Lavaggi	5	1m 35.474s

Race fastest laps
Warm, sunny

Driver	Time	Lap
Gerhard Berger	1m 26.419s	24
Johnny Herbert	1m 26.481s	28
Mark Blundell	1m 26.784s	51
Jean Alesi	1m 26.818s	21
Mika Häkkinen	1m 26.869s	26
David Coulthard	1m 26.936s	11
Damon Hill	1m 26.936s	19
Michael Schumacher	1m 26.969s	21
Rubens Barrichello	1m 26.970s	26
Heinz-Harald Frentzen	1m 27.138s	22
Eddie Irvine	1m 27.472s	23
Olivier Panis	1m 28.710s	20
Mika Salo	1m 28.795s	26
Ukyo Katayama	1m 28.909s	41
Jean-Christophe Boullion	1m 28.976s	49
Luca Badoer	1m 29.175s	19
Massimiliano Papis	1m 29.402s	22
Martin Brundle	1m 29.424s	7
Taki Inoue	1m 29.426s	49
Pedro Diniz	1m 31.563s	17
Giovanni Lavaggi	1m 33.023s	4

CHASSIS LOG BOOK

1	Schumacher	Benetton B195/6
2	Herbert	Benetton B195/5
	spare	Benetton B195/1
3	Katayama	Tyrrell 023/5
4	Salo	Tyrrell 023/6
	spare	Tyrrell 023/2
5	Hill	Williams FW17/6
6	Coulthard	Williams FW17/5
	spare	Williams FW17/2
7	Blundell	McLaren MP4/10B/6
8	Häkkinen	McLaren MP4/10B/5
	spare	McLaren MP4/10B/2
9	Papis	Footwork FA16/3
10	Inoue	Footwork FA16/4
	spare	Footwork FA16/1
14	Barrichello	Jordan 195/4
15	Irvine	Jordan 195/5
	spare	Jordan 195/1
16	Lavaggi	Pacific PR02/1
17	Montermini	Pacific PR02/2
21	Diniz	Forti FG01/4
22	Moreno	Forti FG01/3
	spare	Forti FG01/2
23	Lamy	Minardi M195/3
24	Badoer	Minardi M195/2
	spare	Minardi M195/1
25	Brundle	Ligier JS41/5
26	Panis	Ligier JS41/1
	spare	Ligier JS41/3
27	Alesi	Ferrari 412T2/161
28	Berger	Ferrari 412T2/162
	spares	Ferrari 412T2/159 & 160
29	Boullion	Sauber C14/5
30	Frentzen	Sauber C14/6
	spare	Sauber C14/2

POINTS TABLES

Drivers

1	**Michael Schumacher**	66
2	**Damon Hill**	51
3	**Johnny Herbert**	38
4	**Jean Alesi**	32
5	**David Coulthard**	29
6	**Gerhard Berger**	25
7	**Heinz-Harald Frentzen**	14
8	**Mika Häkkinen**	11
9	**Mark Blundell**	10
10 =	**Rubens Barrichello**	8
10 =	**Olivier Panis**	8
12	**Martin Brundle**	7
13	**Eddie Irvine**	6
14	**Jean-Christophe Boullion**	3
15	**Mika Salo**	2
16 =	**Gianni Morbidelli**	1
16 =	**Aguri Suzuki**	1

Constructors

1	**Benetton**	94
2	**Williams**	74
3	**Ferrari**	57
4	**McLaren**	21
5	**Sauber**	17
6	**Ligier**	16
7	**Jordan**	14
8	**Tyrrell**	2
9	**Footwork**	1

WORLD CHAMPIONSHIP • ROUND 13

PORTUGUESE GRAND PRIX

COULTHARD
SCHUMACHER
HILL
BERGER
ALESI
FRENTZEN

PORTUGUESE GRAND PRIX

Left: David Coulthard locks a front wheel at the absurdly tight hairpin. Putting his disappointments at Spa and Monza behind him, the young Scot notched up the first Grand Prix win of his career with a cool authority that suggested that there will be many more opportunities to waste champagne in the years to come.

As the pack sprinted for the first corner, Damon Hill looked as though he'd got it made. He had slotted his Williams FW17 in tight behind team-mate David Coulthard's sister car, and the Benetton of Michael Schumacher – his key rival – was three lengths back in third place. It was just what Damon needed.

Then came the red flag. Further back down the grid, Ukyo Katayama's Tyrrell had tangled with Luca Badoer's Minardi and all hell had been let loose, the Yamaha-engined car ending up perched on its roll-over bar in the middle of the circuit. Nobody was seriously hurt, but the grid had to be re-formed and the whole affair started again.

At the second start, Coulthard got away cleanly once again. But Schumacher jumped ahead of Hill in the dash to the first corner. It was a crucial manoeuvre which totally dictated the outcome of the battle behind the matchless Coulthard. While the Flying Scot sped to an unchallenged win, it was Michael–Damon in second and third places at the chequered flag. It was precisely the result that Hill had been dreading.

Damon calculated that he must have covered more miles at Estoril in his old job as Williams test driver than at any other circuit in the Grand Prix business. With that in mind, it came as no surprise that he dug deep into those enormous reserves of experience to take a confident pole position at the end of the opening qualifying session. Hill went into the race trailing Michael Schumacher by 15 points with 50 still up for grabs over the remaining five races of the season.

From a strictly mathematical standpoint, time was clearly beginning to run out for Damon's title bid, but the Englishman continued to radiate the steely confidence which he had harnessed to come so close to grasping the championship in 1994. He finished the first session 0.1s ahead of Coulthard with Schumacher trailing by another half-second in third place.

'It's always difficult to get a feel for how things are going to unfold until you get to the first qualifying session,' said Hill. 'I think today we saw the Williams-Renault package working well and that Benetton didn't seem to be as promising, but I expect Michael to get his head down working on it overnight. I'm not counting my chickens, but it is a promising start.'

Hill and Coulthard benefited from aerodynamic revisions to the rear end of their Williams FW17s, the cars consequently being designated 'B' versions, although Chief Designer Adrian Newey claimed this was something of a misnomer as the new configuration really represented the definitive design as originally conceived. The revised car incorporated a new gearbox, rear suspension, diffuser and rear wing mountings.

'The feeling of both David and myself is that the car is more predictable in the slower corners,' said Hill. 'Aerodynamically, it is now better and that is the key to everything in this day and age.'

Hill admitted that he finds driving the Estoril circuit a pretty exhilarating experience – apart from the absurd first-gear ess-bend which was installed in 1994 on safety grounds.

'Every time I get to that corner I think, "Oh no – this is so dreadful,"' he exclaimed. 'The rest of the circuit is blinding. It's probably one of the most dangerous circuits we go to, but I really enjoy it here with these long fast corners. Then you get to this first-gear affair and it's like driving through an obstacle course in a car park.'

Coulthard, whose impending switch to the McLaren-Mercedes team for 1996 was scheduled to be confirmed at the following weekend's Grand Prix of Europe at the Nürburgring, was similarly upbeat about his prospects for the race.

'It's pretty close and considering I only did nine laps in the morning due to hydraulic problems, I'm pretty optimistic,' he said. But with Coulthard still chasing his first Grand Prix victory, the question of Williams team orders was obviously in the back of many people's minds should Schumacher suffer a rare retirement come Sunday.

'I am not scared of team orders at all,' said the Scot. 'If there are any, it will be because I am holding Damon up and the team will request me to move over, which is only fair.'

Behind Schumacher, the Ferraris of Gerhard Berger and Jean Alesi emerged from the first session in fourth and fifth places, both drivers having challenged briefly for fastest time during the course of the afternoon.

During the Friday morning free practice session, both 412T2s were fitted with revised nose cones incorporating new front wings which offered more downforce for no increase in drag. However, the cars were switched back to their 'Monza spec' nose sections for first qualifying.

Berger was guilty of holding up Schumacher's Benetton as the World Champion made his bid for fastest time late in the session. Gerhard chopped across him at the first-gear ess-bend, clearly unwilling to compromise his own efforts by letting the German driver past. Even so, both men affected a politely restrained response to the incident.

'I am a bit angry with my friend Gerhard, who messed up a very good lap of mine,' said Michael. 'I was three-tenths quicker in section one and I was definitely on a very good lap, which he stopped – for no reason.

'When you are on the track the idea is that you always take care of other drivers, but on this occasion he didn't do it, so I am a little disappointed.'

Berger adopted a suitably conciliatory tone: 'I must apologise to Schumacher for having blocked him. I had not seen him and suddenly, in a corner, he was right behind me when I was on my warm-up lap. I don't think it caused him much of a problem as I started my quick lap immediately after the incident.'

Eddie Irvine's Jordan-Peugeot completed the top six on the first day ahead of Mika Häkkinen, with Ligier's Martin Brundle the next Briton in ninth place. Johnny Herbert was a disappointed 12th in the second Benetton, one place ahead of Mark Blundell.

Häkkinen and Blundell were having their first outings in revised C-specification McLaren MP4/10s. This extensively altered version of the Mercedes-engined machine incorporated the third gearbox casing redesign of the season to accommodate further slight rear suspension geometry changes, plus a new undertray and diffusers. However, both drivers finished the first session distinctly unconvinced that these modifications had yielded any significant change for the better.

Meanwhile, the likelihood of Alain Prost making a full-time Grand Prix return with McLaren in 1996 seemed to be steadily receding. The four-times World Champion had been over three seconds slower than Damon Hill's Williams FW17B in testing at Silverstone the previous week, something which further depressed the McLaren workforce. However, it remained possible that Prost would continue to be associated with McLaren in a development role, the team having definitely gleaned some worthwhile technical input from him during his spell behind the wheel of the MP4/10B.

Coulthard's problems on Friday morning meant that he spent the

---

Irvine in surprise move to Ferrari as Brundle signs for Jordan

Over the Portuguese Grand Prix weekend it seemed as though Eddie Jordan's F1 team would have a seamless transition to the 1996 season with drivers and engine supplier remaining unchanged. An official release was circulated confirming that Rubens Barrichello and Eddie Irvine would remain on the team strength and the whole package seemed nicely settled.

What was not obvious from the touchlines was that Eddie Irvine had decided he wanted out; the Ulsterman felt that the team's progress had been lagging disappointingly over the past season. Then the opportunity came up for him to join Ferrari – and Jordan was quite willing to activate Irvine's buy-out clause, reputedly for a figure in the region of $5 million.

Jordan's share of this financial infusion, in addition to a reputed $2.5 million top-up from Peugeot, enabled the Silverstone team to strengthen its financial base at the same time as signing Martin Brundle as Barrichello's new partner for 1996.

'The circumstances and the happenings of the last week, even compared with the previous deals involving Jordan, have been somewhat bizarre,' admitted Eddie Jordan. 'The team is mighty happy to have Martin back. He was the first driver ever to set us on our way; he won our very first F3 race in 1982, and I can tell you that this is a great personal joy for me.'

However, he did concede that his team had to deliver in 1996: 'We must win races next year. There are no excuses and there will be none given. With Rubens and Martin we have the driver package with the talent and know-how to win. We now have to give them the car to do it.'

As far as Irvine's new collaboration with Ferrari was concerned, the Ulsterman's three-year deal takes him one season beyond the end of Michael Schumacher's current commitment to Maranello. The team's Sporting Director Jean Todt emphasised that he will play a clearly defined number two role in 1996.

'Of course I informed Michael about the possibility of Irvine,' said Todt. 'He was very happy about it because he knows that it could be a good pairing. We don't want to rely only on one driver to win races – we want to work for both the constructors' and drivers' championships.'

It was said that Marlboro sponsorship boss John Hogan was keen on Irvine's recruitment because he regarded him as something close to another James Hunt: a talented, irreverent maverick. Since Irvine celebrated his recruitment to Ferrari by telling a media conference 'I don't know a journalist who knows anything about motor racing, so there's not much point listening to them', the new boy had clearly decided to make life difficult for himself right from the outset.

PORTUGUESE GRAND PRIX

rest of the day making up for lost time, but midway through Saturday morning's session he switched to Hill's chassis set-up and immediately felt more confident. Early in second qualifying, David showed what he could do by trimming the pole position time back to 1m 21.239s, just as Mark Blundell briefly raised McLaren spirits with a 1m 22.914s. Unfortunately, while Coulthard continued to joust for fastest time, McLaren's brief resurgence proved an illusion and Blundell was gradually elbowed back down the pack by his rivals.

Then Hill came back to retake pole with 1m 20.905s, but Coulthard had his measure and responded with a 1m 20.537s – amazingly inside Gerhard Berger's 1m 20.608s pole time with the 3.5-litre-engined Ferrari 412T at last year's race.

Brundle briefly showed in sixth place for Ligier before Heinz-Harald Frentzen and Johnny Herbert's Benetton knocked him out of the first three rows, Frentzen in particular being delighted with the handling of his Sauber C14. In the closing moments of the session, Hill went out in an effort to rescue the situation, but caught the two Ligiers coming out of the final right-hander on what he thought would be his quickest run. That meant he had to stay out for another lap, by which time the tyres had lost the fine edge of their grip.

Schumacher also tried everything he could, changing the differential set-up on his Benetton after the Saturday morning session, but despite a heroic effort he simply didn't have sufficient grip to compete with the Williams pair. Berger consolidated fourth place, both he and team-mate Alesi having three runs, improving the set-up on each, but Jean slipped back to a dejected seventh at the end of the day after Frentzen and Herbert had successfully pressed home their attacks.

Rubens Barrichello wound up eighth fastest for Jordan, ahead of a well-satisfied Brundle, Irvine and Panis, leaving the two shell-shocked McLaren drivers trailing in 12th and 13th places, Blundell just ahead of Häkkinen on this occasion.

'We have a lack of balance and rear-end stability which is affecting the front end as well,' reported Mika. 'It doesn't seem to be a set-up problem and we have been making radical changes which produce no solution to the problem.

'There is something fundamentally wrong with the car, and because we have no understanding of it, it is impossible to progress. All our data says that the MP4/10C should be better, but something basic is just not correct with the car.'

This dismal prognosis was shared by Blundell, who also found the car extremely difficult to drive and balance out. By the end of Saturday afternoon it was clear that more testing was needed, so the team decided to stay on at Estoril on the Monday and Tuesday following the race. This left a relay of transporter drivers poised to take the cars on their non-stop 2600-km journey to the Nürburgring, where they were scheduled to arrive the following Thursday, the day before first qualifying for the Grand Prix of Europe.

Behind the McLarens, Jean-Christophe Boullion felt much happier than of late with his Sauber C14, while Mika Salo took 15th place ahead of Ukyo Katayama, the Japanese driver slightly confused that the harder he tried, the slower he seemed to go. The next four places were taken in two-by-two formation by Minardi twins Pedro Lamy and Luca Badoer and Footwork duo Taki Inoue and Max Papis.

Andrea Montermini's Pacific suffered a gearbox breakage on Friday, but this was repaired for the second day and the Italian at least out-qualified both Fortis. Right at the back came Pacific's new pay-driver Jean-Denis Deletraz, who proved more than a little out of his depth, lapping an amazing 12.232s away from Coulthard's pole time. His best lap would have earned him only 22nd place on the grid for the supporting F3000 race!

On Saturday night the Williams team toiled away into the small hours returning their FW17s to the standard specification. The decision to do this was not made until 11.00 p.m. on Saturday evening and the mechanics worked through until 2.00 a.m. on Sunday morning to get the job completed. Team manager Dickie Stanford explained that the team was simply adopting a conservative approach to the race, but rumours were circulating on race morning to the effect that a bearing in one of the FW17B gearboxes had shown signs of excessive wear which persuaded the team to play safe.

Gerhard Berger was fastest in the race morning warm-up from Hill, Häkkinen – now in a McLaren MP4/10B which he felt handled better than the C-spec car – and Coulthard in the other Williams.

The race was initially flagged to a halt at the end of the opening lap after a dramatic accident when Ukyo Katayama's Tyrrell collided with the Minardi of Luca Badoer as the pack accelerated away from the starting grid. Katayama's car was launched into the air over Badoer's right-front wheel and rolled several times before landing upside down in the middle of the track. The Japanese driver was quickly extricated from the wreckage and flown to hospital in Lisbon, where he was kept overnight for observation, but happily his injuries were confined to a strained neck.

This incident turned out to be a bitter tactical blow for Hill, who had accelerated cleanly into second place behind Coulthard at the first start. At the second, Schumacher managed to slip between the two Williams-Renaults to keep Damon bottled up in third place as David made good his escape.

Coulthard slammed across the start/finish line to complete the

PORTUGUESE GRAND PRIX

Mika Häkkinen monitors developments in the McLaren pit garage. The 'C' variant of the disappointing MP4/10 design proved to be a backward step and the team's mechanics were faced with the task of returning the Finn's car to 'B' specification for the race.

Bottom: The Williams-Renault of Damon Hill framed by the steel barriers that line the track. With its long fast corners, Estoril is one of the most demanding circuits on the calendar – and also one of the most dangerous.

Diary

Alain Prost announces on French television that he has more important things to do in 1996 than race F1 cars, putting an end to speculation that he would resume his Grand Prix career with McLaren.

It is revealed that, contrary to earlier indications, Niki Lauda will be continuing in his role as a consultant at Ferrari.

Vincenzo Sospiri clinches FIA International F3000 Championship with seventh place at Estoril.

Williams Touring Car Engineering secures BTCC manufacturers' title for Renault.

opening lap already 1.2s ahead of Schumacher, with Hill right on the World Champion's tail. Already Gerhard Berger was falling back slightly in fourth place, followed by Johnny Herbert's Benetton, Jean Alesi's Ferrari, Martin Brundle's Ligier and Eddie Irvine's Jordan.

By lap five, Coulthard had opened out a 3.4s advantage and the Williams team was beginning to think that Schumacher's Benetton was running to a two-stop schedule. With that in mind, it was decided to switch Hill to a two-stop strategy rather than the three stops which Coulthard was firmly on course to employ.

On lap eight, Coulthard lapped the painfully slow Deletraz, the Swiss soon to retire with leg cramps. Further back in the pack, Olivier Panis's Ligier was signalled in from 12th place to take a ten-second stop-go penalty for jumping the start. The Frenchman duly came in at the end of lap ten, but resumed in such a fury that he spun off for good only two corners after returning to the race!

Behind Brundle's seventh-placed Ligier, Irvine was now a short distance ahead of Jordan team-mate Barrichello, the Brazilian battling to hold station at the head of a jostling bunch comprising the two McLaren-Mercedes and Frentzen's Sauber. The German driver had been forced to start at the back after stalling his Ford Zetec-R V8 at the start of the second parade lap, this setback merely serving to make him doubly determined.

Schumacher came in for his first refuelling stop at the end of lap 18, a fact which made it pretty obvious to the Williams squad that Michael would in fact be stopping three times. Hill followed him in, with Coulthard making his stop next time round.

The Benetton was stationary for only 7.4s, but Hill remained at rest for 16.1s as his Williams was filled up with sufficient fuel to take him through to a second and final refuelling stop later in the race. There was a problem with the sight gauge on the Williams refuelling equipment, causing the team problems in ascertaining whether or not the entire fuel allocation had gone into the tank, and Damon also had to have three tries before the transmission would engage first gear – 'we call it a dog clash' – losing him a few more precious seconds before he could accelerate back into the race.

This delay dropped Hill down into fourth place behind Alesi's Ferrari from lap 19 through to lap 24 when the Frenchman came in for his first refuelling stop. Thus, by the time Damon finally got back into third place, the battle was effectively lost.

Even so, the Williams team leader slogged doggedly onwards, hoping that his readjusted refuelling strategy might in fact reap dividends at the end of the day. On lap 35, Schumacher made his second stop, allowing Damon through into second place, and when Coulthard drew in for the second time on lap 38, Hill surged past into the lead, but with only 3.5s in hand.

He stayed out until lap 44 before making his second stop, dropping back again behind Coulthard and Schumacher. Even allowing for the fact that they both had one more stop to come, Damon was not making ground at a fast enough rate. On lap 54, Coulthard and Schumacher both came in for their final stop, seven seconds apart, and resumed with Hill between them in second place. Michael was 4.6s behind Damon on lap 55, but with the benefit of fresh tyres managed to slash that advantage to 1.9s only four laps later.

On lap 60 the gap was down to 0.85s and it was now only a matter of time. On lap 62, as they braked for the tight first-gear ess-bend, Schumacher caught Hill and sliced

PORTUGUESE GRAND PRIX

decisively up the inside, neatly boxing the Williams out on the wide, slower line. Hill played things absolutely cleanly and fairly, resisting any temptation to close the door.

'It was a tough race,' said Hill. 'We switched to that two-stop strategy on the basis that I was stuck behind Michael at that point. It nearly worked, but I couldn't brake late on my worn tyres on that part of the circuit, he caught me napping and that was the end of it.'

For his part, Coulthard was obviously delighted to have taken his first Grand Prix victory after retiring while in the lead at Spa and Monza. 'It was a warm feeling inside, a fantastic feeling,' he admitted. 'I've had some near-misses and this is the back-end of the season and you can't be sure of how competitive different cars will be next year. It was very important to win a race when I had the opportunity.'

The events of the day suggested that the Scot might find more Grand Prix victories a little harder to come by in 1996. At Estoril, the McLaren-Mercedes were well off the pace and only Blundell managed to get to the finish, one lap down in ninth place.

'We've lost balance and we've lost direction,' said Blundell, who was also in pain from a trapped nerve in his back – caused by lifting a suitcase off his hotel bed! Häkkinen had been beset by acute understeer through the right-hander leading onto the start/finish straight, running eighth between Frentzen and Brundle when he stopped out on the circuit with engine failure on lap 45.

Fourth and fifth were the Ferraris of Gerhard Berger and Jean Alesi, with Frentzen completing the top six after a great recovery in the Sauber-Ford. Alesi finished the race in an absolutely furious mood with Jean Todt, accusing Ferrari's Sporting Director of favouring Berger in terms of race strategy in a particularly candid live interview on Italian television, an outburst which seemed to set the final seal on his split with the team at the end of the year.

The problem had arisen after the two drivers had adopted different strategies, Alesi making two stops and Berger three; Alesi was upset when Berger, running faster on fresh rubber, came up behind him after the Austrian's second stop on lap 33. Despite orders from Todt, Alesi simply would not relinquish the position with the result that Berger was brought in 11 laps ahead of schedule for his third refuelling stop on lap 45 and finally managed to get ahead of Jean when the Frenchman stopped two laps later.

'Todt has been a problem for me all year and he has broken my balls,' raged Alesi. 'If it has to be like this, I would rather not bother.' Yet despite the Ferrari management reportedly imposing a $200,000 fine on Alesi for this tactless outburst, Todt remained conciliatory. 'Jean has a generous nature, but an emotional temperament,' he said. 'We have given him maximum support for five seasons and will continue to do so for the last four races of the season.'

Behind Frentzen, the British trio of Herbert, Brundle and Blundell filled the next three places with a tight-lipped Eddie Irvine and Rubens Barrichello taking tenth and eleventh for the disappointed Jordan-Peugeot squad. Irvine ran a two-stop strategy, but the Brazilian changed to a three-stop schedule after suffering from premature rear tyre wear.

'Right from the start I had a big problem with the rears,' he admitted. 'I was trying to look after them, but the tyres were just no good so I had to go for three stops instead of two. I had a big problem with the brakes as well and they kept locking at the rear.

'It was a bit like karting, really; I had to take risks on the high-speed sections to make up for the slow corners where I was getting completely sideways. That was it really; we were just not quick enough to finish in the top six today.'

In 12th place, Jean-Christophe Boullion's Sauber was followed home by Salo, Badoer, Inoue, Diniz and Moreno – a total of 17 of the 23 drivers who took the restart getting to the chequered flag on this occasion. Badoer struggled with the driving position and handling of the spare Minardi which he had had to race after the collision with Katayama, while Pedro Lamy retired with a hydraulic problem which jammed the gearbox in fourth – resulting in his incurring a suspended one-race ban for inadvertently exceeding the pit lane speed limit as he came in to retire.

From the viewpoint of the World Championship, the result meant that Schumacher had extended his advantage by another two points, Hill going into the Grand Prix of Europe at the Nürburgring 17 points adrift with a maximum of 40 points left to race for. Damon had now reached a crucial fork in the road.

Above: Gerhard Berger appeared in an unfamiliar helmet – the product of a competition run by an Italian newspaper. The Austrian's grid placing and result were much the same as usual, however.

Above far right: Jean-Denis Deletraz levers himself out of the cockpit of the Pacific as the mechanics make their final preparations prior to the start. The Swiss novice was some 12 seconds a lap slower than David Coulthard in qualifying.

As the leaders stream into the first corner Heinz-Harald Frentzen throws away his third-row starting position with a spin. Further back, however, the Tyrrell of Ukyo Katayama has rolled after a collision with the Minardi of Luca Badoer, bringing out the red flags. The Japanese driver was extremely fortunate to escape without serious injury.

Lukas Gorys

Steve Domenjoz

FIA FORMULA ONE WORLD CHAMPIONSHIP ROUND 13

GRANDE PRÉMIO DE PORTUGAL

AUTODROMO DO ESTORIL
22-24 SEPTEMBER 1995

ESTORIL – GRAND PRIX CIRCUIT

CIRCUIT LENGTH: 2.709 MILES/4.360 KM

Race distance: 71 laps, 192.351 miles/309.560 km
Race weather: Bright and sunny

Place	Driver	Nat.	No.	Entrant	Car/Engine	Laps	Time/Retirement	Speed (mph/km/h)
1	**David Coulthard**	GB	6	Rothmans Williams Renault	Williams FW17-Renault RS7C V10	71	1h 41m 52.145s	113.288/182.319
2	**Michael Schumacher**	D	1	Mild Seven Benetton Renault	Benetton B195-Renault RS7C V10	71	1h 41m 59.393s	113.153/182.103
3	**Damon Hill**	GB	5	Rothmans Williams Renault	Williams FW17-Renault RS7C V10	71	1h 42m 14.266s	112.879/181.661
4	**Gerhard Berger**	A	28	Scuderia Ferrari	Ferrari 412T2 044 V12	71	1h 43m 17.024s	111.736/179.822
5	**Jean Alesi**	F	27	Scuderia Ferrari	Ferrari 412T2 044 V12	71	1h 43m 17.574s	111.726/179.806
6	**Heinz-Harald Frentzen**	D	30	Red Bull Sauber Ford	Sauber C14-Ford Zetec-R V8	70		
7	Johnny Herbert	GB	2	Mild Seven Benetton Renault	Benetton B195-Renault RS7C V10	70		
8	Martin Brundle	GB	25	Ligier Gitanes Blondes	Ligier JS41-Mugen Honda MF301 V10	70		
9	Mark Blundell	GB	7	Marlboro McLaren Mercedes	McLaren MP4/10B-Mercedes FO110 V10	70		
10	Eddie Irvine	GB	15	Total Jordan Peugeot	Jordan 195-Peugeot A10 V10	70		
11	Rubens Barrichello	BR	14	Total Jordan Peugeot	Jordan 195-Peugeot A10 V10	70		
12	Jean-Christophe Boullion	F	29	Red Bull Sauber Ford	Sauber C14-Ford Zetec-R V8	70		
13	Mika Salo	SF	4	Nokia Tyrrell Yamaha	Tyrrell 023-Yamaha OX10C V10	69		
14	Luca Badoer	I	24	Minardi Scuderia Italia	Minardi M195-Ford EDM V8	68		
15	Taki Inoue	J	10	Footwork Hart	Footwork FA16-Hart 830 V8	68		
16	Pedro Diniz	BR	21	Parmalat Forti Ford	Forti FG01-Ford ED V8	66		
17	Roberto Moreno	BR	22	Parmalat Forti Ford	Forti FG01-Ford ED V8	64		
	Andrea Montermini	I	17	Pacific Grand Prix Ltd	Pacific PR02-Ford ED V8	53	Gearbox	
	Mika Häkkinen	SF	8	Marlboro McLaren Mercedes	McLaren MP4/10B-Mercedes FO110 V10	44	Engine	
	Jean-Denis Deletraz	CH	16	Pacific Grand Prix Ltd	Pacific PR02-Ford ED V8	14	Driver cramp	
	Olivier Panis	F	26	Ligier Gitanes Blondes	Ligier JS41-Mugen Honda MF301 V10	10	Spun off	
	Pedro Lamy	P	23	Minardi Scuderia Italia	Minardi M195-Ford EDM V8	7	Gearbox	
DNS	Massimiliano Papis	I	9	Footwork Hart	Footwork FA16-Hart 830 V8	0	Gearbox at first start	
DNS	Ukyo Katayama	J	3	Nokia Tyrrell Yamaha	Tyrrell 023-Yamaha OX10C V10	0	Accident at first start	

Fastest lap: Coulthard, on lap 2, 1m 23.220s, 117.195 mph/188.608 km/h.
Lap record: David Coulthard (F1 Williams FW16B-Renault V10), 1m 22.446s, 118.295 mph/190.378 km/h (1994).
All cars used Goodyear tyres

All results and data © FIA 1995

STARTING GRID

6 COULTHARD (1m 20.537s) Williams
5 HILL (1m 20.905s) Williams

1 SCHUMACHER (1m 21.301s) Benetton
28 BERGER (1m 21.970s) Ferrari

30 FRENTZEN* (1m 22.226s) Sauber
2 HERBERT (1m 22.322s) Benetton

27 ALESI (1m 22.391s) Ferrari
14 BARRICHELLO (1m 22.538s) Jordan

25 BRUNDLE (1m 22.588s) Ligier
15 IRVINE (1m 22.831s) Jordan

26 PANIS (1m 22.904s) Ligier
7 BLUNDELL (1m 22.914s) McLaren

8 HÄKKINEN (1m 23.064s) McLaren
29 BOULLION (1m 23.934s) Sauber

4 SALO (1m 23.936s) Tyrrell
3 KATAYAMA** (1m 24.287s) Tyrrell

23 LAMY (1m 24.657s) Minardi
24 BADOER (1m 24.778s) Minardi

10 INOUE (1m 24.883s) Footwork
9 PAPIS** (1m 25.179s) Footwork

17 MONTERMINI (1m 26.172s) Pacific
21 DINIZ (1m 27.292s) Forti

22 MORENO (1m 27.523s) Forti
16 DELETRAZ (1m 32.769s) Pacific

* started from back of grid
** did not take restart

FOR THE RECORD

First Grand Prix win
David Coulthard

TIME SHEETS

Friday free practice
Bright and breezy

Pos.	Driver	Laps	Time
1	Mika Häkkinen	17	1m 23.073s
2	Damon Hill	18	1m 23.162s
3	Michael Schumacher	18	1m 23.231s
4	David Coulthard	9	1m 23.834s
5	Gerhard Berger	17	1m 24.079s
6	Jean Alesi	18	1m 24.540s
7	Eddie Irvine	19	1m 24.644s
8	Rubens Barrichello	17	1m 24.657s
9	Heinz-Harald Frentzen	19	1m 24.903s
10	Johnny Herbert	22	1m 24.933s
11	Olivier Panis	21	1m 25.430s
12	Massimiliano Papis	21	1m 25.737s
13	Mark Blundell	14	1m 26.065s
14	Ukyo Katayama	23	1m 26.091s
15	Martin Brundle	19	1m 26.096s
16	Mika Salo	19	1m 26.356s
17	Jean-Christophe Boullion	17	1m 26.673s
18	Andrea Montermini	17	1m 27.811s
19	Pedro Lamy	22	1m 27.828s
20	Luca Badoer	19	1m 27.870s
21	Taki Inoue	20	1m 27.954s
22	Pedro Diniz	22	1m 29.453s
23	Roberto Moreno	22	1m 30.453s
24	Jean-Denis Deletraz	13	1m 36.805s

Saturday free practice
Sunny and bright

Pos.	Driver	Laps	Time
1	Damon Hill	23	1m 21.443s
2	David Coulthard	18	1m 22.258s
3	Michael Schumacher	21	1m 22.517s
4	Jean Alesi	18	1m 22.854s
5	Gerhard Berger	21	1m 23.046s
6	Heinz-Harald Frentzen	23	1m 23.306s
7	Martin Brundle	22	1m 23.307s
8	Eddie Irvine	15	1m 23.362s
9	Rubens Barrichello	14	1m 23.707s
10	Mark Blundell	23	1m 23.771s
11	Mika Häkkinen	21	1m 23.785s
12	Olivier Panis	21	1m 23.825s
13	Johnny Herbert	23	1m 23.884s
14	Ukyo Katayama	21	1m 24.926s
15	Jean-Christophe Boullion	23	1m 25.092s
16	Mika Salo	19	1m 25.099s
17	Taki Inoue	15	1m 25.390s
18	Massimiliano Papis	20	1m 25.421s
19	Pedro Lamy	23	1m 25.535s
20	Luca Badoer	23	1m 25.811s
21	Andrea Montermini	12	1m 28.023s
22	Roberto Moreno	23	1m 28.040s
23	Pedro Diniz	23	1m 28.606s
24	Jean-Denis Deletraz	19	1m 33.409s

Friday qualifying
Sunny and bright

Pos.	Driver	Laps	Time
1	Damon Hill	11	1m 21.322s
2	David Coulthard	10	1m 21.423s
3	Michael Schumacher	9	1m 21.885s
4	Gerhard Berger	9	1m 22.281s
5	Jean Alesi	11	1m 22.656s
6	Eddie Irvine	6	1m 22.957s
7	**Mika Häkkinen**	10	1m 23.064s
8	Rubens Barrichello	10	1m 23.142s
9	Martin Brundle	11	1m 23.244s
10	Olivier Panis	11	1m 23.284s
11	Heinz-Harald Frentzen	10	1m 23.485s
12	Johnny Herbert	11	1m 23.786s
13	Mark Blundell	10	1m 24.583s
14	Ukyo Katayama	9	1m 24.631s
15	**Taki Inoue**	12	1m 24.883s
16	Mika Salo	11	1m 24.942s
17	Massimiliano Papis	12	1m 25.696s
18	Luca Badoer	11	1m 25.746s
19	Pedro Lamy	11	1m 26.210s
20	Andrea Montermini	4	1m 27.659s
21	Roberto Moreno	12	1m 28.672s
22	Pedro Diniz	4	1m 29.137s
23	Jean-Christophe Boullion	1	14m 20.150s
	Jean-Denis Deletraz		no time

Saturday qualifying
Sunny and bright

Pos.	Driver	Laps	Time
1	David Coulthard	9	1m 20.537s
2	Damon Hill	11	1m 20.905s
3	Michael Schumacher	11	1m 21.301s
4	Gerhard Berger	8	1m 21.970s
5	Heinz-Harald Frentzen	9	1m 22.226s
6	Johnny Herbert	12	1m 22.322s
7	Jean Alesi	9	1m 22.391s
8	Rubens Barrichello	9	1m 22.538s
9	Martin Brundle	12	1m 22.588s
10	Eddie Irvine	12	1m 22.831s
11	Olivier Panis	11	1m 22.904s
12	Mark Blundell	9	1m 22.914s
13	Mika Häkkinen	9	1m 23.114s
14	Jean-Christophe Boullion	11	1m 23.934s
15	Mika Salo	12	1m 23.936s
16	Ukyo Katayama	10	1m 24.287s
17	Pedro Lamy	7	1m 24.657s
18	Luca Badoer	9	1m 24.778s
19	Taki Inoue	10	1m 25.031s
20	Massimiliano Papis	12	1m 25.179s
21	Andrea Montermini	11	1m 26.172s
22	Pedro Diniz	12	1m 27.292s
23	Roberto Moreno	9	1m 27.523s
24	Jean-Denis Deletraz	5	1m 32.769s

Warm-up
Sunny and bright

Pos.	Driver	Laps	Time
1	Gerhard Berger	10	1m 23.037s
2	Damon Hill	15	1m 23.047s
3	Mika Häkkinen	13	1m 23.129s
4	David Coulthard	12	1m 23.669s
5	Heinz-Harald Frentzen	9	1m 23.759s
6	Jean Alesi	12	1m 23.831s
7	Rubens Barrichello	14	1m 24.733s
8	Johnny Herbert	13	1m 24.832s
9	Michael Schumacher	11	1m 24.941s
10	Martin Brundle	15	1m 24.941s
11	Eddie Irvine	10	1m 25.056s
12	Olivier Panis	14	1m 25.223s
13	Jean-Christophe Boullion	15	1m 25.445s
14	Mark Blundell	10	1m 25.531s
15	Mika Salo	14	1m 26.332s
16	Taki Inoue	15	1m 26.733s
17	Ukyo Katayama	6	1m 26.773s
18	Luca Badoer	15	1m 26.908s
19	Massimiliano Papis	11	1m 26.912s
20	Pedro Lamy	15	1m 27.754s
21	Pedro Diniz	13	1m 28.728s
22	Andrea Montermini	9	1m 29.141s
23	Roberto Moreno	9	1m 30.930s
24	Jean-Denis Deletraz	5	1m 32.358s

Fastest race laps
Sunny and bright

Driver	Time	Lap
David Coulthard	1m 23.220s	2
Michael Schumacher	1m 23.702s	37
Damon Hill	1m 23.737s	20
Martin Brundle	1m 24.427s	58
Rubens Barrichello	1m 24.472s	60
Gerhard Berger	1m 24.805s	2
Johnny Herbert	1m 25.128s	8
Heinz-Harald Frentzen	1m 25.283s	56
Jean Alesi	1m 25.544s	8
Mark Blundell	1m 25.646s	24
Mika Häkkinen	1m 25.690s	18
Eddie Irvine	1m 25.767s	54
Olivier Panis	1m 26.123s	4
Jean-Christophe Boullion	1m 26.193s	47
Mika Salo	1m 27.247s	43
Taki Inoue	1m 27.356s	48
Pedro Lamy	1m 27.779s	3
Andrea Montermini	1m 27.801s	22
Luca Badoer	1m 28.043s	32
Pedro Diniz	1m 29.803s	18
Roberto Moreno	1m 31.148s	43
Jean-Denis Deletraz	1m 34.445s	5

CHASSIS LOG BOOK

No.	Driver	Chassis
1	Schumacher	Benetton B195/6
2	Herbert	Benetton B195/5
spare		Benetton B195/1
3	Katayama	Tyrrell 023/6
4	Salo	Tyrrell 023/5
spare		Tyrrell 023/2
5	Hill	Williams FW17B/6*
6	Coulthard	Williams FW17B/5*
spare		Williams FW17/2
7	Blundell	McLaren MP4/10C/4**
8	Häkkinen	McLaren MP4/10C/3**
spare		McLaren MP4/10C/1**
9	Papis	Footwork FA16/3
10	Inoue	Footwork FA16/4
spare		Footwork FA16/1
14	Barrichello	Jordan 195/4
15	Irvine	Jordan 195/5
spare		Jordan 195/1
16	Deletraz	Pacific PR02/1
17	Montermini	Pacific PR02/2
21	Diniz	Forti FG01/4
22	Moreno	Forti FG01/3
spare		Forti FG01/2
23	Lamy	Minardi M195/3
24	Badoer	Minardi M195/2
spare		Minardi M195/1
25	Brundle	Ligier JS41/5
26	Panis	Ligier JS41/1
spare		Ligier JS41/3
27	Alesi	Ferrari 412T2/161
28	Berger	Ferrari 412T2/162
spare		Ferrari 412T2/160
29	Boullion	Sauber C14/1
30	Frentzen	Sauber C14/6
spare		Sauber C14/2

* Williams FW17 for race
** McLaren MP4/10B for race

POINTS TABLES

Drivers

Pos.	Driver	Points
1	Michael Schumacher	72
2	Damon Hill	55
3	David Coulthard	39
4	Johnny Herbert	38
5	Jean Alesi	34
6	Gerhard Berger	28
7	Heinz-Harald Frentzen	15
8	Mika Häkkinen	11
9	Mark Blundell	10
10 =	Rubens Barrichello	8
10 =	Olivier Panis	8
12	Martin Brundle	7
13	Eddie Irvine	6
14	Jean-Christophe Boullion	3
15	Mika Salo	2
16 =	Gianni Morbidelli	1
16 =	Aguri Suzuki	1

Constructors

Pos.	Team	Points
1	Benetton	100
2	Williams	88
3	Ferrari	62
4	McLaren	21
5	Sauber	18
6	Ligier	16
7	Jordan	14
8	Tyrrell	2
9	Footwork	1

WORLD CHAMPIONSHIP • ROUND 14

GRAND PRIX OF EUROPE

GRAND PRIX OF EUROPE

SCHUMACHER
ALESI
COULTHARD
BARRICHELLO
HERBERT
IRVINE

Jumping for joy. An ecstatic Michael Schumacher celebrates a hard-fought victory that had brought the World Championship within his grasp. Runner-up Jean Alesi prepares to take his place in the Benetton star's shadow.

Diary

Indy Car team chief Roger Penske denies that he has any intention of becoming involved in the management of the McLaren F1 team.

Gerhard Berger publicly slams Ferrari F1 public relations man Giancarlo Bacchini for aggravating media speculation over Jean Alesi's post-race outburst at Estoril.

Ford's new Cosworth-built V10 engine, destined for Sauber in 1996, is prepared for its first dynamometer test.

Michael Schumacher came within three points of clinching his second consecutive World Championship with a brilliant victory in the Grand Prix of Europe at the 'new' Nürburgring. It was a triumph which may come to be seen as a decisive moment in Schumacher's career: the day on which he crossed that indistinct dividing line separating the good from the great. In treacherously slippery conditions, he snatched the lead from Jean Alesi's Ferrari only three laps from the chequered flag to claim his second win in front of his home crowd in two months.

The race was once again expected to yield a victory for the Williams team, but neither Damon Hill nor David Coulthard managed to do justice to their technically superior Williams-Renault package. Hill finished the day formally conceding the 1995 World Championship to Schumacher after crashing out of the race. It was a disastrous result which left him 27 points behind his rival with only 30 points to be claimed from the remaining three races. His title hopes were now finished, beyond the most unlikely of mathematical long-shots.

'Well, I am not going to be World Champion this year, but I'll be back,' promised Damon. 'But I don't think I disgraced myself. I put up a good fight, did everything I could to win, and it didn't come off.

'I am in full working order after hitting the barrier, which is good news. The championship is effectively over, but I will have a bloody good go in the last three races. I want to win them all.'

In fact, in the unpredictable conditions it was Alesi who was the hero of the day, opting to use slicks on a damp track surface which never quite dried out all afternoon. When the leading group predictably came in to switch from rain tyres to slicks after a dozen or so laps, Alesi suddenly found himself in the pound seats and with victory almost certainly in the bag. Yet, inexplicably, he seemed to roll off his pace in the closing stages and allowed Schumacher to come at him like a terrier after a bone.

Both Williams drivers again used the B-specification version of the FW17 chassis which had proved so formidably effective during qualifying at Estoril. On that occasion the cars were switched back to original specification for the race in the interests of reliability, but at the Nürburgring Williams gambled on racing them in an effort to bolster Hill's flagging title hopes.

However, it was Coulthard who led the way at the end of first qualifying, the Scot earning provisional pole position with a lap in 1m 18.738s. Hill was a couple of tenths slower, but could console himself with the knowledge that Schumacher had been unable to match the pace of the Williams pair, the Benetton driver having to settle for third place on 1m 19.470s.

'I am very encouraged because today we have a good advantage over the Benettons,' said Damon afterwards. 'I am looking forward to the second session when I hope it is going to be dry because I have got a few things to try on my car which I think will give me more time.'

Meanwhile Coulthard made it clear that he still had his own agenda and would only consider moving over to help Hill should he be asked to do so by the Williams team management. His switch to the McLaren-Mercedes team for 1996 was due to be formally confirmed on race day. The handling problems that continued to beset McLaren's current drivers Mika Häkkinen and Mark Blundell suggested that it might be some time before David was in a position to win a Grand Prix once he had parted with Williams, so to expect him to relinquish any hard-won advantage at this stage of the season seemed unrealistic.

On Saturday it looked as though Coulthard would have no challenge to his fastest time. The Eifel mountains were enveloped in a grey wall of rain which only abated late in the free practice session. But the weather remained extremely cold and, with no sun to dry the circuit, the Nürburgring was still treacherously damp as the clock began ticking into the final hour of timed qualifying.

A handful of tail-enders trickled out onto the circuit early on, but they soon returned to the seclusion of the pit lane. In fact, for the first half-hour of the session almost nothing stirred and the crowd, who had packed into the circuit expecting some frenzied action, began to make their feelings known by booing and jeering vociferously – and understandably.

It was 33 minutes into the session when Hill made his first run, followed in quick succession by Coulthard – anxious to protect his pole position – and Ferrari's Gerhard Berger. With 20 minutes left to go, Alesi joined in the action and suddenly the track was filled with a jostling throng of F1 cars, their drivers all hoping against hope that the circuit would dry sufficiently for them to register an improvement.

With ten minutes to go, the prospects of quicker lap times hung tantalisingly in the balance. Hill was only 0.6s away from Coulthard's best at the second timing split, but would be foiled by a slippery track surface at the final corner. The best he could manage was 1m 19.607s, still 0.9s away from his team-mate's time.

On his final run, Damon managed to avoid the seemingly ever-present spectre of finding a dawdling Pacific on the dry line and felt that pole might be just within his grasp. Then his Williams ran out of fuel and he found himself rolling to a halt out on the circuit. It transpired that an Elf technician had taken a fuel sample earlier during the session and this had not been taken into account when calculating the car's predicted fuel consumption.

There followed a nail-biting few minutes for the British driver. Schumacher, his Benetton's chassis set-up subtly altered since Friday's session, improved his time to 1m 19.444s, but that wasn't sufficient to move him onto the front row. Finally, with little more than a minute to spare as he went into his final flying lap, Michael managed to dip 0.1s under Coulthard's best at the first timing split, but that damp track at the final corner ruined his chances. He strained every sinew to improve to 1m 19.150s, but it wasn't quite enough and he remained in third place – for the second straight weekend.

Hill and Coulthard were both happy and confident about the performance of the Williams FW17B, but David was obviously finding the endless speculation as to whether or not he would defer to Damon come the race increasingly irksome.

'I'm getting rather tired of questions about team orders,' he said, firmly but politely. 'I think what everyone wants to see is a motor race, and my first duty to the team is to try and win the constructors' championship.

'If the circumstances were different, like they were last year, I would think it entirely fair to do as the team requested, and I still do exactly that. But I also think it's fair of Williams not to ask me to slow down if I'm quicker than Damon. That's racing. Damon has the same equipment as I have, so if I'm quicker, I'm

201

Above: Mika Salo's Tyrrell throws up a plume of spray. The race started on a wet track and the circuit remained treacherous throughout.

Brazilian Rubens Barrichello *(above right)* clearly didn't enjoy the weather during his weekend break in the Eifel mountains.

Standing in for a convalescing Ukyo Katayama, touring car ace Gabriele Tarquini *(right)* found it difficult to readjust to the demands of Formula 1.

Opposite top: Johnny Herbert's Benetton tangles with the Jordan of Eddie Irvine. The pair were able to resume their battle and both finished in the points.

David Coulthard *(far right)* finished third in the spare Williams after an embarrassing spin during the pre-race formalities.

Below: A cheerful Olivier Panis manages to keep warm in the Ligier pit garage.

Steve Etherington/Empics

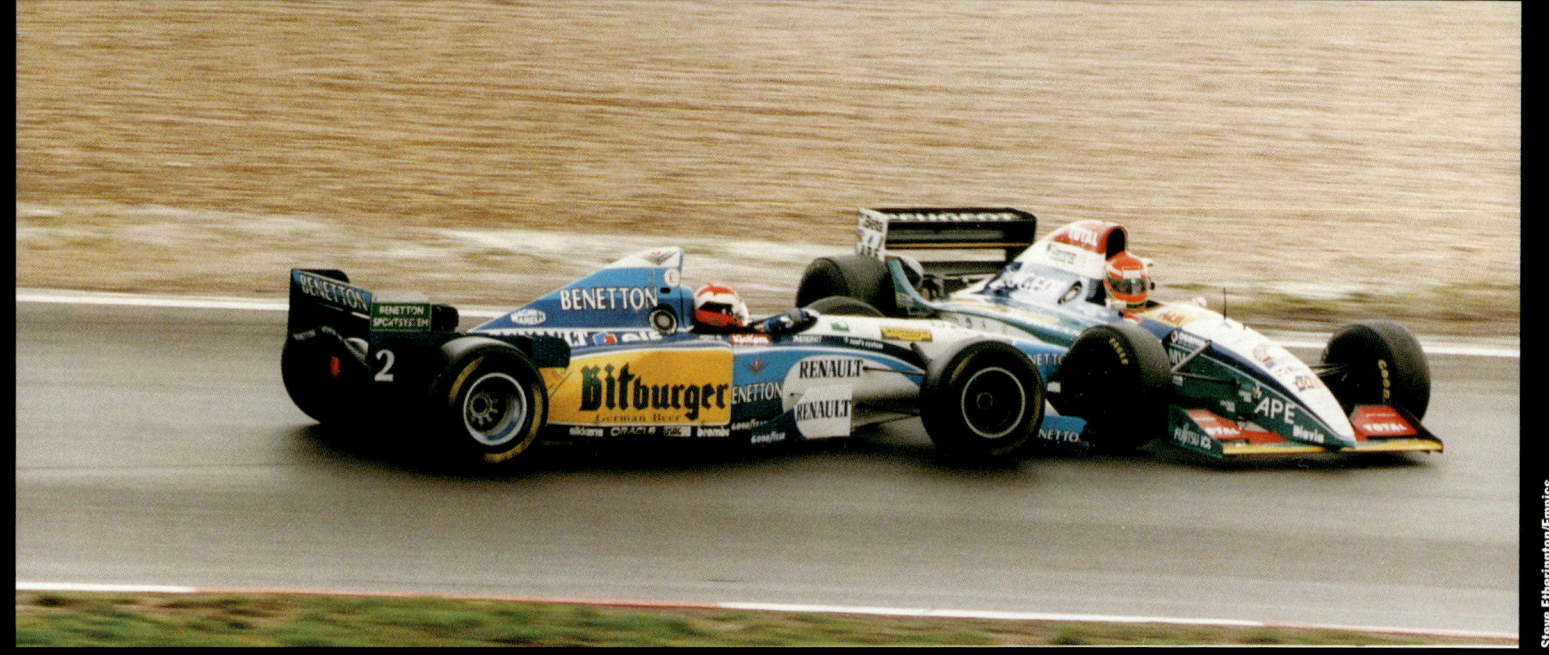

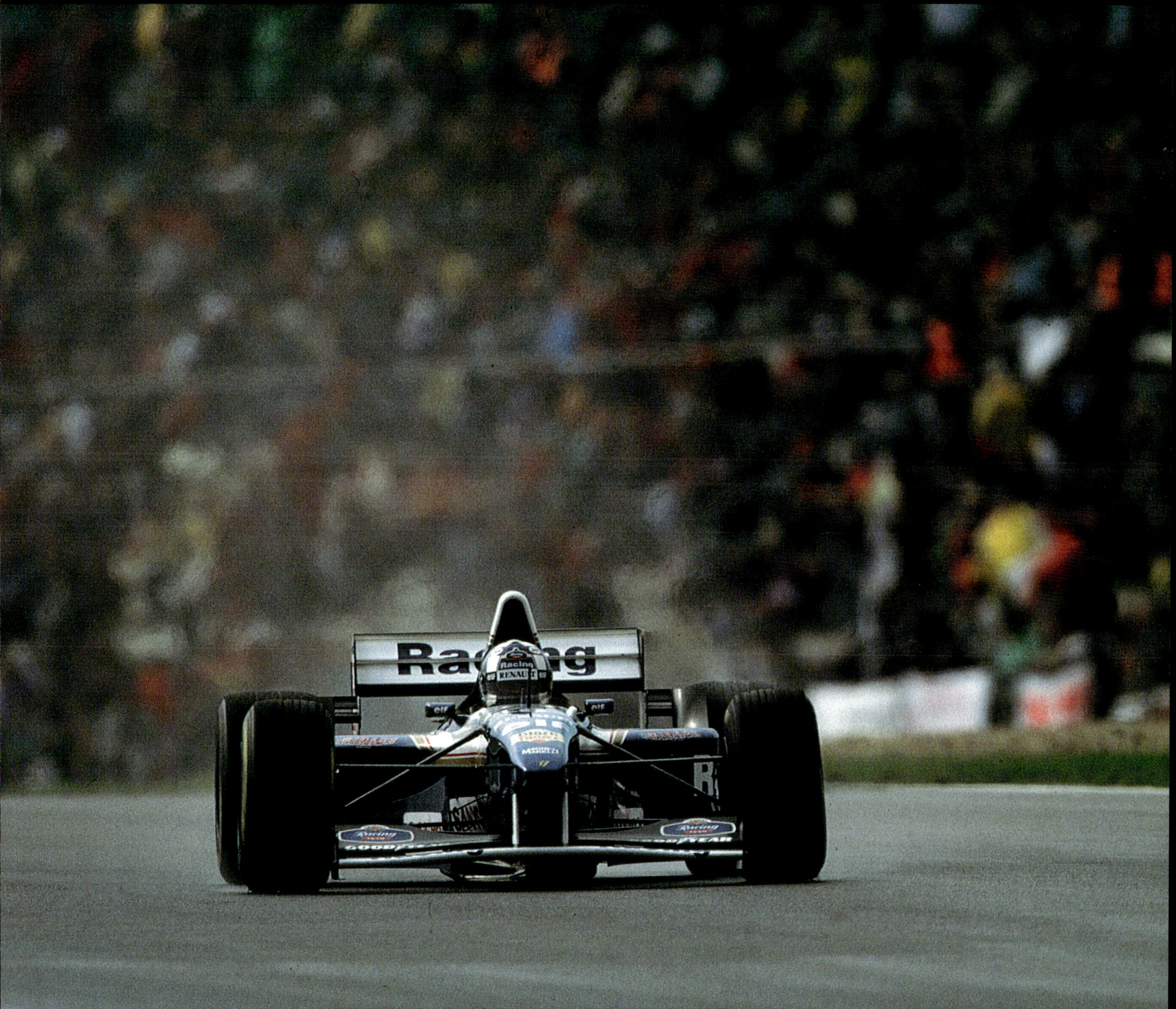

quicker.' Damon remained diplomatically reserved on the matter, only gently pointing out that it would be a pity if the Williams team's chances of winning both the drivers' and constructors' titles were jeopardised. But he admitted that he could see Coulthard's point of view. 'It's a bit of a problem,' he conceded.

Behind the best of the Renault brigade, Gerhard Berger's Ferrari headed the pursuit, separated from his team-mate Jean Alesi by new Maranello recruit Eddie Irvine's Jordan-Peugeot. The Ferraris sported revised side pods and rear wings for this race which both drivers rated as a slight, but definite, improvement.

It might have been expected that Alesi's outburst at Estoril, where he blamed Jean Todt's team management for depriving him of a possible victory by showing partiality towards Berger, would trigger a degree of tension between the two drivers. Not a bit of it; the dial on Alesi's roller-coaster temperament had clearly been set on 'sunny day' and all seemed well with the world.

Irvine was well pleased with his efforts, setting his grid time on his first run on Friday. He then tried a slightly different strategy for his second run only to be slowed by a locking front wheel. Come Saturday afternoon, he was only frustrated that the slippery conditions prevented him trying for an improvement.

Johnny Herbert was a slightly disappointing seventh, but Heinz-Harald Frentzen was simply delighted with eighth place in the Sauber C14-Ford – and reckoned he could have done even better on Saturday.

'I was on a good lap on my second set of tyres when someone got in my way,' said Heinz-Harald. 'I'm really disappointed about that, because, for sure, my time was going to be quicker and I could have moved up the grid.'

In fact, at the end of the day Frentzen was one of only seven drivers to improve their times on Saturday – and only one of those, Taki Inoue, managed to improve his actual grid position.

Over in the McLaren-Mercedes camp there was much optimism that two days of intensive testing at Estoril the previous Monday and Tuesday would produce an improvement in the performance of the latest MP4/10 variant. The team settled on a 10C-spec with a 10B rear end and gearbox, but the message was still the same as usual. Understeer in and oversteer out. Mika Häkkinen and Mark Blundell finished up ninth and tenth on Mercedes' home ground. They had been hoping for much more.

Although Irvine had managed a very respectable fifth place on the grid, Jordan team-mate Rubens Barrichello had a frustrating time on Friday, unable to get his tyres properly warmed up in the cool conditions. He improved his time a little the following day but remained in 11th place overall.

Rubens, together with Footwork driver Max Papis, submitted to a routine drugs test after qualifying, but both were concerned that they would probably fail as they had been taking decongestants for nasal problems and a cold respectively. Barrichello had been taking a treatment which contained Ephedrine since his Imola accident in '94, while Papis used a flu remedy containing the banned pheniphedrine.

'I will fail the test,' shrugged Rubens. 'I took a medicament for a cold this morning which contained a banned substance. I told the FIA doctor before the test and am now praying that I don't have a problem because of it.' No result of the FIA analysis was expected to be made public for at least ten days following the race.

The Brazilian lined up 0.3s ahead of Martin Brundle's Ligier JS41, the Englishman getting the upper hand over team-mate Olivier Panis, who plunged into a tyre barrier on Friday when his Mugen-engined machine suffered a stuck throttle. His car had to be rebuilt round a fresh monocoque for Saturday and he had to settle for 14th, separated from his team-mate by Jean-Christophe Boullion in the second Sauber.

While Frentzen seemed to have worked out a decent chassis balance for his C14, Boullion struggled through both sessions; on Friday his efforts were punctuated by a sideways slide over the chicane kerb and he spent the whole Saturday session struggling for balance. He was not a happy chap.

Mika Salo took 15th place on the grid for Tyrrell. On Friday he had enjoyed good chassis balance, but worryingly little grip. On Saturday morning he reported that the 023 felt nice to drive, but in the progressively drying conditions of second qualifying managed only a single flying lap right at the end of the session.

Tyrrell test driver Gabriele Tarquini stood in for Ukyo Katayama for this race, the little Japanese still recovering from the bruising he sustained when his car flipped during the startline shunt at Estoril, but the Italian touring car ace confessed that he was feeling pretty rusty by F1 standards. He spent the two days' qualifying relearning his single-seater technique and qualified 19th.

In 16th place came Pedro Lamy's Minardi, the Portuguese driver badly balked by a Pacific in Saturday qualifying, while Luca Badoer wound up 18th after losing much of the second session with an engine failure.

The two Minardis were split by Max Papis, who spun off on Friday, damaging the nose of his Footwork. Taki Inoue also spun his Footwork twice in Friday qualifying, but gained a place on Saturday to line up 21st behind Andrea Montermini's Pacific, which lost a rear wheel when the retaining studs sheared during the second qualifying session.

Bringing up the rear were the two Fortis of Pedro Diniz and Roberto Moreno, plus pay-driver Jean-Denis Deletraz, who was having another crack behind the wheel of the second Pacific PR02.

Rain fell steadily on race morning and the track was still treacherous as the field lined up for the start, but Ferrari decided to gamble on slick tyres. Crucially, the Italian team raised the ride heights of the 412T2s on the grid and piled on more downforce, and the audacious strategy very nearly brought Jean Alesi victory. Gerhard Berger would have been right up with his team-mate from the start had it not been for incorrectly pressured tyres which left him battling a handling imbalance. He eventually pulled in with terminal engine electronic problems on lap 40.

Schumacher's outstanding sprint to victory rounded off what was unquestionably the best race in recent memory, with five cars in contention for the lead from the very start.

GRAND PRIX OF EUROPE

Revelling in the testing conditions, Ferrari's Jean Alesi built up what appeared to be a decisive advantage but was unable to resist Michael Schumacher's late-race charge.

Pole position starter David Coulthard incredibly spun off on his first warm-up lap but was able to take over the spare Williams FW17B and opened out a slender advantage in the early stages, pursued by Schumacher and Hill, who had briefly dropped to fourth behind Eddie Irvine's Jordan on the first lap after a slow start from second place on the front row.

Hill made his first scheduled refuelling stop on lap 11, switching from rain tyres to slicks as the track slowly began to dry out. He briefly dropped to seventh, but then came storming back through onto Schumacher's tail in a battle for third.

On lap 12 Coulthard relinquished the lead at his first refuelling stop, allowing Alesi – already on slicks, of course, and planning to refuel only once – through into the lead. David resumed in second place ahead of Schumacher and Hill, but the World Champion was able to slip past the Scot on lap 21. Damon, desperate to maintain the pressure on his rival, passed his team-mate two laps later, and when Michael pulled into the pits for his second refuelling stop at the end of lap 34, Hill moved into second place close behind the Ferrari. Alesi had made his sole refuelling stop on the same lap as the Benetton, but rejoined without surrendering the lead.

Knowing that he still had to make his own second stop, Hill was anxious to force his way past Alesi as quickly as possible and dived up the inside of the tight chicane just before the pits. Alesi chose not to be obliging and the two cars collided, deranging the nose section of Hill's machine. He came straight into the pits for repairs, refuelling and taking on fresh tyres at the same time, but that dropped him to fourth behind Alesi, Schumacher and Coulthard, which is where he would remain for the rest of his race.

'It was touch and go with Alesi,' said Hill, 'but I had to try because Schumacher was closing in and I had a pit stop to come. He [Alesi] knew I was there, and if he'd given me room I'd have gone through without a problem. But there we are. In retrospect, I suppose my mistake was trying to move away from him and get up the kerb.'

The Williams team were just preparing to tell Damon to come in on the next lap when he appeared in the pit lane with a frayed nose section. They had previously been servicing Coulthard and were unable to receive Hill's car any earlier; he was, quite simply, told he could not come in.

Hill was also pressured into his error by the belief that Schumacher was running through non-stop to the finish after his second refuelling stop. In fact, Michael would come in again on lap 52 for a final top-up, so the Williams team's assumptions had been misplaced and Hill's anxiety to get ahead of the Ferrari a touch unnecessary.

'After that incident with Alesi, the steering on my car felt very stiff,' said Hill. 'Later on I was trying to catch Coulthard, but with the steering like that it was difficult and eventually I ran wide over a kerb and hit the barrier.'

Damon was running fourth with only nine of the race's 67 laps remaining when he dropped his right-rear wheel over the kerb exiting a medium-speed left-hander. The car snapped round and charged headlong across the grass into a protective tyre barrier.

Taking his hands off the steering wheel in the final seconds before impact, Hill escaped unscathed apart from his knees being banged firmly together. It was later discovered that he had a suspected cracked bone in one of his legs, but this did not prevent him from setting fastest time at the subsequent Imola test. Earlier in the race he had got precariously close to Schumacher as they battled for third place, lightly tapping the back of the Benetton without damage as the German driver abruptly cut across him.

Damon climbed from the cockpit of the stricken Williams to watch from the trackside as Schumacher staged that blistering late-race surge up onto Alesi's tail. Michael eventually forced his way past with a characteristically decisive move at the chicane with three laps remaining and Jean had to be satisfied with second place. Coulthard finished third after finding that the spare Williams oversteered excessively after that early switch to slick tyres, with the Jordan-Peugeots of Rubens Barrichello and Eddie Irvine sandwiching Johnny Herbert's fifth-placed Benetton.

Early in the race Herbert had slid into Irvine's Jordan shortly after changing to slick rubber and had to come in for a fresh nose to be fitted to his Benetton. Later, Irvine himself had a spin coming up to lap Max Papis in the Footwork, losing the Ulsterman sufficient time for Herbert to get back within striking distance and repass before the chequered flag.

Coulthard confirmed for McLaren-Mercedes

'When Michael went to Ferrari, I became a McLaren driver.' With those words, David Coulthard revealed the nature of the behind-the-scenes dealings which led to his signing to drive for the McLaren-Mercedes team in 1996, the Scot leaving Williams after his first full season.

Coulthard's remarks seemed to confirm that there had been a McLaren option on his services ever since he had signed with Ron Dennis in November 1994 in an effort to get the FIA Contracts Recognition board to adjudicate on the validity of his upcoming deal with Williams.

As things turned out, the board decreed that Frank had first call on David's services. But throughout the season, a cloud of ambiguity had swirled round the precise nature of his commitment to McLaren, the attendant speculation heightened by the fact that he signed for Williams on a one-year deal with no options on either side.

In the middle of the summer, Williams decided not to push for a renewal of Coulthard's contract after failing to get assurances to their satisfaction that he was absolutely free to negotiate. In addition, they felt a trifle cautious about Coulthard's potential after he failed to get on terms with Schumacher's Benetton at Hockenheim after Damon Hill had spun off while in the lead.

'In many ways it is difficult to leave Williams after two and a half years,' said David. 'But I think after Hockenheim the team almost stood back from its inner knowledge to make the decision they took. I was suffering from tonsillitis for the early part of the year and spent most of the time driving in survival mode rather than attacking.'

Coulthard's subsequent upsurge in form would later tempt Frank Williams to observe 'letting him go could have been one of my greatest mistakes'. Yet David remained confident that he would profit from a switch to the McLaren environment. 'I may take a step backwards initially, but I feel I will grow with the team,' he affirmed. Coulthard's recruitment to partner Mika Häkkinen, combined with the news that Jan Magnussen would continue in his testing role, finally closed the door on any prospect of a McLaren F1 return for Alain Prost.

Heinz-Harald Frentzen's chances on home soil with the Sauber-Ford received a setback when he was called in after six laps to take a ten-second stop-go penalty for jumping the start, but the German driver got his head down and had climbed back up to seventh when he was abruptly chopped by Pedro Diniz's Forti on lap 18; the two cars collided and the Sauber spun off into retirement.

Martin Brundle thus took seventh place for Ligier, with Mika Häkkinen eighth after a supremely disappointing race for McLaren in engine supplier Mercedes-Benz's back yard. The team had gambled to run both cars on slicks from the outset, a strategy which clearly worked for the Ferraris but definitely did not have the same effect on the McLarens' prospects.

The ill-handling MP4/10C was just hopeless in the early stages of the race and this, allied to the fact that the Ilmor-built Mercedes V10 had a more abrupt throttle response than the Ferrari V12, meant that Häkkinen and Blundell went sliding down to the back of the pack almost from the start.

Indeed, at one point Häkkinen dropped behind Diniz, this unlikely duo briefly battling for 19th place early in the race. Blundell was at least spared any more suffering when he spun off after 14 laps, but Mika soldiered on to finish a dismally disappointed eighth, a depressing two laps behind the winning Benetton.

'It is easy to be wise after the event,' said Ron Dennis, 'but Alesi demonstrated that starting on slicks could have been the right strategy to win the race. Unfortunately, our calculated decision, which everybody participated in, proved to be wrong. Surprisingly, the circuit never dried up completely, making it an eventful race for everybody.'

In fact, as the track dried out in the closing stages of the race, Häkkinen's lap times improved significantly, offering a tantalising insight into what might have been. Ironically, advice from the Mercedes DTM team to the effect that the Nürburgring track surface dried out quickly in such circumstances had been a factor in making the decision to start on slicks.

At the end of the day Dennis joined Roger Penske and the DTM team boss in a corporate pow-wow to discuss the global Mercedes racing strategy. The German company proved relentlessly supportive even in the face of such a disappointing result, effectively asking the McLaren boss what more they could do to help the team attain a truly competitive pitch.

Behind Häkkinen, Pedro Lamy's Minardi came home ninth, three laps down, ahead of Mika Salo's Tyrrell and Luca Badoer's Minardi. Max Papis, who had earlier been given a ten-second stop-go penalty for taking up an improper grid position, drove consistently to finish 12th ahead of Diniz, Tyrrell deputy Gabriele Tarquini and the uncompetitive Deletraz, whose Pacific was seven laps down at the chequered flag.

Unquestionably, this had been the best race of the season so far and there was no doubting the excellence of Schumacher's achievement. Williams had once again had the best car, but a combination of poor tactics and mistakes by both drivers had resulted in this priceless technical asset being squandered.

FIA FORMULA ONE WORLD CHAMPIONSHIP ROUND 14

EUROPEAN GRAND PRIX

NÜRBURGRING
29 SEPTEMBER – 1 OCTOBER 1995

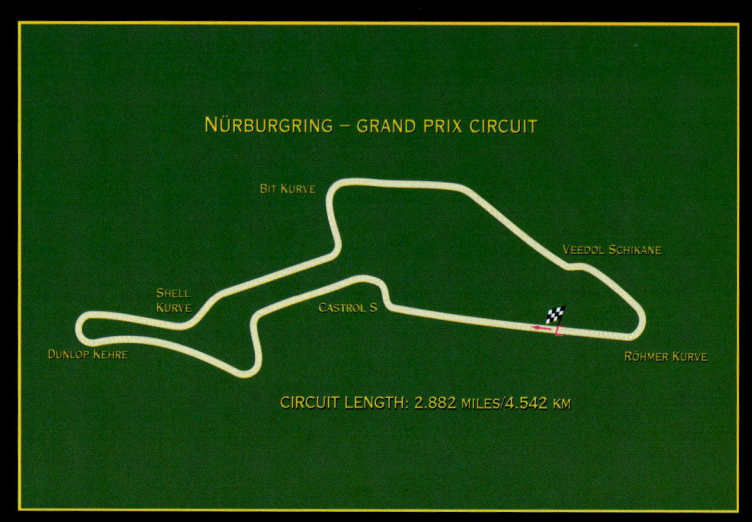

NÜRBURGRING – GRAND PRIX CIRCUIT

CIRCUIT LENGTH: 2.882 MILES/4.542 KM

Race distance: 67 laps, 189.091 miles/304.314 km
Race weather: Damp and overcast

Place	Driver	Nat.	No.	Entrant	Car/Engine	Laps	Time/Retirement	Speed (mph/km/h)
1	**Michael Schumacher**	D	1	Mild Seven Benetton Renault	Benetton B195-Renault RS7C V10	67	1h 39m 59.044s	113.822/183.180
2	**Jean Alesi**	F	27	Scuderia Ferrari	Ferrari 412T2 044 V12	67	1h 40m 01.728s	113.773/183.098
3	**David Coulthard**	GB	6	Rothmans Williams Renault	Williams FW17B-Renault RS7C V10	67	1h 40m 34.426s	113.155/182.106
4	**Rubens Barrichello**	BR	14	Total Jordan Peugeot	Jordan 195-Peugeot A10 V10	66		
5	**Johnny Herbert**	GB	2	Mild Seven Benetton Renault	Benetton B195-Renault RS7C V10	66		
6	**Eddie Irvine**	GB	15	Total Jordan Peugeot	Jordan 195-Peugeot A10 V10	66		
7	Martin Brundle	GB	25	Ligier Gitanes Blondes	Ligier JS41-Mugen Honda MF301 V10	66		
8	Mika Häkkinen	SF	8	Marlboro McLaren Mercedes	McLaren MP4/10C-Mercedes FO110 V10	65		
9	Pedro Lamy	P	23	Minardi Scuderia Italia	Minardi M195-Ford EDM V8	64		
10	Mika Salo	SF	4	Nokia Tyrrell Yamaha	Tyrrell 023-Yamaha OX10C V10	64		
11	Luca Badoer	I	24	Minardi Scuderia Italia	Minardi M195-Ford EDM V8	64		
12	Massimiliano Papis	I	9	Footwork Hart	Footwork FA16-Hart 830 V8	64		
13	Pedro Diniz	BR	21	Parmalat Forti Ford	Forti FG01-Ford ED V8	62		
14	Gabriele Tarquini	I	3	Nokia Tyrrell Yamaha	Tyrrell 023-Yamaha OX10C V10	61		
NC	Jean-Denis Deletraz	CH	16	Pacific Grand Prix Ltd	Pacific PR02-Ford ED V8	60		
	Damon Hill	GB	5	Rothmans Williams Renault	Williams FW17B-Renault RS7C V10	58	Accident	
	Andrea Montermini	I	17	Pacific Grand Prix Ltd	Pacific PR02-Ford ED V8	45	Out of fuel	
	Jean-Christophe Boullion	F	29	Red Bull Sauber Ford	Sauber C14-Ford Zetec-R V8	44	Spun off	
	Gerhard Berger	A	28	Scuderia Ferrari	Ferrari 412T2 044 V12	40	Electronics	
	Roberto Moreno	BR	22	Parmalat Forti Ford	Forti FG01-Ford ED V8	22	Driveshaft	
	Heinz-Harald Frentzen	D	30	Red Bull Sauber Ford	Sauber C14-Ford Zetec-R V8	17	Collision with Diniz	
	Olivier Panis	F	26	Ligier Gitanes Blondes	Ligier JS41-Mugen Honda MF301 V10	14	Spun off	
	Mark Blundell	GB	7	Marlboro McLaren Mercedes	McLaren MP4/10C-Mercedes FO110 V10	14	Spun off	
DNS	Taki Inoue	J	10	Footwork Hart	Footwork FA16-Hart 830 V8	0	Electronics	

Fastest lap: Schumacher, on lap 57, 1m 21.180s, 125.540 mph/202.039 km/h (record).
Lap record: Not previously used for F1 cars in this configuration.
All cars used Goodyear tyres

All results and data © FIA 1995

STARTING GRID

6 COULTHARD (1m 18.738s) Williams		**5 HILL** (1m 18.972s) Williams	
1 SCHUMACHER (1m 19.150s) Benetton		**28 BERGER** (1m 19.821s) Ferrari	
15 IRVINE (1m 20.488s) Jordan		**27 ALESI** (1m 20.510s) Ferrari	
2 HERBERT (1m 20.653s) Benetton		**30 FRENTZEN** (1m 20.749s) Sauber	
8 HÄKKINEN (1m 20.866s) McLaren		**7 BLUNDELL** (1m 20.909s) McLaren	
14 BARRICHELLO (1m 21.211s) Jordan		**25 BRUNDLE** (1m 21.541s) Ligier	
29 BOULLION (1m 22.059s) Sauber		**26 PANIS** (1m 22.062s) Ligier	
4 SALO (1m 23.058s) Tyrrell		**23 LAMY** (1m 23.328s) Minardi	
9 PAPIS (1m 23.689s) Footwork		**24 BADOER** (1m 23.760s) Minardi	
3 TARQUINI (1m 24.286s) Tyrrell		**17 MONTERMINI** (1m 24.696s) Pacific	
10 INOUE* (1m 24.900s) Footwork		**21 DINIZ** (1m 25.157s) Forti	
22 MORENO (1m 26.098s) Forti		**16 DELETRAZ** (1m 27.853s) Pacific	

*did not start

TIME SHEETS

Friday free practice
Breezy, dry and cold

Pos.	Driver	Laps	Time
1	Damon Hill	7	1m 19.343s
2	David Coulthard	10	1m 19.378s
3	Michael Schumacher	16	1m 19.908s
4	Gerhard Berger	7	1m 20.637s
5	Johnny Herbert	14	1m 21.275s
6	Mika Häkkinen	14	1m 21.292s
7	Mark Blundell	18	1m 21.306s
8	Heinz-Harald Frentzen	12	1m 21.356s
9	Eddie Irvine	13	1m 21.513s
10	Jean Alesi	9	1m 21.533s
11	Olivier Panis	17	1m 21.614s
12	Rubens Barrichello	19	1m 21.772s
13	Martin Brundle	16	1m 21.951s
14	Jean-Christophe Boullion	8	1m 23.087s
15	Pedro Lamy	17	1m 23.387s
16	Mika Salo	15	1m 23.415s
17	Massimiliano Papis	13	1m 23.820s
18	Luca Badoer	15	1m 24.379s
19	Gabriele Tarquini	12	1m 24.635s
20	Pedro Diniz	18	1m 25.271s
21	Andrea Montermini	10	1m 25.287s
22	Taki Inoue	13	1m 26.094s
23	Roberto Moreno	2	1m 28.594s
24	Jean-Denis Deletraz	13	1m 28.606s

Saturday free practice
Rain and mist

Pos.	Driver	Laps	Time
1	Damon Hill	23	1m 34.906s
2	David Coulthard	20	1m 35.611s
3	Heinz-Harald Frentzen	23	1m 36.946s
4	Gerhard Berger	14	1m 37.165s
5	Jean Alesi	19	1m 37.219s
6	Michael Schumacher	23	1m 37.374s
7	Johnny Herbert	22	1m 37.488s
8	Rubens Barrichello	22	1m 38.088s
9	Olivier Panis	22	1m 38.693s
10	Mika Salo	23	1m 38.728s
11	Eddie Irvine	12	1m 38.762s
12	Jean-Christophe Boullion	20	1m 38.795s
13	Mika Häkkinen	20	1m 38.977s
14	Martin Brundle	23	1m 38.995s
15	Pedro Lamy	17	1m 39.614s
16	Mark Blundell	21	1m 39.769s
17	Luca Badoer	22	1m 40.144s
18	Andrea Montermini	14	1m 41.821s
19	Massimiliano Papis	13	1m 43.397s
20	Pedro Diniz	14	1m 43.420s
21	Roberto Moreno	23	1m 44.189s
22	Gabriele Tarquini	23	1m 44.554s
23	Jean-Denis Deletraz	18	1m 46.412s
24	Taki Inoue	20	1m 49.666s

Friday qualifying
Windy, slight rain shower

Pos.	Driver	Laps	Time
1	**David Coulthard**	**10**	**1m 18.738s**
2	**Damon Hill**	**11**	**1m 18.972s**
3	Michael Schumacher	11	1m 19.470s
4	**Gerhard Berger**	**9**	**1m 19.821s**
5	**Eddie Irvine**	**9**	**1m 20.488s**
6	Jean Alesi	5	1m 20.521s
7	**Johnny Herbert**	**12**	**1m 20.653s**
8	Heinz-Harald Frentzen	12	1m 20.762s
9	**Mika Häkkinen**	**11**	**1m 20.866s**
10	**Mark Blundell**	**11**	**1m 20.909s**
11	Rubens Barrichello	12	1m 21.350s
12	**Martin Brundle**	**11**	**1m 21.541s**
13	**Jean-Christophe Boullion**	**9**	**1m 22.059s**
14	**Olivier Panis**	**2**	**1m 22.062s**
15	**Mika Salo**	**11**	**1m 23.058s**
16	Pedro Lamy	9	1m 23.328s
17	**Massimiliano Papis**	**5**	**1m 23.689s**
18	**Luca Badoer**	**12**	**1m 23.760s**
19	**Gabriele Tarquini**	**6**	**1m 24.286s**
20	**Andrea Montermini**	**12**	**1m 24.696s**
21	Pedro Diniz	11	1m 25.647s
22	Taki Inoue	4	1m 26.667s
23	Roberto Moreno	12	1m 26.784s
24	**Jean-Denis Deletraz**	**12**	**1m 27.853s**

Saturday qualifying
Cold, damp and overcast

Pos.	Driver	Laps	Time
1	**Michael Schumacher**	**8**	**1m 19.150s**
2	Damon Hill	10	1m 19.607s
3	David Coulthard	7	1m 19.913s
4	**Jean Alesi**	**10**	**1m 20.510s**
5	**Heinz-Harald Frentzen**	**10**	**1m 20.749s**
6	Mika Häkkinen	11	1m 20.968s
7	Gerhard Berger	9	1m 21.083s
8	**Rubens Barrichello**	**11**	**1m 21.211s**
9	Johnny Herbert	8	1m 21.236s
10	Eddie Irvine	10	1m 21.426s
11	Mark Blundell	10	1m 21.583s
12	Martin Brundle	8	1m 22.062s
13	Olivier Panis	9	1m 22.565s
14	Mika Salo	8	1m 23.079s
15	Pedro Lamy	6	1m 24.087s
16	Massimiliano Papis	11	1m 24.134s
17	Gabriele Tarquini	11	1m 24.352s
18	**Taki Inoue**	**9**	**1m 24.900s**
19	**Pedro Diniz**	**8**	**1m 25.157s**
20	**Roberto Moreno**	**8**	**1m 26.098s**
21	Andrea Montermini	4	1m 26.102s
22	Luca Badoer	3	1m 26.406s
23	Jean-Denis Deletraz	6	1m 29.677s
24	Jean-Christophe Boullion	4	1m 34.210s

Warm-up
Initial fog giving way to heavy rain

Pos.	Driver	Laps	Time
1	David Coulthard	11	1m 38.378s
2	Gerhard Berger	13	1m 38.616s
3	Damon Hill	14	1m 38.782s
4	Michael Schumacher	14	1m 38.960s
5	Rubens Barrichello	14	1m 39.205s
6	Jean Alesi	11	1m 39.418s
7	Mika Häkkinen	11	1m 39.943s
8	Johnny Herbert	12	1m 40.056s
9	Heinz-Harald Frentzen	13	1m 40.130s
10	Jean-Christophe Boullion	14	1m 40.315s
11	Eddie Irvine	11	1m 41.347s
12	Martin Brundle	12	1m 41.405s
13	Olivier Panis	13	1m 41.455s
14	Mark Blundell	8	1m 41.499s
15	Pedro Lamy	13	1m 42.440s
16	Mika Salo	8	1m 42.736s
17	Luca Badoer	14	1m 42.967s
18	Massimiliano Papis	17	1m 43.860s
19	Andrea Montermini	12	1m 45.085s
20	Gabriele Tarquini	10	1m 45.500s
21	Roberto Moreno	14	1m 46.409s
22	Taki Inoue	12	1m 46.775s
23	Pedro Diniz	8	1m 49.680s
24	Jean-Denis Deletraz	10	1m 50.131s

Fastest race laps
Damp and overcast

Driver	Time	Lap
Michael Schumacher	1m 21.180s	57
David Coulthard	1m 21.739s	60
Damon Hill	1m 21.933s	58
Johnny Herbert	1m 22.544s	56
Mika Häkkinen	1m 22.760s	65
Jean Alesi	1m 22.814s	58
Martin Brundle	1m 23.801s	64
Gerhard Berger	1m 24.239s	38
Eddie Irvine	1m 24.775s	63
Rubens Barrichello	1m 25.018s	37
Jean-Christophe Boullion	1m 25.385s	43
Mika Salo	1m 25.516s	61
Luca Badoer	1m 25.962s	62
Gabriele Tarquini	1m 26.160s	61
Massimiliano Papis	1m 26.332s	55
Andrea Montermini	1m 26.566s	44
Pedro Lamy	1m 26.832s	59
Pedro Diniz	1m 27.555s	57
Jean-Denis Deletraz	1m 31.253s	59
Heinz-Harald Frentzen	1m 37.423s	16
Roberto Moreno	1m 37.763s	21
Olivier Panis	1m 39.347s	12
Mark Blundell	1m 40.613s	14

CHASSIS LOG BOOK

1	Schumacher	Benetton B195/6
2	Herbert	Benetton B195/5
	spare	Benetton B195/1
3	Tarquini	Tyrrell 023/3
4	Salo	Tyrrell 023/5
	spare	Tyrrell 023/2
5	Hill	Williams FW17B/6
6	Coulthard	Williams FW17B/5
	spare	Williams FW17/2
7	Blundell	McLaren MP4/10C/4
8	Häkkinen	McLaren MP4/10C/1
	spare	McLaren MP4/10C/3
9	Papis	Footwork FA16/3
10	Inoue	Footwork FA16/4
	spare	Footwork FA16/1
14	Barrichello	Jordan 195/4
15	Irvine	Jordan 195/5
	spare	Jordan 195/1
16	Deletraz	Pacific PR02/1
17	Montermini	Pacific PR02/2
21	Diniz	Forti FG01/4
22	Moreno	Forti FG01/3
	spare	Forti FG01/2
23	Lamy	Minardi M195/3
24	Badoer	Minardi M195/2
	spare	Minardi M195/1
25	Brundle	Ligier JS41/5
26	Panis	Ligier JS41/1
	spare	Ligier JS41/3
27	Alesi	Ferrari 412T2/161
28	Berger	Ferrari 412T2/162
	spare	Ferrari 412T2/160
29	Boullion	Sauber C14/5
30	Frentzen	Sauber C14/6
	spare	Sauber C14/2

POINTS TABLES

Drivers

1	Michael Schumacher	82
2	Damon Hill	55
3	David Coulthard	43
4 =	Johnny Herbert	40
4 =	Jean Alesi	40
6	Gerhard Berger	28
7	Heinz-Harald Frentzen	15
8 =	Mika Häkkinen	11
8 =	Rubens Barrichello	11
10	Mark Blundell	10
11	Olivier Panis	8
12 =	Martin Brundle	7
12 =	Eddie Irvine	7
14	Jean-Christophe Boullion	3
15	Mika Salo	2
16 =	Gianni Morbidelli	1
16 =	Aguri Suzuki	1

Constructors

1	Benetton	112
2	Williams	92
3	Ferrari	68
4	McLaren	21
5 =	Jordan	18
5 =	Sauber	18
7	Ligier	16
8	Tyrrell	2
9	Footwork	1

WORLD CHAMPIONSHIP • ROUND 15

PACIFIC GRAND PRIX

SCHUMACHER
COULTHARD
HILL
BERGER
ALESI
HERBERT

A schedule of three long-haul races in the space of four weekends presented the F1 circus with a considerable logistical challenge. Even luminaries such as Eddie Jordan *(bottom)* found themselves pushing luggage trolleys.

Right: One down, 23 to go. Mark Blundell has signed the flag, but there is still a lot of space to be filled . . .

Michael Schumacher became the youngest driver in the history of the official World Championship to win back-to-back titles with a tactically brilliant victory in the second Pacific Grand Prix to be held at millionaire Hajime Tanaka's tight and tortuous TI Circuit Aida, Japan's second current F1 circuit near Osaka.

It was a brilliant team triumph for both Schumacher and Benetton, the young German having dropped as low as fifth place after a barging match with Damon Hill's Williams at the first corner. Yet as Hill and his Williams team-mate David Coulthard found their qualifying advantage dramatically evaporating for a variety of reasons throughout the race, Schumacher seemed to perform the F1 equivalent of a card trick to trump his key opposition decisively after his third and final refuelling stop.

'It was a bit difficult at the beginning,' admitted Michael, 'because I was in fifth place and at that stage didn't think I was in a position to win. I was sure that I would be able to score the points I needed, and that was it.

'But as the race developed, and because my pit crew was able to do the first stop in a perfect way, I was able to pull out in front of Damon and Alesi. That helped me to catch David and our strategy worked out. I never saw anything like this team [Benetton] and its ability to come up with strategies. They have been unbelievable. Not one mistake this season from these guys.'

Coulthard, who had started commandingly from pole position and amassed almost half a minute's lead before his first refuelling stop, found a switch from three to two stops working against him at the end of the day. He had to settle for second place, with Hill, frustrated by a poor first refuelling stop, a slight collision with Eddie Irvine's Jordan and a generally bad time in traffic, trailing home third, the last unlapped runner.

From the outset the Williams-Renaults displayed their customary outstanding form in high-downforce trim, just as they had at circuits such as Monaco and the Hungaroring. Coulthard dominated qualifying once again, setting quickest time in each of the timed sessions to clinch his fourth pole in succession by 0.2s from Hill's sister car.

Coulthard's confidence seemed to be soaring, the unquenchable enthusiasm with which he viewed his imminent move to McLaren boosted by news that he would be taking top Williams race engineer David Brown, who was currently working on Hill's car, along for the ride. Brown was thus set to become the latest in a long line of McLaren acquisitions at Williams's expense that included TAG and Honda.

His transfer to the Woking team, reputedly for a massive threefold salary hike, came at a time when Hill again seemed to be under psychological assault from all sides. Having realistically conceded the championship after the Grand Prix of Europe at the Nürburgring, Hill found Coulthard observing critically, 'I cannot ever see myself giving up. If you give up once, you always give up.'

Martin Brundle added, 'Damon has to re-establish himself as a racer. More than a few of us think that, wheel-to-wheel, he is lacking something. It might be that he needs to lose a front wheel or two to do so.'

Finally, Schumacher remarked, 'Damon's biggest problem is that he doesn't appear to be in control when he is trying to overtake. He makes half-hearted attempts which land him in trouble – with no way out.'

To top it all, there were wild rumours that Williams wanted to tear up his contract for 1996 and engineer a swap deal with Gerhard Berger. This was firmly denied by all concerned.

Hill just shrugged, kept his counsel and his head down. Like Coulthard, he preferred to conserve tyres for the race and covered only six laps in second qualifying.

Schumacher, benefiting from revised rear suspension geometry on his Benetton B195, progressively backed off on downforce during the second session and luridly inched closer to the Williams duo. With a final fling on fresh rubber, he got to within a tenth of pushing Damon off the front row.

'Michael got close,' acknowledged Hill, 'and in a way I would have preferred him to have been ahead of me, because then I would have been on the cleaner line going down to the first corner.' With this in mind, come race morning, Hill would briefly take the spare Williams out in an effort to clean up the dusty inside line on the start/finish straight.

One crucial factor was the fact that Schumacher went into the race with three brand-new sets of rubber, the Williams drivers only two. All three front-runners set their best times in second qualifying, Coulthard privately regretting that he had wasted another set of rubber right at the end of Saturday afternoon as Schumacher went out to bid for pole.

'For me it was just a case of going out for my last run and trying to do better just in case Michael improved,' he explained. 'But it was so close to the end of the session that I had to be out on the circuit; there wasn't time to see if Michael went quicker, then go out and try for a time if he did.'

Fourth and fifth on the grid were the two Ferrari 412T2s of Jean Alesi and Gerhard Berger, suffering respectively from flu and jet lag, both of whom set their best times on Friday. Alesi used only two sets on Saturday, but Gerhard decided to use a third in his efforts to improve, but spun and slightly damaged his car's undertray over a kerb.

In the Jordan camp Eddie Irvine had a trouble-free run to sixth place, setting his best time on Saturday after grappling with a touch of understeer in the morning. 'That was a good session, no major mistakes at all and I gradually refined the lap with each new set of tyres,' said Eddie.

'Starting near the front is very important here because it's so difficult to overtake. It could have been even better except for a touch of understeer at the last corner.'

Only 0.4s separated Irvine from his team-mate Rubens Barrichello down in 11th place. The Brazilian ran with less wing on Saturday and was quite satisfied with his efforts, although he was in a slightly distant and depressed frame of mind after the death of his friend and compatriot Marco Campos in the previous weekend's F3000 finale at Magny-Cours.

Leading the bunch between the two Jordans were Johnny Herbert's Benetton B195 and an on-form Heinz-Harald Frentzen with the Sauber C14. 'We made some changes to the car and, like yesterday, the balance was good but this time we had more grip,' said Frentzen. 'Both my runs this afternoon were exactly the same. I couldn't have gone any quicker.'

His team-mate Jean-Christophe Boullion stuck with used tyres for Saturday's free practice session. However, his C14 had been fitted with the latest-spec Zetec-R V8 overnight and he complained that the additional power made the car feel completely different, with the result that he went the wrong way on set-up. Unfortunately, when he put on new tyres for final qualifying he spun off on his third lap and failed to better his Friday time as a result. He would start from 15th place on the grid.

Olivier Panis, on this occasion partnered by Aguri Suzuki, was quite pleased with the feel of his Ligier JS41 on the way to ninth place in the final line-up.

'Although it may not be the best in terms of grid placing, it was certainly

PACIFIC GRAND PRIX

one of my most satisfying qualifying performances of the year,' said the Frenchman. 'Less than a tenth of a second quicker would have netted me seventh-fastest time!'

Tenth place fell to Mark Blundell's McLaren-Mercedes, the team using the MP4/10B specification for this race, but the Englishman was disappointed not to have improved on his 1m 15.652s Friday best which had left him an overnight seventh.

Mark lost a lot of time on Saturday morning when his car stopped on the circuit after only nine laps when the engine failed. This left the Englishman standing by his machine in a vulnerable position on the outside of a left-hand corner, apparently protected by no waved yellow flags as he attempted to re-fix the McLaren's removable steering wheel. It also meant that he lost crucial laps during which he'd hoped to assess some set-up changes for second qualifying. As it was, he was still struggling for balance by the end of the second session.

With Mika Häkkinen out of action recuperating from the effects of an appendix operation, test driver Jan Magnussen was given his F1 chance in the second car. The 22-year-old Dane handled himself with an impressive assurance, never putting a wheel wrong on the slippery track surface throughout the two days' qualifying. He lined up an extremely respectable 12th, separated from Blundell only by Barrichello's Jordan.

Next came Suzuki's Ligier, followed by Pedro Lamy, two places ahead of his Minardi team-mate Luca Badoer. Both were delighted with the handling of their M195s on this tight circuit. 'Qualifying so close behind a Ligier is like pole position for us,' said the Portuguese driver.

Tyrrell's 023s had a bad time for much of the weekend and it was a great disappointment for Ukyo Katayama that he could not manage a better showing on his home turf. Both he and Mika Salo were beset by lack of grip in the slow corners and, while Katayama improved his time in the second session, Salo was unable to beat his Friday best and lined up 18th, one place and 0.2s behind the Japanese driver.

Gianni Morbidelli returned to the Arrows line-up to pick up the threads of his relationship with the team, replacing Max Papis for the moment and playing himself in steadily as he got to grips with F1 for the first time since the French Grand Prix. His Footwork FA16 was equipped with experimental revised suspension geometry, but the team reverted to the original set-up for the race after Morbidelli was unable to qualify better than 19th, one place ahead of team-mate Taki Inoue.

Pedro Diniz and Roberto Moreno buttoned up the penultimate row of the grid for Forti Corse with Andrea Montermini and Pacific old hand Bertrand Gachot completing the grid in their Cosworth ED-engined PR02s.

In the race morning warm-up, Coulthard set fastest lap some 0.7s ahead of an on-form Jean-Christophe Boullion, although the Sauber driver had the benefit of fresh rubber, which David most certainly did not, bearing in mind he only had two new sets left for the race. As if to emphasise just how marginal the situation was for the Williams team, Coulthard did a few laps early in the warm-up on rain tyres in the dry so that he could run in a freshly installed gearbox.

Schumacher was another not to use new tyres during the warm-up, preferring to slide about on used rubber and settle for eighth-fastest time, secure in the knowledge that he had saved three fresh sets of tyres for the race.

Michael had an anxious few moments before the start when his Benetton began to develop a worrying vibration which had briefly troubled him during the warm-up, but it did not take long to confirm that all was well and he duly accelerated away on the parade lap behind the two Williams FW17Bs.

At the green light, Coulthard got away cleanly from pole position, with Schumacher drawing level with Hill on the outside as they sprinted to the first corner. Michael attempted to go round the outside of his old sparring partner, but Damon slid slightly wide, almost forcing the Benetton up onto the left-hand kerb and allowing Alesi's Ferrari to nip past into second place as they hurtled down the hill to the first hairpin.

Schumacher lost more time as he dropped back to fifth behind Berger and David was able to make good his escape, completing the opening lap 2.7s ahead of Alesi's Ferrari. Third was Hill from Berger, Schumacher, Herbert, Irvine, Frentzen and the McLaren-Mercedes duo, Blundell and Magnussen.

Schumacher was not happy with Hill's first-corner tactics. 'I wasn't upset about it,' he said. 'But I was disappointed that he concentrated a bit too much on me and allowed the Ferraris past. We should have been second and third and continued to race, but that's the way it was and still entertaining.'

With Alesi neatly boxing in Hill, Coulthard looked set to walk away with the race. On the next seven laps the young Scot's advantage increased in the following sequence: 4.2s, 5.2s, 7.1s, 8.4s, 9.8s, 11.0s and 12.5s.

Schumacher got past Berger to take fourth place on lap five and quickly closed in on Hill. Midway round lap 11, Michael got a run up close behind the Williams as they went onto the long back straight, but as they approached the tight right-hand hairpin at the end, Damon moved over to the right to monopolise the inside line.

The two cars got extremely close as they slid wide, nose to tail, away from the apex of the corner. Later, as Hill walked over to congratulate Schumacher on clinching the World Championship after the race, he was amazed when Michael lost his temper and began accusing him of unethical behaviour in respect of that particular manoeuvre.

Hill responded robustly at the post-race press conference to this criticism from Schumacher.

McLaren test driver Jan Magnussen made a highly accomplished Grand Prix debut as a stand-in for appendicitis victim Mika Häkkinen, the former British Formula 3 Champion following his much more experienced team-mate Mark Blundell home in tenth place.

Bottom: Aguri Suzuki catches up on the F1 gossip with Ligier boss Tom Walkinshaw *(right)*. Back in the team for the first time since the German GP in July, the Japanese driver spun out of the race after only ten laps.

No new rules on F1 driving tactics

On the Thursday immediately prior to the Pacific Grand Prix the FIA World Council debated the issue of F1 driver etiquette but stopped short of laying down any fresh rules governing overtaking manoeuvres after a season of continual controversy. However, the FIA emphasised that the International Sporting Code will be enforced on the basis that drivers are free to drive as they wish 'provided they do not deliberately endanger another driver or repeatedly obstruct him on a straight'.

Commenting on this decision, FIA President Max Mosley said, 'Racing is different to the road in one sense – when competing, you drive to the limit of your abilities.

'We held a meeting earlier this month with leading F1 drivers and they agreed that no driver should endanger another driver, but otherwise should be allowed to compete freely. The World Council has accepted this view. The drivers are top professionals, so we will let them get on with it.'

The FIA also formalised new rules for practice and qualifying to be introduced at the start of the 1996 season. Free practice will now take place on Friday (Thursday at Monaco) from 11 a.m. to 12 noon and from 1.00 to 2.00 p.m., then on Saturday from 9.00 to 9.45 a.m. and from 10.15 to 11.00 a.m. Each driver will be allowed a maximum of 30 laps on each day as opposed to this year's 23-lap allowance.

There will be a single qualifying session, which will take place on Saturday from 1.00 to 2.00 p.m., during which the maximum of 12 laps per competitor will remain unchanged. Spare cars may be used in qualifying, but not in the free practice sessions.

'Michael wasn't happy with what I did a couple of times in the race and he has told me that he is unhappy with my driving,' said Damon. 'I find that extraordinary, completely extraordinary. The situation now [under the clarified rules] is that we are completely free to drive as we like as long as it is not deliberately dangerous. So I drove in that style and he didn't like it. He should have no complaints.'

Hill described Schumacher as 'a hypocrite' for adopting such an attitude. The strong implication was that it was Michael who had raised the subject of driving ethics in the first place; now the FIA had deliberated on it and Hill was only following what he understood to be the new rules.

Schumacher complained that Hill had moved to the right across him on the back straight 'and that, somehow or other, when we got into the braking area at the end of the back straight I did something wrong. But I can't see what I did wrong.

'It seems there is one rule for him and another for everybody else at times. I just think that either you agree to that, and there should be no complaints, or there are rules and you should stick to them.

'I think I am a better, stronger driver this year than I was last year and can build on that for next year. Clearly Michael has an advantage over everyone and if I want to win, then I am going to have to overhaul him.'

Coulthard, meanwhile, remained in the lead, looking relaxed and assured. Further back, the first retirement had been Gachot, whose Pacific rolled to a halt with gearbox hydraulic failure on the third lap, while Boullion's Sauber spun out of 15th place on lap eight, the irritated Frenchman later accusing Minardi driver Pedro Lamy of having weaved across his C14 and caused his exit from the race.

Coulthard had been scheduled to run a three-stop strategy from the start, but by lap 18 he was simply flying away from the field some 14 seconds ahead. 'At that point I thought, "I can do this with a two-stop strategy," and immediately told the pits to delay my stop, because I was originally due to come in at the end of lap 18,' he said. 'In retrospect, I wish I could blame somebody else for this decision, but I can't.'

So while David pressed on in the lead, at the end of lap 19 Alesi, Hill and Schumacher came hurtling into the pit lane in nose-to-tail formation.

Schumacher was serviced in 6.3s, but Damon – who now had to change onto worn rubber as he had had only two new sets left – found himself stationary for 12.1s due to a sticking refuelling valve. This was the start of his undoing. By the time he got back into the race, Schumacher was off and away in second place with Irvine briefly third, then Alesi and Damon's Williams back in fifth.

On lap 24 Alesi dived inside Irvine to take third at the end of the back straight and Damon went to follow the Ferrari through. Unfortunately Eddie came back across him and hit Hill's left-front aerofoil and wheel quite hard. Fortunately the slight damage sustained did not affect the handling of his car.

Then on lap 25 Coulthard came in for his first stop, also having to switch to used rubber for the middle stint of his race.

When Coulthard resumed, he was 7.5s ahead of Schumacher, but Michael gradually trimmed that advantage back to under a second by the time he brought the Benetton in for its second stop on lap 38, switching to used rubber for his next stint. Nevertheless, he was able to post the race's fastest lap on a clear track only two laps later.

Meanwhile, Hill remained boxed in behind the unhelpful Alesi's Ferrari right through to lap 39 when he made his second stop. Although Jean came in next time round, Damon briefly found himself behind

Diary

Minardi opens negotiations with Yamaha for customer versions of Japanese company's OX10C engine for its 1996 programme as all-new OX11 V10 is unveiled for Tyrrell's exclusive use.

Forti team driver Pedro Diniz is linked with Ligier-Mugen team as possible second driver in 1996.

Michael Schumacher and Eddie Irvine scheduled to have their first Ferrari F1 test at Fiorano on the Friday following the Australian Grand Prix.

Berger in fourth place and only moved through to third again when Gerhard came in to refuel at the end of lap 42.

As for Ferrari strategy, both men pitted on three occasions. On lap 45 Berger moved ahead of his team-mate going down the back straight when Jean was handicapped by the worst of his four tyre sets. 'There's not really a lot to say,' shrugged Jean after finishing a disappointing fifth. 'At the start I managed to fight it out with the leaders mainly because I had started on a new set of tyres and had good grip. Then my tyres were not so good and I just did the best I could.'

Berger, meanwhile, was happy to get through to fourth at the chequered flag, despite suffering from a misfire which he thought might have been caused by a cut-off sensor.

The crucial turning-point for Coulthard's victory prospects came after his second refuelling stop at the end of lap 50. He fitted fresh rubber, but found himself badly bogged down in traffic and was thus unable fully to capitalise on the three or four laps' enhanced grip it would offer.

Schumacher had gone through into the lead while David's FW17B was making its final refuelling stop, but the Williams driver found himself dropping back from 14.3s adrift on lap 51 to over 21 seconds by the time Michael came in for a quick, final 8.2s stop at the end of lap 60.

Coulthard just failed to retake the lead by four seconds and Schumacher was able to retain his advantage to the chequered flag, despite worrying gearchange problems which bugged him over the final 20 laps of the race. The German finished almost 15 seconds ahead to clinch his second World Championship, becoming the youngest driver ever to retain the crown.

In the Williams camp there was nothing but a perceptible air of acute disappointment, the team feeling – perhaps rather harshly – that the drivers had let them down.

Behind the two Ferraris, Herbert drove steadily to sixth place ahead of Frentzen's Sauber, Panis's Ligier and the McLaren-Mercs of Blundell and the impressive Magnussen. Both MP4/10Bs were two laps behind at the chequered flag – not something from which Coulthard could take much solace as he looked forward to his 1996 season with his new team.

PACIFIC GRAND PRIX

Left: This one's for you. Michael Schumacher clinched his second World Championship with another well-judged victory.

The German's Ferrari team-mate in 1996, Eddie Irvine *(above)*, shone in qualifying, taking sixth place on the grid with the Jordan-Peugeot, but was unable to repeat that form on race day.

It was a frustrating weekend for Damon Hill *(above right)*. Outpaced by his team-mate David Coulthard, he then became embroiled in another futile dispute with the new World Champion.

Jean Alesi *(right)* once again found that his Ferrari was no match for the Renault-powered cars and had to settle for fifth place, one lap down.

Steve Etherington/Empics

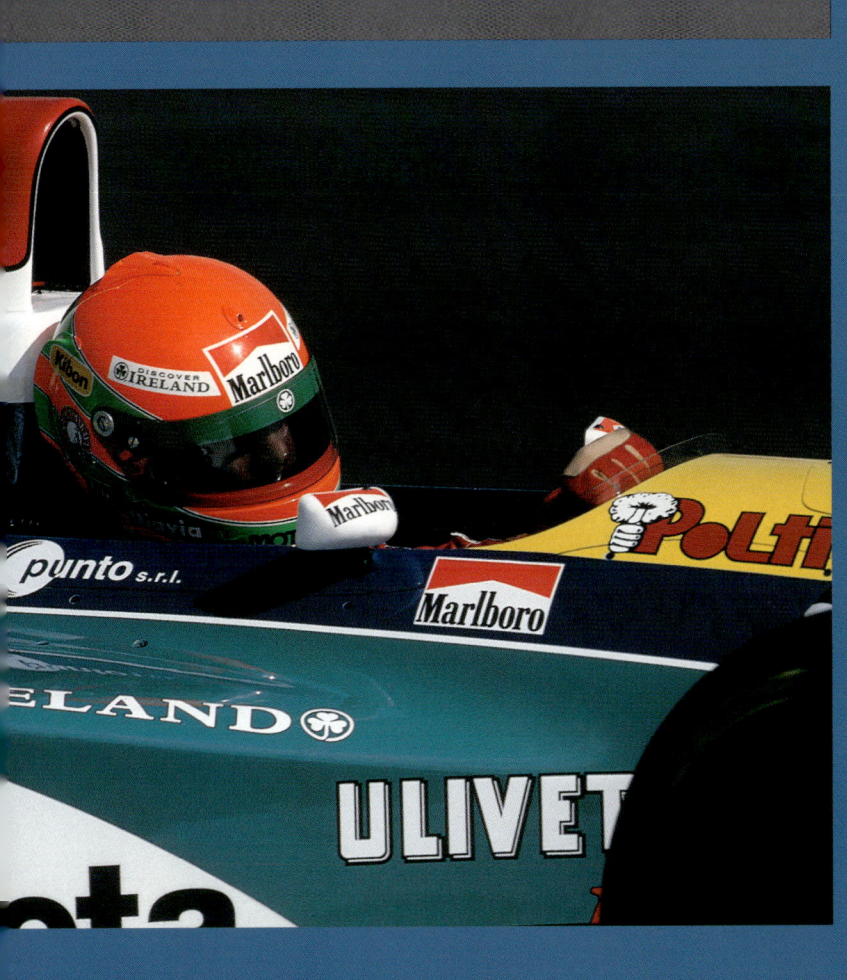

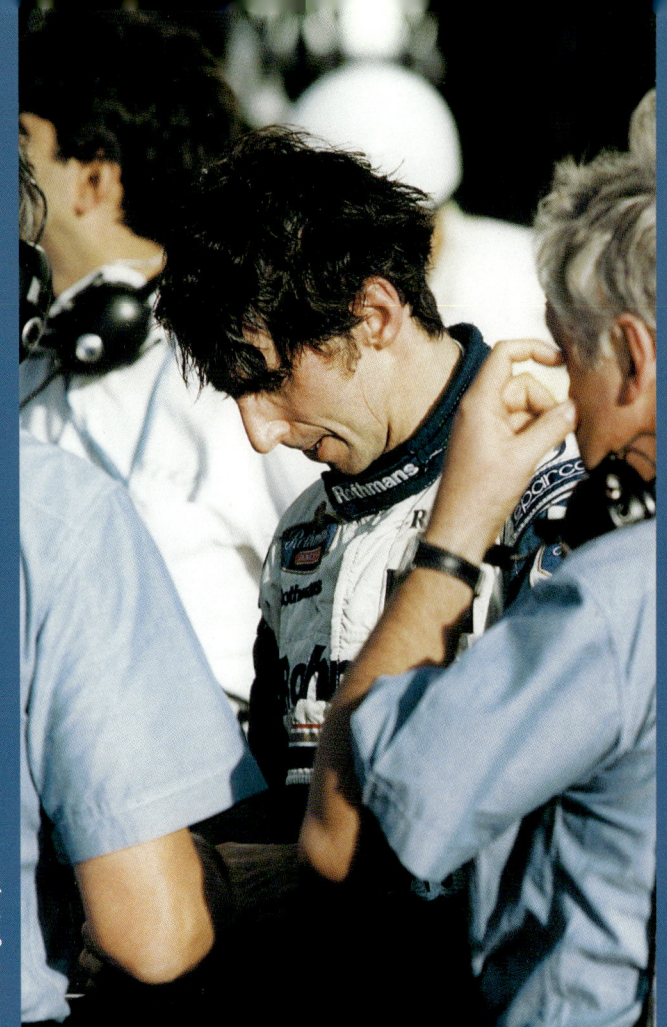

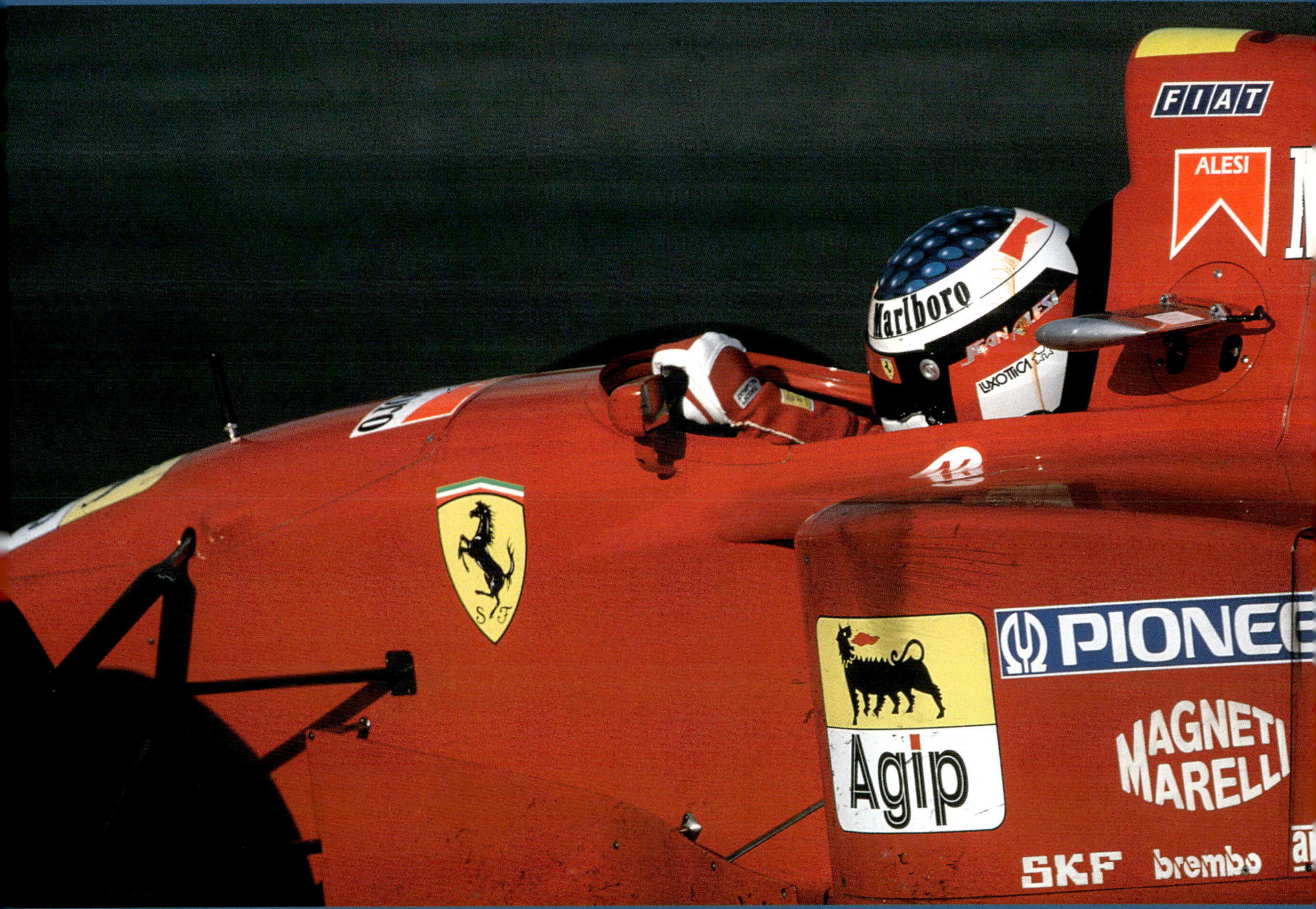

FIA FORMULA ONE WORLD CHAMPIONSHIP ROUND 15

T I AIDA PACIFIC GRAND PRIX
T I CIRCUIT
20–22 OCTOBER 1995

T I Circuit – Aida, Japan
Circuit length: 2.300 miles / 3.702 km

Race distance: 83 laps, 190.925 miles / 307.266 km
Race weather: Sunny and bright

Place	Driver	Nat.	No.	Entrant	Car/Engine	Laps	Time/Retirement	Speed (mph/km/h)
1	**Michael Schumacher**	D	1	Mild Seven Benetton Renault	Benetton B195-Renault RS7C V10	83	1h 48m 49.972s	105.286/169.442
2	**David Coulthard**	GB	6	Rothmans Williams Renault	Williams FW17B-Renault RS7C V10	83	1h 49m 04.892s	105.046/169.056
3	**Damon Hill**	GB	5	Rothmans Williams Renault	Williams FW17B-Renault RS7C V10	83	1h 49m 38.305s	104.512/168.197
4	**Gerhard Berger**	A	28	Scuderia Ferrari	Ferrari 412T2 044 V12	82		
5	**Jean Alesi**	F	27	Scuderia Ferrari	Ferrari 412T2 044 V12	82		
6	**Johnny Herbert**	GB	2	Mild Seven Benetton Renault	Benetton B195-Renault RS7C V10	82		
7	Heinz-Harald Frentzen	D	30	Red Bull Sauber Ford	Sauber C14-Ford Zetec-R V8	82		
8	Olivier Panis	F	26	Ligier Gitanes Blondes	Ligier JS41-Mugen Honda MF301 V10	81		
9	Mark Blundell	GB	7	Marlboro McLaren Mercedes	McLaren MP4/10B-Mercedes FO110 V10	81		
10	Jan Magnussen	DK	8	Marlboro McLaren Mercedes	McLaren MP4/10B-Mercedes FO110 V10	81		
11	Eddie Irvine	GB	15	Total Jordan Peugeot	Jordan 195-Peugeot A10 V10	81		
12	Mika Salo	SF	4	Nokia Tyrrell Yamaha	Tyrrell 023-Yamaha OX10C V10	80		
13	Pedro Lamy	P	23	Minardi Scuderia Italia	Minardi M195-Ford EDM V8	80		
14	Ukyo Katayama	J	3	Nokia Tyrrell Yamaha	Tyrrell 023-Yamaha OX10C V10	80		
15	Luca Badoer	I	24	Minardi Scuderia Italia	Minardi M195-Ford EDM V8	80		
16	Roberto Moreno	BR	22	Parmalat Forti Ford	Forti FG01-Ford ED V8	78		
17	Pedro Diniz	BR	21	Parmalat Forti Ford	Forti FG01-Ford ED V8	77		
	Rubens Barrichello	BR	14	Total Jordan Peugeot	Jordan 195-Peugeot A10 V10	67	Engine	
	Gianni Morbidelli	I	9	Footwork Hart	Footwork FA16-Hart 830 V8	53	Engine	
	Taki Inoue	J	10	Footwork Hart	Footwork FA16-Hart 830 V8	38	Engine	
	Andrea Montermini	I	17	Pacific Grand Prix Ltd	Pacific PR02-Ford ED V8	14	Gearbox	
	Aguri Suzuki	J	25	Ligier Gitanes Blondes	Ligier JS41-Mugen Honda MF301 V10	10	Spun off	
	Jean-Christophe Boullion	F	29	Red Bull Sauber Ford	Sauber C14-Ford Zetec-R V8	7	Spun off	
	Bertrand Gachot	F	16	Pacific Grand Prix Ltd	Pacific PR02-Ford ED V8	2	Hydraulics	

Fastest lap: Schumacher, on lap 40, 1m 16.374s, 108.457 mph/174.546 km/h.
Lap record: Michael Schumacher (F1 Benetton B194-Ford V8), 1m 14.023s, 111.872 mph/180.041 km/h (1994).
All cars used Goodyear tyres

All results and data © FIA 1995

STARTING GRID

Pos	Driver	Time	Team
	6 COULTHARD	(1m 14.013s)	Williams
	5 HILL	(1m 14.213s)	Williams
	1 SCHUMACHER	(1m 14.284s)	Benetton
	27 ALESI	(1m 14.919s)	Ferrari
	28 BERGER	(1m 14.974s)	Ferrari
	15 IRVINE	(1m 15.354s)	Jordan
	2 HERBERT	(1m 15.556s)	Benetton
	30 FRENTZEN	(1m 15.561s)	Sauber
	26 PANIS	(1m 15.621s)	Ligier
	7 BLUNDELL	(1m 15.652s)	McLaren
	14 BARRICHELLO	(1m 15.774s)	Jordan
	8 MAGNUSSEN	(1m 16.339s)	McLaren
	25 SUZUKI	(1m 16.519s)	Ligier
	23 LAMY	(1m 16.596s)	Minardi
	29 BOULLION	(1m 16.646s)	Sauber
	24 BADOER	(1m 16.887s)	Minardi
	3 KATAYAMA	(1m 17.014s)	Tyrrell
	4 SALO	(1m 17.213s)	Tyrrell
	9 MORBIDELLI	(1m 18.114s)	Footwork
	10 INOUE	(1m 18.212s)	Footwork
	21 DINIZ	(1m 19.579s)	Forti
	22 MORENO	(1m 19.745s)	Forti
	17 MONTERMINI	(1m 20.093s)	Pacific
	16 GACHOT	(1m 21.405s)	Pacific

FOR THE RECORD

100th Grand Prix start
Jean Alesi

TIME SHEETS

Friday free practice
Bright and sunny

Pos.	Driver	Laps	Time
1	Michael Schumacher	21	1m 16.057s
2	Damon Hill	23	1m 16.417s
3	David Coulthard	22	1m 16.480s
4	Gerhard Berger	14	1m 17.126s
5	Jean Alesi	17	1m 17.303s
6	Mark Blundell	23	1m 17.995s
7	Eddie Irvine	22	1m 18.002s
8	Heinz-Harald Frentzen	20	1m 18.059s
9	Jean-Christophe Boullion	23	1m 18.292s
10	Johnny Herbert	22	1m 18.372s
11	Rubens Barrichello	18	1m 18.377s
12	Olivier Panis	23	1m 18.839s
13	Pedro Lamy	23	1m 19.125s
14	Mika Salo	20	1m 19.137s
15	Jan Magnussen	23	1m 19.394s
16	Aguri Suzuki	20	1m 19.647s
17	Ukyo Katayama	23	1m 19.904s
18	Luca Badoer	23	1m 20.266s
19	Gianni Morbidelli	21	1m 20.323s
20	Andrea Montermini	5	1m 20.926s
21	Taki Inoue	8	1m 21.292s
22	Roberto Moreno	23	1m 21.963s
23	Pedro Diniz	23	1m 21.992s
24	Bertrand Gachot	2	1m 42.770s

Saturday free practice
Bright and warm

Pos.	Driver	Laps	Time
1	David Coulthard	22	1m 15.730s
2	Damon Hill	23	1m 16.086s
3	Jean Alesi	22	1m 16.408s
4	Eddie Irvine	22	1m 16.468s
5	Gerhard Berger	19	1m 16.488s
6	Michael Schumacher	23	1m 16.681s
7	Johnny Herbert	23	1m 16.833s
8	Heinz-Harald Frentzen	23	1m 16.959s
9	Rubens Barrichello	20	1m 17.560s
10	Jean-Christophe Boullion	23	1m 17.735s
11	Mark Blundell	9	1m 17.744s
12	Jan Magnussen	23	1m 17.872s
13	Olivier Panis	15	1m 17.982s
14	Ukyo Katayama	22	1m 18.003s
15	Aguri Suzuki	23	1m 18.226s
16	Pedro Lamy	23	1m 18.556s
17	Mika Salo	21	1m 18.933s
18	Gianni Morbidelli	17	1m 19.025s
19	Luca Badoer	23	1m 19.352s
20	Taki Inoue	21	1m 20.218s
21	Andrea Montermini	4	1m 21.281s
22	Pedro Diniz	23	1m 21.304s
23	Roberto Moreno	22	1m 21.626s
24	Bertrand Gachot	3	1m 24.195s

Friday qualifying
Bright and sunny

Pos.	Driver	Laps	Time
1	David Coulthard	10	1m 14.182s
2	Damon Hill	11	1m 14.289s
3	Michael Schumacher	12	1m 14.524s
4	**Jean Alesi**	9	**1m 14.919s**
5	**Gerhard Berger**	8	**1m 14.974s**
6	Johnny Herbert	12	1m 15.561s
7	**Mark Blundell**	10	**1m 15.652s**
8	Eddie Irvine	12	1m 15.696s
9	Heinz-Harald Frentzen	8	1m 15.942s
10	Rubens Barrichello	11	1m 16.263s
11	**Jan Magnussen**	11	**1m 16.339s**
12	**Jean-Christophe Boullion**	10	**1m 16.646s**
13	Aguri Suzuki	11	1m 17.019s
14	Olivier Panis	8	1m 17.071s
15	**Mika Salo**	12	**1m 17.213s**
16	Pedro Lamy	12	1m 17.224s
17	Ukyo Katayama	12	1m 17.265s
18	Luca Badoer	12	1m 17.612s
19	Gianni Morbidelli	12	1m 18.288s
20	Taki Inoue	12	1m 19.471s
21	**Roberto Moreno**	11	**1m 19.745s**
22	Pedro Diniz	10	1m 20.555s
23	Andrea Montermini	4	1m 22.096s
24	Bertrand Gachot	7	1m 22.710s

Saturday qualifying
Fine and bright

Pos.	Driver	Laps	Time
1	**David Coulthard**	6	**1m 14.013s**
2	**Damon Hill**	6	**1m 14.213s**
3	**Michael Schumacher**	12	**1m 14.284s**
4	Gerhard Berger	8	1m 15.125s
5	Jean Alesi	6	1m 15.131s
6	**Eddie Irvine**	12	**1m 15.354s**
7	**Johnny Herbert**	12	**1m 15.556s**
8	**Heinz-Harald Frentzen**	6	**1m 15.561s**
9	**Olivier Panis**	12	**1m 15.621s**
10	**Rubens Barrichello**	12	**1m 15.774s**
11	Mark Blundell	12	1m 16.166s
12	Jan Magnussen	8	1m 16.368s
13	**Aguri Suzuki**	9	**1m 16.519s**
14	**Pedro Lamy**	10	**1m 16.596s**
15	**Luca Badoer**	12	**1m 16.887s**
16	**Ukyo Katayama**	12	**1m 17.014s**
17	Mika Salo	12	1m 17.235s
18	**Gianni Morbidelli**	12	**1m 18.114s**
19	**Taki Inoue**	12	**1m 18.212s**
20	**Pedro Diniz**	12	**1m 19.579s**
21	Roberto Moreno	12	1m 19.779s
22	**Andrea Montermini**	7	**1m 20.093s**
23	**Bertrand Gachot**	10	**1m 21.405s**
24	Jean-Christophe Boullion	2	1m 23.791s

Warm-up
Sunny and bright

Pos.	Driver	Laps	Time
1	David Coulthard	14	1m 16.831s
2	Jean-Christophe Boullion	14	1m 17.531s
3	Damon Hill	18	1m 17.534s
4	Olivier Panis	16	1m 17.613s
5	Heinz-Harald Frentzen	13	1m 17.662s
6	Eddie Irvine	17	1m 17.970s
7	Gerhard Berger	11	1m 18.082s
8	Michael Schumacher	17	1m 18.181s
9	Jean Alesi	13	1m 18.183s
10	Mark Blundell	17	1m 18.293s
11	Johnny Herbert	15	1m 18.316s
12	Rubens Barrichello	15	1m 18.486s
13	Jan Magnussen	12	1m 18.972s
14	Gianni Morbidelli	15	1m 19.014s
15	Pedro Lamy	16	1m 19.502s
16	Mika Salo	13	1m 19.716s
17	Aguri Suzuki	19	1m 19.727s
18	Luca Badoer	18	1m 19.892s
19	Taki Inoue	17	1m 19.969s
20	Ukyo Katayama	16	1m 20.173s
21	Andrea Montermini	5	1m 20.992s
22	Pedro Diniz	15	1m 22.429s
23	Roberto Moreno	10	1m 22.985s
24	Bertrand Gachot	4	1m 23.580s

Fastest race laps
Sunny and bright

Driver	Time	Lap
Michael Schumacher	1m 16.374s	40
Damon Hill	1m 16.444s	72
David Coulthard	1m 16.674s	4
Eddie Irvine	1m 16.927s	76
Gerhard Berger	1m 17.795s	63
Jean Alesi	1m 17.854s	8
Heinz-Harald Frentzen	1m 17.913s	56
Johnny Herbert	1m 18.164s	65
Rubens Barrichello	1m 18.326s	43
Olivier Panis	1m 18.335s	29
Jan Magnussen	1m 18.631s	68
Mark Blundell	1m 18.983s	46
Ukyo Katayama	1m 19.574s	61
Aguri Suzuki	1m 19.816s	3
Mika Salo	1m 19.878s	69
Gianni Morbidelli	1m 19.975s	23
Pedro Lamy	1m 20.055s	4
Jean-Christophe Boullion	1m 20.099s	6
Luca Badoer	1m 20.299s	77
Andrea Montermini	1m 21.355s	4
Taki Inoue	1m 21.503s	7
Roberto Moreno	1m 22.102s	60
Pedro Diniz	1m 22.528s	32
Bertrand Gachot	1m 26.608s	2

CHASSIS LOG BOOK

No.	Driver	Chassis
1	Schumacher	Benetton B195/6
2	Herbert	Benetton B195/5
	spare	Benetton B195/1
3	Katayama	Tyrrell 023/6
4	Salo	Tyrrell 023/5
	spare	Tyrrell 023/2
5	Hill	Williams FW17B/4
6	Coulthard	Williams FW17B/5
	spare	Williams FW17B/3
7	Blundell	McLaren MP4/10B/4
8	Magnussen	McLaren MP4/10B/5
	spare	McLaren MP4/10B/3
9	Papis	Footwork FA16/3
10	Inoue	Footwork FA16/4
	spare	Footwork FA16/1
14	Barrichello	Jordan 195/4
15	Irvine	Jordan 195/5
	spare	Jordan 195/1
16	Gachot	Pacific PR02/1
17	Montermini	Pacific PR02/2
21	Diniz	Forti FG01/4
22	Moreno	Forti FG01/3
	spare	Forti FG01/2
23	Lamy	Minardi M195/3
24	Badoer	Minardi M195/2
	spare	Minardi M195/1
25	Suzuki	Ligier JS41/5
26	Panis	Ligier JS41/6
	spare	Ligier JS41/3
27	Alesi	Ferrari 412T2/161
28	Berger	Ferrari 412T2/162
	spare	Ferrari 412T2/160
29	Boullion	Sauber C14/5
30	Frentzen	Sauber C14/7
	spare	Sauber C14/6

POINTS TABLES

Drivers

1	Michael Schumacher	92
2	Damon Hill	59
3	David Coulthard	49
4	Jean Alesi	42
5	Johnny Herbert	41
6	Gerhard Berger	31
7	Heinz-Harald Frentzen	15
8 =	Mika Häkkinen	11
8 =	Rubens Barrichello	11
10	Mark Blundell	10
11	Olivier Panis	8
12 =	Martin Brundle	7
12 =	Eddie Irvine	7
14	Jean-Christophe Boullion	3
15	Mika Salo	2
16 =	Gianni Morbidelli	1
16 =	Aguri Suzuki	1

Constructors

1	Benetton	123
2	Williams	102
3	Ferrari	73
4	McLaren	21
5 =	Jordan	18
5 =	Sauber	18
7	Ligier	16
8	Tyrrell	2
9	Footwork	1

JAPANESE GRAND PRIX

Diary

Bernie Ecclestone celebrates 65th birthday by missing Japanese Grand Prix.

Jos Verstappen set to sign for Footwork team.

Ligier boss Tom Walkinshaw denies approach to Pedro Diniz.

Emerson Fittipaldi to race for newly established Hogan-Penske Indy Car team in 1996.

Thumbs-up from an exultant Michael Schumacher after recording his ninth win of the season. Together with team-mate Johnny Herbert's third place, the German's latest triumph gave the Benetton team its first constructors' championship, to the intense satisfaction of team boss Flavio Briatore, who waits to congratulate his star driver.

As at Aida the previous weekend, Damon Hill's hopes of a late-season renaissance collapsed in chaos during the Japanese Grand Prix as Michael Schumacher breezed to his ninth win of the year, equalling Nigel Mansell's record established in 1992. It was a success which gave Benetton its first-ever constructors' championship title, the Enstone team taking this prestigious crown from Williams, who had shared it with McLaren since 1984.

Ironically, Hill took the lead briefly on lap 32 of the 53-lap race after Schumacher made his second scheduled refuelling stop. But when Damon came in for his own second stop at the end of lap 35, allowing Schumacher back ahead, everything began to go wrong for the Williams driver.

Two laps later, during a light rain shower, he slid off the circuit and had to come into the pits for a replacement nose section to be fitted to his car. In doing so, he exceeded the pit lane speed limit and, having dropped to fifth, was on his way back to the pits to take the penalty when he spun off for good.

Despite then being hit with a $10,000 fine in lieu of his stop-go penalty, Hill finished the day looking remarkably upbeat for a man apparently surrounded by gossip that Williams would really like to replace him.

'Just when you think it couldn't get any worse, it does,' he said. 'There is no easy way out of this, you just have to keep pressing on. The easiest thing to do is to give up, and it would probably be less painful that way, but that is not an option.'

Mika Häkkinen finished the race a strong second after the most convincing performance yet from the McLaren-Mercedes alliance, with Johnny Herbert third to put the icing on the cake of Benetton's constructors' title.

Damon Hill's pursuit of Michael Schumacher followed its now firmly established, familiar pattern when the Englishman again played second fiddle to the newly crowned World Champion in the first qualifying session at Suzuka. Schumacher went into the race with two aims in mind – to equal Nigel Mansell's one-season record of nine Grand Prix wins and then set a new bench-mark with a tenth victory in the final race of the season, the Australian GP at Adelaide on 12 November.

After a struggle with his car's handling balance which left him grim-faced and non-committal at the end of the morning's free practice session, Hill made key changes to the chassis set-up of his Williams FW17B-Renault to vault up to second place.

'I think our car is competitive and capable of getting pole position,' he predicted. 'It is just a question of getting more out of it tomorrow. On my qualifying run today I had a problem with the car running too low, so my backside got roasted as the underside scraped along the ground.

'As far as fastest time is concerned, it is a trademark of Michael's that he always manages to pull out something extra, so you just have to go back to your reserves and find something extra yourself.'

At the end of the Friday free practice session Hill had stormed back to the Williams team office without offering a word to the assembled British media contingent waiting behind the team's pit. It wasn't a surprising reaction; in the aftermath of his Pacific GP debacle, the armchair tabloid press back in England had once again written his career obituary in an unforgiving style they would never have dared employ with Nigel Mansell. Small wonder he gave them short shrift.

But there was something else. Struggling to change damper settings, fiddling with springs and rear wing adjustments, Damon had come close to exasperating the Williams team management with the amount of time he took to work out a decent chassis balance. Just like he'd done in the same session exactly 12 months earlier.

Third-fastest time fell to Mika Häkkinen in the hitherto disappointing McLaren MP4/10B, which benefited from a revised-specification Mercedes V10 engine offering further-enhanced driveability and slightly more power. Häkkinen, who was returning to the cockpit after missing the Pacific Grand Prix while recovering from an appendectomy, more than made up for the disappointment suffered by his team-mate Mark Blundell, who slid off into a gravel trap on only his second lap, breaking the MP4/10B's left-rear suspension pushrod in the process, and ended up languishing 24th and slowest overnight.

Jean Alesi's Ferrari was fourth ahead of Suzuka first-timer David Coulthard in the other Williams-Renault, Heinz-Harald Frentzen in the Sauber-Ford and Eddie Irvine's Jordan-Peugeot.

Further back, Johnny Herbert celebrated the first anniversary of his promotion to the position of Schumacher's Benetton team-mate in unfortunate fashion when he lost control and crashed heavily into a tyre barrier. He was unhurt, although taken briefly to the circuit medical centre for a check-up.

'On my first run, I got one lap in but went off over the kerb when pushed,' he explained. 'On the next lap I was held up a bit, then I managed to clock a time, but decided I was not doing enough and pushed harder.

'But the car was very snappy and nervous. It just went off. It was a fairly heavy impact, but I was OK.'

In the Sauber team, Austrian Karl Wendlinger made his second F1 return of the season, now hopefully fully recovered from the practice accident at Monaco last year which had left him in a coma for 19 days. He could only manage 17th-fastest time, 3.6s slower than team-mate Frentzen. It was not a promising start.

If Williams had been disappointed with Hill on Friday, this was as nothing compared to the look on Patrick Head's face after Damon spun into a gravel trap exiting the Spoon Curve during free practice on Saturday. Then, right at the end of the session, Coulthard followed suit but just managed to coax his FW17B back onto the circuit.

A few minutes later, Mark Blundell's misfortunes continued when he slammed off the road at around 170 mph on the fast left-hand kink before the start/finish chicane. The MP4/10B hurtled into the tyre barrier, shedding its nosebox, and Blundell was fortunate to be able to stagger away from the wreck, shaken but not stirred. After a medical check-up, Blundell was advised to sit out the second qualifying session, but the McLaren monocoque, amazingly, was deemed repairable.

Despite cooler temperatures, track conditions were not significantly quicker in final qualifying, largely because the cars had benefited from a tail wind on the long straight on Friday – the most significant improvement in the opening exchanges coming from Gerhard Berger, who posted a 1m 39.040s best to push Häkkinen's McLaren-Merc out of third place.

Then with ten minutes of the session left, Aguri Suzuki dropped his Ligier's right-front wheel onto the grass going into one of the fast ess-bends behind the paddock. Instantly the Mugen-engined car snapped out of control and pirouetted at almost undiminished speed into the tyre barrier.

The moment the JS41 slid to rest on the side of the circuit, Suzuki undid the removable steering wheel, hurling it overboard as if he were about to get out of the car. But it soon became clear that he had sustained some injury and the session was red-flagged to a halt, allowing FIA Medical Delegate Professor Watkins to come out and attend to him.

Suzuki was immediately taken by ambulance to the circuit medical centre, then by helicopter on to hospital where he was diagnosed as suffering from a cracked vertebra and internal lung bleeding. The session was delayed for around 20 minutes until the medical helicopter returned and then resumed with Häkkinen's McLaren the first car back onto the circuit.

With six minutes of the session left, Hill went out in an attempt to get on terms with Schumacher, but his Williams lacked its customary handling poise on this low-downforce circuit. In particular, Damon dropped his right-rear wheel over the kerb at the point where Blundell had lost control during the morning, but was fortunate enough to get away with it.

Suddenly Alesi popped up in second place with a 1m 38.888s best, the Frenchman taking the chequered flag then braking hard and pulling over to the right, where he stopped, knowing full well that he had insufficient fuel to complete another lap. Hill was now feeling the pressure more than ever.

A few moments later Häkkinen turned a 1m 38.954s to move up into third place, just as Berger's Ferrari pushed in ahead of David Coulthard's Williams, the Scot now demoted to sixth. Finally, starting his last lap barely seven seconds before the chequered flag came out, Schumacher rubbed in the message with a 1m 38.023s. It was the final word.

Coulthard was able to articulate what he felt was wrong with his car. 'I had a touch of understeer yesterday, but it wasn't too difficult to manage because the rear end felt pretty stable,' he explained. 'Today the rear end felt loose, which made it more difficult to keep control of the understeer.'

Hill was less specific. 'Nobody is more disappointed than myself and the team. We have to investigate

JAPANESE GRAND PRIX

Williams gives vote of confidence to Hill

Team chief Frank Williams offered an unequivocal vote of confidence to Damon Hill in the run-up to Suzuka after a difficult week during which he had seemed more than usually under critical siege from the British daily press. Hill had been the subject of several attacks following his failure to challenge Michael Schumacher in the previous weekend's Pacific Grand Prix. However, Williams made it clear that Damon continued to enjoy his complete confidence.

'If he's getting a slagging [in the media] that must mean he is as good as Nigel Mansell used to be – he must have attained Nigel's eminence.

'You say he has taken a bit of a pounding. Before Aida, I read for the second time a marvellous book by Elizabeth Longford about Wellington and Waterloo. He said, "By God, we are taking a pounding." But let's see who can pound the hardest. Do you see what I mean?

'I am sure he [Damon] will give as good as he gets and in the next race he could turn round and piss on everyone.

'I have had doubts about him of course; you cannot ignore your problems, and he has obviously gone off the boil a couple of times. But he is improving all the time. We have made our decision and are happy with that.'

Williams's ringing endorsement came after speculation had suggested he was keen to terminate Hill's 1996 contract, perhaps swapping him with Gerhard Berger at Benetton or Heinz-Harald Frentzen at Sauber. However, such allegations were specifically denied yet again.

Hill remained remarkably sanguine about the whole business. 'As far as thinking about the championship is concerned, that's history,' he said. 'I am now thinking about the last two races of the season and looking forward to next season already.'

He was not impressed when he was told that Michael Schumacher, having examined the video of the Pacific GP, no longer blames him for what happened in that race. 'I don't want to comment on that at all. I've not got any views I want to expand on here. I want to forget all that.'

As far as prospects for 1996 are concerned, Hill admits that he will take a rest from driving immediately after the end of the season. 'I think I need to stand back from it for a while,' he said, 'but I'll be back in the car before Christmas. It will be Jacques [Villeneuve] and Jules [Boullion] doing the testing to start with.'

Asked whether he detected any diminution in confidence from the Williams team, he replied: 'I can't really comment on what other people might feel and think unless they come up to me and say it.

'But I tell you this: it has been a tough season. It hasn't gone all to plan; there have been more downs than ups and I understand more about the pressures involved in trying to win a championship than I did last year.'

why we were not competitive. I was surprised by the performance of the McLaren and even more impressed by Michael's performance right at the end of the session.' He had no explanations or excuses to offer for failing to improve his time.

With Irvine seventh, Jordan continued its steady progress immediately outside the established top six front-runners. Eddie had less understeer on the second day and prudently saved his second set of new rubber for Sunday's race.

By contrast, Rubens Barrichello experimented with his chassis set-up and finally reverted to the one he had employed on Friday. He managed to go quicker, but the time was aborted due to the red flag for the Suzuki accident. It was extremely frustrating for the young Brazilian, who would line up in tenth place on the grid, separated from his team-mate by the Sauber of Heinz-Harald Frentzen and Johnny Herbert's Benetton.

Olivier Panis found the handling balance of his Ligier-Mugen not so good on the second day, failing to improve. He started 11th ahead of Mika Salo's Tyrrell-Yamaha, both the Finn and team-mate Ukyo Katayama suffering from too much time-consuming understeer at the start/finish chicane.

The two Tyrrells were split by the luckless Suzuki, with Footwork returnee Gianni Morbidelli winding up 15th after struggling to make up his mind whether or not to persist with a new floor, the revised exhaust on which kept breaking. Karl Wendlinger was 16th, improving on the second day but still remaining almost three seconds slower than Frentzen's best.

Frentzen had problems on Saturday morning, stopping out on the circuit with engine trouble, his car then being refitted with the Zetec-R V8 he had used on Friday for final qualifying. The bottom line was that he had too much understeer, slipping from sixth to eighth in the final order as Berger and Irvine went quicker.

In the Minardi camp Pedro Lamy and Luca Badoer were a well-matched 17th and 18th, ahead of Taki Inoue's Footwork and Andrea Montermini's Pacific, which briefly caught fire in the pit garage on Saturday morning due to an oil leak onto an exhaust.

Diniz, Moreno and Gachot completed the last two rows in company with Blundell, although there was a question mark over the McLaren driver's participation as he had completed only a single qualifying lap over the two days.

The start took place in wet conditions and, although the rain had stopped, the field was on rain tyres as Schumacher accelerated away into an immediate lead from Alesi, Häkkinen and Hill. Morbidelli's Footwork spun in the middle of the pack at the first corner after being tapped from behind by Karl Wendlinger's Sauber, the Italian stalling the engine and retiring on the spot.

Even before this, Moreno's Forti had been pushed back into the pits with a malfunctioning gearbox sensor. Roberto started from the pit lane but, with the system running no better, came in to retire after a single lap.

Meanwhile, at the end of the opening lap, Schumacher led by 1.5s from Alesi, Häkkinen, Hill, Irvine, Coulthard, Berger, Barrichello and Herbert. Further back, Blundell's McLaren had already made seven places from 24th to 17th and was closing on Inoue's Footwork.

By lap four, Schumacher had opened a 2.7s gap, just as the Ferrari team was advised that both its drivers had incurred a ten-second stop-go penalty for jumping the start. Next time round, Alesi duly came in to take his penalty, dropping from second to tenth behind Frentzen's Sauber.

On lap six Berger came in for his

JAPANESE GRAND PRIX

Heinz-Harald Frentzen aims his Sauber C14 down the inside of Johnny Herbert's Benetton-Renault. While the Englishman's gift for staying out of trouble allowed him to pick up another rostrum finish, Frentzen could manage no better than eighth place.

Bottom: Karl Wendlinger swoops down on the Footwork of Taki Inoue. Restored to the Sauber line-up in an attempt to revive his fading F1 career, the Austrian was again unable to approach the pace of his highly regarded team-mate.

stop-go penalty, losing nine places. On the following lap Alesi came in for slicks and fuel, resuming in 15th place. Jean's arrival in the pits was a typically emotional affair, the Frenchman jinking right across the bows of Herbert's Benetton to enter the pit lane a split-second after overtaking the Englishman coming through the immediately preceding flat-out left-hander. One could only speculate as to precisely what Alesi had been thinking about . . .

Schumacher was now 12.5s ahead of Häkkinen with Hill third, but Ferrari's decision to bring Alesi in for slicks immediately after his stop-go had been a tactical master-stroke which gave him a terrific advantage as the racing line was now drying out very quickly. He was soon climbing through the field, although his meteoric progress was briefly interrupted when he was forced into a spin down the grass as Lamy's Minardi moved over on him coming out of the start/finish chicane. Undaunted, Jean continued and held position.

With nine laps completed, Hill came in for a routine refuelling stop and slicks (8.2s), dropping from third to fifth. A lap later Schumacher followed suit (8.4s), allowing Häkkinen into the lead.

At the same moment, Alesi came storming up onto Hill's tail as they braked for the pits chicane. Without a second's hesitation, Jean slammed down the outside and cut across Damon's bows going into the tight right-hander. Hill gave him racing room in a disciplined manner.

Predictably, opinion was subsequently divided. Was Damon acting ethically? Or did he simply cave in under pressure? It seems you can't please even some of the people even some of the time in this business.

Either way, with Coulthard making his first stop, Alesi and Hill moved from fifth and sixth to fourth and fifth, which became second and third when Häkkinen came in for his first stop at the end of lap 11 after a brief moment of glory in the lead, followed by Irvine. Mika spent 6.5s refuelling and fitting slicks, dropping to fourth behind Schumacher, Alesi and Hill.

On lap 16 Barrichello's seventh-placed Jordan somehow contrived to spin into team-mate Irvine under braking for the chicane, but while Eddie continued, Rubens pirouetted to a stop in the gravel.

'The first time I tried to come in and change tyres, I was a bit too quick, so I had to do another lap and that cost me a lot of time,' explained Rubens.

'My car was set up more for slicks than wets, so I was a bit faster than Eddie when the track dried. I could see Coulthard pulling away ahead, and I thought I could overtake Eddie easily at the chicane, but I put a wheel on the wet and spun. Thankfully he kept going, because I knew it would be very big trouble for me if he didn't!'

Immediately afterwards a dejected Berger retired from ninth place with engine electronic sensor problems.

'I don't know what to say,' he fumed. 'That was the same sensor which had given me problems in other races. As for my penalty, I really think the control system is not very good.

'I realised that the car had started to move as the track slopes downhill, and so I braked. Because of that I made a bad start and dropped two places. And they call that a jumped start?'

The battle for the lead was shaping up nicely now. On lap 19 Alesi closed to within a second of Schumacher as Hill was gently easing away from Häkkinen's fourth-placed McLaren.

Irvine had more problems in store; Frentzen took a turn to ram his Jordan under braking for the hairpin as they battled for sixth. Irvine spun and recovered, but Frentzen's C14 lost its nose section and the German

came in for a replacement, resuming in tenth place.

On lap 25 the gallant Alesi retired from second place out on the circuit with apparent differential failure. On closer examination it was discovered that a driveshaft joint had failed inside the gearbox, possibly as a result of Jean's wild spin across the run-off as he avoided Lamy's Minardi. It was a bitter pill for the Frenchman to swallow. Together with Schumacher, he had been the absolute star of the show. But not blessed with the Benetton's mechanical reliability, his Ferrari had now wilted yet again.

'It would be presumptuous of me to say I could have won,' shrugged Alesi, 'but I would certainly have fought for it, all the way to the end. I tried again to win today and I was in a bad mood, because I was convinced I did not jump the start. The grid slopes downhill and, although the car crept forwards by a few centimetres, it was certainly not intentional.'

Schumacher now led by 19.5s from Hill with Häkkinen third ahead of Coulthard, Irvine and Herbert. On lap 28 Häkkinen made a second refuelling stop, dropping from third to fourth behind Coulthard. Three laps later, Schumacher made his second refuelling stop (12.1s), resuming in second behind Hill.

Everything began to go wrong for Williams the moment Coulthard and Hill had made their second refuelling stops. David came in on lap 34 for an 11.5s stop and just squeezed out in third place ahead of Häkkinen's McLaren. On the following lap Damon came in, was stationary for 10.5s and dropped from first to second behind Schumacher again.

Suddenly on lap 37 Hill went autocrossing into the gravel at Spoon Curve as a light rain shower doused the circuit, dropping to fourth and coming in for a replacement nose section. In the process, he exceeded the pit lane speed limit and was given a ten-second stop-go. Now back in fifth place, he was not to remain in the race long enough to take the penalty.

On lap 40 Coulthard imitated Hill's autocrossing at the Spoon Curve, regained the circuit and then spun off with gravel on his rear tyres at the same spot which had claimed Blundell in practice.

'The rain was spitting a little round here, but when I got round the back [of the circuit] there was a lot of rain at that corner and I just ran wide into the gravel,' explained Coulthard.

219

JAPANESE GRAND PRIX

Mika Häkkinen's McLaren-Mercedes leads the pursuit of Michael Schumacher and Jean Alesi in the early stages, with Damon Hill, Eddie Irvine, David Coulthard, Gerhard Berger, Rubens Barrichello, Johnny Herbert and Heinz-Harald Frentzen completing the top ten.

'Then when I got to the fast corner, as I dabbed my brakes all the gravel came out of the side pods and I spun on it. It's a disappointing way to end the weekend especially after the guys did a brilliant job in the pits to get me out in front of Mika.'

The Williams personnel were by now pretty depressed, but then their frustration was compounded when Hill spun off for good at Spoon Curve – just as he had done on Saturday morning – while running fourth. The final straw was when he was fined $10,000 for his pit lane speeding infringement.

'While we were in the race we were competitive and I was in with a shout, I suppose, all the time I was on the track,' said Hill. 'But things took a massive turn for the worse, I am afraid.

'I drove through the rain and the second time I spun off I think it was oil rather than rain. It is not a glorious end to the season but the ingredients are all there and there is no reason why we should not get into the winning habit again.'

And so it came to pass after 53 laps that Michael Schumacher won his ninth Grand Prix of the season from Häkkinen and Herbert with Irvine the only other unlapped runner. Panis was fifth for Ligier with Blundell just failing – by 1.8s – to catch Salo's Tyrrell for sixth place and the last championship point.

Frentzen was a disappointed eighth with the Minardis of Badoer and Lamy sandwiching Wendlinger's tenth-placed Sauber. The only other runner to make the finish was Taki Inoue in the Footwork, the Japanese driver reporting that the FA16 seemed to have an extremely good handling balance on slick tyres.

As Benetton celebrated its first constructors' championship title with suitable gusto, McLaren was equally buoyed by Häkkinen's second place. 'For us it was almost as good as a win,' grinned Norbert Haug, the Mercedes-Benz motor sport manager.

Meanwhile, Schumacher was ecstatic. 'It's a really great feeling now, because I fulfilled the promises that I made to the team at the beginning of the season to get both titles.'

It had been another sparkling demonstration of Michael Schumacher's genius, although Alesi's performance certainly gave Benetton a boost when they looked ahead to 1996. For Hill and Williams it was more than a little difficult to see a path through the trees.

FIA FORMULA ONE WORLD CHAMPIONSHIP ROUND 16

FUJI TELEVISION JAPANESE GRAND PRIX
SUZUKA CIRCUIT
27–29 OCTOBER 1995

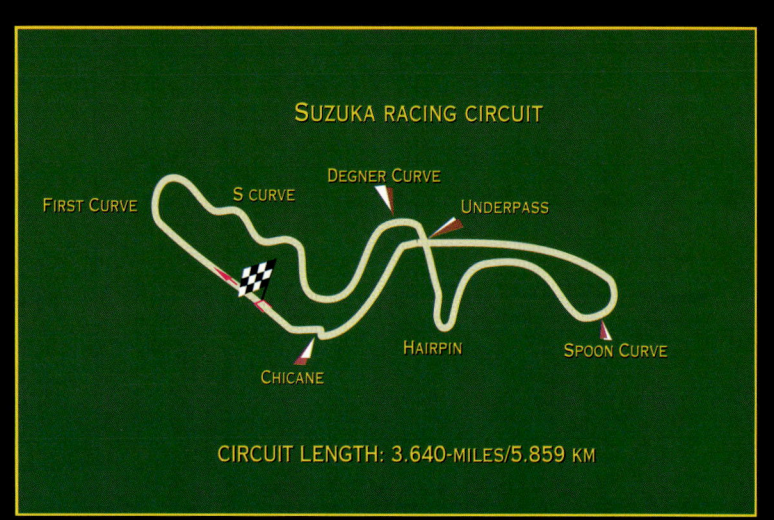

Suzuka Racing Circuit — First Curve, S Curve, Degner Curve, Underpass, Hairpin, Spoon Curve, Chicane

CIRCUIT LENGTH: 3.640-MILES/5.859 KM

Race distance: 53 laps, 192.952 miles/310.527 km
Race weather: Overcast, then dry

Place	Driver	Nat.	No.	Entrant	Car/Engine	Laps	Time/Retirement	Speed (mph/km/h)
1	**Michael Schumacher**	D	1	Mild Seven Benetton Renault	Benetton B195-Renault RS7C V10	53	1h 36m 52.930s	119.519/192.349
2	**Mika Häkkinen**	SF	8	Marlboro McLaren Mercedes	McLaren MP4/10B-Mercedes FO110 V10	53	1h 37m 12.267s	119.124/191.712
3	**Johnny Herbert**	GB	2	Mild Seven Benetton Renault	Benetton B195-Renault RS7C V10	53	1h 38m 16.734s	117.821/189.616
4	**Eddie Irvine**	GB	15	Total Jordan Peugeot	Jordan 195-Peugeot A10 V10	53	1h 38m 35.066s	117.456/189.028
5	Olivier Panis	F	26	Ligier Gitanes Blondes	Ligier JS41-Mugen Honda MF301 V10	52		
6	Mika Salo	SF	4	Nokia Tyrrell Yamaha	Tyrrell 023-Yamaha OX10C V10	52		
7	Mark Blundell	GB	7	Marlboro McLaren Mercedes	McLaren MP4/10B-Mercedes FO110 V10	52		
8	Heinz-Harald Frentzen	D	30	Red Bull Sauber Ford	Sauber C14-Ford Zetec-R V8	52		
9	Luca Badoer	I	24	Minardi Scuderia Italia	Minardi M195-Ford EDM V8	51		
10	Karl Wendlinger	A	29	Red Bull Sauber Ford	Sauber C14-Ford Zetec-R V8	51		
11	Pedro Lamy	P	23	Minardi Scuderia Italia	Minardi M195-Ford EDM V8	51		
12	Taki Inoue	J	10	Footwork Hart	Footwork FA16-Hart 830 V8	51		
	Damon Hill	GB	5	Rothmans Williams Renault	Williams FW17B-Renault RS7C V10	40	Spun off	
	David Coulthard	GB	6	Rothmans Williams Renault	Williams FW17B-Renault RS7C V10	39	Spun off	
	Pedro Diniz	BR	21	Parmalat Forti Ford	Forti FG01-Ford ED V8	32	Spun off	
	Jean Alesi	F	27	Scuderia Ferrari	Ferrari 412T2 044 V12	24	Differential	
	Andrea Montermini	I	17	Pacific Grand Prix Ltd	Pacific PR02-Ford ED V8	23	Spun off	
	Gerhard Berger	A	28	Scuderia Ferrari	Ferrari 412T2 044 V12	16	Electronic sensor	
	Rubens Barrichello	BR	14	Total Jordan Peugeot	Jordan 195-Peugeot A10 V10	15	Spun off	
	Ukyo Katayama	J	3	Nokia Tyrrell Yamaha	Tyrrell 023-Yamaha OX10C V10	12	Spun off	
	Bertrand Gachot	F	16	Pacific Grand Prix Ltd	Pacific PR02-Ford ED V8	6	Driveshaft bearing	
	Roberto Moreno	BR	22	Parmalat Forti Ford	Forti FG01-Ford ED V8	1	Gearbox	
	Gianni Morbidelli	I	9	Footwork Hart	Footwork FA16-Hart 830 V8	0	Spun off	
DNS	Aguri Suzuki	J	25	Ligier Gitanes Blondes	Ligier JS41-Mugen Honda MF301 V10	0	Qualifying accident	

Fastest lap: Schumacher, on lap 33, 1m 42.976s, 127.382 mph/205.003 km/h.
Lap record: Nigel Mansell (F1 Williams FW14B-Renault V10), 1m 40.646s, 130.332 mph/209.749 km/h (1992).
All cars used Goodyear tyres

All results and data © FIA 1995

Grid order		1	2	3	4	5	6	7	8	9	10	11	12	13	14	15	16	17	18	19	20	21	22	23	24	25	26	27	28	29	30	31	32	33	34	35	36	37	38	39	40
1	SCHUMACHER	1	1	1	1	1	1	1	1	1	1	8	1	1	1	1	1	1	1	1	1	1	1	1	1	1	1	1	1	1	1	1	1	5	5	5	5	1	1	1	1
27	ALESI	27	27	27	27	27	8	8	8	8	8	1	27	27	27	27	27	27	27	27	27	27	27	27	27	5	5	5	5	5	5	5	1	1	1	1	1	6	6	6	8
8	HÄKKINEN	8	8	8	8	8	5	5	5	15	15	15	5	5	5	5	5	5	5	5	5	5	5	5	5	8	8	8	8	6	6	6	6	6	6	6	6	8	8	8	2
5	HILL	5	5	5	5	5	15	15	15	5	6	27	8	8	8	8	8	8	8	8	8	8	8	8	8	6	6	6	6	8	8	8	8	8	8	8	5	2	2	5	
28	BERGER	15	15	15	15	15	6	6	6	6	5	5	15	15	15	6	6	6	6	6	6	6	6	6	6	15	15	2	2	2	2	2	2	2	2	2	2	5	5	15	
6	COULTHARD	6	6	6	6	6	28	14	30	30	30	6	6	6	6	15	15	15	15	15	15	15	15	15	15	2	2	15	15	15	15	15	15	15	15	15	15	30	30	30	
15	IRVINE	28	28	28	28	28	14	2	4	4	24	14	14	14	14	30	30	30	30	30	2	2	2	2	2	26	26	26	26	4	4	30	30	30	30	30	30	15	15	26	
30	FRENTZEN	14	14	14	14	14	2	30	14	24	14	2	2	30	30	2	2	2	2	2	4	4	4	4	4	4	4	4	4	30	30	4	26	26	26	26	26	26	26		
2	HERBERT	2	2	2	2	2	30	4	2	27	2	30	30	2	2	28	4	4	4	4	26	26	26	26	26	30	30	30	30	7	7	7	4	4	4	4	4	4	7		
14	BARRICHELLO	30	30	30	30	30	27	27	24	28	30	24	28	28	28	4	26	26	26	26	30	30	30	30	30	7	7	7	7	26	26	26	7	7	7	7	7	7	24		
26	PANIS	26	26	26	26	26	4	26	28	2	28	28	4	4	4	26	7	7	7	7	7	7	7	7	7	24	24	24	24	24	24	24	24	24	24	29	29	29	23		
4	SALO	4	4	4	4	4	26	28	26	3	4	4	24	26	26	7	23	23	23	23	23	23	23	23	23	29	29	29	29	29	29	29	29	29	29	24	24	24	29		
25	SUZUKI	24	24	24	24	24	3	3	14	4	7	23	26	24	24	23	29	29	29	29	29	29	29	29	29	23	23	23	23	23	23	23	23	10	10	10	10	10	10		
3	KATAYAMA	3	3	3	3	3	23	23	27	7	27	7	7	7	7	29	17	17	17	17	17	17	17	17	10	10	10	10	10	10	10	10	10								
9	MORBIDELLI	23	23	23	23	23	29	29	7	14	3	3	10	10	10	17	10	10	10	10	10	10	10	10	21	21	21	21	21	21	21	21									
29	WENDLINGER	10	7	7	7	7	7	7	29	26	10	23	7	29	29	17	10	10	10	10	10	10	10	21																	
23	LAMY	7	10	10	10	10	10	10	10	29	10	29	7	10	10	10	21	21	21	21	21	21	21																		
24	BADOER	17	17	17	17	29	17	17	17	29	7	17	10	21																											
10	INOUE	16	16	29	29	17	17	17	17	26	17	17	21																												
17	MONTERMINI	29	29	16	16	16	21	21	21	21	21																														
21	DINIZ	21	21	21	21	21																																			
22	MORENO	22																																							
16	GACHOT																																								
7	BLUNDELL																																								

Pit stop
One lap behind leader

STARTING GRID

1	SCHUMACHER (1m 38.023s) Benetton	27	ALESI (1m 38.888s) Ferrari
8	HÄKKINEN (1m 38.954s) McLaren	5	HILL (1m 39.032s) Williams
28	BERGER (1m 39.040s) Ferrari	6	COULTHARD (1m 39.155s) Williams
15	IRVINE (1m 39.621s) Jordan	30	FRENTZEN (1m 40.010s) Sauber
2	HERBERT (1m 40.349s) Benetton	14	BARRICHELLO (1m 40.381s) Jordan
26	PANIS (1m 40.838s) Ligier	4	SALO (1m 41.355s) Tyrrell
25	SUZUKI* (1m 41.592s) Ligier	3	KATAYAMA (1m 41.977s) Tyrrell
9	MORBIDELLI (1m 42.059s) Footwork	29	WENDLINGER (1m 42.912s) Sauber
23	LAMY (1m 43.102s) Minardi	24	BADOER (1m 43.542s) Minardi
10	INOUE (1m 44.074s) Footwork	17	MONTERMINI (1m 46.097s) Pacific
21	DINIZ (1m 46.654s) Forti	22	MORENO (1m 48.267s) Forti
16	GACHOT (1m 48.289s) Pacific	7	BLUNDELL (16m 42.640s) McLaren

did not start due to qualifying accident

TIME SHEETS

Friday free practice
Bright and sunny

Pos.	Driver	Laps	Time
1	Michael Schumacher	19	1m 40.410s
2	Mika Häkkinen	19	1m 40.694s
3	Damon Hill	22	1m 41.024s
4	Jean Alesi	14	1m 41.283s
5	David Coulthard	23	1m 41.492s
6	Gerhard Berger	15	1m 41.952s
7	Rubens Barrichello	17	1m 42.147s
8	Heinz-Harald Frentzen	12	1m 42.294s
9	Johnny Herbert	21	1m 42.381s
10	Mark Blundell	21	1m 42.910s
11	Olivier Panis	23	1m 43.045s
12	Eddie Irvine	16	1m 43.660s
13	Mika Salo	21	1m 44.414s
14	Ukyo Katayama	21	1m 44.443s
15	Karl Wendlinger	23	1m 44.810s
16	Gianni Morbidelli	9	1m 44.906s
17	Aguri Suzuki	20	1m 45.377s
18	Taki Inoue	21	1m 45.871s
19	Pedro Lamy	22	1m 45.901s
20	Luca Badoer	16	1m 47.371s
21	Andrea Montermini	9	1m 48.657s
22	Pedro Diniz	23	1m 48.877s
23	Bertrand Gachot	17	1m 49.655s
24	Roberto Moreno	2	2m 17.198s

Saturday free practice
Dry, overcast

Pos.	Driver	Laps	Time
1	Mika Häkkinen	12	1m 40.389s
2	Eddie Irvine	14	1m 40.674s
3	Damon Hill	15	1m 40.741s
4	Michael Schumacher	20	1m 40.765s
5	Jean Alesi	17	1m 40.899s
6	Heinz-Harald Frentzen	8	1m 41.116s
7	David Coulthard	21	1m 41.151s
8	Gerhard Berger	22	1m 41.699s
9	Mark Blundell	20	1m 41.789s
10	Rubens Barrichello	21	1m 41.924s
11	Olivier Panis	23	1m 42.017s
12	Johnny Herbert	22	1m 42.749s
13	Aguri Suzuki	20	1m 43.084s
14	Ukyo Katayama	22	1m 43.309s
15	Mika Salo	22	1m 43.324s
16	Karl Wendlinger	23	1m 44.177s
17	Gianni Morbidelli	16	1m 44.231s
18	Taki Inoue	21	1m 44.892s
19	Pedro Lamy	23	1m 45.010s
20	Luca Badoer	20	1m 45.956s
21	Andrea Montermini	10	1m 46.860s
22	Roberto Moreno	13	1m 48.048s
23	Pedro Diniz	21	1m 48.203s
24	Bertrand Gachot	17	1m 49.184s

Friday qualifying
Bright and sunny

Pos.	Driver	Laps	Time
1	Michael Schumacher	9	1m 38.428s
2	**Damon Hill**	**11**	**1m 39.032s**
3	Mika Häkkinen	9	1m 39.127s
4	Jean Alesi	11	1m 39.142s
5	**David Coulthard**	**11**	**1m 39.155s**
6	**Heinz-Harald Frentzen**	**10**	**1m 40.010s**
7	Eddie Irvine	9	1m 40.153s
8	Gerhard Berger	4	1m 40.305s
9	**Johnny Herbert**	**6**	**1m 40.349s**
10	**Rubens Barrichello**	**11**	**1m 40.381s**
11	**Olivier Panis**	**10**	**1m 40.838s**
12	**Mika Salo**	**11**	**1m 41.355s**
13	**Ukyo Katayama**	**9**	**1m 41.977s**
14	Aguri Suzuki	11	1m 42.561s
15	Gianni Morbidelli	7	1m 42.623s
16	Pedro Lamy	12	1m 43.387s
17	Karl Wendlinger	12	1m 43.634s
18	Luca Badoer	11	1m 43.940s
19	Taki Inoue	11	1m 44.386s
20	**Pedro Diniz**	**12**	**1m 46.654s**
21	Andrea Montermini	9	1m 46.869s
22	Bertrand Gachot	8	1m 48.824s
23	Roberto Moreno	5	1m 50.097s
24	**Mark Blundell**		**1 16m 42.640s**

Saturday qualifying
Dry, overcast

Pos.	Driver	Laps	Time
1	**Michael Schumacher**	**8**	**1m 38.023s**
2	**Jean Alesi**	**5**	**1m 38.888s**
3	**Mika Häkkinen**	**7**	**1m 38.954s**
4	**Gerhard Berger**	**11**	**1m 39.040s**
5	Damon Hill	8	1m 39.158s
6	David Coulthard	10	1m 39.368s
7	**Eddie Irvine**	**6**	**1m 39.621s**
8	Heinz-Harald Frentzen	7	1m 40.380s
9	Johnny Herbert	9	1m 40.391s
10	Rubens Barrichello	12	1m 40.413s
11	Olivier Panis	9	1m 41.081s
12	**Aguri Suzuki**	**9**	**1m 41.592s**
13	Mika Salo	10	1m 41.637s
14	**Gianni Morbidelli**	**9**	**1m 42.059s**
15	Ukyo Katayama	10	1m 42.273s
16	**Karl Wendlinger**	**9**	**1m 42.912s**
17	**Pedro Lamy**	**10**	**1m 43.102s**
18	**Luca Badoer**	**9**	**1m 43.542s**
19	**Taki Inoue**	**10**	**1m 44.074s**
20	**Andrea Montermini**	**7**	**1m 46.097s**
21	Pedro Diniz	3	1m 47.166s
22	**Roberto Moreno**	**5**	**1m 48.267s**
23	**Bertrand Gachot**	**7**	**1m 48.289s**
	Mark Blundell	0	no time

Warm-up
Cloudy and wet

Pos.	Driver	Laps	Time
1	Damon Hill	11	2m 00.025s
2	Michael Schumacher	9	2m 00.414s
3	David Coulthard	9	2m 00.659s
4	Jean Alesi	9	2m 00.850s
5	Heinz-Harald Frentzen	8	2m 01.069s
6	Eddie Irvine	8	2m 01.957s
7	Gerhard Berger	9	2m 02.231s
8	Johnny Herbert	8	2m 03.071s
9	Mika Häkkinen	10	2m 03.465s
10	Ukyo Katayama	11	2m 03.470s
11	Mark Blundell	12	2m 03.686s
12	Olivier Panis	12	2m 03.808s
13	Pedro Lamy	10	2m 04.050s
14	Mika Salo	9	2m 04.236s
15	Rubens Barrichello	10	2m 04.313s
16	Luca Badoer	11	2m 04.530s
17	Karl Wendlinger	10	2m 05.237s
18	Gianni Morbidelli	11	2m 06.223s
19	Andrea Montermini	8	2m 08.562s
20	Taki Inoue	9	2m 10.531s
21	Bertrand Gachot	6	2m 10.651s
22	Pedro Diniz	8	2m 14.072s
23	Roberto Moreno	1	11m 07.750s

Fastest race laps
Overcast, then dry

Driver	Time	Lap
Michael Schumacher	1m 42.976s	33
David Coulthard	1m 43.079s	33
Damon Hill	1m 43.193s	31
Mika Häkkinen	1m 43.369s	38
Johnny Herbert	1m 43.404s	37
Eddie Irvine	1m 43.477s	30
Heinz-Harald Frentzen	1m 44.211s	35
Mark Blundell	1m 44.287s	50
Jean Alesi	1m 44.370s	23
Mika Salo	1m 45.625s	51
Olivier Panis	1m 45.661s	47
Karl Wendlinger	1m 45.824s	43
Taki Inoue	1m 46.600s	42
Pedro Lamy	1m 46.954s	44
Luca Badoer	1m 47.025s	47
Andrea Montermini	1m 49.985s	21
Pedro Diniz	1m 50.261s	30
Rubens Barrichello	1m 51.343s	13
Gerhard Berger	1m 52.165s	12
Ukyo Katayama	1m 56.404s	12
Bertrand Gachot	2m 06.927s	5

CHASSIS LOG BOOK

1	Schumacher	Benetton B195/6
2	Herbert	Benetton B195/5
spare		Benetton B195/1
3	Katayama	Tyrrell 023/6
4	Salo	Tyrrell 023/5
spare		Tyrrell 023/2
5	Hill	Williams FW17B/4
6	Coulthard	Williams FW17B/5
spare		Williams FW17B/3
7	Blundell	McLaren MP4/10B/4
8	Häkkinen	McLaren MP4/10B/5
spare		McLaren MP4/10B/3
9	Morbidelli	Footwork FA16/3
10	Inoue	Footwork FA16/4
spare		Footwork FA16/1
14	Barrichello	Jordan 195/4
15	Irvine	Jordan 195/5
spare		Jordan 195/1
16	Gachot	Pacific PR02/1
17	Montermini	Pacific PR02/2
21	Diniz	Forti FG01/4
22	Moreno	Forti FG01/3
spare		Forti FG01/2
23	Lamy	Minardi M195/2
24	Badoer	Minardi M195/2
spare		Minardi M195/1
25	Suzuki	Ligier JS41/5
26	Panis	Ligier JS41/6
spare		Ligier JS41/3
27	Alesi	Ferrari 412T2/161
28	Berger	Ferrari 412T2/162
spare		Ferrari 412T2/160
29	Wendlinger	Sauber C14/5
30	Frentzen	Sauber C14/7
spare		Sauber C14/6

POINTS TABLES

Drivers

1	Michael Schumacher	102
2	Damon Hill	59
3	David Coulthard	49
4	Johnny Herbert	45
5	Jean Alesi	42
6	Gerhard Berger	31
7	Mika Häkkinen	17
8	Heinz-Harald Frentzen	15
9	Rubens Barrichello	11
10 =	Eddie Irvine	10
10 =	Olivier Panis	10
10 =	Mark Blundell	10
13	Martin Brundle	7
14 =	Jean-Christophe Boullion	3
14 =	Mika Salo	3
16 =	Gianni Morbidelli	1
16 =	Aguri Suzuki	1

Constructors

1	Benetton	137
2	Williams	102
3	Ferrari	73
4	McLaren	27
5	Jordan	21
6 =	Ligier	18
6 =	Sauber	18
8	Tyrrell	3
9	Footwork	1

FOR THE RECORD

50th Grand Prix start
Damon Hill

WORLD CHAMPIONSHIP • ROUND 17

AUSTRALIAN GRAND PRIX

HILL
PANIS
MORBIDELLI
BLUNDELL
SALO
LAMY

Above: With most of the usual front-runners falling by the wayside, winner Damon Hill was joined on the podium by Ligier's Olivier Panis and Footwork stalwart Gianni Morbidelli, who had managed just one previous top-three finish between them.

Michael Schumacher's attempt to better Nigel Mansell's tally of nine wins in a season ended in a controversial collision with Jean Alesi's Ferrari.

AUSTRALIAN GRAND PRIX

Häkkinen survives head injuries in high-speed accident

Disaster yet again brushed against the hem of the Formula 1 business when Mika Häkkinen's McLaren-Mercedes crashed heavily in the first qualifying session at Adelaide and the 27-year-old Finn was taken to hospital with serious head injuries. Thankfully, after an initial period of acute nervousness about his condition, Mika was confirmed as out of immediate danger and is expected to make a complete recovery in time to resume racing at the start of 1996.

Häkkinen lost control of his McLaren MP4/10B after a sudden deflation of its left-rear tyre – due to running over debris on the circuit – as it approached the 110 mph, fourth-gear right-hander leading onto Adelaide's long Brabham Straight. The car spun wildly over a high kerb and was launched at high speed into a single row of protective tyres facing the concrete barrier on the outside of the corner.

Häkkinen's life was saved in the immediate aftermath of the impact by the prompt and efficient intervention of track marshals and doctors at the scene. His head was held straight to prevent him choking on his own blood and a tracheotomy performed at the trackside to prevent any brain damage through oxygen loss. He was then transferred to the Royal Adelaide Hospital where his recovery was duly monitored by Professor Syd Watkins, the FIA Medical Delegate.

It was later discovered that similarly cut rear tyres had been sustained in the same session by Johnny Herbert's Benetton and Pedro Lamy's Minardi.

Professor Watkins *(seen above with Ron Dennis)* explained that an airbag might well have saved Häkkinen from sustaining such a serious injury. 'We are not sure whether the helmet struck the steering wheel or the side of the cockpit,' he said, 'but we have the in-car television tape which we will study in slow motion in order to relate the site of the impact to the area of the crash helmet where there is some local damage.'

He went on to explain that technical research on F1 airbags was continuing at Britain's Motor Industry Research Association. 'We are working to determine the optimum size and shape and the best site in which to place it in an F1 car,' he continued.

'The technology to inflate the bag in the time required is available, but, following its inflation, we need to control the rate at which it deflates so that the bag will not obstruct the cockpit and interfere with the extrication or escape of the driver.'

Additional tyres were used to build up the barrier at the accident site following a track inspection by Michael Schumacher, Damon Hill and Gerhard Berger in their role as members of the Grand Prix Drivers' Association. Increased lateral cockpit protection is being incorporated into the 1996 F1 technical regulations with a view to reducing the possibility of drivers suffering injuries like those Häkkinen sustained in the future.

Damon Hill signed off at the end of the season with the kind of performance that had been so conspicuously missing for much of 1995 up to that point. The Australian Grand Prix was a race of survival: of keeping away from the walls and barriers, of avoiding other cars and eliminating errors on the slippery track surface. Hill did all this and more, inheriting the lead when team-mate David Coulthard slid into the pit wall as he came in for his first refuelling stop, then keeping his cool as the opposition fell away and the greatest pressure was that which came from within.

Damon eventually won by over two laps from Olivier Panis's smoking Ligier-Mugen and the reliable Footwork-Hart of Gianni Morbidelli, a result which at least gave the winner's rostrum a distinctly different look for this final race of the season.

With Australia's round of the World Championship heading for Melbourne at the start of the 1996 season, the final Adelaide race was staged in a mood of reflective nostalgia and more than a passing degree of bewilderment as to precisely why the race was being taken away from this successful venue.

FOCA President Bernie Ecclestone very firmly laid the blame on the Adelaide media for a campaign of criticism surrounding the event over the past few years, but this was firmly refuted by the local newspapers, who blasted back at Grand Prix motor racing's most powerful figure.

Ecclestone told the *Adelaide Advertiser* that he did not want the race to leave Adelaide, but claimed there had been endless media criticism of the event. However, these allegations were firmly rebutted by Peter Blunden, the newspaper's editor. 'The Adelaide media has supported the Grand Prix more than any city in the world, and Mr Ecclestone knows it,' he replied.

'The *Advertiser* has always been totally committed to the Grand Prix, and has devoted much more space than any newspaper in any host city. We have quite properly asked questions about some financial arrangements, but to use us as a scapegoat is absurd.'

Meanwhile, in the Adelaide pit lane there was a distinct end-of-term feeling surrounding the race. This seemed to be more than usually evident in the Williams-Renault garage, where neither Technical Director Patrick Head nor Chief Designer Adrian Newey could be bothered to make the trip. It could hardly be interpreted as an unqualified vote of confidence in drivers Damon Hill and David Coulthard.

Nevertheless, the British pairing were in fine form, Damon securing pole position with a time in cool conditions on Friday that remained unbeaten in Saturday's second session.

'Provisional pole position is really good news here,' said Hill on Friday evening, 'although the car felt very nice this morning and I think we may back-track slightly on set-up tomorrow.'

Coulthard was frustrated by understeer and poor throttle response during the Friday morning free practice session, but battled confidently in the face of slippery track conditions to set second-fastest time in first qualifying. Like his team-mate, David was unable to improve on Saturday, but his place on the front row of the grid remained secure.

Of course, Mika Häkkinen's accident during the first qualifying session (see sidebar) had an understandably dampening effect on pit lane morale, but by the time the Williams duo went out to defend their provisional front row times on Saturday the news from the Royal Adelaide Hospital was much more encouraging.

Overnight there had been a significant improvement in Häkkinen's condition, which had remained stable, and the Finn was slowly regaining consciousness. He had started to move all his limbs to command and understood what was being said to him, although he remained under sedation and was breathing on a ventilator.

This was certainly welcome news, but Damon was vividly reminded of the narrow tightrope between success and disaster when his Williams strayed over the same kerb midway through qualifying and came within a few metres of hitting the same tyre barrier before he coaxed it back onto the circuit.

'In the ordinary course of events this would have been scary, but bearing in mind Mika's accident yesterday, it was twice as frightening,' said Hill.

'It is this first-hand experience which the Grand Prix Drivers' Association is bringing to bear on these issues of circuit safety which is so valuable. The problems simply do not look the same when you are going round in a road car.'

Hill was well satisfied with the seventh pole position of his '95 season – the 11th of his career all told – with Adelaide first-timer Coulthard equally pleased to be on the front row yet again.

Michael Schumacher had finished Friday qualifying in fourth place, fitting stiffer front and softer rear springs as he fine-tuned the set-up during the course of the session. But on Saturday morning everything seemed to go wrong.

First he spun gently into a gravel trap exiting a slow left-hander on the final leg of the circuit. He wasn't quite sure why, but after the car was extricated at the mid-session break, he continued to try various chassis set-ups with heavy fuel loads and used tyres. He was satisfied, but not totally content.

Only midway through second qualifying, when he found the Benetton was almost a second slower than it had been on Friday, did a detailed examination reveal a faulty shock absorber. This was duly changed and he vaulted forward to take third place on the grid.

Fourth and fifth were the Ferraris of Gerhard Berger and Jean Alesi. Gerhard suffered an engine failure on Friday morning and then found his brakes locking up intermittently during second qualifying.

Alesi effectively lost the entire first qualifying session due to a problem with an electrical cable to the engine management sensor. This was finally sorted out in time for second qualifying and Jean went out to post a representative time early in the session before realising that he wasn't likely to go much quicker in the hotter conditions.

Jean spent the rest of the session working on his race set-up with a heavy fuel load, finishing up 0.3s ahead of Heinz-Harald Frentzen's sixth-placed Sauber C14-Ford, which was consistently quick throughout both days.

Frentzen stopped on the final lap of Friday's session with a Ford Zetec-R engine failure, but continued to run strongly the following day and set his grid time in final qualifying despite a touch of unwanted understeer.

By sad contrast, his team-mate Karl Wendlinger had a thoroughly miserable time, crashing his C14 heavily at the tricky chicane after the pits on Friday morning. The car was repairable, but Karl sustained a sprained wrist and later reported feeling a whiplash-like sensation when he was out in the car. He missed Saturday qualifying as a result, slipping one place to 18th

225

AUSTRALIAN GRAND PRIX

> **Diary**
>
> *British F3 Champion Oliver Gavin's hopes of driving a Pacific in the Australian GP are thwarted by a mix-up with the RAC over his F1 Superlicence.*
>
> *Rumours that Paul Stewart Racing will graduate to F1 in 1997 with Ford power resurface again at Adelaide.*
>
> *Damon Hill named as Britain's highest-paid sportsman on £3 million, beating Chris Eubank (£2.75 million) into second place.*
>
> *Mercedes hope to help Mark Blundell obtain a seat alongside Heinz-Harald Frentzen at Sauber for 1996.*

Restored to the Footwork line-up for the last three races of the season, popular Italian Gianni Morbidelli scored the team's first podium finish since 1989.

Below: Heinz-Harald Frentzen locks up his right-front wheel as he finally finds a way past the obstructive Mark Blundell. Johnny Herbert follows, hoping to profit from the situation.

overall, but hoped to feel sufficiently recovered to take the start.

Rubens Barrichello lost a lot of time on Saturday morning with serious gearbox trouble, then found himself prevented from improving further when his Peugeot V10 began to lose power and trail smoke. He wound up seventh in the final order ahead of Johnny Herbert, who changed springs, ride heights and roll bar settings in second qualifying after crashing during the Friday session, possibly due to a cut rear tyre similar to Häkkinen's. The Englishman's Benetton monocoque was written off in the impact, which drove a left-front suspension member into the chassis, so he had to use the spare car for the balance of the weekend.

Eddie Irvine claimed ninth place after correcting a touch of understeer, while the top ten was completed by Mark Blundell in the surviving McLaren MP4/10B, which suffered from particularly poor grip on the slow final section of the lap, despite using the central aerofoil in an attempt to enhance the car's grip level.

Martin Brundle lined up 11th for Ligier, moderately happy with his JS41, while team-mate Olivier Panis, one place further back, was a little discouraged.

'I'm disappointed that I haven't found a balance which has allowed me to attack as hard as I would have liked,' explained Olivier. 'Whenever I tried to raise the pace, I found myself faced with an understeer problem into the medium-fast corners.'

Gianni Morbidelli made good use of the revised suspension and undertray on his Footwork FA16 – which worked well on this occasion – to post 13th-fastest time overall, despite being forced to spin to avoid Pedro Diniz's Forti FG01.

Mika Salo took 14th place, complaining ceaselessly of poor grip with the Tyrrell 023, a couple of tenths ahead of Luca Badoer's Minardi, with the Tyrrell of a highly frustrated Ukyo Katayama and Pedro Lamy in the other Minardi slotting in ahead of Wendlinger.

Taki Inoue did a respectable job to capitalise on the revised undertray and exhaust configuration on his Footwork, setting 19th-fastest time ahead of Roberto Moreno and Diniz in their Fortis.

Andrea Montermini was 22nd fastest despite a major gearbox oil leak in the second session, while Bertrand Gachot brought up the back of the grid in the other Pacific PR02.

There was a holiday mood in the Adelaide paddock on race day, for although this was the final Grand Prix to take place in the South Australia city, an all-time record crowd well in excess of 200,000 people had turned out to say goodbye to the event which had been part of their lives for 11 seasons.

The race morning warm-up saw Hill and Coulthard heading the times, but Schumacher was worryingly close to the Williams duo in third place and the two British drivers appreciated that they would have a fight on their hands.

With Häkkinen out of the equation for the weekend, only 23 cars lined up for the start and this became 22 when Badoer's Minardi failed to fire up on the grid prior to the parade lap and was pushed away with electrical trouble.

Damon felt confident that he had the legs of the opposition, but Coulthard opted to gamble and reduced downforce on his Williams FW17B at the last minute. When the green light came on, David surged away from second spot to squeeze into the lead as the pack scrambled through the first tricky chicane.

Behind the Williams duo, Schumacher made an uncharacteristically poor start and was overtaken by the Ferraris of Berger and Alesi even before he reached the first chi-

cane. Round onto the back straight, Michael tucked himself tightly into Alesi's slipstream and took a perfectly timed tow from the Ferrari, popping out to pass the Frenchman under braking for the tight right-hander at the end.

However, the Williams-Renaults were already pulling away commandingly by the end of the first lap and Schumacher still had to deal with Berger if he was going to have a hope of challenging for the lead. Sixth was Frentzen's Sauber, chased by Herbert's Benetton, the Jordan-Peugeots of Irvine and Barrichello, Martin Brundle's Ligier and Mark Blundell's McLaren.

Coulthard's last-minute aerodynamic change ensured that his Williams was slightly quicker than Hill's on the straight, while it took until midway round lap five for the Benetton team leader to find a way past Berger's Ferrari.

With ten laps completed Coulthard was 1.6s ahead of Hill with Schumacher steadying his deficit at around 11 seconds – effectively the full length of the back straight. The Benetton certainly looked much more of a handful than the Williams opposition over the bumps and Michael was having to drive absolutely flat out to keep in touch. This was beginning to look like one race he would not win after all.

At the end of lap 19, Hill came in for his first refuelling stop, his Williams being stationary for 9.1s. He resumed in third place, but this soon became second as Coulthard found himself eliminated in an incident which, on the face of it, looked remarkably stupid, but which the Scot explained away with confident conviction.

'What happened was that I slowed for the pits sufficiently, but when I came down into second gear the low idle strategy of the engine suddenly picked up and drove me forward,' he explained.

'I should have dipped the clutch, but I was so surprised that I hit the brakes and slid into the wall. I am very disappointed, but I'm not embarrassed; I was caught out by something which has been a problem in the pit lane all year. It's just one of those things – a shame, because I felt very comfortable and happy.'

This simply amazing lapse left Schumacher 2.3s ahead of Damon, but with the Benetton still to make its first refuelling stop. Michael duly came in at the end of lap 22, surrendering the lead after a quick 6.9s top-up, and the race settled down with Hill comfortably ahead and under no pressure.

As Schumacher accelerated back into the race, Alesi's Ferrari slammed past the pit exit to get ahead of the Benetton going into the chicane. On fresh tyres, Michael reasoned that he could not afford to be held up behind Alesi if he was to have a chance of catching Hill, so he dived down the inside of the Frenchman at the end of the long back straight on lap 23.

As the Benetton pulled level, Alesi abruptly swung into the German's car, hooking his right-front wheel inside Michael's left-rear. The Ferrari's front wings were shredded in the collision and, although Jean stayed ahead, they flew off completely a couple of corners later and he came straight into the pits.

Schumacher soldiered on for another lap before coming into the pits to investigate a damaged tyre and suspension. He resumed, but returned at the end of lap 26 to retire for good.

Schumacher was extremely annoyed. 'It was a very unnecessary action that Alesi took, because I was clearly faster than him,' said Michael. 'I don't understand what was going on in his brain. Was it switched off? He'd better keep out of my way at the Benetton party tonight, because this wasn't the way I wanted to finish the season. OK, the Williams were quicker, but I would have been happy to finish second here today.'

Alesi had no explanation for the incident. 'As a result of the collision, I had to make my first refuelling stop one lap earlier than expected,' he commented. 'The team did a good job to quickly change my damaged front wing, but after I returned to the race the car was pulling badly to the right, so there was nothing I could do but retire.'

This now left Hill over half a minute clear of Johnny Herbert's Benetton, Berger's Ferrari and Frentzen's Sauber, which had made its first refuelling stop at the end of lap 22, dropping from fourth to seventh and then pulling back to fourth as the runners ahead of him hit trouble.

AUSTRALIAN GRAND PRIX

Mika Salo *(left)* scored points for Tyrrell for the second race in succession.

Below: Olivier Panis nursed his smoking Ligier-Mugen Honda to the finish and was rewarded with second place.

Pedro Lamy took sixth for Minardi, earning the first World Championship point of his career and the Italian team's first of the season.

The next major drama occurred after Brundle brought his Ligier in for its first refuelling stop after holding fifth place at the end of lap 27. He resumed in eighth place, then moved back to seventh on the tail of Blundell's McLaren.

Martin suddenly found himself catching his former Ligier teammate at a prodigious speed at the end of the back straight, running into the back of the Mercedes-engined car and spinning it off midway round lap 30. Mark managed to get going again, his McLaren's aerodynamic performance now ruined due to the fact that several of its underfloor supporting stays had been broken in the impact, but Martin stalled his engine and went no further. It was a particularly unfortunate episode, because the 'Brundell Brothers' were due to go out to celebrate the end of the season together that same evening!

Herbert was on a two-stop strategy and didn't bring his Benetton in for the first time until lap 31 when he was stationary for 9.1s. This allowed Berger through to second place, but the Austrian's promising run lasted only another three laps before the Italian V12 blew up spectacularly and he coasted to a halt out on the circuit.

The race was now effectively falling apart in Damon's wake. By the time he brought the Williams in for its second stop (8.7s) at the end of lap 40, he was easily able to rejoin without being remotely threatened.

Frentzen had pulled back to a magnificent second after Berger's retirement, the German driver expertly dealing with both pressure from Herbert and the unfortunate balking performance from Blundell which lasted from laps 35 to 37.

When Heinz-Harald finally squeezed ahead of Mark at the end of the back straight, he let his true feelings be known by raising a single finger aloft in a very public gesture of disapproval. Blundell later explained that, in the absence of totally convincing flag signals or a radio message from his pit, he was unsure whether or not the Sauber was about to lap him.

On lap 40 Frentzen suddenly slowed and pulled off at the side of the circuit with gearbox failure. This cruel blow promoted Herbert to second place ahead of Irvine's Jordan, Panis's Ligier, Morbidelli's Footwork and Blundell.

The next casualty was Irvine, his being the sole surviving Jordan since Barrichello unaccountably drove off the road into a tyre barrier on lap 21 after grappling with understeer in the opening stages. Irvine, meanwhile, had come in for fresh tyres on laps 25, 41 and 58, but then came back in for an unscheduled stop on lap 62 after the engine developed a top-end misfire.

'This gradually began to happen at lower and lower revs,' explained Irvine. 'We topped the air up a couple of times, but [the system] was leaking so badly I would have had to come in every other lap.' The car was finally retired at the end of lap 63.

Now it seemed as though Herbert would have an unchallenged run through to take second place but, having made his second refuelling stop on lap 54, he rolled to a halt out on the circuit on lap 70. Flames were licking round the rear end of the Benetton, which had been sidelined by a driveshaft problem.

Next Olivier Panis went into second place, but with four laps to go his Ligier began trailing an ominous cloud of smoke. Only nine laps from the finish the Frenchman had come in for an 8.1s precautionary fuel top-up, but now it seemed there was no way he would make the finish.

Olivier eased back, secure in the knowledge that he was sufficiently far ahead of Morbidelli's Footwork to take it easy. In the closing moments, Hill came up to lap the stricken Ligier, Panis's team telling him over the radio to drop back and allow Damon through as this would mean he had one fewer lap to cover to the finish.

In the end, Hill was two laps ahead – matching the previous biggest winning margin, achieved when Jackie Stewart's Matra beat Bruce McLaren's McLaren in the 1969 Spanish GP at Montjuich Park.

However, Damon was fortunate to be under so little pressure in the closing stages that he was able to accommodate a nail-biting 22.1s stop on lap 60 when the front-left wheel nut cross-threaded and took an enormous amount of effort before it was eventually freed. Had anyone been closer in second place, it would have been a major drama.

Panis struggled home second with Morbidelli a fighting third, followed by Blundell and Salo, with Pedro Lamy scoring the first point of the season for Minardi. It was the end of a memorable day.

FIA FORMULA ONE WORLD CHAMPIONSHIP ROUND 17

EDS AUSTRALIAN GRAND PRIX

ADELAIDE CIRCUIT
10-12 NOVEMBER 1995

Race distance: 81 laps, 190.150 miles/306.018 km
Race weather: Warm and sunny

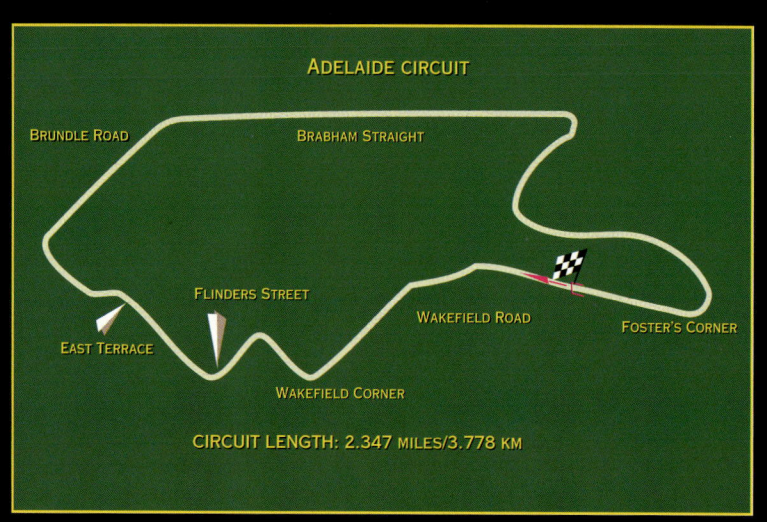

ADELAIDE CIRCUIT
CIRCUIT LENGTH: 2.347 MILES/3.778 KM

Place	Driver	Nat.	No.	Entrant	Car/Engine	Laps	Time/Retirement	Speed (mph/km/h)
1	**Damon Hill**	GB	5	Rothmans Williams Renault	Williams FW17B-Renault RS7C V10	81	1h 49m 15.946s	104.470/168.129
2	**Olivier Panis**	F	26	Ligier Gitanes Blondes	Ligier JS41-Mugen Honda MF301 V10	79		
3	**Gianni Morbidelli**	I	9	Footwork Hart	Footwork FA16-Hart 830 V8	79		
4	**Mark Blundell**	GB	7	Marlboro McLaren Mercedes	McLaren MP4/10B-Mercedes FO110 V10	79		
5	**Mika Salo**	SF	4	Nokia Tyrrell Yamaha	Tyrrell 023-Yamaha OX10C V10	78		
6	**Pedro Lamy**	P	23	Minardi Scuderia Italia	Minardi M195-Ford EDM V8	78		
7	Pedro Diniz	BR	21	Parmalat Forti Ford	Forti FG01-Ford ED V8	77		
8	Bertrand Gachot	F	16	Pacific Grand Prix Ltd	Pacific PR02-Ford ED V8	76		
	Ukyo Katayama	J	3	Nokia Tyrrell Yamaha	Tyrrell 023-Yamaha OX10C V10	70	Engine	
	Johnny Herbert	GB	2	Mild Seven Benetton Renault	Benetton B195-Renault RS7C V10	69	Driveshaft	
	Eddie Irvine	GB	15	Total Jordan Peugeot	Jordan 195-Peugeot A10 V10	62	Engine	
	Heinz-Harald Frentzen	D	30	Red Bull Sauber Ford	Sauber C14-Ford Zetec-R V8	39	Gearbox	
	Gerhard Berger	A	28	Scuderia Ferrari	Ferrari 412T2 044 V12	34	Engine	
	Martin Brundle	GB	25	Ligier Gitanes Blondes	Ligier JS41-Mugen Honda MF301 V10	29	Spun off	
	Michael Schumacher	D	1	Mild Seven Benetton Renault	Benetton B195-Renault RS7C V10	25	Collision damage	
	Jean Alesi	F	27	Scuderia Ferrari	Ferrari 412T2 044 V12	23	Collision damage	
	Roberto Moreno	BR	22	Parmalat Forti Ford	Forti FG01-Ford ED V8	21	Accident	
	Rubens Barrichello	BR	14	Total Jordan Peugeot	Jordan 195-Peugeot A10 V10	20	Accident	
	David Coulthard	GB	6	Rothmans Williams Renault	Williams FW17B-Renault RS7C V10	19	Accident	
	Taki Inoue	J	10	Footwork Hart	Footwork FA16-Hart 830 V8	15	Accident	
	Karl Wendlinger	A	29	Red Bull Sauber Ford	Sauber C14-Ford Zetec-R V8	8	Driver withdrew	
	Andrea Montermini	I	17	Pacific Grand Prix Ltd	Pacific PR02-Ford ED V8	2	Gearbox	
DNS	Luca Badoer	I	24	Minardi Scuderia Italia	Minardi M195-Ford EDM V8	0	Electrics	
DNS	Mika Häkkinen	SF	8	Marlboro McLaren Mercedes	McLaren MP4/10B-Mercedes FO110 V10	0	Qualifying accident	

Fastest lap: Hill, on lap 16, 1m 17.943s, 108.484 mph/174.589 km/h.
Lap record: Damon Hill (F1 Williams FW15C-Renault V10), 1m 15.381s, 112.172 mph/180.523 km/h (1993).
All cars used Goodyear tyres

All results and data © FIA 1995

Pit stop
One lap behind leader

STARTING GRID

5 HILL (1m 15.505s) Williams	**6 COULTHARD** (1m 15.628s) Williams
1 SCHUMACHER (1m 15.839s) Benetton	**28 BERGER** (1m 15.932s) Ferrari
27 ALESI (1m 16.305s) Ferrari	**30 FRENTZEN** (1m 16.647s) Sauber
14 BARRICHELLO (1m 16.725s) Jordan	**2 HERBERT** (1m 16.950s) Benetton
15 IRVINE (1m 17.116s) Jordan	**7 BLUNDELL** (1m 17.348s) McLaren
25 BRUNDLE (1m 17.624s) Ligier	**26 PANIS** (1m 18.033s) Ligier
9 MORBIDELLI (1m 18.391s) Footwork	**4 SALO** (1m 18.604s) Tyrrell
24 BADOER* (1m 18.810s) Minardi	**3 KATAYAMA** (1m 18.828s) Tyrrell
23 LAMY (1m 18.875s) Minardi	**29 WENDLINGER** (1m 19.561s) Sauber
10 INOUE (1m 19.677s) Footwork	**22 MORENO** (1m 20.657s) Forti
21 DINIZ (1m 20.878s) Forti	**17 MONTERMINI** (1m 21.659s) Pacific
16 GACHOT (1m 21.998s) Pacific	

* did not start

FOR THE RECORD
First Grand Prix point
Pedro Lamy

TIME SHEETS

Friday free practice
Humid and overcast

Pos.	Driver	Laps	Time
1	Damon Hill	23	1m 15.396s
2	Jean Alesi	23	1m 16.236s
3	Gerhard Berger	23	1m 16.319s
4	Mika Häkkinen	22	1m 16.408s
5	David Coulthard	23	1m 16.538s
6	Michael Schumacher	19	1m 16.551s
7	Heinz-Harald Frentzen	23	1m 17.170s
8	Mark Blundell	23	1m 17.241s
9	Rubens Barrichello	23	1m 17.327s
10	Johnny Herbert	22	1m 17.378s
11	Olivier Panis	23	1m 17.970s
12	Martin Brundle	23	1m 17.972s
13	Eddie Irvine	20	1m 17.980s
14	Ukyo Katayama	22	1m 18.548s
15	Mika Salo	23	1m 18.805s
16	Gianni Morbidelli	23	1m 18.965s
17	Karl Wendlinger	21	1m 19.093s
18	Luca Badoer	23	1m 19.646s
19	Pedro Lamy	23	1m 19.723s
20	Taki Inoue	19	1m 20.506s
21	Roberto Moreno	23	1m 20.865s
22	Bertrand Gachot	13	1m 21.795s
23	Andrea Montermini	12	1m 21.929s
24	Pedro Diniz	23	1m 22.617s

Saturday free practice
Cloudy and warm

Pos.	Driver	Laps	Time
1	Damon Hill	23	1m 15.394s
2	David Coulthard	23	1m 15.659s
3	Jean Alesi	19	1m 15.905s
4	Heinz-Harald Frentzen	23	1m 16.309s
5	Gerhard Berger	14	1m 16.499s
6	Michael Schumacher	23	1m 17.025s
7	Eddie Irvine	20	1m 17.033s
8	Martin Brundle	23	1m 17.155s
9	Mark Blundell	23	1m 17.267s
10	Johnny Herbert	23	1m 17.528s
11	Olivier Panis	23	1m 17.697s
12	Gianni Morbidelli	21	1m 18.154s
13	Mika Salo	22	1m 18.335s
14	Rubens Barrichello	10	1m 18.548s
15	Ukyo Katayama	20	1m 18.733s
16	Taki Inoue	22	1m 18.942s
17	Pedro Lamy	23	1m 19.451s
18	Luca Badoer	23	1m 19.453s
19	Karl Wendlinger	8	1m 19.508s
20	Pedro Diniz	23	1m 20.716s
21	Roberto Moreno	23	1m 20.917s
22	Andrea Montermini	9	1m 21.635s
23	Bertrand Gachot	11	1m 21.678s

Friday qualifying
Humid and overcast

Pos.	Driver	Laps	Time
1	**Damon Hill**	**12**	**1m 15.505s**
2	**David Coulthard**	**12**	**1m 15.628s**
3	**Gerhard Berger**	**12**	**1m 15.932s**
4	Michael Schumacher	9	1m 16.039s
5	**Rubens Barrichello**	**11**	**1m 16.725s**
6	Heinz-Harald Frentzen	11	1m 16.837s
7	Eddie Irvine	11	1m 17.197s
8	Johnny Herbert	5	1m 17.289s
9	**Mark Blundell**	**8**	**1m 17.348s**
10	Martin Brundle	12	1m 17.788s
11	**Olivier Panis**	**11**	**1m 18.033s**
12	**Mika Salo**	**11**	**1m 18.604s**
13	Gianni Morbidelli	12	1m 18.814s
14	**Ukyo Katayama**	**12**	**1m 18.828s**
15	**Pedro Lamy**	**12**	**1m 18.875s**
16	Luca Badoer	12	1m 19.285s
17	**Karl Wendlinger**	**12**	**1m 19.561s**
18	Taki Inoue	10	1m 19.764s
19	Roberto Moreno	12	1m 21.419s
20	**Andrea Montermini**	**5**	**1m 21.659s**
21	Pedro Diniz	12	1m 22.154s
22	Bertrand Gachot	6	1m 22.881s
23	Mika Häkkinen	2	1m 37.998s
24	Jean Alesi	2	32m 21.400s

Saturday qualifying
Cloudy and bright

Pos.	Driver	Laps	Time
1	David Coulthard	11	1m 15.792s
2	**Michael Schumacher**	**12**	**1m 15.839s**
3	Damon Hill	12	1m 15.988s
4	**Jean Alesi**	**12**	**1m 16.305s**
5	Heinz-Harald Frentzen	9	1m 16.647s
6	**Johnny Herbert**	**12**	**1m 16.950s**
7	Rubens Barrichello	12	1m 16.971s
8	Gerhard Berger	5	1m 16.994s
9	**Eddie Irvine**	**12**	**1m 17.116s**
10	**Martin Brundle**	**11**	**1m 17.624s**
11	Mark Blundell	11	1m 17.721s
12	Olivier Panis	10	1m 18.065s
13	**Gianni Morbidelli**	**12**	**1m 18.391s**
14	**Luca Badoer**	**12**	**1m 18.810s**
15	Mika Salo	12	1m 19.083s
16	Ukyo Katayama	11	1m 19.114s
17	Pedro Lamy	12	1m 19.484s
18	**Taki Inoue**	**7**	**1m 19.677s**
19	**Roberto Moreno**	**12**	**1m 20.657s**
20	**Pedro Diniz**	**11**	**1m 20.878s**
21	Andrea Montermini	6	1m 21.870s
22	**Bertrand Gachot**	**6**	**1m 21.998s**
	Mika Häkkinen		no time
	Karl Wendlinger		no time

Warm-up
Bright and sunny

Pos.	Driver	Laps	Time
1	Damon Hill	13	1m 16.875s
2	David Coulthard	14	1m 17.197s
3	Michael Schumacher	15	1m 17.205s
4	Johnny Herbert	14	1m 18.031s
5	Heinz-Harald Frentzen	15	1m 18.156s
6	Rubens Barrichello	15	1m 18.171s
7	Jean Alesi	12	1m 18.283s
8	Eddie Irvine	11	1m 18.595s
9	Olivier Panis	19	1m 18.630s
10	Gerhard Berger	12	1m 18.699s
11	Martin Brundle	14	1m 19.119s
12	Gianni Morbidelli	16	1m 19.126s
13	Mark Blundell	17	1m 19.395s
14	Mika Salo	16	1m 20.057s
15	Pedro Lamy	16	1m 20.181s
16	Luca Badoer	14	1m 20.442s
17	Ukyo Katayama	13	1m 20.617s
18	Taki Inoue	18	1m 20.774s
19	Andrea Montermini	7	1m 21.335s
20	Pedro Diniz	15	1m 21.656s
21	Karl Wendlinger	6	1m 22.019s
22	Roberto Moreno	12	1m 22.145s
23	Bertrand Gachot	3	1m 23.085s

Fastest race laps
Warm and sunny

Driver	Time	Lap
Damon Hill	1m 17.943s	16
David Coulthard	1m 18.025s	5
Michael Schumacher	1m 18.199s	7
Johnny Herbert	1m 19.056s	33
Gerhard Berger	1m 19.493s	7
Jean Alesi	1m 19.503s	12
Heinz-Harald Frentzen	1m 19.861s	20
Olivier Panis	1m 20.305s	26
Eddie Irvine	1m 20.563s	14
Rubens Barrichello	1m 20.643s	14
Martin Brundle	1m 20.835s	29
Mark Blundell	1m 21.363s	53
Mika Salo	1m 21.392s	45
Gianni Morbidelli	1m 21.418s	12
Pedro Lamy	1m 21.677s	48
Taki Inoue	1m 22.641s	14
Karl Wendlinger	1m 22.784s	4
Ukyo Katayama	1m 22.790s	4
Roberto Moreno	1m 22.944s	7
Pedro Diniz	1m 23.253s	4
Bertrand Gachot	1m 24.139s	7
Andrea Montermini	2m 25.242s	2
Luca Badoer	no time	

CHASSIS LOG BOOK

1	Schumacher	Benetton B195/6
2	Herbert	Benetton B195/5
	spare	Benetton B195/1
3	Katayama	Tyrrell 023/6
4	Salo	Tyrrell 023/5
	spare	Tyrrell 023/2
5	Hill	Williams FW17B/4
6	Coulthard	Williams FW17B/5
	spare	Williams FW17B/2
7	Blundell	McLaren MP4/10B/6
8	Häkkinen	McLaren MP4/10B/5
	spare	McLaren MP4/10B/3
9	Morbidelli	Footwork FA16/3
10	Inoue	Footwork FA16/4
	spare	Footwork FA16/1
14	Barrichello	Jordan 195/4
15	Irvine	Jordan 195/5
	spare	Jordan 195/1
16	Gachot	Pacific PR02/1
17	Montermini	Pacific PR02/2
21	Diniz	Forti FG01/4
22	Moreno	Forti FG01/3
	spare	Forti FG01/2
23	Lamy	Minardi M195/3
24	Badoer	Minardi M195/2
	spare	Minardi M195/1
25	Brundle	Ligier JS41/4
26	Panis	Ligier JS41/6
	spare	Ligier JS41/3
27	Alesi	Ferrari 412T2/161
28	Berger	Ferrari 412T2/163
	spare	Ferrari 412T2/164
29	Wendlinger	Sauber C14/5
	Frentzen	Sauber C14/7
	spare	Sauber C14/6

POINTS TABLES

Drivers

1	Michael Schumacher	102
2	Damon Hill	69
3	David Coulthard	49
4	Johnny Herbert	45
5	Jean Alesi	42
6	Gerhard Berger	31
7	Mika Häkkinen	17
8	Olivier Panis	16
9	Heinz-Harald Frentzen	15
10	Mark Blundell	13
11	Rubens Barrichello	11
12	Eddie Irvine	10
13	Martin Brundle	7
14 =	Gianni Morbidelli	5
14 =	Mika Salo	5
16	Jean-Christophe Boullion	3
17 =	Aguri Suzuki	1
17 =	Pedro Lamy	1

Constructors

1	Benetton	137
2	Williams	112
3	Ferrari	73
4	McLaren	30
5	Ligier	24
6	Jordan	21
7	Sauber	18
8 =	Footwork	5
8 =	Tyrrell	5
10	Minardi	1

1995 FIA WORLD CHAMPIONSHIP

Compiled by Nick Henry

Driver	Nationality	Date of birth	Car	Brazil	Argentina	San Marino	Spain	Monaco	Canada	France	Britain	Germany	Hungary	Belgium	Italy	Portugal	Europe	Pacific	Japan	Australia	Points total
Michael Schumacher	D	3/1/69	Benetton-Renault	1f	3f	Rp	1p	1	5pf	1f	R	1f	11*	1	R	2	1f	1f	1pf	R	102
Damon Hill	GB	17/9/60	Williams-Renault	Rp	1	1	4f	2p	R	2p	Rpf	Rp	1pf	2	R	3	R	3	R	1pf	69
David Coulthard	GB	27/3/71	Williams-Renault	2	Rp	4	R	R	R	3	3	2	2	Rf	Rp	1pf	3p	2p	R	R	49
Johnny Herbert	GB	25/6/64	Benetton-Renault	R	4	7	2	4	R	R	1	4	4	7	1	7	5	6	3	R	45
Jean Alesi	F	11/6/64	Ferrari	5	2	2	R	Rf	1	5	2	R	R	R	R	5	2	5	R	R	42
Gerhard Berger	A	27/8/59	Ferrari	3	6	3f	3	3	R	12	R	3	3	Rp	Rf	4	R	4	R	R	31
Mika Häkkinen	SF	28/9/68	McLaren-Mercedes	4	R	5	R	R	R	7	R	R	R	R	2	R	8	–	2	DNS	17
Olivier Panis	F	2/9/66	Ligier-Mugen Honda	R	7	9	6	R	4	8	4	R	6	9	R	R	8	5	2		16
Heinz-Harald Frentzen	D	18/5/67	Sauber-Ford	R	5	6	8	6	R	10	6	R	5	4	3	6	R	7	8	R	15
Mark Blundell	GB	8/4/66	McLaren-Mercedes	6	R	–	–	5	R	11	5	R	R	5	4	9	R	9	7	4	13
Rubens Barrichello	BR	23/5/72	Jordan-Peugeot	R	R	R	7	R	2	6	11*	R	7	6	R	11	4	R	R	R	11
Eddie Irvine	GB	10/11/65	Jordan-Peugeot	R	R	8	5	R	3	9	R	9*	13*	R	R	10	6	11	4	R	10
Martin Brundle	GB	1/6/59	Ligier-Mugen Honda	–	–	–	9	R	R	4	R	R	R	3	R	8	7	–	–	R	7
Gianni Morbidelli	I	31/1/68	Footwork-Hart	R	R	13	11	9	6	14	–	–	–	–	–	–	–	R	R	3	5
Mika Salo	SF	30/11/66	Tyrrell-Yamaha	7	R	R	10	R	7	15	8	R	R	8	5	13	10	12	6	5	5
Jean-Christophe Boullion	F	27/12/69	Sauber-Ford	–	–	–	8*	R	R	R	9	5	10	11	6	12	R	–	–	–	3
Pedro Lamy	P	20/3/72	Minardi-Ford	–	–	–	–	–	–	–	–	9	10	R	R	9	13	11	6		1
Aguri Suzuki	J	8/9/60	Ligier-Mugen Honda	8	R	11	–	–	–	–	–	6	–	–	–	–	–	R	DNS	–	1
Luca Badoer	I	25/1/71	Minardi-Ford	R	DNS	14	R	R	8	13	10	R	8	R	R	14	11	15	9	DNS	0
Jean-Denis Deletraz	CH	1/10/63	Pacific-Ford	–	–	–	–	–	–	–	–	–	–	–	–	R	NC	–	–	–	0
Pedro Diniz	BR	22/5/70	Forti-Ford	10	NC	NC	R	10	R	R	R	R	13	9	16	13	17	R	7		0
Bertrand Gachot	F	23/12/62	Pacific-Ford	R	R	R	R	R	R	R	12	–	–	–	–	–	–	R	R	8	0
Taki Inoue	J	5/9/63	Footwork-Hart	R	R	R	R	R	9	R	R	R	R	R	12	8	15	DNS	R	12	R	0
Ukyo Katayama	J	29/5/63	Tyrrell-Yamaha	R	8	R	R	R	R	R	R	7	R	R	NC	DNS	–	14	R	R	0
Giovanni Lavaggi	I	18/2/58	Pacific-Ford	–	–	–	–	–	–	–	–	R	R	R	R	–	–	–	–	–	0
Jan Magnussen	DK	4/7/73	McLaren-Mercedes	–	–	–	–	–	–	–	–	–	–	–	–	–	–	10	–	–	0
Nigel Mansell	GB	8/8/53	McLaren-Mercedes	–	–	10	R	–	–	–	–	–	–	–	–	–	–	–	–	–	0
Pierluigi Martini	I	23/4/61	Minardi-Ford	R	R	12	14	7	R	R	7	R	–	–	–	–	–	–	–	–	0
Andrea Montermini	I	30/5/64	Pacific-Ford	9	R	R	DNS	DQ	R	NC	R	8	12	R	DNS	R	R	R	R	R	0
Roberto Moreno	BR	11/2/59	Forti-Ford	R	NC	NC	R	R	R	16	R	R	14	DNS	17	R	16	R	R		0
Massimiliano Papis	I	3/10/69	Footwork-Hart	–	–	–	–	–	–	–	R	DNS	R	R	7	DNS	12	–	–	–	0
Domenico Schiattarella	I	17/11/67	Simtek-Ford	R	9	R	15	DNS	–	–	–	–	–	–	–	–	–	–	–	–	0
Gabriele Tarquini	I	2/3/62	Tyrrell-Yamaha	–	–	–	–	–	–	–	–	–	–	–	–	–	14	–	–	–	0
Jos Verstappen	NL	4/3/72	Simtek-Ford	R	R	R	12	DNS	–	–	–	–	–	–	–	–	–	–	–	–	0
Karl Wendlinger	A	20/12/68	Sauber-Ford	R	R	R	13	–	–	–	–	–	–	–	–	–	–	10	R		0

KEY

p	pole position	*	classified but not running at the finish	DQ	disqualified
f	fastest lap	R	retired	DNS	did not start
		NC	not classified		

POINTS & PERCENTAGES
Compiled by DAVID HAYHOE

CAREER PERFORMANCES: 1995 DRIVERS

Driver	Nationality	Races	Championships	Wins	2nd places	3rd places	4th places	5th places	6th places	Pole positions	Fastest laps	Points
Jean Alesi	F	102	–	1	8	9	9	9	3	1	2	142
Luca Badoer	F	29	–	–	–	–	–	–	–	–	–	–
Rubens Barrichello	BR	48	–	–	1	1	6	1	2	1	–	32
Gerhard Berger	A	180	–	9	15	20	20	8	9	11	18	338*
Mark Blundell	GB	61	–	–	–	3	2	6	2	–	–	32
Jean-Christophe Boullion	F	11	–	–	–	–	–	1	1	–	–	3
Martin Brundle	GB	142	–	–	–	2	7	7	11	7	–	90
David Coulthard	GB	25	–	1	5	3	2	2	1	5	4	63
Jean-Denis Deletraz	F	3	–	–	–	–	–	–	–	–	–	–
Pedro Diniz	BR	17	–	–	–	–	–	–	–	–	–	–
Heinz-Harald Frentzen	D	32	–	–	–	1	2	3	6	–	–	22
Bertrand Gachot	F	47	–	–	–	–	–	1	3	–	1	5
Mika Häkkinen	SF	63	–	–	3	6	3	3	3	–	–	60
Johnny Herbert	GB	80	–	2	1	1	8	3	3	–	–	63
Damon Hill	GB	51	–	13	12	5	2	–	1	11	14	229
Taki Inoue	J	18	–	–	–	–	–	–	–	–	–	–
Eddie Irvine	GB	32	–	–	–	1	1	2	2	3	–	17
Ukyo Katayama	J	62	–	–	–	–	–	2	1	–	–	5
Pedro Lamy	P	16	–	–	–	–	–	–	1	–	–	1
Giovanni Lavaggi	I	4	–	–	–	–	–	–	–	–	–	–
Jan Magnussen	DK	1	–	–	–	–	–	–	–	–	–	–
Nigel Mansell	GB	187	1	31	17	11	8	6	9	32	30	482
Pierluigi Martini	I	119	–	–	–	–	2	4	4	–	–	18
Andrea Montermini	I	17	–	–	–	–	–	–	–	–	–	–
Gianni Morbidelli	I	60	–	–	–	1	–	1	3	–	–	8.5
Roberto Moreno	BR	42	–	–	1	–	2	1	1	–	1	15
Olivier Panis	F	33	–	–	2	–	2	2	3	–	–	25
Massimiliano Papis	I	7	–	–	–	–	–	–	–	–	–	–
Mika Salo	J	19	–	–	–	–	–	2	1	–	–	5
Domenico Schiattarella	I	7	–	–	–	–	–	–	–	–	–	–
Michael Schumacher	D	69	2	19	11	8	3	2	10	23	–	303
Aguri Suzuki	J	64	–	–	–	1	–	–	4	–	–	8
Gabriele Tarquini	I	38	–	–	–	–	–	1	–	–	–	1
Jos Verstappen	NL	15	–	–	–	2	–	1	–	–	–	10
Karl Wendlinger	A	41	–	–	–	–	3	1	3	–	–	14

includes 1 point from 1984 that was not valid for the championship

GRID POSITIONS: 1995

	Driver	Starts	Best	Worst	Average
1	Damon Hill	17	1	8	2.47
2	David Coulthard	17	1	6	2.65
3	Michael Schumacher	17	1	16	2.94
4	Gerhard Berger	17	1	8	4.18
5	Jean Alesi	17	2	10	5.06
6	Mika Häkkinen	15	3	13	6.87
7	Johnny Herbert	17	4	11	7.35
8	Eddie Irvine	17	4	12	7.59
9	Nigel Mansell	2	9	10	9.50
10	Rubens Barrichello	17	5	16	9.53
11	Heinz-Harald Frentzen	17	5	14	10.35
12	Martin Brundle	11	8	14	10.64
13	Mark Blundell	15	6	23	11.33
14	Olivier Panis	17	6	18	11.65
15	Jan Magnussen	1	12	12	12.00
16	Gianni Morbidelli	10	11	19	13.80
17	Mika Salo	17	7	23	14.35
18	Jean-Christophe Boullion	11	13	19	15.55
19	Ukyo Katayama	16	11	19	15.63
20	Aguri Suzuki	5	13	19	16.20
21	Pedro Lamy	8	14	19	16.37
22	Luca Badoer	17	12	21	17.12
23	Massimiliano Papis	7	15	20	17.71
24	Pierluigi Martini	9	15	20	17.78
25	Jos Verstappen	5	14	24	18.80
26=	Gabriele Tarquini	1	19	19	19.00
26=	Karl Wendlinger	6	15	21	19.00
28	Taki Inoue	17	18	26	20.06
29=	Andrea Montermini	17	19	25	22.00
29=	Bertrand Gachot	11	20	24	22.00
31	Domenico Schiattarella	5	20	26	22.20
32	Roberto Moreno	17	20	25	22.71
33	Pedro Diniz	17	20	26	22.82
34	Giovanni Lavaggi	4	23	24	23.75
35	Jean-Denis Deletraz	2	24	24	24.00

UNLAPPED: 1995

Number of cars on same lap as leader

Grand Prix	Starters	at ¼ distance	at ½ distance	at ¾ distance	at full distance
Brazil	26	12	8	4	2
Argentina	26	11	5	3	3
San Marino	26	11	4	4	4
Spain	26	18	8	4	4
Monaco	26	13	6	3	3
Canada	24	15	6	5	5
France	24	17	9	6	5
Britain	24	19	7	7	5
Germany	24	18	11	5	4
Hungary	24	16	13	3	2
Belgium	24	21	13	10	10
Italy	24	19	10	7	4
Portugal	24	14	7	8	5
Europe	24	14	7	4	3
Pacific	24	16	9	7	3
Japan	23	18	8	5	4
Australia	23	18	11	11	1

LAP LEADERS: 1995

Grand Prix	Michael Schumacher	Damon Hill	David Coulthard	Jean Alesi	Johnny Herbert	Gerhard Berger	Mika Häkkinen	Rubens Barrichello
Brazil	47	12	12	–	–	–	–	–
Argentina	6	53	5	8	–	–	–	–
San Marino	9	42	1	–	11	–	–	–
Spain	65	–	–	–	–	–	–	–
Monaco	54	23	–	1	–	–	–	–
Canada	57	–	–	12	–	–	–	–
France	51	21	–	–	–	–	–	–
Britain	13	32	2	–	14	–	–	–
Germany	40	1	4	–	–	–	–	–
Hungary	–	77	–	–	–	–	–	–
Belgium	25	6	8	2	3	–	–	–
Italy	–	–	13	17	10	11	–	1
Portugal	–	5	66	–	–	–	–	–
Europe	3	–	12	52	–	–	–	–
Pacific	34	–	49	–	–	–	–	–
Japan	48	4	–	–	–	–	1	–
Australia	2	60	19	–	–	–	–	–
Total	454	336	191	92	27	22	2	1
Percentage	(40.4%)	(29.9%)	(17.0%)	(8.2%)	(2.4%)	(2.0%)	(0.2%)	(0.1%)

RETIREMENTS: 1995

Number of cars to have retired

Grand Prix	Starters	at ¼ distance	at ½ distance	at ¾ distance	at full distance
Brazil	26	8	11	15	16
Argentina	26	8	10	15	15
San Marino	26	4	7	10	10
Spain	26	1	5	8	11
Monaco	26	5	9	12	16
Canada	24	4	7	11	15
France	24	4	6	7	7
Britain	24	2	9	11	13
Germany	24	6	10	15	16
Hungary	24	4	5	9	13
Belgium	24	2	7	10	10
Italy	24	6	10	11	14
Portugal	24	5	5	7	7
Europe	24	4	5	8	9
Pacific	24	4	5	6	7
Japan	23	4	8	10	11
Australia	23	6	12	12	15

FORMULA 3000 REVIEW

PLAYING THE PERCENTAGES
by Andrew Benson

'The problem for me has been that my father sells chickens – he's not Graham Hill or Gilles Villeneuve!' It was the quote of the season, and it was the way Vincenzo Sospiri justified taking four up-and-down years to win the Formula 3000 International Championship. 'I never had a huge budget to do F3000 with a proper team,' he said. 'But I never gave up, and this has been the first year when I've had the best car. I think I've done a good job.'

In many ways, Sospiri was right. It was his first year with the best car in the field, and he did make good use of it, but even in his moment of glory, Sospiri remains an enigma.

Although he won more races than anyone else in 1995 – and three victories out of eight races is pretty good by anyone's standards – Sospiri played the percentages on his way to the title.

'When I had to win, I did,' was the way the genial, wiry Italian shrugged off the critics. 'Which is better,' he asks, 'starting from pole or winning the race? If I don't feel it is better to go for pole position, that I can more easily win the day after if I start from second or third, then I won't go for pole.'

Sospiri was never on the front row, but that was never a problem, because his racing ability is from the top drawer. He set out to do a job, and he completed it with the minimum of fuss. His season was one of admirable consistency, and in the end he won the title a race early.

The way he won it in many ways reflected the way he approached the season. The Super Nova Reynard 95D-Cosworth AC was by far the most competitive proposition at the start of the year, and rival team bosses admitted that the team had used its time over the winter better than anyone else – aided immeasurably by sticking with Sospiri for a second consecutive season.

The result was a supremely user-friendly car which, while it was not always the fastest, allowed the drivers always to get the most out of it. And that they did. Sospiri and team-mate Ricardo Rosset left rival teams reeling with their absolute domination of the first half of the season, each winning two of the first four races – including three 1-2s – and by that time Sospiri was already in an almost unassailable position at the top of the championship.

So good a shape was he in, in fact, that a no-score at the German Grand Prix round did little to harm his position, and he all but tied up the title with a superbly controlled win at the Belgian GP, which ensured that only Rosset could now beat him – and even that would be a long shot.

After that, the team dropped off. Sospiri clinched the championship with a comfortable cruise to seventh place in Portugal, gauging his race on Rosset, who was only a couple of places ahead of him, and ended the year with a low-key fifth at Magny-Cours.

It was Sospiri's experience that put him ahead of Rosset. Before the title was sewn up, when Sospiri had an off-race he would still usually finish second. When Rosset did, generally because he did not know a track, he would not get any points at all.

Rosset was, in many ways, the season's outstanding driver. We already knew that Sospiri was good; Rosset we were less sure of. But most of the doubts that may have been in the mind after two unconvincing years in British Formula 3 were firmly dispelled when he dominated the first round from pole position. OK, it was at Silverstone, a track he knew well, but Rosset confirmed his talent with a second place to Sospiri at the next round in Barcelona.

That he did not mount a stronger challenge for the title was solely down to inexperience on circuits he did not know. But otherwise he was at least a match for Sospiri, proving quicker than his team-mate on several occasions despite this being only his first season in F3000.

He did enough in 1995 to convince that he has developed into a fine racing driver. A calm, phlegmatic, friendly man, Rosset will surely adapt to F1 without problem, as long as he can wriggle into a drive. He certainly has nothing left to prove in F3000.

In Super Nova's wake, Belgian Marc Goossens rewarded some serious hard work by chassis manufacturer Lola and his team Nordic Racing with third place in the championship. A tough, feisty racer, once Goossens had finally got the hang of qualifying – at Hockenheim in July – he became a constant feature in the battle for victory. A dominant win in Germany was followed by a tigerish drive behind Sospiri at Spa, which ended in the wall, a less convincing performance at Estoril, and then second at Magny-Cours, where he spent most of the race on the tail of race-winner Kenny Bräck. Third place was no less than he deserved.

Lola, in fact, bounced back to competitiveness after three years in the wilderness with a vengeance, and into the bargain won the contract to supply next year's one-make F3000 chassis.

Had the Danielson team had a chance to do any pre-season testing, and had its lead driver, Christophe Bouchut, managed to get his hands on a Lola rather than an engineerless Reynard before the third round, he could perhaps have pushed Goossens for the best Lola driver slot.

Bouchut, whose fiery personality and irreverent approach provided many light-hearted moments on and off the track, rapidly gained speed in the second half of the season, and he did more than enough to prove that he has what it takes to make it at the sport's highest level.

Bräck, too, had a good season with Madgwick International. He got off to a slow start, but his race-winning potential began to show at Enna-Pergusa, the fourth round, where he qualified on pole but squandered a possible win with a poor start and then excessive kerb-climbing which resulted in broken suspension. But from then on, he was a constant feature at the front,

FORMULA 3000 REVIEW

Left: Fortune smiled on Vincenzo Sospiri at last and the experienced Italian made the most of his opportunity.

Right: Looking ahead. Paul Stewart and his father Jackie have yet to crack F3000 but it is assumed they have their sights set on F1.

Few had expected Ricardo Rosset *(below)* to be a title contender.

Marc Goossens *(below right)* restored Lola's credibility with a commanding victory at Hockenheim.

Bottom right: Sweden's Kenny Bräck made impressive progress, taking a win in the final race at Magny-Cours.

and his season ended in impressive fashion with third at Estoril being followed by a lights-to-flag win at the final round.

Seventh overall with no wins, however, was a lot less than Allan McNish had been hoping for. Perhaps the driver potentially closest to the pace of the Super Nova men, the former Benetton test driver was desperate to re-establish himself in the forefront of F1 team managers' minds. But while he and Paul Stewart Racing certainly did not lack for pace, McNish's season fell apart around him.

Impressive poles at Barcelona and Spa were wasted by a spin and an engine problem, and while he qualified right up at the front in all but two of the races, annoying problems – bad starts, engine failures, assaults by out-of-control Frenchmen (Emmanuel Clérico at Enna) or Brazilians (Tarso Marques in Magny-Cours), for example – left him with a meagre score and, once again, an uncertain future.

The French DAMS and Apomatox teams also had a comparatively miserable time. Having finished first and second in 1994 with five wins between them, only DAMS won a race this year, courtesy of the mercurial Brazilian, Tarso Marques.

A combination of the 19-year-old and the champion team of the last two years was always likely to be fast, but what was less sure was how long the car would stay on the road. Sure enough, while Marques took his first win in convincing style at the penultimate round at Estoril, and was strong and consistent in other places, he still showed at times a waywardness that will need to be curbed if he is to make it in F1. However, if Marques can be controlled, he has the speed to go a long way.

His team-mate Guillaume Gomez was occasionally impressive – pole and third place at Hockenheim, third at Spa, front row at Pau – but crashed too much. And Apomatox's lead driver Emmanuel Clérico spent much of the year close to the pace, but not close enough. He has the natural speed, as he proved in 1994, but for much of the time in 1995 he seemed a little bored. Still, he has the money to make it to F1 if he chooses to do so.

Marco Campos looked like he had the talent to do the same, but his death at the end of the season robbed the sport of a promising young star. It was a horrifying accident, Campos's car taking off over the back of a rival and coming down upside down on a concrete wall. But it was generally accepted that there were no safety implications. One experienced observer suggested that the accident would have been unsurvivable in any single-seater. The tragic irony is that in a series which had not seen a driver fatality in its 11-year existence, Campos's was the last car racing on the last lap of the last race.

The crash left a terribly bitter taste in the mouth at the end of F3000's last year as a free-chassis, free-engine formula. Next year, the F3000 International Championship retains its name, but switches to a cost-cutting one-make concept, about which the jury is still out.

Some think it will be a great step forward, and a number of new teams have already pledged their support, including the Arrows F1 team, which will run a satellite operation. But some insiders worry that the new F3000 is so restrictive that it will fail to provide a sensible technical challenge for drivers and engineers before F1. At this early stage, whether it will work is unclear. We can only hope that it starts on a better note than that on which its predecessor finished.

FORMULA THREE REVIEW

VICTORY FOR OLIVER'S ARMY

by Gary Watkins

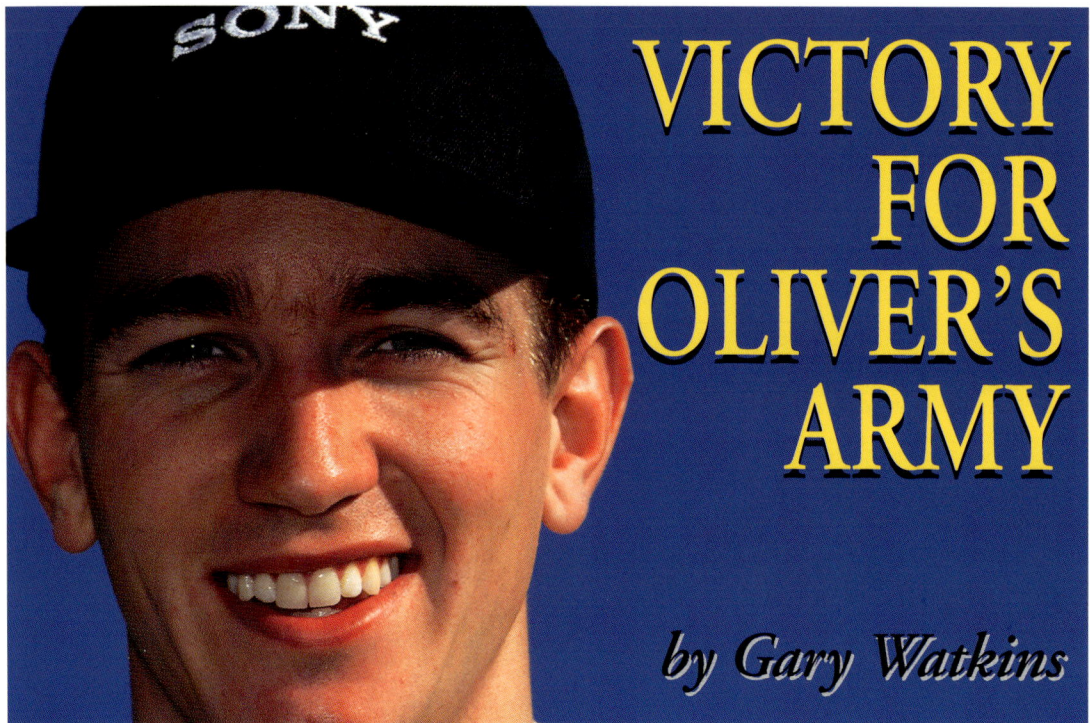

Paul Stewart Racing claimed it was Ralph Firman's ten-second penalty for jumping the start at Oulton Park in August; the Edenbridge Racing team said it came at Snetterton three weeks later, when its driver Oliver Gavin dominated and Firman made an unforced error and ended up with a zero score.

It's difficult to identify the exact turning point of the 1995 British Formula 3 Championship, but one thing is for certain – the mid-season dominance that had seen Firman become almost a dead cert for the title came to an end and allowed series returnee Gavin to pinch the crown from right under his nose. The turnaround was dramatic, but perhaps not altogether unexpected – it provided a thrilling final twist in a topsy-turvy season that saw the fortunes of the leading protagonists rise and fall like the tide.

High watermark for Firman came at the height of the summer. In the five races in four weeks from the last weekend in July to the last weekend in August, the 20-year-old notched up five straight pole positions aboard his Dallara-Mugen Honda. Firman won three of them, though he lost certain victory in another, courtesy of that stop-go penalty.

After the Brands Hatch August Bank Holiday double-header, where he was probably at his most dominant, Firman was 36 points clear of PSR team-mate Helio Castro Neves, nigh on the equivalent of two maximum scores – and with just six races to go. Gavin, meanwhile, was a further two points behind and utterly demoralised by the dominance of his fellow Brit.

When the F3 circus rolled into Snetterton a fortnight later, Gavin looked a changed man, especially after he put his Vauxhall-engined Dallara on pole. With Firman only third on the grid, it seemed, just maybe, that the tide was beginning to turn.

Confirmation of this came in the race: Gavin produced a display of Firmanesque authority, stretching his lead at will and claiming the bonus point for fastest lap along the way. Firman, meanwhile, made another of the unnecessary errors that punctuated his season, crashing out of third place.

A 38-point deficit had been reduced to 17, but that gap promptly went out to 37 points when Firman led home a PSR 1-2 in the first of the two races at Pembrey two weeks later with Gavin failing to score.

Within an hour, however, the smile was wiped off the faces of the PSR team when their lead driver had ten seconds added to his race time for, said the clerk of the course, failing to observe the correct procedure behind the pace car. Before the start of the second race a few hours later, PSR managed to get the decision overturned, something that was still subject to an appeal by Edenbridge at the season's end.

But Firman's sixth win of the year was to be his last. From that moment on, the snap went out of his driving. He could only watch from seventh place as Gavin won the second part of the Pembrey double-header.

This downhill trend continued in rounds 16 and 17 of the 18-race series at Silverstone. With part of his front wing lost against a marker cone, Firman tried every trick in the book to keep his championship rival behind, even though they were fighting for eighth place. Inevitably it ended in tears, with Gavin spinning down to 19th, but not before Firman's actions had caught the attention of the clerk of the course, who subsequently disqualified him from the race.

With Gavin cantering away to his sixth win of the season in the second race, Firman again saw red as he made an optimistic bid for fifth place, clouting the car ahead. His left-front tyre punctured, the Norfolk driver dropped out of the points, but again the officials took umbrage, endorsing the driver's licence. With three black marks against his name, Firman was lucky to keep his racing licence and had to sweat for three days before finding out that he would actually be able to race in the Thruxton finale the following week.

It wasn't the perfect preparation for a head-to-head battle. And on a circuit at which PSR hadn't had the best of days earlier in the year, Firman was unable to present an effective challenge. Level on points going into the race (with Castro Neves a further nine behind), it was effectively a straight race to the flag between the two Brits. And it was a battle that 23-year-old Gavin won hands down with a measured drive to third position, four places ahead of his lacklustre rival.

When it was all over, Firman admitted that he had felt the pressure at Silverstone, explaining his loss of the title thus: 'We didn't pick up enough minor positions, the fourths, fifths and sixths.' But even then, Firman's F3 decline looked set to continue. With Edenbridge's appeal of the Pembrey results pending, the six-times winner was faced with the prospect of dropping to fourth in the points behind Castro Neves and Warren Hughes.

If the pressure got to Firman at the final reckoning, then it was Gavin who got the jitters at the beginning of the year. He stalled at the start of round one, before bouncing back in perfect style at Thruxton with two victories – one fortuitous, one dominant. But there were more mistakes along the way, most notably at the most important race of the year. In front of the Formula 1 circus at Silverstone in July, Gavin should have repeated his 1993 British Grand Prix supporter victory. On pole by a massive three-tenths of a second, he succumbed to relentless pressure from Brazilian Gualter Salles on the opening lap of the race, taking a trip across the grass at Club Corner. Then with Firman stretching his legs in the month of August, Gavin stalled again at Oulton Park.

As the fortunes of Firman and Gavin rose and fell, a consistent season from Castro Neves brought him to the verge of his first title success. After a false start at the Silverstone season-openers, when his racing lasted two corners, he bounced back with a string of top-six results, which included no fewer than five seconds and five fourths. But the fact that he could only win a solitary race meant he could never quite get on terms with Firman and Gavin.

Jérémie Dufour failed to score points in just one round of the championship, and then only after he had been excluded from the results for dangerous driving. But to describe his season with the Ligier Junior team as consistent would be incorrect. The Frenchman – still only 20, yet in his third season of British F3 – showed all the traits that had characterised his efforts in previous seasons, except that this time he actually won a championship race, at Silverstone in May. He would impress at some point during the weekend, but all too often via an impressive drive to make up for a poor qualifying position. No fewer than five fastest laps are a testament to that.

Unlike Dufour, fellow F3 veteran Warren Hughes had previously won a race, but you needed a long memory to recall his solitary victory in the class back in 1992. Hughes almost returned to the winner's circle at Thruxton in April, before tangling with James Matthews in an optimistic manoeuvre to take the lead.

Through the year, Hughes kept his name in the limelight by virtue of some flying starts and astounding first laps, which quite often converted poor grid positions into podium finishes. But when it all came right at the end of the season, the 28-year-old was virtually unbeatable, notching up two victories for the HKS Mitsubishi-engined Alan Docking Racing team.

FORMULA THREE REVIEW

Far left: Oliver Gavin's decision to return to F3 represented a considerable gamble but it paid off when he snatched the title at the last gasp.

Left: Brazilian quartet Cristiano da Matta, Luiz Garcia Jnr, Helio Castro Neves and Gualter Salles made less of an impression than many had expected.

Above left: Ralph Firman leads the pack at Oulton Park. The ten-second penalty that cost him victory marked a turning point in the Norfolk driver's fortunes.

Above: Gavin gave Edenbridge Racing its first F3 title, breaking PSR's grip on the championship.

Luca Rangoni *(left)* overcame strong opposition to take the Italian title.

Below: Drivers competing in the German series came out on top in the Marlboro Masters of F3 at Zandvoort. Winner Norberto Fontana is flanked by runner-up Ralf Schumacher *(left)* and Brazilian Helio Castro Neves.

After Castro Neves and Salles, a third Brazilian took to the top step of the podium in 1995. His name was Cristiano da Matta, and he'd arrived in Britain as reigning Brazilian F3 Champion, quickly boosting his reputation with a series of impressive pre-season tests.

But his year never truly recovered from a big crash at Thruxton in April. Da Matta's next points finish came an amazing five months later, although he ended this barren run with a victory at Oulton, albeit after Firman was penalised.

Unlike a string of Brazilians, including the late Ayrton Senna and Rubens Barrichello, who have come knocking on the door of the West Surrey Racing team, da Matta never gelled with its boss, Dick Bennetts. In fact, on one of the many occasions he ended a race in the tyre barrier, da Matta promptly disappeared for several hours.

That race was the Marlboro Masters of F3 at Zandvoort in the Netherlands, the annual chance for the cream of Europe's F3 talent to race on something approaching equal terms. As it has done before, the German F3 Championship came out on top, with Norberto Fontana leading home Ralf Schumacher, while Castro Neves upheld 'British' honour with a distant third.

Fontana, already the Sauber Formula 1 team's test driver, also had the better of Schumacher, younger brother of you-know-who, over the course of the year. Ten wins from the 16 races gave the diminutive Argentinian the title, despite a mid-season burst of three victories from four starts from Schumacher.

The sternest challenge to the two German series runners at Zandvoort should have come from Italian Gianantonio Pacchioni, who had already notched up his second victory in Europe's other big race, the Monaco F3 Grand Prix. But after qualifying a close third, he lost any chance of victory when he spun on the opening lap after being hit from behind.

Despite his vast F3 experience, Pacchioni couldn't win the Italian title for the Prema Power Team. Instead, that honour fell to Luca Rangoni, who finally overcame a stiff challenge from Andrea Boldrini at the final meeting of the year, despite winning one race fewer.

The French stayed away from the big races in 1995, thanks to cost-cutting rules which outlawed the new breed of F3 car. But Laurent Redon still claimed that the French F3 crown, which he'd narrowly won from Nicolas Minassian, was as prestigious as any other in Europe.

He was wrong on that count. While the championship protagonists in the well-promoted German series were at least a match for any driver in the category, the British championship retained the strength in depth that has made sure it is the most prestigious prize in F3 over the past decade. Well done, Oliver Gavin.

237

SUPERCAR SUPREME

by Adam Cooper

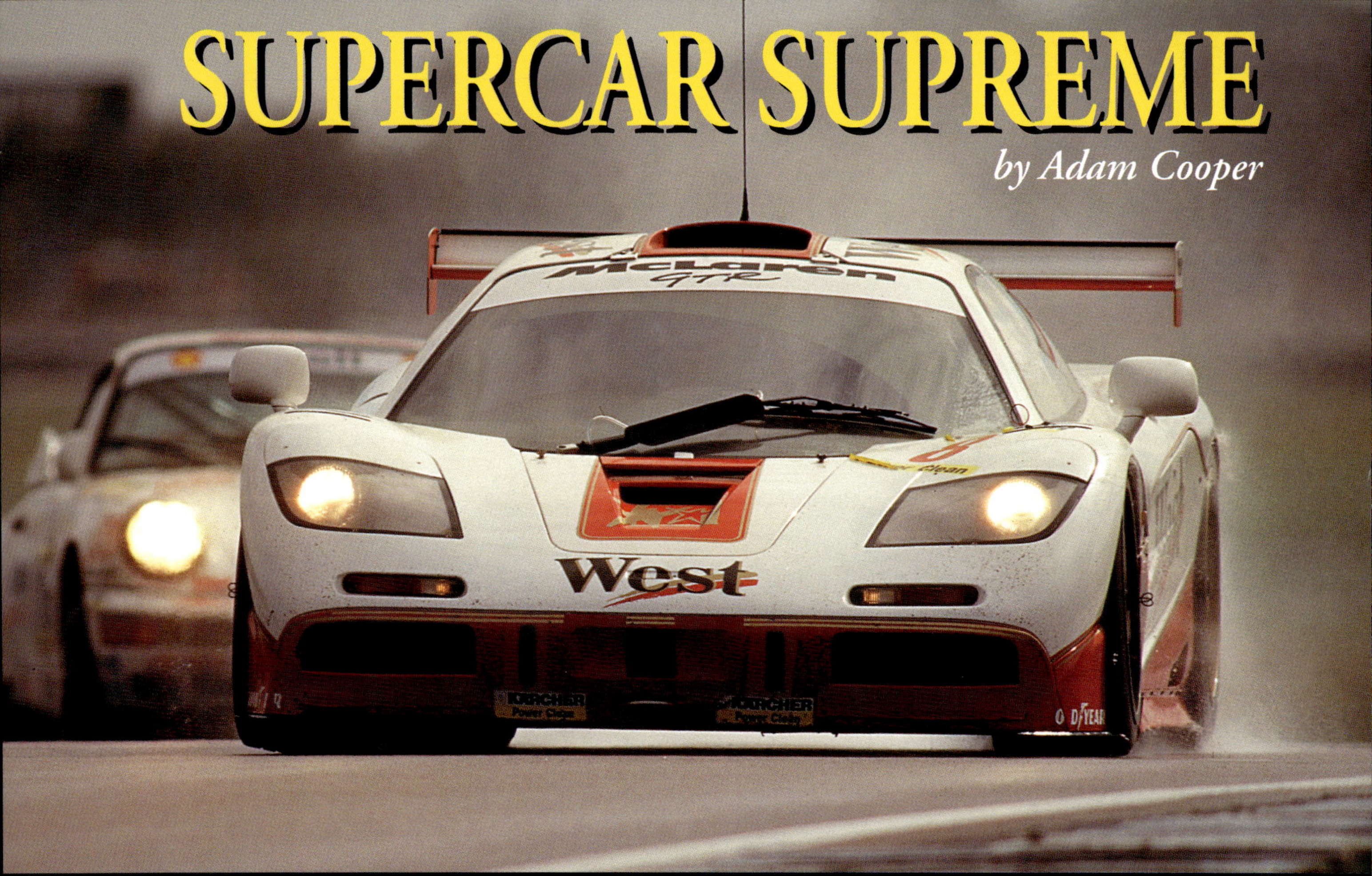

John Overton

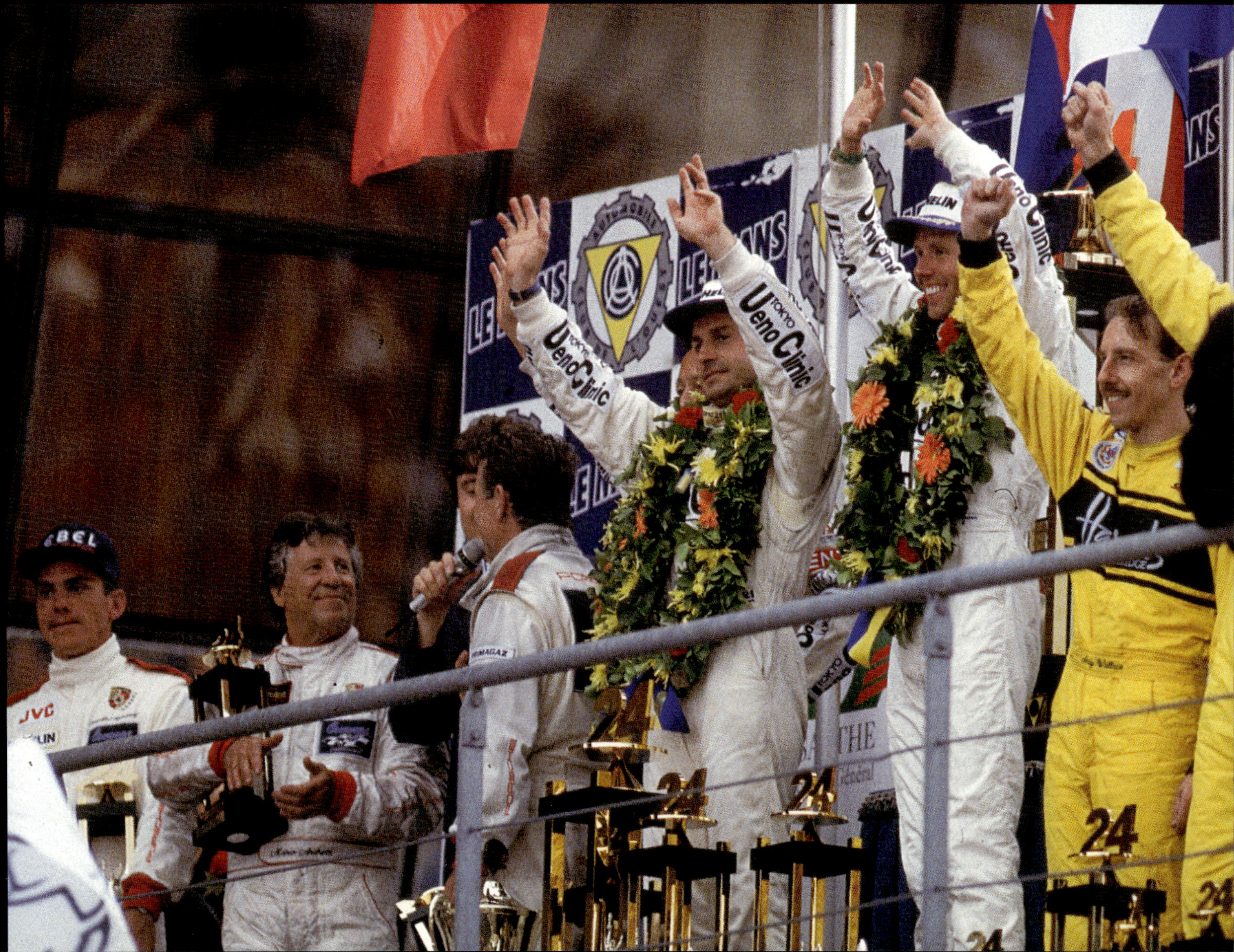

Nigel Snowdon

SPORTS CAR RACING REVIEW

The consistent West McLaren of John Nielsen and Thomas Bscher *(left)* won the BPR-organised GT series after a close-fought contest with the Gulf-backed GTR of Ray Bellm and Maurizio Sala.

Below: What might have been. While the victorious McLaren trio Sekiya, Dalmas and Lehto *(centre)* take the applause, Mario Andretti wears a rueful smile as he talks with Courage team-mate Bob Wollek, having finished second at Le Mans and thus failed to equal the late Graham Hill's unique achievement of winning the World Championship, the Indianapolis 500 and Le Mans 24 Hours.

Above right: The IMSA championship saw an intriguing battle between the Ferrari of Fermin Velez *(left)* and the Ford R&S of British expat racer James Weaver. The Spaniard took the title at the final round.

Against all the odds, sports car racing has emerged from the shadows. International GT racing flourished in 1995, and seems to have a healthy future, albeit not at the heady level predicted a few years ago.

The days of massive manufacturer involvement are gone, the big budgets going to touring cars or, in the case of Peugeot and Mercedes, to F1. The emphasis is now on private teams funded by wealthy amateurs, and small, specialist marques.

This year Le Mans ran its own, totally independent show, but next season the French race was due to join forces with Daytona and Suzuka in what promised to be a prestigious, FIA-approved 'Triple Crown'.

However, as is usual in this form of racing, getting the parties to agree on regulations proved difficult, and in October the World Motor Sport Council postponed the idea until at least 1997. One of the main problems was the continued presence of prototypes both in the IMSA series and at Le Mans at a time when the FIA is trying to push GTs.

The catalyst for the sports car revival is not the FIA nor even the Automobile Club de l'Ouest, but a small, Paris-based organisation called BPR. After a modest start with a series of non-championship GT races in 1994, Jurgen Barth and his colleagues announced an ambitious schedule for '95, with four-hour events all over Europe supplemented by visits to Suzuka and the Zhuhai street track in China.

After the season started, BPR gained FIA approval to award points at its events, and so the Global GT Endurance Series came into being. It was generally adjudged a success, although many felt there were too many races, especially in the first half of the year.

In its maiden season in 1994, BPR attracted mainly Porsches, Venturis and a few Ferraris, but '95 saw the arrival of an eagerly awaited contender in the form of the McLaren F1 GTR. Ron Dennis gave in to pressure to turn the BMW-powered supercar into a racing machine, and designer Gordon Murray did an excellent conversion job. It may have been a very expensive purchase, but no one who forked out for a GTR could complain. It was a superbly engineered machine, and an instant race winner.

The four-hour 'sprints' were usually battles between two British McLaren teams. Former Spice owner and Group C2 World Champion Ray Bellm put together a two-car, Gulf-sponsored effort, with himself and Maurizio Sala in one car, and Pierre-Henri Raphanel and gentleman racer Lindsay Owen-Jones in the other.

Ex-Sauber team manager David Price ran cars for two wealthy owners. Thomas Bscher raced alongside John Nielsen in his West entry, while Moody Fayed preferred to watch and hire two pros for his Harrods-backed car. Andy Wallace was his anchorman, along with a variety of co-drivers. Another very competitive car was run by the French Jacadi team.

After dominating the four-hour events, the real test for the McLaren came at Le Mans. There, the GTR faced reliability worries and extra opposition in the form of open 'Le Mans Prototypes', inspired by IMSA's World Sports Car class. The quickest of these were former Group C cars with their roofs chopped and both downforce and power severely restricted.

One of these cars nearly produced what would have been one of the most romantic results of the season. Having retired from Indy cars, Mario Andretti returned to the Sarthe with the Courage-Porsche team, and came within a whisker of joining Graham Hill as the only man to win Le Mans, Indy and the World Championship.

Mario had only himself to blame, for the car lost vital minutes after he crashed when caught up in traffic. A superb comeback drive, aided by fellow veteran Bob Wollek and '93 winner Eric Hélary, brought the car back to runner-up spot.

No one knew if the McLarens could survive the rigours of the race, but they did. Victory went to the least troubled car, handled by JJ Lehto, Yannick Dalmas and Masanori Sekiya. The winning car was a factory-owned machine, leased to a Japanese sponsor and run by a mixed bag of a crew.

The other McLarens, all regulars in the BPR series, had a variety of problems, including several accidents in what was the wettest and slowest Le Mans in years. Unluckiest of the lot was probably the Harrods machine, in which Derek Bell came close to winning his sixth Le Mans in the company of Wallace and son Justin. Late transmission problems dropped them to third.

The BPR points race was close, but eventually the title went to Bscher and his vastly experienced co-driver Nielsen, even though Bellm and Sala won more races in the lead Gulf entry.

The only cars to seriously challenge the McLarens for overall victories were Ferrari F40s. They were fast but proved rather fragile, although one took the honours at Anderstorp. The race at Montlhéry – boycotted by the McLarens – went to a Porsche.

Both at Le Mans and in the BPR races, a large number of other marques appeared, and many interesting future projects were announced. The possibilities seem endless.

In Japan, GT racing went its own successful way, Nissan, Toyota and Honda all supporting it strongly. Toyota's Supra was very competitive, its drivers including F1 refugee Erik Comas. The title went to Nissan's Skyline, which also appeared at Le Mans as the first step in a serious effort to win the race within three years.

Meanwhile IMSA continued to promote the open WSC cars as its main class. The season saw a fascinating battle between the Ferrari 333SPs and the new Ford-powered R&S chassis. Brit James Weaver came close to stealing the title from Maranello with the latter, but he was pipped at the final round by Spaniard Fermin Velez in Scandia's works-supported 333SP.

The Ferraris failed at Daytona, and Kremer's visiting Porsche 962 Spyder scooped the honours with a steady run. The Italian marque made amends with a historic triumph at Sebring, where Velez was joined by Eric van de Poele and team owner Andy Evans.

While there was interest at the front, IMSA suffered from a serious lack of strength in depth. The series faces an uncertain future, although the organisation continues to make optimistic noises about larger grids. It also continues to frustrate competitors, something it did most notably at Daytona, where a full factory effort from Porsche was cancelled after a late rule change. The marque later canned its Le Mans plans as well.

Porsche's stillborn, TWR-built car could yet be dusted off for a shot at Le Mans, where turbo-powered prototypes are still welcome. Ferrari's next target is also the 24 Hours. The company took pains to avoid official involvement in this year's race, although privateer Massimo Sigala went under his own steam and regretted it after experiencing an awful weekend. A full factory effort, the first for 23 years, will be a different story.

Meanwhile the BPR series goes from strength to strength. Races at Interlagos and Laguna Seca in California have been added to the '96 schedule, and it will be a GT World Championship in all but name.

Main photo: The winning McLaren of JJ Lehto, Yannick Dalmas and Masanori Sekiya takes the chequered flag at Le Mans.

Inset right: Moody Fayed's Harrods-backed car ran into late-race transmission problems which dropped it to third, denying veteran Derek Bell the chance of a sixth win.

The second Gulf Racing McLaren of Raphanel/Owen-Jones/Alliot *(inset far right)* was halted by an accident, but the sister car of Blundell/Bellm/Sala reached the finish in fourth place.

Photos: Bryn Williams/Words & Pictures

BRITISH TOURING CAR CHAMPIONSHIP REVIEW

DOMESTIC BLISS

by Laurence Foster

BRITISH TOURING CAR CHAMPIONSHIP REVIEW

Headlights ablaze, the Vauxhall Cavalier of John Cleland leads the pack in the early stages of the British Grand Prix support race. The Scot went on to take his fourth win in a row, establishing a firm grip on the championship.

After two years of domination by raiders from the Continent, 1995 was the year when the home-grown establishment finally got its act together again in the British Touring Car Championship.

In 1993, BMW Team Schnitzer and Jo Winkelhock had looted 2-litre tin-top racing's glittering prize, thanks to Germanic efficiency and a staggering attention to detail. A year later, Alfa Corse and Gabriele Tarquini brought Italian guile and a new perspective on rulebooks, and left with the silverware.

But in 1995, the oldest double-act in the business – 43-year-old Scottish motor trader John Cleland and the venerable Vauxhall Cavalier – showed how the indigenous species were now just as capable of cutting it too. As Cleland himself succinctly put it after claiming the BTCC crown with two races still to run: 'not bad for an old-timer in an old fleet car, eh?'

As well as shifting the balance back to the British-based teams, Cleland's title was also significant in showing there's still room for a dyed-in-the-wool saloon specialist in the BTCC, despite the tidal wave of single-seater talent that has poured into the series in recent seasons.

Cleland served notice of intent with victory in April's Donington Park season-opener, and backed that up with a trio of second places as the series rolled to its mid-point. But it was four victories on the trot at the height of summer, including the prestigious British Grand Prix support race and a crushing Donington Park double, that effectively put the title in the Scot's pocket.

After that, one more victory and a conveyor belt of podium spots ensured that a second BTCC crown, adding to the one he claimed in the class-riddled days of 1989, was his before the mid-September Silverstone finale.

Perhaps the title could have been Cleland's even sooner had he not spent his first Brands Hatch visit of the season exploring the scenery with almost metronomic regularity? That glitch aside, however, it was an almost flawless season, with Cleland always ready to adapt himself to the most realistic option on any given day – win, podium or points – as he looked at the bigger title picture.

If there was a slight niggle for him at the end of it all, it was only that Cleland had failed to achieve his self-set goal of equalling Tarquini's BTCC record of eight wins the previous season. That and the fact that Vauxhall failed to take the manufacturers' crown and make it a clean sweep of titles.

Looking back to the two years of foreign domination that had gone before, the Cleland/Cavalier combination was never totally out of the picture, as a pair of fourth places in the final championship points testified. But it took a change of the Super Touring aerodynamic regulations and a switch of tyre manufacturer to give the Ray Mallock-built Cavalier, with its outstanding chassis and bullet-proof four-in-line engine, the final impetus to be a genuine title contender in its swan-song season.

For 1995, the FIA allowed every manufacturer to run a rear wing and front air dam of strictly controlled dimensions, the plan being to stop any single marque from buying success with ultra-expensive homologation specials.

Spectacle-wise, the consensus was that the wings, and the shorter braking distances they brought about, actually reduced the amount of *banzai* overtaking seen. But for Vauxhall, the wings meant it was able to genuinely compete in the downforce stakes, while the switch to Michelin from Dunlop brought the team in line with the majority of the other front-runners and removed an unknown from the equation. Sure, Volvo showed Dunlop could produce race-winning rubber. But for Cleland at least, the change was a positive step psychologically.

Ah yes, Cleland and psychology. Two years of finishing outside the top three had brought about a major change in the Scot's make-up. Granted, he'd never been a shrinking violet when it came to extolling his own virtues. But for 1995, the determination and self-belief was almost frightening. Getting Cleland to admit any shortcomings in himself or the package was like trying to outstare a dog – impossible.

At the start of the season, Cleland's main opposition was basically Volvo's Rickard Rydell and Renault's Alain Menu. By the end, it was just Menu.

Looking at Rydell first, the Swede was the dominant force in the early part of the season – even more so than Cleland during the opening spring skirmishes. But whereas Cleland and Vauxhall were able to build a solid platform in the opening races, then find something extra and sprint ahead come mid-season, Rydell and the TWR Racing-run Volvo came out of the starting stalls fully up to

Keeping the customer satisfied

Will the BTCC bubble eventually burst? How long can a series continue to keep nine manufacturers happy, given that not everybody can be a winner?

At the moment, it seems that the skin of the Super Touring bubble remains fairly resilient to slings and arrows. Sure, Alfa has decided to throw its resources wholeheartedly into Class 1 racing, Toyota and Peugeot continue their annual close-season game of find-the-budget, and BMW's long-term plans remain fluid.

But with Audi ready to enter the BTCC arena – forget about 1995's aborted plans, it is for real this time – and Chrysler, Hyundai, Mitsubishi and even Daewoo waiting in the wings, the class looks as healthy as it has ever been.

What could eventually knock the BTCC off the rails is the notoriously fickle nature of the British TV audience when it comes to sports outside the established football, cricket, rugby and horse racing cartel which has traditionally dominated coverage.

Perhaps Grand Prix racing can feel fairly confident that its feet are under the TV table, but can the BTCC? Remember darts and snooker and ice dancing and their all too brief reigns as the brightest stars in televised sport's firmament? Granted, their definition as 'sport' is a tenuous one indeed, but it's still something to bear in mind. And those fickle TV viewers who got sick of the sight of Eric Bristow and Steve Davis are the same people buying the Cavaliers, Mondeos and Lagunas seen rubbing door handles on *Grandstand*.

The bottom line is that the BTCC's success relies on its ability to sell cars, and if touring car racing doesn't retain its TV audience by keeping it fresh and in-your-face, then manufacturer interest will diminish accordingly. The harsh reality of supply and demand says the BTCC cannot afford to rest on its laurels.

Too much of a good thing?

A good idea, but one that went a little too far. That was the general consensus on the FIA's decision to allow everybody in Super Touring to use wings and front air dams of carefully controlled dimensions in 1995 and beyond.

On the plus side, it removed in one fell swoop the gap between the haves and the have-nots – those with the cash and the backing of the board to produce a 'homologation special' base road car, and those without. Performance-wise, it closed the field up even more and considerably increased fast and medium corner speeds.

On the downside, the actual size of the wings and the amount of downforce they produced has been detrimental to the overall spectacle of Super Touring, with braking distances, and hence overtaking opportunities, well down. Super Touring still provides good racing – excellent racing even. But the sort of *banzai*, act in haste, repent at leisure moves that are trademarks of the BBC *Grandstand* coverage were less frequently seen.

Among the drivers, reaction to the wings was mixed.

'I think it's made us into more thinking drivers,' said 1995 BTCC champion John Cleland, 'but if you want to win races in the dry, you've got to qualify on the front row now.'

'Anybody can go quickly now,' rued Ford's Super Touring star Paul Radisich. 'It makes ordinary drivers into competitive drivers, which isn't really the point.'

FIA President Max Mosley was quick to voice his opinion that the wings in their current guise maybe had gone too far – on aesthetic grounds, as well as actual performance. But with the manufacturers already well down the line in developing their packages for 1996, it was decided to stick with the devil you know for at least one more season.

---

speed, but never really found another gear after that.

For 1995, with its learning year over, Volvo decided to ditch the publicity-grabbing 850 estate and go the saloon route instead – the new FIA wing regulations pretty much decided that for them anyway. But with the engine and mechanicals known quantities and the 1995-spec car up and running as early as February (compared to two weeks before the first race for Vauxhall and even less for Renault) it looked like Volvo might be the team to beat.

Three victories for Rydell from the first nine races, backed up by two for his team-mate Tim Harvey, added weight to that theory. But after that, things began to go a little awry and progress seemed to temporarily stagnate. For a while in the middle of the season, the 850 saloon wasn't a front row car – a situation not helped by Rydell's inability to make consistently good starts.

The former Formula 3 star and sophomore Super Touring driver added one more win to his tally. But that was more than outweighed by a series of problematical late-season performances, including brake failure while leading at Snetterton and a disastrous qualifying performance at Oulton Park's penultimate round that finally handed the title to Cleland.

On the plus side, TWR Racing will doubtless learn from its mistakes and come back stronger next year, while Rydell has shown himself to be

243

BRITISH TOURING CAR CHAMPIONSHIP REVIEW

Radiating seemingly impregnable self-belief, John Cleland *(right)* saw off the challenge of his younger rivals to clinch his second BTCC title.

Below, top to bottom:
Johnny Cecotto endured a frustrating season in the BMW, which was no longer a match for the best of the front-wheel drive opposition.
The rapid progress made by the Honda Accord in the hands of David Leslie *(pictured)* and James Kaye bodes well for 1996.
Former Grand Prix driver Julian Bailey plugged away in the Toyota Carina but success remained elusive.

Decline and fall

It's always harder to defend a championship than to win it in the first place. But few expected such a spectacular decline as that seen from Alfa Romeo in the BTCC in 1995.

One season before, the Italian-based Alfa Corse had taken a hat-trick of drivers', manufacturers' and teams' titles, scoring ten victories *en route*. For 1996, Alfa Corse and its champion returned to Italy, but were replaced by what seemed, on paper at least, an equally strong combination – the Banbury-based Prodrive team and former Formula 1 racer and Sports Car World Champion Derek Warwick. Tarquini's '94 team-mate Giampiero Simoni, a BTCC race winner himself, was kept on the roster for continuity and as a bench-mark for Warwick. It looked good.

The problem was the car. Alfa Romeo revised its 155 TS over the winter, homologating a shell with wider wheel arches for wider suspension and kitting itself with the new-for-1995 FIA-approved wings. But most of its off-season efforts went into its Class 1 machines for the DTM. Little was done on the engine or the chassis and, frankly, Alfa totally underestimated the leap in performance its opposition would make during the winter months. For the first time since becoming a major force in touring cars, Alfa had got it wrong in a big, big way.

After the Grand Prix support, with the cars still not performing, Tarquini was drafted back in to partner Warwick for the rest of the season. The Italian picked up a trio of fourth-place finishes, but couldn't sneak the podium he'd set his sights on.

Frustratingly for Warwick, the situation with Alfa meant he had little opportunity to quell the doubters in his first season of tin-top racing. As well as a below-par car, Warwick was thrown into the deep end of mastering front-wheel drive and a 'mere' 300 bhp and suffered as a result.

'I've got unfinished business,' said Warwick. 'This is the most competitive championship I've ever raced in and I want to show people that I can be a winner in it. I know I can.'

To finish the business, it's likely Warwick will have to move elsewhere: at the end of the season, Alfa announced it was withdrawing its factory backing from Super Touring racing, and at the time of writing it looked unlikely that the blood-red cars would race again in the BTCC.

one of the true aces of 2-litre races – 13 poles from 25 attempts, as well as those four victories, testify to that.

When the Volvo attack ran out of steam, Renault and the Williams Touring Car Engineering team were ready to pick up the baton and take on the challenge of the Vauxhalls. Glimpses of what was to come were shown by Menu's three early-season wins. But it was the final run-in that showed the Lagunas as a real force to be reckoned with. The team took an incredible seven victories from the last nine races – four for eventual championship runner-up Menu, three for his team-mate Will Hoy – and stole the manufacturers' title from under Vauxhall's nose at the final race.

For Menu, the season added further weight to the theory that the Swiss ex-Formula 3000 driver is the best Super Touring driver around – a fair point – while for Williams Touring Car Engineering, a title in what was ostensibly its learning year was a fairly stunning debut for the offspring of a rather more famous parent.

Prior to its entry into the BTCC, many had expected WTCE to change the face of Super Touring racing and take it flying off on some hyper-expensive tangent. In reality, all WTCE did was take a strong existing package – the Renault Laguna – and turn it into a stronger one by attention to detail and sound engineering practice. Nothing earth-shattering there.

Cleland and the Volvo and Renault pairings aside, three other drivers tasted victory during 1995.

Cleland's young team-mate James Thompson became the youngest-ever BTCC race winner and pole-sitter when he took victory at Thruxton in May. It was vindication of Vauxhall's decision to take on the flamboyant 21-year-old, but it was all to end in tears when Thompson suffered an enormous testing accident at Knockhill and was forced to sit out the rest of the season.

South African champion Mike Briggs did a good job standing in for the injured rookie, but the break in continuity could have cost Vauxhall the manufacturers' title.

Ford's pairing of double tin-top World Cup winner Paul Radisich and 1993 British Formula 3 Champion and touring car newcomer Kelvin Burt both took a single victory. But whatever way you looked at it, the season was a disaster for the Blue Oval.

In theory, the Ford Mondeo, with its powerful V6 engine, wide track, good aerodynamics and sound mechanical layout, should be the car the others aspire to. But a real penchant for devouring front tyres meant the Andy Rouse-built machines were rarely a factor over a full race distance.

Ford did salvage some lesser glory when Matt Neal and Richard Kaye took a 1-2 in the Total Cup for privateers. But that's small reward for a multi-million-pound investment, and Ford is set to bring in some major

244

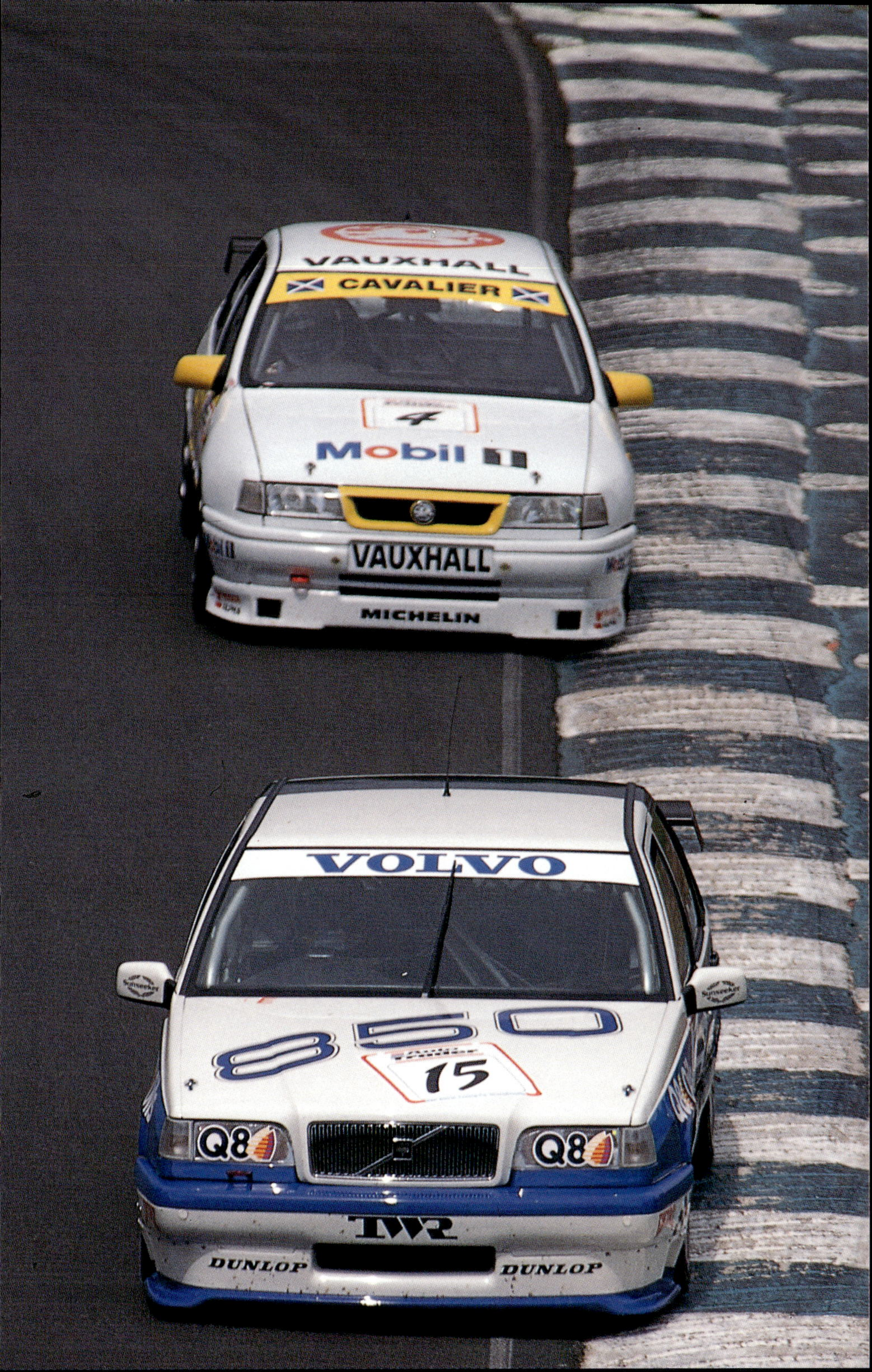

John Marsh/Action Images

Colin McMaster/Words & Pictures

John Marsh/Action Images

John Marsh/Action Images

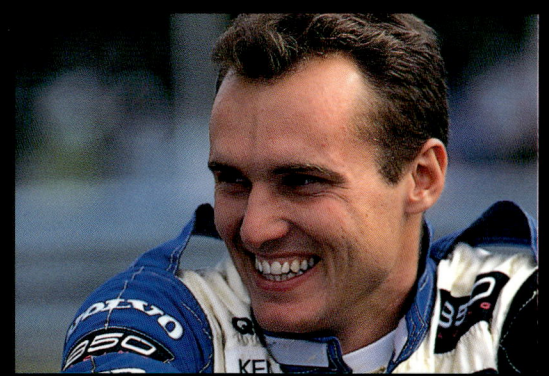

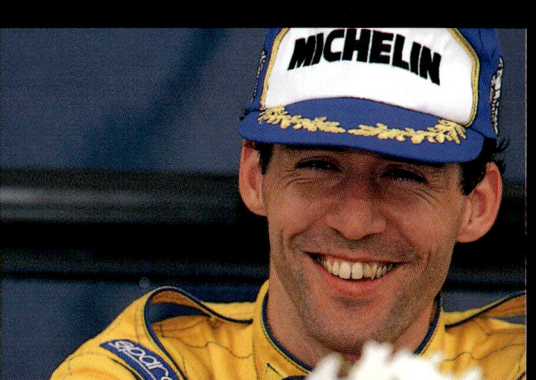

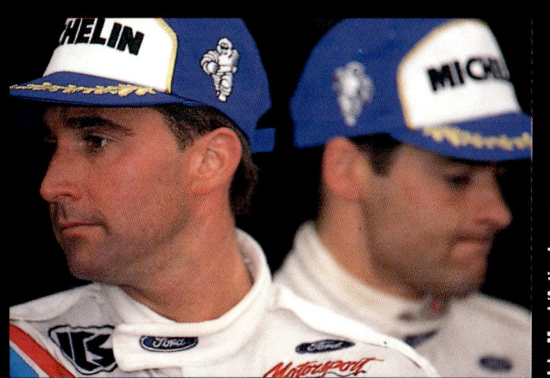

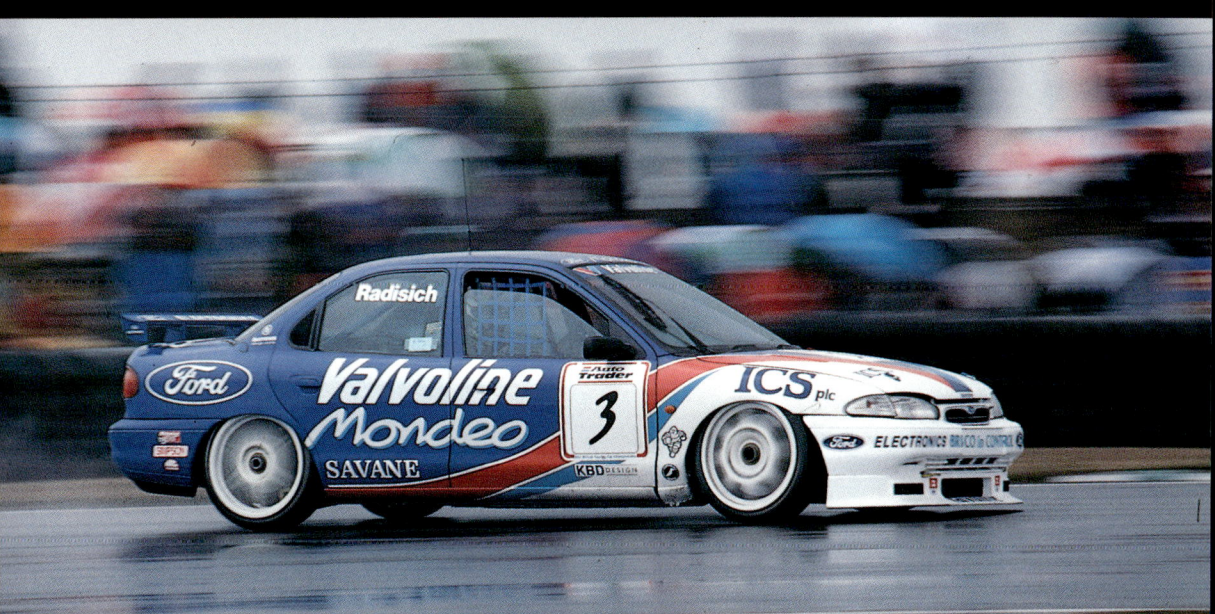

Above: **Rickard Rydell leads John Cleland at Brands Hatch. Volvo set the pace in the early stages of the season but could not sustain its challenge.**

Far right, top to bottom: **Rydell notched up 13 pole positions out of 25 but could not always translate his practice speed into race victories. Renault's Alain Menu was the driver to beat at season's end. Ford duo Paul Radisich and Kelvin Burt scored a single win apiece.**

Right: **The Mondeo seemed to possess all the ingredients for success but failed to fulfil its potential.**

John Overton

BRITISH TOURING CAR CHAMPIONSHIP REVIEW

Renault became the end-of-year pacesetters, Alain Menu and Will Hoy scoring seven wins in the last nine races to clinch the manufacturers' title.

changes to its operation over the winter break.

Of those who didn't win, perhaps the biggest surprise was the decline of Alfa Romeo. The Banbury-based Prodrive team took over from Alfa Corse, with former Formula 1 driver Derek Warwick making his tin-top debut as a replacement for the Italian series-bound Tarquini. Sadly though, the 1995-spec Alfa 155 TS was a bit of a pig at the start of the year and shed few of its porcine qualities as the season wore on.

Tarquini was brought back to replace Giampiero Simoni in the later races, and did manage to claim a trio of fourth-place finishes. But for everybody involved, it was an extremely disappointing year, and one unlikely to be repeated as Alfa puts its full budgetary weight behind the Class 1 International Touring Car series in 1996.

For Alfa's tribulations, read BMW's too. The 1993 champions finished 1994 off strongly. But again, the 1995-spec car was never quite up to the job. Schnitzer was replaced by the full-factory BMW Motorsport Team, with a strong driver line-up of BMW golden boy Johnny Cecotto and Formula 1 refugee David Brabham. But for all concerned, 1995 turned into a recurring nightmare.

Three other manufacturers – Toyota, Peugeot and Honda – fielded full works-backed efforts in 1995, with varying fortunes.

Toyota's Carina E and Peugeot's 405 Mi16 again failed to find the winner's circle – although Peugeot's Patrick Watts did manage to take a pair of podiums, to possibly ease Peugeot Sport's task in justifying its budget to the board for yet another season.

Honda, the BTCC's new kid on the block, did all that could have been expected of it in its first year, short of an actual win or pole position. As the season unwound, David Leslie and James Kaye steadily untapped the huge potential of the Accord and could be dark horses for some serious success in 1996.

Others looking for success next season will include newcomers Audi, who finally take the BTCC plunge after a last-minute change of plan saw the marque scrubbing its 1995 British plans.

But for Audi, or Honda, or anybody else to break into the BTCC big time, first they must break the three-way stranglehold imposed this season by Renault, Vauxhall (equipped with the all-new mutt's nuts Vectra for 1996) and Volvo. Judging by the current state of play, that's definitely going to be easier said than done.

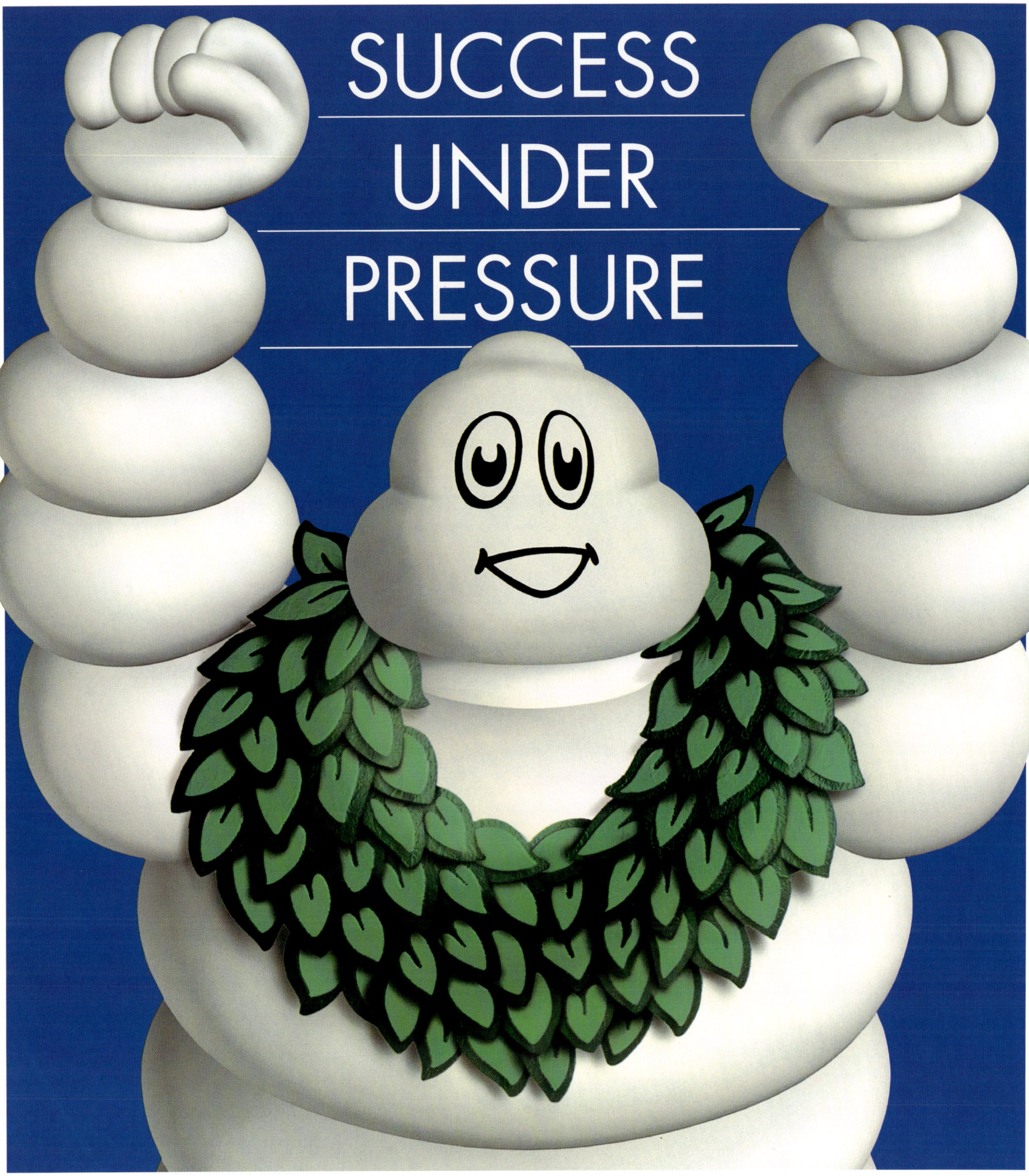

SUCCESS UNDER PRESSURE

MICHELIN PILOTS FLY IN FIRST AGAIN.

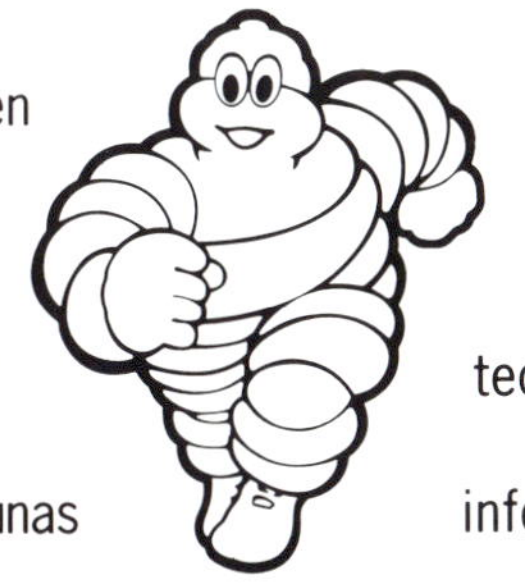

For the second year running, Michelin Pilot tyres have taken top honours in the British Touring Car Championship. John Cleland in the Vauxhall Cavalier won the drivers' championship and Alain Menu and Will Hoy in the Renault Lagunas won the constructors' title on Pilots. Fit Pilots to your car and you'll benefit from the same investment in technology that led to this sporting achievement. For more information about Pilot tyres, contact your local dealer.

INTERNATIONAL TOURING CAR RACING REVIEW

SCHNEIDER'S TROPHIES

by Laurence Foster

INTERNATIONAL TOURING CAR RACING REVIEW

A transitional season for Class 1 touring car racing was dominated by the AMG Mercedes of Bernd Schneider, who won both the last DTM championship and the newly introduced ITC series.

The times they are a-changing in Class 1 touring car racing, and Bernd Schneider's 1995 feat of winning the Deutsche Tourenwagen Meisterschaft and the International Touring Car series was both the beginning and the end of an era.

Next year, the DTM is dead, long live the International Touring Car Championship (see sidebar). But in 1995's transitional year, when a five-round international series was grafted at short notice onto a shrunken DTM schedule, Schneider and Mercedes-Benz utterly dominated both.

Protracted wranglings between the FIA, the three Class 1 manufacturers (Alfa Romeo, Mercedes and Opel) and DTM organiser ITR meant the ITC wasn't actually confirmed until just days before the opening round at Mugello. After that, a constantly changing calendar, loosely alternating between DTM and ITC events, served merely to confuse the casual observer. But amid all the upheaval, there was always one constant – Schneider.

Of the 23 Class 1 races run in 1995, Schneider was victorious in 11 and could have added a further win had he not clouted the wall in Helsinki. That number is even more impressive when one considers that, in the DTM and ITC, success on the track is rewarded not only with points, but also with 'success ballast'. In the latter stages of the season, the 31-year-old former Formula 1 driver managed to shrug off a maximum 50 kilos of the stuff in his C-Class and still keep on winning.

Schneider wrapped up his DTM crown at Singen, with the Hockenheim finale still to spare, and added the ITC crown at Magny-Cours three weeks later – scoring almost double the points of his nearest rival. It was the sort of domination last seen in 1993, when Alfa Romeo first entered the series, caught everybody on the hop and ushered in the modern era of Class 1 racing.

Schneider's unstoppable season came as a marked contrast to the one that had gone before, when the German led almost half the races, yet took the chequered flag first only twice.

But to some extent, it was Schneider's failures in 1994 that led to his position of strength this year. The German's hard-driving style discovered the flaws and weaknesses in the C-Class's debut season and Mercedes and AMG responded with a virtually bullet-proof car in 1995.

Added to that, refined aerodynamics on the rear-wheel drive, traction-controlled C-Class, plus a stiffer chassis and near enough 500 bhp from Merc's 2.5-litre V6, gave Schneider and the other six works drivers a package that no longer played second best to the four-wheel drive Alfas and Opels in the tight stuff and was superior in a straight line.

The introduction of a pneumatically valved engine halfway through the season merely reinforced Stuttgart's power advantage, while a semi-automatic gearbox waited in the wings, but was never required.

There were also changes in Schneider's way of going racing. At the end of the 1994 season, Merc's newly crowned DTM champ Klaus Ludwig switched to Opel, leaving Schneider with the weight of team leadership on his shoulders. That extra responsibility didn't temper the raw speed of Mercedes motor sport boss Norbert Haug's 'favourite son' too much. But it did control his natural aggression and force him to think more tactically. Balls-out became balls-in when necessary.

Ludwig's move, along with the release of Mercedes stalwart Roland Asch, allowed the three-pointed star to resurrect its junior team concept in 1995. A trio consisting of British Formula 3 Champion and McLaren test driver Jan Magnussen, his Paul Stewart Racing team-mate Dario Franchitti and former Mercedes privateer Sandy Grau were duly signed for what should have been little more than a learning year. In reality, AMG twins Franchitti and Magnussen were the revelations of the series.

Schneider's AMG team-mate Franchitti shocked the establishment with a pole and a podium at the Hockenheim season-opener, took his maiden Class 1 win at the Mugello ITC race and rounded the season off with another pole at Hockenheim. In between, the 22-year-old Scot took the brunt of the team's bad luck, with mechanical failures and unexpected variables such as errant Eifel hares preventing further wins in an otherwise superlative first tin-top campaign.

Magnussen took a little longer to get up to speed, citing an unwillingness to compromise his single-seater techniques, but was on the verge of a first win when he broke a leg in a freak paddock scooter accident at Norisring. Two rounds later he was back, finally picking up his first ITC win at Estoril and taking second overall in the final standings.

World stage for Class 1 touring cars

The DTM has gone, absorbed by the experimental International Touring Car offspring it spawned in 1995.

For 1996, Class 1 touring car racing will consist of a single 14-round International Touring Car Championship (ITCC) – six rounds to be held in Germany, eight more as far afield as Japan and Brazil – with the television rights owned by Bernie Ecclestone.

To all intents and purposes, that's how the three manufacturers involved – Alfa Romeo (above), Mercedes and Opel – envisaged the series would eventually develop, with Class 1 as tin-top racing's international high-tech flagship and the Super Touring class providing strong domestic championships below it. What wasn't in the plan was quite how quickly the young pretender has usurped its established parent.

How the ITCC fares in practice remains to be seen. In its final couple of seasons, the DTM was champing at the bit to be released onto a wider stage, but with its three manufacturers in cosy alliance and phenomenal interest from the German motor sport public, it had a solid bedrock to dream its dreams from.

Now, pushed out into the wide, wide world with barely time to blink – albeit with that German-biased safety net in place for the moment – and with the possibility of other manufacturers entering the series to raise the stakes, just how will it cope with the harsh new realities?

The product is there, as is a growing international interest in the series and its all-singing, all-dancing machinery. The biggest question is how far will it be allowed to grow when its new standing allows it to potentially pose a threat to the continued well-being of Grand Prix racing?

It's a fine line between being a complement and being a rival to Formula 1. The defunct Group C Sports Car World Championship and the one-off 1987 Touring Car World Championship stand as testimony to what the ITCC must avoid.

Grau's year was more circumspect, with a huge accident at Mugello leaving his confidence eroded in the first half of the season. But podiums at AVUS, Helsinki and the Nürburgring further reinforced the logic of Mercedes' policy.

Grau's team-mate and Zakspeed number one Kurt Thiim was the pundits' choice to be fighting with Schneider for the titles. But although the speed was there – possibly more so even than with Schneider – the Dane had inherited Schneider's mantle of non-finish magnet. Three wins, but little else to support them, scuppered his title chances.

In contrast, AMG's Jörg van Ommen had the consistency, but not always the speed, and it was he who eventually finished second in the DTM points – equalling team-mate Magnussen's ITC feat.

Ellen Lohr completed the seven-car works Merc line-up, driving a third Zakspeed car. Hers was a difficult and confusing season, with the semi-works Persson cars of Uwe Alzen – who finished an incredible second overall at the Hockenheim DTM finale – and Bernd Mayländer often getting the better of her.

But for a *really* difficult and confusing season, one must look to Alfa Romeo and its seven-car works squad split among four different teams. Alfa overstretched itself technically over the winter in order to keep up with Mercedes, finished its 1995-spec cars far too late for any reasonable pre-season testing, then found itself in a quagmire of its own making as it tried desperately to play catch-up.

Alfa Corse fielded cars for 1993 DTM champ Nicola Larini and Alessandro Nannini; Euroteam chipped in with cars for Stefano Modena and Michael Bartels; Schübel ran Christian Danner and Grand Prix retiree Michele Alboreto, and Alfa Corse 2 were charged with Alfa junior and Italian Formula 3 Champion Giancarlo Fisichella. That was the simple bit – the complications came with the actual racing.

A pre-season car-destroying accident for Larini didn't help matters. But come the Hockenheim opener, it was obvious that wasn't the *raison d'être* for Alfa's maladies. The Italians had concocted two levels of 1995 car: the interim Step 1 car, with modifications to such things as weight distribution and aerodynamics, and the all-singing Step 2 car, which boasted wishbone suspension and electronically controlled differentials for its four-wheel drive – and, erm, didn't work very well.

Larini and Nannini suffered with the Step 2 car at Hockenheim, before switching to '94 cars at AVUS. After that, Nannini bit the bullet and concentrated on developing the Step 2 car, while Larini doggedly took the fight to Mercedes with the older car, until switching to a Step 2 machine with but a handful of races still to run.

Larini took a single win on the streets of Helsinki and even kept himself in the ITC and DTM title hunts until each series' penultimate round, but it was a deeply frustrating season for the Ferrari test driver. Ditto for Nannini, except that

The unique Norisring street circuit remained a feature of the DTM calendar. Menacing skies offer an evocative backdrop as Klaus Ludwig's Opel Calibra sweeps past the sinister relics of another, darker age.

Manuel Reuter *(right)* was part of a six-car effort from the Russelsheim marque but for most of the season real success seemed as far away as ever.

Faced with the task of developing the recalcitrant Step 2 Alfa, former Benetton star Alessandro Nannini *(below right)* had little chance to shine.

Far right: Leaving no margin for error, Bernd Schneider hustles the Mercedes C-Class around the barrier-lined Singen street track.

photos: matthias schneider

INTERNATIONAL TOURING CAR RACING REVIEW

Anti-clockwise from above: Keke Rosberg shows protégé JJ Lehto around the Class 1 paddock; Dario Franchitti quickly adapted to Class 1 racing under the tutelage of AMG team-mate Bernd Schneider, but fellow Mercedes junior Jan Magnussen's progress was interrupted by injury; reigning DTM champion Klaus Ludwig spearheaded Opel's late-season return to form; Michele Alboreto bore a wretched season with as much grace as he could muster; Alfa's endless problems prevented Nicola Larini from mounting a title challenge.

INTERNATIONAL TOURING CAR RACING REVIEW

he was rarely at the sharp end of a race when his endless list of gearbox and engine failures usually struck.

The nadir for the pair of them came at Magny-Cours' ITC finale. Larini took pole, with Nannini second on the grid, but neither completed even the first corner after identical gearbox failures. It just about summed up the year.

For Alfa and fellow four-wheel drivers Opel, a small chink of light did come with a mid-season decision to equalise the Class 1 weights at 1040 kilos, adding 20 kilos to the Mercs and taking 20 off everybody else. But as an effective gesture and with so much else that needed fixing too, it was too little, too late to salvage the 1995 season.

At the end of it all, Larini took fourth in the ITC and sixth in the DTM, the top Alfa man in each. But in terms of wins, it was the German duo of Michael Bartels and Christian Danner who led the standings with two each in the DTM.

Bartels' victories were the most impressive, coming from pole at the fast/slow/fast/slow airfield circuit at Diepholz – the first meeting held to the new weight regulations. Sure, Mercedes was caught a little on the hop by its extra weight, but that shouldn't detract from Bartels' achievement.

Danner's, in contrast, were of a more opportunistic nature. At Helsinki, with a high attrition rate and several stop-go penalties dished out to the front-runners, Danner was in the right place at the right time, while the Norisring saw an inspired choice of slicks on a damp, but drying, track give victory number two.

One of the most laborious and heartbreaking tasks to carry out at any DTM or ITC round was trying to work out which combination of Step, aerodynamics, gearbox and differential control any given works car was running at any given time. And that endlessly changing roster served to hamper more than one driver: Minardi test driver Fisichella and Modena had the odd promising weekend, but the constant chopping and changing meant the rhythm that comes with familiarity was never quite there. Alboreto fared even worse, slipping into the role of Step 2 guinea pig and never having a chance to really shine.

By the end of the season, Alfa sports chief Giorgio Pianta had increased his factory roster to eight cars and brought 1994 BTCC champ Gabriele Tarquini into the line-up, prior to a full Class 1 programme in 1996. But an excellent end of season, when his pace was second only to the Alfa Corse duo, was stymied by . . . you guessed it – car problems.

And so to Opel, a manufacturer that promised so much, but failed to deliver until the dying moments of the season. The Russelsheim mar-

Below: Kurt Thiim's Zakspeed Mercedes throws up a shower of sparks at Donington Park. The Dane was expected to be Bernd Schneider's closest challenger, but a sequence of non-finishes ruined his chances.

Manufacturers share Super Touring spoils

Besides the hugely popular DTM for Class 1 cars, Germany's almost insatiable desire for roofed racing has also given it a 2-litre Super Touring series second only to the BTCC in terms of crowds and coverage.

With BMW and Audi not currently active in the DTM, the German Super Touring Cup is their major chance to race on home territory. Not surprisingly, with BMW fielding six works cars and Audi four, it boiled down to a straight fight between the two.

Audi's Frank Biela *(above)* held the early advantage. But a late-season development surge by BMW and Michelin saw Schnitzer star and '93 BTCC champion Jo Winkelhock take the title at the Nürburgring finale. Winkelhock's team-mate Peter Kox rubbed in the Schnitzer domination with second in the points in only his first full season in a works team.

Sadly, the closing stages of the season were overshadowed by a fatal accident to Nissan's Kieth Odor. The British driver had just begun to unlock the potential of the Primera when he was involved in a high-speed accident at Berlin's AVUS circuit.

Audi's failure to take the German title was compensated for to some extent by a second successive Italian Superturismo crown for Emanuele Pirro. However, Audi's Italian opposition was somewhat weakened by Alfa Corse's pull-out halfway through the season and there was little real challenge from anybody bar the semi-works Nordauto Alfa Romeo team and the three-car works-backed CiBiEmme BMW team.

For 1996, Pirro swaps to the German series, with Biela spearheading Audi's first-ever attack on the BTCC.

Other significant Super Touring series winners included Opel's Mike Briggs in the burgeoning South African Touring Car Championship; Yvan Muller and the ORECA BMW team in France, beating works squads from Opel and Peugeot; and Paul Morris's Gardner BMW in Australia.

Steve Soper and Schnitzer BMW also put up a strong fight against the massed ranks of Toyota in Japan, which has the biggest Super Touring series outside Europe. In fact, had the bench-mark BTCC not been such a disaster for the Munich marque, it would have been an excellent season for BMW and its 318i.

INTERNATIONAL TOURING CAR RACING REVIEW

que, under the patronage of motor sports boss Walter Treser, had spent 1994 trading speed for reliability, but finally looked to have both together in 1995. Its four-wheel drive Calibra V6 was slightly down on power compared to Merc or the best Alfa pneumatic-valved motors, but its purposeful aerodynamics and excellent handling were meant to offset that.

The three-car effort of '94 was doubled to six, with Joest running four cars and newcomers Opel Team Rosberg taking on two more. Keke Rosberg and Manuel Reuter stayed on from the previous season and were joined by shock transferee and reigning DTM champ Klaus Ludwig from Mercedes, plus former F1 drivers JJ Lehto and Yannick Dalmas. Oh, and Portuguese tin-top champ Ni Amorim was given his Class 1 chance. Ludwig teamed up with Rosberg in the 1982 World Champion's team, with the remaining four forming Joest's attack.

It all looked good on paper. But from the start of the season the cars proved problematical, especially in the transmission department, and a series of car-destroying accidents put a massive added drain on Opel's resources.

Ludwig took a podium at Hockenheim and second at the Norisring, Finland's Lehto briefly led on his home tarmac in Helsinki and Reuter put up a number of promising, but ultimately unrewarded, performances. But on the whole, the opening three-quarters of the season was the sort of bad trip that must have made Alfa breathe a collective sigh of relief.

The breakthrough came at Magny-Cours, when a second for Reuter and a third for Ludwig – but both on merit, not just attrition – pointed to better things at the Hockenheim DTM finale. Sure enough, one week later, Ludwig took a double victory, with Reuter picking up second and fourth. Doubters pointed to the rather trick, moveable rear wings fitted to the cars of Ludwig, Reuter and Rosberg as the reason for Opel's late-season success. But a more charitable – and accurate – view says it was methodical trouble-shooting and hard work. The trick now is to keep up the momentum through the winter and into 1996.

As a footnote to the Class 1 season, Rosberg took his final bow from international racing at the Hockenheim finale – or rather his latest in a long line of final bows.

Rosberg, who will concentrate on Opel Team Rosberg and his management company from now on, scored only one DTM win in a tin-top career spanning four seasons. But as Class 1 racing prepares to step up another gear next year, the part played by the amazing popularity of the Flying Finn in bringing it to its current position shouldn't be underestimated.

Audis dominate low-key World Cup

As a concept, the FIA Touring Car World Cup is undoubtedly an excellent idea. The best Super Touring cars and drivers from around the world converge for a one-off pair of races to determine who – unofficially at least – carries the title of tin-top World Champion for the next 12 months.

In practice, however, a certain reluctance on the part of the FIA to give the event the promotion it deserves, plus a less than enthusiastic response from the main Super Touring series outside Europe, has up to now served to dilute the impact of the World Cup.

The 1995 event – held at Paul Ricard in France – was no different from the previous two, in that TV coverage was minuscule and the top runners from Japan, Australia and South Africa were largely notable by their absence.

For the manufacturers, the lack of promotion and TV is a cause of growing consternation. As one put it this year: 'I feel sorry for those who do well, because they then have to spend millions letting people know it's happened.'

Talk is of the manufacturers getting together and trying to promote the event along with a third party such as the BTCC organiser TOCA. But would that sit easily with the FIA and Bernie Ecclestone – especially since conspiracy theorists believe the stunted growth of the World Cup is a deliberate ploy to keep Super Touring in its place?

At the end of play at Ricard, the four-wheel drive Audi A4s had turned the perceived form book on its head, with Frank Biela taking the drivers' title, ahead of Emanuele Pirro, and Audi lifting the manufacturers' crown.

BMW, mostly in the shape of Steve Soper, local star Yvan Muller and Johnny Cecotto, provided the nearest thing to opposition with its rear-wheel drive 318i. But the biggest shock of the weekend was the ineffectiveness of the front-wheel drive cars of the BTCC.

As the series that all others aspire to, the BTCC was expected to provide the bench-mark in France. In reality, an incompatibility with the long Signes corner, rear tyre cooling problems on the long Mistral straight and a lack of Ricard-specific tyre testing by the top British teams left them frankly embarrassed.

Renault, Volvo, Vauxhall, Honda, Ford et al. will doubtless learn hard lessons from their pasting at Paul Ricard. But with the growing disillusionment among the manufacturers, will they get the chance for revenge in 1996?

Mark Bothwell/Bothwell Photographic

UNITED STATES RACING REVIEW

VILLENEUVE
A NEW STAR RISES IN THE WEST

by Gordon Kirby

Main photograph. Displaying a maturity that will serve him well in Formula 1, Jacques Villeneuve claimed the PPG Cup in only his second year in Indy Car racing with Barry Green's Reynard-Ford.

A season of glorious unpredictability threw up more than a dozen potential race winners. Villeneuve, Paul Tracy, Al Unser Jnr, Emerson Fittipaldi and Gil de Ferran *(opposite, anti-clockwise from top left)* all tasted victory, as did Andre Ribeiro, Scott Pruett and Robby Gordon *(anti-clockwise from left),* while Bobby Rahal *(centre)* managed to sustain a title challenge without a single success.

UNITED STATES RACING REVIEW

Robby Gordon scored a couple of wins in one of Derrick Walker's Reynards but fifth place in the final points table was less than he had expected.

Bottom: Michael Andretti leads Gordon and Al Unser Jnr at Vancouver. Andretti was the early-season pacesetter but a number of unforced errors blighted his championship chances.

This was a vintage season for American motor sport as a whole and Indy Car racing in particular. Television and spectator turnouts for all of America's major forms of motor sport have set records steadily over the past two decades and that reliable growth continued in 1995.

NASCAR's Winston Cup championship, brilliantly managed over more than forty years and two generations by Bill France Snr and his son Bill Jnr, maintains a firm hold as the most popular form of motor racing in the USA. The 31-race Winston Cup series was hailed this summer on the cover of America's *Sports Illustrated* magazine as 'America's Hottest Sport', and there was even a fresh-faced new champion this year in 24-year-old Jeff Gordon, who toppled the Man in Black, seven-times champion Dale Earnhardt, in a classic battle.

At the same time Indy Car racing has been growing by leaps and bounds in both domestic and international markets, and under new President and Chief Executive Officer Andrew Craig, the IndyCar organisation itself has shaken off years of political infighting and emerged as an extremely strong, united group. With Craig at the helm over the past two years, IndyCar has got itself into enough of a position of strength to compete head-to-head with the Indianapolis Motor Speedway in 1996 (see sidebar).

Ultra-competitive

Meanwhile, the PPG Indy Car World Series enjoyed its most competitive season on record in 1995. Nine different drivers, two rookies included, won the year's 17 races and no fewer than 17 different faces made the podium. A popular myth about Indy Car racing was also exploded this year. Ten of the season's races were won by five drivers in their twenties, and only one race winner – Emerson Fittipaldi – was in his forties.

The championship was won by the brilliantly talented Jacques Villeneuve in only his second season in Indy cars, at a mere 24 years of age. Jacques was made to work very hard for his PPG Cup title by defending champion Al Unser Jnr, who recovered from failing to qualify at Indianapolis to launch a tenacious comeback drive over the second half of the season.

Villeneuve and Unser won four races apiece and their records of second to sixth places were almost identical. In fact, using the F1 points system, Villeneuve and Unser would have been tied, each with 60 points, and Unser would have won the title with two second places to Villeneuve's single second! Indy Car scores points down to 12th place, however, and also awards bonus points for pole positions and the driver who leads the most laps in each race, so that Villeneuve beat Unser by 11 points. Six poles for Villeneuve, and none for Unser, was therefore a key element in Villeneuve's title.

Although we didn't know it at the time, the character of the year was established at the opening race. Villeneuve wasn't absolutely the fastest thing in the streets of Miami in March but he and Barry Green's tightly knit little team were definitely the cleanest and coolest. A very fast second pit stop gave Jacques the lead and he drove perfectly to the finish under fierce pressure to win from Mauricio Gugelmin, Bobby Rahal and Scott Pruett, all four covered by two seconds.

Michael Andretti was on the pole in Miami and led strongly until running into the wayward Eliseo Salazar as he tried to lap him. It was probably an eager move to make on a guy like Salazar who was in his first Indy Car race. Andretti said he mistook Salazar for Christian Fittipaldi and might not have tried the manoeuvre had he known who was driving the other car – a classic, slightly misanthropic incident for Michael. When he crashed on the last lap in Surfers Paradise two weeks later after again taking the pole and leading the early going, the die was somehow cast for Andretti's 1995 season.

At the same time defending champion Unser struggled for grip and speed with Penske's latest PC24 in Miami's season-opener. In the race he plugged on through a series of pit stops to try to solve an engine electronic problem, eventually finishing many laps behind in 15th place, out of the points. In Australia, Al Jnr qualified third but was given two

VALVOLINE
THE WINNINGEST OIL OF THE 1995 INDY SEASON.

6592.531 MILES.
6 POLES.
6 VICTORIES.
INDY 500 VICTORY.
PPG INDYCAR CHAMPION.

ALSO AVAILABLE FOR RUSH HOUR GRIDLOCKS, FAMILY VACATIONS, AND FRIDAY NIGHT CRUISING.

 PEOPLE WHO KNOW USE VALVOLINE.®

©1995 The Valvoline Company, Marketers of ZEREX and PYROIL

UNITED STATES RACING REVIEW

A routine pit stop for Teo Fabi's Forsythe Racing Reynard at Milwaukee. The Italian veteran showed impressive speed at times but didn't enjoy the best of fortune.

Below: Al Unser Jnr defended his PPG Cup title with characteristic tenacity, keeping Villeneuve under pressure until the last race of the season.

stop-and-go penalties for jumping a restart and speeding in the pit lane, finally finishing sixth. Here too, after two races, the tone seemed to have been set for the rest of Team Penske's season.

Villeneuve, meanwhile, showed he was a serious contender by qualifying second in Australia and third at Phoenix in April. He ran strongly in the early laps in Australia but didn't finish after a transmission failure. He was fifth, a lap down, in Phoenix and fell out again with transmission problems at Long Beach. Drivetrain problems hit most Reynard teams in this year's earliest street races and after Long Beach the Reynard people leaped into performing the necessary corrective surgery.

As that was happening, Villeneuve's championship chase began in earnest at Nazareth in the middle of April. Jacques finished a very strong second to Emerson Fittipaldi, who enjoyed his best race and only win of the year on the furious little sub-mile trioval. Then at Indianapolis Jacques truly fomented his championship attack. He was a front-runner all month at Indy, qualifying fifth and emerging unfazed from an accident while doing race tests with his back-up car at the end of the second week. In the race he drove brilliantly to come back from an early two-lap penalty for passing the pace car. Using the subsequent yellows to best effect, Villeneuve made up the deficit and was ready to score a surprise win after leaders Scott Pruett and Scott Goodyear were eliminated in the last 15 laps.

First Pruett crashed on unacknowledged oil in the fourth turn. Then Goodyear made a terrible mistake, jumping ahead of the languidly driven pace car on the final restart, handing the race to Villeneuve. Goodyear was black-flagged. After he ignored the flag, USAC stopped scoring him. Villeneuve rather than Goodyear therefore became the first Canadian to win the Indy 500. It was a charmed but hard-won victory and from that day on Villeneuve and Team Green, like other Indy winners before them, were motivated, focused and essentially unchallenged in winning the PPG Cup title.

Penske's nightmare

In fact, Indianapolis was truly the determining point in the season. In the 500, Andretti crashed again while leading after misjudging a pass of Mauricio Gugelmin, who was heading for the pits. Unser and team-mate Fittipaldi inexplicably failed to qualify at Indianapolis. It was the first time a defending Indy 500 champion had attempted to qualify for the race and not made the field. For Al Jnr, Emerson and Roger Penske it was probably the lowest, darkest day of their vast careers. Unser came back strongly at Milwaukee the following weekend, however, leading most of the race and finishing second to Paul Tracy.

By that point of the season the only thing that was clear was that the next race was unlikely to be anything like the one just finished. Race after race produced not only different winners but entirely dissimilar story lines and featured players. Amid that setting, which produced a record nine winners, Villeneuve's championship quest took a little while to take shape.

He fought his way to sixth in Milwaukee and hung on for ninth in Detroit. Points but nothing more. A good test the following week at Mid-Ohio brought Team Green's Reynard back to life and, starting at Portland at the end of June, Jacques was a contender to win every race. He took his first pole of the year at Portland and battled with the resurgent Al Jnr before a suspension bracket broke. Unser went on to score a dominant victory only to be disqualified two hours after the race when IndyCar officials judged his car's side pods to be too low. Coming a month after Indianapolis, this was a deep blow to Unser and the Penske team, although the victory was ultimately restored by an appeal court three months later.

Meanwhile, Villeneuve's season took off, starting at Road America in July. Jacques had scored his first Indy Car victory the previous autumn on the majestic four-mile Wisconsin road circuit, and won again, from the pole, this year. He was on the pole again in Toronto's streets the next

No such thing as a winnable war: IndyCar and the Indy Racing League

weekend, led the early going and finished third behind Andretti and Bobby Rahal after a hard race.

This was literally the heat of the season with four races in July at successively hot and humid midwestern venues. Cleveland's fast, open and bumpy airport track the next weekend brought us the wildest race of the year with Villeneuve winning from Bryan Herta and Jimmy Vasser after a series of late-race bumping incidents. Robby Gordon was fined, and he and Michael Andretti were put on probation while Villeneuve emerged from an incredibly fierce race to win. With twenty laps to go that day Jacques looked like finishing fourth or fifth but a combination of good luck and cool confidence in the most hectic heat of battle gave him his fourth and last win of the year.

At that stage of the season Villeneuve looked suddenly like a shoo-in for the PPG Cup title. He was 32 points ahead of Bobby Rahal with Gordon and Andretti a further seven and ten points adrift. After crashing with Andretti at Road America, crashing again in Toronto and failing to finish at Cleveland after a transmission failure, Unser was ninth, 77 points behind and apparently unable to defend his championship.

Over the last five races, however, with his disqualification from Portland under protest and then appeal, Al Jnr mounted a mighty impressive come-from-behind attack. Starting with a tremendous drive to second place behind Scott Pruett in the Michigan 500, Unser hauled his way from ninth to a close second in the final points. He won at Mid-Ohio two weeks later after Andretti dropped out with a failed engine just four laps from the end. He finished a good third on the New Hampshire oval the next week and won again with a superb, jackal-like performance in Vancouver. At Laguna's season-closer Al Jnr could only qualify 14th and finish sixth, so that Villeneuve took the title despite troubles of his own.

In fact those last five races were full of trouble for Villeneuve. At the Michigan 500 he lost 15 laps changing a failed wheel bearing (a not uncommon problem on the high-banked superspeedway) and made the finish in tenth place. He then flew to England for his highly successful Williams test, signing to drive in F1 in 1996 before the next race, at Mid-Ohio. In his last four Indy Car races Jacques was very impressive in

As *Autocourse* closed for press, IndyCar seemed set to stage its own 500-mile race at Michigan International Speedway on 26 May in direct competition with the Indianapolis 500. This dramatic turn of events has come about because Indianapolis Motor Speedway President Tony George has decided to create his own Indy Car series, separate and distinct from IndyCar's PPG Indy Car World Series. George says he wants to make Indy Car racing cheaper and more accessible to American drivers with short-track oval racing backgrounds. George has argued with IndyCar since he took over the presidency of Indianapolis in 1990, announcing in 1994 that he was going his own way in 1996. This past year George announced his own, inaugural 1996 Indy Racing League (IRL) series, comprising five races, all on ovals. In midsummer, George made another announcement, reserving 25 of the 33 places in the field for next year's 80th Indianapolis 500 for IRL drivers and teams. George's new qualifying rules leave only eight places open to 'at large' (a.k.a. IndyCar) competitors.

George maintains his new ruling is 'an incentive' to encourage people to compete in the IRL. IndyCar's team owners view the move as 'a lockout' and say they will not enter the 1996 Indy 500. Instead they plan to run their own 500-mile race on the same day at Roger Penske's Michigan International Speedway, about an hour's drive west from Detroit.

'We have a very united board of directors who have little real interest in the IRL,' declared IndyCar President Craig in October. 'The board is very united and very resolute. They have a purpose, a direction, and they know what they want to do. Perhaps more importantly, they know what they're not prepared to do.

'Our teams have worked too hard, too long. It is our teams that have made this sport what it is today. I think that's a very important point. Anybody who looks back to 15 years ago would have to agree that it's CART [IndyCar] and its board of directors and its teams that have created the growth of the sport, given the sport some leadership and direction. We're absolutely not about to back away from that and give up those things and, frankly, return the sport to the very narrow world in which it used to exist years back.'

The PPG Indy Car World Series drew an accumulative total of 56 million domestic television viewers in 1995 in 43 million homes, up dramatically from 30 million homes in '94. That's one in every four homes in the country. 'A remarkable achievement', noted Craig, 'which underscores the popularity of Indy Car and motor sports in general in America.' IndyCar's best 1995 domestic TV audiences were the Michigan 500 with 4.8 million viewers and Detroit with 3.8 million.

At-the-track spectator numbers weren't available until after *Autocourse*'s deadline, but Craig was sure that similarly strong increases will be shown by all but one of 1995's PPG Cup races. 'In our discussions with our promoters in every case, with the exception of Phoenix,' noted Craig, 'we had a report of substantially higher audiences. In many cases we had record crowds. In some cases, a sell-out. Even New Hampshire, which has proven to be a difficult race, we saw an increase this year. When the Goodyear results come out at the end of the year I think we're going to see some very significant increases. I think we have a group of race promoters out there who are very happy with the achievements of this year.'

IndyCar is convinced, therefore, that it can move forward without the Indianapolis 500 as part of its championship. IMS President George meanwhile, is equally confident that he can go his own way, without IndyCar's drivers and teams. 'They have to decide what's best for them,' commented George in October. 'If that's their decision, then so be it. It's totally up to them if they choose to do something else. We have been around for eighty years and we'll be running our race as usual next May, and we're trying to develop a series around our race. That's our intention.'

Craig said he believes most major sponsors will support IndyCar and its teams wherever they race. 'Most sponsors are saying to their teams,' commented Craig in October, ' "Look, we sponsor your team and we support you. You determine what you as a team want to do and we'll go with you." So they're leaving the decision in the hands of the teams. I think the popular wisdom a few months back was that the sponsors are bound to instruct their teams to go to the Indy 500. Well, that's not happening. For the most part the sponsors are saying, "It's your call." '

IndyCar's President said he believes most sponsors are not happy with The Speedway trying to assume a dictatorial position through the IRL. 'There is a significant reluctance', said Craig, 'to put themselves in a position where effectively they would be supporting a series that is going to be run by an organisation that is intent on dominating the sport. That's not attractive to sponsors. They don't want to be in a situation where one party will direct them what to do. It's just not what the sponsors like. They're customers and they want to be treated like customers.'

Craig said he also believes a race run opposite the Indianapolis 500 will do equally well for the sponsors. 'I've no reason to think otherwise,' he declared. 'We're very experienced promoters at IndyCar. We have very good resources and I have no reason whatsoever to think that we couldn't do a highly effective job. Just because one organisation by virtue really of the benevolence of the competitors has been allowed to take over a position on one month for the last seventy-odd years does not mean that it's impossible for another party to come along with the right skills, the right abilities, the right resources, and do a better job.'

George remained almost dismissive of IndyCar's proposed, rival 500-mile race. 'With regard to a proposed or a suggested race up in Michigan,' said George in October, 'we have absolutely no control over that. We've never had any kind of guarantees in the past that certain entrants or drivers were going to be competing in our series [sic]. On more than one occasion in the past we have not benefited from some really great names that were not able to participate in our race for reasons that were beyond our control. This is another situation that may be out of our control, or we have no control over.'

The IMS President also commented on reports that Indianapolis mayor Steven Goldsmith had been asked to act as a mediator between IndyCar and the IRL. 'I think the mayor has been put in an unfortunate position of being cast as a potential mediator,' commented George. 'I think his efforts have led to attracting a number of people [teams] that are involved in the sport to the community. Those people are quite happy to be here. I think, more to the point, one of the reasons they're here is because of the IMS, and geographically, it makes sense. I think he feels an obligation to listen to their perspective.

'As far as this situation requiring mediation, I don't know. I think there has been plenty of time for meaningful discussions and negotiations to occur, but at this point in time I think we're well past the window of opportunity. We're just a couple of months away from Orlando and the Indy 200 at Walt Disney World and, certainly, we've been trying to sit down and have meaningful dialogue on the issues for eighteen months. And it just hasn't been well received, so I don't know that, ninety days out, a lot can be accomplished. The issues are few but they were important and we're at such opposite ends of the spectrum, I don't know what mediation might lend to this, at this point.'

Sunday, 26 May 1996 shapes up, therefore, as a remarkable day in the history of American automobile racing. Instead of racing at Indianapolis that day, the likes of Al Unser Jnr, Michael Andretti, Bobby Rahal, Emerson Fittipaldi, Paul Tracy, Scott Pruett and Robby Gordon will be racing at MIS, two hundred miles to the north-east. The 80th Indy 500, meanwhile, will feature the likes of Eddie Cheever, Scott Brayton, Davey Hamilton, Eliseo Salazar and Fermin Velez. It will all be very interesting, to say the least.

UNITED STATES RACING REVIEW

Rookie of the Year Gil de Ferran threatened to win a race long before recording his maiden Indy Car victory in the season's finale at Laguna Seca.

qualifying, taking three poles, but he wasn't able to translate those poles into wins. Despite leading the early laps in three of those four races he wound up third at Mid-Ohio, fourth on the New Hampshire oval and then had transmission and tyre trouble in the last two races, scraping home 12th in Vancouver and 11th at Laguna Seca.

With Unser finishing no better than sixth, Villeneuve was far enough ahead to take the PPG Cup title regardless of the outcome of Penske's appeal against Unser's Portland disqualification. When Unser was reinstated two weeks after the end of the season as the winner at Portland, it meant Villeneuve won the championship in the end by just 11 points. It was on consistency and a slightly better finishing record that Jacques beat Al, as well as the points from six poles. Unser took not a single pole in '95, although he did lead half as many laps again as Villeneuve. There's no question therefore that Villeneuve's success and Unser's failure at Indianapolis were critical to the outcome of the championship.

It's interesting that Penske won more races – five – with Unser and Fittipaldi than any other team. Villeneuve and Team Green won four races. Paul Tracy and Michael Andretti combined at Newman-Haas to win three times. Robby Gordon scored two wins for Walker Racing. One-time winners were Patrick Racing with Scott Pruett, Tasman Motorsports with rookie Andre Ribeiro and Jim Hall Racing with Rookie of the Year Gil de Ferran.

Ready for F1

Cool and analytical, Villeneuve is a very bright young man who can be as aggressive as anyone when required. Jacques drove many excellent races in 1995 and didn't make a single serious mistake. He was superb in qualifying in the second half of the year, and is a great talent – perfectly nurtured by team owner Barry Green and chief engineer Tony Cicale – who is ready to show a thing or two to the world in F1.

Al Jnr showed even his most ardent doubters in 1995 that he may well be the world's greatest race car driver. He bounced back from repeated setbacks and came unbelievably close to making a silk purse out of a sow's ear of a season. Teammate Fittipaldi won at Nazareth in April, but after failing to qualify at Indy he struggled through one of the toughest seasons of his long career. He had only one other podium finish and ended the year 11th in points.

Three-times champion Bobby Rahal hung in there with persistence and a handful of impressive street racing performances, most notably in Toronto and Vancouver, to take third in the championship. Rahal failed to win a race for the third successive year, but beat his younger rivals to third in points through savvy and consistency. Rahal also split with partner Carl Hogan at the end of the year, and goes it alone as Team Rahal in '96 with a new five-year sponsorship deal with the Miller Brewing Co.

Michael Andretti was a disappointing fourth in points. The early-season championship favourite, Michael made too many mistakes this year and was also hurt by poor reliability, engines in particular. As fast as ever, Andretti's inestimable racer's spirit continues to burn fiercely, but he badly needs a good year in '96.

Finishing only two points behind Andretti was the mercurial Robby Gordon. In his third season, Gordon finally won his first race, then won again two months later. Much of the year, however, was lost in the doldrums, thrashing with a mishandling car. It was a bit disappointing for one with so much talent. Gordon continues with Derrick Walker's organisation in '96, and Walker must sharpen up his team if consistent results are to come.

Paul Tracy was sixth in the championship. Teamed for one year only with Andretti at Newman-Haas, Tracy was right in the thick of things, given half a chance. He was held back, however, by a lack of testing and poor engine reliability. He and Michael actually worked very well together but it was a transient season for the talented Tracy, who returns to his home at Penske for '96 with Unser and Fittipaldi.

Seventh in points was taken by Scott Pruett, who finally established himself at 35 with that elusive first win and a series of other feisty performances. Pruett led the championship early in the year and is enjoying another full winter test programme with Firestone. He should be even stronger in '96.

Jimmy Vasser really found his feet in 1995, his first year with Chip Ganassi's team, and emerged in the season's second half as a regular front-runner. He finished eighth in points ahead of veterans Teo Fabi, Mauricio Gugelmin and Emerson Fittipaldi. Vasser has served a tough apprenticeship; continuing with Ganassi's team with Honda engines next year, the cool, aggressive Californian has a tremendous chance to shine.

Rookie of the Year and most impressive of the newcomers was Gil de Ferran. An extremely smooth, precise driver, de Ferran was frequently impressive in Jim Hall's Reynard but was damned for most of the year with the worst kind of luck. Surprisingly, he snatched the Rookie of the Year award by finishing second in the year's penultimate race, then scoring his first win in the season finale. De Ferran is a great talent, and with Hall's team switching to Honda engines in '96, he might establish himself as a regular winner.

Two other Brazilian drivers, Christian Fittipaldi and Andre Ribeiro, finished second and third in IndyCar's 1995 rookie ratings. Fittipaldi moved from F1 to Indy cars with Derrick Walker's team and frequently ran well. His best race of the year was second to Villeneuve at Indianapolis, but the rest of his season was ruined by terrible reliability. Nevertheless, young Fittipaldi got the break of his life at the end of the year, signing with Newman-Haas to replace the departing Tracy as Michael Andretti's team-mate.

Ribeiro showed his stuff with a great win at New Hampshire in August, helped for sure that day by

104 PPG World Championship Victories

Emerson Fittipaldi marked Ilmor's 100th win at Nazareth, 23 April 1995.

1 Long Beach, Mario Andretti 2 Cleveland, Emerson Fittipaldi 3 Toronto, Emerson Fittipaldi 4 Pocono, Rick Mears 5 Elkhart Lake, Mario Andretti 6 Phoenix, Mario Andretti 7 Long Beach, Al Unser Jr 8 Indy 500, Rick Mears 9 Milwaukee, Rick Mears 10 Portland, Danny Sullivan 11 Cleveland, Mario Andretti 12 Toronto, Al Unser Jr 13 Meadowlands, Al Unser Jr 14 Michigan 500, Danny Sullivan 15 Mid-Ohio, Emerson Fittipaldi 16 Elkhart Lake, Emerson Fittipaldi 17 Nazareth, Danny Sullivan 18 Laguna Seca, Danny Sullivan 19 Miami, Al Unser Jr 20 Phoenix, Rick Mears 21 Long Beach, Al Unser Jr 22 Indy 500, Emerson Fittipaldi 23 Milwaukee, Rick Mears 24 Detroit, Emerson Fittipaldi 25 Portland, Emerson Fittipaldi 26 Cleveland, Emerson Fittipaldi 27 Toronto, Michael Andretti 28 Michigan 500, Michael Andretti 29 Pocono, Danny Sullivan 30 Elkhart Lake, Danny Sullivan 31 Nazareth, Emerson Fittipaldi 32 Laguna Seca, Rick Mears 33 Phoenix, Rick Mears 34 Long Beach, Al Unser Jr 35 Indy 500, Arie Luyendyk 36 Milwaukee, Al Unser Jr 37 Detroit, Michael Andretti 38 Portland, Michael Andretti 39 Cleveland, Danny Sullivan 40 Meadowlands, Michael Andretti 41 Toronto, Al Unser Jr 42 Michigan 500, Al Unser Jr 43 Denver, Al Unser Jr 44 Vancouver, Al Unser Jr 45 Mid-Ohio, Michael Andretti 46 Elkhart Lake, Michael Andretti 47 Nazareth, Emerson Fittipaldi 48 Laguna Seca, Danny Sullivan 49 Surfers Paradise, John Andretti 50 Long Beach, Al Unser Jr 51 Phoenix, Arie Luyendyk 52 Indy 500, Rick Mears 53 Milwaukee, Michael Andretti 54 Detroit, Emerson Fittipaldi 55 Portland, Michael Andretti 56 Cleveland, Michael Andretti 57 Meadowlands, Bobby Rahal 58 Toronto, Michael Andretti 59 Michigan 500, Rick Mears 60 Denver, Al Unser Jr 61 Vancouver, Michael Andretti 62 Mid-Ohio, Michael Andretti 63 Elkhart Lake, Michael Andretti 64 Nazareth, Arie Luyendyk 65 Laguna Seca, Michael Andretti 66 Surfers Paradise, Emerson Fittipaldi 67 Phoenix, Bobby Rahal 68 Long Beach, Danny Sullivan 69 Indy 500, Al Unser Jr 70 Detroit, Bobby Rahal 71 New Hampshire, Bobby Rahal 72 Michigan 500, Scott Goodyear 73 Cleveland, Emerson Fittipaldi 74 Elkhart Lake, Emerson Fittipaldi 75 Mid-Ohio, Emerson Fittipaldi 76 Nazareth, Bobby Rahal 77 Long Beach, Paul Tracy 78 Indy 500, Emerson Fittipaldi 79 Detroit, Danny Sullivan 80 Portland, Emerson Fittipaldi 81 Cleveland, Paul Tracy 82 Toronto, Paul Tracy 83 Elkhart Lake, Paul Tracy 84 Vancouver, Al Unser Jr 85 Mid-

in 156 IndyCar World Series Races

Ohio, Emerson Fittipaldi 86 Laguna Seca, Paul Tracy 87 Phoenix, Emerson Fittipaldi 88 Long Beach, Al Unser Jr 89 Indy 500, Al Unser Jr 90 Milwaukee, Al Unser Jr 91 Detroit, Paul Tracy 92 Portland, Al Unser Jr 93 Cleveland, Al Unser Jr 94 Mid-Ohio, Al Unser Jr 95 Loudon, Al Unser Jr 96 Vancouver, Al Unser Jr 97 Nazareth, Paul Tracy 98 Laguna Seca, Paul Tracy 99 Long Beach, Al Unser Jr 100 Nazareth, Emerson Fittipaldi 101 Portland, Al Unser Jr 102 Mid-Ohio, Al Unser Jr 103 Vancouver, Al Unser Jr 104 Laguna Seca, Gil de Ferran

ILMOR ENGINEERING, LTD — Racing Engines

UNITED STATES RACING REVIEW

Tasman's Andre Ribeiro was one of four drivers to win races for Reynard, helping the Bicester company to the inaugural constructors' championship.

Popular 24-year-old Californian Jeff Gordon *(below right)* deservedly took the NASCAR crown at the wheel of Rick Hendrick's Chevrolet Monte Carlo.

Honda power and Firestone rubber. He had some other good showings as well, at Indianapolis, Michigan and Road America, but needs more consistency to realise his potential. Ribeiro continues with Tasman Motorsports, Honda and Firestone in '96.

Plenty of other drivers had their days or moments in the sun. Among these were Bryan Herta, Mauricio Gugelmin, Teo Fabi, Stefan Johansson, Parker Johnstone and Scott Goodyear. Herta was very fast and impressive in some races, taking a strong second at Cleveland, but was much less competitive in others. Gugelmin and Fabi were surprisingly strong on occasion but unable to show consistent speed. Johansson had a handful of good races, and finished third at Nazareth, but is among those hoping for a better year in '96. Johnstone and Goodyear led the Michigan and Indy 500s respectively, with Honda engines and Firestone tyres, and both of them hope to transform their heartbreaks of '95 into results next year.

Reynard's constructors' title

In IndyCar's new constructors' championship, Reynard was an impressive winner with eight wins and no fewer than 13 poles. Lola was second with four wins and four poles while Penske trailed in third place with five wins and no poles. This was a real triumph for Reynard in only its second season in Indy cars. There's no question that the Reynard 95I was the quickest and most useful car of the year, winning races with with four different drivers and teams and all three types of engine – Ford, Mercedes-Benz and Honda.

Much of the credit for Reynard's success goes to street-smart chief designer Malcolm Oastler, who helps Jim Hall and de Ferran on race weekends. Oastler himself praises chief aerodynamicist Andrew Macauley and it certainly seemed evident at most races this past season that the 95I had the best aero package. It made more downforce than its competitors and reacted less critically to changes in temperature and track conditions. Reynard also did a great job of fixing its transmission troubles during April and May, the credit there due to an extremely hard-working and committed workforce.

IndyCar's inaugural manufacturers' championship was won by Ford with ten wins and 13 poles. The wins came with four different teams – Team Green, Newman-Haas, Walker and Patrick – and the poles with no fewer than seven teams. Mercedes-Benz won six races with two teams – Penske and Hall – and had but one pole, with Hall and de Ferran at Laguna. Honda scored its first Indy Car victory with rookie Ribeiro and Tasman Motorsports at New Hampshire in August and also had two poles with Ribeiro in New Hampshire and Parker Johnstone at the Michigan 500. The Indy 500 pole was taken by Scott Brayton with one of John Menard's Buick-based big-boost, rocker arm V6s.

The unofficial tyre war was taken by Goodyear with 15 wins and 15 poles to Firestone's tally of two each. Both tyre companies did an outstanding job with not a single serious tyre failure during the year. Rather surprisingly, Firestone was more competitive and successful on ovals than road and street circuits, coming within a heartbeat or two of winning at Indianapolis, and then pulling it off for the first time in 21 years to win the Michigan 500.

And the Nations' Cup, also in its inaugural year, was won by the United States from Canada, Brazil and Italy. Unser, Rahal, Andretti, Gordon, Pruett and Jimmy Vasser contributed to the USA's victory, mustering eight wins between them to Canada's six and Brazil's three, so, despite the protestations of Tony George and the IRL, there's plenty of excellent homegrown talent racing Indy cars. On all fronts then, the competition in the PPG Indy Car World Series is very tough. With or without the Indianapolis 500, its great popularity and steady domestic and worldwide growth is sure to continue.

Gordon beats Earnhardt

NASCAR's 31-round 1995 Winston Cup championship featured a season-long battle between seven-times champion Dale Earnhardt and Jeff Gordon, who was in only his third year in NASCAR's premier league. Earnhardt had won the championship in four of the previous five years, equalling NASCAR legend Richard Petty's tally of seven titles in 1994. Californian Gordon moved as a teenager with his family to Indiana to race midget and sprint cars with great success, but instead of going Indy Car racing, he chose NASCAR. Gordon competed for two years in the second division Busch Grand National series before winning the Winston Cup Rookie of the Year award in 1993. He won his first Winston Cup race in '94, and got off

UNITED STATES RACING REVIEW

The main challenge to Gordon came from the Man in Black, seven-times champion Dale Earnhardt.

Below: Typical nose-to-tail Winston Cup action at Pocono. Ricky Rudd (10), Terry Labonte (5) and Morgan Shepherd (21) battle it out at close quarters.

to a great start in '95, winning three of the first six races.

Gordon made the jump into Winston Cup with Rick Hendrick's three-car Chevrolet team, the biggest operation in NASCAR. His team-mates are veterans Terry Labonte and Ken Schrader, and each car is run separately from its own shop. Until this year, Hendrick's cars had won races but never a championship. Gordon changed all that, however, working closely with crew chief Ray Evernham, himself a former Modified driver from New Jersey. One of the favourites to win the championship in '95, Gordon quickly established himself as *the* favourite, taking command of the points standings in the middle of NASCAR's marathon season.

In the end, only Earnhardt could offer any kind of a challenge to

UNITED STATES RACING REVIEW

Young Canadian Greg Moore dominated the Indy Lights series with ten wins from twelve races and graduates to the PPG Cup in '96.

Tom Kendall *(bottom)* claimed the TransAm title for Ford, but Chevrolet took the manufacturers' crown.

Gordon, who led all but two of the 31 races. Gordon led more than 2600 laps in 1995, more than a quarter of the 12,000-mile season. He won seven races, took eight poles and was clearly the year's dominant driver. Known as 'Wonder Boy', Gordon is tremendously popular and was married two years ago to a former Miss Winston. Gordon and his wife live on Lake Norman in central North Carolina outside Charlotte like many other NASCAR stars, and in company with Hendrick's well-funded team and crew chief Evernham, he appears to have the world at his feet.

Earnhardt, now 44, won five races in 1995, and had six second places, but he took just three poles and led only half as many laps as Gordon. In the closing months of the season Earnhardt was at least able to keep the pressure on Gordon, taking the championship decision down to the final race of the season. Earnhardt has won all but one of his seven championships with Richard Childress's Chevrolet team and continues with the team for a 13th season in 1996. He and Gordon will again start the new year as championship co-favourites.

A surprising championship contender this past year was Sterling Marlin, who started the season in great style, winning the Daytona 500 for the second year in a row. Marlin won again at Darlington in April, and once more at Talladega in July. He also defied his critics by staying in the battle for the championship through the first half of the year, and winding up third in points, by far his best year. The 38-year-old Tennesseean has raced Winston Cup cars regularly for nine years and made his first Winston Cup start in his father's car back in 1976.

Fourth in the championship was Mark Martin, who completed his eighth year with Jack Roush's Ford team. Martin and Roush have finished either second or third in the Winston Cup championship four times, but they've yet to win it. There's no question that the wiry little 36-year-old from Arkansas is one of NASCAR's top drivers. Martin has won 18 races during his eight years with Roush, and took four poles and four wins in '95, occasionally being the class of the field. But he just wasn't consistently strong enough, week in and out, to match Gordon or Earnhardt. Roush ran a second car for the second year for Ted Musgrave, who took his first pole, led some races, and finished second twice in '95, but couldn't quite make the winner's circle. Nevertheless, Illinoisan Musgrave had a good year, finishing seventh in points.

Rusty Wallace is much like Martin in that he's usually right in the hunt and frequently challenges for the win. Yet for some reason, there are some races where he's a little off the pace, nor is Wallace's luck often very good. Rusty won the Winston Cup title in 1989, beating Earnhardt by a handful of points while driving for drag racer Raymond Beadle. For the past five years Wallace has been an owner-driver, a partner in Penske South, with long-time partner Don Miller and Roger Penske. Wallace finished second and third in the 1993 and '94 Winston Cup championships, winning a total of 18 races. In '95 he was fifth with two wins and nine other finishes in the top three, but never a championship threat.

The other driver who was almost always up front this past year was Terry Labonte. Winston Cup champion back in 1984 with Billy Hagan's team, Labonte has been with Rick Hendrick's three-car operation the past two years. The 39-year-old Texan was very strong in 1995, winning three races, leading more than 400 laps and finishing sixth in points.

Other drivers to win Winston Cup races in '95 were Labonte's younger brother Bobby, Dale Jarrett, Ricky Rudd, Kyle Petty and Ward Burton. The younger Labonte and Burton are newcomers to Winston Cup racing in the past two and three years, both scoring their first victories in NASCAR's top league this year. Thirty-year-old Labonte in particular is seen as a superstar of the future, driving for NFL football coach Joe Gibbs's team. Rookie of the Year in 1995 was Ricky Craven, who hails from Maine in the USA's far northeast, and came up through the Busch Grand National and Grand National North series. The second division Busch Grand National championship was won in 1995 by Johnny Benson Jnr, another newcomer from outside the American South. Benson comes from the upper-midwestern state of Michigan.

Near the end of the season, in late September, everyone was delighted to see Ernie Irvan make a successful return to racing. In the summer of '94, Irvan was challenging Earnhardt for the year's Winston Cup title when he suffered a serious head injury in a head-on collision with the wall while practising at Michigan International Speedway in August. Irvan wasn't expected by his doctors to be able to return to racing but, miraculously, he fought his way back to complete fitness and made his return to Winston Cup racing at North Wilkesboro, North Carolina on 1 October 1995. Despite wearing an eye patch over his left eye, Irvan finished a very competitive sixth, and led more than one hundred laps at Phoenix at the end of October before his engine failed. Irvan will run the full season again in '96 with Robert Yates's team.

Moore, Hearn, Kendall & Velez

Other notable American champions in 1995 included Canadian Greg Moore in the Indy Lights series and Californian Richie Hearn in the Toyota/Atlantic championship. Young Moore, who turned 20 during the season, was the most dominant Indy Lights champion ever seen, winning ten of twelve races. The gifted Moore moves up to Indy cars in '96 with Forsythe Racing and the Player's sponsorship that served Jacques Villeneuve so well in the past three years. Hearn triumphed in Atlanta after a great season-long battle with defending champion David Empringham and Patrick Carpentier.

The SCCA's TransAm series was won for the second time by Tom Kendall, driving a Ford, although the manufacturers' title was won by Chevrolet. Kendall's primary competitors were TransAm veterans Ron Fellows and Dorsey Schroeder and newcomer Boris Said III.

IMSA's World Sports Car championship was won by Spaniard Fermin Velez driving one of Andy Evans's Ferrari 333SPs. Ferrari also won the manufacturers' championship thanks to Evans's two-car operation and Gianpiero Moretti's single-car team. James Weaver won five races, more than anyone else, with Rob Dyson's Ford-powered Riley & Scott Mk3, but was beaten to the title by Velez's more reliable Ferrari.

Near-disaster struck IMSA when Jeremy Dale and Fabrizio Barbazza were badly injured in a multi-car accident at Road Atlanta in April. Dale is battling to overcome severe leg injuries while Barbazza was lucky to recover from a closed-head injury. For IMSA, struggling as it is for fields and spectators, it wasn't a good year.

OTHER MAJOR 1995 RESULTS

Compiled by David Hayhoe

FIA International Formula 3000 Championship

BRDC INTERNATIONAL TROPHY, Silverstone Grand Prix Circuit, Towcester, Northamptonshire, Great Britain, 7 May. Round 1. 40 laps of the 3.142-mile/5.057-km circuit, 125.680 miles/202.262 km.

1 Ricardo Rosset, BR (Reynard 95D-Cosworth AC), 1h 08m 13.35s, 110.532 mph/177.885 km/h.

2 Vincenzo Sospiri, I (Reynard 95D-Cosworth AC), 1h 08m 21.12s; 3 Allan McNish, GB (Reynard 95D-Cosworth AC), 1h 08m 21.71s; 4 Marc Goossens, B (Lola T95/50-Cosworth AC), 1h 08m 24.48s; 5 Kenny Bräck, S (Reynard 95D-Zytek Judd KV), 1h 08m 41.07s; 6 Christian Pescatori, I (Reynard 95D-Cosworth AC), 1h 09m 03.90s; 7 Fabrizio de Simone, I (Reynard 95D-Zytek Judd KV), 1h 09m 21.12s; 8 Jean-Philippe Belloc, F (Reynard 95D-Cosworth AC), 1h 09m 26.41s; 9 Christophe Tinseau, F (Reynard 95D-Zytek Judd KV), 1h 09m 32.68s; 10 Wim Eyckmans, B (Reynard 95D-Cosworth AC), 1h 09m 33.32s; 11 Jan Lammers, NL (Reynard 95D-Cosworth AC), 1h 10m 13.85s; 12 Tarso Marques, BR (Reynard 95D-Cosworth AC), 39 laps; 13 Guillaume Gomez, F (Reynard 95D-Cosworth AC), 39; 14 Gary Formato, ZA (Reynard 95D-Cosworth AC), 38; 15 Marcos Gueiros, BR (Reynard 95D-Zytek Judd KV), 37 (DNF – electrics); 16 Alain Filhol, F (Reynard 93D-Cosworth DFY), 36; 17 Emmanuel Clérico, F (Reynard 95D-Cosworth AC), 34 (DNF – gear selection); 18 Jérôme Policand, F (Lola T95/50-Cosworth AC), 24 (DNF – accident); 19 Stephen Watson, ZA (Lola T95/50-Cosworth AC), 12 (DNF – accident); 20 Didier Cottaz, F (Reynard 95D-Cosworth AC), 3 (DNF – accident); 21 Mikke van Hool, B (Reynard 95D-Zytek Judd KV), 3 (DNF – accident); 22 Marco Campos, BR (Lola T95/50-Cosworth AC), 0 (DNF – stalled); 23 Gareth Rees, GB (Reynard 95D-Zytek Judd KV), 0 (DNF – stalled); 24 Dino Morelli, GB (Reynard 95D-Zytek Judd KV), 0 (DNF – gearbox).

Fastest race lap: Marques, 1m 40.95s, 112.048 mph/180.323 km/h.

Fastest qualifying lap: Rosset, 1m 38.023s, 115.393 mph/185.708 km/h.

Did not start: Christophe Bouchut, F (Reynard 95D-Cosworth DFY), disqualified; Claude-Yves Gosselin, F (Reynard 93D-Cosworth DFY), did not qualify.

Championship points: 1 Rosset, 9; 2 Sospiri, 6; 3 McNish, 4; 4 Goossens, 3; 5 Bräck, 2; 6 Pescatori, 1.

FIA INTERNATIONAL FORMULA 3000 CHAMPIONSHIP, Circuit de Catalunya, Montmelo, Barcelona, Spain, 13 May. Round 2. 43 laps of the 2.937-mile/4.727-km circuit, 126.301 miles/203.261 km.

1 Vincenzo Sospiri, I (Reynard 95D-Cosworth AC), 1h 06m 56.018s, 113.217 mph/182.205 km/h.

2 Ricardo Rosset, BR (Reynard 95D-Cosworth AC), 1h 06m 58.248s; 3 Tarso Marques, BR (Reynard 95D-Cosworth AC), 1h 07m 00.215s; 4 Emmanuel Clérico, F (Reynard 95D-Cosworth AC), 1h 07m 03.397s; 5 Marc Goossens, B (Lola T95/50-Cosworth AC), 1h 07m 21.676s; 6 Christophe Tinseau, F (Reynard 95D-Zytek Judd KV), 1h 07m 26.992s; 7 Gareth Rees, GB (Reynard 95D-Zytek Judd KV), 1h 07m 41.584s; 8 Mikke van Hool, B (Reynard 95D-Zytek Judd KV), 1h 07m 52.373s; 9 Guillaume Gomez, F (Reynard 95D-Cosworth AC), 1h 07m 52.611s; 10 Jan Lammers, NL (Reynard 95D-Cosworth AC), 1h 08m 18.398s; 11 Stephen Watson, ZA (Lola T95/50-Cosworth AC), 42 laps; 12 Wim Eyckmans, B (Reynard 95D-Cosworth AC), 42; 13 Kenny Bräck, S (Reynard 95D-Zytek Judd KV), 41 (DNF – accident); 14 Gary Formato, ZA (Reynard 95D-Cosworth AC), 41; 15 Christian Pescatori, I (Reynard 95D-Cosworth AC), 39 (DNF – accident damage/wing); 16 Alain Filhol, F (Reynard 93D-Cosworth DFY), 39; 17 Marcos Gueiros, BR (Reynard 95D-Zytek Judd KV), 34 (DNF – accident); 18 Jérôme Policand, F (Lola T95/50-Cosworth AC), 25 (DNF spin); 19 Fabrizio de Simone, I (Reynard 95D-Zytek Judd KV), 18 (DNF – spin); 20 Didier Cottaz, F (Reynard 95D-Cosworth AC), 11 (DNF – accident damage, wing); 21 Allan McNish, GB (Reynard 95D-Cosworth AC), 6 (DNF – spin); 22 Dino Morelli, GB (Reynard 95D-Zytek Judd KV), 5 (DNF – brakes, accident); 23 Marco Campos, BR (Lola T95/50-Cosworth AC), 0 (DNF – accident).

Jean-Philippe Belloc, F (Reynard 95D-Cosworth AC), 16th and Christophe Bouchut, F (Reynard 95D-Cosworth AC), 19th but disqualified.

Fastest race lap: Clérico, 1m 31.597s, 115.440 mph/185.783 km/h.

Fastest qualifying lap: McNish, 1m 29.922s, 117.591 mph/189.244 km/h.

Did not start: Claude-Yves Gosselin, F (Reynard 93D-Cosworth DFY), did not qualify.

Championship points: 1= Sospiri, 15; 1= Rosset, 15; 3 Goossens, 5; 4= McNish, 4; 4= Marques, 4; 6 Clérico, 3.

55th GRAND PRIX AUTOMOBILE DE PAU, Circuit de Pau, France, 5 June. Round 3. 72 laps of the 1.715-mile/2.760-km circuit, 123.479 miles/198.720 km.

1 Vincenzo Sospiri, I (Reynard 95D-Cosworth AC), 1h 26m 47.823s, 85.357 mph/137.369 km/h.

2 Allan McNish, GB (Reynard 95D-Cosworth AC), 1h 26m 50.614s; 3 Marc Goossens, B (Lola T95/50-Cosworth AC), 1h 26m 51.453s; 4 Kenny Bräck, S (Reynard 95D-Zytek Judd KV), 1h 26m 59.347s; 5 Jean-Philippe Belloc, F (Reynard 95D-Cosworth AC), 1h 27m 14.707s; 6 Didier Cottaz, F (Reynard 95D-Cosworth AC), 1h 27m 15.767s; 7 Emmanuel Clérico, F (Reynard 95D-Cosworth AC), 1h 27m 16.214s; 8 Christophe Bouchut, F (Lola T95/50-Cosworth AC), 1h 27m 20.504s; 9 Ricardo Rosset, BR (Reynard 95D-Cosworth AC), 1h 27m 28.154s; 10 Jan Lammers, NL (Reynard 95D-Cosworth AC), 1h 27m 49.915s; 11 Fabrizio de Simone, I (Reynard 95D-Zytek Judd KV), 1h 27m 50.131s; 12 Stephen Watson, ZA (Lola T95/50-Cosworth AC), 70 laps; 13 Marco Campos, BR (Lola T95/50-Cosworth AC), 69; 14 Wim Eyckmans, B (Reynard 95D-Cosworth AC), 69 (DNF – transmission); 15 Christian Pescatori, I (Reynard 95D-Cosworth AC), 51 (DNF – suspension); 16 Christophe Tinseau, F (Reynard 95D-Zytek Judd KV), 46 (DNF – accident); 17 Gareth Rees, GB (Reynard 95D-Zytek Judd KV), 21 (DNF – suspension); 18 Gary Formato, ZA (Reynard 95D-Cosworth AC), 3 (DNF – accident); 19 Marcos Gueiros, BR (Reynard 95D-Zytek Judd KV), 1 (DNF – accident); 20 Tarso Marques, BR (Reynard 95D-Cosworth AC), 0 (DNF – accident); 21 Guillaume Gomez, F (Reynard 95D-Cosworth AC), 0 (DNF – accident); 22 Jérôme Policand, F (Lola T95/50-Cosworth AC), 0 (DNF – accident).

Fastest race lap: Clérico, 1m 10.801s, 87.201 mph/140.337 km/h.

Fastest qualifying lap: Marques, 1m 09.171s, 89.256 mph/143.644 km/h.

Did not start: Mikke van Hool, B (Reynard 95D-Zytek Judd KV), did not qualify; Hans Fertl, D (Reynard 95D-Cosworth AC), did not qualify; Alain Filhol, F (Reynard 93D-Cosworth DFY), did not qualify; Claude-Yves Gosselin, F (Reynard 93D-Cosworth DFY), did not qualify.

Championship points: 1 Sospiri, 24; 2 Rosset, 15; 3 McNish, 10; 4 Goossens, 9; 5 Bräck, 5; 6 Marques, 4.

33rd GRAN PREMIO del MEDITERRANEO, Ente Autodromo di Pergusa, Enna-Pergusa, Sicily, Italy, 23 July. Round 4. 40 laps of the 3.076-mile/4.950-km circuit, 123.031 miles/198.000 km.

1 Ricardo Rosset, BR (Reynard 95D-Cosworth AC), 1h 02m 15.387s, 118.572 mph/190.824 km/h.

2 Vincenzo Sospiri, I (Reynard 95D-Cosworth AC), 1h 02m 27.601s; 3 Christian Pescatori, I (Reynard 95D-Cosworth AC), 1h 02m 33.290s; 4 Marco Campos, BR (Lola T95/50-Cosworth AC), 1h 02m 46.200s; 5 Fabrizio de Simone, I (Reynard 95D-Zytek Judd KV), 1h 02m 50.253s; 6 Jérôme Policand, F (Reynard 95D-Cosworth AC), 1h 03m 03.222s; 7 Stephen Watson, ZA (Lola T95/50-Cosworth AC), 1h 03m 04.794s; 8 Gareth Rees, GB (Reynard 95D-Zytek Judd KV), 1h 03m 10.564s; 9 Gary Formato, ZA (Reynard 95D-Cosworth AC), 39 laps; 10 Peter Olsson, S (Reynard 93D-Cosworth AC), 39; 11 Severino Nardozi, I (Reynard 95D-Zytek Judd KV), 37; 12 Allan McNish, GB (Reynard 95D-Cosworth AC), 27 (DNF – accident); 13 Emmanuel Clérico, F (Reynard 95D-Cosworth AC), 27 (DNF – accident); 14 Marc Goossens, B (Lola T95/50-Cosworth AC), 26 (DNF – accident); 15 Didier Cottaz, F (Reynard 95D-Cosworth AC), 18 (DNF – accident); 16 Kenny Bräck, S (Reynard 95D-Zytek Judd KV), 9 (DNF steering); 17 Mikke van Hool, B (Reynard 95D-Zytek Judd KV), 5 (DNF – accident); 18 Jean-Philippe Belloc, F (Reynard 95D-Cosworth AC), 5 (DNF – accident); 19 Tarso Marques, BR (Reynard 95D-Cosworth AC), 5 (DNF – engine); 20 Marcos Gueiros, BR (Reynard 95D-Zytek Judd KV), 5 (DNF – accident); 21 Christophe Tinseau, F (Reynard 95D-Zytek Judd KV), 5 (DNF); 22 Claude-Yves Gosselin, F (Reynard 93D-Cosworth DFY), 5 (DNF – suspension); 23 Christophe Bouchut, F (Reynard 95D-Cosworth AC), 2 (DNF – accident); 24 Guillaume Gomez, F (Reynard 95D-Cosworth AC), 0 (DNF – accident).

Fastest race lap: Rosset, 1m 31.149s, 121.481 mph/195.504 km/h.

Fastest qualifying lap: Bräck, 1m 29.853s, 123.233 mph/198.324 km/h.

Championship points: 1 Sospiri, 30; 2 Rosset, 24; 3 McNish, 10; 4 Goossens, 9; 5= Bräck, 5; 5= Pescatori, 5.

FIA INTERNATIONAL FORMULA 3000 CHAMPIONSHIP, Hockenheimring, Heidelberg, Germany, 29 July. Round 5. 29 laps of the 4.240-mile/6.823-km circuit, 122.949 miles/197.867 km.

1 Marc Goossens, B (Lola T95/50-Cosworth AC), 58m 04.329s, 127.030 mph/204.436 km/h.

2 Kenny Bräck, S (Reynard 95D-Zytek Judd KV), 58m 08.063s; 3 Guillaume Gomez, F (Reynard 95D-Cosworth AC), 58m 16.513s; 4 Emmanuel Clérico, F (Reynard 95D-Cosworth AC), 58m 17.928s; 5 Marcos Gueiros, BR (Reynard 95D-Zytek Judd KV), 58m 28.362s; 6 Allan McNish, GB (Reynard 95D-Cosworth AC), 58m 33.598s; 7 Christophe Tinseau, F (Reynard 95D-Zytek Judd KV), 58m 38.247s; 8 Jérôme Policand, F (Lola T95/50-Cosworth AC), 58m 39.716s; 9 Ricardo Rosset, BR (Reynard 95D-Cosworth AC), 58m 53.092s; 10 Mikke van Hool, B (Reynard 95D-Zytek Judd KV), 58m 56.932s; 11 Didier Cottaz, F (Reynard 95D-Cosworth AC), 59m 04.747s; 12 Wim Eyckmans, B (Reynard 95D-Cosworth AC), 1h 00m 02.676s; 13 Peter Olsson, S (Reynard 94D-Cosworth DFY), 28 laps; 14 Severino Nardozi, I (Reynard 95D-Zytek Judd KV), 28; 15 Tarso Marques, BR (Reynard 95D-Cosworth AC), 19 (DNF – accident); 16 Vincenzo Sospiri, I (Reynard 95D-Cosworth AC), 18 (DNF – accident); 17 Christophe Bouchut, F (Lola T95/50-Cosworth AC), 18 (DNF – accident); 18 Marco Campos, BR (Lola T95/50-Cosworth AC), 18 (DNF – accident); 19 Stephen Watson, ZA (Lola T95/50-Cosworth AC), 17 (DNF – transmission); 20 Gary Formato, ZA (Reynard 95D-Cosworth AC), 12 (DNF – engine); 21 Christian Pescatori, I (Reynard 95D-Cosworth AC), 10 (DNF – accident damage); 22 Hans Fertl, D (Reynard 95D-Cosworth AC), 3 (DNF – accident); 23 Jean-Philippe Belloc, F (Reynard 95D-Cosworth AC), 0 (DNF accident); 24 Fabrizio de Simone, I (Reynard 95D-Zytek Judd KV), 0 (DNF – accident); 25 Claude-Yves Gosselin, F (Reynard 93D-Cosworth DFY), 0 (DNF – driveshaft).

Fastest race lap: Rosset, 1m 58.633s, 128.654 mph/207.049 km/h.

Fastest qualifying lap: Gomez, 1m 55.843s, 131.753 mph/212.035 km/h.

Championship points: 1 Sospiri, 30; 2 Rosset, 24; 3 Goossens, 18; 4= Bräck, 11; 4= McNish, 11; 6 Clérico, 6.

FIA INTERNATIONAL FORMULA 3000 CHAMPIONSHIP, Circuit de Spa-Francorchamps, Stavelot, Belgium, 27 August. Round 6. 28 laps of the 4.333-mile/6.974-km circuit, 121.336 miles/195.272 km.

1 Vincenzo Sospiri, I (Reynard 95D-Cosworth AC), 59m 03.485s, 123.272 mph/198.386 km/h.

2 Christophe Bouchut, F (Lola T95/50-Cosworth AC), 59m 06.830s; 3 Guillaume Gomez, F (Reynard 95D-Cosworth AC), 59m 07.324s; 4 Ricardo Rosset, BR (Reynard 95D-Cosworth AC), 59m 29.433s; 5 Tarso Marques, BR (Reynard 95D-Cosworth AC), 59m 34.082s; 6 Emmanuel Clérico, F (Reynard 95D-Cosworth AC), 59m 41.850s; 7 Christophe Tinseau, F (Reynard 95D-Zytek Judd KV), 59m 43.829s; 8 Marco Campos, BR (Lola T95/50-Cosworth AC), 59m 44.419s; 9 Mikke van Hool, B (Reynard 95D-Zytek Judd KV), 1h 00m 20.162s; 10 Jérôme Policand, F (Lola T95/50-Cosworth AC), 1h 00m 24.241s; 11 Didier Cottaz, F (Reynard 95D-Cosworth AC), 1h 00m 43.773s; 12 Stephen Watson, ZA (Lola T95/50-Cosworth AC), 1h 00m 51.918s; 13 Jean-Philippe Belloc, F (Reynard 95D-Cosworth AC), 27 laps; 14 Severino Nardozi, I (Reynard 94D-Zytek Judd KV), 27; 15 James Taylor, GB (Reynard 95D-Cosworth AC), 26; 16 Marc Goossens, B (Lola T95/50-Cosworth AC), 25 (DNF – accident); 17 Allan McNish, GB (Reynard 95D-Cosworth AC), 21 (DNF – engine); 18 Stefan de Groodt, B (Reynard 95D-Cosworth AC), 20 (DNF – gearbox); 19 Christian Pescatori, I (Reynard 95D-Cosworth AC), 13 (DNF – accident); 20 Naoki Hattori, J (Reynard 95D-Cosworth AC), 10 (DNF – accident); 21 Fabrizio de Simone, I (Reynard 95D-Zytek Judd KV), 2 (DNF – accident); 22 Kenny Bräck, S (Reynard 95D-Zytek Judd KV), 2 (DNF – accident); 23 Marcos Gueiros, BR (Reynard 95D-Zytek Judd KV), 2 (DNF – accident); 24 Gary Formato, ZA (Reynard 95D-Cosworth AC), 1 (DNF – spin).

Fastest race lap: Gomez, 2m 04.022s, 125.787 mph/202.435 km/h.

Fastest qualifying lap: McNish, 2m 03.989s, 125.821 mph/202.489 km/h.

Championship points: 1 Sospiri, 39; 2 Rosset, 27; 3 Goossens, 18; 4= Bräck, 11; 4= McNish, 11; 6 Gomez, 8.

FIA INTERNATIONAL FORMULA 3000 CHAMPIONSHIP, Autodromo do Estoril, Alcabideche, Portugal, 24 September. Round 7. 46 laps of the 2.709-mile/4.360-km circuit, 124.622 miles/200.560 km.

1 Tarso Marques, BR (Reynard 95D-Cosworth AC), 1h 11m 49.521s, 104.104 mph/167.540 km/h.

2 Emmanuel Clérico, F (Reynard 95D-Cosworth AC), 1h 11m 56.200s; 3 Kenny Bräck, S (Reynard 95D-Zytek Judd KV), 1h 12m 05.565s; 4 Jérôme Policand, F (Lola T95/50-Cosworth AC), 1h 12m 17.750s; 5 Ricardo Rosset, BR (Reynard 95D-Cosworth AC), 1h 12m 18.845s; 6 Christian Pescatori, I (Reynard 95D-Cosworth AC), 1h 12m 42.809s; 7 Vincenzo Sospiri, I (Reynard 95D-Cosworth AC), 1h 12m 46.564s; 8 Marc Goossens, B (Lola T95/50-Cosworth AC), 1h 13m 04.970s; 9 Marco Campos, BR (Lola T95/50-Cosworth AC), 45 laps; 10 Christophe Tinseau, F (Reynard 95D-Zytek Judd KV), 45; 11 Fabrizio de Simone, I (Reynard 95D-Zytek Judd KV), 45; 12 Gary Formato, ZA (Reynard 95D-Cosworth AC), 45; 13 Peter Olsson, S (Reynard 94D-Zytek Judd KV), 45; 14 Christophe Bouchut, F (Lola T95/50-Cosworth AC), 44 (DNF – engine); 15 Severino Nardozi, I (Reynard 94D-Zytek Judd KV), 44; 16 Marc Rostan, F (Reynard 95D-Cosworth AC), 43; 17 James Taylor, GB (Reynard 95D-Cosworth AC), 43; 18 Jean-Philippe Belloc, F (Reynard 95D-Cosworth AC), 36 (DNF – gearbox); 19 Guillaume Gomez, F (Reynard 95D-Cosworth AC), 35 (DNF – accident); 20 Didier Cottaz, F (Reynard 95D-Cosworth AC), 26 (DNF – accident); 21 Stephen Watson, ZA (Lola T95/50-Cosworth AC), 21 (DNF – spin); 22 Allan McNish, GB (Reynard 95D-Cosworth AC), 17 (DNF – accident); 23 Naoki Hattori, J (Reynard 95D-Cosworth AC), 16 (DNF – accident); 24 Marcos Gueiros, BR (Reynard 95D-Zytek Judd KV), 4 (DNF – accident); 25 Mikke van Hool, B (Reynard 95D-Zytek Judd KV), 4 (DNF – accident).

Fastest race lap: Gomez, 1m 32.421s, 105.528 mph/169.832 km/h.

Fastest qualifying lap: Marques, 1m 28.938s, 109.661 mph/176.482 km/h.

Championship points: 1 Sospiri, 39; 2 Rosset, 29; 3 Goossens, 18; 4= Bräck, 15; 4= Marques, 15; 6 Clérico, 13.

FIA INTERNATIONAL FORMULA 3000 CHAMPIONSHIP, Circuit de Nevers, Magny-Cours, France, 15 October. Round 8. 47 laps of the 2.641-mile/4.250-km circuit, 124.119 miles/199.750 km.

1 Kenny Bräck, S (Reynard 95D-Zytek Judd KV), 1h 08m 59.65s, 107.939 mph/173.710 km/h.

2 Marc Goossens, B (Lola T95/50-Cosworth AC), 1h 09m 08.15s; 3 Jean-Philippe Belloc, F (Reynard 95D-Cosworth AC), 1h 09m 14.64s; 4 Vincenzo Sospiri, I (Reynard 95D-Cosworth AC), 1h 09m 14.82s; 5 Emmanuel Clérico, F (Reynard 95D-Cosworth AC), 1h 09m 15.54s; 6 Christian Pescatori, I (Reynard 95D-Cosworth AC), 1h 09m 30.02s; 7 Allan McNish, GB (Reynard 95D-Cosworth AC), 1h 09m 32.74s; 8 Marcos Gueiros, BR (Reynard 95D-Zytek Judd KV), 1h 09m 37.68s; 9 Thomas Biagi, I (Reynard 95D-Cosworth AC), 1h 10m 24.61s; 10 Marco Campos†, BR (Lola T95/50-Cosworth AC), 46 laps (DNF – fatal accident); 11 Didier Cottaz, F (Reynard 95D-Cosworth AC), 46; 12 Stephen Watson, ZA (Lola T95/50-Cosworth AC), 46; 13 Gary Formato, ZA (Reynard 95D-Cosworth AC), 46; 14 Christophe Tinseau, F (Reynard 95D-Zytek Judd KV), 46; 15 Severino Nardozi, I (Reynard 94D-Zytek Judd KV), 45; 16 Marc Rostan, F (Reynard 95D-Cosworth AC), 45; 17 Stephane de Groodt, B (Lola T95/50-Cosworth AC), 37 (DNF – accident); 18 Claude-Yves Gosselin, F (Reynard 94D-Cosworth AC), 34 (DNF – gearbox); 19 Fabrizio de Simone, I (Reynard 95D-Zytek Judd KV), 33 (DNF – accident); 20 Tarso Marques, BR (Reynard 95D-Cosworth AC), 33 (DNF – accident); 21 Peter Olsson, S (Reynard 94D-Zytek Judd KV), 20 (DNF – transmission); 22 Mikke van Hool, B (Reynard 95D-Zytek Judd KV), 20 (DNF – withdrew); 23 Ricardo Rosset, BR (Reynard 95D-Cosworth AC), 11 (DNF – accident); 24 Jérôme Policand, F (Lola T95/50-Cosworth AC), 11 (DNF – engine); 25 Christophe Bouchut, F (Lola T95/50-Cosworth AC), 1 (DNF – clutch).

Fastest race lap: Marques, 1m 26.88s, 109.427 mph/176.105 km/h.

Fastest qualifying lap: Bräck, 1m 25.10s, 111.715 mph/179.788 km/h.

Did not start: James Taylor, GB (Reynard 95D-Cosworth AC), too slow; Guillaume Gomez, F (Reynard 95D-Cosworth AC), accident.

Final championship points

1	Vincenzo Sospiri, I	42
2	Ricardo Rosset, BR	29
3=	Marc Goossens, B	24
3=	Kenny Bräck, S	24
5=	Tarso Marques, BR	15
5=	Emmanuel Clérico, F	15

7 Allan McNish, GB, 11; 8 Guillaume Gomez, F, 8; 9 Christian Pescatori, I, 7; 10= Jean-Philippe Belloc, F, 6; 10= Christophe Bouchut, F, 6; 12 Jérôme Policand, F, 4; 13 Marco Campos†, BR, 3; 14= Marcos Gueiros, BR, 2; 14= Fabrizio de Simone, I, 2; 16= Christophe Tinseau, F, 1; 16= Didier Cottaz, F, 1.

International Touring Car Series

AvD MUGELLO CUP 1995, Autodromo Internazionale del Mugello, Scarperia, Firenze (Florence), Italy, 21 May. 2 x 20 laps of the 3.259-mile/5.245-km circuit.

Round 1 (65.182 miles/104.900 km)

1 Bernd Schneider, D (AMG Mercedes C-Klasse), 37m 39.67s, 103.845 mph/167.122 km/h.

2 Nicola Larini, I (Alfa Romeo 155 V6 TI), 37m 45.10s; 3 Jan Magnussen, DK (AMG Mercedes C-Klasse), 37m 54.13s; 4 Dario Franchitti, GB (AMG Mercedes C-Klasse), 37m 54.77s; 5 Alessandro Nannini, I (Alfa Romeo 155 V6 TI), 37m 56.24s; 6 Stefano Modena, I (Alfa Romeo 155 V6 TI), 37m 56.70s; 7 Giancarlo Fisichella, I (Alfa Romeo 155 V6 TI), 38m 02.64s; 8 Klaus Ludwig, D (Opel Calibra V6), 38m 07.90s; 9 Manuel Reuter, D (Opel Calibra V6), 38m 08.26s; 10 Ellen Lohr, D (AMG Mercedes C-Klasse), 38m 20.55s.

Fastest race lap: Schneider, 1m 50.47s, 106.207 mph/170.924 km/h.

Fastest qualifying lap: Schneider, 1m 48.63s, 108.006 mph/173.819 km/h.

Round 2 (65.182 miles/104.900 km)

1 Dario Franchitti, GB (AMG Mercedes C-Klasse), 37m 27.74s, 104.396 mph/168.009 km/h.

2 Giancarlo Fisichella, I (Alfa Romeo 155 V6 TI), 37m 28.74s; 3 Bernd Schneider, D (AMG Mercedes C-Klasse), 37m 29.42s; 4 Kurt Thiim, DK (AMG Mercedes C-Klasse), 37m 40.73s; 5 Nicola Larini, I (Alfa Romeo 155 V6 TI), 37m 40.74s; 6 Jan Magnussen, DK (AMG Mercedes C-Klasse), 37m 41.99s; 7 Jörg van Ommen, D (AMG Mercedes C-Klasse), 37m 52.31s; 8 JJ Lehto, SF (Opel Calibra V6), 37m 52.71s; 9 Uwe Alzen, D (AMG Mercedes C-Klasse), 38m 07.67s; 10 Bernd Mayländer, D (AMG Mercedes C-Klasse), 38m 07.94s.

Fastest race lap: Stefano Modena, 1m 50.19s, 106.477 mph/171.359 km/h.

C1 THUNDER IN HELSINKI, Helsinki Street Circuit, Finland, 4 June. 2 x 31 laps of the 2.051-mile/3.300-km circuit.

Round 3 (63.566 miles/102.300 km)

1 Christian Danner, D (Alfa Romeo 155 V6 TI), 52m 21.07s, 72.854 mph/117.247 km/h.

2 Stefano Modena, I (Alfa Romeo 155 V6 TI), 52m

28.01s; **3** JJ Lehto, SF (Opel Calibra V6), 52m 34.09s; **4** Manuel Reuter, D (Opel Calibra V6), 52m 36.43s; **5** Bernd Schneider, D (AMG Mercedes C-Klasse), 52m 36.84s; **6** Gianni Giudici, I (Alfa Romeo 155 V6 TI), 52m 55.21s; **7** Nicola Larini, I (Alfa Romeo 155 V6 TI), 52m 55.86s; **8** Alexander 'Sandy' Grau, D (AMG Mercedes C-Klasse), 53m 03.79s; **9** Bernd Mayländer, D (AMG Mercedes C-Klasse), 53m 04.27s; **10** Stig Amthor, D (Alfa Romeo 155 V6 TI), 53m 06.77s.
Fastest race lap: Larini, 1m 26.39s, 85.448 mph/137.516 km/h.
Fastest qualifying lap: Michael Bartels, D (Alfa Romeo 155 V6 TI), 1m 26.20s, 85.637 mph/137.819 km/h.

Round 4 (63.566 miles/102.300 km)
1 Nicola Larini, I (Alfa Romeo 155 V6 TI), 53m 56.31s, 70.710 mph/113.796 km/h.
2 Jan Magnussen, DK (AMG Mercedes C-Klasse), 54m 07.92s; **3** Alexander 'Sandy' Grau, D (AMG Mercedes C-Klasse), 54m 10.39s; **4** Uwe Alzen, D (AMG Mercedes C-Klasse), 54m 12.33s; **5** Ellen Lohr, D (AMG Mercedes C-Klasse), 54m 26.80s; **6** Kurt Thiim, DK (AMG Mercedes C-Klasse), 54m 31.82s; **7** Manuel Reuter, D (Opel Calibra V6), 54m 43.20s; **8** Gianni Giudici, I (Alfa Romeo 155 V6 TI), 54m 46.20s; **9** Bernd Mayländer, D (AMG Mercedes C-Klasse), 54m 59.43s; **10** Markku Alén, SF (Alfa Romeo 155 V6 TI), 55m 15.43s.
Fastest race lap: Stefano Modena, I (Alfa Romeo 155 V6 TI), 1m 25.93s, 85.906 mph/138.252 km/h.

DONINGTON GOLD CUP, Donington Park Grand Prix Circuit, Derbyshire, Great Britain, 9 July. 2 x 25 laps of the 2.500-mile/4.023-km circuit.
Round 5 (62.494 miles/100.575 km)
1 Bernd Schneider, D (AMG Mercedes C-Klasse), 42m 06.19s, 89.059 mph/143.327 km/h.
2 Dario Franchitti, GB (AMG Mercedes C-Klasse), 42m 07.88s; **3** Kurt Thiim, DK (AMG Mercedes C-Klasse), 42m 13.05s; **4** Jörg van Ommen, D (AMG Mercedes C-Klasse), 42m 14.03s; **5** Giancarlo Fisichella, I (Alfa Romeo 155 V6 TI), 42m 14.72s; **6** Stefano Modena, I (Alfa Romeo 155 V6 TI), 42m 22.25s; **7** Uwe Alzen, D (AMG Mercedes C-Klasse), 42m 24.89s; **8** Klaus Ludwig, D (Opel Calibra V6), 42m 27.08s; **9** Alexander 'Sandy' Grau, D (AMG Mercedes C-Klasse), 42m 29.25s; **10** Manuel Reuter, D (Opel Calibra V6), 42m 29.62s.
Fastest race lap: Schneider, 1m 32.93s, 96.838 mph/155.847 km/h.
Fastest qualifying lap: Schneider, 1m 30.44s, 99.505 mph/160.137 km/h.

Round 6 (62.494 miles/100.575 km)
1 Bernd Schneider, D (AMG Mercedes C-Klasse), 38m 59.27s, 96.175 mph/154.779 km/h.
2 Dario Franchitti, GB (AMG Mercedes C-Klasse), 38m 59.87s; **3** Jörg van Ommen, D (AMG Mercedes C-Klasse), 39m 04.71s; **4** Kurt Thiim, DK (AMG Mercedes C-Klasse), 39m 07.89s; **5** Alexander 'Sandy' Grau, D (AMG Mercedes C-Klasse), 39m 09.13s; **6** Manuel Reuter, D (Opel Calibra V6), 39m 21.14s; **7** Uwe Alzen, D (AMG Mercedes C-Klasse), 39m 27.56s; **8** Bernd Mayländer, D (AMG Mercedes C-Klasse), 39m 37.11s; **9** Christian Danner, D (Alfa Romeo 155 V6 TI), 39m 38.29s; **10** Ellen Lohr, D (AMG Mercedes C-Klasse), 39m 41.79s.
Fastest race lap: Schneider, 1m 32.03s, 97.785 mph/157.370 km/h.

ESTORIL GOLDEN CUP, Autodromo do Estoril, Alcabideche, Portugal, 6 August. 2 x 23 laps of the 2.709-mile/4.360-km circuit.
Round 7 (62.311 miles/100.280 km)
1 Bernd Schneider, D (AMG Mercedes C-Klasse), 40m 30.52s, 92.293 mph/148.531 km/h.
2 Jan Magnussen, DK (AMG Mercedes C-Klasse), 40m 32.95s; **3** Nicola Larini, I (Alfa Romeo 155 V6 TI), 40m 35.19s; **4** Giancarlo Fisichella, I (Alfa Romeo 155 V6 TI), 40m 35.52s; **5** Dario Franchitti, GB (AMG Mercedes C-Klasse), 40m 36.18s; **6** Kurt Thiim, DK (AMG Mercedes C-Klasse), 40m 39.39s; **7** Alexander 'Sandy' Grau, D (AMG Mercedes C-Klasse), 40m 51.04s; **8** Alessandro Nannini, I (Alfa Romeo 155 V6 TI), 40m 51.77s; **9** Ellen Lohr, D (AMG Mercedes C-Klasse), 41m 03.84s; **10** Yannick Dalmas, F (Opel Calibra V6), 41m 04.44s.
Fastest race lap: Larini, 1m 43.96s, 93.815 mph/150.981 km/h.

Round 8 (62.311 miles/100.280 km)
1 Jan Magnussen, DK (AMG Mercedes C-Klasse), 40m 01.65s, 93.402 mph/150.317 km/h.
2 Bernd Schneider, D (AMG Mercedes C-Klasse), 40m 03.85s; **3** Dario Franchitti, GB (AMG Mercedes C-Klasse), 40m 04.86s; **4** Alexander 'Sandy' Grau, D (AMG Mercedes C-Klasse), 40m 16.39s; **5** Stefano Modena, I (Alfa Romeo 155 V6 TI), 40m 16.87s; **6** Jörg van Ommen, D (AMG Mercedes C-Klasse), 40m 24.18s; **7** Alessandro Nannini, I (Alfa Romeo 155 V6 TI), 40m 25.97s; **8** Klaus Ludwig, D (Opel Calibra V6), 40m 29.00s; **9** Manuel Reuter, D (Opel Calibra V6), 40m 30.19s; **10** Ellen Lohr, D (AMG Mercedes C-Klasse), 40m 31.37s.
Fastest race lap: Nicola Larini, I (Alfa Romeo 155 V6 TI), 1m 42.65s, 95.013 mph/152.908 km/h.

INTERNATIONAL TOURING CAR SERIES, Circuit de Nevers, Magny-Cours, France, 8 October. 22 and 24 laps of the 2.641-mile/4.250-km circuit.
Round 9 (58.098 miles/93.500 km)
1 Bernd Schneider, D (AMG Mercedes C-Klasse), 36m 41.14s, 95.021 mph/152.921 km/h.
2 Jan Magnussen, DK (AMG Mercedes C-Klasse), 36m 56.40s; **3** Klaus Ludwig, D (Opel Calibra V6), 36m 56.40s; **4** Manuel Reuter, D (Opel Calibra V6), 37m 00.25s; **5** Stefano Modena, I (Alfa Romeo 155 V6 TI), 37m 01.02s; **6** Jörg van Ommen, D (AMG Mercedes C-Klasse), 37m 01.59s; **7** Yannick Dalmas, F (Opel Calibra V6), 37m 01.87s; **8** JJ Lehto, SF (Opel Calibra V6), 37m 02.78s; **9** Uwe Alzen, D (AMG Mercedes C-Klasse), 37m 11.62s; **10** Kurt Thiim, DK (AMG Mercedes C-Klasse), 37m 16.65s.
Fastest race lap: Schneider, 1m 39.08s, 95.953 mph/154.421 km/h.
Fastest qualifying lap: Larini, 1m 35.61s, 99.435 mph/160.025 km/h.

Round 10 (63.380 miles/102.000 km)
1 Bernd Schneider, D (AMG Mercedes C-Klasse), 39m 41.71s, 95.800 mph/154.175 km/h.
2 Manuel Reuter, D (Opel Calibra V6), 39m 47.37s; **3** Jörg van Ommen, D (AMG Mercedes C-Klasse), 39m 47.94s; **4** Yannick Dalmas, F (Opel Calibra V6), 39m 50.49s; **5** JJ Lehto, SF (Opel Calibra V6), 39m 59.42s; **6** Stefano Modena, I (Alfa Romeo 155 V6 TI), 40m 05.30s; **7** Uwe Alzen, D (AMG Mercedes C-Klasse), 40m 05.82s; **8** Keke Rosberg, SF (Opel Calibra V6), 40m 10.36s; **9** Alessandro Nannini, I (Alfa Romeo 155 V6 TI), 40m 11.35s; **10** Philippe Gache, F (Alfa Romeo 155 V6 TI), 40m 14.58s.
Fastest race lap: Schneider, 1m 38.40s, 96.616 mph/155.488 km/h.

Final championship points
Drivers

1	Bernd Schneider, D	155
2	Jan Magnussen, DK	83
3	Dario Franchitti, GB	80
4	Nicola Larini, I	59
5=	Jörg van Ommen, D	50
5=	Manuel Reuter, D	50

7 Stefano Modena, I, 49; **8** Kurt Thiim, DK, 45; **9** Alexander 'Sandy' Grau, D, 39; **10** Giancarlo Fisichella, I, 37; **11=** Uwe Alzen, D, 26; **11=** JJ Lehto, SF, 26; **13** Christian Danner, D, 22; **14** Klaus Ludwig, D, 21; **15** Alessandro Nannini, I, 17; **16** Yannick Dalmas, F, 15; **17** Ellen Lohr, D, 13; **18** Gianni Giudici, I, 9; **19** Bernd Mayländer, D, 8; **20** Keke Rosberg, SF, 3; **21=** Markku Alén, SF, 1; **21=** Stig Amthor, D, 1; **21=** Philippe Gache, F, 1.

Manufacturers
1 Mercedes Benz, 183; **2** Alfa Romeo, 114; **3** Opel, 62.

German Touring Car Championship (Deutsche Tourenwagen Meisterschaft – DTM)

AvD-MAC RENNSPORTFESTIVAL, Hockenheimring, Heidelberg, Germany, 23 April. 2 x 38 laps of the 1.639-mile/2.638-km circuit.
Round 1 (62.289 miles/100.244 km)
1 Bernd Schneider, D (AMG Mercedes C-Klasse), 40m 45.07s, 91.711 mph/147.594 km/h.
2 Jörg van Ommen, D (AMG Mercedes C-Klasse), 40m 52.23s; **3** Dario Franchitti, GB (AMG Mercedes C-Klasse), 40m 57.93s; **4** Jan Magnussen, DK (AMG Mercedes C-Klasse), 40m 59.59s; **5** Klaus Ludwig, D (Opel Calibra V6), 41m 21.53s; **6** Giancarlo Fisichella, I (Alfa Romeo 155 V6 TI), 41m 24.81s; **7** Keke Rosberg, SF (Opel Calibra V6), 41m 35.73s; **8** JJ Lehto, SF (Opel Calibra V6), 41m 36.81s; **9** Yannick Dalmas, F (Opel Calibra V6), 41m 38.28s; **10** Nicola Larini, I (Alfa Romeo 155 V6 TI), 41m 50.19s.
Fastest race lap: Schneider, 1m 02.86s, 93.876 mph/151.079 km/h.
Fastest qualifying lap: Franchitti, 1m 01.07s, 96.627 mph/155.507 km/h.

Round 2 (62.289 miles/100.244 km)
1 Bernd Schneider, D (AMG Mercedes C-Klasse), 40m 36.94s, 92.017 mph/148.087 km/h.
2 Jörg van Ommen, D (AMG Mercedes C-Klasse), 41m 02.95s; **3** Klaus Ludwig, D (Opel Calibra V6), 41m 18.69s; **4** JJ Lehto, SF (Opel Calibra V6), 41m 28.38s; **5** Kurt Thiim, DK (AMG Mercedes C-Klasse), 41m 31.80s; **6** Alexander 'Sandy' Grau, D (AMG Mercedes C-Klasse), 37 laps; **7** Michele Alboreto, I (Alfa Romeo 155 V6 TI), 37; **8** Ni Amorim, P (Opel Calibra V6), 37; **9** Christian Danner, D (Alfa Romeo 155 V6 TI), 37; **10** Stig Amthor, D (Alfa Romeo 155 V6 TI), 37.
Fastest race lap: Schneider, 1m 02.62s, 94.236 mph/151.658 km/h (record).

INTERNATIONALER ADAC AVUS-RENNEN, AVUS Street Circuit, Berlin, Germany, 7 May. 35 and 13 laps of the 1.640-mile/2.640-km circuit.
Round 3 (57.415 miles/92.400 km)
1 Kurt Thiim, DK (AMG Mercedes C-Klasse), 31m 52.40s, 108.080 mph/173.939 km/h.
2 Alexander 'Sandy' Grau, D (AMG Mercedes C-Klasse), 31m 56.80s; **3** Alessandro Nannini, I (Alfa Romeo 155 V6 TI), 32m 01.59s; **4** Giancarlo Fisichella, I (Alfa Romeo 155 V6 TI), 32m 05.47s; **5** Stefano Modena, I (Alfa Romeo 155 V6 TI), 32m 07.52s; **6** Michael Bartels, D (Alfa Romeo 155 V6 TI), 32m 12.82s; **7** Jörg van Ommen, D (AMG Mercedes C-Klasse), 32m 16.08s; **8** Christian Danner, D (Alfa Romeo 155 V6 TI), 32m 19.30s; **9** Keke Rosberg, SF (Opel Calibra V6), 32m 23.55s; **10** JJ Lehto, SF (Opel Calibra V6), 32m 32.59s.
Fastest race lap: Thiim, 53.66s, 110.054 mph/177.115 km/h.
Fastest qualifying lap: Thiim, 53.24s, 110.922 mph/178.512 km/h.

Round 4 (21.325 miles/34.320 km)
1 Kurt Thiim, DK (AMG Mercedes C-Klasse), 18m 39.56s, 68.573 mph/110.358 km/h.
2 Stefano Modena, I (Alfa Romeo 155 V6 TI), 18m 41.24s; **3** Christian Danner, D (Alfa Romeo 155 V6 TI), 18m 42.53s; **4** Keke Rosberg, SF (Opel Calibra V6), 18m 42.68s; **5** Ellen Lohr, D (AMG Mercedes C-Klasse), 18m 44.96s; **6** Nicola Larini, I (Alfa Romeo 155 V6 TI), 18m 45.85s; **7** Jan Magnussen, DK (AMG Mercedes C-Klasse), 18m 46.87s; **8** Michele Alboreto, I (Alfa Romeo 155 V6 TI), 18m 47.48s; **9** Stig Amthor, D (Alfa Romeo 155 V6 TI), 18m 48.25s; **10** Yannick Dalmas, F (Opel Calibra V6), 18m 50.00s.
Fastest race lap: Thiim, 53.95s, 109.463 mph/176.163 km/h.

200 MEILEN VON NÜRNBERG, Norisring, Nürnberg, Germany, 25 June. 2 x 44 laps of the 1.429-mile/2.300-km circuit.
Round 5 (62.883 miles/101.200 km)
1 Christian Danner, D (Alfa Romeo 155 V6 TI), 40m 24.08s, 93.387 mph/150.292 km/h.
2 Klaus Ludwig, D (Opel Calibra V6), 40m 30.88s; **3** Alessandro Nannini, I (Alfa Romeo 155 V6 TI), 40m 41.50s; **4** Bernd Schneider, D (AMG Mercedes C-Klasse), 40m 41.86s; **5** Stefano Modena, I (Alfa Romeo 155 V6 TI), 40m 46.55s; **6** Dario Franchitti, GB (AMG Mercedes C-Klasse), 40m 51.98s; **7** JJ Lehto, SF (Opel Calibra V6), 40m 58.78s; **8** Nicola Larini, I (Alfa Romeo 155 V6 TI), 41m 10.11s; **9** Ni Amorim, P (Opel Calibra V6), 40m 59.23s; **10** Michael Bartels, D (Alfa Romeo 155 V6 TI), 43 laps.
Fastest race lap: Schneider, 51.46s, 99.980 mph/160.902 km/h.
Fastest qualifying lap: Schneider, 50.61s, 101.659 mph/163.604 km/h.

Round 6 (62.883 miles/101.200 km)
1 Bernd Schneider, D (AMG Mercedes C-Klasse), 37m 49.34s, 99.755 mph/160.540 km/h.
2 Dario Franchitti, GB (AMG Mercedes C-Klasse), 38m 07.14s; **3** Jörg van Ommen, D (AMG Mercedes C-Klasse), 38m 09.99s; **4** Stefano Modena, I (Alfa Romeo 155 V6 TI), 38m 10.79s; **5** Alexander 'Sandy' Grau, D (AMG Mercedes C-Klasse), 38m 35.95s; **6** Christian Danner, D (Alfa Romeo 155 V6 TI), 43 laps; **7** Bernd Mayländer, D (AMG Mercedes C-Klasse), 43; **8** Louis Krages, D (AMG Mercedes C-Klasse), 43; **9** Alessandro Nannini, I (Alfa Romeo 155 V6 TI), 42; **10** Nicola Larini, I (Alfa Romeo 155 V6 TI), 41.
Fastest race lap: Schneider, 50.96s, 100.961 mph/162.480 km/h.

INTERNATIONALER 28th ADAC-FLUGPLATZRENNEN, Diepholz Airfield Circuit, Osnabruck, Germany, 23 July. 2 x 37 laps of the 1.690-mile/2.720-km circuit.
Round 7 (62.535 miles/100.640 km)
1 Michael Bartels, D (Alfa Romeo 155 V6 TI), 37m 54.11s, 98.995 mph/159.317 km/h.
2 Dario Franchitti, GB (AMG Mercedes C-Klasse), 37m 55.17s; **3** Nicola Larini, I (Alfa Romeo 155 V6 TI), 37m 55.41s; **4** Alessandro Nannini, I (Alfa Romeo 155 V6 TI), 38m 02.13s; **5** Jörg van Ommen, D (AMG Mercedes C-Klasse), 38m 03.27s; **6** Giancarlo Fisichella, I (Alfa Romeo 155 V6 TI), 38m 10.20s; **7** Bernd Schneider, D (AMG Mercedes C-Klasse), 38m 19.51s; **8** Christian Danner, D (Alfa Romeo 155 V6 TI), 38m 40.80s; **9** Bernd Mayländer, D (AMG Mercedes C-Klasse), 38m 55.82s; **10** Ellen Lohr, D (AMG Mercedes C-Klasse), 38m 58.15s.
Fastest race lap: Larini, 1m 00.44s, 100.670 mph/162.012 km/h.
Fastest qualifying lap: Bartels, 59.40s, 102.432 mph/164.848 km/h.

Round 8 (62.535 miles/100.640 km)
1 Michael Bartels, D (Alfa Romeo 155 V6 TI), 37m 40.72s, 99.581 mph/160.260 km/h.
2 Nicola Larini, I (Alfa Romeo 155 V6 TI), 37m 41.03s; **3** Jörg van Ommen, D (AMG Mercedes C-Klasse), 37m 50.07s; **4** Dario Franchitti, GB (AMG Mercedes C-Klasse), 37m 51.82s; **5** Jan Magnussen, DK (AMG Mercedes C-Klasse), 38m 08.19s; **6** Bernd Schneider, D (AMG Mercedes C-Klasse), 38m 13.46s; **7** Manuel Reuter, D (Opel Calibra V6), 38m 18.92s; **8** JJ Lehto, SF (Opel Calibra V6), 38m 35.00s; **9** Ellen Lohr, D (AMG Mercedes C-Klasse), 38m 38.98s; **10** Bernd Mayländer, D (AMG Mercedes C-Klasse), 38m 39.08s.
Fastest race lap: Magnussen, 59.90s, 101.577 mph/163.472 km/h.

INTERNATIONALER ADAC GROSSER PREIS DER TOURENWAGEN, Nürburgring, Nürburg/Eifel, Germany, 20 August. 2 x 23 laps of the 2.831-mile/4.556-km circuit.
Round 9 (65.112 miles/104.788 km)
1 Bernd Schneider, D (AMG Mercedes C-Klasse), 39m 18.08s, 99.405 mph/159.976 km/h.
2 Nicola Larini, I (Alfa Romeo 155 V6 TI), 39m 20.61s; **3** Alexander 'Sandy' Grau, D (AMG Mercedes C-Klasse), 39m 25.84s; **4** Keke Rosberg, SF (Opel Calibra V6), 39m 28.70s; **5** Jörg van Ommen, D (AMG Mercedes C-Klasse), 39m 32.80s; **6** Giancarlo Fisichella, I (Alfa Romeo 155 V6 TI), 39m 33.20s; **7** Klaus Ludwig, D (Opel Calibra V6), 39m 43.96s; **8** Ellen Lohr, D (AMG Mercedes C-Klasse), 39m 48.40s; **9** Uwe Alzen, D (AMG Mercedes C-Klasse), 39m 50.66s; **10** Michael Bartels, D (Alfa Romeo 155 V6 TI), 40m 07.40s.
Fastest race lap: Kurt Thiim, DK (AMG Mercedes C-Klasse), 1m 41.35s, 100.557 mph/161.831 km/h.
Fastest qualifying lap: Schneider, 1m 38.92s, 103.028 mph/165.807 km/h.

Round 10 (65.112 miles/104.788 km)
1 Bernd Schneider, D (AMG Mercedes C-Klasse), 39m 01.63s, 100.103 mph/161.100 km/h.
2 Alexander 'Sandy' Grau, D (AMG Mercedes C-Klasse), 39m 02.11s; **3** Nicola Larini, I (Alfa Romeo 155 V6 TI), 39m 04.13s; **4** Kurt Thiim, DK (AMG Mercedes C-Klasse), 39m 15.84s; **5** Ellen Lohr, D (AMG Mercedes C-Klasse), 39m 21.00s; **6** Jörg van Ommen, D (AMG Mercedes C-Klasse), 39m 21.94s; **7** Jan Magnussen, DK (AMG Mercedes C-Klasse), 39m 22.40s; **8** Uwe Alzen, D (AMG Mercedes C-Klasse), 39m 26.81s; **9** Manuel Reuter, D (Opel Calibra V6), 39m 27.05s; **10** Klaus Ludwig, D (Opel Calibra V6), 39m 28.92s.
Fastest race lap: Grau, 1m 40.26s, 101.651 mph/163.591 km/h.

INTERNATIONALER ADAC-PREIS SINGEN ALEMANNENRING, Singen Street Circuit, Germany, 17 September. 36 and 28 laps of the 1.740-mile/2.800-km circuit.
Round 11 (62.634 miles/100.800 km)
1 Kurt Thiim, DK (AMG Mercedes C-Klasse), 46m 40.61s, 80.512 mph/129.572 km/h.
2 Dario Franchitti, GB (AMG Mercedes C-Klasse), 46m 41.12s; **3** Nicola Larini, I (Alfa Romeo 155 V6 TI), 46m 54.28s; **4** Jan Magnussen, DK (AMG Mercedes C-Klasse), 46m 58.24s; **5** Manuel Reuter, D (Opel Calibra V6), 47m 05.00s; **6** Bernd Schneider, D (AMG Mercedes C-Klasse), 47m 07.72s; **7** Christian Danner, D (Alfa Romeo 155 V6 TI), 47m 20.99s; **8** Jörg van Ommen, D (AMG Mercedes C-Klasse), 47m 34.10s; **9** Yannick Dalmas, F (Opel Calibra V6), 47m 37.86s; **10** Keke Rosberg, SF (Opel Calibra V6), 47m 39.89s.
Fastest race lap: Thiim, 1m 15.49s, 82.970 mph/133.528 km/h.
Fastest qualifying lap: Franchitti, 1m 14.84s, 83.691 mph/134.687 km/h.

Round 12 (48.716 miles/78.400 km)
1 Kurt Thiim, DK (AMG Mercedes C-Klasse), 36m 14.12s, 80.665 mph/129.818 km/h.
2 Jan Magnussen, DK (AMG Mercedes C-Klasse), 36m 15.51s; **3** Bernd Schneider, D (AMG Mercedes C-Klasse), 36m 21.23s; **4** Christian Danner, D (Alfa Romeo 155 V6 TI), 36m 28.07s; **5** Jörg van Ommen, D (AMG Mercedes C-Klasse), 36m 31.05s; **6** Yannick Dalmas, F (Opel Calibra V6), 36m 34.69s; **7** Ellen Lohr, D (AMG Mercedes C-Klasse), 37m 00.18s; **8** JJ Lehto, SF (Opel Calibra V6), 37m 00.75s; **9** Uwe Alzen, D (AMG Mercedes C-Klasse), 37m 05.50s; **10** Dario Franchitti, GB (AMG Mercedes C-Klasse), 37m 13.78s.
Fastest race lap: Franchitti, 1m 14.53s, 84.039 mph/135.248 km/h.

INTERNATIONALER DTM-PREIS VON HOCKENHEIM, Hockenheimring, Heidelberg, Germany, 15 October. 2 x 15 laps of the 4.240-mile/6.823-km circuit.
Round 13 (63.594 miles/102.345 km)
1 Klaus Ludwig, D (Opel Calibra V6), 32m 51.62s, 116.117 mph/186.873 km/h.
2 Manuel Reuter, D (Opel Calibra V6), 32m 51.98s; **3** Uwe Alzen, D (AMG Mercedes C-Klasse), 32m 56.23s; **4** Jörg van Ommen, D (AMG Mercedes C-Klasse), 32m 56.60s; **5** Alessandro Nannini, I (Alfa Romeo 155 V6 TI), 32m 58.61s; **6** JJ Lehto, SF (Opel Calibra V6), 32m 58.86s; **7** Alexander 'Sandy' Grau, D (AMG Mercedes C-Klasse), 33m 04.44s; **8** Yannick Dalmas, F (Opel Calibra V6), 33m 04.80s; **9** Bernd Mayländer, D (AMG Mercedes C-Klasse), 33m 05.36s; **10** Giancarlo Fisichella, I (Alfa Romeo 155 V6 TI), 33m 08.84s.
Fastest race lap: Kurt Thiim, DK (AMG Mercedes C-Klasse), 2m 09.55s, 117.813 mph/189.601 km/h.
Fastest qualifying lap: Dario Franchitti, GB (AMG Mercedes C-Klasse), 2m 07.61s, 119.604 mph/192.483 km/h.

Round 14 (63.594 miles/102.345 km)
1 Klaus Ludwig, D (Opel Calibra V6), 32m 43.70s, 116.586 mph/187.626 km/h.
2 Uwe Alzen, D (AMG Mercedes C-Klasse), 32m 47.56s; **3** Jörg van Ommen, D (AMG Mercedes C-Klasse), 32m 50.05s; **4** Manuel Reuter, D (Opel Calibra V6), 32m 50.19s; **5** Alexander 'Sandy' Grau, D (AMG Mercedes C-Klasse), 32m 50.88s; **6** JJ Lehto, SF (Opel Calibra V6), 32m 51.04s; **7** Yannick Dalmas, F (Opel Calibra V6), 32m 52.00s; **8** Bernd Mayländer, D (AMG Mercedes C-Klasse), 32m 55.44s; **9** Jan Magnussen, DK (AMG Mercedes C-Klasse), 32m 58.73s; **10** Giancarlo Fisichella, I (Alfa Romeo 155 V6 TI), 33m 02.74s.
Fastest race lap: Dalmas, 2m 09.86s, 117.531 mph/189.148 km/h.

Final championship points
Drivers

1	Bernd Schneider, D	138
2	Jörg van Ommen, D	113
3	Klaus Ludwig, D	80
4	Kurt Thiim, DK	78
5	Dario Franchitti, GB	74
6	Nicola Larini, I	71

7 Alexander 'Sandy' Grau, D, 68; **8** Jan Magnussen, DK, 49; **9** Christian Danner, D, 48; **10** Michael Bartels, D, 47; **11** Alessandro Nannini, I, 44; **12** Manuel Reuter, D, 39; **13** JJ Lehto, SF, 36; **14** Uwe Alzen, D, 34; **15** Giancarlo Fisichella, I, 30; **16** Stefano Modena, I, 26; **17** Ellen Lohr, D, 18; **18=** Yannick Dalmas, F, 17; **18=** Keke Rosberg, SF, 17; **20** Bernd Mayländer, D, 12; **21** Ni Amorim, P, 5; **22** Michele Alboreto, I, 4; **23** Louis Krages, D, 3; **24** Stig Amthor, D, 1.

Manufacturers
1 Mercedes Benz, 224; **2** Alfa Romeo, 150; **3** Opel, 107.

British Formula 3 Championship

BRITISH FORMULA 3 CHAMPIONSHIP, Silverstone Club Circuit, Towcester, Northamptonshire, Great Britain, 26 March. 2 x 15 laps of the 1.642-mile/2.643-km circuit.
Round 1 (24.630 miles/39.638 km)
1 Ralph Firman, GB (Dallara F395-Mugen Honda), 14m 59.35s, 98.591 mph/158.667 km/h.
2 Cristiano da Matta, BR (Dallara F395-Mugen Honda), 15m 01.55s; **3** Steve Arnold, GB (Dallara F395-Vauxhall), 15m 02.52s; **4** Warren Hughes, GB (Dallara F395-HKS Mitsubishi), 15m 05.32s; **5** Jamie Davies, GB (Dallara F395-TOM'S Toyota), 15m 07.30s; **6** Jérémie Dufour, F (Dallara F395-Mugen Honda), 15m 09.92s; **7** Gualter Salles, BR (Dallara F395-Mugen Honda), 15m 12.19s; **8** Gonzalo Rodriguez, U (Dallara F395-HKS Mitsubishi), 15m 13.17s; **9** Oliver Gavin, GB (Dallara F395-Vauxhall), 15m 13.65s; **10** Brian Cunningham, USA (Dallara F395-Mugen Honda), 15m 16.88s.
Fastest race lap: Arnold, 57.31s, 103.144 mph/165.995 km/h.
Class B winner: Johnny Mowlem, GB (Dallara F393-Vauxhall), 15m 24.34s.
Fastest qualifying lap: Firman, 56.86s, 103.961 mph/167.308 km/h.

Round 2 (24.630 miles/39.638 km)
1 Ralph Firman, GB (Dallara F395-Mugen Honda), 14m 24.94s, 102.513 mph/164.979 km/h.
2 Steve Arnold, GB (Dallara F395-Vauxhall), 14m 25.99s; **3** Warren Hughes, GB (Dallara F395-HKS Mitsubishi), 14m 26.80s; **4** Cristiano da Matta, BR (Dallara F395-Mugen Honda), 14m 27.36s; **5** James Matthews, GB (Dallara F395-Mugen Honda), 14m 33.52s; **6** Gualter Salles, BR (Dallara F395-Mugen Honda), 14m 34.49s; **7** Jérémie Dufour, F (Dallara F395-Mugen Honda), 14m 34.80s; **8** Brian Cunningham, USA (Dallara F395-Mugen Honda), 14m 35.48s; **9** Oliver Gavin, GB (Dallara F395-Vauxhall), 14m 36.49s; **10** Marc Gene, E (Dallara F395-Mugen Honda), 14m 37.05s.
Fastest race lap: da Matta, 56.93s, 103.833 mph/167.103 km/h.
Class B winner: Martin Byford, GB (Dallara F394-Vauxhall), 14m 45.99s.
Fastest qualifying lap: Firman, 56.68s, 103.961 mph/167.308 km/h.

Championship points. Class A: 1 Firman, 40; **2** Arnold, 28; **3** da Matta, 26; **4** Hughes, 22; **5=** Dufour, 10; **5=** Salles, 10. **Class B: 1** Mowlem, 37; **2** Byford, 30; **3** Yokoyama, 27.

BRITISH FORMULA 3 CHAMPIONSHIP, Thruxton Circuit, Andover, Hampshire, Great Britain, 17 April. 2 x 10 laps of the 2.356-mile/3.792-km circuit.
Round 3 (23.560 miles/37.916 km)
1 Oliver Gavin, GB (Dallara F395-Vauxhall), 12m 01.82s, 117.503 mph/189.103 km/h.
2 Helio Castro Neves, BR (Dallara F395-Mugen Honda), 12m 05.98s; **3** Gualter Salles, BR (Dallara F395-Mugen Honda), 12m 08.19s; **4** Jérémie Dufour, F (Dallara F395-Mugen Honda), 12m 08.59s; **5** Warren Hughes, GB (Dallara F395-HKS Mitsubishi), 12m 12.02s; **6** Marc Gene, E (Dallara F395-Mugen Honda), 12m 12.68s; **7** Brian Cunningham, USA (Dallara F395-Mugen Honda), 12m 14.91s; **8** Garth Waberski, ZA (Dallara F395-Mugen Honda), 12m 16.78s; **9** Christian Horner, GB (Dallara F395-Mugen Honda), 12m 19.04s; **10** Jamie Davies, GB (Dallara F395-TOM'S Toyota), 12m 22.66s.
Fastest race lap: Gavin, 1m 10.70s, 119.966 mph/193.067 km/h.
Class B winner: Martin Byford, GB (Dallara F394-Vauxhall), 12m 24.29s.
Fastest qualifying lap: Hughes, 1m 10.65s, 120.051 mph/193.203 km/h.

Round 4 (23.560 miles/37.916 km)
1 Oliver Gavin, GB (Dallara F395-Vauxhall), 14m 06.33s, 100.216 mph/161.282 km/h.
2 Ralph Firman, GB (Dallara F395-Mugen Honda), 14m 09.20s; **3** James Matthews, GB (Dallara F395-Mugen Honda), 14m 23.06s; **4** Jérémie Dufour, F (Dallara F395-Mugen Honda), 14m 25.99s; **5** Steve Arnold, GB (Dallara F395-Vauxhall), 14m 28.40s; **6** Helio Castro Neves, BR (Dallara F395-Mugen Honda), 14m 33.96s; **7** Marc Gene, E (Dallara F395-Mugen Honda), 14m 35.49s; **8** Gualter Salles, BR (Dallara F395-Mugen Honda), 14m 40.25s; **9** Johnny Mowlem, GB (Dallara F394-Mugen Honda), 14m 41.79s (1st Class B); **10** Gonzalo Rodriguez, U (Dallara F395-HKS Mitsubishi), 14m 42.12s.
Fastest race lap: Gavin, 1m 22.08s, 103.333 mph/166.299 km/h.
Fastest qualifying lap: Warren Hughes, GB (Dallara F395-HKS Mitsubishi), 1m 10.20s, 120.821 mph/194.442 km/h.
Championship points. Class A: 1 Firman, 55; **2** Gavin, 46; **3** Arnold, 36; **4=** Dufour, 30; **4=** Hughes, 30; **6** da Matta, 26. **Class B: 1** Mowlem, 73; **2** Byford, 62; **3** Yokoyama, 39.

BRITISH FORMULA 3 CHAMPIONSHIP, Donington Park Club Circuit, Derbyshire, Great Britain, 23 April. Round 5. 25 laps of the 1.957-mile/3.149-km circuit, 48.925 miles/78.737 km.
1 Helio Castro Neves, BR (Dallara F395-Mugen Honda), 28m 08.53s, 104.310 mph/167.870 km/h.
2 Warren Hughes, GB (Dallara F395-HKS Mitsubishi), 28m 11.77s; **3** Gonzalo Rodriguez, U (Dallara F395-HKS Mitsubishi), 28m 19.81s; **4** Oliver Gavin, GB (Dallara F395-Vauxhall), 28m 22.12s; **5** Steve Arnold, GB (Dallara F395-Vauxhall), 28m 30.90s; **6** Jamie Spence, GB (Dallara F395-Mugen Honda), 28m 45.02s; **7** Jérémie Dufour, F (Dallara F395-Mugen Honda), 28m 50.66s; **8** Mark Shaw, GB (Dallara F395-Fiat), 28m 54.90s; **9** James Matthews, GB (Dallara F395-Mugen Honda), 28m 55.45s; **10** Geoffroy Horion, B (Dallara F395-Mugen Honda), 28m 55.69s.
Fastest race lap: Gavin, 1m 06.74s, 105.562 mph/169.885 km/h (record).
Class B winner: Martin Byford, GB (Dallara F394-Vauxhall), 28m 55.92s.
Fastest qualifying lap: Castro Neves, 1m 15.077s, 93.840 mph/151.020 km/h.
Championship points. Class A: 1 Gavin, 57; **2** Firman, 55; **3** Hughes, 45; **4** Arnold, 44; **5** Castro Neves, 41; **6** Dufour, 34. **Class B: 1** Byford, 83; **2** Mowlem, 77; **3** Yokoyama, 54.

BRITISH FORMULA 3 CHAMPIONSHIP, Silverstone Club Circuit, Towcester, Northamptonshire, Great Britain, 29 May. Round 6. 25 laps of the 1.642-mile/2.643-km circuit, 41.050 miles/66.064 km.
1 Jérémie Dufour, F (Dallara F395-Mugen Honda), 23m 57.78s, 102.783 mph/165.414 km/h.
2 Ralph Firman, GB (Dallara F395-Mugen Honda), 23m 58.81s; **3** Jamie Spence, GB (Dallara F395-Mugen Honda), 23m 59.99s; **4** Helio Castro Neves, BR (Dallara F395-Mugen Honda), 24m 01.62s; **5** Warren Hughes, GB (Dallara F395-HKS Mitsubishi), 24m 02.13s; **6** Gonzalo Rodriguez, U (Dallara F395-HKS Mitsubishi), 24m 14.05s; **7** Gualter Salles, BR (Dallara F395-Mugen Honda), 24m 14.78s; **8** Marc Gene, E (Dallara F395-Mugen Honda), 24m 15.25s; **9** Geoffroy Horion, B (Dallara F395-Mugen Honda), 24m 17.07s; **10** Luiz Garcia Jnr, BR (Dallara F395-Mugen Honda), 24m 17.55s.
Pedro de la Rosa, E (Dallara F395-TOM'S Toyota) finished 6th in 24m 03.64s and Cristiano da Matta, BR (Dallara F395-Mugen Honda) finished 7th in 24m 09.62s, but were disqualified.
Fastest race lap: Dufour, 56.79s, 104.089 mph/167.515 km/h.
Class B winner: Takashi Yokoyama, J (Dallara F394-TOM'S Toyota), 24m 29.37s.
Fastest qualifying lap: Firman, 56.663s, 104.322 mph/167.890 km/h.
Championship points. Class A: 1 Firman, 70; **2** Gavin, 57; **3** Dufour, 55; **4** Hughes, 53; **5** Castro Neves, 51; **6** Arnold, 44. **Class B: 1** Byford, 83; **2** Mowlem, 77; **3** Yokoyama, 75.

BRITISH FORMULA 3 CHAMPIONSHIP, Silverstone Grand Prix Circuit, Towcester, Northamptonshire, Great Britain, 15 July. Round 7. 15 laps of the 3.142-mile/5.057-km circuit, 47.130 miles/75.848 km.
1 Gualter Salles, BR (Dallara F395-Mugen Honda), 30m 16.08s, 93.425 mph/150.354 km/h.
2 Jérémie Dufour, F (Dallara F395-Mugen Honda), 30m 16.77s; **3** Ralph Firman, GB (Dallara F395-Mugen Honda), 30m 17.40s; **4** Steve Arnold, GB (Dallara F395-Vauxhall), 30m 21.32s; **5** Jamie Spence, GB (Dallara F395-TOM'S Toyota), 30m 22.89s; **6** Helio Castro Neves, BR (Dallara F395-Mugen Honda), 30m 23.51s; **7** Alexander Wurz, A (Dallara F395-Opel), 30m 25.76s; **8** Oliver Gavin, GB (Dallara F395-Vauxhall), 30m 26.20s; **9** James Matthews, GB (Dallara F395-Mugen Honda), 30m 27.35s; **10** Luiz Garcia Jnr, BR (Dallara F395-Mugen Honda), 30m 30.08s.
Fastest race lap: Marc Gene, E (Dallara F395-Mugen Honda), 1m 50.43s, 102.429 mph/164.843 km/h.
Class B winner: Martin Byford, GB (Dallara F394-Vauxhall), 30m 39.18s.
Fastest qualifying lap: Gavin, 1m 49.206s, 103.577 mph/166.691 km/h.
Championship points. Class A: 1 Firman, 82; **2** Dufour, 70; **3** Gavin, 60; **4** Castro Neves, 57; **5** Arnold, 54; **6** Hughes, 53. **Class B: 1** Byford, 103; **2** Mowlem, 77; **3** Yokoyama, 75.

BRITISH FORMULA 3 CHAMPIONSHIP, Donington Park Grand Prix Circuit, Derbyshire, Great Britain, 30 July. 2 x 12 laps of the 2.500-mile/4.023-km circuit.
Round 8 (30.000 miles/48.280 km)
1 Oliver Gavin, GB (Dallara F395-Vauxhall), 18m 29.83s, 97.312 mph/156.609 km/h.
2 Jérémie Dufour, F (Dallara F395-Mugen Honda), 18m 34.72s; **3** Marc Gene, E (Dallara F395-Mugen Honda), 18m 36.32s; **4** Helio Castro Neves, BR (Dallara F395-Mugen Honda), 18m 36.80s; **5** Gualter Salles, BR (Dallara F395-Mugen Honda), 18m 40.01s; **6** Warren Hughes, GB (Dallara F395-HKS Mitsubishi), 18m 41.56s; **7** Jamie Davies, GB (Dallara F395-Mugen Honda), 18m 42.67s; **8** Garth Waberski, ZA (Dallara F395-Mugen Honda), 18m 46.05s; **9** Kurt Mollekens, B (Dallara F395-Mugen Honda), 18m 47.84s; **10** Gonzalo Rodriguez, U (Dallara F395-HKS Mitsubishi), 18m 48.63s.
Fastest race lap: Dufour, 1m 31.78s, 98.061 mph/157.813 km/h.
Class B winner: Martin Byford, GB (Dallara F394-Vauxhall), 18m 57.44s.
Fastest qualifying lap: Ralph Firman, GB (Dallara F395-Mugen Honda), 1m 30.914s, 98.995 mph/159.316 km/h.

Round 9 (30.000 miles/48.280 km)
1 Ralph Firman, GB (Dallara F395-Mugen Honda), 20m 17.91s, 88.677 mph/142.711 km/h.
2 Jamie Davies, GB (Dallara F395-Mugen Honda), 20m 18.94s; **3** Warren Hughes, GB (Dallara F395-HKS Mitsubishi), 20m 21.72s; **4** Helio Castro Neves, BR (Dallara F395-Mugen Honda), 20m 22.84s; **5** Oliver Gavin, GB (Dallara F395-Vauxhall), 20m 23.03s; **6** Gualter Salles, BR (Dallara F395-Mugen Honda), 20m 26.90s; **7** Jérémie Dufour, F (Dallara F395-Mugen Honda), 20m 29.40s; **8** Jamie Spence, GB (Dallara F395-TOM'S Toyota), 20m 32.28s; **9** Marc Gene, E (Dallara F395-Mugen Honda), 20m 32.94s; **10** Luiz Garcia Jnr, BR (Dallara F395-Mugen Honda), 20m 36.89s.
Fastest race lap: Firman, 1m 31.05s, 98.847 mph/159.078 km/h.
Class B winner: Martin Byford, GB (Dallara F394-Vauxhall), 20m 45.95s,
Fastest qualifying lap: Firman, 1m 30.990s, 98.912 mph/159.183 km/h.
Championship points. Class A: 1 Firman, 103; **2** Dufour, 90; **3** Gavin, 88; **4** Castro Neves, 77; **5** Hughes, 71; **6** Salles, 63. **Class B: 1** Byford, 145; **2** Lupberger, 83; **3** Mowlem, 77.

BRITISH FORMULA 3 CHAMPIONSHIP, Oulton Park Circuit, Tarporley, Cheshire, Great Britain, 19 August. Round 10. 15 laps of the 2.775-mile/4.466-km circuit, 41.625 miles/66.989 km.
1 Cristiano da Matta, BR (Dallara F395-Mugen Honda), 23m 55.70s, 104.374 mph/167.974 km/h.
2 Gualter Salles, BR (Dallara F395-Mugen Honda), 23m 56.44s; **3** Warren Hughes, GB (Dallara F395-HKS Mitsubishi), 24m 02.72s; **4** Helio Castro Neves, BR (Dallara F395-Mugen Honda), 24m 03.44s; **5** Marc Gene, E (Dallara F395-Mugen Honda), 24m 05.18s; **6** Jamie Davies, GB (Dallara F395-Mugen Honda), 24m 05.48s; **7** Steve Arnold, GB (Dallara F395-Vauxhall), 24m 06.85s; **8** Christian Horner, GB (Dallara F395-TOM'S Toyota), 24m 07.85s; **9** Ralph Firman, GB (Dallara F395-Mugen Honda), 24m 08.31s; **10** Mark Shaw, GB (Dallara F395-Fiat), 24m 10.69s.
Fastest race lap: Firman, 1m 33.68s, 106.640 mph/171.620 km/h.
Class B winner: Martin Byford, GB (Dallara F394-Vauxhall), 24m 28.21s.
Fastest qualifying lap: Firman, 1m 33.277s, 107.100 mph/172.361 km/h.
Championship points. Class A: 1 Firman, 106; **2** Dufour, 90; **3** Gavin, 88; **4** Castro Neves, 87; **5** Hughes, 83; **6** Salles, 78. **Class B: 1** Byford, 165; **2** Lupberger, 98; **3** Mowlem, 77.

BRITISH FORMULA 3 CHAMPIONSHIP, Brands Hatch Indy Circuit, Dartford, Kent, Great Britain, 27/28 August. 2 x 25 laps of the 1.2036-mile/1.9370-km circuit.
Round 11 (30.090 miles/48.425 km)
1 Ralph Firman, GB (Dallara F395-Mugen Honda), 17m 59.12s, 100.382 mph/161.549 km/h.
2 Helio Castro Neves, BR (Dallara F395-Mugen Honda), 17m 59.90s; **3** Cristiano da Matta, BR (Dallara F395-Mugen Honda), 18m 00.14s; **4** Oliver Gavin, GB (Dallara F395-Vauxhall), 18m 00.54s; **5** Jamie Davies, GB (Dallara F395-Mugen Honda), 18m 01.53s; **6** Jérémie Dufour, F (Dallara F395-Mugen Honda), 18m 02.24s; **7** Marc Gene, E (Dallara F395-Mugen Honda), 18m 04.47s; **8** Kurt Mollekens, B (Dallara F395-Mugen Honda), 18m 06.26s; **9** Mark Shaw, GB (Dallara F395-Fiat), 18m 07.90s; **10** James Matthews, GB (Dallara F395-Mugen Honda), 18m 14.21s.
Fastest race lap: Firman, 42.17s, 102.750 mph/165.360 km/h.
Class B winner: Johnny Mowlem, GB (Dallara F394-Mugen Honda), 18m 27.82s.
Fastest qualifying lap: Firman, 42.042s, 103.063 mph/165.863 km/h.

Round 12 (30.090 miles/48.425 km)
1 Ralph Firman, GB (Dallara F395-Mugen Honda), 17m 50.51s, 101.189 mph/162.848 km/h.
2 Jamie Davies, GB (Dallara F395-Mugen Honda), 17m 54.08s; **3** Oliver Gavin, GB (Dallara F395-Vauxhall), 17m 54.47s; **4** Helio Castro Neves, BR (Dallara F395-Mugen Honda), 17m 57.16s; **5** Steve Arnold, GB (Dallara F395-Vauxhall), 17m 58.27s; **6** Cristiano da Matta, BR (Dallara F395-Mugen Honda), 17m 58.78s; **7** Jérémie Dufour, F (Dallara F395-Mugen Honda), 17m 59.25s; **8** Kurt Mollekens, B (Dallara F395-Mugen Honda), 18m 02.01s; **9** Marc Gene, E (Dallara F395-Mugen Honda), 18m 02.45s; **10** Gualter Salles, BR (Dallara F395-Mugen Honda), 18m 05.12s.
Fastest race lap: Firman, 42.00s, 103.166 mph/166.029 km/h.
Class B winner: Johnny Mowlem, GB (Dallara F394-Mugen Honda), 18m 19.70s.
Fastest qualifying lap: Firman, 42.046s, 103.053 mph/165.847 km/h.
Championship points. Class A: 1 Firman, 148; **2** Castro Neves, 112; **3** Gavin, 110; **4** Dufour, 100; **5** Hughes, 83; **6** Salles, 79. **Class B: 1** Byford, 191; **2** Lupberger, 125; **3** Mowlem, 118.

BRITISH FORMULA 3 CHAMPIONSHIP, Snetterton Circuit, Norfolk, Great Britain, 10 September. Round 13. 19 laps of the 1.952-mile/3.141-km circuit, 37.088 miles/59.687 km.
1 Oliver Gavin, GB (Dallara F395-Vauxhall), 21m 30.17s, 103.488 mph/166.547 km/h.
2 Helio Castro Neves, BR (Dallara F395-Mugen Honda), 21m 35.64s; **3** Jérémie Dufour, F (Dallara F395-Mugen Honda), 21m 37.17s; **4** Luiz Garcia Jnr, BR (Dallara F395-Mugen Honda), 21m 44.89s; **5** James Matthews, GB (Dallara F395-Mugen Honda), 21m 45.39s; **6** Gualter Salles, BR (Dallara F395-Mugen Honda), 21m 45.63s; **7** Steve Arnold, GB (Dallara F395-Vauxhall), 21m 46.99s; **8** Kurt Mollekens, B (Dallara F395-Mugen Honda), 21m 47.40s; **9** Gonzalo Rodriguez, U (Dallara F395-HKS Mitsubishi), 21m 49.21s; **10** Jamie Davies, GB (Dallara F395-Mugen Honda), 21m 49.53s.
Fastest race lap: Gavin, 1m 06.83s, 105.150 mph/169.223 km/h.
Class B winner: Martin Byford, GB (Dallara F394-Vauxhall), 22m 05.89s.
Fastest qualifying lap: Gavin, 1m 06.468s, 105.723 mph/170.145 km/h.
Championship points. Class A: 1 Firman, 148; **2** Gavin, 131; **3** Castro Neves, 127; **4** Dufour, 112; **5** Salles, 85; **6** Hughes, 83. **Class B: 1** Byford, 211; **2** Lupberger, 125; **3** Mowlem, 118.

BRITISH FORMULA 3 CHAMPIONSHIP, Pembrey Circuit, Llanelli, Dyfed, Great Britain, 24 September. 2 x 18 laps of the 1.456-mile/2.343-km circuit.
Round 14 (26.208 miles/42.178 km)
1 Ralph Firman, GB (Dallara F395-Mugen Honda), 18m 30.28s, 84.977 mph/136.758 km/h.
2 Helio Castro Neves, BR (Dallara F395-Mugen Honda), 18m 30.94s; **3** Warren Hughes, GB (Dallara F395-HKS Mitsubishi), 18m 32.06s; **4** Marc Gene, E (Dallara F395-Mugen Honda), 18m 34.75s; **5** Gualter Salles, BR (Dallara F395-Mugen Honda), 18m 37.64s; **6** Christian Horner, GB (Dallara F395-TOM'S Toyota), 18m 38.24s; **7** Kurt Mollekens, B (Dallara F395-Mugen Honda), 18m 38.91s; **8** Jérémie Dufour, F (Dallara F395-Mugen Honda), 18m 39.13s; **9** Gonzalo Rodriguez, U (Dallara F395-HKS Mitsubishi), 18m 41.86s; **10** James Matthews, GB (Dallara F395-Mugen Honda), 18m 43.99s.
Fastest race lap: Dufour, 52.66s, 99.537 mph/160.189 km/h.
Class B winner: Martin Byford, GB (Dallara F394-Vauxhall), 18m 47.35s.
Fastest qualifying lap: Firman, 51.661s, 101.461 mph/163.286 km/h.

Round 15 (26.208 miles/42.178 km)
1 Oliver Gavin, GB (Dallara F395-Vauxhall), 18m 49.17s, 83.556 mph/134.470 km/h.
2 Jérémie Dufour, F (Dallara F395-Mugen Honda), 18m 49.84s; **3** Jamie Davies, GB (Dallara F395-Mugen Honda), 18m 51.78s; **4** Warren Hughes, GB (Dallara F395-HKS Mitsubishi), 18m 53.54s; **5** Cristiano da Matta, BR (Dallara F395-Mugen Honda), 18m 55.38s; **6** Helio Castro Neves, BR (Dallara F395-Mugen Honda), 18m 56.85s; **7** Ralph Firman, GB (Dallara F395-Mugen Honda), 18m 59.60s; **8** Gualter Salles, BR (Dallara F395-Mugen Honda), 19m 00.59s; **9** Kurt Mollekens, B (Dallara F395-Mugen Honda), 19m 01.03s; **10** Christian Horner, GB (Dallara F395-TOM'S Toyota), 19m 05.10s.
Fastest race lap: Gavin, 52.28s, 100.260 mph/161.353 km/h.
Class B winner: Takashi Yokoyama, J (Dallara F394-TOM'S Toyota), 19m 15.59s.
Fastest qualifying lap: Dufour, 51.578s, 101.625 mph/163.549 km/h.
Championship points. Class A: 1 Firman, 172; **2** Gavin, 152; **3** Castro Neves, 148; **4** Dufour, 131; **5** Hughes, 105; **6** Salles, 96. **Class B: 1** Byford, 248; **2** Yokoyama, 134; **3** Lupberger, 125.

AUTUMN GOLD CUP, Silverstone Club Circuit, Towcester, Northamptonshire, Great Britain, 8 October. 14 and 18 laps of the 1.642-mile/2.643-km circuit.
Round 16 (22.988 miles/36.996 km)
1 Warren Hughes, GB (Dallara F395-HKS Mitsubishi), 13m 27.67s, 102.464 mph/164.899 km/h.
2 Helio Castro Neves, BR (Dallara F395-Mugen Honda), 13m 28.34s; **3** Jamie Davies, GB (Dallara F395-Mugen Honda), 13m 32.67s; **4** James Matthews, GB (Dallara F395-Mugen Honda), 13m 39.30s; **5** Gonzalo Rodriguez, U (Dallara F395-HKS Mitsubishi), 13m 40.69s; **6** Marc Gene, E (Dallara F395-Mugen Honda), 13m 40.99s; **7** Brian Cunningham, USA (Dallara F395-Mugen Honda), 13m 49.26s; **8** Takashi Yokoyama, J (Dallara F394-TOM'S Toyota), 13m 52.87s (1st Class B); **9** Cristiano da Matta, BR (Dallara F395-Mugen Honda), 13m 53.45s; **10** Martin Byford, GB (Dallara F394-Vauxhall), 13m 53.64s.
Fastest race lap: Jérémie Dufour, F (Dallara F395-Mugen Honda), 56.82s, 104.034 mph/167.426 km/h.
Fastest qualifying lap: Hughes, 1m 04.205s, 92.068 mph/148.168 km/h.

Round 17 (29.556 miles/47.566 km)
1 Oliver Gavin, GB (Dallara F395-Vauxhall), 17m 20.55s, 102.255 mph/164.564 km/h.
2 James Matthews, GB (Dallara F395-Mugen Honda), 17m 23.10s; **3** Warren Hughes, GB (Dallara F395-HKS Mitsubishi), 17m 23.46s; **4** Jamie Davies, GB (Dallara F395-Mugen Honda), 17m 23.73s; **5** Owen McAuley, GB (Dallara F395-HKS Mitsubishi), 17m 28.17s; **6** Cristiano da Matta, BR (Dallara F395-Mugen Honda), 17m 29.36s; **7** Gonzalo Rodriguez, U (Dallara F395-HKS Mitsubishi), 17m 32.92s; **8** Kurt Mollekens, B (Dallara F395-Mugen Honda), 17m 33.49s; **9** Steve Arnold, GB (Dallara F395-Vauxhall), 17m 34.16s; **10** Christian Horner, GB (Dallara F395-TOM'S Toyota), 17m 35.95s.
Fastest race lap: Jérémie Dufour, F (Dallara F395-Mugen Honda), 57.03s, 103.651 mph/166.810 km/h.
Class B winner: Martin Byford, GB (Dallara F394-Vauxhall), 17m 40.80s.
Fastest qualifying lap: Gavin, 1m 05.118s, 90.777 mph/146.091 km/h.
Championship points. Class A: 1= Firman, 172; **2=** Gavin, 172; **3** Castro Neves, 163; **4** Hughes, 137; **5** Dufour, 133; **6** Salles, 96. **Class B: 1** Byford, 248; **2** Yokoyama, 134; **3** Lupberger, 125.

BRITISH FORMULA 3 CHAMPIONSHIP, Thruxton Circuit, Andover, Hampshire, Great Britain, 15 October. Round 18. 20 laps of the 2.356-mile/3.792-km circuit, 47.120 miles/75.832 km.
1 Warren Hughes, GB (Dallara F395-HKS Mitsubishi), 23m 51.17s, 118.527 mph/190.750 km/h.
2 Jamie Davies, GB (Dallara F395-Mugen Honda), 23m 55.41s; **3** Oliver Gavin, GB (Dallara F395-Vauxhall), 23m 57.24s; **4** Gualter Salles, BR (Dallara F395-Mugen Honda), 23m 57.71s; **5** Jérémie Dufour, F (Dallara F395-Mugen Honda), 23m 59.23s; **6** Helio Castro Neves, BR (Dallara F395-Mugen Honda), 24m 02.28s; **7** Ralph Firman, GB (Dallara F395-Mugen Honda), 24m 06.05s; **8** Luiz Garcia Jnr, BR (Dallara F395-Mugen Honda), 24m 11.26s; **9** Gonzalo Rodriguez, U (Dallara F395-HKS Mitsubishi), 24m 11.67s; **10** James Matthews, GB (Dallara F395-Mugen Honda), 24m 15.99s.
Fastest race lap: Hughes, 1m 10.71s, 119.949 mph/193.039 km/h.
Class B winner: Takashi Yokoyama, J (Dallara F394-TOM'S Toyota), 24m 30.26s.
Fastest qualifying lap: Hughes, 1m 10.237s, 120.757 mph/194.339 km/h.

Final championship points
Class A

1	Oliver Gavin, GB	184
2	Ralph Firman, GB	176
3	Helio Castro Neves, BR	169
4	Warren Hughes, GB	158
5	Jérémie Dufour, F	141
6	Jamie Davies, GB	107

7 Gualter Salles, BR, 106; **8** Cristiano da Matta, BR, 81; **9** Steven Arnold, GB, 72; **10** James Matthews, GB, 60; **11** Marc Gene, E, 59; **12** Gonzalo Rodriguez, U, 42; **13** Jamie Spence, GB, 29; **14** Kurt Mollekens, B, 20; **15** Luiz Garcia Jnr, BR, 16; **16** Christian Horner, GB, 14; **17** Brian Cunningham, USA, 12; **18** Owen McAuley, GB, 10; **19** Mark Shaw, GB, 7; **20** Garth Waberski, ZA, 6; **21** Alexander Wurz, A, 4; **22** Geoffroy Horion, B, 3.

Class B

1 Martin Byford, GB	284
2 Takashi Yokoyama, J	190
3 Werner Lupberger, ZA	150
4 Johnny Mowlem, GB	118
5 Philip Hopkins, GB	115
6 Jim Carney, USA	102

7 Tavo Hellmund, USA, 64; **8** Tony Renna, USA, 63; **9** Alan Berkov, RUS, 61; **10** Paula Cook, GB, 32; **11=** Steve Allen, GB, 24; **11=** Daoud Abou Daye, SAU, 24; **13** Zak Brown, USA, 16; **14** Jason Rolf, GB, 14.

French Formula 3 Championship

COUPES DE PRINTEMPS, Circuit de Lédenon, Remoulins, Nimes, France, 2 April. Round 1. 24 laps of the 1.957-mile/3.150-km circuit, 46.976 miles/75.600 km.
1 Alexandre Janoray, F (Dallara F394-Opel), 32m 37.02s, 86.413 mph/139.069 km/h.
2 David Dussau, F (Dallara F394-Renault), 32m 44.52s; **3** Laurent Redon, F (Dallara F394-Fiat), 32m 48.20s; **4** Nicolas Minassian, F (Dallara F394-Fiat), 32m 48.44s; **5** Stéphane Sarrazin, F (Dallara F394-Fiat), 32m 49.00s; **6** Jesse Bouhet, F (Dallara F394-Fiat), 32m 53.27s; **7** Benjamin Roy, F (Dallara F394-Seymaz Honda), 33m 03.09s; **8** Soheil Ayari, F (Dallara F394-Seymaz Honda), 33m 12.19s; **9** Fabrice Walfisch, F (Dallara F394-Fiat), 33m 13.03s; **10** Didier Andre, F (Dallara F394-Fiat), 33m 13.13s.
Fastest race lap: Janoray, 1m 20.73s, 87.283 mph/140.468 km/h.

COUPES DE PAQUES, Circuit Automobile Paul Armagnac, Nogaro, France, 16/17 April. 2 x 13 laps of the 2.259-mile/3.636-km circuit.
Round 2 (29.371 miles/47.268 km)
1 David Dussau, F (Dallara F394-Renault), 18m 34.97s, 94.833 mph/152.618 km/h.
2 Laurent Redon, F (Dallara F394-Fiat), 18m 39.73s; **3** Nicolas Minassian, F (Dallara F394-Fiat), 18m 41.82s; **4** Alexandre Janoray, F (Dallara F394-Opel), 18m 42.89s; **5** Jesse Bouhet, F (Dallara F394-Fiat), 18m 43.71s; **6** Benjamin Roy, F (Dallara F394-Seymaz Honda), 18m 51.10s; **7** Fabrice Walfisch, F (Dallara F394-Fiat), 18m 52.06s; **8** James Ruffier, F (Dallara F394-Fiat), 18m 52.31s; **9** Anthony Beltoise, F (Dallara F394-Seymaz Honda), 18m 57.14s; **10** Didier Andre, F (Dallara F394-Fiat), 19m 01.61s.
Fastest race lap: Dussau, 1m 25.15s, 95.525 mph/153.724 km/h.

Round 3 (29.371 miles/47.268 km)
1 David Dussau, F (Dallara F394-Renault), 18m 31.79s, 95.104 mph/153.055 km/h.
2 Laurent Redon, F (Dallara F394-Fiat), 18m 32.30s; **3** Alexandre Janoray, F (Dallara F394-Opel), 18m 34.63s; **4** Nicolas Minassian, F (Dallara F394-Fiat), 18m 37.15s; **5** Benjamin Roy, F (Dallara F394-Seymaz Honda), 18m 45.55s; **6** Jesse Bouhet, F (Dallara F394-Fiat), 18m 45.86s; **7** Fabrice Walfisch, F (Dallara F394-Fiat), 18m 46.14s; **8** James Ruffier, F (Dallara F394-Fiat), 18m 47.49s; **9** Stéphane Sarrazin, F (Dallara F394-Fiat), 18m 49.66s; **10** Soheil Ayari, F (Dallara F394-Seymaz Honda), 18m 52.22s.

Fastest race lap: Redon, 1m 24.62s, 96.118 mph/154.687 km/h.

TROPHÉES JEAN BERNIGAUD, Circuit de Nevers, Magny-Cours, France, 30 April. 2 x 13 laps of the 2.641-mile/4.250-km circuit.
Round 4 (34.331 miles/55.250 km)
1 Nicolas Minassian, F (Dallara F394-Fiat), 20m 37.26s, 99.891 mph/160.758 km/h.
2 Laurent Redon, F (Dallara F394-Fiat), 20m 39.13s; **3** David Dussau, F (Dallara F394-Renault), 20m 45.74s; **4** Benjamin Roy, F (Dallara F394-Seymaz Honda), 20m 54.65s; **5** Stéphane Sarrazin, F (Dallara F394-Fiat), 20m 54.82s; **6** Jesse Bouhet, F (Dallara F394-Fiat), 20m 57.67s; **7** James Ruffier, F (Dallara F394-Fiat), 20m 58.07s; **8** Fabrice Walfisch, F (Dallara F394-Fiat), 20m 58.40s; **9** Jérémy Charon, F (Dallara F394-Fiat), 21m 13.51s; **10** Philippe Sinault, F (Dallara F393-Fiat), 21m 20.97s.
Fastest race lap: Minassian, 1m 33.92s, 101.224 mph/162.905 km/h.

Round 5 (34.331 miles/55.250 km)
1 Nicolas Minassian, F (Dallara F394-Fiat), 20m 35.39s, 100.042 mph/161.002 km/h.
2 Alexandre Janoray, F (Dallara F394-Opel), 20m 36.38s; **3** David Dussau, F (Dallara F394-Renault), 20m 40.76s; **4** Jesse Bouhet, F (Dallara F394-Fiat), 20m 51.99s; **5** James Ruffier, F (Dallara F394-Fiat), 20m 56.60s; **6** Ivan Arias, E (Dallara F394-Fiat), 20m 57.81s; **7** Laurent Redon, F (Dallara F394-Fiat), 21m 09.32s; **8** Anthony Beltoise, F (Dallara F394-Seymaz Honda), 21m 09.96s; **9** Didier Andre, F (Dallara F394-Fiat), 21m 17.34s; **10** Grégoire de Galzain, F (Dallara F394-Opel), 21m 17.52s.
Fabrice Walfisch, F (Dallara F394-Fiat), finished 4th in 20m 51.51s but was disqualified for failing to obey order to return to the pits.
Fastest race lap: Janoray, 1m 34.13s, 100.998 mph/162.541 km/h.

GRAND PRIX DIJON-BOURGOGNE, Circuit de Dijon-Prenois, Fontaine-les-Dijon, France, 21 May. Round 6. 20 laps of the 2.361-mile/3.800-km circuit, 47.224 miles/76.000 km.
1 Laurent Redon, F (Dallara F394-Fiat), 25m 25.13s, 111.471 mph/179.395 km/h.
2 Alexandre Janoray, F (Dallara F394-Opel), 25m 27.24s; **3** Jesse Bouhet, F (Dallara F394-Fiat), 25m 28.24s; **4** Nicolas Minassian, F (Dallara F394-Fiat), 25m 28.71s; **5** James Ruffier, F (Dallara F394-Fiat), 25m 34.91s; **6** Soheil Ayari, F (Dallara F394-Opel), 25m 40.91s; **7** Didier Andre, F (Dallara F394-Fiat), 25m 41.88s; **8** Benjamin Roy, F (Dallara F394-Seymaz Honda), 25m 43.04s; **9** Anthony Beltoise, F (Dallara F394-Seymaz Honda), 25m 46.51s; **10** Jérémy Charon, F (Dallara F393-Fiat), 25m 46.76s.
Fastest race lap: Fabrice Walfisch, F (Dallara F394-Fiat), 1m 15.27s, 112.932 mph/181.746 km/h.

FRENCH FORMULA 3 CHAMPIONSHIP, Circuit de Pau, France, 5 June. Round 7. 28 laps of the 1.715-mile/2.760-km circuit, 48.020 miles/77.280 km.
1 Alexandre Janoray, F (Dallara F393-Opel), 35m 13.02s, 81.812 mph/131.664 km/h.
2 Laurent Redon, F (Dallara F394-Fiat), 35m 22.64s; **3** Soheil Ayari, F (Dallara F394-Opel), 35m 24.40s; **4** Nicolas Minassian, F (Dallara F394-Fiat), 35m 26.48s; **5** Jesse Bouhet, F (Dallara F394-Fiat), 35m 26.92s; **6** David Dussau, F (Dallara F394-Renault), 35m 27.21s; **7** Anthony Beltoise, F (Dallara F394-Seymaz Honda), 35m 36.09s; **8** James Ruffier, F (Dallara F394-Fiat), 35m 36.60s; **9** Jérémy Charon, F (Dallara F393-Fiat), 35m 51.39s; **10** Benjamin Roy, F (Dallara F394-Seymaz Honda), 35m 55.00s.
Fastest race lap: Stéphane Sarrazin, F (Dallara F393-Fiat), 1m 13.96s, 83.477 mph/134.343 km/h.

4th COUPE DU VAL DE VIENNE, Circuit du Val de Vienne, Le Vigeant, France, 25 June. Round 8. 24 laps of the 2.334-mile/3.757-km circuit, 56.028 miles/90.168 km.
1 Jesse Bouhet, F (Dallara F394-Fiat), 38m 56.74s, 86.317 mph/138.914 km/h.
2 David Dussau, F (Dallara F394-Renault), 38m 58.26s; **3** Nicolas Minassian, F (Dallara F394-Fiat), 39m 01.62s; **4** Stéphane Sarrazin, F (Dallara F393-Fiat), 39m 10.80s; **5** Laurent Redon, F (Dallara F394-Fiat), 39m 11.25s; **6** Alexandre Janoray, F (Dallara F393-Opel), 39m 12.17s; **7** Jeremy Charon, F (Dallara F393-Fiat), 39m 23.11s; **8** Angel Burgueno, F (Dallara F394-Renault), 39m 30.13s; **9** Boris Derichebourg, F (Dallara F394-Seymaz Honda), 39m 35.75s; **10** Didier Andre, F (Dallara F394-Fiat), 39m 39.28s.
Fastest race lap: Minassian, 1m 36.50s, 87.090 mph/140.158 km/h.

22nd PRIX DU PAS DE CALAIS, Circuit Auto-Moto Croix-en-Ternois, France, 9 July. Round 9. 40 laps of the 1.181-mile/1.900-km circuit, 47.224 miles/76.000 km.
1 Laurent Redon, F (Dallara F394-Fiat), 34m 56.82s, 81.079 mph/130.483 km/h.
2 Jesse Bouhet, F (Dallara F394-Fiat), 34m 58.23s; **3** Alexandre Janoray, F (Dallara F393-Opel), 35m 03.04s; **4** Nicolas Minassian, F (Dallara F394-Fiat), 35m 15.08s; **5** Jean-Claude de Castelli, F (Elise 393-Fiat), 35m 18.94s; **6** Jérémy Charon, F (Dallara F393-Fiat), 35m 19.32s; **7** Angel Burgueno, F (Dallara F394-Renault), 35m 21.06s; **8** Xavier Pompidou, F (Dallara F394-Fiat), 35m 29.13s; **9** Fabrice Walfisch, F (Dallara F394-Fiat), 35m 30.06s; **10** Steeve Hiesse, F (Dallara F393-Fiat), 35m 31.87s.
Fastest race lap: Janoray, 51.89s, 81.907 mph/131.817 km/h.

FRENCH FORMULA 3 CHAMPIONSHIP, Circuit ASA Paul Ricard, Le Beausset, France, 23 July. Round 10. 19 laps of the 2.353-mile/3.786-km circuit, 44.698 miles/71.934 km.
1 Laurent Redon, F (Dallara F394-Fiat), 25m 49.44s, 103.852 mph/167.133 km/h.
2 Jérémy Charon, F (Dallara F393-Fiat), 25m 55.68s; **3** Jesse Bouhet, F (Dallara F394-Fiat), 26m 00.49s; **4** Soheil Ayari, F (Dallara F394-Opel), 26m 01.40s; **5** David Dussau, F (Dallara F394-Renault), 26m 04.44s; **6** Nicolas Minassian, F (Dallara F394-Fiat), 26m 04.77s; **7** Alexandre Janoray, F (Dallara F393-Opel), 26m 13.99s; **8** James Ruffier, F (Dallara F394-Fiat), 26m 21.51s; **9** Philippe Sinault, F (Dallara F393-Fiat), 26m 26.58s; **10** Didier Andre, F (Dallara F394-Fiat), 26m 27.80s.
Fastest race lap: Redon, 1m 20.74s, 104.893 mph/168.809 km/h.

53rd GRAND PRIX D'ALBI, Circuit d'Albi, France, 2/3 September. 2 x 12 laps of the 2.206-mile/3.551-km circuit.
Round 11 (26.478 miles/42.612 km)
1 Laurent Redon, F (Dallara F394-Fiat), 14m 20.71s, 110.746 mph/178.229 km/h.
2 Nicolas Minassian, F (Dallara F394-Fiat), 14m 21.43s; **3** David Dussau, F (Dallara F394-Renault), 14m 23.74s; **4** Alexandre Janoray, F (Dallara F393-Opel), 14m 25.45s; **5** Soheil Ayari, F (Dallara F394-Opel), 14m 29.27s; **6** Jesse Bouhet, F (Dallara F394-Fiat), 14m 30.69s; **7** Fabrice Walfisch, F (Dallara F394-Fiat), 14m 33.21s; **8** Stéphane Sarrazin, F (Dallara F393-Fiat), 14m 33.47s; **9** Didier Andre, F (Dallara F394-Fiat), 14m 39.11s; **10** Stéphane Daoudi, F (Elise 392-Fiat), 14m 53.43s.
Fastest race lap: Minassian, 1m 10.71s, 112.337 mph/180.789 km/h.

Round 12 (26.478 miles/42.612 km)
1 Nicolas Minassian, F (Dallara F394-Fiat), 14m 25.33s, 110.155 mph/177.277 km/h.
2 David Dussau, F (Dallara F394-Renault), 14m 28.37s; **3** Benjamin Roy, F (Dallara F394-Mugen Honda), 14m 37.37s; **4** Xavier Pompidou, F (Dallara F394-Fiat), 14m 42.07s; **5** Jérémy Charon, F (Dallara F393-Fiat), 14m 45.78s; **6** Didier Andre, F (Dallara F394-Fiat), 14m 45.97s; **7** Anthony Beltoise, F (Dallara F394-Seymaz Honda), 14m 49.94s; **8** Grégoire de Galzain, F (Dallara F394-Opel), 14m 54.37s; **9** Stéphane Daoudi, F (Elise 392-Seymaz Honda), 14m 55.18s; **10** Daniel Derichebourg, F (Dallara F394-Seymaz Honda), 14m 55.81s.
Fastest race lap: Minassian, 1m 11.14s, 111.658 mph/179.696 km/h.

COUPES D'AUTOMNE, Circuit Le Mans-Bugatti, France, 24 September. Round 13. 11 laps of the 2.752-mile/4.430-km circuit, 30.279 miles/48.730 km.
1 Soheil Ayari, F (Dallara F394-Opel), 22m 15.50s, 81.622 mph/131.358 km/h.
2 Jesse Bouhet, F (Dallara F394-Fiat), 22m 28.69s; **3** Nicolas Minassian, F (Dallara F394-Fiat), 22m 31.98s; **4** Stéphane Sarrazin, F (Dallara F393-Fiat), 22m 37.62s; **5** Anthony Beltoise, F (Dallara F394-Seymaz Honda), 22m 47.36s; **6** Laurent Redon, F (Dallara F394-Fiat), 22m 50.60s; **7** Grégoire de Galzain, F (Dallara F394-Opel), 22m 53.16s; **8** David Dussau, F (Dallara F394-Renault), 23m 53.75s; **9** Benjamin Roy, F (Dallara F394-Mugen Honda), 23m 11.31s; **10** Angel Burgueno, F (Dallara F394-Renault), 23m 20.14s.
Fastest race lap: Ayari, 1m 59.92s, 82.635 mph/132.989 km/h.

Final championship points

1	Laurent Redon, F	131
2	Nicolas Minassian, F	123
3	David Dussau, F	111
4	Alexandre Janoray, F	102
5	Jesse Bouhet, F	94
6	Soheil Ayari, F	49

7 Benjamin Roy, F, 39; **8** Stéphane Sarrazin, F, 34; **9** Jérémy Charon, F, 33; **10** James Ruffier, F, 28; **11** Anthony Beltoise, F, 22; **12** Fabrice Walfisch, F, 21; **13** Didier Andre, F, 17; **14** Xavier Pompidou, F, 12; **15** Angel Burgueno, F, 9; **16** Grégoire de Galzain, F, 8; **17** Ivan Arias, E, 5; **18=** Philippe Sinault, F, 3; **18=** Boris Derichebourg, F, 3; **18=** Stéphane Daoudi, F, 3.

German Formula 3 Championship

GERMAN FORMULA 3 CHAMPIONSHIP, Hockenheimring, Heidelberg, Germany, 22/23 April. 2 x 31 laps of the 1.639-mile/2.638-km circuit.
Round 1 (50.814 miles/81.778 km)
1 Norberto Fontana, RA (Dallara F395-Opel), 31m 13.97s, 97.617 mph/157.100 km/h.
2 Ralf Schumacher, D (Dallara F395-Opel), 31m 19.51s; **3** Pedro Couceiro, P (Dallara F395-Fiat), 31m 28.13s; **4** Alexander Wurz, A (Dallara F395-Opel), 31m 28.93s; **5** Vincent Radermecker, B (Dallara F395-Fiat), 31m 45.56s; **6** Paolo Coloni, I (Dallara F395-Opel), 31m 45.83s; **7** Rui Aguas, P (Dallara F395-Opel), 31m 47.12s; **8** Arnd Meier, D (Dallara F395-Fiat), 31m 47.93s; **9** Klaus Graf, D (Dallara F395-Opel), 31m 54.03s; **10** Wolf Henzler, D (Dallara F394-Opel), 32m 06.99s (1st Class II).
Fastest race lap: Schumacher, 59.26s, 99.579 mph/160.256 km/h.

Round 2 (50.814 miles/81.778 km)
1 Norberto Fontana, RA (Dallara F395-Opel), 31m 28.83s, 96.849 mph/155.864 km/h.
2 Ralf Schumacher, D (Dallara F395-Opel), 31m 33.65s; **3** Alexander Wurz, A (Dallara F395-Opel), 31m 44.41s; **4** Pedro Couceiro, P (Dallara F395-Fiat), 31m 46.13s; **5** Paolo Coloni, I (Dallara F395-Opel), 31m 46.76s; **6** Rui Aguas, P (Dallara F395-Opel), 31m 47.74s; **7** Klaus Graf, D (Dallara F395-Opel), 31m 51.36s; **8** Wolf Henzler, D (Dallara F394-Opel), 32m 05.01s (1st Class II); **9** Marcel Tiemann, D (Dallara F395-Fiat), 32m 05.37s; **10** Sandro Zani, NL (Dallara F394-Opel), 32m 22.79s.
Fastest race lap: Schumacher, 1m 00.34s, 97.796 mph/157.388 km/h.

GERMAN FORMULA 3 CHAMPIONSHIP, AVUS Street Circuit, Berlin, Germany, 6/7 May. 2 x 31 laps of the 1.640-mile/2.640-km circuit.
Round 3 (50.853 miles/81.840 km)
1 Norberto Fontana, RA (Dallara F395-Opel), 28m 44.13s, 106.182 mph/170.883 km/h.
2 Massimiliano 'Max' Angelelli, MC (Dallara F395-Opel), 28m 47.73s; **3** Arnd Meier, D (Dallara F395-Fiat), 28m 49.86s; **4** Rui Aguas, P (Dallara F395-Opel), 28m 51.28s; **5** Ralf Schumacher, D (Dallara F395-Opel), 28m 52.48s; **6** Pedro Couceiro, P (Dallara F395-Fiat), 28m 56.61s; **7** Oliver Tichy, A (Dallara F395-Opel), 29m 05.75s; **8** Marcel Tiemann, D (Dallara F395-Fiat), 29m 07.08s; **9** Tom Coronel, NL (Dallara F395-Opel), 29m 09.68s; **10** Ralf Kalaschek, D (Dallara F395-Opel), 29m 10.33s.
Fastest race lap: Aguas, 54.44s, 108.477 mph/174.578 km/h.
Class II winner: Tim Bergmeister, D (Dallara F393-Opel), 29m 15.61s.

Round 4 (50.853 miles/81.840 km)
1 Norberto Fontana, RA (Dallara F395-Opel), 28m 31.12s, 106.989 mph/172.182 km/h.
2 Massimiliano 'Max' Angelelli, MC (Dallara F395-Opel), 28m 42.54s; **3** Oliver Tichy, A (Dallara F395-Opel), 28m 46.96s; **4** Arnd Meier, D (Dallara F395-Fiat), 28m 47.54s; **5** Alexander Wurz, A (Dallara F395-Opel), 28m 47.91s; **6** Ralf Schumacher, D (Dallara F395-Opel), 28m 49.28s; **7** Marcel Tiemann, D (Dallara F395-Fiat), 28m 53.28s; **8** Paolo Coloni, I (Dallara F395-Opel), 28m 56.62s; **9** Pedro Couceiro, P (Dallara F395-Fiat), 29m 01.62s; **10** Ralf Kalaschek, D (Dallara F395-Opel), 29m 01.86s.
Fastest race lap: Fontana, 54.33s, 108.697 mph/174.931 km/h.
Class II winner: Tim Bergmeister, D (Dallara F393-Opel), 29m 16.68s.

GERMAN FORMULA 3 CHAMPIONSHIP, Norisring, Nürnberg, Germany, 24/25 June. 35 and 30 laps of the 1.429-mile/2.300-km circuit.
Round 5 (50.020 miles/80.500 km)
1 Ralf Schumacher, D (Dallara F395-Opel), 30m 27.52s, 98.534 mph/158.576 km/h.
2 Massimiliano 'Max' Angelelli, MC (Dallara F395-Opel), 30m 31.65s; **3** Norberto Fontana, RA (Dallara F395-Opel), 30m 36.21s; **4** Tom Coronel, NL (Dallara F395-Opel), 30m 36.72s; **5** Oliver Tichy, A (Dallara F395-Opel), 30m 40.42s; **6** Arnd Meier, D (Dallara F395-Fiat), 30m 49.45s; **7** Rui Aguas, P (Dallara F395-Opel), 30m 52.53s; **8** Jarno Trulli, I (Dallara F394-Opel), 30m 59.50s; **9** Vincent Radermecker, B (Dallara F395-Fiat), 31m 00.17s; **10** Klaus Graf, D (Dallara F395-Opel), 31m 01.11s.
Fastest race lap: Schumacher, 51.50s, 99.902 mph/160.777 km/h.
Class II winner: Tim Bergmeister, D (Dallara F393-Opel).

Round 6 (42.875 miles/69.000 km)
1 Massimiliano 'Max' Angelelli, MC (Dallara F395-Opel), 26m 48.47s, 95.960 mph/154.432 km/h.
2 Ralf Schumacher, D (Dallara F395-Opel), 26m 54.81s; **3** Tom Coronel, NL (Dallara F395-Opel), 26m 56.58s; **4** Norberto Fontana, RA (Dallara F395-Opel), 26m 59.20s; **5** Marcel Tiemann, D (Dallara F395-Fiat), 27m 06.25s; **6** Jarno Trulli, I (Dallara F394-Opel), 27m 12.09s (1st Class II); **7** Pedro Couceiro, P (Dallara F395-Fiat), 27m 17.54s; **8** Alexander Wurz, A (Dallara F395-Opel), 27m 21.16s; **9** Tim Bergmeister, D (Dallara F393-Opel), 27m 40.96s; **10** Jakob Sund, CZ (Dallara F394-Opel), 27m 50.57s.
Fastest race lap: Schumacher, 51.83s, 99.266 mph/159.753 km/h.

GERMAN FORMULA 3 CHAMPIONSHIP, Diepholz Airfield Circuit, Osnabruck, Germany, 23 July. 2 x 30 laps of the 1.690-mile/2.720-km circuit.
Round 7 (50.704 miles/81.600 km)
1 Ralf Schumacher, D (Dallara F395-Opel), 30m 20.75s, 100.252 mph/161.340 km/h.
2 Massimiliano 'Max' Angelelli, MC (Dallara F395-Opel), 30m 22.75s; **3** Norberto Fontana, RA (Dallara F395-Opel), 30m 34.25s; **4** Arnd Meier, D (Dallara F395-Fiat), 30m 42.03s; **5** Oliver Tichy, A (Dallara F395-Opel), 30m 48.01s; **6** Ralf Kalaschek, D (Dallara F395-Opel), 30m 59.80s; **7** Pedro Couceiro, P (Dallara F395-Fiat), 31m 03.90s; **8** Jakob Sund, CZ (Dallara F394-Opel), 31m 08.47s (1st Class II); **9** Marcel Tiemann, D (Dallara F395-Fiat), 31m 09.78s; **10** Johan Stureson, S (Dallara F394-Opel), 29 laps.
Fastest race lap: Fontana, 59.45s, 102.346 mph/164.710 km/h.

Round 8 (50.704 miles/81.600 km)
1 Ralf Schumacher, D (Dallara F395-Opel), 30m 09.22s, 100.891 mph/162.368 km/h.
2 Massimiliano 'Max' Angelelli, MC (Dallara F395-Opel), 30m 13.97s; **3** Norberto Fontana, RA (Dallara F395-Opel), 30m 23.13s; **4** Arnd Meier, D (Dallara F395-Fiat), 30m 29.90s; **5** Oliver Tichy, A (Dallara F395-Opel), 30m 30.28s; **6** Jarno Trulli, I (Dallara F394-Opel), 30m 30.90s (1st Class II); **7** Pedro Couceiro, P (Dallara F395-Fiat), 30m 42.09s; **8** Klaus Graf, D (Dallara F395-Opel), 30m 42.46s; **9** Tom Coronel, NL (Dallara F395-Opel), 30m 43.85s; **10** Jakob Sund, CZ (Dallara F394-Opel), 30m 48.00s.
Fastest race lap: Fontana, 59.45s, 102.346 mph/164.710 km/h.

GERMAN FORMULA 3 CHAMPIONSHIP, Nürburgring, Nürburg/Eifel, Germany, 19 August. 15 and 18 laps of the 2.831-mile/4.556-km circuit.
Round 9 (42.465 miles/68.340 km)
1 Norberto Fontana, RA (Dallara F395-Opel), 24m 39.86s, 103.302 mph/166.248 km/h.
2 Ralf Schumacher, D (Dallara F395-Opel), 24m 40.79s; **3** Tom Coronel, NL (Dallara F395-Opel), 24m 48.81s; **4** Jarno Trulli, I (Dallara F394-Opel), 24m 49.07s; **5** Philipp Peter, A (Dallara F395-Fiat), 24m 54.26s; **6** Klaus Graf, D (Dallara F395-Opel), 25m 01.89s; **7** Alexander Wurz, A (Dallara F395-Opel), 25m 05.61s; **8** Pedro Couceiro, P (Dallara F395-Fiat), 25m 08.68s; **9** Christian Abt, D (Dallara F395-Opel), 25m 09.02s; **10** Wolf Henzler, D (Dallara F394-Opel), 25m 21.95s (1st Class II).
Fastest race lap: Fontana, 1m 37.73s, 104.282 mph/167.826 km/h.

Round 10 (50.957 miles/82.008 km)
1 Norberto Fontana, RA (Dallara F395-Opel), 29m 55.11s, 102.192 mph/164.463 km/h.
2 Jarno Trulli, I (Dallara F395-Opel), 30m 00.66s; **3** Ralf Schumacher, D (Dallara F395-Opel), 30m 01.25s; **4** Tom Coronel, NL (Dallara F395-Opel), 30m 02.80s; **5** Philipp Peter, A (Dallara F395-Fiat), 30m 12.64s; **6** Massimiliano 'Max' Angelelli, MC (Dallara F395-Opel), 30m 13.35s; **7** Pedro Couceiro, P (Dallara F395-Fiat), 30m 21.75s; **8** Alexander Wurz, A (Dallara F395-Opel), 30m 21.80s; **9** Klaus Graf, D (Dallara F395-Opel), 30m 21.84s; **10** Christian Abt, D (Dallara F395-Opel), 30m 29.89s.
Fastest race lap: Schumacher, 1m 38.44s, 103.530 mph/166.615 km/h.
Class II winner: Wolf Henzler, D (Dallara F394-Opel), 30m 32.15s.

GERMAN FORMULA 3 CHAMPIONSHIP, Singen Street Circuit, Germany, 17 September. 29 and 27 laps of the 1.740-mile/2.800-km circuit.
Round 11 (50.455 miles/81.200 km)
1 Norberto Fontana, RA (Dallara F395-Opel), 37m 18.71s, 81.136 mph/130.575 km/h.
2 Pedro Couceiro, P (Dallara F395-Fiat), 37m 23.13s; **3** Ralf Schumacher, D (Dallara F395-Opel), 37m 23.77s; **4** Rui Aguas, P (Dallara F395-Opel), 37m 25.02s; **5** Christian Abt, D (Dallara F395-Opel), 37m 25.37s; **6** Klaus Graf, D (Dallara F395-Opel), 37m 28.57s; **7** Philipp Peter, A (Dallara F395-Fiat), 37m 29.44s; **8** Jarno Trulli, I (Dallara F395-Opel), 37m 31.06s; **9** Arnd Meier, D (Dallara F395-Fiat), 37m 31.59s; **10** Frank Krämer, D (Dallara F394-Opel), 37m 46.75s (1st Class II).
Fastest race lap: Fontana, 1m 14.50s, 84.073 mph/135.302 km/h.

Round 12 (46.976 miles/75.600 km)
1 Norberto Fontana, RA (Dallara F395-Opel), 35m 40.33s, 79.012 mph/127.158 km/h.
2 Pedro Couceiro, P (Dallara F395-Fiat), 35m 41.90s; **3** Ralf Schumacher, D (Dallara F395-Opel), 35m 43.49s; **4** Jarno Trulli, I (Dallara F395-Opel), 35m 44.38s; **5** Christian Abt, D (Dallara F395-Opel), 35m 47.35s; **6** Philipp Peter, A (Dallara F395-Fiat), 35m 51.59s; **7** Alexander Wurz, A (Dallara F395-Opel), 35m 56.49s; **8** Tim Bergmeister, D (Dallara F393-Opel), 36m 12.75s (1st Class II); **9** Massimiliano 'Max' Angelelli, MC (Dallara F395-Opel), 36m 19.92s; **10** Jakob Sund, CZ (Dallara F394-Opel), 36m 22.85s.
Fastest race lap: Angelelli, 1m 13.73s, 84.951 mph/136.715 km/h.

GERMAN FORMULA 3 CHAMPIONSHIP, Hockenheimring, Heidelberg, Germany, 15 October. 2 x 12 laps of the 4.235-mile/6.815-km circuit.
Round 13 (50.816 miles/81.780 km)
1 Jarno Trulli, I (Dallara F395-Opel), 26m 32.05s, 114.906 mph/184.924 km/h.
2 Massimiliano 'Max' Angelelli, MC (Dallara F395-Opel), 26m 34.24s; **3** Wolf Henzler, D (Dallara F394-Opel), 26m 36.07s (1st Class II); **4** Norberto Fontana, RA (Dallara F395-Opel), 26m 36.69s; **5** Philipp Peter, A (Dallara F395-Fiat), 26m 42.01s; **6** Rui Aguas, P (Dallara F395-Opel), 26m 42.75s; **7** Marcel Tiemann, D (Dallara F395-Opel), 26m 42.95s; **8** Tom Coronel, D (Dallara F395-Fiat), 26m 45.32s; **9** Tim Bergmeister, D (Dallara F393-Opel), 26m 48.67s; **10** Klaus Graf, D (Dallara F395-Opel), 26m 50.65s.
Fastest race lap: Fontana, 2m 10.45s, 116.863 mph/188.072 km/h.

Round 14 (50.816 miles/81.780 km)
1 Jarno Trulli, I (Dallara F395-Opel), 26m 44.18s, 114.037 mph/183.526 km/h.
2 Rui Aguas, P (Dallara F395-Opel), 26m 47.82s; **3** Philipp Peter, A (Dallara F395-Fiat), 26m 50.10s; **4** Tim Bergmeister, D (Dallara F393-Opel), 26m 50.69s (1st Class II); **5** Jakob Sund, CZ (Dallara F394-Opel), 26m 53.17s; **6** Jason Watt, DK (Dallara F395-Opel), 26m 58.38s; **7** Wolf Henzler, D (Dallara F394-Opel), 27m 00.65s; **8** Martin Albrecht, A (Dallara F393-Opel), 27m 01.05s; **9** Steffen Widmann, D (Dallara F394-Opel), 27m 06.59s; **10** Marcel Tiemann, D (Dallara F395-Fiat), 27m 09.02s.
Fastest race lap: Wolf Henzler, D (Dallara F394-Opel), 2m 12.12s, 115.385 mph/185.695 km/h.

Final championship points

1	Norberto Fontana, RA	216
2	Ralf Schumacher, D	170
3	Massimiliano 'Max' Angelelli, MC	118
4	Jarno Trulli, I	87
5	Pedro Couceiro, P	79
6	Rui Aguas, P	55

7 Arnd Meier, D, 53; **8** Tom Coronel, NL, 51; **9** Philipp Peter, A, 46; **10** Alexander Wurz, A, 44; **11** Oliver Tichy, A, 40; **12** Klaus Graf, D, 25; **13** Marcel Tiemann, D, 24; **14** Wolf Henzler, D, 21; **15** Christian Abt, D, 19; **16=** Paolo Coloni, I, 17; **16=** Tim Bergmeister, D, 17; **18** Jakob Sund, CZ, 14; **19** Vincent Radermecker, B, 10; **20** Ralf Kalaschek, D, 8.

Italian Formula 3 Championship

ITALIAN FORMULA 3 CHAMPIONSHIP, Autodromo Nazionale di Monza, Milan, Italy, 25/26 March. 2 x 16 laps of the 3.604-mile/5.800-km circuit.
Round 1 (57.663 miles/92.800 km)
1 Andrea Boldrini, I (Dallara F395-Fiat), 29m 02.846s, 119.108 mph/191.686 km/h.
2 Luca Rangoni, I (Dallara F395-Fiat), 29m 04.902s; **3** Luca Riccitelli, I (Dallara F395-Fiat), 29m 14.172s; **4** Maurizio Mediani, I (Dallara F395-Fiat), 29m 20.668s; **5** Oliver Martini, I (Dallara F395-Fiat), 29m 43.069s; **6** Danilo Tomassini, RSM (Dallara F395Fiat), 29m 45.682s; **7** Fabrizio Gollin, I (Dallara F395-Fiat), 29m 45.807s; **8** Paolo Ruberti, I (Dallara F395-Fiat), 29m 53.236s; **9** Gianantonio Pacchioni, I (Dallara F395-Fiat), 29m 53.815s; **10** Pietro Antonelli, I (Dallara F395-Mugen Honda), 29m 54.965s.
Fastest race lap: Boldrini, 1m 47.390s, 120.814 mph/194.432 km/h.
Fastest qualifying lap: Thomas Biagi, I (Dallara F395-Opel), 1m 47.323s, 120.890 mph/194.553 km/h.

Round 2 (57.663 miles/92.800 km)
1 Andrea Boldrini, I (Dallara F395-Fiat), 29m 05.861s, 118.903 mph/191.355 km/h.
2 Luca Rangoni, I (Dallara F395-Fiat), 29m 06.777s; **3** Antoine 'Tony' Kanaan, BR (Dallara F395-Fiat), 29m 21.347s; **4** Oliver Martini, I (Dallara F395-Fiat), 29m 23.180s; **5** Maurizio Mediani, I (Dallara F395-Fiat), 29m 28.205s; **6** Cesare Manfredini, I (Dallara F395-Fiat), 29m 29.020s; **7** Danilo Rossi, I (Dallara F395-Fiat), 29m 29.372s; **8** Gianluca Paglicci, I (Dallara F395-Fiat), 29m 34.552s; **9** Michele Gasparini, I (Dallara F395-Fiat), 29m 35.508s; **10** Fabrizio Gollin, I (Dallara F395-Fiat), 29m 37.847s.

Fastest race lap: Kanaan, 1m 47.628s, 120.547 mph/194.002 km/h.

ITALIAN FORMULA 3 CHAMPIONSHIP, Autodromo Magione, Perugia, Italy, 16/17 April. 2 x 42 laps of the 1.025-mile/1.650-km circuit.
Round 3 (43.061 miles/69.300 km)
1 Gianluca Paglicci, I (Dallara F395-Fiat), 33m 43.940s, 76.593 mph/123.265 km/h.
2 Antoine 'Tony' Kanaan, BR (Dallara F395-Fiat), 33m 56.431s; **3** Gianantonio Pacchioni, I (Dallara F395-Fiat), 33m 57.194s; **4** Luca Rangoni, I (Dallara F395-Fiat), 33m 57.660s; **5** Fabrizio Gollin, I (Dallara F395-Fiat), 34m 03.140s; **6** Luca Riccitelli, I (Dallara F395-Fiat), 34m 05.474s; **7** Danilo Rossi, I (Dallara F395-Fiat), 34m 08.446s; **8** Maurizio Mediani, I (Dallara F395-Fiat), 34m 09.458s; **9** Andrea Boldrini, I (Dallara F395-Fiat), 34m 09.651s; **10** Thomas Biagi, I (Dallara F395-Opel), 34m 15.745s.
Fastest race lap: Paglicci, 47.358s, 77.937 mph/125.428 km/h.
Fastest qualifying lap: Paglicci, 47.514s, 77.681 mph/125.016 km/h.

Round 4 (43.061 miles/69.300 km)
1 Gianluca Paglicci, I (Dallara F395-Fiat), 33m 56.747s, 76.111 mph/122.489 km/h.
2 Luca Rangoni, I (Dallara F395-Fiat), 34m 05.887s; **3** Antoine 'Tony' Kanaan, BR (Dallara F395-Fiat), 34m 13.131s; **4** Gianantonio Pacchioni, I (Dallara F395-Fiat), 34m 13.715s; **5** Luca Riccitelli, I (Dallara F395-Fiat), 34m 14.233s; **6** Andrea Boldrini, I (Dallara F395-Fiat), 34m 14.904s; **7** Fabrizio Gollin, I (Dallara F395-Fiat), 34m 15.490s; **8** Danilo Rossi, I (Dallara F395-Fiat), 34m 16.871s; **9** Oliver Martini, I (Dallara F395-Fiat), 34m 17.318s; **10** Michele Gasparini, I (Dallara F395-Fiat), 34m 19.222s.
Fastest race lap: Paglicci, 47.702s, 77.375 mph/124.523 km/h.

39th GRAN PREMIO PERGUSA, Ente Autodromo di Pergusa, Enna-Pergusa, Sicily, 6/7 May. 2 x 18 laps of the 3.076-mile/4.950-km circuit.
Round 5 (55.364 miles/89.100 km)
1 Andrea Boldrini, I (Dallara F395-Fiat), 29m 23.644s, 113.011 mph/181.873 km/h.
2 Luca Riccitelli, I (Dallara F395-Fiat), 29m 31.396s; **3** Omar Bettin, I (Dallara F395-Fiat), 29m 35.577s; **4** Maurizio Mediani, I (Dallara F395-Fiat), 29m 36.165s; **5** Oliver Martini, I (Dallara F395-Fiat), 29m 39.030s; **6** Gianantonio Pacchioni, I (Dallara F395-Fiat), 29m 40.741s; **7** Gianluca Paglicci, I (Dallara F395-Fiat), 29m 46.466s; **8** Thomas Biagi, I (Dallara F395-Opel), 29m 48.019s; **9** Danilo Rossi, I (Dallara F395-Fiat), 29m 48.247s; **10** Fabrizio Gollin, I (Dallara F395-Fiat), 29m 53.829s.
Fastest race lap: Boldrini, 1m 36.799s, 114.390 mph/184.093 km/h.
Fastest qualifying lap: Riccitelli, 1m 36.631s, 114.589 mph/184.413 km/h.

Round 6 (55.364 miles/89.100 km)
1 Andrea Boldrini, I (Dallara F395-Fiat), 29m 26.162s, 112.850 mph/181.614 km/h.
2 Omar Bettin, I (Dallara F395-Fiat), 29m 33.786s; **3** Gianantonio Pacchioni, I (Dallara F395-Fiat), 29m 35.121s; **4** Cesare Manfredini, I (Dallara F395-Fiat), 29m 36.217s; **5** Oliver Martini, I (Dallara F395-Fiat), 29m 36.627s; **6** Thomas Biagi, I (Dallara F395-Opel), 29m 42.945s; **7** Michele Gasparini, I (Dallara F395-Fiat), 29m 49.474s; **8** Luca Rangoni, I (Dallara F395-Fiat), 29m 51.135s; **9** Danilo Rossi, I (Dallara F395-Fiat), 29m 51.724s; **10** Pietro Antonelli, I (Dallara F395-Mugen Honda), 29m 54.231s.
Fastest race lap: Boldrini, 1m 36.689s, 114.520 mph/184.302 km/h.

GRAN PREMIO CAMPAGNANO – TROFEO IGNAZIO GIUNTI, Autodromo di Vallelunga, Campagnano di Roma, Italy, 3/4 June. 2 x 26 laps of the 1.988-mile/3.200-km circuit.
Round 7 (51.698 miles/83.200 km)
1 Luca Rangoni, I (Dallara F395-Fiat), 30m 58.332s, 100.151 mph/161.177 km/h.
2 Gianantonio Pacchioni, I (Dallara F395-Fiat), 31m 01.185s; **3** Andrea Boldrini, I (Dallara F395-Fiat), 31m 03.843s; **4** Maurizio Mediani, I (Dallara F395-Fiat), 31m 07.251s; **5** Gianluca Paglicci, I (Dallara F395-Fiat), 31m 13.147s; **6** Danilo Rossi, I (Dallara F395-Fiat), 31m 20.964s; **7** Antoine 'Tony' Kanaan, BR (Dallara F395-Fiat), 31m 23.066s; **8** Thomas Biagi, I (Dallara F395-Opel), 31m 30.764s; **9** Pietro Antonelli, I (Dallara F395-Mugen Honda), 31m 32.516s; **10** Luca Riccitelli, I (Dallara F395-Fiat), 31m 40.979s.
Fastest race lap: Rangoni, 1m 10.704s, 101.242 mph/162.933 km/h.
Fastest qualifying lap: Pacchioni, 1m 10.319s, 101.796 mph/163.825 km/h.

Round 8 (51.698 miles/83.200 km)
1 Luca Rangoni, I (Dallara F395-Fiat), 31m 05.023s, 99.791 mph/160.599 km/h.
2 Andrea Boldrini, I (Dallara F395-Fiat), 31m 11.038s; **3** Gianantonio Pacchioni, I (Dallara F395-Fiat), 31m 11.544s; **4** Maurizio Mediani, I (Dallara F395-Fiat), 31m 12.420s; **5** Danilo Rossi, I (Dallara F395-Fiat), 31m 12.574s; **6** Gianluca Paglicci, I (Dallara F395-Fiat), 31m 18.760s; **7** Thomas Biagi, I (Dallara F395-Opel), 31m 24.032s; **8** Luca Riccitelli, I (Dallara F395-Fiat), 31m 25.715s; **9** Antoine 'Tony' Kanaan, BR (Dallara F395-Fiat), 31m 33.156s; **10** Paolo Ruberti, I (Dallara F395-Fiat), 31m 34.640s.
Fastest race lap: Rangoni, 1m 11.124s, 100.644 mph/161.971 km/h.

ITALIAN FORMULA 3 CHAMPIONSHIP, Autodromo Riccardo Paletti, Varano, Parma, Italy, 17/18 June. 2 x 41 laps of the 1.118-mile/1.800-km circuit.
Round 9 (45.857 miles/73.800 km)
1 Gianantonio Pacchioni, I (Dallara F395-Fiat), 30m 41.261s, 89.659 mph/144.292 km/h.
2 Oliver Martini, I (Dallara F395-Fiat), 30m 41.949s; **3** Luca Rangoni, I (Dallara F395-Fiat), 30m 42.660s; **4** Luca Riccitelli, I (Dallara F395-Fiat), 30m 43.614s; **5** Andrea Boldrini, I (Dallara F395-Fiat), 30m 43.869s; **6** Thomas Biagi, I (Dallara F395-Opel), 30m 45.711s; **7** Michele Gasparini, I (Dallara F395-Fiat), 30m 48.993s; **8** Paolo Ruberti, I (Dallara F395-Fiat), 30m 55.418s; **9** Gianluca Paglicci, I (Dallara F395-Fiat), 30m 55.748s; **10** Gaston Mazzacane, RA (Dallara F395-Mugen Honda), 30m 58.953s.
Fastest race lap: Paglicci, 44.062s, 91.382 mph/147.065 km/h.
Fastest qualifying lap: Pacchioni, 43.945s, 91.626 mph/147.457 km/h.

Round 10 (45.857 miles/73.800 km)
1 Gianantonio Pacchioni, I (Dallara F395-Fiat), 30m 43.426s, 89.554 mph/144.123 km/h.
2 Gianluca Paglicci, I (Dallara F395-Fiat), 30m 51.852s; **3** Oliver Martini, I (Dallara F395-Fiat), 30m 52.396s; **4** Thomas Biagi, I (Dallara F395-Opel), 30m 56.032s; **5** Luca Riccitelli, I (Dallara F395-Fiat), 30m 56.787s; **6** Michele Gasparini, I (Dallara F395-Fiat), 30m 57.996s; **7** Paolo Ruberti, I (Dallara F395-Fiat), 31m 01.948s; **8** Gaston Mazzacane, RA (Dallara F395-Mugen Honda), 31m 08.809s; **9** Andrea Boldrini, I (Dallara F395-Fiat), 31m 09.700s; **10** Danilo Rossi, I (Dallara F395-Fiat), 31m 21.023s.
Fastest race lap: Paglicci, 44.421s, 90.644 mph/145.877 km/h.

36th GRAN PREMIO LOTTERIA DI MONZA, Autodromo Nazionale di Monza, Milan, Italy, 24/25 June. 16 and 15 laps of the 3.604-mile/5.800-km circuit.
Round 11 (57.663 miles/92.800 km)
1 Andrea Boldrini, I (Dallara F395-Fiat), 29m 04.405s, 119.002 mph/191.515 km/h.
2 Antoine 'Tony' Kanaan, BR (Dallara F395-Fiat), 29m 08.590s; **3** Thomas Biagi, I (Dallara F395-Opel), 29m 09.261s; **4** Maurizio Mediani, I (Dallara F395-Fiat), 29m 09.304s; **5** Gianantonio Pacchioni, I (Dallara F395-Fiat), 29m 09.793s; **6** Luca Riccitelli, I (Dallara F395-Fiat), 29m 11.451s; **7** Gianluca Paglicci, I (Dallara F395-Fiat), 29m 15.677s; **8** Luca Rangoni, I (Dallara F395-Fiat), 29m 17.130s; **9** Cesare Manfredini, I (Dallara F395-Fiat), 29m 18.925s; **10** Paolo Ruberti, I (Dallara F395-Fiat), 29m 19.515s.
Fastest race lap: Biagi, 1m 47.962s, 120.174 mph/193.401 km/h.
Fastest qualifying lap: Boldrini, 1m 47.433s, 120.766 mph/194.354 km/h.

Round 12 (54.059 miles/87.000 km)
1 Andrea Boldrini, I (Dallara F395-Fiat), 27m 20.776s, 118.611 mph/190.885 km/h.
2 Antoine 'Tony' Kanaan, BR (Dallara F395-Fiat), 27m 23.849s; **3** Thomas Biagi, I (Dallara F395-Opel), 27m 25.907s; **4** Gianluca Paglicci, I (Dallara F395-Fiat), 27m 26.515s; **5** Luca Rangoni, I (Dallara F395-Fiat), 27m 27.454s; **6** Maurizio Mediani, I (Dallara F395-Fiat), 27m 34.813s; **7** Cesare Manfredini, I (Dallara F395-Fiat), 27m 34.849s; **8** Paolo Ruberti, I (Dallara F395-Fiat), 27m 35.956s; **9** Gaston Mazzacane, RA (Dallara F395-Mugen Honda), 27m 36.230s; **10** Danilo Rossi, I (Dallara F395-Fiat), 27m 36.642s.
Fastest race lap: Boldrini, 1m 48.308s, 119.790 mph/192.784 km/h.

ITALIAN FORMULA 3 CHAMPIONSHIP, Autodromo Internazionale del Mugello, Scarperia, Firenze (Florence), Italy, 22/23 July. 2 x 16 laps of the 3.259-mile/5.245-km circuit.
Round 13 (52.145 miles/83.920 km)
1 Thomas Biagi, I (Dallara F395-Opel), 28m 44.359s, 108.866 mph/175.202 km/h.
2 Luca Rangoni, I (Dallara F395-Fiat), 28m 44.846s; **3** Omar Bettin, I (Dallara F395-Fiat), 29m 02.262s; **4** Michele Gasparini, I (Dallara F395-Fiat), 29m 11.707s; **5** Paolo Ruberti, I (Dallara F395-Fiat), 29m 12.116s; **6** Antoine 'Tony' Kanaan, BR (Dallara F395-Fiat), 29m 12.439s; **7** Danilo Rossi, I (Dallara F395-Fiat), 29m 14.405s; **8** Maurizio Mediani, I (Dallara F395-Fiat), 29m 17.202s; **9** Pietro Antonelli, I (Dallara F395-Mugen Honda), 29m 20.816s; **10** Danilo Tomassini, RSM (Dallara F395-Fiat), 29m 28.319s.
Fastest race lap: Rangoni, 1m 46.800s, 109.857 mph/176.798 km/h.
Fastest qualifying lap: Gasparini, 1m 46.965s, 109.688 mph/176.525 km/h.

Round 14 (52.145 miles/83.920 km)
1 Luca Rangoni, I (Dallara F395-Fiat), 29m 01.064s, 107.821 mph/173.521 km/h.
2 Thomas Biagi, I (Dallara F395-Opel), 29m 05.885s; **3** Omar Bettin, I (Dallara F395-Fiat), 29m 11.268s; **4** Gianantonio Pacchioni, I (Dallara F395-Fiat), 29m 12.258s; **5** Andrea Boldrini, I (Dallara F395-Fiat), 29m 21.974s; **6** Michele Gasparini, I (Dallara F395-Fiat), 29m 24.384s; **7** Maurizio Mediani, I (Dallara F395-Fiat), 29m 31.598s; **8** Gianluca Paglicci, I (Dallara F395-Fiat), 29m 31.780s; **9** Danilo Rossi, I (Dallara F395-Fiat), 29m 32.462s; **10** Pietro Antonelli, I (Dallara F395-Mugen Honda), 29m 32.979s.
Fastest race lap: Rangoni, 1m 47.471s, 109.171 mph/175.694 km/h.

ITALIAN FORMULA 3 CHAMPIONSHIP, Autodromo di Binetto, Bari, Italy, 2/3 September. 2 x 42 laps of the 0.980-mile/1.577-km circuit.
Round 15 (41.156 miles/66.234 km)
1 Luca Rangoni, I (Dallara F395-Fiat), 31m 28.702s, 78.446 mph/126.247 km/h.
2 Gianantonio Pacchioni, I (Dallara F395-Fiat), 31m 29.883s; **3** Gianluca Paglicci, I (Dallara F395-Fiat), 31m 30.434s; **4** Andrea Boldrini, I (Dallara F395-Fiat), 31m 30.723s; **5** Michele Gasparini, I (Dallara F395-Fiat), 31m 33.041s; **6** Luca Riccitelli, I (Dallara F395-Fiat), 31m 45.543s; **7** Gaston Mazzacane, RA (Dallara F395-Fiat), 31m 48.167s; **8** Antoine 'Tony' Kanaan, BR (Dallara F395-Fiat), 31m 48.530s; **9** Thomas Biagi, I (Dallara F395-Opel), 31m 53.832s; **10** Oliver Martini, I (Dallara F395-Fiat), 31m 56.597s.
Fastest race lap: Boldrini, 43.979s, 80.212 mph/129.089 km/h.
Fastest qualifying lap: Pacchioni, 43.638s, 80.839 mph/130.098 km/h.

Round 16 (41.156 miles/66.234 km)
1 Luca Rangoni, I (Dallara F395-Fiat), 31m 21.967s, 78.727 mph/126.699 km/h.
2 Gianantonio Pacchioni, I (Dallara F395-Fiat), 31m 22.533s; **3** Gianluca Paglicci, I (Dallara F395-Fiat), 31m 26.110s; **4** Andrea Boldrini, I (Dallara F395-Fiat), 31m 26.316s; **5** Luca Riccitelli, I (Dallara F395-Fiat), 31m 34.822s; **6** Gaston Mazzacane, RA (Dallara F395-Fiat), 31m 36.547s; **7** Danilo Tomassini, RSM (Dallara F395-Fiat), 31m 40.547s; **8** Danilo Rossi, I (Dallara F395-Fiat), 31m 43.072s; **9** Michele Gasparini, I (Dallara F395-Fiat), 31m 43.583s; **10** Thomas Biagi, I (Dallara F395-Opel), 31m 43.935s.
Fastest race lap: Rangoni, 44.115s, 79.965 mph/128.691 km/h.

ITALIAN FORMULA 3 CHAMPIONSHIP, Autodromo Enzo e Dino Ferrari, Imola, Italy, 17 September. 17 and 15 laps of the 3.042-mile/4.895-km circuit.
Round 17 (51.707 miles/83.215 km)
1 Thomas Biagi, I (Dallara F395-Opel), 31m 19.032s, 99.065 mph/159.430 km/h.
2 Antoine 'Tony' Kanaan, BR (Dallara F395-Fiat), 31m 19.316s; **3** Gianluca Paglicci, I (Dallara F395-Fiat), 31m 35.390s; **4** Luca Riccitelli, I (Dallara F395-Fiat), 31m 37.539s; **5** Esteban Tuero, RA (Dallara F395-Opel), 31m 39.568s; **6** Gianantonio Pacchioni, I (Dallara F395-Fiat), 31m 46.981s; **7** Oliviero Saleri, I (Dallara F395-Fiat), 31m 48.679s; **8** Oliver Martini, I (Dallara F395-Fiat), 31m 51.001s; **9** Paolo Ruberti, I (Dallara F395-Fiat), 31m 51.337s; **10** Omar Bettin, I (Dallara F395-Fiat), 31m 51.813s.
Luca Rangoni, I (Dallara F395-Fiat), finished 7th in 31m 48.575s but was disqualified.
Fastest race lap: Tuero, 1m 49.080s, 100.383 mph/161.551 km/h.
Fastest qualifying lap: Tuero, 1m 48.893s, 100.556 mph/161.829 km/h.

Round 18 (45.624 miles/73.425 km)
1 Antoine 'Tony' Kanaan, BR (Dallara F395-Fiat), 27m 49.271s, 98.394 mph/158.351 km/h.
2 Thomas Biagi, I (Dallara F395-Opel), 27m 55.055s; **3** Esteban Tuero, RA (Dallara F395-Opel), 27m 55.755s; **4** Gianantonio Pacchioni, I (Dallara F395-Fiat), 27m 56.157s; **5** Luca Riccitelli, I (Dallara F395-Fiat), 27m 56.641s; **6** Paolo Ruberti, I (Dallara F395-Fiat), 27m 59.415s; **7** Luca Rangoni, I (Dallara F395-Fiat), 28m 00.196s; **8** Danilo Tomassini, RSM (Dallara F395-Fiat), 28m 04.575s; **9** Maurizio Mediani, I (Dallara F395-Fiat), 28m 06.917s; **10** Gaston Mazzacane, RA (Dallara F395-Fiat), 28m 14.168s.
Fastest race lap: Andrea Boldrini, I (Dallara F395-Fiat), 1m 49.894s, 99.640 mph/160.355 km/h.

ITALIAN FORMULA 3 CHAMPIONSHIP, Autodromo Santamonica, Misano Adriatico, Rimini, Italy, 8 October. 2 x 20 laps of the 2.523-mile/4.060-km circuit.
Round 19 (50.455 miles/81.200 km)
1 Gianantonio Pacchioni, I (Dallara F395-Fiat), 29m 49.539s, 101.501 mph/163.349 km/h.
2 Antoine 'Tony' Kanaan, BR (Dallara F395-Fiat), 29m 51.532s; **3** Luca Rangoni, I (Dallara F395-Fiat), 29m 55.575s; **4** Oliver Martini, I (Dallara F395-Fiat), 30m 07.390s; **5** Gianluca Paglicci, I (Dallara F395-Alfa Romeo), 30m 11.484s; **6** Pietro Antonelli, I (Dallara F395-Mugen Honda), 30m 12.903s; **7** Oliviero Saleri, I (Dallara F395-Fiat), 20m 21.934s; **8** Luca Riccitelli, I (Dallara F395-Fiat), 30m 24.637s; **9** Danilo Tomassini, RSM (Dallara F395-Fiat), 30m 27.903s; **10** Omar Bettin, I (Dallara F395-Fiat), 30m 30.587s.
Fastest race lap: Pacchioni, 1m 28.657s, 102.439 mph/164.860 km/h.
Fastest qualifying lap: Pacchioni, 1m 28.292s, 102.863 mph/165.542 km/h.

Round 20 (50.455 miles/81.200 km)
1 Gianantonio Pacchioni, I (Dallara F395-Fiat), 29m 49.839s, 101.484 mph/163.322 km/h.
2 Luca Rangoni, I (Dallara F395-Fiat), 29m 55.068s; **3** Antoine 'Tony' Kanaan, BR (Dallara F395-Fiat), 29m 56.670s; **4** Andrea Boldrini, I (Dallara F395-Fiat), 29m 57.357s; **5** Pietro Antonelli, I (Dallara F395-Mugen Honda), 30m 04.328s; **6** Luca Riccitelli, I (Dallara F395-Fiat), 30m 04.983s; **7** Gianluca Paglicci, I (Dallara F395-Fiat), 30m 05.912s; **8** Paolo Ruberti, I (Dallara F395-Fiat), 30m 12.753s; **9** Oliver Martini, I (Dallara F395-Fiat), 30m 13.024s; **10** Oliviero Saleri, I (Dallara F395-Fiat), 30m 15.062s.
Fastest race lap: Pacchioni, 1m 28.592s, 102.514 mph/164.981 km/h.

Final championship points
(rounds 17 and 18 invalid and not counted)

1	Luca Rangoni, I	223
2	Andrea Boldrini, I	203
3	Gianantonio Pacchioni, I	197
4	Gianluca Paglicci, I	139
5	Antoine 'Tony' Kanaan, BR	100
6	Thomas Biagi, I	95

7 Luca Riccitelli, I, 92; **8** Oliver Martini, I, 76; **9** Maurizio Mediani, I, 74; **10** Omar Bettin, I, 52; **11** Michele Gasparini, I, 43; **12** Danilo Rossi, I, 40; **13** Paolo Ruberti, I, 26; **14** Cesare Manfredini, I, 22; **15** Pietro Antonelli, I, 21; **16** Fabrizio Gollin, I, 18; **17** Gaston Mazzacane, RA, 16; **18** Danilo Tomassini, RSM, 13; **19** Oliviero Saleri, I, 4.

Major Non-Championship Formula 3 Results

1994 Results

The Macau Formula 3 race was run after *Autocourse 1994/95* went to press .

FIA F3 WORLD CUP, 41st MACAU GP, Circuito Da Guia, Macau, 20 November. 12 and 15 laps of the 3.801-mile/6.117-km circuit, 102.625 miles/165.159 km.
First heat stopped after an accident, and run over an aggregate of 7 and 5 laps.
1 Sascha Maassen, D (Dallara F394-Opel), 1h 06m 03.75s, 93.207 mph/150.002 km/h.
2 Kelvin Burt, GB (Dallara F394-Mugen Honda), 1h 06m 07.05s; **3** Jan Magnussen, DK (Dallara F394-Mugen Honda), 1h 06m 10.20s; **4** Ralf Schumacher, D (Dallara F394-Opel), 1h 06m 19.33s; **5** Michael Krumm, D (TOM'S 034-Toyota), 1h 06m 19.68s; **6** Dario Franchitti, GB (Dallara F394-Mugen Honda), 1h 06m 37.16s; **7** Philipp Peter, A (Dallara F394-Fiat), 1h 06m 39.62s; **8** Ricardo Rosset, BR (Dallara F394-Mugen Honda), 1h 06m 48.35s; **9** Thomas Biagi, I (Dallara F393-Opel), 1h 07m 01.41s; **10** Arnd Meier, D (Dallara F394-Opel), 1h 07m 20.77s.
Fastest race lap: Gualter Salles, BR (Dallara F394-Mugen Honda), 2m 18.52s, 98.782 mph/158.975 km/h.
Fastest qualifying lap: Giancarlo Fisichella, I (Dallara F394-Opel), 2m 17.96s, 99.183 mph/159.620 km/h.

1995 Results

37th GRAND PRIX DE 'MONACO FORMULA 3', Monte Carlo Street Circuit, Monaco, 27 May. 24 laps of the 2.068-mile/3.328-km circuit, 49.630 miles/79.872 km.
1 Gianantonio Pacchioni, I (Dallara F395-Fiat), 38m 55.755s, 76.493 mph/123.103 km/h.
2 Ralf Schumacher, D (Dallara F395-Opel), 38m 56.278s; **3** Massimilaino 'Max' Angelelli, MC (Dallara F395-Opel), 39m 14.707s; **4** Gianluca Paglicci, I (Dallara F395-Fiat), 39m 14.746s; **5** Paolo Coloni, I (Dallara F395-Opel), 39m 22.555s; **6** Alexander Wurz, A (Dallara F395-Opel), 39m 23.103s; **7** Oliver Tichy, A (Dallara F395-Opel), 39m 30.864s; **8** Norberto Fontana, RA (Dallara F395-Opel), 39m 51.501s; **9** Klaus Graf, D (Dallara F395-Opel), 40m 09.542s; **10** Oliver Martini,I (Dallara F395-Fiat), 40m 24.928s.
Fastest race lap: Paglicci, 1m 36.01s, 77.539 mph/124.787 km/h.
Fastest qualifying lap: Pacchioni, 1m 35.702s, 77.789 mph/125.189 km/h.

INTERNATIONAL FORMULA 3 CHALLENGE, Donington Park Grand Prix Circuit, Derbyshire, Great Britain, 9 July. 20 laps of the 2.500-mile/4.023-km circuit, 50.000 miles/80.467 km.
1 Ralph Firman, GB (Dallara F395-Mugen Honda), 30m 32.48s, 98.228 mph/158.082 km/h.
2 Gualter Salles, BR (Dallara F395-Mugen Honda), 30m 36.14s; **3** Warren Hughes, GB (Dallara F395-HKS Mitsubishi), 30m 38.32s; **4** Alexander Wurz, A (Dallara F395-Opel), 30m 45.63s; **5** James Matthews, GB (Dallara F395-Mugen Honda), 30m 46.98s; **6** Thomas Biagi, I (Dallara F395-Opel), 30m 49.53s; **7** Marc Gene, E (Dallara F395-Mugen Honda), 30m 55.28s; **8** Luiz Garcia Jnr, BR (Dallara F395-Mugen Honda), 30m 56.71s; **9** Kurt Mollekens, B (Dallara F395-Mugen Honda), 30m 58.65s; **10** Oliver Gavin, GB (Dallara F395-Vauxhall), 30m 59.32s.
Fastest race lap: Hughes, 1m 30.89s, 99.021 mph/159.359 km/h.
Fastest qualifying lap: Firman, 1m 29.425s, 100.643 mph/161.969 km/h.

5th MARLBORO MASTERS OF FORMULA 3, Circuit van Zandvoort, Holland, 6 August. 32 laps of the 1.565-mile/2.519-km circuit, 50.087 miles/80.608 km.
1 Norberto Fontana, RA (Dallara F395-Opel), 34m 47.532s, 86.377 mph/139.010 km/h.
2 Ralf Schumacher, D (Dallara F395-Opel), 34m 48.163s; **3** Helio Castro Neves, BR (Dallara F395-Mugen Honda), 34m 49.810s; **4** Oliver Gavin, GB (Dallara F395-Vauxhall), 34m 51.874s; **5** Tom Coronel, NL (Dallara F395-Opel), 35m 05.603s; **6** Massimiliano 'Max' Angelelli, MC (Dallara F395-Opel), 35m 06.512s; **7** Luca Rangoni, I (Dallara F395-Fiat), 35m 07.461s; **8** Kurt Mollekens, B (Dallara F395-Mugen Honda), 35m 14.649s; **9** Paolo Coloni, I (Dallara F395-Fiat), 35m 16.298s; **10** Ralph Firman, GB (Dallara F395-Mugen Honda), 35m 16.730s.
Fastest race lap: Schumacher, 1m 04.196s, 87.776 mph/141.261 km/h.
Fastest qualifying lap: Fontana, 1m 02.747s, 89.803 mph/144.523 km/h.

NON-CHAMPIONSHIP GERMAN FORMULA 3, Circuit de Nevers, Magny-Cours, France, 8 October. 2 x 19 laps of the 2.641-mile/4.250-km circuit.
Race 1 (50.176 miles/80.750 km)
1 Norberto Fontana, RA (Dallara F395-Opel), 30m 07.35s, 99.943 mph/160.843 km/h.
2 Alexander Wurz, A (Dallara F395-Opel), 30m 16.60s; **3** Tom Coronel, NL (Dallara F395-Opel), 30m 23.95s; **4** Massimiliano 'Max' Angelelli, MC (Dallara F395-Opel), 30m 25.15s; **5** Jarno Trulli, I (Dallara F395-Opel), 30m 25.39s; **6** Rui Aguas, P (Dallara F395-Opel), 30m 26.60s; **7** Max Wilson, BR (Dallara F395-Opel), 30m 32.99s; **8** Arnd Meier, D (Dallara F395-Fiat), 30m 33.67s; **9** Frank Krämer, D (Dallara F394-Opel), 30m 36.05s (1st Class II); **10** Ralf Schumacher, D (Dallara F395-Opel), 30m 36.53s.
Fastest race lap: Fontana, 1m 34.66s, 100.433 mph/161.631 km/h.

Race 2 (50.176 miles/80.750 km)
1 Norberto Fontana, RA (Dallara F395-Opel), 30m 20.75s, 99.208 mph/159.659 km/h.
2 Alexander Wurz, A (Dallara F395-Opel), 30m 24.50s; **3** Massimiliano 'Max' Angelelli, MC (Dallara F395-Opel), 30m 31.34s; **4** Tom Coronel, NL (Dallara F395-Opel), 30m 32.44s; **5** Max Wilson, BR (Dallara F395-Opel), 30m 33.88s; **6** Pedro Couceiro, P (Dallara F395-Fiat), 30m 34.31s; **7** Arnd Meier, D (Dallara F395-Fiat), 30m 40.10s; **8** Jakob Sund, CZ (Dallara F394-Opel), 30m 45.60s (1st Class II); **9** Philipp Peter, A (Dallara F395-Fiat), 30m 57.82s; **10** Christian Menzel, D (Dallara F395-Opel), 31m 07.14s.
Fastest race lap: Trulli, 1m 34.82s, 100.263 mph/161.358 km/h.

INTERNATIONAL FORMULA 3 CUP, Donington Park Club Circuit, Derbyshire, Great Britain, 22 October. 20 laps of the 1.957-mile/3.149-km circuit, 39.140 miles/62.990 km.
1 Owen McAuley, GB (Dallara F395-HKS Mitsubishi), 22m 48.739s, 102.944 mph/165.673 km/h.
2 Jason Elliott, GB (Dallara F395-Fiat), 22m 50.458s; **3** Takashi Yokoyama, J (Dallara F395-TOM'S Toyota), 22m 52.117s; **4** Scott Lakin, GB (Dallara F395-Mugen Honda), 22m 56.352s; **5** Paula Cook, GB (Dallara F394-Mugen Honda), 22m 58.805s (1st Class B); **6** Laurent Redon, GB (Dallara F395-Mugen Honda), 22m 58.939s; **7** Jonny Kane, GB (Dallara F395-Mugen Honda), 22m 59.050s; **8** Martin O'Connell, GB (Dallara F394-TOM'S Toyota), 23m 03.122s; **9** Juan Pablo Montoya, CO (Dallara F395-Mugen Honda), 23m 12.497s; **10** Brian Smith, RA (Dallara F395-Mugen Honda), 23m 25.534s.
Fastest race lap: Redon, 1m 07.659s, 104.128 mph/167.578 km/h.
Fastest qualifying lap: McAuley, 1m 05.961s, 106.809 mph/171.892 km/h.

The result of the Macau Formula 3 race will be given in *Autocourse 1996/97.*

Sports Car Racing

63rd 24 HEURES DU MANS, Circuit de la Sarthe, Le Mans, France, 17-18 June. 298 laps of the 8.451-mile/13.600-km circuit, 2518.293 miles/4052.800 km.
1 Yannick Dalmas/JJ Lehto/Masanori Sekiya, F/SF/J (McLaren F1 GTR), 24h 00m 000s, 105.007 mph/168.992 km/h (1st LM GT1 class).
2 Bob Wollek/Mario Andretti/Éric Hélary, F/USA/F (Courage C34-Porsche), 298 laps (1st WSC class); **3** Andy Wallace/Justin Bell/Derek Bell, GB/GB/GB (McLaren F1 GTR), 296; **4** Ray Bellm/Maurizio Sandro Sala/Mark Blundell, GB/BR/GB (McLaren F1 GTR), 291; **5** Fabien Giroix/Olivier Grouillard/Jean-Denis Deletraz, F/F/CH (McLaren F1 GTR), 290; **6** Hans Stuck/Thierry Boutsen/Christophe Bouchut, D/B/F (Kremer K8-Porsche), 289; **7** Yojiro Terada/Jim Downing/Franck Fréon, J/USA/F (Kudzu DG3-Mazda), 283; **8** Kunimitsu Takahashi/Keiichi Tsuchiya/Akira Iida, J/J/J (Honda NSX GT), 275 (1st LM GT2 class); **9** Johnny Unser/Frank Jelinski/Enrico Bertaggia, USA/D/I (Callaway Corvette-Chevrolet), 273; **10** Hideo Fukuyama/Masahiko Kondo/Shunji Kasuya, J/J/J (Nissan Skyline GT-R LM), 271; **11** Riccardo 'Rocky' Agusta/Eugene O'Brien/Robin Donovan, I/GB/GB (Callaway Corvette-Chevrolet), 270; **12** Michel Ferté/Olivier Thevenin/Carlos Palau, F/F/E (Ferrari F40 LM), 270; **13** Jean-Luc Maury-Laribiere/Marc Sourd/Hervé Poulain, F/F/F (McLaren F1 GTR), 266; **14** Jeff Krosnoff/Mauro Martini/Marco Apicella, USA/I/I (Toyota Supra GT LM), 264; **15** Guy Kuster/Karel Dolejsi/Peter Seikel, F/CZ/D (Porsche 911GT2), 263; **16** Éric van de Vyver/Didier Ortion/Jean-François Veroux, F/F/F (Porsche 911GT2), 262; **17** Richard Jones/Nick Adams/Gerard MacQuillan, GB/GB/GB (Porsche 911GT2), 250; **18** Fabio Mancini/Massimo Monti/Gary Ayles, I/I/GB (Ferrari F40 GT-E), 237; **19** Wolfgang Kaufmann/Yukihiro Hane/Michel Lignonet, D/J/F (Porsche 993 Bi-turbo), 229; **20** Patrice Roussel/Bernard Santal/Edouard Sezionale, F/CH/F (Bonnet Debora LMP295-Ford), 222 (1st LMP2 class); **21** Jean-Marc Gounon/Paul Belmondo/Arnaud Trevisiol, F/F/F (Venturi 600 LM), 193; **22** Chris Marsh/François Migault/David Leslie, F/F/GB (Marcos LM600), 184; **23** Philippe Favre/Hideki Okada/Naoki Hattori, CH/J/J (Honda NSX GTI), 121; **24** William David/Jean-Bernard Bouvet/Richard Balendras, F/F/F (WR LM94-Peugeot), 196 (DNF – fuel feed); **25** Éric Graham/François Birbeau/Ferdinand de Lesseps, F/F/F (Venturi 600 LM), 178 (DNF – electrics); **26** Jürgen Laessig/Franz Konrad/Antonio Hermann, D/A/BR (Kremer K8-Porsche), 163 (DNF – electrics); **27** Kazuyoshi Hoshino/Toshio Suzuki/Masahiko Kageyama, J/J/J (Nissan Skyline GT-R LM), 157 (DNF – gearbox); **28** Richard Piper/Tiff Needell/James Weaver, GB/GB/GB (Jaguar XJ 220), 135 (DNF – crankshaft); **29** Chris Hodgetts/Cor Euser/Thomas Erdos, GB/NL/BR (Marcos LM600), 133 (DNF – transmission); **30** John Nielsen/Thomas Bscher/Jochen Mass, DK/D/D (McLaren F1 GTR), 131 (DNF – accident); **31** Emmanuel Clérico/Bernard Chauvin/Laurent Lecuyer, F/F/CH (Venturi 600LM), 130 (DNF – ignition); **32** Win Percy/Olindo Iacobelli/Bernard Thuner, GB/I/CH (Jaguar XJ 220), 123 (DNF – accident damage); **33** Almo Coppelli/Thorkild Thyrring/Patrick Bourdais, I/DK/F (Callaway Corvette-Chevrolet), 96 (DNF – accident); **34** Dominique Dupuy/Emmanuel Collard/Stéphane Ortelli, F/F/F (Porsche 911 RSR GT1), 82 (DNF – accident); **35** Enzo Calderari/Lillian Bryner/Andreas Fuchs, CH/CH/D (Porsche 911 GT2), 81 (DNF – accident); **36** Lindsay Owen-Jones/Pierre-Henri Raphanel/Philippe Alliot, GB, F/F (McLaren F1 GTR), 77 (DNF – accident); **37** Tomas Saldana/Alfonso de Orleans/Angel Miguel de Castro, E/E/E (Porsche 911 GT2), 63 (DNF – accident); **38** Jean-Pierre Jarier/Erik Comas/Jesus Pareja, F/F/E (Porsche 911 RSR GT1), 58 (DNF – accident); **39** John Paul Jnr/Chris McDougall/James Mero, USA/CDN/USA (Chevrolet Corvette ZR1), 57 (DNF – engine); **40** Luciano della Noce/Anders Olofsson/Tetsuya Ota, I/S/J (Ferrari F40 GT-E), 42 (DNF – gearbox); **41** Geoff Lees/Rupert Keegan/Dominic Chappell, GB/GB/GB (Lister Storm), 40 (DNF – transmission); **42** Pierre Yver/Jean-Luc Chereau/Jack Leconte, F/F/F (Porsche 911 RSR GT1), 40 (DNF – accident); **43** Patrick Gonin/Pierre Petit/Marc Rostan, F/F/F (WR LM94-Peugeot), 33 (DNF – accident); **44** Henri Pescarolo/Franck Lagorce/Éric Bernard, F/F/F (Courage C41-Chevrolet), 26 (DNF – electrics); **45** Alain Ferté/Kenneth Acheson, F/GB (SARD MC8R), 14 (DNF – brakes); **46** Charles Margueron/Philippe Siffert/Pierre de Thoisy, CH/CH/F (Porsche 911 GT2), 13 (DNF – accident); **47** Jay Cochran/René Arnoux/Massimo Sigala, USA/F/I (Ferrari 333SP), 7 (DNF – engine); **48** Bertrand Gachot/Armin Hahne/Ivan Capelli, F/D/I (Honda NSX GT1), 7 (DNF – gearbox).
Fastest race lap: Gonin, 3m 51.41s, 131.465 mph/211.573 km/h.
Fastest qualifying lap: David, 3m 46.05s, 134.582 mph/216.589 km/h.
Did not qualify: Eric van de Poele/Olivier Beretta/Matjaz Tomljem B/MC/SLO (Courage C41-Chevrolet); Dominique Lacaud/JeanPaul Libert/Pascal Dro, F/F/F (Norma M14-Buick); John Jones/Jean-Marc Masse/François Provost, CDN/F/F (Tiga FJ94-Buick); Christian Heinkele/Lucien Guitteny/François O'Born, F/F/F (Ferrari F355).

PPG Indy Car World Series

MARLBORO GRAND PRIX OF MIAMI PRESENTED BY TOYOTA, Miami Street Circuit, Florida, USA, 5 March. Round 1. 90 laps of the 1.843-mile/2.966-km circuit, 165.870 miles/266.942 km.
1 Jacques Villeneuve, CDN (Reynard 95I-Ford Cosworth XB), 1h 59m 16.863s, 82.801 mph/133.255 km/h.
2 Mauricio Gugelmin, BR (Reynard 95I-Ford Cosworth XB), 1h 59m 17.915s; **3** Bobby Rahal, USA (Lola T95/00-Mercedes Benz), 90 laps; **4** Scott Pruett, USA (Lola T95/00-Ford Cosworth XB), 90; **5** Christian Fittipaldi, BR (Reynard 95I-Ford Cosworth XB), 90; **6** Raul Boesel, BR (Lola T95/00-Mercedes Benz), 90; **7** Christian Danner, D (Lola T93/00-Ford Cosworth XB), 90; **8** Jimmy Vasser, USA (Reynard 95I-Ford Cosworth XB), 90; **9** Danny Sullivan, USA (Reynard 95I-Ford Cosworth XB), 89; **10** Bryan Herta, USA (Reynard 95I-Ford Cosworth XB), 87.
Most laps led: Michael Andretti, USA (Lola T95/00-Ford Cosworth XB), 48.
Fastest qualifying lap: Andretti, 1m 03.254s, 104.891 mph/168.806 km/h (record).
Championship points: **1** Villeneuve, 20; **2** Gugelmin, 16; **3** Rahal, 14; **4** Pruett, 12; **5** Fittipaldi (Christian), 10; **6** Boesel, 8.

INDY CAR AUSTRALIA, Surfers Paradise Street Circuit, Queensland, Australia, 19 March. Round 2. 65 laps of the 2.804-mile/4.513km circuit, 181.675 miles/292.378 km.
1 Paul Tracy, CDN (Lola T95/00-Ford Cosworth XB), 1h 58m 26.054s, 92.335 mph/148.598 km/h.
2 Bobby Rahal, USA (Lola T95/00-Mercedes Benz), 1h 58m 33.037s; **3** Scott Pruett, USA (Lola T95/00-Ford Cosworth XB), 65 laps; **4** Mauricio Gugelmin, BR (Reynard 95I-Ford Cosworth XB), 65; **5** Danny Sullivan, USA (Reynard 95I-Ford Cosworth XB), 65; **6** Al Unser Jnr, USA (Penske PC24-Mercedes Benz), 65; **7** Eddie Cheever, USA (Lola T95/00-Ford Cosworth XB), 65; **8** Raul Boesel, BR (Lola T95/00-Mercedes Benz), 65; **9** Michael Andretti, USA (Lola T95/00-Ford Cosworth XB), 64 (DNF – accident); **10** Eliseo Salazar, RCH (Lola T95/00-Ford Cosworth XB), 64.
Most laps led: Andretti, 51.
Fastest qualifying lap: Andretti, 1m 36.770s, 104.313 mph/167.876 km/h.
Championship points: **1** Rahal, 30; **2** Gugelmin, 28; **3** Pruett, 26; **4=** Villeneuve, 20; **4=** Tracy, 20; **6** Sullivan, 14.

SLICK-50 200 PRESENTED BY LCI INTERNATIONAL, Phoenix International Raceway, Arizona, USA, 2 April. Round 3. 200 laps of the 1.000-mile/1.609-km circuit, 200.000 miles/321.869 km.
1 Robby Gordon, USA (Reynard 95I-Ford Cosworth XB), 1h 29m 33.930s, 133.980 mph/215.620 km/h.
2 Michael Andretti, USA (Lola T95/00-Ford Cosworth XB), 1h 29m 34.718s; **3** Emerson Fittipaldi, BR (Penske PC24-Mercedes Benz), 200 laps; **4** Paul Tracy, CDN (Lola T95/00-Ford Cosworth XB), 200; **5** Jacques Villeneuve, CDN (Reynard 95I-Ford Cosworth XB), 200; **6** Raul Boesel, BR (Lola T95/00-Mercedes Benz), 198; **7** Teo Fabi, I (Reynard 95I-Ford Cosworth XB), 198; **8** Al Unser Jnr, USA (Penske PC24-Mercedes Benz), 197; **9** Scott Pruett, USA (Lola T95/00-Ford Cosworth XB), 197; **10** Christian Fittipaldi, BR (Reynard 95I-Ford Cosworth XB), 195.
Most laps led: Fittipaldi (Emerson), 78.
Fastest qualifying lap: Bryan Herta, USA (Reynard 95I-Ford Cosworth XB), 19.785s, 181.956 mph/292.830 km/h (record).
Championship points: **1** Tracy, 32; **2=** Villeneuve, 30; **2=** Rahal, 30; **2=** Pruett, 30; **5** Gugelmin, 28; **6** Andretti, 24.

TOYOTA GRAND PRIX OF LONG BEACH, Long Beach Street Circuit, California, USA, 9 April. Round 4. 105 laps of the 1.590-mile/2.559-km circuit, 166.950 miles/268.680 km.
1 Al Unser Jnr, USA (Penske PC24-Mercedes Benz), 1h 49m 32.667s, 91.442 mph/147.162 km/h.
2 Scott Pruett, USA (Lola T95/00-Ford Cosworth XB), 1h 49m 55.792s; **3** Teo Fabi, I (Reynard 95I-Ford Cosworth XB), 105 laps; **4** Eddie Cheever, USA (Lola T95/00-Ford Cosworth XB), 104 (DNF – fuel feed); **5** Mauricio Gugelmin, BR (Reynard 95I-Ford Cosworth XB), 104; **6** Stefan Johansson, S (Penske PC23-Mercedes Benz), 104; **7** Eric Bachelart, B (Lola T94/00-Ford Cosworth XB), 104; **8** Alessandro Zampedri, I (Lola T94/00-Ford Cosworth XB), 104; **9** Michael Andretti, USA (Lola T95/00-Ford Cosworth XB), 104; **10** Danny Sullivan, USA (Reynard 95I-Ford Cosworth XB), 104.
Most laps led: Unser Jnr, 74.
Fastest qualifying lap: Andretti, 52.482s, 109.066 mph/175.525 km/h (record).
Championship points: **1** Pruett, 46; **2** Gugelmin, 38; **3** Unser Jnr, 34; **4** Tracy, 32; **5** Villeneuve, 30; **6** Rahal, 30.

BOSCH SPARK PLUG GRAND PRIX, Pennsylvania International Raceway, Nazareth, Pennsylvania, USA, 23 April. Round 5. 200 laps of the 1.000-mile/1.609-km circuit, 200.000 miles/321.869 km.
1 Emerson Fittipaldi, BR (Penske PC24-Mercedes Benz), 1h 31m 23.410s, 131.305 mph/211.315 km/h.
2 Jacques Villeneuve, CDN (Reynard 95I-Ford Cosworth XB), 1h 31m 23.719s; **3** Stefan Johansson, S (Penske PC23-Mercedes Benz), 200 laps; **4** Robby Gordon, USA (Reynard 95I-Ford Cosworth XB), 200; **5** Eddie Cheever, USA (Lola T95/00-Ford Cosworth XB), 199 (DNF – out of fuel); **6** Bobby Rahal, USA (Lola T95/00-Mercedes Benz), 199; **7** Teo Fabi, I (Reynard 95I-Ford Cosworth XB), 199; **8** Scott Pruett, USA (Lola T95/00-Ford Cosworth XB), 199; **9** Adrian Fernandez, MEX (Lola T95/00-Mercedes Benz), 199; **10** Raul Boesel, BR (Lola T95/00-Mercedes Benz), 199.
Most laps led: Villeneuve, 45.
Fastest qualifying lap: Gordon, 19.206s, 187.441 mph/301.658 km/h (record).
Championship points: **1** Pruett, 51; **2** Villeneuve, 47; **3=** Rahal, 38; **3=** Gugelmin, 38; **5** Fittipaldi (Emerson), 35; **6** Unser Jnr, 34.

79th INDIANAPOLIS 500, Indianapolis Motor Speedway, Indiana, USA, 28 May. Round 6. 200 laps of the 2.500-mile/4.023-km circuit, 500.000 miles/804.672 km.
1 Jacques Villeneuve, CDN (Reynard 95I-Ford Cosworth XB), 3h 15m 17.561s, 153.616 mph/247.220 km/h*.
2 Christian Fittipaldi, BR (Reynard 95I-Ford Cosworth XB), 3h 15m 20.042s; **3** Bobby Rahal, USA (Lola T95/00-Mercedes Benz), 3h 15m 20.527s; **4** Eliseo Salazar, RCH (Lola T95/00-Ford Cosworth XB), 3h 15m 22.329s; **5** Robby Gordon, USA (Reynard 95I-Ford Cosworth XB), 3h 15m 32.466s; **6** Mauricio Gugelmin, BR (Reynard 95I-Ford Cosworth XB), 3h 15m 34.638s; **7** Arie Luyendyk, NL (Lola T95/00-Menard Buick), 3h 15m 59.520s; **8** Teo Fabi, I (Reynard 95I-Ford Cosworth XB), 199 laps; **9** Danny Sullivan, USA (Reynard 95I-Ford Cosworth XB), 199; **10** Hiro Matsushita, J (Reynard 95I-Ford Cosworth XB), 199; **11** Alessandro Zampedri, I (Lola T94/00-Ford Cosworth XB), 198; **12** Roberto Guerrero, USA (Reynard 94I-Mercedes Benz), 198; **13** Bryan Herta, USA (Reynard 95I-Ford Cosworth XB), 198; **14** Scott Goodyear, CDN (Reynard 95I-Honda), 195; **15** Hideshi Matsuda, J (Lola T94/00-Ford Cosworth XB), 194; **16** Stefan Johansson, S (Reynard 94I-Ford Cosworth XB), 192; **17** Scott Brayton, USA (Lola T95/00-Menard Buick), 190; **18** Andre Ribeiro, BR (Reynard 95I-Honda), 187; **19** Scott Pruett, USA (Lola T95/00-Ford Cosworth XB), 184 (DNF – accident); **20** Raul Boesel, BR (Lola T95/00-Mercedes Benz), 184 (DNF – oil line); **21** Adrian Fernandez, MEX (Lola T95/00-Mercedes Benz), 176 (DNF – engine); **22** Jimmy Vasser, USA (Reynard 95I-Ford Cosworth XB), 170 (DNF – accident); **23** Davy Jones, USA (Lola T95/00-Ford Cosworth XB), 161 (DNF – accident); **24** Paul Tracy, CDN (Lola T95/00-Ford Cosworth XB), 136 (DNF – electrics); **25** Michael Andretti, USA (Lola T95/00-Ford Cosworth XB), 77 (DNF – suspension); **26** Scott Sharp, USA (Lola T95/00-Ford Cosworth XB), 74 (DNF – accident); **27** Buddy Lazier, USA (Lola T95/00-Menard Buick), 45 (DNF – fuel system); **28** Eric Bachelart, B (Lola T94/00-Ford Cosworth XB), 6 (DNF – mechanical); **29** Gil de Ferran, BR (Reynard 95I-Mercedes Benz), 1 (DNF – accident); **30** Stan Fox, USA (Reynard 95I-Ford Cosworth XB), 0 (DNF – accident); **31** Eddie Cheever, USA (Lola T95/00-Ford Cosworth XB), 0 (DNF – accident); **32** Lyn St James, USA (Lola T95/00-Ford Cosworth XB), 0 (DNF – accident); **33** Carlos Guerrero, MEX (Lola T95/00-Ford Cosworth XB), 0 (DNF accident).
** includes 2-lap penalty for passing under a yellow flag.*
Most laps led: Gugelmin, 59.
Fastest qualifying lap: Brayton, 2m 35.438s, 231.604 mph/372.731 km/h (over four laps).
Did not qualify: Emerson Fittipaldi, BR (Lola T95/00-Mercedes Benz); Franck Fréon, F (Lola T92/00-Menard Buick); Al Unser Jnr, USA (Lola T95/00-Mercedes Benz); Marco Greco, BR (Lola T95/00-Mercedes Benz); Davey Hamilton, USA (Reynard 94I-Ford Cosworth XB); Jeff Ward, USA (Lola T94/00-Ford Cosworth XB); Johnny Parsons, USA (Reynard 94I-Ford Cosworth XB).
Championship points: **1** Villeneuve, 67; **2** Rahal, 52; **3** Pruett, 51; **4** Gugelmin, 47; **5** Gordon, 43; **6** Fittipaldi (Emerson), 35.

MILLER GENUINE DRAFT 200, Wisconsin State Fair Park Speedway, West Allis, Milwaukee, Wisconsin, USA, 4 June. Round 7. 200 laps of the 1.000-mile/1.609-km circuit, 200.000 miles/321.869 km.
1 Paul Tracy, CDN (Lola T95/00-Ford Cosworth XB), 1h 27m 23.853s, 137.304 mph/220.969 km/h.
2 Al Unser Jnr, USA (Penske PC24-Mercedes Benz), 1h 27m 24.699s; **3** Michael Andretti, USA (Lola T95/00-Ford Cosworth XB), 199 laps; **4** Teo Fabi, I (Reynard 95I-Ford Cosworth XB), 198; **5** Robby Gordon, USA (Reynard 95I-Ford Cosworth XB), 197; **6** Jacques Villeneuve, CDN (Reynard 95I-Ford Cosworth XB), 197; **7** Christian Fittipaldi, BR (Reynard 95I-Ford Cosworth XB), 196; **8** Gil de Ferran, BR (Reynard 95I-Mercedes Benz), 195; **9** Jimmy Vasser, USA (Reynard 95I-Ford Cosworth XB), 195; **10** Adrian Fernandez, MEX (Lola T95/00-Mercedes Benz), 195.
Most laps led: Unser Jnr, 120.
Fastest qualifying lap: Fabi, 22.160s, 162.455 mph/261.446 km/h.
Championship points: **1** Villeneuve, 75; **2** Gordon, 53; **3=** Tracy, 52; **3=** Rahal, 52; **3=** Pruett, 52; **6** Unser Jnr, 51.

ITT AUTOMOTIVE DETROIT GRAND PRIX, Belle Isle Park Circuit, Detroit, Michigan, USA, 11 June. Round 8. 77 laps of the 2.100-mile/3.380-km circuit, 161.700 miles/260.231 km.
1 Robby Gordon, USA (Reynard 95I-Ford Cosworth XB), 1h 56m 11.607s, 83.499 mph/134.378 km/h.
2 Jimmy Vasser, USA (Reynard 95I-Ford Cosworth XB), 1h 56m 11.952s; **3** Scott Pruett, USA (Lola T95/00-Ford Cosworth XB), 77 laps; **4** Michael Andretti, USA (Lola T95/00-Ford Cosworth XB), 77; **5** Al Unser Jnr, USA (Penske PC24-Mercedes Benz), 77; **6** Adrian Fernandez, MEX (Lola T95/00-Mercedes Benz), 77; **7** Teo Fabi, I (Reynard 95I-Ford Cosworth XB), 77; **8** Paul Tracy, CDN (Lola T95/00-Ford Cosworth XB), 77; **9** Jacques Villeneuve, CDN (Reynard 95I-Ford Cosworth XB), 77; **10** Emerson Fittipaldi, BR (Penske PC24-Mercedes Benz), 77.
Most laps led: Gordon, 43.
Fastest qualifying lap: Gordon, 1m 09.795s, 108.317 mph/174.320 km/h.
Championship points: **1** Villeneuve, 79; **2** Gordon, 75; **3** Pruett, 66; **4** Unser Jnr, 61; **5** Tracy, 57; **6** Andretti, 55.

BUDWEISER/G.I.JOE'S 200 PRESENTED BY TEXACO/HAVOLINE, Portland International Raceway, Oregon, USA, 25 June. Round 9. 102 laps of the 1.950-mile/3.138-km circuit, 198.900 miles/320.099 km.
1 Al Unser Jnr, USA (Penske PC24-Mercedes Benz), 1h 54m 49.410s, 103.933 mph/167.265 km/h*.
2 Jimmy Vasser, USA (Reynard 95I-Ford Cosworth XB), 1h 55m 17.971s; **3** Bobby Rahal, USA (Lola T95/00-Mercedes Benz), 102 laps; **4** Michael Andretti, USA (Lola T95/00-Ford Cosworth XB), 102; **5** Raul Boesel, BR (Lola T95/00-Mercedes Benz), 102; **6** Stefan Johansson, S (Penske PC23-Mercedes Benz), 101 (DNF – out of fuel); **7** Mauricio Gugelmin, BR (Reynard 95I-Ford Cosworth XB), 101; **8** Robby Gordon, USA (Reynard 95I-Ford Cosworth XB), 101; **9** Adrian Fernandez, MEX (Lola T95/00-Mercedes Benz), 101; **10** Gil de Ferran, BR (Reynard 95I-Mercedes Benz), 100.
** Initially disqualified for a technical infringement, but re-instated as winner after appeal hearing in September.*
Most laps led: Unser Jnr, 76.
Fastest qualifying lap: Villeneuve, 59.687s, 117.614 mph/189.281 km/h (record).
Championship points: **1=** Villeneuve, 81; **1=** Gordon, 81; **3** Andretti, 69; **4** Rahal, 68; **5** Pruett, 67; **6** Unser Jnr, 61.

TEXACO/HAVOLINE 200, Road America Circuit, Elkhart Lake, Wisconsin, USA, 9 July. Round 10. 50 laps of the 4.000-mile/6.437-km circuit, 200.000 miles/321.869 km.
1 Jacques Villeneuve, CDN (Reynard 95I-Ford Cosworth XB), 1h 55m 29.659s, 103.901 mph/167.213 km/h.
2 Paul Tracy, CDN (Lola T95/00-Ford Cosworth XB), 1h 55m 30.624s; **3** Jimmy Vasser, USA (Reynard 95I-Ford Cosworth XB), 50 laps; **4** Andre Ribeiro, BR (Reynard 95I-Honda), 50; **5** Bobby Rahal, USA (Lola T95/00-Mercedes Benz), 50; **6** Adrian Fernandez, MEX (Lola T95/00-Mercedes Benz), 50; **7** Scott Pruett, USA (Lola T95/00-Ford Cosworth XB), 50; **8** Christian Fittipaldi, BR (Reynard 95I-Ford Cosworth XB), 50; **9** Teo Fabi, I (Reynard 95I-Ford Cosworth XB), 50; **10** Stefan Johansson, S (Penske PC23-Mercedes Benz), 50.
Most laps led: Villeneuve, 46.
Fastest qualifying lap: Villeneuve, 1m 41.261s, 142.207 mph/228.860 km/h (record).
Championship points: **1** Villeneuve, 103; **2** Gordon, 81; **3** Rahal, 78; **4=** Tracy, 73; **4=** Pruett, 73; **6** Andretti, 69.

MOLSON INDY TORONTO, Exhibition Place Circuit, Toronto, Ontario, Canada, 16 July. Round 11. 98 laps of the 1.780-mile/2.865-km circuit, 174.440 miles/280.734 km.
1 Michael Andretti, USA (Lola T95/00-Ford Cosworth XB), 1h 50m 25.202s, 94.787 mph/152.545 km/h.
2 Bobby Rahal, USA (Lola T95/00-Mercedes Benz), 1h 50m 25.627s; **3** Jacques Villeneuve, CDN (Reynard 95I-Ford Cosworth XB), 98 laps; **4** Teo Fabi, I (Reynard 95I-Ford Cosworth XB), 98; **5** Robby Gordon, USA (Reynard 95I-Ford Cosworth XB), 98; **6** Raul Boesel, BR (Lola T95/00-Mercedes Benz), 98; **7** Adrian Fernandez, MEX (Lola T95/00-Mercedes Benz), 98; **8** Paul Tracy, CDN (Lola T95/00-Ford Cosworth XB), 98; **9** Christian Fittipaldi, BR (Reynard 95I-Ford Cosworth XB), 98; **10** Emerson Fittipaldi, BR (Penske PC24-Mercedes Benz), 98.
Most laps led: Andretti (Michael), 74.
Fastest qualifying lap: Villeneuve, 58.046s, 110.395 mph/177.664 km/h (record).
Championship points: **1** Villeneuve, 118; **2** Rahal, 94; **3** Gordon, 91; **4** Andretti, 90; **5** Tracy, 78; **6** Pruett, 73.

MEDIC DRUG GRAND PRIX OF CLEVELAND PRESENTED BY DAIRY MART, Burke Lakefront Airport Circuit, Cleveland, Ohio, USA, 23 July. Round 12. 90 laps of the 2.369-mile/3.813-km circuit, 213.210 miles/343.128 km.
1 Jacques Villeneuve, CDN (Reynard 95I-Ford Cosworth XB), 1h 38m 19.151s, 130.113 mph/209.397 km/h.
2 Bryan Herta, USA (Reynard 95I-Ford Cosworth XB), 1h 38m 20.308s; **3** Jimmy Vasser, USA (Reynard 95I-Ford Cosworth XB), 90 laps; **4** Bobby Rahal, USA (Lola T95/00-Mercedes Benz), 90; **5** Danny Sullivan, USA (Reynard 95I-Ford Cosworth XB), 90; **6** Robby Gordon, USA (Reynard 95I-Ford Cosworth XB), 90; **7** Michael Andretti, USA (Lola T95/00-Ford Cosworth XB), 90; **8** Stefan Johansson, S (Penske PC23-Mercedes Benz), 89; **9** Alessandro Zampedri, I (Lola T94/00-Ford Cosworth XB), 89; **10** Eliseo Salazar, RCH (Lola T95/00-Ford Cosworth XB), 88.
Most laps led: Gil de Ferran, BR (Reynard 95I-Mercedes Benz), 67.
Fastest qualifying lap: de Ferran, 57.815s, 147.512 mph/237.397 km/h (record).
Championship points: **1** Villeneuve, 138; **2** Rahal, 106; **3** Gordon, 99; **4** Andretti, 96; **5** Tracy, 78; **6=** Vasser, 73; **6=** Pruett, 73.

MARLBORO MICHIGAN 500 PRESENTED BY SPEED STICK, Michigan International Speedway, Brooklyn, Michigan, USA, 30 July. Round 13. 250 laps of the 2.000-mile/3.219-km circuit, 500.000 miles/804.672 km.
1 Scott Pruett, USA (Lola T95/00-Ford Cosworth XB), 3h 07m 52.826s, 159.676 mph/256.974 km/h.
2 Al Unser Jnr, USA (Penske PC24-Mercedes Benz), 3h 07m 52.882s; **3** Adrian Fernandez, MEX (Lola T95/00-Mercedes Benz), 249 laps; **4** Teo Fabi, I (Reynard 95I-Ford Cosworth XB), 247; **5** Emerson Fittipaldi, BR (Penske PC24-Mercedes Benz), 245; **6** Stefan Johansson, S (Penske PC23-Mercedes Benz), 244; **7** Jimmy Vasser, USA (Reynard 95I-Ford Cosworth XB), 241; **8** Bobby Rahal, USA (Lola T95/00-Mercedes Benz), 240; **9** Christian Fittipaldi, BR (Reynard 95I-Ford Cosworth XB), 239; **10** Jacques Villeneuve, CDN (Reynard 95I-Ford Cosworth XB), 235.
Most laps led: Andre Ribeiro, BR (Reynard 95I-Honda), 68.
Fastest qualifying lap: Parker Johnstone, USA (Reynard 95I-Honda), 31.242s, 230.459 mph/370.888 km/h.
Championship points: **1** Villeneuve, 141; **2** Rahal, 111; **3** Gordon, 99; **4** Andretti, 96; **5** Pruett, 93; **6** Vasser, 79.

MILLER GENUINE DRAFT 200, Mid-Ohio Sports Car Course, Lexington, Ohio, USA, 13 August. Round 14. 83 laps of the 2.250-mile/3.621-km circuit, 185.800 miles/299.016 km.
1 Al Unser Jnr, USA (Penske PC24-Mercedes Benz), 1h 44m 04.774s, 107.110 mph/172.377 km/h.
2 Paul Tracy, CDN (Lola T95/00-Ford Cosworth XB), 1h 44m 06.811s; **3** Jacques Villeneuve, CDN (Reynard 95I-Ford Cosworth XB), 83 laps; **4** Adrian Fernandez, MEX (Lola T95/00-Mercedes Benz), 83; **5** Bryan Herta, USA (Reynard 95I-Ford Cosworth XB), 83; **6** Mauricio Gugelmin, BR (Reynard 95I-Ford Cosworth XB), 83; **7** Juan Manuel Fangio II, RA (Reynard 95I-Ford Cosworth XB), 83; **8** Robby Gordon, USA (Reynard 95I-Ford Cosworth XB), 83; **9** Jimmy Vasser, USA (Reynard 95I-Ford Cosworth XB), 83; **10** Eddie Cheever, USA (Lola T95/00-Ford Cosworth XB), 83.
Most laps led: Michael Andretti, USA (Lola T95/00-Ford Cosworth XB), 38.
Fastest qualifying lap: Villeneuve, 1m 06.836s, 121.192 mph/195.040 km/h (record).
Championship points: **1** Villeneuve, 156; **2** Rahal, 111; **3** Gordon, 104; **4=** Unser Jnr, 97; **4=** Andretti, 97; **6** Pruett, 95.

NEW ENGLAND 200, New Hampshire International Speedway, Loudon, New Hampshire, USA, 20 August. Round 15. 200 laps of the 1.058-mile/1.703-km circuit, 211.600 miles/340.537 km.
1 Andre Ribeiro, BR (Reynard 95I-Honda), 1h 34m 36.192s, 134.203 mph/215.978 km/h (under caution).
2 Michael Andretti, USA (Lola T95/00-Ford Cosworth XB), 1h 34m 50.674s; **3** Al Unser Jnr, USA (Penske PC24-Mercedes Benz), 199 laps; **4** Jacques Villeneuve, CDN (Reynard 95I-Ford Cosworth XB), 199; **5** Emerson Fittipaldi, BR (Penske PC24-Mercedes

Benz), 199; **6** Jimmy Vasser, USA (Reynard 95I-Ford Cosworth XB), 198; **7** Gil de Ferran, BR (Reynard 95I-Mercedes Benz), 198; **8** Christian Fittipaldi, BR (Reynard 95I-Ford Cosworth XB), 198; **9** Robby Gordon, USA (Reynard 95I-Ford Cosworth XB), 197; **10** Bobby Rahal, USA (Lola T95/00-Mercedes Benz), 197.
Most laps led: Ribeiro, 96.
Fastest qualifying lap: Ribeiro, 21.466s, 177.434 mph/285.552 km/h (record).
Championship points: 1 Villeneuve, 168; **2** Rahal, 114; **3** Andretti, 113; **4** Unser Jnr, 111; **5** Gordon, 108; **6** Pruett, 95.

MOLSON INDY VANCOUVER, Vancouver Street Circuit, Pacific Place, Vancouver, British Columbia, Canada, 3 September. Round 16. 100 laps of the 1.703-mile/2.741-km circuit, 170.300 miles/274.071 km.
1 Al Unser Jnr, USA (Penske PC24-Mercedes Benz), 1h 46m 54.900s, 95.571 mph/153.807 km/h.
2 Gil de Ferran, BR (Reynard 95I-Mercedes Benz), 1h 47m 09.913s; **3** Robby Gordon, USA (Reynard 95I-Ford Cosworth XB), 100 laps; **4** Stefan Johansson, S (Penske PC23-Mercedes Benz), 100; **5** Bobby Rahal, USA (Lola T95/00-Mercedes Benz), 100; **6** Scott Pruett, USA (Lola T95/00-Ford Cosworth XB), 100; **7** Emerson Fittipaldi, BR (Penske PC24-Mercedes Benz), 100; **8** Paul Tracy, CDN (Lola T95/00-Ford Cosworth XB), 99; **9** Alessandro Zampedri, I (Lola T94/00-Ford Cosworth XB), 99; **10** Raul Boesel, BR (Lola T95/00-Mercedes Benz), 99.
Most laps led: Unser Jnr, 40.
Fastest qualifying lap: Jacques Villeneuve, CDN (Reynard 95I-Ford Cosworth XB), 55.226s, 111.013 mph/178.658 km/h (record).
Championship points: 1 Villeneuve, 170; **2** Unser Jnr, 132; **3** Rahal, 124; **4** Gordon, 122; **5** Andretti, 113; **6** Pruett, 103.

TOYOTA GRAND PRIX OF MONTEREY FEATURING THE BANK OF AMERICA 300, Laguna Seca Raceway, Monterey, California, USA, 10 September. Round 17. 84 laps of the 2.214-mile/3.563-km circuit, 185.976 miles/299.299 km.
1 Gil de Ferran, BR (Reynard 95I-Mercedes Benz), 1h 53m 17.579s, 98.493 mph/158.509 km/h.
2 Paul Tracy, CDN (Lola T95/00-Ford Cosworth XB), 1h 53m 25.538s; **3** Mauricio Gugelmin, BR (Reynard 95I-Ford Cosworth XB), 84 laps; **4** Michael Andretti, USA (Lola T95/00-Ford Cosworth XB), 84; **5** Scott Pruett, USA (Lola T95/00-Ford Cosworth XB), 84; **6** Al Unser Jnr, USA (Penske PC24-Mercedes Benz), 84; **7** Bobby Rahal, USA (Lola T95/00-Mercedes Benz), 84; **8** Jimmy Vasser, USA (Reynard 95I-Ford Cosworth XB), 84; **9** Teo Fabi, I (Reynard 95I-Ford Cosworth XB), 84; **10** Adrian Fernandez, MEX (Lola T95/00-Mercedes Benz), 84.
Most laps led: de Ferran, 54.
Fastest qualifying lap: Jacques Villeneuve, CDN (Reynard 95I-Ford Cosworth XB), 1m 09.625s, 114.476 mph/184.231 km/h (record).

Final championship points following the reinstatement of Al Unser Jnr as the winner at Portland

1	Jacques Villeneuve, CDN	172
2	Al Unser Jnr, USA	161
3	Bobby Rahal, USA	128
4	Michael Andretti, USA	123
5	Robby Gordon, USA	121
6	Paul Tracy, CDN	115

7 Scott Pruett, USA, 112; **8** Jimmy Vasser, USA, 92; **9** Teo Fabi, I, 83; **10** Mauricio Gugelmin, BR, 80; **11** Emerson Fittipaldi, BR, 67; **12** Adrian Fernandez, MEX, 66; **13** Stefan Johansson, S, 60; **14** Gil de Ferran, BR, 56; **15** Christian Fittipaldi, BR, 54; **16** Raul Boesel, BR, 48; **17** Andre Ribeiro, BR, 38; **18** Eddie Cheever, USA, 33; **19** Danny Sullivan, USA, 32; **20** Bryan Herta, USA, 30; **21** Eliseo Salazar, RCH, 19; **22** Alessandro Zampedri, I, 15; **23** Eric Bachelart, B, 8; **24=** Christian Danner, D, 6; **24=** Arie Luyendyk, NL, 6; **24=** Juan Manuel Fangio II, RA, 6; **24=** Parker Johnstone, USA, 6; **28** Hiro Matsushita, J, 5; **29=** Marco Greco, BR, 2; **29=** Carlos Guerrero, MEX, 2; **29=** Dean Hall, USA, 2; **32=** Scott Goodyear, CDN, 1; **32=** Roberto Guerrero, USA, 1; **32=** Scott Brayton, USA, 1.

Nations' Cup
1 United States, 290; **2** Canada, 219; **3** Brazil, 201; **4** Italy, 90; **5** Mexico, 68; **6** Sweden, 60; **7** Chile, 19; **8** Belgium, 8; **9=** Germany, 6; **9=** Netherlands, 6; **9=** Argentina, 6; **12** Japan, 5; **13** Colombia, 1.

Manufacturers' Championship
1 Ford Cosworth, 310; **2** Mercedes Benz, 272; **3** Honda, 40; **4** Menard Buick, 6.

Constructors' Championship
1 Reynard, 286; **2** Lola, 264; **3** Penske, 197.

Jim Trueman Rookie of the Year
1 Gil de Ferran, BR, 57; **2** Christian Fittipaldi, BR, 55; **3** Andre Ribeiro, BR, 38; **4** Eliseo Salazar, RCH, 19; **5** Juan Manuel Fangio II, RA, 6; **6** Carlos Guerrero, MEX, 2.

NASCAR Winston Cup

DAYTONA 500, Daytona International Speedway, Daytona Beach, Florida, USA, 19 February. Round 1. 200 laps of the 2.500-mile/4.023-km circuit, 500.000 miles/804.672 km.
1 Sterling Marlin, USA (Chevrolet Monte Carlo), 3h 31m 42s, 141.710 mph/228.060 km/h.
2 Dale Earnhardt, USA (Chevrolet Monte Carlo), 3h 31m 42.61s; **3** Mark Martin, USA (Ford Thunderbird), 200 laps; **4** Ted Musgrave, USA (Ford Thunderbird), 200; **5** Dale Jarrett, USA (Ford Thunderbird), 200; **6** Michael Waltrip, USA (Pontiac Grand Prix), 200; **7** Steve Grissom, USA (Chevrolet Monte Carlo), 200; **8** Terry Labonte, USA (Chevrolet Monte Carlo), 200; **9** Ken Schrader, USA (Chevrolet Monte Carlo), 200; **10** Morgan Shepherd, USA (Ford Thunderbird), 200.
Fastest qualifying lap: Jarrett, 46.512s, 193.498 mph/311.406 km/h.
Drivers Championship points: 1 Marlin, 185; **2** Earnhardt, 175; **3** Martin, 170; **4** Musgrave, 160; **5=** Jarrett, 155; **5=** Waltrip, 155.

GOODWRENCH 500, North Carolina Motor Speedway, Rockingham, North Carolina, USA, 26 February. Round 2. 492 laps of the 1.017-mile/1.637-km circuit, 500.364 miles/805.258 km.
1 Jeff Gordon, USA (Chevrolet Monte Carlo), 3h 59m 15s, 125.483 mph/201.946 km/h.
2 Bobby Labonte, USA (Chevrolet Monte Carlo), 3h 59m 16.19s; **3** Dale Earnhardt, USA (Chevrolet Monte Carlo), 492 laps; **4** Ricky Rudd, USA (Ford Thunderbird), 492; **5** Dale Jarrett, USA (Ford Thunderbird), 491; **6** Steve Grissom, USA (Chevrolet Monte Carlo), 491; **7** Mark Martin, USA (Ford Thunderbird), 490; **8** Derrike Cope, USA (Ford Thunderbird), 489; **9** Ward Burton, USA (Chevrolet Monte Carlo), 489; **10** Kyle Petty, USA (Pontiac Grand Prix), 489.
Fastest qualifying lap: Gordon, 23.228s, 157.620 mph/253.665 km/h (record).
Drivers Championship points: 1 Earnhardt, 345; **2** Martin, 316; **3** Marlin, 312; **4** Jarrett, 310; **5** Grissom, 296; **6** Rudd, 289.

PONTIAC EXCITEMENT 400, Richmond International Raceway, Virginia, USA, 5 March. Round 3. 400 laps of the 0.750-mile/1.207-km circuit, 300.000 miles/482.803 km.
1 Terry Labonte, USA (Chevrolet Monte Carlo), 2h 49m 08s, 106.425 mph/171.274 km/h.
2 Dale Earnhardt, USA (Chevrolet Monte Carlo), 2h 49m 09.25s; **3** Rusty Wallace, USA (Ford Thunderbird), 400 laps; **4** Ken Schrader, USA (Chevrolet Monte Carlo), 400; **5** Sterling Marlin, USA (Chevrolet Monte Carlo), 400; **6** Derrike Cope, USA (Ford Thunderbird), 400; **7** Darrell Waltrip, USA (Chevrolet Monte Carlo), 400; **8** Mark Martin, USA (Ford Thunderbird), 399; **9** Bobby Hamilton, USA (Pontiac Grand Prix), 399; **10** John Andretti, USA (Ford Thunderbird), 399.
Fastest qualifying lap: Jeff Gordon, USA (Chevrolet Monte Carlo), 21.642s, 124.757 mph/200.778 km/h (record).
Drivers Championship points: 1 Earnhardt, 520; **2** Marlin, 467; **3** Martin, 458; **4** Labonte (Terry), 412; **5** Jarrett, 398; **6** Rudd, 389.

PUROLATOR 500, Atlanta Motor Speedway, Hampton, Georgia, USA, 12 March. Round 4. 328 laps of the 1.522-mile/2.449-km circuit, 499.216 miles/803.410 km.
1 Jeff Gordon, USA (Chevrolet Monte Carlo), 3h 19m 32s, 150.115 mph/241.587 km/h.
2 Bobby Labonte, USA (Chevrolet Monte Carlo), 3h 19m 32.19s; **3** Terry Labonte, USA (Chevrolet Monte Carlo), 328 laps; **4** Dale Earnhardt, USA (Chevrolet Monte Carlo), 328; **5** Dale Jarrett, USA (Ford Thunderbird), 328; **6** Morgan Shepherd, USA (Ford Thunderbird), 327; **7** Sterling Marlin, USA (Chevrolet Monte Carlo), 327; **8** Ricky Rudd, USA (Ford Thunderbird), 327; **9** Mark Martin, USA (Ford Thunderbird), 326; **10** Rusty Wallace, USA (Ford Thunderbird), 326.
Fastest qualifying lap: Earnhardt, 29.605s, 185.077 mph/297.852 km/h.
Drivers Championship points: 1 Earnhardt, 685; **2** Marlin, 613; **3** Martin, 596; **4** Labonte (Terry), 582; **5** Jarrett, 553; **6** Gordon, 532.

TRANSOUTH FINANCIAL 400, Darlington Raceway, South Carolina, USA, 26 March. Round 5. 293 laps of the 1.366-mile/2.198-km circuit, 400.238 miles/644.121 km.
1 Sterling Marlin, USA (Chevrolet Monte Carlo), 3h 35m 35s, 111.392 mph/179.268 km/h.
2 Dale Earnhardt, USA (Chevrolet Monte Carlo), 3h 35m 36.05s; **3** Ted Musgrave, USA (Ford Thunderbird), 293 laps; **4** Todd Bodine, USA (Ford Thunderbird), 293; **5** Derrike Cope, USA (Ford Thunderbird), 293; **6** Steve Grissom, USA (Chevrolet Monte Carlo), 293; **7** Michael Waltrip, USA (Pontiac Grand Prix), 293; **8** Morgan Shepherd, USA (Ford Thunderbird), 293; **9** Bobby Hamilton, USA (Pontiac Grand Prix), 293; **10** John Andretti, USA (Ford Thunderbird), 292.
Fastest qualifying lap: Jeff Gordon, USA (Chevrolet Monte Carlo), 28.786s, 170.833 mph/274.929 km/h (record).
Drivers Championship points: 1 Earnhardt, 860; **2** Marlin, 793; **3** Martin, 648; **4** Cope, 646; **5** Labonte (Terry), 643; **6** Musgrave, 624.

FOOD CITY 500, Bristol International Raceway, Tennessee, USA, 2 April. Round 6. 500 laps of the 0.533-mile/0.858-km circuit, 266.500 miles/428.890 km.
1 Jeff Gordon, USA (Chevrolet Monte Carlo), 2h 53m 47s, 92.011 mph/148.078 km/h.
2 Rusty Wallace, USA (Ford Thunderbird), 2h 53m 52.74s; **3** Darrell Waltrip, USA (Chevrolet Monte Carlo), 500 laps; **4** Bobby Hamilton, USA (Pontiac Grand Prix), 500; **5** Ricky Rudd, USA (Ford Thunderbird), 500; **6** Dale Jarrett, USA (Ford Thunderbird), 500; **7** Terry Labonte, USA (Chevrolet Monte Carlo), 499; **8** Mark Martin, USA (Ford Thunderbird), 499; **9** Sterling Marlin, USA (Chevrolet Monte Carlo), 499; **10** Robert Pressley, USA (Chevrolet Monte Carlo), 498.
Fastest qualifying lap: Martin, 15.399s, 124.605 mph/200.533 km/h.
Drivers Championship points: 1 Earnhardt, 948; **2** Marlin, 931; **3** Martin, 795; **4** Gordon, 794; **5** Labonte (Terry), 789; **6** Cope, 770.

FIRST UNION 400, North Wilkesboro Speedway, North Carolina, USA, 9 April. Round 7. 400 laps of the 0.625-mile/1.006-km circuit, 250.000 miles/402.336 km.
1 Dale Earnhardt, USA (Chevrolet Monte Carlo), 2h 26m 27s, 102.424 mph/164.836 km/h.
2 Jeff Gordon, USA (Chevrolet Monte Carlo), 2h 26m 40.48s; **3** Mark Martin, USA (Ford Thunderbird), 400 laps; **4** Rusty Wallace, USA (Ford Thunderbird), 400; **5** Steve Grissom, USA (Chevrolet Monte Carlo), 400; **6** Ted Musgrave, USA (Ford Thunderbird), 399; **7** Sterling Marlin, USA (Chevrolet Monte Carlo), 399; **8** Rick Mast, USA (Ford Thunderbird), 399; **9** Brett Bodine, USA (Ford Thunderbird), 399; **10** Darrell Waltrip, USA (Chevrolet Monte Carlo), 398.
Fastest qualifying lap: Gordon, 18.945s, 118.765 mph/191.133 km/h.
Drivers Championship points: 1 Earnhardt, 1133; **2** Marlin, 1077; **3** Gordon, 969; **4** Martin, 965; **5** Labonte (Terry), 904; **6** Wallace, 895.

HANES 500, Martinsville Speedway, Virginia, USA, 23 April. Round 8. 356 laps of the 0.526-mile/0.847-km circuit, 187.256 miles/301.359 km.
Scheduled for 500 laps, but stopped early due to bad weather.
1 Rusty Wallace, USA (Ford Thunderbird), 2h 35m 44s, 72.145 mph/116.106 km/h.
2 Ted Musgrave, USA (Ford Thunderbird), 2h 35m 44.81s; **3** Jeff Gordon, USA (Chevrolet Monte Carlo), 356 laps; **4** Darrell Waltrip, USA (Chevrolet Monte Carlo), 356; **5** Mark Martin, USA (Ford Thunderbird), 356; **6** Ken Schrader, USA (Chevrolet Monte Carlo), 356; **7** Dale Jarrett, USA (Ford Thunderbird), 356; **8** Bobby Hamilton, USA (Pontiac Grand Prix), 356; **9** Kyle Petty, USA (Pontiac Grand Prix), 356; **10** Bobby Labonte, USA (Chevrolet Monte Carlo), 355.
Fastest qualifying lap: Labonte (Bobby), 20.294s, 93.308 mph/150.165 km/h.
Drivers Championship points: 1 Earnhardt, 1209; **2** Marlin, 1201; **3** Gordon, 1139; **4** Martin, 1120; **5** Wallace, 1080; **6** Musgrave, 1058.

WINSTON SELECT 500, Talladega Superspeedway, Alabama, USA, 30 April. Round 9. 188 laps of the 2.660-mile/4.281-km circuit, 500.080 miles/804.801 km.
1 Mark Martin, USA (Ford Thunderbird), 2h 47m 43s, 178.902 mph/287.914 km/h.
2 Jeff Gordon, USA (Chevrolet Monte Carlo), 2h 47m 43.18s; **3** Morgan Shepherd, USA (Ford Thunderbird), 188 laps; **4** Darrell Waltrip, USA (Chevrolet Monte Carlo), 188; **5** Bobby Labonte, USA (Chevrolet Monte Carlo), 188; **6** Bill Elliott, USA (Ford Thunderbird), 188; **7** Geoff Bodine, USA (Ford Thunderbird), 188; **8** Todd Bodine, USA (Ford Thunderbird), 188; **9** Jimmy Spencer, USA (Ford Thunderbird), 188; **10** Loy Allen, USA (Ford Thunderbird), 188.
Fastest qualifying lap: Terry Labonte, USA (Chevrolet Monte Carlo), 48.725s, 196.532 mph/316.287 km/h.
Drivers Championship points: 1= Gordon, 1314; **1=** Earnhardt, 1314; **3** Martin, 1305; **4** Marlin, 1252; **5=** Wallace, 1188; **5=** Musgrave, 1188.

SAVE MART SUPERMARKETS 300, Sears Point Raceway, Sonoma, California, USA, 7 May. Round 10. 74 laps of the 2.520-mile/4.056-km circuit, 186.480 miles/300.110 km.
1 Dale Earnhardt, USA (Chevrolet Monte Carlo), 2h 38m 18s, 70.681 mph/113.750 km/h.
2 Mark Martin, USA (Ford Thunderbird), 2h 38m 18.32s; **3** Jeff Gordon, USA (Chevrolet Monte Carlo), 74 laps; **4** Ricky Rudd, USA (Ford Thunderbird), 74; **5** Terry Labonte, USA (Chevrolet Monte Carlo), 74; **6** Ted Musgrave, USA (Ford Thunderbird), 74; **7** Sterling Marlin, USA (Chevrolet Monte Carlo), 74; **8** Todd Bodine, USA (Ford Thunderbird), 74; **9** Ken Schrader, USA (Chevrolet Monte Carlo), 74; **10** Michael Waltrip, USA (Pontiac Grand Prix), 74.
Fastest qualifying lap: Rudd, 1m 32.132s, 98.467 mph/158.468 km/h (record).
Drivers Championship points: 1 Earnhardt, 1494; **2** Martin, 1485; **3** Gordon, 1479; **4** Marlin, 1398; **5** Musgrave, 1338; **6** Wallace, 1291.

COCA-COLA 600, Charlotte Motor Speedway, North Carolina, USA, 28 May. Round 11. 400 laps of the 1.500-mile/2.414-km circuit, 600.000 miles/965.606 km.
1 Bobby Labonte, USA (Chevrolet Monte Carlo), 3h 56m 55s, 151.952 mph/244.543 km/h.
2 Terry Labonte, USA (Chevrolet Monte Carlo), 3h 57m 01.28s; **3** Michael Waltrip, USA (Pontiac Grand Prix), 400 laps; **4** Sterling Marlin, USA (Chevrolet Monte Carlo), 399; **5** Ricky Rudd, USA (Ford Thunderbird), 399; **6** Dale Earnhardt, USA (Chevrolet Monte Carlo), 399; **7** Hut Stricklin, USA (Ford Thunderbird), 399; **8** Lake Speed, USA (Ford Thunderbird), 398; **9** Bobby Hamilton, USA (Pontiac Grand Prix), 398; **10** Ricky Craven, USA (Chevrolet Monte Carlo), 397.
Fastest qualifying lap: Jeff Gordon, USA (Chevrolet Monte Carlo), 29.370s, 183.861 mph/295.896 km/h.
Drivers Championship points: 1 Earnhardt, 1649; **2** Martin, 1569; **3** Marlin, 1563; **4** Gordon, 1548; **5** Musgrave, 1456; **6** Labonte (Terry), 1379.

MILLER GENUINE DRAFT 500, Dover Downs International Speedway, Dover, Delaware, USA, 4 June. Round 12. 500 laps of the 1.000-mile/1.609-km circuit, 500.000 miles/804.672 km.
1 Kyle Petty, USA (Pontiac Grand Prix), 4h 10m 15s, 119.880 mph/192.928 km/h.
2 Bobby Labonte, USA (Chevrolet Monte Carlo), 4h 10m 15.22s; **3** Ted Musgrave, USA (Ford Thunderbird), 500 laps; **4** Hut Stricklin, USA (Ford Thunderbird), 500; **5** Dale Earnhardt, USA (Chevrolet Monte Carlo), 500; **6** Jeff Gordon, USA (Chevrolet Monte Carlo), 499; **7** Sterling Marlin, USA (Chevrolet Monte Carlo), 499; **8** Michael Waltrip, USA (Pontiac Grand Prix), 499; **9** Rusty Wallace, USA (Ford Thunderbird), 499; **10** Joe Nemechek, USA (Chevrolet Monte Carlo), 499.
Fastest qualifying lap: Gordon, 23.427s, 153.669 mph/247.306 km/h (record).
Drivers Championship points: 1 Earnhardt, 1809; **2** Marlin, 1709; **3** Gordon, 1703; **4** Martin, 1627; **5** Musgrave, 1626; **6** Labonte (Bobby), 1531.

UAW-GM TEAMWORK 500, Pocono Raceway, Pennsylvania, USA, 11 June. Round 13. 200 laps of the 2.500-mile/4.023-km circuit, 500.000 miles/804.672 km.
1 Terry Labonte, USA (Chevrolet Monte Carlo), 3h 37m 50s, 137.720 mph/221.639 km/h.
2 Ted Musgrave, USA (Ford Thunderbird), 3h 37m 51.64s; **3** Ken Schrader, USA (Chevrolet Monte Carlo), 200 laps; **4** Sterling Marlin, USA (Chevrolet Monte Carlo), 200; **5** Hut Stricklin, USA (Ford Thunderbird), 200; **6** Bill Elliott, USA (Ford Thunderbird), 200; **7** Morgan Shepherd, USA (Ford Thunderbird), 200; **8** Dale Earnhardt, USA (Chevrolet Monte Carlo), 200; **9** Michael Waltrip, USA (Pontiac Grand Prix), 200; **10** Brett Bodine, USA (Ford Thunderbird), 200.
Fastest qualifying lap: Schrader, 55.088s, 163.375 mph/262.927 km/h.
Drivers Championship points: 1 Earnhardt, 1951; **2** Marlin, 1874; **3** Gordon, 1828; **4** Musgrave, 1801; **5** Martin, 1757; **6** Labonte (Bobby), 1618.

MILLER GENUINE DRAFT 400, Michigan International Speedway, Brooklyn, Michigan, USA, 18 June. Round 14. 200 laps of the 2.000-mile/3.219-km circuit, 400.000 miles/643.738 km.
1 Bobby Labonte, USA (Chevrolet Monte Carlo), 2h 58m 58s, 134.103 mph/215.818 km/h.
2 Jeff Gordon, USA (Chevrolet Monte Carlo), 2h 58m 58.27s; **3** Rusty Wallace, USA (Ford Thunderbird), 200 laps; **4** John Andretti, USA (Ford Thunderbird), 200; **5** Morgan Shepherd, USA (Ford Thunderbird), 200; **6** Dale Jarrett, USA (Ford Thunderbird), 200; **7** Sterling Marlin, USA (Chevrolet Monte Carlo), 200; **8** Mark Martin, USA (Ford Thunderbird), 200; **9** Terry Labonte, USA (Chevrolet Monte Carlo), 200; **10** Ted Musgrave, USA (Ford Thunderbird), 200.
Fastest qualifying lap: Gordon, 38.583s, 186.611 mph/300.321 km/h (record).
Drivers Championship points: 1 Marlin, 2020; **2** Earnhardt, 2014; **3** Gordon, 2008; **4** Musgrave, 1935; **5** Martin, 1899; **6** Labonte (Bobby), 1798.

PEPSI 400, Daytona International Speedway, Daytona Beach, Florida, USA, 1 July. Round 15. 160 laps of the 2.500-mile/4.023-km circuit, 400.000 miles/643.738 km.
1 Jeff Gordon, USA (Chevrolet Monte Carlo), 2h 23m 44s, 166.976 mph/268.722 km/h.
2 Sterling Marlin, USA (Chevrolet Monte Carlo), 2h 23m 44.21s; **3** Dale Earnhardt, USA (Chevrolet Monte Carlo), 160 laps; **4** Mark Martin, USA (Ford Thunderbird), 160; **5** Ted Musgrave, USA (Ford Thunderbird), 160; **6** Ken Schrader, USA (Chevrolet Monte Carlo), 160; **7** Kyle Petty, USA (Pontiac Grand Prix), 160; **8** Ricky Rudd, USA (Ford Thunderbird), 160; **9** Jimmy Spencer, USA (Ford Thunderbird), 160; **10** Bill Elliott, USA (Ford Thunderbird), 160.
Fastest qualifying lap: Earnhardt, 47.033s, 191.355 mph/307.956 km/h.
Drivers Championship points: 1 Marlin, 2200; **2** Gordon, 2193; **3** Earnhardt, 2184; **4** Musgrave, 2090; **5** Martin, 2059; **6** Wallace, 1859.

SLICK 50 300, New Hampshire International Speedway, Loudon, New Hampshire, USA, 9 July. Round 16. 300 laps of the 1.058-mile/1.703-km circuit, 317.400 miles/510.806 km.
1 Jeff Gordon, USA (Chevrolet Monte Carlo), 2h 57m 56s, 107.029 mph/172.246 km/h.
2 Morgan Shepherd, USA (Ford Thunderbird), 2h 57m 57.23s; **3** Mark Martin, USA (Ford Thunderbird), 300 laps; **4** Terry Labonte, USA (Chevrolet Monte Carlo), 300; **5** Ricky Rudd, USA (Ford Thunderbird), 300; **6** Rusty Wallace, USA (Ford Thunderbird), 300; **7** Derrike Cope, USA (Ford Thunderbird), 300; **8** Ted Musgrave, USA (Ford Thunderbird), 300; **9** Sterling Marlin, USA (Chevrolet Monte Carlo), 300; **10** Ken Schrader, USA (Chevrolet Monte Carlo), 300.
Fastest qualifying lap: Martin, 29.568s, 128.815 mph/207.308 km/h (record).
Drivers Championship points: 1 Gordon, 2378; **2** Marlin, 2338; **3** Earnhardt, 2286; **4** Musgrave, 2232; **5** Martin, 2229; **6** Labonte (Terry), 2020.

MILLER GENUINE DRAFT 500, Pocono Raceway, Pennsylvania, USA, 16 July. Round 17. 200 laps of the 2.500-mile/4.023-km circuit, 500.000 miles/804.672 km.
1 Dale Jarrett, USA (Ford Thunderbird), 3h 43m 49s, 134.038 mph/215.714 km/h.
2 Jeff Gordon, USA (Chevrolet Monte Carlo), 3h 43m 49.19s; **3** Ricky Rudd, USA (Ford Thunderbird), 200 laps; **4** Ted Musgrave, USA (Ford Thunderbird), 200; **5** Bill Elliott, USA (Ford Thunderbird), 200; **6** Geoff Bodine, USA (Ford Thunderbird), 200; **7** Mark Martin, USA (Ford Thunderbird), 200; **8** Jeremy Mayfield, USA (Ford Thunderbird), 200; **9** Joe Nemechek, USA (Chevrolet Monte Carlo), 200; **10** Dick Trickle, USA (Ford Thunderbird), 200.
Fastest qualifying lap: Elliott, 55.386s, 162.496 mph/261.512 km/h.
Drivers Championship points: 1 Gordon, 2553; **2** Martin, 2447; **3** Musgrave, 2397; **4** Earnhardt, 2389; **5** Martin, 2380; **6** Labonte (Terry), 2141.

DIEHARD 500, Talladega Superspeedway, Alabama, USA, 23 July. Round 18. 188 laps of the 2.660-mile/4.281-km circuit, 500.080 miles/804.801 km.
1 Sterling Marlin, USA (Chevrolet Monte Carlo), 2h 53m 15s, 173.188 mph/278.719 km/h.
2 Dale Jarrett, USA (Ford Thunderbird), 2h 53m 15.05s; **3** Dale Earnhardt, USA (Chevrolet Monte Carlo), 188 laps; **4** Morgan Shepherd, USA (Ford Thunderbird), 188; **5** Bill Elliott, USA (Ford Thunderbird), 188; **6** Kyle Petty, USA (Pontiac Grand Prix), 188; **7** Mark Martin, USA (Ford Thunderbird), 188; **8** Jeff Gordon, USA (Chevrolet Monte Carlo), 188; **9** Michael Waltrip, USA (Pontiac Grand Prix), 188; **10** Jimmy Spencer, USA (Ford Thunderbird), 187.
Fastest qualifying lap: Marlin, 49.307s, 194.212 mph/312.554 km/h.
Drivers Championship points: 1 Gordon, 2705; **2** Marlin, 2627; **3** Earnhardt, 2559; **4** Martin, 2531; **5** Musgrave, 2527; **6** Shepherd, 2225.

BRICKYARD 400, Indianapolis Motor Speedway, Speedway, Indiana, USA, 5 August. Round 19. 160 laps of the 2.500-mile/4.023-km circuit, 400.000 miles/643.738 km.
1 Dale Earnhardt, USA (Chevrolet Monte Carlo), 2h 34m 38s, 155.206 mph/249.780 km/h.
2 Rusty Wallace, USA (Ford Thunderbird), 2h 34m 38.37s; **3** Dale Jarrett, USA (Ford Thunderbird), 160 laps; **4** Bill Elliott, USA (Ford Thunderbird), 160; **5** Mark Martin, USA (Ford Thunderbird), 160; **6** Jeff Gordon, USA (Chevrolet Monte Carlo); 160; **7** Sterling Marlin, USA (Chevrolet Monte Carlo), 160; **8** Rick Mast, USA (Ford Thunderbird), 160; **9** Bobby Labonte, USA (Chevrolet Monte Carlo), 160; **10** Morgan Shepherd, USA (Ford Thunderbird), 160.
Fastest qualifying lap: Gordon, 52.163s, 172.536 mph/277.670 km/h (record).
Drivers Championship points: 1 Gordon, 2860; **2** Marlin, 2778; **3** Earnhardt, 2739; **4** Martin, 2686; **5** Musgrave, 2642; **6** Wallace, 2387.

THE BUD AT THE GLEN, Watkins Glen International 'Short' Course, New York, USA, 13 August. Round 20. 90 laps of the 2.454-mile/3.949-km circuit, 220.860 miles/355.440 km.

1 Mark Martin, USA (Ford Thunderbird), 2h 11m 54s, 100.467 mph/161.686 km/h.
2 Wally Dallenbach, USA (Pontiac Grand Prix), 2h 11m 55.01s; 3 Jeff Gordon, USA (Chevrolet Monte Carlo), 90 laps; 4 Ricky Rudd, USA (Ford Thunderbird), 90; 5 Terry Labonte, USA (Chevrolet Monte Carlo), 90; 6 Bobby Labonte, USA (Chevrolet Monte Carlo), 90; 7 John Andretti, USA (Ford Thunderbird), 90; 8 Darrell Waltrip, USA (Chevrolet Monte Carlo), 90; 9 Geoff Bodine, USA (Ford Thunderbird), 90; 10 Ricky Craven, USA (Chevrolet Monte Carlo), 90.
Fastest qualifying lap: Martin, 1m 11.249s, 123.993 mph/199.548 km/h (record).
Drivers Championship points: 1 Gordon, 3030; 2 Marlin, 2878; 3 Martin, 2871; 4 Earnhardt, 2833; 5 Musgrave, 2766; 6 Labonte (Terry), 2484.

GM GOODWRENCH DEALER 400, Michigan International Speedway, Brooklyn, Michigan, USA, 20 August. Round 21. 200 laps of the 2.000-mile/3.219-km circuit, 400.000 miles/643.738 km.
1 Bobby Labonte, USA (Chevrolet Monte Carlo), 2h 32m 09s, 157.739 mph/253.856 km/h.
2 Terry Labonte, USA (Chevrolet Monte Carlo), 2h 32m 15.8s; 3 Jeff Gordon, USA (Chevrolet Monte Carlo), 200 laps; 4 Sterling Marlin, USA (Chevrolet Monte Carlo), 200; 5 Rusty Wallace, USA (Ford Thunderbird), 200; 6 Ward Burton, USA (Chevrolet Monte Carlo), 200; 7 Ricky Craven, USA (Chevrolet Monte Carlo), 200; 8 Bobby Hamilton, USA (Pontiac Grand Prix), 200; 9 Bill Elliott, USA (Ford Thunderbird), 199; 10 Hut Stricklin, USA (Ford Thunderbird), 199.
Fastest qualifying lap: Labonte (Bobby), 39.045s, 184.403 mph/296.767 km/h.
Drivers Championship points: 1 Gordon, 3205; 2 Marlin, 3038; 3 Martin, 2920; 4 Earnhardt, 2891; 5 Musgrave, 2845; 6 Labonte (Terry), 2654.

GOODY'S 500, Bristol International Raceway, Tennessee, USA, 26 August. Round 22. 500 laps of the 0.533-mile/0.858-km circuit, 266.500 miles/428.890 km.
1 Terry Labonte, USA (Chevrolet Monte Carlo), 3h 15m 03s, 81.979 mph/131.932 km/h.
2 Dale Earnhardt, USA (Chevrolet Monte Carlo), 3h 15m 03.10s; 3 Dale Jarrett, USA (Ford Thunderbird), 500 laps; 4 Darrell Waltrip, USA (Chevrolet Monte Carlo), 500; 5 Mark Martin, USA (Ford Thunderbird), 500; 6 Jeff Gordon, USA (Chevrolet Monte Carlo), 500; 7 Sterling Marlin, USA (Chevrolet Monte Carlo), 500; 8 Mike Wallace, USA (Ford Thunderbird), 500; 9 Jeff Burton, USA (Ford Thunderbird), 500; 10 Derrike Cope, USA (Ford Thunderbird), 499.
Fastest qualifying lap: Martin, 15.339s, 125.093 mph/201.318 km/h (record).
Drivers Championship points: 1 Gordon, 3360; 2 Marlin, 3184; 3 Martin, 3080; 4 Earnhardt, 3066; 5 Musgrave, 2969; 6 Labonte (Terry), 2834.

MOUNTAIN DEW SOUTHERN 500, Darlington Raceway, South Carolina, USA, 3 September. Round 23. 367 laps of the 1.366-mile/2.198-km circuit, 501.322 miles/806.800 km.
1 Jeff Gordon, USA (Chevrolet Monte Carlo), 4h 08m 07s, 121.231 mph/195.102 km/h.
2 Dale Earnhardt, USA (Chevrolet Monte Carlo), 4h 08m 07.66s; 3 Rusty Wallace, USA (Ford Thunderbird), 367 laps; 4 Ward Burton, USA (Chevrolet Monte Carlo), 367; 5 Michael Waltrip, USA (Pontiac Grand Prix), 367; 6 Ricky Rudd, USA (Ford Thunderbird), 367; 7 Hut Stricklin, USA (Ford Thunderbird), 367; 8 Bobby Labonte, USA (Chevrolet Monte Carlo), 367; 9 Lake Speed, USA (Ford Thunderbird), 367; 10 Sterling Marlin, USA (Chevrolet Monte Carlo), 367.
Fastest qualifying lap: John Andretti, USA (Ford Thunderbird), 29.380s, 167.379 mph/269.371 km/h.
Drivers Championship points: 1 Gordon, 3540; 2 Marlin, 3323; 3 Earnhardt, 3246; 4 Martin, 3144; 5 Musgrave, 3066; 6 Labonte (Terry), 2940.

MILLER GENUINE DRAFT 400, Richmond International Raceway, Virginia, USA, 9 September. Round 24. 400 laps of the 0.750-mile/1.207-km circuit, 300.000 miles/482.803 km.
1 Rusty Wallace, USA (Ford Thunderbird), 2h 52m 19s, 104.459 mph/168.110 km/h.
2 Terry Labonte, USA (Chevrolet Monte Carlo), 2h 52m 24.6s; 3 Dale Earnhardt, USA (Chevrolet Monte Carlo), 400 laps; 4 Dale Jarrett, USA (Ford Thunderbird), 400; 5 Bobby Hamilton, USA (Pontiac Grand Prix), 400; 6 Jeff Gordon, USA (Chevrolet Monte Carlo), 400; 7 John Andretti, USA (Ford Thunderbird), 399; 8 Ricky Rudd, USA (Ford Thunderbird), 399; 9 Ken Schrader, USA (Chevrolet Monte Carlo), 399; 10 Ted Musgrave, USA (Ford Thunderbird), 399.
Fastest qualifying lap: Earnhardt, 22.033s, 122.543 mph/197.215 km/h.
Drivers Championship points: 1 Gordon, 3695; 2 Earnhardt, 3416; 3 Marlin, 3387; 4 Martin, 3262; 5 Musgrave, 3200; 6 Labonte (Terry), 3115.

MBNA 500, Dover Downs International Speedway, Dover, Delaware, USA, 17 September. Round 25. 500 laps of the 1.000-mile/1.609-km circuit, 500.000 miles/804.672 km.
1 Jeff Gordon, USA (Chevrolet Monte Carlo), 4h 00m 30s, 124.740 mph/200.750 km/h.
2 Bobby Hamilton, USA (Pontiac Grand Prix), 4h 00m 32.34s; 3 Rusty Wallace, USA (Ford Thunderbird), 500 laps; 4 Joe Nemechek, USA (Chevrolet Monte Carlo), 500; 5 Dale Earnhardt, USA (Chevrolet Monte Carlo), 500; 6 Sterling Marlin, USA (Chevrolet Monte Carlo), 500; 7 Derrike Cope, USA (Ford Thunderbird), 499; 8 Mark Martin, USA (Ford Thunderbird), 499; 9 Bobby Labonte, USA (Chevrolet Monte Carlo), 498; 10 Ricky Rudd, USA (Ford Thunderbird), 498.
Fastest qualifying lap: Rick Mast, USA (Ford Thunderbird), 23.461s, 153.446 mph/246.948 km/h.
Drivers Championship points: 1 Gordon, 3880; 2 Earnhardt, 3571; 3 Marlin, 3537; 4 Martin, 3404; 5 Musgrave, 3330; 6 Wallace, 3257.

GOODY'S 500, Martinsville Speedway, Virginia, USA, 24 September. Round 26. 500 laps of the 0.526-mile/0.847-km circuit, 263.000 miles/423.257 km.
1 Dale Earnhardt, USA (Chevrolet Monte Carlo), 3h 33m 24s, 73.946 mph/119.004 km/h.
2 Terry Labonte, USA (Chevrolet Monte Carlo), 3h 33m 25.3s; 3 Rusty Wallace, USA (Ford Thunderbird), 500 laps; 4 Bobby Hamilton, USA (Pontiac Grand Prix), 500; 5 Geoff Bodine, USA (Ford Thunderbird), 500; 6 Bill Elliott, USA (Ford Thunderbird), 500; 7 Jeff Gordon, USA (Chevrolet Monte Carlo), 500; 8 Darrell Waltrip, USA (Chevrolet Monte Carlo), 500; 9 Derrike Cope, USA (Ford Thunderbird), 500; 10 Dale Jarrett, USA (Ford Thunderbird), 500.
No qualifying due to bad weather.
Drivers Championship points: 1 Gordon, 4031; 2 Earnhardt, 3756; 3 Marlin, 3631; 4 Martin, 3531; 5 Wallace, 3427; 6 Labonte (Terry), 3408.

TYSON HOLLY FARMS 400, North Wilkesboro Speedway, North Carolina, USA, 1 October. Round 27. 400 laps of the 0.625-mile/1.006-km circuit, 250.000 miles/402.336 km.
1 Mark Martin, USA (Ford Thunderbird), 2h 25m 38s, 102.998 mph/165.760 km/h.
2 Rusty Wallace, USA (Ford Thunderbird), 2h 25m 38.86s; 3 Jeff Gordon, USA (Chevrolet Monte Carlo), 400 laps; 4 Terry Labonte, USA (Chevrolet Monte Carlo), 400; 5 Ricky Rudd, USA (Ford Thunderbird), 400; 6 Ernie Irvan, USA (Ford Thunderbird), 400; 7 Dale Jarrett, USA (Ford Thunderbird), 400; 8 Ken Schrader, USA (Chevrolet Monte Carlo), 399; 9 Dale Earnhardt, USA (Chevrolet Monte Carlo), 399; 10 Bill Elliott, USA (Ford Thunderbird), 399.
Fastest qualifying lap: Ted Musgrave, USA (Ford Thunderbird), 19.004s, 118.396 mph/190.540 km/h.
Drivers Championship points: 1 Gordon, 4201; 2 Earnhardt, 3899; 3 Marlin, 3749; 4 Martin, 3716; 5 Wallace, 3597; 6 Labonte (Terry), 3568.

UAW-GM 500, Charlotte Motor Speedway, North Carolina, USA, 8 October. Round 28. 334 laps of the 1.500-mile/2.414-km circuit, 501.000 miles/806.281 km.
1 Mark Martin, USA (Ford Thunderbird), 3h 26m 48s, 145.358 mph/233.931 km/h.
2 Dale Earnhardt, USA (Chevrolet Monte Carlo), 3h 26m 48.97s; 3 Terry Labonte, USA (Chevrolet Monte Carlo), 334 laps; 4 Ricky Rudd, USA (Ford Thunderbird), 334; 5 Dale Jarrett, USA (Ford Thunderbird), 334; 6 Sterling Marlin, USA (Chevrolet Monte Carlo), 334; 7 Ward Burton, USA (Chevrolet Monte Carlo), 334; 8 Bobby Labonte, USA (Chevrolet Monte Carlo), 334; 9 Rusty Wallace, USA (Ford Thunderbird), 334; 10 Bobby Hamilton, USA (Pontiac Grand Prix), 334.
Fastest qualifying lap: Rudd, 29.904s, 180.578 mph/290.612 km/h.
Drivers Championship points: 1 Gordon, 4279; 2 Earnhardt, 4074; 3 Marlin, 3904; 4 Martin, 3896; 5 Labonte (Terry), 3738; 6 Wallace, 3735.

AC-DELCO 400, North Carolina Motor Speedway, Rockingham, North Carolina, USA, 22 October. Round 29. 393 laps of the 1.017-mile/1.637-km circuit, 399.681 miles/643.224 km.
1 Ward Burton, USA (Chevrolet Monte Carlo), 3h 28m 56s, 114.778 mph/184.717 km/h.
2 Rusty Wallace, USA (Ford Thunderbird), 3h 28m 57.9s; 3 Mark Martin, USA (Ford Thunderbird), 393 laps; 4 Terry Labonte, USA (Chevrolet Monte Carlo), 393; 5 Jeff Burton, USA (Ford Thunderbird), 393; 6 Sterling Marlin, USA (Chevrolet Monte Carlo), 393; 7 Dale Earnhardt, USA (Chevrolet Monte Carlo), 393; 8 Ricky Craven, USA (Chevrolet Monte Carlo), 393; 9 Joe Nemechek, USA (Chevrolet Monte Carlo), 393; 10 Bill Elliott, USA (Ford Thunderbird), 393.
Fastest qualifying lap: Hut Stricklin, USA (Ford Thunderbird), 23.563s, 155.379 mph/250.059 km/h.
Drivers Championship points: 1 Gordon, 4387; 2 Earnhardt, 4225; 3 Martin, 4066; 4 Marlin, 4059; 5 Wallace, 3910; 6 Labonte (Terry), 3898.

SLICK 50 500, Phoenix International Raceway, Arizona, USA, 29 October. Round 30. 312 laps of the 1.000-mile/1.609-km circuit, 312.000 miles/502.115 km.
1 Ricky Rudd, USA (Ford Thunderbird), 3h 03m 18s, 102.128 mph/164.359 km/h.
2 Derrike Cope, USA (Ford Thunderbird), 3h 03m 18.53s; 3 Dale Earnhardt, USA (Chevrolet Monte Carlo), 312 laps; 4 Rusty Wallace, USA (Ford Thunderbird), 312; 5 Jeff Gordon, USA (Chevrolet Monte Carlo), 312; 6 Ted Musgrave, USA (Ford Thunderbird), 312; 7 Morgan Shepherd, USA (Ford Thunderbird), 312; 8 Mark Martin, USA (Ford Thunderbird), 312; 9 Rick Mast, USA (Ford Thunderbird), 312; 10 Ken Schrader, USA (Chevrolet Monte Carlo), 312.
Fastest qualifying lap: Bill Elliott, USA (Ford Thunderbird), 27.668s, 130.020 mph/209.247 km/h (record).
Drivers Championship points: 1 Gordon, 4542; 2 Earnhardt, 4395; 3 Martin, 4208; 4 Marlin, 4186; 5 Wallace, 4075; 6 Labonte (Terry), 4022.

NAPA 500, Atlanta Motor Speedway, Hampton, Georgia, USA, 12 November. Round 31. 328 laps of the 1.522-mile/2.449-km circuit, 499.216 miles/803.410 km.
1 Dale Earnhardt, USA (Chevrolet Monte Carlo), 3h 03m 03s, 163.633 mph/263.341 km/h.
2 Sterling Marlin, USA (Chevrolet Monte Carlo), 3h 03m 06.74s; 3 Rusty Wallace, USA (Ford Thunderbird), 328; 4 Bill Elliott, USA (Ford Thunderbird), 328; 5 Ward Burton, USA (Pontiac Grand Prix), 328; 6 Jimmy Spencer, USA (Ford Thunderbird), 328; 7 Ernie Irvan, USA (Ford Thunderbird), 327; 8 Bobby Labonte, USA (Chevrolet Monte Carlo), 327; 9 Bobby Hillin, USA (Ford Thunderbird), 327; 10 Ricky Rudd, USA (Ford Thunderbird), 327.
Fastest qualifying lap: Darrell Waltrip, USA (Chevrolet Monte Carlo), 29.610s, 185.046 mph/297.803 km/h.

Final championship points
Drivers

1	Jeff Gordon, USA	4614
2	Dale Earnhardt, USA	4580
3	Sterling Marlin, USA	4361
4	Mark Martin, USA	4320
5	Rusty Wallace, USA	4240
6	Terry Labonte, USA	4146

7 Ted Musgrave, USA, 3949; 8 Bill Elliott, USA, 3746; 9 Ricky Rudd, USA, 3734; 10 Bobby Labonte, USA, 3718; 11 Morgan Shepherd, USA, 3618; 12 Michael Waltrip, USA, 3601; 13 Dale Jarrett, USA, 3584; 14 Bobby Hamilton, USA, 3576; 15 Derrike Cope, USA, 3384; 16 Geoff Bodine, USA, 3357; 17 Ken Schrader, USA, 3221; 18 John Andretti, USA, 3140; 19 Darrell Waltrip, USA, 3078; 20 Brett Bodine, USA, 2988.

Manufacturers
1 Chevrolet, 245; 2 Ford, 204 ; 3 Pontiac, 140.

Other NASCAR Results

BUSCH CLASH OF '95, Daytona International Speedway, Daytona Beach, Florida, USA, 12 February, 2 x 10 laps of the 2.500-mile/4.023-km circuit.
Segment 1
1 Jeff Gordon, USA (Chevrolet Monte Carlo), 10 laps.
2 Sterling Marlin, USA (Chevrolet Monte Carlo), 10; 3 Dale Earnhardt, USA (Chevrolet Monte Carlo), 10; 4 Bill Elliott, USA (Ford Thunderbird), 10; 5 Ted Musgrave, USA (Ford Thunderbird), 10; 6 Todd Bodine, USA (Ford Thunderbird), 10; 7 Jimmy Spencer, USA (Ford Thunderbird), 10; 8 Rusty Wallace, USA (Ford Thunderbird), 10; 9 Ricky Rudd, USA (Ford Thunderbird), 10; 10 Geoff Bodine, USA (Ford Thunderbird), 10.

Segments 1 & 2 overall (50.000 miles/80.467 km)
1 Dale Earnhardt, USA (Chevrolet Monte Carlo), 15m 55s, 188.482 mph/303.332 km/h.
2 Sterling Marlin, USA (Chevrolet Monte Carlo), 20 laps; 3 Bill Elliott, USA (Ford Thunderbird), 20; 4 Jeff Gordon, USA (Chevrolet Monte Carlo), 20; 5 Todd Bodine, USA (Ford Thunderbird), 20; 6 Ricky Rudd, USA (Ford Thunderbird), 20; 7 Ted Musgrave, USA (Ford Thunderbird), 20; 8 Rusty Wallace, USA (Ford Thunderbird), 20; 9 Jimmy Spencer, USA (Ford Thunderbird), 20; 10 Rick Mast, USA (Ford Thunderbird), 20.

THE WINSTON SELECT, Charlotte Motor Speedway, North Carolina, USA, 21 May. 70 laps of the 1.500-mile/2.414-km circuit, 105.000 miles/168.981 km.
Run over two segments. Aggregate results given.
1 Jeff Gordon, USA (Chevrolet Monte Carlo), 42m 27s, 148.410 mph/238.843 km/h.
2 Sterling Marlin, USA (Chevrolet Monte Carlo), 42m 28.07s; 3 Ricky Rudd, USA (Ford Thunderbird), 70 laps; 4 Rusty Wallace, USA (Ford Thunderbird), 70; 5 Geoff Bodine, USA (Ford Thunderbird), 70; 6 Bill Elliott, USA (Ford Thunderbird), 70; 7 Robert Pressley, USA (Chevrolet Monte Carlo), 70; 8 Mike Wallace, USA (Ford Thunderbird), 70; 9 Jimmy Spencer, USA (Ford Thunderbird), 70; 10 Brett Bodine, USA (Ford Thunderbird), 70.

PPG Firestone Indy Lights Championship

All cars are Lola T93/20-Buick GS.

MIAMI PPG FIRESTONE INDY LIGHTS RACE, Miami Street Circuit, Florida, USA, 5 March. Round 1. 25 laps of the 1.843-mile/2.966-km circuit, 46.075 miles/74.151 km.
1 Greg Moore, CDN, 47m 00.675s, 58.358 mph/93.919 km/h.
2 Jeff Ward, USA, 47m 02.892s; 3 Pedro Chaves, P, 25 laps; 4 Robbie Buhl, USA, 25; 5 Doug Boyer, USA, 25; 6 Jose Luis di Palma, RA, 25; 7 Claude Bourbonnais, CDN, 25; 8 Affonso Giaffone, BR, 25; 9 Buzz Calkins, USA, 25; 10 Nick Firestone, USA, 25.
Most laps led: Moore, 25.
Fastest qualifying lap: Moore, 1m 09.743s, 95.132 mph/153.100 km/h.

PHOENIX PPG FIRESTONE INDY LIGHTS RACE, Phoenix International Raceway, Arizona, USA, 2 April. Round 2. 75 laps of the 1.000-mile/1.609-km circuit, 75.000 miles/120.701 km.
1 Greg Moore, CDN, 42m 56.113s, 104.809 mph/168.674 km/h.
2 Robbie Buhl, USA, 42m 59.192s; 3 Buzz Calkins, USA, 75 laps; 4 Doug Boyer, USA, 75; 5 Affonso Giaffone, BR, 74*; 6 Niko Palhares, BR, 74; 7 Mark Hotchkis, USA, 74; 8 Beaux Barfield, USA, 74; 9 Juan Carbonell, RCH, 74; 10 David LaCroix, USA, 74.
** includes 1-minute penalty for passing the pace car.*
Most laps led: Giaffone, 66.
Fastest qualifying lap: Claude Bourbonnais, CDN, 22.887s, 157.295 mph/253.141 km/h.

LONG BEACH PPG FIRESTONE INDY LIGHTS RACE, Long Beach Street Circuit, California, USA, 9 April. Round 3. 47 laps of the 1.590-mile/2.559-km circuit, 74.730 miles/120.266 km.
1 Greg Moore, CDN, 58m 23.255s, 76.794 mph/123.588 km/h.
2 Robbie Buhl, USA, 58m 25.562s; 3 Dave DeSilva, USA, 47 laps; 4 Alex Padilla, USA, 47; 5 Pedro Chaves, P, 47; 6 Bob Reid, USA, 47; 7 Jeff Ward, USA, 47; 8 Enrique Contreras, MEX, 47; 9 Peter Faucetta, USA, 46; 10 Akira Ishikawa, J, 46.
Most laps led: Moore, 47.
Fastest qualifying lap: Moore, 57.496s, 99.555 mph/160.218 km/h.

NAZARETH PPG FIRESTONE INDY LIGHTS RACE, Pennsylvania International Raceway, Nazareth, Pennsylvania, USA, 23 April. Round 4. 75 laps of the 1.000-mile/1.609-km circuit, 75.000 miles/120.701 km.
1 Greg Moore, CDN, 44m 23.382s, 101.375 mph/163.147 km/h.
2 Affonso Giaffone, BR, 44m 30.702s; 3 Robbie Buhl, USA, 75 laps; 4 Buzz Calkins, USA, 75; 5 Doug Boyer, USA, 75; 6 Alex Padilla, USA, 74 (DNF – accident); 7 Jeff Ward, USA, 74; 8 Diego Guzman, CO, 74; 9 Pedro Chaves, P, 74; 10 Jeff Andretti, USA, 74.
Most laps led: Moore, 44.
Fastest qualifying lap: Bob Dorricott Jnr, USA, 22.883s, 157.322 mph/253.185 km/h.

MILWAUKEE PPG FIRESTONE INDY LIGHTS RACE, Wisconsin State Fair Park Speedway, West Allis, Milwaukee, Wisconsin, USA, 4 June. Round 5. 75 laps of the 1.000-mile/1.609-km circuit, 75.000 miles/120.701 km.
1 Greg Moore, CDN, 39m 29.386s, 113.954 mph/183.390 km/h.
2 Affonso Giaffone, BR, 39m 36.821s; 3 Buzz Calkins, USA, 75 laps; 4 Robbie Buhl, USA, 75; 5 Mark Hotchkis, USA, 75; 6 Jeff Ward, USA, 74; 7 Dave DeSilva, USA, 74; 8 Mike Borkowski, USA, 74; 9 Doug Boyer, USA, 74; 10 Pedro Chaves, P, 73.
Most laps led: Moore, 52.
Fastest qualifying lap: Buhl, 25.712s, 140.012 mph/225.328 km/h.

DETROIT PPG FIRESTONE INDY LIGHTS RACE, Belle Isle Park Circuit, Detroit, Michigan, USA, 11 June. Round 6. 24 laps of the 2.100-mile/3.380-km circuit, 50.400 miles/81.111 km.
1 Robbie Buhl, USA, 50m 05.993s, 60.359 mph/97.139 km/h.
2 Greg Moore, CDN, 50m 06.163s; 3 Jeff Ward, USA, 24 laps; 4 Nick Firestone, USA, 24; 5 Affonso Giaffone, BR, 24; 6 Diego Guzman, CO, 24; 7 Buzz Calkins, USA, 24; 8 Doug Boyer, USA, 24; 9 Mike Borkowski, USA, 24; 10 Mark Hotchkis, USA, 24.
Most laps led: Buhl, 24.
Fastest qualifying lap: Buhl, 1m 17.460s, 97.599 mph/157.070 km/h.

PORTLAND PPG FIRESTONE INDY LIGHTS RACE, Portland International Raceway, Oregon, USA, 25 June. Round 7. 39 laps of the 1.950-mile/3.138-km circuit, 76.050 miles/122.391 km.
1 Greg Moore, CDN, 51m 28.388s, 88.907 mph/143.082 km/h.
2 Affonso Giaffone, BR, 51m 30.471s; 3 Nick Firestone, USA, 39 laps; 4 Mike Borkowski, USA, 39; 5 Buzz Calkins, USA, 39; 6 Pedro Chaves, P, 39; 7 Jose Luis di Palma, RA, 39; 8 Doug Boyer, USA, 39; 9 Mark Hotchkis, USA, 39; 10 David LaCroix, USA, 39.
Most laps led: Moore, 39.
Fastest qualifying lap: Moore, 1m 06.080s, 106.235 mph/170.968 km/h.

TORONTO PPG FIRESTONE INDY LIGHTS RACE, Exhibition Place Circuit, Toronto, Ontario, Canada, 16 July. Round 8. 42 laps of the 1.780-mile/2.865-km circuit, 74.760 miles/120.315 km.
1 Greg Moore, CDN, 52m 41.622s, 85.126 mph/136.997 km/h.
2 Robbie Buhl, USA, 52m 42.406s; 3 Doug Boyer, USA, 42 laps; 4 Affonso Giaffone, BR, 42; 5 Jose Luis di Palma, RA, 42; 6 Mark Hotchkis, USA, 42; 7 Bertrand Godin, CDN, 42; 8 Buzz Calkins, USA, 42; 9 Dave DeSilva, USA, 42; 10 Mike Borkowski, USA, 42.
Most laps led: Moore, 42.
Fastest qualifying lap: Moore, 1m 03.845s, 100.368 mph/161.527 km/h.

BUICK CHALLENGE OF CLEVELAND, Burke Lakefront Airport Circuit, Cleveland, Ohio, USA, 23 July. Round 9. 32 laps of the 2.369-mile/3.813-km circuit, 75.808 miles/122.001 km.
1 Greg Moore, CDN, 48m 37.497s, 93.542 mph/150.541 km/h.
2 Pedro Chaves, P, 48m 40.683s; 3 Doug Boyer, USA, 32 laps; 4 Mark Hotchkis, USA, 32; 5 Buzz Calkins, USA, 32; 6 Bertrand Godin, CDN, 32; 7 Diego Guzman, CO, 32; 8 Mike Borkowski, USA, 32; 9 Dave DeSilva, USA, 32; 10 Nick Firestone, USA, 32.
Most laps led: Moore, 32.
Fastest qualifying lap: Moore, 1m 05.752s, 129.706 mph/208.741 km/h.

LOUDON PPG FIRESTONE INDY LIGHTS RACE, New Hampshire International Speedway, Loudon, New Hampshire, USA, 20 August. Round 10. 71 laps of the 1.058-mile/1.703-km circuit, 75.118 miles/120.891 km.
1 Greg Moore, CDN, 34m 29.131s, 130.695 mph/210.333 km/h.
2 Claude Bourbonnais, CDN, 34m 29.785s; 3 Robbie Buhl, USA, 71 laps; 4 Pedro Chaves, P, 71; 5 Mark Hotchkis, USA, 71; 6 Affonso Giaffone, BR, 71; 7 Jeff Andretti, USA, 70; 8 Trevor Seibert, CDN, 70; 9 Doug Boyer, USA, 69; 10 Nick Firestone, USA, 69.
Most laps led: Buhl, 40.
Fastest qualifying lap: Buhl, 25.126s, 151.588 mph/243.957 km/h.

VANCOUVER PPG FIRESTONE INDY LIGHTS RACE, Vancouver Street Circuit, Pacific Place, Vancouver, British Columbia, Canada, 3 September. Round 11. 44 laps of the 1.703-mile/2.741-km circuit, 74.932 miles/120.591 km.
1 Pedro Chaves, P, 51m 29.013s, 87.327 mph/140.540 km/h.
2 Doug Boyer, USA, 51m 37.516s; 3 Robbie Buhl, USA, 44 laps; 4 Affonso Giaffone, BR, 44; 5 Greg Moore, CDN, 44; 6 Alex Padilla, USA, 44; 7 Bob Reid, USA, 44; 8 Diego Guzman, CO, 44; 9 Nick Firestone, USA, 43; 10 Trevor Seibert, CDN, 43.
Most laps led: Moore, 29.
Fastest qualifying lap: Moore, 1m 01.243s, 100.106 mph/161.105 km/h.

MONTEREY PPG FIRESTONE INDY LIGHTS RACE, Laguna Seca Raceway, Monterey, California, USA, 10 September. Round 12. 34 laps of the 2.214-mile/3.563-km circuit, 75.276 miles/121.145 km.
1 Greg Moore, CDN, 48m 09.053s, 93.800 mph/150.957 km/h.
2 Affonso Giaffone, BR, 48m 12.370s; 3 Doug Boyer, USA, 34 laps; 4 Pedro Chaves, P, 34; 5 Nick Firestone, USA, 34; 6 Trevor Seibert, CDN, 34; 7 Claude Bourbonnais, CDN, 34; 8 Diego Guzman, CO, 34; 9 Mark Hotchkis, USA, 34; 10 Jeff Ward, USA, 34.
Most laps led: Moore, 34.
Fastest qualifying lap: Moore, 1m 16.968s, 103.555 mph/166.655 km/h.

Final championship points

1 Greg Moore, CDN	242
2 Robbie Buhl, USA	140
3 Affonso Giaffone, BR	122
4 Doug Boyer, USA	108
5 Pedro Chaves, P	99
6 Buzz Calkins, USA	77

7 Mark Hotchkis, USA, 57; 8 Jeff Ward, USA, 56; 9 Nick Firestone, USA, 52; 10 Dave DeSilva, USA, 33.